IIS 6

Administration

Mitch Tulloch

McGraw-Hill/Osborne

New York   Chicago   San Francisco
Lisbon   London   Madrid   Mexico City   Milan
New Delhi   San Juan   Seoul   Singapore   Sydney   Toronto

The McGraw·Hill Companies

McGraw-Hill/Osborne
2100 Powell Street, Floor 10
Emeryville, California 94608
U.S.A.

To arrange bulk purchase discounts for sales promotions, premiums, or fund-raisers, please contact **McGraw-Hill/Osborne** at the above address. For information on translations or book distributors outside the U.S.A., please see the International Contact Information page immediately following the index of this book.

IIS 6 Administration

67890 CUS CUS 01987

ISBN 0-07-219485-5

Publisher
  Brandon A. Nordin
Vice President & Associate Publisher
  Scott Rogers
Acquisitions Editor
  Francis Kelly
Project Editor
  Julie M. Smith
Acquisitions Coordinator
  Jessica Wilson
Technical Editor
  Patrick Santry
Copy Editor
  Sally Engelfried

Proofreader
  Linda Medoff
Indexer
  Claire Splan
Computer Designers
  George Toma Charbak, Tara A. Davis
Illustrators
  Melinda Moore Lytle, Michael Mueller,
  Lyssa Wald
Series Design
  Lyssa Wald, Peter F. Hancik
Cover Series Design
  Jeff Weeks

This book was composed with Corel VENTURA™ Publisher.

Dedicated to myself—why not? ☺

About the Author

Mitch Tulloch, MSCE, is a consultant, trainer, and author of over a dozen computing books including *Administering IIS 4*, *Administering IIS 5*, *Administering Exchange Server 5.5*, and *Administering Exchange 2000 Server*, all from Osborne/McGraw-Hill.

CONTENTS

Part IV   Advanced Administration

ACKNOWLEDGMENTS

Thanks to Franny, Martin, Julie, Jessica, and the rest of the team at Osborne/McGraw-Hill (www.osborne.com) for their tireless editorial work in helping me write this, my seventh book, for Osborne.

Thanks to Patrick Santry who as technical editor made many helpful comments and suggestions.

Thanks to Neil Salkind my friend and agent, and to the whole crew at Studio B (www.studiob.com).

Thanks to MTS Communications Inc. (www.mts.ca) for providing Internet services and web hosting for my company (www.mtit.com)

And thanks to Ingrid, my wife and colleague, for her support, encouragement, and patience as I worked on this project.

INTRODUCTION

This book is about IIS 6—how to plan, deploy, administer, maintain, and troubleshoot Microsoft's web services component for the Windows Server 2003 operating system. IIS 6 is not just the latest in a long series of versions of IIS; it's a radically redesigned platform for hosting highly scalable and reliable web applications. In fact, installing IIS means adding a whole new role called Application Server that can leverage the powerful features of ASP.NET for creating dynamic web applications with greater ease than ever before.

I'm excited about this new version of IIS, as you will be too once you start reading this book. Not only has the internal architecture of IIS changed to provide better reliability and improved performance, security is built right into the platform. Instead of leaving the responsibility of securing IIS to you after you install it, the platform now installs in a totally locked-down state right out-of-the-box. Administration is simpler too, with an improved IIS Manager console, a brand-new HTML administration tool, and new WMI scripts for administering IIS from the command-line. And the IIS metabase is now an XML file that can be read and modified using a text editor even when IIS is running. Whether you are an experienced IT professional familiar with previous versions of IIS, or a newbie looking for step-by-step instructions on how to implement and manage IIS, this book is for you.

OVERVIEW OF CHAPTERS

The sixteen chapters of this book have been organized into four parts: Overview (chapters 1 and 2), Deployment (chapters 3 and 4), Basic Administration (chapters 5 through 9) and Advanced Administration (chapters 10 through 16). There are also two appendices, one outlining the similarities and differences between IIS 6 and the previous version IIS 5, and the other listing useful IIS resources on the Internet.

Here's a breakdown of what's covered in each chapter:

Chapter 1 Introducing IIS 6 looks at the history of Microsoft's Internet Information Services (IIS) and outlines the new features and enhancements in version 6 of IIS.

Chapter 2 IIS 6 Architecture takes a detailed look at the internal architecture and operation of IIS 6 and compares this with the architecture of previous IIS 4 and 5 versions. Topics covered in this chapter include isolation modes, worker processes, application pools, kernel mode listener, and caching.

Chapter 3 Planning Deployment explains the various tools and methods you can use for deploying IIS 6 in your enterprise. Topics covered include manual and automated deployment methods, clean installs vs. upgrades, Windows Server 2003 editions, hardware compatibility, licensing, product activation, and other planning issues.

Chapter 4 Installing IIS 6 walks you through several examples of installing IIS 6 including clean install from product CD, clean install from network distribution point, unattended install, upgrade from IIS 4, and upgrade from IIS 5.

Chapter 5 Administering Standard/Enterprise Edition looks at tools and procedures for administering IIS 6 on Windows Server 2003, Standard Edition and Enterprise Edition. Tools covered in this chapter include the IIS Manager console, Remote Desktop (formerly called Terminal Services in Administration Mode), and Remote Desktop Web Connection. Administrative tasks covered here include restarting IIS, saving configuration to disk, and configuring general server properties.

Chapter 6 Administering Web Edition examines additional tools for administering IIS 6 including the Web Interface for Server Administration and Telnet.

Chapter 7 Creating and Configuring Websites looks at how to create websites using the Web Site Creation Wizard and how to perform basic configuration tasks such as configuring website identity, creating virtual directories for storing content, specifying default documents, configuring MIME types, and stopping/starting individual sites.

Chapter 8 Creating and Configuring Applications examines how the ASP, ASP.NET, ISAPI, and CGI application models are implemented in IIS 6. Topics covered include selecting an isolation mode, enabling dynamic content, creating application pools, assigning applications to application pools, and configuring application settings including starting points, mappings, options, and debugging. Also covered are ISAPI filters and wildcard application mappings.

Chapter 9 Creating and Configuring FTP Sites looks at basic FTP site administration tasks including configuring site identity, content location, FTP messages, and directory listing style. Also covered are enhancements to FTP in IIS 6 including server-to-server transfer and FTP user isolation.

Chapter 10 Securing IIS is an important chapter covering various aspects of IIS security, including NTFS permission, web permissions, authentication methods (Anonymous, Basic, Digest, Advanced Digest, Integrated Windows, and Passport), IP address and domain name restrictions, Web Service Extensions (WSE), application execute permissions, application pool identity, parent paths, and SSL.

Chapter 11 Working From the Command-Line examines how to administer various aspects of IIS from a command prompt using the administration scripts included with the platform. Tasks covered include creating and managing websites, FTP sites, virtual directories, applications, and web service extensions.

Chapter 12 Performance Tuning and Monitoring looks at tuning IIS for maximum performance by configuring application pool features like health monitoring, worker process recycling, demand start, idle timeout, web gardens, processor affinity, and CPU monitoring. Also covered are quality of service features like bandwidth throttling, HTTP keep-alives, HTTP compression, connection limits, and connection timeouts. The chapter concludes with a potpourri of tips for do's and don'ts for ensuring optimal performance from your IIS 6 machines.

Chapter 13 Maintenance and Troubleshooting examines in detail HTTP error messages and how they can be used for troubleshooting problems with IIS. Also covered are topics like IIS logging, event logs, and various troubleshooting tips.

Chapter 14 Working with the Metabase outlines the organization of the new XML metabase of IIS 6 and how to edit it directly while IIS is running. Also covered are metabase administration tasks like saving changes to disk, backing up and restoring the metabase, how the metabase history feature works, and how to export and import portions of the metabase.

Chapter 15 SMTP and NNTP looks at how to configure the optional Simple Mail Transfer Protocol (SMTP) and Network News Transfer Protocol (NNTP) services in IIS 6 including how to test SMTP forwarding and NNTP newsgroups.

Chapter 16 Publishing with IIS concludes with a detailed look at how Web Distributed Authoring and Versioning (WebDAV) can be used to publish content to IIS. Also covered are FrontPage Server Extensions (FPSE), redirection, content expiration, and content ratings.

PART 1

Overview

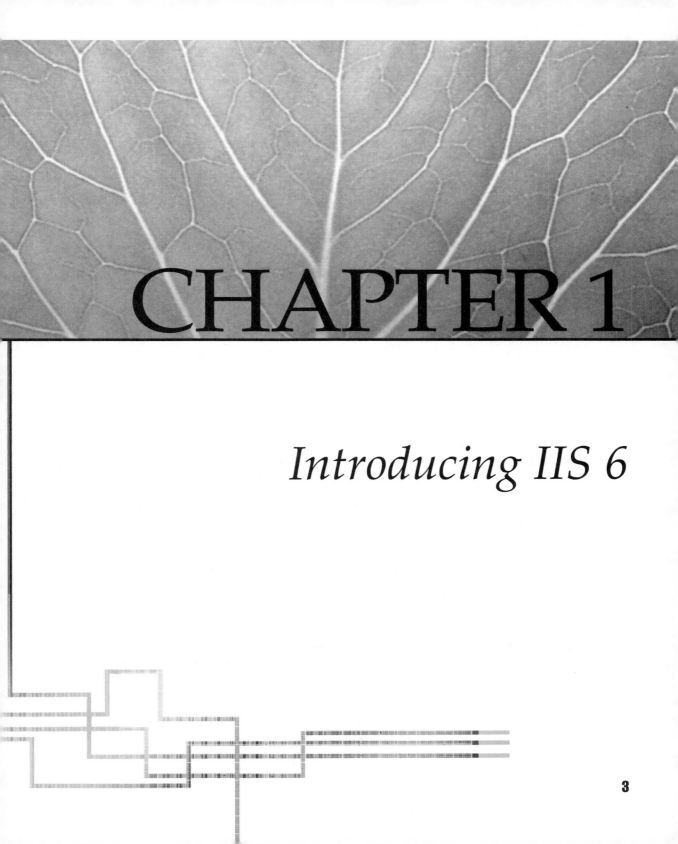

CHAPTER 1

Introducing IIS 6

W e'll begin our overview of IIS 6 by examining the many new features and enhancements Microsoft has included in the latest version of their popular web server platform. These enhancements were designed to increase the security, reliability, scalability, performance, and manageability of the product, and they range from fundamental changes in underlying architecture and operation to cosmetic improvements in the user interface for administration.

This chapter and the next ("IIS 6 Architecture") will provide the background necessary for later chapters dealing with issues such as deployment, configuration, management, monitoring, maintenance, and troubleshooting IIS. Also included in this chapter is a brief history of the different versions of IIS and an overview of Microsoft's new Windows Server 2003 operating system family (of which IIS is a component) and how the different flavors of Windows Server 2003 relate to IIS.

THE IIS STORY

Those of us who have been working in the IT field for a while may remember the abrupt about-face Microsoft made in 1995 with regard to the Internet. Realizing that they were about to be left behind by companies like Netscape, Microsoft suddenly shifted gears from a position of "The Internet? Who cares?" to a policy of building Internet functionality into all of their products and giving this functionality away for free. It was one of the smartest business moves in all history, and an incredibly fast move for a company as large as Microsoft. To the popular mind, the centerpiece of Microsoft's strategy was the Internet Explorer web browser, which Microsoft gave away for free and soon incorporated into their 16- and 32-bit Microsoft Windows operating system platforms. The result of this action was the infamous "Browser Wars" of the late 1990s, where Microsoft and Netscape furiously competed with each other by incorporating more and more features in their browser platforms as new versions came out with breakneck speed. No one doubts now that Microsoft won the war, though at the time some parties thought they did so unfairly, which resulted in a series of lawsuits that culminated in the famous legal battle between Microsoft and the U.S. Department of Justice during the Clinton era. Microsoft seems to have won that battle, though a number of states decided that the Department of Justice let Microsoft off too lightly and are still pursuing legal action against the company at the time of writing this book.

While the battle between browsers may have captivated the public imagination, a far more earnest battle began taking place in IT shops during the same time period, and has continued to this day. This is the battle for server supremacy, or: who will control the content on the Internet? Microsoft has been waging this war on several fronts, including web servers (IIS vs. Apache), Internet mail servers (Exchange vs. Sendmail), web application programming (Active Server Pages vs. Perl), and web portals (MSN vs. AOL). Any of these topics could form the basis of a whole book in itself, but it's the first of these, the battle for web server supremacy, that provides the underlying excitement for this new release of IIS. Will the new features and enhancements found in version 6 finally make IIS the server of choice for enterprise environments? Can IIS recover from its checkered reputation in earlier versions as a product full of security holes? Has Linux built up enough momentum in the enterprise to convince IT decision makers to start switching from IIS back to Apache? And is version 6 of IIS secure and reliable enough to enable Microsoft to regain the trust of IT departments after its mistakes and oversights in earlier versions?

Exciting, isn't it? Makes you want to learn all about IIS 6, doesn't it? Well if it does, read on!

IIS RISING

Version 6 of IIS is both the culmination of a long history of development for the product and an important new beginning from the standpoint of performance, reliability, and security. It's worthwhile to take a few moments to review the history of IIS and how it has evolved over the last six years. That's right, six versions of the product in six years, a new version each year. That's a hectic pace for an upgrade cycle from the enterprise point of view, and in fact many industry pundits have taken Microsoft to task for this, saying things like, "Why couldn't Microsoft have gotten it right in the first place?" and "Why release versions of the product that were inferior, lacked security, and had performance and scalability problems?" On the other hand, you can only admire a company that turns itself completely around and hits the ground running.

Perhaps the corporate world has been the world's biggest beta testing environment for IIS, and perhaps, as such, it has complained bitterly about holes and leaks being discovered almost daily and about the steady stream of fixes and patches coming out of Redmond. But the corporate world has nevertheless embraced IIS with enthusiasm, as various statistics demonstrate:

- Netcraft (www.netcraft.com) has maintained statistics on websites connected to the Internet since August 1995. While Apache continues to be the dominant platform used with a 56.5 percent share of hosted sites as of February 2002, growth in market share for this platform has flattened out in the last two years and may even be starting to decrease. Meanwhile, after flattening for several years, market share for IIS has been increasing in the last year and stands at a 30.25 percent market share at the time of this writing. The results of the Netcraft survey are well known in the Internet community (especially among Apache enthusiasts!) but a lesser known fact is that Netcraft also conducts surveys of web server platforms used for secure e-commerce, and in this area IIS excels. For example, a January 2001 survey of over 100,000 web servers using SSL indicated that almost half (48.76 percent) of these sites ran on IIS, while only 28.21 percent employed Apache and 6.79 percent used Netscape/iPlanet. The Netcraft statistics, when considered overall, say clearly that while Apache is still favored for simple web hosting purposes, IIS is popular for web applications and particularly for hosting e-commerce sites.

- ENT Magazine (www.entmag.com) surveyed the sites of Fortune 500 companies in July 2000 and found that IIS was the most popular platform used with a 41 percent market share. Sun-Netscape Alliance's iPlanet server came in second with a 35 percent share, while Apache came in third with only a 15 percent share. Large companies like Compaq, Ford Motor Company, Phillip Morris, and many others use IIS exclusively as their web server platform, primarily because using IIS simplifies the process of developing large-scale web applications.

HISTORY OF IIS

Let's now take a closer look at how IIS evolved since its inception in 1995. This will help you understand the significance of some of the new features of IIS 6 and how this version can be considered a quantum leap forward from earlier versions. It's also an interesting story of how a large company develops a new product on-the-fly, and how advances come in fits and starts.

IIS 1

The initial version of IIS was released in February 1996 for the Microsoft Windows NT 3.51 Server platform. Microsoft migrated their own microsoft.com site to IIS 1 for testing purposes prior to commercially releasing the product. This is a little-known fact to most people who complain about bugs and instabilities in Microsoft products and say they feel like beta testers who have to pay for Microsoft software prior to testing it. The reality is that Microsoft tests all new software they develop on their own in-house servers prior to releasing it commercially, and since microsoft.com is one of the largest sites in the world, this means each version of IIS gets thorough in-house testing prior to shipping. In fact, many Microsoft employees end up working with release candidates of current Microsoft Windows platforms and Microsoft Office products prior to general product release, and thus end up being (sometimes unwillingly, I suspect) beta testers for new software!

Anyway, IIS 1 included support for three popular Internet protocols: Hypertext Transfer Protocol (HTTP) for delivering web content, File Transfer Protocol (FTP) for hosting FTP sites for uploading and downloading files, and Gopher (not an acronym) for hierarchical storage and retrieval of files. It also included support for the Common Gateway Interface (GCI), a UNIX programming environment for implementing dynamic features like forms on web pages using scripting languages like Perl. Everything worked fine, but performance was less than stellar, despite Microsoft's claim that it was the fastest web server around. Some of the features of IIS 1 included

- Internet Services Manager, a GUI tool for managing IIS (see Figure 1-1).
- Integration with the Windows NT platform (IIS was implemented as a collection of Windows NT services).

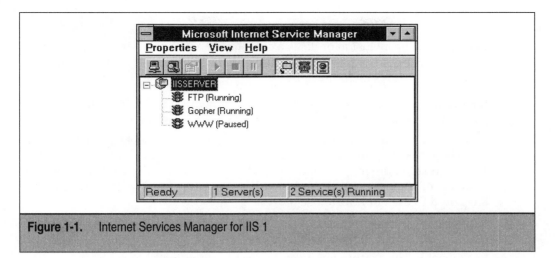

Figure 1-1.   Internet Services Manager for IIS 1

- Virtual servers, a method for hosting multiple websites on a single physical IIS machine. This feature was particularly useful for Internet Service Providers (ISPs) who needed to host thousands of sites for their clients, and it obviated the need of deploying a new physical server each time a new client wanted to set up a website.

- Virtual directories, a method for locating website content in a directory located outside of the web root directory (\wwwroot) or on a network file server instead of on the web server itself, which provides added security and flexibility to publish content easily.

- Internet Server API (ISAPI), an application programming interface that allowed dynamic web applications to be written using a high-level language like C++ and incorporated into static HTML pages.

- Internet Database Connector (IDC), Microsoft's first attempt at tying website content to back-end databases running Microsoft SQL Server or some other commercial database program like Oracle.

- Support for both Basic Authentication (an RFC-compliant authentication scheme compatible with UNIX platforms) and Windows NT LAN Manager (NTLM) Challenge/Response Authentication for extra security in a corporate intranet environment.

- Support for Secure Sockets Layer (SSL) version 1 protocol for building secure e-commerce sites.

- Text file and ODBC logging for troubleshooting problems and tracking traffic.

Not bad for a first try!

IIS 2

This release marked the inclusion of IIS as a component of the new Microsoft Windows NT 4 Server platform, with its new services and enhanced Windows 95–like GUI. IIS 2 added several new features including

- Integration of IIS into Windows NT Setup, allowing for IIS to be configured as part of the default installation of a Windows NT system.

- Support for host header names in order to allow multiple websites to be hosted on a single server using only a single IP address and the default TCP port 80. This is great feature for ISPs and web hosting providers who want to host large numbers of sites on a single machine—but unfortunately, in this early release, few could figure out how to use it!

- Support for both NCS- and CERN-style image maps.

- Enhanced logging features for logging both successful and failed HTTP transactions. This feature was useful in troubleshooting browser/server communication problems.

- HTTP byte range, a feature that allowed its supported client (Internet Explorer, naturally) to recover from interruptions and resume download.

- Enhanced syntax for Internet Data Query (IDQ) and Hypertext Extension (HTX), which were early file formats used for connecting IIS to back-end database engines to allow clients to issue queries against databases.

- HTML Administrator, an ISAPI application that supported administering IIS from a standard web browser (like Internet Explorer) as an alternative to the Internet Services Manager application in Administrative Tools. Using HTML Administrator, you could manage an IIS server remotely over the Internet using only a web browser. It was clunky, but it worked.

- Key Manager, a tool for generating key pairs for acquiring digital certificates to implement the Secure Sockets Layer (SSL) protocol. For history's sake, note that SSL was actually developed by Netscape!

- Index Server, a tool for creating content indexes to allow users to perform full-text queries of web content hosted on IIS.

IIS 3

Released in December 1996 (that's the third version released in less than a year!), Microsoft quickly touted version 3 of IIS as "40 percent faster than IIS 1" based on tests conducted by Shiloh Consulting and Haynes & Co. using SGI's WebStone performance tool. Other tests showed that it also outperformed Netscape's FastTrack Server and

Novell's NetWare Web Server, two other popular platforms used in enterprise environments.

Perhaps the most significant development with version 3 was the release of Microsoft's server-side web scripting engine called Active Server Pages (ASP). ASP enabled developers to build dynamic web applications that had all the functionality of standard client/server applications while using a standard web browser for its client interface. Together with Microsoft's powerful new ActiveX component technology (developed in reaction to the rising popularity of Sun's Java programming environment) and two new scripting languages, Visual Basic Scripting Edition (VBScript) and JScript, essentially a knock-off of Netscape's JavaScript, ASP was quickly embraced by the large Microsoft developer community as the wave of the future with regard to application development. ASP also supported connectivity with databases using the Open Database Connectivity (ODBC) standard and Microsoft's new ActiveX Data Objects (ADO) technology. Because of the ease of developing ASP-enabled websites using VBScript and ODBC compared with the difficulty of creating ISAPI applications using C++ and the limitations of older Common Gateway Interface (CGI) technology, ASP became (and still is) the dominant development platform for writing dynamic web applications for IIS.

Version 3 represented a quantum leap forward for IIS, from web server to web application development platform, and it was widely embraced by businesses for this purpose. Netcraft's statistics suggest that the popularity of IIS continued to rise after version 3 was released, while Apache began to plateau and other web servers declined in use. Other enhancements to Microsoft's web platform strategy that appeared in version 3 included

- Microsoft Transaction Server (MTS), for providing the underlying "plumbing" for distributed web applications

- Microsoft Visual InterDev (part of Microsoft Visual Studio), for developing web applications using Visual Basic, Visual J++, and Visual C++

- Microsoft NetShow, to provide streaming audio and video support for IIS

- Microsoft FrontPage 97 Server Extensions, to enable FrontPage to be used as a development tool for websites on IIS

Microsoft had gone from offering a bare-bones web server to a full web application development platform and associated tools in under a year. Not bad for a big company! Who says inertia is proportional to size?

At that time, Microsoft also expanded its line of Internet server products with the release of the initial versions of Microsoft Site Server (now Content Management Server) and Merchant Server (now Commerce Server), both of its BackOffice line of server products (now replaced by the newer .NET Enterprise Server family of products). However, these products are beyond the scope of this book.

IIS 4

Microsoft soon improved on version 3 with the Windows NT 4 Option Pack, released in March 1998. The Option Pack provided a number of enhancements both to the underlying Windows NT 4 Server operating system and to the IIS platform, including

- Version 4 of IIS itself
- Version 2 of Microsoft Transaction Server (MTS)
- Version 1 of Microsoft Message Queue Server (MSMQ), which provided the underlying plumbing for asynchronous communications within distributed applications on a network
- Version 2 of Index Server
- Version 1 of Microsoft Certificate Server, a tool for establishing a public key infrastructure (PKI) to support secure e-commerce
- Site Server Express 2, a tool for helping manage large amounts of web content on IIS machines
- Microsoft Internet Explorer 4.01, which helped Microsoft finally win the Browser Wars with Netscape
- Personal Web Server (PWS), a scaled-down version of IIS for the Microsoft Windows 95 platform
- Service Pack 3 for Windows NT 4
- Microsoft Management Console (MMC) version 1, Microsoft's first attempt at creating a single unified interface for administering all aspects of their Windows NT 4 Server platform (and later the basic administration interface for Windows 2000, Windows XP, and Windows .NET Server family)

IIS 4 marked a watershed in IIS development, with many administrators balking at the frequent upgrades and large numbers of new features they needed to cope with when deploying IIS. Many chose to stay with IIS 3 since it was stable and ran smoothly, rather than take the chance of upgrading to version 4 and seeing something break. Others saw the Option Pack enhancements as so many bells and whistles and also decided to stick with IIS 3. There were just too many service packs coming out of Redmond in the opinion of many people, though in fact all Microsoft was trying to do was make the Windows NT 4 platform more secure and reliable. Nevertheless, those who were forward-looking could see the writing on the wall and chose to upgrade, and in most cases this went smoothly enough.

Some of the enhancements that were rolled into version 4 included

- An entirely new version of Internet Service Manager, implemented as a series of snap-ins for the new Microsoft Management Console (MMC) interface. This was probably the biggest change from the point of view of IIS administration, as it meant learning an unfamiliar interface for performing familiar tasks.

- Implementation of the new HTTP 1.1 standard from the IETF, which made HTTP transfers more reliable and efficient.

- Upgrading SSL to the new version 3 standard for greater security and support for 128-bit encryption (where allowed).

- Use of MTS for developing transactional ASP applications that employed persistence to maintain state information across multiple HTTP requests. This allowed for much more complex web applications to be developed using ASP/IIS.

- Improved browser-based administration of IIS using an ASP application called HTML Administrator (HTMLA).

- The ability to manage certain aspects of IIS configuration by running scripts from the command line or desktop shortcuts. These scripts were typically written using JScript and executed using the new Windows Script Host (WSH).

- The metabase, a new binary file that was used instead of the Registry for storing IIS configuration information. The most common question most administrators had after installing IIS 4 was, "Where's the metabase, and how can I edit it directly?"

- Host headers that actually worked, enabling multiple websites to be hosted on a single IIS machine using a single IP address and the default TCP port 80 (host headers were introduced into version 2 of IIS but needed support for HTTP 1.1 to work effectively).

- Bare-bones support for two additional Internet standard protocols, Simple Mail Transport Protocol (SMTP), which was implemented in IIS 4 as an SMTP mail forwarder for use by ASP applications, and Network News Transport Protocol (NNTP), which forms the basis of USENET but was implemented in IIS 4 mainly to provide discussion group functionality for advanced websites.

There were various other enhancements as well, including a new Website Operators group for assigning users privileges for administering IIS, per-site bandwidth throttling (important in multihoming environments), configuration backup and rollback for greater reliability when IIS configurations were modified, W3C Extended Logging format (an industry standard finally adopted by Microsoft), the ability to run an ASP application in a separate memory space from the web server and from IIS itself (this helped ensure the stability of a web server running an unstable application), an improved Microsoft Virtual Machine to provide better Java support, a script debugger to facilitate debugging of ASP applications, domain blocking to restrict access to content based on domain or IP address, custom error messages for greater user usability, and so on.

IIS 5

Development of IIS on the Windows NT platform basically halted after the Option Pack was released (though several more service packs appeared for the platform to correct bugs and fix things that didn't work in IIS). Instead, the next development in the history of the platform was version 5, which was released as part of the new Windows 2000 Server operating system two years later. The biggest difference between versions 4 and 5 was the name change: previously IIS stood for "Internet Information Server" and was considered almost a separate server application in Windows NT (though in fact it was really just an optional component), but with Windows 2000 the acronym now represented "Internet Information Services," probably to indicate more clearly that Internet functionality was something that Microsoft had built into their new operating system from the ground up (just like Internet Explorer was supposed to be an "integrated" part of the operating system).

Apart from the name change, the most important enhancements in version 5 included

- A new application model called Pooled Process that allowed multiple web applications to run within a shared memory space separate from the In Process space of Inetinfo.exe

- CPU throttling, which allowed administrators to specify the share of CPU time that could be assigned to a site

- Integration with Windows 2000's Active Directory service, which provided greater security and the ability to delegate IIS administration at a more granular level than earlier versions

- New wizards to simplify the job of setting up and managing IIS, including permissions wizards for securing access to sites

- Support for Web Distributed Authoring and Versioning (WebDAV), an extension to HTTP 1.1 that allowed users to share documents over the Internet more easily

In addition, there were a few other enhancements, such as new ASP capabilities, support for the U.S. Government's Fortezza security architecture, enhancements in scalability, and so on. IIS 5 was clearly nothing revolutionary, but it did represent a polishing and fine-tuning of the product that led some to upgrade from earlier versions.

IIS 5.1

Before I get to version 6, which is what this book is all about, we'll briefly mention an interim release called IIS 5.1. This version is essentially a scaled-down and slightly enhanced version of IIS 5 and is available only on the Windows XP Professional desktop platform. It's a little hard to know why Microsoft released this version, as few people need a stripped-down web server on their desktop machine. Web developers using FrontPage 2002 are probably about the only ones who would use this version, but any real web production company would prefer tying their developers into a real IIS 5 server. Basically, IIS 5.1 on Windows XP is to IIS 6 on Windows Server 2003 as Personal Web Server (PWS) on Windows NT Workstation is to IIS 4 on Windows NT Server. In other words, IIS 5.1 is about as unnecessary for the Windows XP/ 2003 platform as PWS was for the Windows NT platform. For the sake of being complete, I should mention that Windows 2000 Professional also had a scaled-down version of IIS 5 included with it, which was unfortunately also called IIS 5.

FEATURES OF IIS 6

This brings us to the current incarnation of IIS, version 6, which is what the rest of this book is about. Having surveyed the evolution of IIS up to the present, let's now take a look at some of the exciting new features and enhancements that make version 6 a must-have upgrade for any serious Microsoft shop.

Improved Architecture

The biggest changes in IIS 6 are hidden from view under the hood of the product. These are changes in the basic architecture of how IIS serves out content in response to HTTP requests, and they have a significant impact on how IIS performs. In IIS 5 there was one main service called Inetinfo.exe, and web applications could either run In Process (together with Inetinfo.exe) or Out of Process (isolated from Inetinfo.exe and running in a separate memory space). In IIS 6 this architecture has been completely redesigned by moving all HTTP listening into the kernel for greater performance and reliability. Incoming HTTP requests are now handled by a kernel-mode component called Http.sys, which responds to each request by placing it into the appropriate queue for each website or application on IIS. Because of the isolation of Http.sys within the kernel, it is no longer possible for the failure of one web application to bring down other applications on the server. And because Http.sys runs in kernel mode, it can handle greater numbers of HTTP requests more efficiently than the previous architecture in IIS 5. I'll talk more about Http.sys and other aspects of the new IIS 6 architecture in the next chapter.

New Mode

Previous versions of IIS separated web applications into different memory pools, including In Process (runs within the context of the main Inetinfo.exe service), Out of Process (runs in isolation from Inetinfo.exe within the context of a helper dllhost.exe process), or Pooled Process (runs collectively as a group of applications within an isolated helper dllhost.exe process). With IIS 6, this distinction between in-process and out-of-process execution no longer applies. Instead, all user-developed application code is now run within isolated processes in a mode of operation called worker process isolation mode. In other words, all third-party application code is completely isolated from the core web server processes (such as Http.sys). As a result, the failure or crash of one web application cannot affect the operation of other applications on the server or corrupt any of the core IIS configuration information and bring down the server itself. In addition, multiple applications can be grouped together if needed into separate application pools, with each pool being serviced by a separate Http.sys queue. Worker process isolation mode also means that management of IIS applications is simplified, since sites can now be taken offline or brought online independently and can be modified or debugged without affecting other sites running on the server. This is a great feature in today's web development environment where application development cycles are measured in weeks instead of years, with the result that bugs are often never completely worked out of a program before the next release appears. I'll talk more about Worker Process Isolation Mode and application pools in Chapter 2 and in Chapter 8, "Configuring Applications."

Web Gardens

Just as IIS 6 allows multiple web applications to run within the same application pool (for example, applications that need to share information with each other), it also lets you configure multiple worker processes to service a single application pool. A worker process is a host process that contains the web service DLLs used to service the needs of a web application. The executable associated with a worker process is w3wp.exe, and it handles tasks like processing of HTTP requests forwarded from the kernel, loading and unloading ISAPI extensions and filters, performing authentication and authorization, andso on. Normally, each application pool has a single worker process assigned to it to service the needs of the applications within the pool, but IIS 6 also lets you configure an application pool to be serviced by multiple worker processes. It's sort of like a web farm where multiple physical web servers can respond to incoming HTTP requests, except here multiple worker processes respond to requests submitted to a single http.sys queue. The end result is reliability, because if one worker process becomes congested or fails, other processes take up the load and the responsiveness of the application is unaffected. I'll talk more about this feature in Chapters 2 and 8. Note that IIS 6 even allows you to assign worker processes to individual CPUs on SMP systems!

IIS 5 Compatibility

For applications that work well under IIS 5 but break when run within the new worker process isolation mode, IIS 6 gives you the option of switching to the old model of IIS 5 using an emulation called IIS 5 isolation mode. In this mode, the underlying architecture with kernel mode HTTP listening and response cache is still the same as IIS 6, but the user mode architecture changes to that of IIS 5 to ensure that applications developed for that platform still work in IIS 6.

New Metabase

The IIS metabase was the bane of administrators in earlier versions of this product. The metabase was designed to improve upon the Registry as a location for storing IIS configuration information. The Registry itself is a hierarchical structure that replaced the earlier System.ini and Win.ini files, which were plain text files in good old Windows 3.1. The problem with the metabase in IIS 4 and 5 was that it was a binary file that was not directly modifiable by administrators (even the Registry could be modified directly using Regedit.exe or Regedt32.exe). The reason for having a metabase at all was to speed up access to IIS configuration information by isolating this information from the Windows Registry. Searching the Registry on disk was too slow, and the Registry was often quite large and would have been unwieldy to load into memory just to have fast access to the IIS portion of it. So a hierarchical binary structure called the metabase was created and stored in the \system32\inetsrv directory, and this metabase.bin was then loaded by IIS into memory to give it fast access to its properties. To be fair, Microsoft did later provide a command-line tool called Mdutil for directly editing metabase properties, with the caveat that it was just as dangerous to do this as edit the Windows Registry by hand using Regedit. They also provided a GUI version of this tool called MetaEdit in the Windows 2000 Resource Kit.

Well, with IIS 6 we've come full circle with regard to the metabase: namely, it's a text file once again! Shades of Win.ini! The proprietary binary format of the IIS 4 and 5 metabase has been abandoned in favor of plain text files formatted using Extensible Markup Language (XML), the wave of the future as far as interprocess communications is concerned. This makes it easy to edit the metabase using tools as simple as Notepad (something you want to be careful about doing, however, because one slip up and your metabase is corrupted and your web server may not start). I'm assuming you can read native XML directly, of course—but perhaps in a few years, children will learn XML in kindergarten, right after they learn how to draw the letters of the alphabet!

There are other enhancements besides the basic format of the metabase:

- A metabase history feature that keeps track of all changes made to the metabase, creating a version history of different Metabase.xml files for your server. This is terrific in case you need to revert to a previous stable metabase configuration if you mess up your web server settings.

- The ability to edit the metabase while IIS is still running without having to stop and restart websites or services. This is cool.

- The ability to programmatically export and import branches of the metabase. This feature allows you to copy a directory, site, or entire server collection from one physical machine to another using the admin scripts included with IIS 6, Active Directory Services Interface (ADSI) scripts, or Windows Management Instrumentation (WMI) tools.

I'll talk more about the metabase and its new features in Chapter 18.

Enhanced Security

Lack of security has probably been the number one issue brought against the Microsoft Windows platform, and against IIS in particular. In part this was due to the high visibility of Microsoft, which made its products a tempting target for hackers and disaffectionados.

The reality is that IIS is probably the most secure web server platform around, simply because it has been hacked from this way through Sunday. The result is that most of its security vulnerabilities have been exposed and are well known and easily fixed using service packs and hot fixes available from Microsoft. Nevertheless, in one aspect of the security issue, Microsoft really did fall down: when you installed earlier versions of IIS out of the box it was basically "wide open" instead of "locked down." This meant every service was enabled and started, permissions were assigned their least restrictive values, and service accounts had high system privileges. The result was that when an inexperienced administrator set up IIS sites on a server, these sites were likely to be easily compromised or taken down by knowledgeable hackers. In response to this, Microsoft began to get serious about security, and in late 2001 they released a Security Toolkit on their website that contained some important additions to IIS 4 and 5— namely, the IIS Security Lockdown Wizard, a tool that implemented the security recommendations Microsoft previously published in its Security Checklists for these products, and UrlScan, an ISAPI filter that blocked malicious HTTP requests that attempted to destabilize IIS through buffer overflows and other programming tricks.

What's new with IIS 6 is that the functionality of the Lockdown Wizard has now been incorporated into the product in the form of a new feature called Web Service Extensions (WSE). Furthermore, IIS is now installed in a locked-down state instead of a wide-open configuration, with ASP and FrontPage extensions disabled, permissions set at high levels, no ISAPI extensions or filters installed, and sample content that consists only of harmless static HTML pages. In fact, you need to use WSE after you install IIS, not to lock it up further, but to open it up to the degree necessary to meet your needs. This is a big improvement, and Microsoft deserves kudos for finally taking this step because it flies in the face of their common goal of giving users "features, features, features!" That goal might be acceptable for end users and desktop applications, but the server room is something far different.

 SECURITY ALERT! We'll examine WSE in more detail later in Chapter 7, "Creating and Configuring Web Sites," and Chapter 10, "Securing IIS"; but if you've already installed and started playing with IIS 6 and find that the web applications you've migrated to this new version no longer work, try playing with the WSE node in IIS Manager. Out of the box, IIS 6 will only serve up static HTML files to clients; in order for ISAPI, CGI, or ASP.NET applications to work, these features must first be unlocked using the wizard.

There are other security improvements Microsoft made in IIS 6, including

- Configurable worker process identity, a method for ensuring that an administrator of one web application deployed on IIS is completely isolated from and cannot interfere with the configuration or operation of web applications managed by other administrators on the same server.

- Low privileges for IIS 6 worker processes, which by default use a special built-in identity called NetworkService as the context in which they run, instead of the more-powerful LocalSystem account used in previous versions of IIS.

- Digest Authentication, an authentication method that sends a hash value across the network and can work through firewalls and proxy servers. Integrated Windows Authentication is also still available (as are Basic Authentication and Anonymous Access) when less security is required.

- Integration with Microsoft .NET Passport to allow IIS to use Passport as an authentication method.

- The ability for cryptographic processing to be offloaded to a suitable cryptographic service provider (CSP) for strong security.

- The ability to configure the metabase to cause IIS to respond with an Access Denied message when requests for files with unknown file extensions are received.

- In an Active Directory environment, Group Policy can be used to block IIS from being installed in order to prevent users from deploying unauthorized web servers on a company's network.

I'll cover these various security features in more detail later in Chapter 10.

Improved Performance

I've already talked about how moving the HTTP listener into the kernel dramatically increases performance of IIS and allows more applications and websites to be hosted on a single machine (which means lower costs). IIS 6 includes other enhancements that also contribute to improved performance over earlier versions, including

- Large memory support for caching up to 64GB of data on 32-bit Intel platforms. Cached data can now be retrieved more quickly, and this boosts the performance of the web server.

- Advanced caching heuristics that determine when content (static or dynamic) should be cached and when it should be discarded. This includes caching of ASP templates (when an ASP file is processed, it is first compiled into an ASP template prior to execution). The most requested ASP templates are held in memory while others are persisted to disk.

- Web gardens (mentioned earlier) that can reduce blocking by binding worker processes to specific processors on SMP machines.

- Improved thread management to make more efficient user of concurrency when executing processor-bound requests.

- Improved allocation of resources, now allocated as required instead of being allocated during initialization.

- Compression of HTTP responses to improve performance on congested networks. This feature was first included in IIS 5 but only as a global ISAPI filter. In IIS 6, however, it can be configured at the server, site, directory, or even file level.

- Improved management of server resources for individual sites and application pools, including configurable connection limits and timeouts, bandwidth throttling, process accounting, memory recycling, and queue length limits.

The net result of all these performance enhancements is that a single IIS 6 machine can host thousands more sites than an earlier IIS 5 one could. This is especially good news for service providers like ISPs and web hosting companies, and it may give them just the reason they need to migrate their systems away from Apache. I'll cover these performance enhancements in Chapter 2, as well as Chapter 12.

Improved Management

In addition to being able to manage IIS using the Internet Services Manager snap-in, there are several other ways you can manage IIS 6 machines:

- A WMI provider is included to allow IIS configuration information stored in the metabase to be remotely accessed and manipulated using Windows Management Instrumentation (WMI). This complements the already-existing way of accomplishing this using Active Directory Services Interfaces (ADSI) in IIS 5.

- A collection of administration scripts written in VBScript are included, which allow administrators to manage IIS from the command line to create, delete, start, stop, and list web and FTP sites; create and delete virtual directories; export and import IIS configuration into a text file formatted with XML; back up and restore IIS configuration information; and so on.

- A brand new browser-based administration tool much superior in ease of use to the old HTMLA of earlier IIS versions (see Figure 1-2 for a peek at this new tool).

You can also administer IIS remotely using Terminal Services, which has been enhanced and improved in Windows Server 2003. I'll talk more about these various administration tools in Chapter 5, "Administering Standard/Enterprise Edition"; Chapter 6, "Administering Web Server Edition"; Chapter 11, "Working from the Command-Line"; and Chapter 12, "Performance Tuning and Monitoring."

Other Enhancements

Few changes were made to the FTP, SMTP, and NNTP services in this version, as IIS is really a web application platform. One change that's worth mentioning is FTP User Isolation, which isolates users' top-level FTP directories from each other, making them appear as if they are the root directory of the server. This helps prevent FTP users from

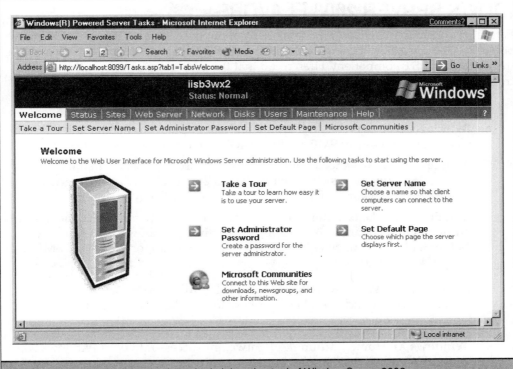

Figure 1-2.   The new browser-based administration tool of Window Server 2003.

nosing around in other peoples' home directories and enhances the security of IIS as an FTP server platform. Another FTP improvement is FTP Restart, which allows interrupted file transfers to be resumed where they left off.

Other enhancements in this version include:

- The ability to restart IIS without rebooting your machine (in fact, very few reboots are required in Windows Server 2003).

- Enhanced IIS W3SVC logging feature that supports Unicode and UTF-8 and not just ASCII.

- Improved custom HTTP error messages, which you can further customize if you desire.

- Improved ISAPI functionality, including Unicode support, custom errors, COM+ services, and so on. This is pretty heavy stuff and basically of interest only to high-level programmers.

WINDOWS SERVER 2003 FLAVORS

Before we conclude this chapter, I'll talk briefly about the different "flavors" of Windows Server 2003 because they impact to a degree the capabilities (and sometimes the features) of the platform's IIS 6 component. First, recall that the previous platform in this series from Microsoft, Windows 2000, came in four flavors:

- **Windows 2000 Professional**   The desktop version of the platform

- **Windows 2000 Server**   A departmental server platform that included IIS 5 and supported 4-way SMP and up to 4GB of memory

- **Windows 2000 Advanced Server**   An enterprise-level server that included everything Windows 2000 Server had, plus 2-node clustering and network load balancing; and it supported 8-way SMP and up to 8GB of memory.

- **Windows 2000 Datacenter Server**   A high-availability platform available only through OEM channels that included everything Windows 2000 Advanced Server had, plus 4-node failover clustering; and it supported 32-way SMP and up to 64GB of memory.

In Microsoft's new Windows XP/2003 Server family platform, which is the successor to the earlier Windows 2000 line, these four earlier products have now evolved into six new ones:

- **Windows XP Home Edition**   A lightweight successor to both Windows 98/ Me and Windows 2000 Professional.

- **Windows XP Professional Edition**   Replaces Windows 2000 Professional on the corporate desktop.

- **Windows Server 2003, Standard Edition**   Includes IIS 6 and is the natural successor to Windows 2000 Server as a basic departmental file, print, and application server. Standard Server supports four-way SMP and up to 4GB of memory.

- **Windows Server 2003, Enterprise Edition**   The natural descendant of Windows 2000 Advanced Server. Enterprise Server includes everything found in Standard plus 8-node Edition clustering and support for 8-way SMP and up to 32GB of memory (Windows 2000 Advanced Server supported only 8GB of memory).

- **Windows Server 2003, Datacenter Edition**   The super high-end mission-critical platform that you can only buy direct from an OEM. Features are similar to Windows 2000 Datacenter Server with advanced clustering support.

- **Windows Server 2003, Web Edition**   A.k.a. "Blade" (with apologies to Wesley Snipes), this is the new baby in the evolutionary tree and represents a radical (and refreshing) departure for Microsoft: it's a version of their server operating system specifically intended for use as a web server. the Web Edition is easy to deploy and manage and is intended primarily for running on rack-mountable "blade servers" where multiple physical servers, each the size of a peripheral card, are mounted inside a chassis for greater density of server resources. As a result of its intended use, the Web Edition lacks many of the features found on the other Windows Server 2003 family members, such as Internet Connection Sharing and Services for Macintosh. In addition, the Web Edition cannot be deployed as a domain controller, does not support clustering, and supports 2-way SMP and up to 2GB of memory, making it the most lightweight of the Windows Server 2003 family.

In addition, I should mention that two members of the family—namely, Enterprise and Datacenter Servers—are also available in 64-bit versions that run on Intel's new Itanium processor architecture. Enterprise Server supports up to 64GB of memory on Itanium, while Datacenter Server can go up to 512GB of memory on this platform. For a closer comparison of the features supported by the four Windows Server 2003 family members, see Table 1-1. The hardware requirements for these different platforms will be specified in detail in Chapter 3, "Planning Deployment."

NOTE   I've omitted coverage of Windows Datacenter Edition from Table 1-1 as this is an OEM product whose specifications depend in part on hardware support. Because it is unlikely that Datacenter Server would be used as a web application server (it is intended mainly as a back-end database server), it is not covered in this book.

Feature	Web	Standard	Enterprise
Clustering Technologies			
Cluster Service			Yes
Network Load Balancing (NLB)	Yes	Yes	Yes
Directory Services			
Active Directory	Partial	Yes	Yes
Metadirectory Services (MMS) Support			Yes
File and Print Services			
Distributed File System (Dfs)	Yes	Yes	Yes
Encrypting File System (EFS)	Yes	Yes	Yes
Fax Service		Yes	Yes
Removable and Remote Storage		Yes	Yes
Services for Macintosh		Yes	Yes

Table 1-1.   Differences Between Web, Standard, and Enterprise Editions

Feature	Web	Standard	Enterprise
Shadow Copy Restore	Yes	Yes	Yes
SharePoint Team Services		Yes	Yes
Management Services			
IntelliMirror	Yes	Yes	Yes
Remote Installation Services (RIS)		Yes	Yes
Remote OS Installation	Yes	Yes	Yes
Resultant Set of Policy (RSoP)	Yes	Yes	Yes
Windows Management Instrumentation (WMI) Command Line	Yes	Yes	Yes
Multimedia Services			
Windows Media Services		Yes	Yes
.NET Application Services			
ASP.NET	Yes	Yes	Yes
Enterprise UDDI Services		Yes	Yes
Internet Information Services 6	Yes	Yes	Yes
.NET Framework	Yes	Yes	Yes
Networking Services			
Internet Authentication Service (IAS)		Yes	Yes
Internet Connection Sharing (ICS)		Yes	Yes
IPv6 support	Yes	Yes	Yes
Network Bridge		Yes	Yes
Session Initiation Protocol (SIP)		Yes	Yes
Virtual Private Networking (VPN)	Partial	Yes	Yes
Scalability			
64-bit Support for Itanium Platform			Yes
Hot Add Memory			Possible
Non-Uniform Memory Access (NUMA)			Possible
Security Services			
Certificate Services, PKI, and Smart Cards	Partial	Yes	Yes
Internet Connection Firewall		Yes	Yes
Terminal Services			
Remote Desktop for Administration	Yes	Yes	Yes
Terminal Server		Yes	Yes
Terminal Server Session Directory			Yes

Table 1-1.   Differences Between Windows Server 2003 Web, Standard, and Enterprise Servers *(continued)*

Challenge

You are currently running your company's website on a combination of IIS 4 and 5 machines and are considering upgrading to IIS 6. What reasons can you give your boss to justify the cost of the upgrade? What benefits do you expect to achieve with IIS 6 over previous versions? How concerned are you about your legacy web applications running on the new platform? Which flavors of Windows Server 2003 would you utilize for running IIS 6?

CHECKLIST: FEATURES OF IIS 6

The following is a checklist for familiarizing yourself with the new features of version 6 of IIS. Read them through and check off which ones are important to you when considering migrating your existing IIS 4 and 5 servers to IIS 6:

- ☐ HTTP request handling has been moved to the kernel for greater reliability and better performance.

- ☐ User-developed code is completely isolated from core web server processes for improved stability and reliability.

- ☐ Web applications can be grouped together into multiple application pools for simplified administration and greater flexibility.

- ☐ Multiple worker processes can be assigned to the same application pool for improved reliability and greater responsiveness.

- ☐ A special IIS 5 compatibility mode can be used for older applications that have trouble running under the new IIS 6 architecture.

- ☐ A new XML metabase provides administrators with the flexibility of configuring IIS 6 by manually editing the metabase file using a text editor like Notepad, even while IIS is running.

- ☐ A metabase history feature allows you to revert to previous metabase versions easily to recover from problems arising from configuration changes.

- ☐ Portions of the metabase can be imported and exported easily, providing administrators with the flexibility of copying directories, sites, or entire servers from one physical machine to another.

- ☐ IIS 6 installs in a locked-down mode by default that serves up only static HTML files, and it must be opened up using the Web Service Extensions (WSE) node before web applications can work. This makes IIS 6 a more secure platform than earlier versions that were installed in a wide-open mode by default.

☐   Worker processes are assigned the NetworkService identity as their security context by default. This identity has few privileges in order to make web applications more secure.

☐   Worker process identities can be manually configured to completely isolate web applications on an IIS 6 machine, providing enhanced security and greater reliability.

☐   IIS 6 supports .NET Passport as an authentication method, providing greater flexibility for developing secure, scalable web applications.

☐   Improved caching heuristics and support for cache sizes up to 64GB allow both static and dynamic content to be cached by IIS, providing a significant performance boost over earlier versions.

☐   For greater flexibility, IIS 6 can be administered a variety of ways including MMC console, WMI, ADSI, Terminal Services, scripts, and improved browser-based administration.

☐   Fewer reboots are required after configuration changes, resulting in less downtime for mission-critical applications running on IIS.

☐   Improvements in ISAPI to allow developers to create better web applications running on IIS.

☐   A new "Blade" version of Windows Server 2003 has been designed for high-availability rack-mountable servers running in large datacenters.

CHAPTER 2

IIS 6 Architecture

In the previous chapter, we looked at the new features and enhancements Microsoft has incorporated into their latest version of IIS. These enhancements are intended to increase the security, reliability, scalability, performance, and manageability of the platform.

This chapter complements the previous one by providing an in-depth examination of the internal workings or architecture of IIS. Understanding this information is crucial to being able to effectively deploy, configure, manage, monitor, maintain, and troubleshoot IIS web applications in the real world.

THE EVOLUTION OF IIS ARCHITECTURE

The inner workings of IIS have evolved a great deal since the initial version IIS 1 was released in February 1996. In fact, the internals of IIS have undergone significant redesign several times. It will help you understand the enhancements and new features of the current version IIS 6 if we trace the evolution of IIS architecture from the early days to today. I touched on some of the new architectural features of IIS 6 in the previous chapter and will now cover them in detail.

Prior to IIS 4

The original architecture of IIS could best be described as monolithic: everything was based on *in-process execution*. In other words, a developer who wanted to write a web application would typically use Microsoft's Internet Services Application Programming Interface (ISAPI) and the C programming language to write DLLs that would add dynamic functionality to their website. These DLLs would then be loaded into the main IIS web server process (inetinfo.exe) and run within that process. This was very different from the original UNIX web server model, as you'll see next.

ISAPI was developed for IIS 1 as the Windows NT alternative to the Common Gateway Interface (CGI) of UNIX web servers. CGI uses an *out-of-process* execution model whereby a CGI application (typically a Perl script) runs within its own CGI process, separate from the web server process or Httpd daemon. While CGI works well enough for simple applications like form handlers (the code that handles information submitted from a form on a web page), performance is usually poor because each time a CGI application is invoked, a new instance of the CGI application is started on the web server. So, if a site with a form is experiencing heavy traffic, it is possible that a dozen or more instances of the same CGI process might be simultaneously running on the server, each consuming its own memory resources. The process of creating and destroying CGI processes also consumes processor and memory resources, further degrading performance and limiting CGI's ability to scale.

Because CGI scaled so poorly, Microsoft developed the ISAPI approach based on in-process execution as an alternative. In-process means that an ISAPI DLL runs within the main web server process inetinfo.exe, not within its own separate process as in the CGI model. Like CGI, these ISAPI DLLs can be loaded into memory when needed and unloaded when no longer required. Unlike CGI, however, a single ISAPI DLL can satisfy requests from multiple clients simultaneously (in the CGI model, a new CGI process must be started to handle each client request). This means that ISAPI applications are more scalable because they use memory more efficiently than CGI does. Another advantage is that the overhead of constantly switching between processes (a problem with the CGI model) is eliminated, because IIS also allowed ISAPI DLLs to be loaded into memory at server runtime.

On the whole, ISAPI was a terrific idea and made IIS a powerful platform on which to develop dynamic web applications. For example, ISAPI filters could be used to preprocess HTTP requests from web browser clients to perform functions such as customized authentication, access control, and logging. An ISAPI filter is an ISAPI DLL that receives an HTTP request, processes it in some fashion, and then forwards it to the World Wide Web Publishing Service (WWW Service) for further action. ISAPI filters could also be used to post-process HTTP responses received from the WWW Service before they are returned to the browser client. Alternatively, ISAPI applications could be written to enable database lookups from web pages. In this scenario, the client sends an HTTP request that's received by the WWW Service and passed to the ISAPI application. The application then uses the Internet Database Connector (IDC) to issue a query against the database. It receives a response and forwards this response to the WWW Service, which returns the result to the client (the IDC is now legacy technology, having been replaced by ADO and other technologies). See Figure 2-1 for an illustration of how ISAPI worked in early versions of IIS.

NOTE   ISAPI applications were often called ISAPI extensions because they "extended" the functionality of the WWW Service, making IIS a more powerful platform than one that simply served up static HTML pages. IIS also supported the CGI model used by UNIX to make it easier for developers to port web applications written with Perl scripts from Apache to IIS. However, Microsoft recommended using ISAPI wherever possible because of its greater scalability and better performance. IIS 2 also included another programming model called server-side includes, which supported only the #INCLUDE directive and not #EXEC (this is rarely used now so we won't discuss it here).

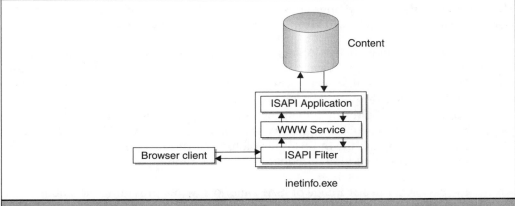

Figure 2-1.   The in-process execution model of IIS 1, 2, and 3.

This all sounded great in theory, but in practice ISAPI was difficult to use because it generally required C programming expertise to develop the appropriate DLLs. (By contrast, Perl, used in CGI programming, is an interpreted scripting language and is much easier to learn than C.) Another, more serious disadvantage was that one malfunctioning ISAPI DLL could bring down the entire web server and require a reboot to correct. This was particularly frustrating for developers, as C programs are often difficult to debug, and there was no way of isolating a buggy application from other ISAPI applications running on the server.

Microsoft then introduced a powerful new model for developing dynamic web applications with IIS 3. This new model was called Active Server Pages (ASP) and involved combining ActiveX scripts with ActiveX server components to create powerful web applications using scripting languages like Visual Basic Scripting Edition (VBScript) and JScript (an offshoot of Netscape's JavaScript). In fact, both these scripting languages were developed by Microsoft primarily for use in ASP on IIS 3, and the resulting IIS/ASP combination rapidly soared in popularity. It remains the most popular way of developing web applications for IIS today. VBScript in particular enabled Microsoft to leverage the talent of millions of Visual Basic programmers around the world, giving them a brand new platform to develop applications for: the Internet.

The architecture of IIS remained essentially unchanged in version 3 with the introduction of ASP, because ASP itself was implemented as an ISAPI extension called Asp.dll. This meant, however, that ASP on IIS 3 suffered the same problems that other ISAPI applications experienced, which was that one malfunctioning ASP application could bring down the entire server. While the in-process execution model of IIS 3 increased performance of web applications, it decreased reliability because ASP applications also ran within the same inetinfo.exe process as the WWW Service. However, this was about to change with version 4 of IIS.

IIS 4

IIS 4 was the first version of IIS to undergo a significant change in its internal architecture. There were two significant changes that occurred in IIS 4, which involved both how web applications ran and how IIS configuration information was stored:

- Web applications such as ASP scripts and ISAPI extensions could now optionally be run out-of-process from the main web server process inetinfo.exe. With IIS 4, you could specify which applications should be loaded in-process with inetinfo.exe and run in the same process as the WWW Service, and which applications should run in their own separate processes (see Figure 2-2). This new feature was known as *process isolation* and could be used to enhance the stability and reliability of IIS applications because an application running out-of-process could fail without affecting the running of other in-process applications on the server. Essentially, process isolation allowed IIS to maintain the performance advantage of ISAPI and ASP while providing the stability of GGI. I'll talk more about process isolation in a moment.

- Most IIS configuration settings were moved from the Windows Registry where they were in previous versions to a new memory-resident data store called the *metabase*. The reason for this was performance: the metabase was faster, more flexible, and more easily expanded than the Registry. The only IIS configuration settings not migrated to the metabase were those Registry keys involved in starting up IIS services, plus a few others for maintaining backward compatibility with earlier versions of IIS. I'll talk more about the metabase in Chapter 14, "Working with the Metabase."

Process Isolation

The ability of IIS 4 to run applications out-of-process offered several advantages compared to the monolithic in-process execution model of previous versions:

- An out-of-process application that crashed had no effect on other applications running on the server. This was different from the monolithic architecture of earlier versions where all applications ran in-process with the main IIS process, and the crash of one application meant all applications went down on the server.

- An out-of-process application could be stopped and restarted independent of other applications on the server without affecting the other applications. This simplified the task of application maintenance on IIS. For example, if a component of an isolated web application needed to be updated, the application could be stopped, upgraded, and restarted without affecting anything else running on the server. This was great for administrators who needed to upgrade web applications with as little downtime as possible.

- An out-of-process application could be configured to restart automatically after it failed. If an in-process application failed, the entire web server was down until inetinfo.exe could be restarted or the server rebooted.

The downside of process isolation was that out-of-process applications tended to run much more slowly than in-process ones. This meant that process isolation was mainly suited toward testing and debugging applications on IIS. Once they were bug-free, they could be moved in-process for better performance. Another disadvantage was that

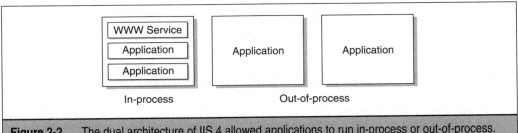

Figure 2-2.   The dual architecture of IIS 4 allowed applications to run in-process or out-of-process.

out-of-process applications could not access IIS metabase properties using built-in IIS admin objects (this could be worked around but was not recommended for security reasons). Finally, out-of-process applications consume more memory resources than in-process ones. Every ASP application running in its own process requires resources to run; and if you needed to run a dozen of them on a single machine, you would need a very large machine!

NOTE Process isolation on IIS 4 was a feature of ISAPI *applications*, which included ASP applications. It was not a feature of ISAPI *filters*, however, as these could only be run in-process.

MTS and WAM

The ability to run web applications out-of-process within their own separate memory space was made possible because of the integration of Microsoft Transaction Server (MTS) into the IIS 4 architecture. MTS worked as a middle layer that provided automatic thread and process management for IIS components. A component of MTS called the Web Application Manager (WAM) was responsible for enabling IIS applications to run out-of-process. The WAM was essentially a COM wrapper that could be used as a container for ISAPI functionality. In other words, web applications like ISAPI extensions and ASP pages were wrapped in WAM objects, which themselves were hosted by the MTS runtime environment and registered as COM objects by MTS. The WAM object encapsulated all the ISAPI functionality of the application, enabling the appropriate ISAPI DLL to be located and loaded when required (each IIS application had its corresponding WAM object in one-to-one fashion).

The MTS Executive (mtxex.dll) ultimately hosted all of the web applications on the IIS machine, whether they ran in-process (within inetinfo.exe) or out-of-process (within an MTS proxy process called mtx.exe spawned by the IWAM_*computername* account). The WAM Director received each incoming HTTP request and forwarded it to the appropriate MTS package, as shown in Figure 2-3.

By default, on IIS 4 all applications were initially configured to run as in-process applications. Once an application was installed on the server it could be configured to run out-of-process by selecting the Run In Separate Memory Space (Isolated Process) check box on the properties sheet for the application's virtual directory (see Figure 2-4). Selecting this check box caused IIS to automatically create a new MTS package for this application and run it within the proxy mtx.exe process.

NOTE Process isolation in IIS 4 applied to dynamic web content (ISAPI extensions or ASP pages) only. All static web content was serviced by the core inetinfo.exe web server process, regardless of what application it was a part of.

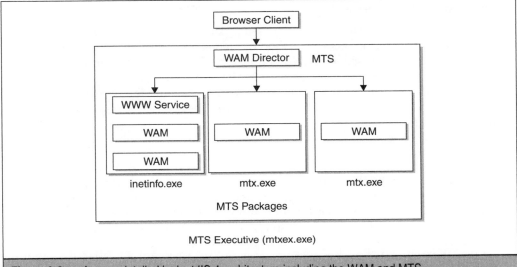

Figure 2-3. A more-detailed look at IIS 4 architecture including the WAM and MTS

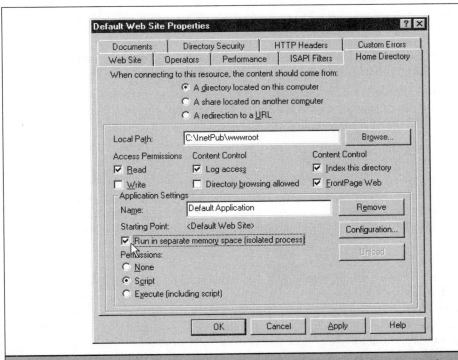

Figure 2-4. Configuring an IIS 4 application to run out-of-process within its own isolated memory space

IIS Admin Service

I should mention here one additional under-the-hood component of IIS 4, the IIS Admin Service. This service acted as a kind of manager of all other IIS services, and these services, like the World Wide Web Publishing Service (WWW Service or W3SVC, a component of inetinfo.exe), FTP Service, SMTP Service, and NNTP Service all are dependent on the IIS Admin Service. In other words, stopping the IIS Admin Service stops all these other services as well. The IIS Admin Service is also responsible for maintaining the metabase.

IIS 5

Microsoft again changed the architecture of IIS in version 5. The reason was that the process isolation feature of IIS 4 had an additional limitation I haven't mentioned: an out-of-process web application could not communicate with any other applications on the same machine. Unfortunately, certain types of applications needed to cooperate with each other, and this was impossible in the IIS 4 model unless such applications ran within the core web server process (inetinfo.exe), which of course affected stability and reliability of the server. Clearly, something different was needed, and the architecture of IIS was modified to meet this need.

Whereas IIS 4 offered only two levels of application protection (in-process and out-of-process), IIS 5 was designed to provide three different levels of application protection:

- **Low (IIS Process)**   The application runs in-process as part of the core web server process (inetinfo.exe) as in the original monolithic architecture of IIS versions 1–3.

- **Medium (Pooled)**   The application runs out-of-process from inetinfo.exe as a separate *pooled process*, that is, as one of several applications running within a new COM+ host process called dllhost.exe.

- **High (Isolated)**   The application runs out-of-process alone within its own isolated dllhost.exe host process.

NOTE   The newer COM+ architecture of Windows 2000 means that all out-of-process IIS 5 execution takes place within surrogate dllhost.exe processes instead of the mtx.exe proxy processes used in MTS 2 on IIS 4. These dllhost.exe processes are spawned by the same IWAM_*computername* account used in IIS 4.

The Medium (Pooled) option was new to IIS 5, and it allowed multiple ISAPI and ASP applications to run within a shared memory space for greater cooperative interaction between them. Note that the Medium and High options use out-of-process execution while Low is in-process. The advantage of this new architecture was that pooled out-of-process applications run with better performance than isolated out-of-process applications. Also, while a single IIS machine could typically host only a dozen or so isolated applications (because of the huge memory requirements), it could host hundreds or even thousands of pooled ones. Figure 2-5 shows the revised architecture of this version 5 of IIS.

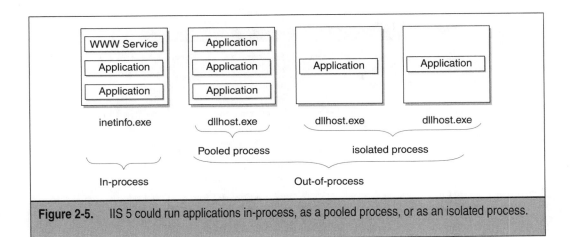

Figure 2-5.   IIS 5 could run applications in-process, as a pooled process, or as an isolated process.

NOTE   An obvious disadvantage of running thousands of sites or applications within a single pooled process is that if one application crashes, the entire pool goes down. Microsoft anticipated this problem, however, and IIS 5 was structured so that when the pool went down, it automatically restarted when the next request sent to any application in the pool was received. Windows 2000 also included a new feature called the Service Control Manager (SCM) that provided automatic recovery options for services that failed, allowing IIS services to be restarted without user intervention when a crash occurred. For example, the IIS Admin Service can be configured to restart or a reboot can occur should the service fail. Finally, administrators could manually run a command-line utility called iisreset.exe to restart IIS 5 after a crash. With all these various options, IIS 5 was certainly a more robust and reliable platform for web application development than previous versions!

Medium (Pooled) was the default setting for all applications on IIS 5, which meant by default the web server process inetinfo.exe ran by itself, serving up static content while all dynamic web applications ran within the same pooled process. When a new application was created, it was automatically assigned to this pool and could be moved to an isolated process or made part of the core web server process by selecting the Application Protection list box on the properties sheet for the application's virtual directory (see Figure 2-6). Note that this could only be set at the application's starting-point directory (you needed to define the application starting point first).

The main problem with the IIS 5 architecture was the issue of performance. Applications running with Low (IIS Process) application protection ran in-process with inetinfo.exe and performed well, but led to instability because a failed application could bring down the core web server process. For greater reliability, either Medium (Pooled) or High (Isolated) application protection could be used, but this often led to a performance penalty, particularly when an out-of-process web application had to retrieve an ISAPI server variable from the core inetinfo.exe process. To accomplish this, data marshalling had to be used, an inherently slow procedure that employed RPCs over COM between the WAM process and inetinfo.exe. As you'll see shortly, the new architecture of IIS 6 eliminates this bottleneck with the result that out-of-process applications run much quicker on IIS 6 than they did on IIS 5.

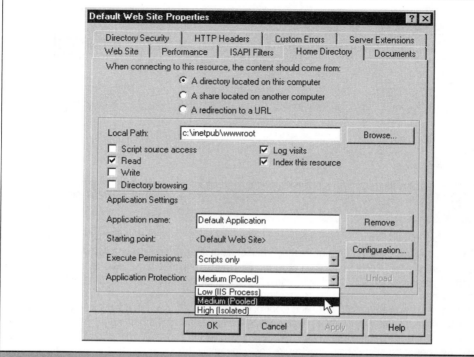

Figure 2-6. Selecting the Application Protection level in IIS 5

NOTE Microsoft recommended in IIS 5 that inetinfo.exe be run as its own separate process with no applications configured in it. This way a single application failure can't bring down the entire web server; even if all dynamic applications crash, the server can still serve up static HTML content. Applications that are either under development or mission-critical should be run as isolated processes, while all remaining applications can be run within the pooled process for greater performance. Microsoft further recommends that the number of isolated applications be limited to ten or less to reduce the impact on web server performance these applications have.

IIS 6 CORE COMPONENTS

Now that we've reviewed in detail how the architecture of IIS has evolved from versions 1 through 5, it's time to move on and examine the inner workings of version 6, the latest incarnation of IIS. I'll do this by first providing an overview of the differences between version 6 and the previous version 5, and then going into detail about the components and operation of version 6.

Differences from IIS 5

First, here is a summary of the key differences between IIS 6 and earlier versions:

- Handling of HTTP requests has been moved from the main inetinfo.exe process directly into the kernel for better performance.

- Two new application isolation models are supported: *worker process isolation mode* (totally new), which fully isolates all user-developed application code from the core IIS services, and *IIS 5 isolation mode*, which is provided for backward compatibility with older applications designed for IIS 5.

- Support for multiple application pools is now included, with each pool being independently configurable.

- The WWW Service (W3SVC) has been restructured to include a new configuration and process management portion called the Web Administration Service (WAS).

The IIS 6 architecture also supports other enhanced features including processor affinity, health monitoring, web gardens, demand start, idle timeout, rapid-fail protection, recycling of worker processes, XML metabase, and so on. Many of these features are discussed in the following sections, while some (like the XML metabase) are explained elsewhere in this book.

Let's now look at each of these new features in detail, building your knowledge of the IIS 6 architecture block by block.

Kernel Mode HTTP Listener (http.sys)

Earlier versions of IIS had their architecture built around the core inetinfo.exe process. This process contained the IIS Admin Services plus four protocol services dependent upon IIS Admin:

- W3SVC, the World Wide Web Publishing Service
- MSFTPSVC, the FTP Publishing Service
- NNTPSVC, the Microsoft NNTP Service
- SMTPSVC, the Microsoft SMTP Service

Incoming HTTP requests were received by the IIS Admin Service and handed off to either

- W3SVC, if the request was for either static HTML content or dynamic content from a web application running in-process (within inetinfo.exe).

- A dllhost.exe helper process, if the request was for dynamic content from a web application running out-of-process, either as an isolated process in IIS 4 and 5 or as a pooled process in IIS 5.

In other words, the core inetinfo.exe process functioned as

- **Listener**   Waiting for incoming HTTP requests
- **Router**   Forwarding such requests to the appropriate protocol service or helper process

The problem with earlier versions of IIS was that inetinfo.exe, which handled these two functions, ran as a pageable user mode process. The term *user mode* is one of two processor modes in which code can execute; the other is *kernel mode*. Because user mode processes can contain user-developed code, which may be buggy, a single misbehaving web application could bring inetinfo.exe down and thus prevent incoming HTTP requests from being received and handled.

To overcome this problem, Microsoft has moved the HTTP listening and routing functions of IIS 6 from the user mode inetinfo.exe process to a kernel mode process called the *Kernel Mode HTTP Listener*. This new component is implemented as a kernel mode device driver called http.sys that is part of the TCP/IP networking subsystem of Windows Server 2003. Architecturally, http.sys sits as a network driver on top of TCP and listens for HTTP requests that want to connect to IP addresses and port numbers used by websites running on IIS. In other words, http.sys is not really part of IIS at all, it's part of the TCP/IP stack of Windows Server 2003. Its main purpose is to be used by IIS for handling HTTP requests, but it also fulfills several other functions including caching HTTP responses in kernel mode, managing TCP connections, implementing connection limits and time-outs, managing bandwidth throttling, and handling text-based logging for the WWW Publishing service.

Modifying the architecture of IIS in this fashion has several significant benefits:

- IIS performance is improved because kernel mode processes execute with a higher level of priority than user mode processes. In essence, http.sys acts to tune IIS throughput by speeding up response to incoming HTTP requests.

- IIS reliability is improved because http.sys contains no user-developed code and thus cannot be crashed by a buggy web application.

- IIS responsiveness is improved because http.sys can continue to receive and queue HTTP requests even when the applications for which it is queuing these requests crashes.

Kernel Vs. User Mode

Kernel mode and user mode refer to the two levels of privilege in which routines can run on the Windows Server 2003 platform. Applications running in kernel mode have full access to hardware and to system data, while those running in user mode have nonprivileged access to system data and no direct hardware access. Kernel mode applications are generally components of the operating system itself, and they run in the highly privileged ring 0 mode of the Intel x86 processor architecture. User mode applications include operating system components that display a user interface as well as programs developed by users, and they run in the less-privileged ring 3 mode. IIS includes components running in both kernel and user mode.

http.sys and Paging

The fact that inetinfo.exe is pageable means that having insufficient physical memory (RAM) on an IIS machine can significantly affect performance. If there is insufficient RAM, IIS may page part of inetinfo.exe to disk, which can severely affect the response of web applications. In IIS 6, insufficient memory can result in http.sys queues filling up and requests being dropped, so ensure that your IIS machines have enough RAM to keep the entire inetinfo.exe process in memory at all times. Use the Performance console to monitor the size of the working set and number of page faults per second for inetinfo.exe to determine whether you have enough RAM installed.

In addition to listening for and parsing incoming HTTP requests and routing (forwarding) them to the appropriate worker process for further processing, http.sys does a few other important things:

- It queues such requests for processing by IIS. Each application pool in IIS has a corresponding in-memory *kernel mode queue* associated with it, and http.sys routes requests to these queues where they can wait for user mode worker processes to service these requests. I'll talk more about worker processes and application pools in the sections "Worker Processes" and "Application Pools," later in this chapter.

- It manages all TCP connections, both setup and tear-down, for incoming HTTP requests and outgoing HTTP responses.

- It caches HTTP responses using a kernel mode cache so that frequently requested content can be served without needing to switch from kernel mode to user mode and invoke inetinfo.exe. http.sys can cache HTTP responses for both static and dynamic content. Kernel mode caching is discussed further later in this chapter.

- It handles other IIS functions previously performed by inetinfo.exe, including IIS logging services and quality of service (QoS) functions like bandwidth throttling, connection limits, and connection timeouts. IIS logging is discussed in more detail in the section "Logging," later in this chapter.

Note that http.sys does not actually process HTTP requests; it simply routes these requests to the appropriate IIS worker process, receives HTTP responses from these processes, and forwards them back to the requesting client. The only exception to this is if the response can be retrieved from its internal kernel mode cache, in which case http.sys appears to be "processing" the request and returning a response.

Let's now look at this kernel mode queuing by http.sys in a bit more detail.

CAUTION   Be careful running third-party network applications on IIS machines if these applications make use of the same port numbers used by IIS. Such third-party applications (such as another web server) would likely have their own HTTP parsers and would not utilize http.sys for this purpose, and the result will be a conflict that will prevent either IIS 6 or the third-party application from starting and running properly. This conflict will occur even if IIS and the application use different IP addresses and server bindings. It's the conflicting port numbers that affect this—IIS bindings cannot be restricted to a single IP address. However, this problem will not arise if IIS and the application utilize different port numbers.

Kernel Mode Queuing

Kernel mode queuing will continue even if the web applications that HTTP requests are being queued for crashes. That's really the purpose of queuing, of course: to allow requests to be collected until they can be serviced. For example, a print job is queued (spooled) so that if the printer runs out of paper, the job can be held until the situation is corrected. With IIS 6, this queuing of HTTP requests will continue until each queue is full (the size of these queues can be configured by the administrator). Each application pool (pool of web applications serviced by a dllhost.exe process) has its own separate queue, and http.sys routes incoming requests to the appropriate pool (see Figure 2-7). The advantage of these kernel mode queues is that pending HTTP requests are not lost when a web application crashes on IIS 6, and normally IIS 6 will recover and restart the application so queued requests will not be lost (the client may not even notice that the application crashed, just that it took a little longer to respond than normal).

NOTE   If the core IIS service inetinfo.exe crashes, queuing of HTTP requests stops until the service is restarted. If a pooled dllhost.exe process crashes, however, queuing continues for that pool and IIS automatically restarts the application pool.

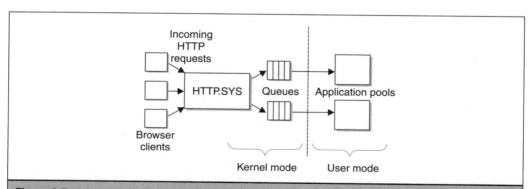

Figure 2-7.   http.sys forwards incoming HTTP requests to a queue to await processing by an application pool.

IIS Admin Service

If the HTTP listening and routing functions have been removed from the main IIS process inetinfo.exe in IIS 6, what functions still remain for this process? In previous versions, inetinfo.exe has contained both the IIS Admin Service and protocol services like the WWW and FTP Services. But with IIS 6, this model has changed: the IIS Admin Service now handles everything IIS does that is *not* connected with the Web. In other words, in IIS 6 the IIS Admin Service is responsible for FTP, NNTP, and SMTP, but not HTTP. When you create an FTP site on IIS 6, the IIS Admin Service handles the configuration and operation of that site. But if you create a website, a different service called the Web Administration Service (WAS) is employed instead of IIS Admin.

An important consequence of the fact that the IIS Admin Service is no longer directly associated with the WWW service in IIS 6 is that *in-process web applications are no longer allowed*. Remember that in IIS 5 you could run web applications either in-process (within inetinfo.exe, which hosts the IIS Admin Service) or out-of-process (either as a singled pooled process or multiple isolated processes, both running within a dllhost.exe proxy process). Well, in IIS 6 things have changed: web applications can no longer run in-process, that is, in the same memory space as inetinfo.exe. All web applications instead now run out-of-process as pooled processes called application pools. Actually, to be more correct, IIS 6 usually runs in this fashion, but as you'll see there is an exception when IIS 6 is run in a special mode called *IIS 5 isolation mode*. We'll talk more about the two IIS 6 modes in the section entitled "IIS 6 Application Modes" later in this chapter.

TIP   Despite the fact that in IIS 6 the IIS Admin Service no longer manages web applications directly, stopping the IIS Admin Service (either using the Services console or by using **net stop iisadmin** from the command line) also stops the WWW Service and thus all web applications on the machine.

Services Console

You can see which processes are associated with each IIS protocol by using the Services console in Administrative tools. Open the Services console and double-click IIS Admin to open its properties sheet, and you'll see that the executable associated with this service is inetinfo.exe, which resides in the System32\inetsrv\ directory. Do the same with the FTP Publishing Service, and you'll see that the associated executable is again inetinfo.exe. The same is true for the Network News Transfer Protocol (NNTP) and Simple Mail Transfer Protocol (SMTP) Services. But if you open the properties sheet of the World Wide Web Publishing Service, you'll see that the corresponding executable is svchost.exe instead. svchost.exe was introduced in Windows 2000 and Windows XP as a generic host process for those kinds of services that run from dynamic link libraries (DLLs) instead of from executable files. In the case of the WWW Service, the associated executable is listed as svchost -k iissvcs. Here iissvcs indirectly identifies the DLL that runs the WWW Publishing Service, as you'll see in the next section.

NOTE The IIS Admin Service also has another function: managing the memory-resident IIS metabase, the XML file that contains IIS configuration information for the machine. I'll talk more about the metabase later in Chapter 14.

Web Administration Service (WAS)

If the IIS Admin Service (which lives within inetinfo.exe) is no longer responsible for the creation and operation of websites on IIS 6, which service handles this function? The answer is the *Web Administration Service (WAS)*, a new component in IIS 6. This new service has two components:

- **Configuration Manager**   Responsible for interacting with the metabase to store or retrieve website configuration information when needed. It is also responsible for initializing the namespace routing table for the Kernel Mode HTTP Listener (http.sys) at startup—it creates one entry in the http.sys routing table for each application pool so queued HTTP requests can be routed to the appropriate pool. Also, as new pools are created for new web applications, the WAS Configuration Manager notifies http.sys to update its routing table accordingly. http.sys needs this information so that if an application fails, it can be restarted; and if an application pool requires an additional worker process to handle the load, it can create one on demand.

- **Application Pool Manager**   Responsible for managing the worker processes associated with IIS application pools. These include starting, stopping, restarting, and recycling worker processes, and monitoring their health and maintaining their configuration and how they interact with their kernel mode queue associated with http.sys.

The WAS is an essential component of the WWW Publishing Service (W3SVC) and is implemented, like the IIS Admin Service, in user mode. WAS is not responsible for running any user-developed code, however, such as a web application. Instead, web applications are run within separate processes called worker processes, which I'll discuss next.

As I mentioned in the Note in the preceding section, unlike the IIS Admin Service, which runs as an executable (inetinfo.exe), the WAS (and hence W3SVC itself) runs instead as a DLL within a host process called svchost.exe. You saw earlier that the associated executable for the WWW Service was svchost.exe -k iissvcs and that the actual DLL for the WAS could be determined from this parameter iissvcs. You can do this by examining the Registry. Select the following key:

HKLM\Software\Microsoft\WindowsNT\CurrentVersion\Svchost

The values under this key show the names of the various groups of services that can run within svchost.exe host processes on Windows Server 2003. (If you open Task Manager and select the Processes tab, you may see several instances of svchost.exe running at any given time, where each instance represents a service or group of services that are run as DLLs instead of executables.) Find the value named iissvcs and note that the data for this value reads w3svc. Now go to the following key:

HKLM\System\CurrentControlSet\Services\W3SVC

Select the Parameters key under this and open the value named ServiceDLL. The data for this value is as follows:

%systemroot%\System32\inetsrv\iisw3adm.dll

You've discovered that the DLL for the WAS is named iisw3adm.dll and is located in the \inetsrv directory, where inetinfo.exe is also found. For more information on svchost.exe, see Knowledge Base article 314056 on support.microsoft.com.

Worker Processes

I mentioned that the WAS is responsible for managing worker processes and that worker processes are associated with application pools on IIS 6, but I haven't explained either of these terms yet. I'll do that now.

In IIS 6, all user-developed application code runs in special user mode processes called *worker processes*. These worker processes act as host processes within which user-developed code such as ASP applications can run. They are called "worker processes" because their job (work) is to process user requests received from kernel mode http.sys queues and return the results (either a static or dynamic page) to the user (again via http.sys).

The executable w3wp.exe implements an instance of a worker process, and IIS 6 typically has multiple worker processes running at any given moment, each servicing different applications or pools of applications. A worker process can host ISAPI applications and filters, ASP applications, CGI applications, and static content. ISAPI filters and extensions are loaded into w3wp.exe via a web service DLL, which also handles authentication and authorization for applications running within the worker process.

NOTE   While an IIS 5 pooled process or isolated process ran within a host process called dllhost.exe, the architecture in IIS 6 uses the executable w3wp.exe as the host process for running worker processes.

Worker processes are themselves controlled by the WAS, which I just discussed. The WAS manages the health of worker processes and can restart or recycle them when needed. This "health monitoring" feature of IIS 6 works by having the WAS periodically ping each worker process to determine whether they are active (can respond to the ping) or blocked (either crashed or too busy to respond). When a worker process becomes blocked, the WAS automatically terminates the worker process and starts a new one to replace it. This might happen, for example, if an ISAPI filter within the worker process causes a memory access violation, causing the worker process to crash. Should this happen, the WAS automatically starts a new worker process to replace the failed one. This is certainly better than the old IIS 5 model, where ISAPI filters typically ran in-process within inetinfo.exe and their failure resulted in IIS going down completely.

TIP   When the health monitoring system of IIS 6 detects a problem with a worker process, it can also be configured to log an event in Event Viewer so the administrator can have a record of the occurrence.

The purpose of these worker processes is thus to ensure the greatest possible reliability for IIS 6 as a web application hosting platform. This is accomplished by enabling user-developed applications to be separated both from each other via process boundaries and from core IIS code such as inetinfo.exe and http.sys. Application isolation is ensured because each worker process can service only a single application pool, and each worker process has its own corresponding kernel mode queue within http.sys.

The role of worker processes in this is illustrated in Figure 2-8. An incoming HTTP request is received by http.sys and queued in kernel mode until the worker process for the application called can pull the request from the queue and process it. The results are returned by the worker process to http.sys, which caches the response (in case it is requested again shortly) and sends it to the requesting client.

Processor Affinity

An additional feature of worker processes is that on symmetric multiprocessing (SMP) machines an individual worker process can be assigned to a specific CPU for processing. This feature is known as *processor affinity* and makes IIS 6 a powerful platform for running large mission-critical web database applications. Processor affinity for IIS 6 applications can be configured using Active Directory Services Interface (ADSI) or Windows Management Instrumentation (WMI).

Application Pools

The final piece of the puzzle for IIS 6 architecture is the *application pool*, which is essentially one level of abstraction higher than worker processes. Whereas a worker process is a host process named w3wp.exe within which user-developed web application code can run, an application pool consists of the following:

- One kernel mode http.sys request queue
- One or more worker processes (instances of w3wp.exe)

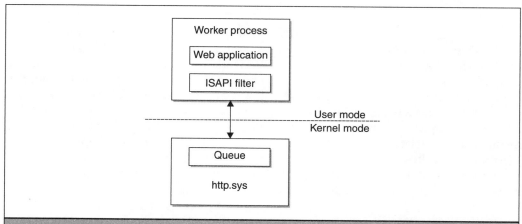

Figure 2-8. A worker process acts as a host process within which a web application or ISAPI filter can run.

Combining together the ideas of worker processes and application pools, there are three possible configurations for running applications on IIS 6:

- An application pool consisting of one worker process hosting a single web application isolated from all other applications by process boundaries (see Figure 2-9A). This corresponds to the concept of an out-of-process application in IIS 4 or an isolated process in IIS 5, but the performance is much improved in IIS 6 because all user-developed code such as ASP pages or ISAPI extensions run in-process within the worker process servicing the pool, eliminating the need for processor context changes from user mode to user mode, which are inherently slow to implement.

- An application pool consisting of one worker process hosting two or more web applications (see Figure 2-9B). This is the analog of default Medium (Pooled) process setting in IIS 5 but has no corresponding analog in IIS 4. This approach to using application pools is the default in IIS 6, where multiple ASP applications and ISAPI extensions or filters are run within the same application pool. Each application running within the pool shares the worker process servicing the pool (pulling HTTP requests from the kernel into the pool and returning responses to http.sys). As you'll see in the section called "Application Pools" later in this chapter, you can create as many of these application pools as desired, something you couldn't do with IIS 5, which allowed only one pooled process to run.

- An application pool consisting of multiple worker processes hosting one or more web applications (see Figure 2-9C). This configuration is new to IIS 6 and is referred to by the new name of *web garden*. A web garden is a special feature of IIS 6 that allows multiple worker processes to service a single application pool. In other words, a web garden is an application pool serviced by several worker processes, as opposed to the default single worker process per pool. The name "web garden" is derived from "web farm," which refers to multiple web servers running a single application; but in the case of web gardens, this all takes place on a single physical machine. When an incoming HTTP request arrives for an application running in a web garden, the kernel mode HTTP listener (http.sys) decides on which worker process (that is, which particular instance of w3wp.exe) within the web garden to forward the request to. Web gardens increase the reliability of IIS 6 even further by ensuring that if a worker process servicing an application becomes bogged down, the load can be taken up by the other worker processes in the garden. Web gardens can be configured for application pools that have either a single application running in them (for enhanced performance and fault tolerance) or multiple applications (for better reliability and to prevent application thread blocking from occurring).

The default type of application pool on IIS is one that has a single worker process servicing it. In other words, web gardens must be planted and grown, they don't just spring up by themselves!

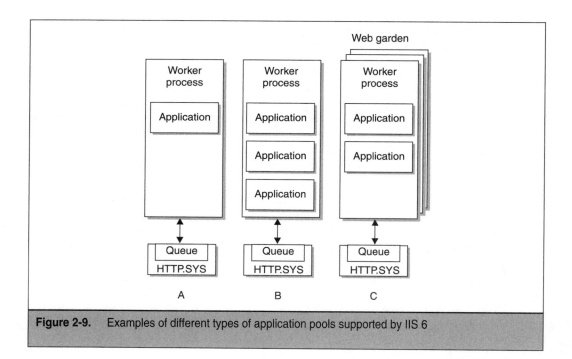

Figure 2-9.   Examples of different types of application pools supported by IIS 6

NOTE   Processor affinity, a feature of IIS 6 on multiprocessor machines just discussed, is particularly useful when used with web gardens. For example, an application pool with two worker processes servicing it can have each instance of w3wp.exe assigned to a separate CPU on a 4-way SMP machine. This can significantly increase the performance, availability, and reliability of the application running in the pool.

As I already mentioned, a major difference between IIS 5 and the current version is that in IIS 6 there can be multiple application pools running on a single machine, while in IIS 5 there was only one pooled process. In addition, each application pool in IIS 6 can be configured differently, and applications can easily be moved from one pool to another. When you install IIS 6, a default application pool is created that you can use to run as many applications as you wish, or you can create additional pools to isolate groups of applications (or individual applications) from one another. You can also rename the default pool if desired.

Application pools are a great advantage in IIS 6 because they increase reliability by allowing sites to be grouped together and isolated from other sites. For example, should one application within a pool crash, the only applications affected are others within that pool—applications in other pools remain unaffected. The application pool model is also less memory intensive than the process isolation model of IIS 5 and allows many more (possibly thousands) of sites to be hosted on a single IIS 6 machine with good performance resulting, thus greatly increasing the scalability of IIS over previous versions. Finally, application pools simplify the administration of web applications on IIS 6 by allowing configuration settings to be applied simultaneously to a group of web applications residing within the same pool.

An exception to the application isolation offered by having different applications run in different application pools can exist with regard to COM+ objects. Normally a COM+ object will be written to run in-process. Such a COM+ object can run as a component of multiple applications hosted by multiple pools. If the COM+ object fails in one application pool, other applications in different pools will remain unaffected. If the COM+ object is a singleton (designed to run as a single instance object), however, then all worker processes hosting this object will be affected and all applications using this object will fail, regardless of which pool they run in. In this case, the best solution from the administrator's point of view is to put all web applications that use this singleton COM+ object in the same application pool and disable overlapped recycling because of the concurrency issues. COM+ is pretty esoteric stuff and mainly of interest to developers. I won't go into it further in this book except to mention that the main thing for developers to remember when creating COM+ objects for IIS applications is that they need to be designed to run in-process as local servers.

Application pools are managed by the same WAS that manages the lifecycle of worker processes associated with these pools. These settings for application pools and worker processes are configurable in IIS 6 and include a number of advanced features. Let's discuss these briefly while we're on the topic of application pools.

Demand Start

The new Demand Start feature of IIS 6 allows worker processes to be started to service an application pool when the first HTTP request for an application within the pool is received. This means valuable memory is not used by pools until the first request directed toward an application in the pool is received. Demand Start also allows additional worker processes to be started to serve the pool should this be required. This is a big improvement over earlier versions of IIS and means that more sites can be hosted on a single machine. It also speeds up the startup and shutdown time for a machine hosting large numbers of sites because worker processes don't need to be instantiated during startup, they can instead be started when the first HTTP request is received for the applications they service.

Demand Start also means that IIS 6 manages its processor, memory, and disk resources much better than previous versions. It does this by allocating resources as needed when HTTP requests are received rather than pre-allocating them at startup. Using Demand Start, an IIS machine can start up with numerous applications ready to run but not a single worker process running. As soon as an incoming HTTP request arrives for an application, IIS allocates the resources to start a worker process for the application.

Demand Start is managed by the WAS component of IIS 6 and, together with the new Idle Timeout feature discussed next, makes IIS 6 a much more resource-efficient application-hosting platform than earlier versions.

Idle Timeout

If a worker process servicing an application pool has been idle for a specified amount of time, the WAS can automatically shut down the process, saving valuable memory on the machine. This means IIS 6 can actually tune itself to utilize only those memory and processor resources needed to service websites and applications that are actually actively being used by clients.

Taken together, the Demand Start and Idle Timeout features mean that IIS 6 is much more efficient in its use of memory resources than previous versions, which enhances the scalability and performance of the platform. Idle Timeout can cause problems in certain situations, however, such as when used in conjunction with process recycling discussed next.

Recycling

Sometimes a web application developed by a user will contain faulty code leading to conditions like memory leaks or violations. It may not be feasible to correct this situation (the coder may be on vacation). In previous versions of IIS, the web server had to be rebooted periodically to keep the application up and running. In IIS 6, however, this can be accomplished through recycling worker processes associated with the pool instead of manually rebooting the server.

Recycling (also called process recycling) is managed in IIS 6 by the WAS, which is the parent process of all worker processes running on the machine. Recycling is accomplished by configuring the pool so that its worker processes are scheduled to restart periodically whether the application has failed or not. This can be done on the basis of settings like the elapsed time running, a specific scheduled time of day, the number of HTTP requests received by the pool, virtual memory growing beyond specified limits, or manually on demand. When a worker process is recycled, the old process is notified to shut down, after which a brief period of time is allowed for any remaining requests in the queue to be serviced (this wait period is configurable). Then a new worker process spins up (that is, is started) to take the place of the old. The new process starts before the old shuts down, so there is no interruption in service from the client's viewpoint. If the old process doesn't respond to the shutdown command, it is forcibly terminated after a specified time interval. This type of recycling is called Overlapped Recycle because the new process is stopped before the old one is terminated. It is also possible to configure recycling so that overlap doesn't occur, where the old process is first terminated and then a new one is started to replace it.

It's generally better to use overlapped recycling because it ensures no interruption of service from the client's perspective. However, in some instances, overlapped recycling can cause concurrency issues from multiple instances of the same ASP or ISAPI application running simultaneously, a condition known as multi-instancing. If you experience problems running an application with overlapped recycling enabled, try disabling this feature to see if the problem disappears. Alternatively, you can ask your developer to recode the application so that it can properly handle a multi-instanced execution environment, but this may be more trouble than it's worth for older applications. A typical situation where this problem can arise is when a custom logging module is included as part of an application.

Idle Timeout together with recycling can cause problems for web applications like ASP applications where Session objects are used for storing state information between page views. In this scenario, the worker process times out, shuts down, and state information is lost and not transferred to the new process started by recycling. From the administrator's point of view, the way around this is to disable the idle timeout and process recycling features for the application pool under consideration. An alternative would be to run IIS 6 in IIS 5 isolation mode (discussed later in the chapter in the section "IIS 5 Isolation Mode"), but this is a poor solution because it entails a performance hit. From a developer's viewpoint, however, the workaround is to modify the application so that it persists such state information externally, for example, within an XML-formatted text file or SQL database. An alternative for the developer is to use the enhanced Session Service of ASP.NET, but discussion of this is beyond the scope of this book.

Orphaning

I mentioned earlier that the WAS periodically monitors the health of worker processes associated with application pools. Should a worker process be found unresponsive, the WAS normally forces termination of the process and starts a new process to replace it. However, IIS 6 can be configured instead to leave the unresponsive worker process running while it starts a new process to take over the load. This is accomplished by enabling a feature called orphaning, which is used mainly in a development context. For example, a debugger could be configured to connect to an orphaned process to determine what went wrong, since shutting down the offending process would prevent the developer from debugging the problem.

Rapid Fail Protection

Sometimes things go very wrong with applications, and they may be so buggy that the pool hosting them repeatedly shuts down. The rapid fail protection feature of IIS 6 allows pools to be configured so that if frequent multiple failures occur (more than a threshold number), the pool is switched to an out-of-service mode instead of being restarted. In this scenario, http.sys returns an HTTP 503 Service Unavailable message to clients making requests to applications in the pool. Administrators can manually produce the same effect by stopping the application pool using the Management console. You'll see how to do this later in Chapter 8, "Creating and Configuring Applications."

NOTE   There's another issue regarding application pools and how they isolate application processes in IIS 6 that I should mention here: security. By default in IIS 6, worker processes associated with application pools run in the security context of a built-in system identity called NetworkService. This identity is an account with very low privileges on the local system to ensure the security of IIS applications should they be compromised. However, since all worker processes use this identity, the isolation of applications in separate pools is not complete. You can completely isolate application pools by creating and assigning your own special low-privilege user accounts to each worker process, using a different account for each pool. I'll discuss this issue further in Chapter 10.

IIS 6 APPLICATION MODES

It turns out that everything you've learned so far about IIS 6 architecture is really only half the story. IIS 6 is a kind of chameleon that can change its colors to meet the needs of its environment, and it actually has two possible architectures that are quite different from one another. These architectures are referred to as the *application isolation modes* because they determine how applications are isolated from one another for greater reliability and scalability. The two application isolation modes of IIS 6 are as follows:

- **Worker process isolation mode**   This is the main operating mode of IIS 6 and involves the core components we have been discussing so far, in the way I have described them. Everything I've said so far about IIS 6 architecture refers to its architecture when running in worker process isolation mode.

- **IIS 5 isolation mode**   This secondary mode of operation employs a modified IIS 6 architecture designed to be backward compatible with applications developed specifically for the IIS 5 platform. If an application built for IIS 5 won't run on IIS 6 in worker process isolation mode, you can run IIS 6 in IIS 5 isolation mode instead to support it.

Let's look at these two modes in detail now to get the big picture.

Worker Process Isolation Mode

This is the primary mode of operation for IIS 6 and implements all of the new and enhanced architectural features we've discussed so far, including worker processes, application pools, health monitoring, demand start, rapid fail protection, and so on. Figure 2-10 shows the architectural big picture when IIS 6 is running in worker process isolation mode:

- User mode worker processes pull HTTP requests from the Kernel Mode HTTP Listener http.sys. Each application pool also has its own corresponding kernel mode queue in http.sys.

- Application pools may contain either single or multiple web applications and be serviced by either a single worker process or, in the case of a web garden, multiple worker processes. This means that applications can be isolated from each other in separate pools so that the failure of one application can be prevented from affecting other applications. Another way of saying this is that applications are isolated from each other by process boundaries.

- User-developed code such as ASP or ASP.NET applications and ISAPI extensions are loaded only into worker processes, not into IIS core components like inetinfo.exe or http.sys. This means core IIS processes can never be brought down by a failed user application.

- Application pools and their worker processes are managed by the new Web Administration Service (WAS).

- The FTP, NNTP, and SMTP Services and the XML metabase are managed by inetinfo.exe.

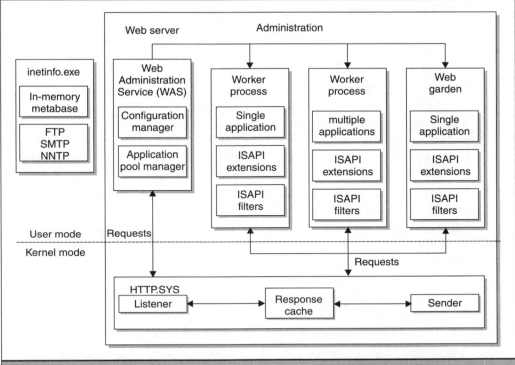

Figure 2-10. Big picture of IIS 6 architecture when running in worker process isolation mode

TIP Although a crashed web application in IIS 6 will not affect the FTP, NNTP, and SMTP Services running in inetinfo.exe, the reverse is unfortunately not true. If something happens to bring down the FTP, NNTP, or SMTP Service, web applications can be adversely affected as well. The reason is that inetinfo.exe also manages the metabase, which contains the configuration information for (among other things) websites and applications running on IIS. Failure of FTP, for example, could bring down inetinfo.exe, which would bring to a halt all web applications running on the server. This single point of failure will probably be fixed in future versions of IIS. In the meantime, it might be best if IIS machines used for hosting mission-critical web applications were not also used to host FTP sites, NNTP discussion groups, or SMTP mail relay sites. In other words, offload these functions to a separate IIS machine for greater reliability.

To understand Figure 2-10 fully, I'll walk you through the process of a client web browser requesting an ASP page from IIS 6:

1. The client sends the HTTP GET request.
2. The request is detected by http.sys, which verifies it as a valid request. If the request is invalid, http.sys returns the appropriate HTTP error code to the client.

3. http.sys checks the kernel mode response cache to see if the requested page has been cached from a recent request. If the response is in the cache, http.sys returns the cached response to the client. This happens very fast because everything takes place in kernel mode. Note that http.sys is capable of caching both static and dynamic content.

4. Http.sys routes the request to the appropriate kernel mode queue associated with the application pool for the ASP page being requested.

5. As soon as a thread becomes available, a worker process for the application pool pulls the request from the kernel mode cache. If there is currently no worker process servicing the application pool, http.sys notifies the WAS, which starts a worker process for the pool.

6. The ASP page is executed within the worker process using the ISAPI filter for the ASP script engine, which also runs within the worker process.

7. The worker process sends the response to http.sys, which caches it for future use and returns it to the client. http.sys may also log the action if IIS logging is enabled.

Worker process isolation mode is the recommended mode of operation when using IIS 6 because of its increased reliability, availability, and performance. For applications that break when run in this mode, however (such as applications developed for earlier versions of IIS), an alternate mode of operation can be used called IIS 5 isolation mode, which I'll discuss next.

IIS 5 Isolation Mode

If applications developed for IIS 5 don't run properly on IIS 6, you can make them run properly by running IIS 6 in a second application isolation mode called IIS 5 isolation mode. This mode of IIS 6 operation basically emulates the IIS 5 architecture to ensure backward compatibility for legacy applications to run on IIS 6. The architecture of IIS 5 isolation mode is quite different from that of worker process isolation mode, as can be seen from Figure 2-11.

From an examination of Figure 2-11, you can determine the following architectural features of IIS 6 when running in IIS 5 isolation mode:

- The WWW Service process w3svc.dll, which runs in-process within a svchost.exe host process, pulls HTTP requests from the request queue of the Kernel Mode HTTP Listener http.sys. A single worker process within w3svc.dll acts as a process pool for running in-process web applications.

- Applications can alternatively be run out-of-process within dllhost.exe host processes.

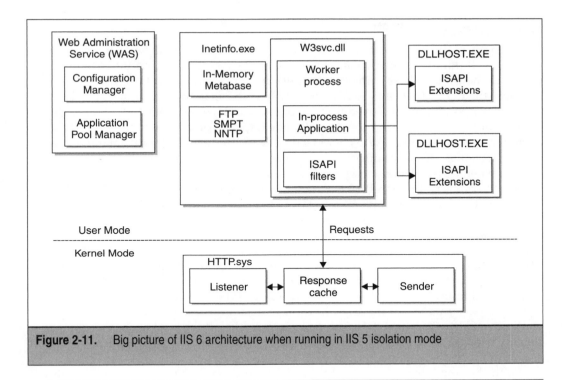

Figure 2-11. Big picture of IIS 6 architecture when running in IIS 5 isolation mode

---

NOTE Note that in IIS 5 isolation mode there is only one kernel mode request queue servicing http.sys. This means all HTTP requests are routed through inetinfo.exe regardless of whether the requested applications are running in-process (within inetinfo.exe) or out-of-process (within dllhost.exe). This means that routing of HTTP requests is slower in IIS 5 isolation mode than in worker process isolation mode. If you want the best possible performance out of IIS 6, you must run it in worker process isolation mode.

Examples of applications that require IIS 6 to be running in IIS 5 isolation mode in order to function properly include the following:

- ISAPI applications that can be loaded multiple times and run concurrently
- ISAPI filters that perform read-raw data filtering
- Any applications that need to call processes located outside the application pool where the application resides
- Any application that needs to persist session state information (with the exception of ASP.NET applications)

NOTE IIS 5 isolation mode is also sometimes known as compact mode or compatibility mode.

Comparison with IIS 5

If you compare the IIS 5 isolation mode of IIS 6 (Figure 2-11) with the earlier architecture of IIS 5 itself (Figure 2-5), you can see that in both cases the core inetinfo.exe process manages the IIS metabase; runs ISAPI filters and in-process ISAPI extensions; and manages the FTP, NNTP, and SMTP Services. In IIS 5 isolation mode, however, HTTP protocol support has been moved from inetinfo.exe (which used Winsock to manage HTTP requests in IIS 5) to the new kernel mode http.sys component of IIS 6, which is itself managed by the new WAS component of IIS 6. The actual operational differences are slight enough that any application designed to run on IIS 5 will run without problem on IIS 6 when IIS 5 isolation mode is being used.

When IIS 6 is running in IIS 5 isolation mode, it offers the same three application protection levels offered by IIS 5 itself: Low (IIS Process), Medium (Pooled), and High (Isolated). When you run a legacy IIS 5 application on IIS 6 in this mode, configure the application protection level to the same setting used on the downlevel Windows 2000 Server running IIS 5. An additional point to mention is that when IIS 6 is configured in IIS 5 isolation mode, applications running as either Medium (Pooled) or High (Isolated) will experience the same kind of performance hit such out-of-process applications experienced in IIS 5. This is due to the same issue of data marshalling that negatively impacted performance for these application protection levels in IIS 5. When IIS 6 is configured in worker process isolation mode, however, there is no such performance penalty because all applications and their associated ISAPI filters run in-process within a worker process w3wp.exe.

So the bottom line is, don't run IIS 6 in IIS 5 isolation mode unless there's absolutely no other way to get your applications working!

Comparison of IIS 6 Application Isolation Modes

Now that we've looked in detail at the two application isolation modes in IIS 6, let's make sure you understand them by comparing their features at the process level. Table 2-1 lists the key architectural features of IIS 6 in each mode and the corresponding process managing or implementing each feature.

Another difference between the two application isolation modes of IIS 6 is that certain features are *not* available when running in IIS 5 isolation mode:

- Health detection
- Process recycling
- Processor affinity
- Rapid fail protection
- Web gardens

IIS Feature	Worker Process Isolation Mode	IIS 5 Isolation Mode
HTTP	http.sys	http.sys
FTP	inetinfo.exe	inetinfo.exe
NNTP	inetinfo.exe	inetinfo.exe
SMTP	inetinfo.exe	inetinfo.exe
Metabase	inetinfo.exe	inetinfo.exe
http.sys configuration	WAS	WAS
Worker process	w3wp.exe	N/A
ISAPI filters	w3wp.exe	inetinfo.exe
In-process ISAPI extensions	w3wp.exe	inetinfo.exe
Out-of-process ISAPI extensions	N/A	dllhost.exe

Table 2-1.   Comparison of IIS 6 Application Isolation Modes at the Process Level

Availability of Modes

The default application isolation mode for IIS 6 depends on whether installation or upgrade has been performed, specifically,

- New (clean) installations of Windows Server 2003 where the IIS 6 component has been selected will result in IIS 6 being installed to run by default in worker process isolation mode.

- Upgrading from Windows NT Server (IIS 4) or Windows 2000 Server (IIS 5) to Windows Server 2003 will result in IIS 6 being installed to run by default in IIS 5 isolation mode.

I'll discuss IIS 6 deployment further in the next chapter, "Planning Deployment."

NOTE   You cannot run IIS 6 in both modes simultaneously. If you have some applications that can only run on IIS 5, you could migrate your remaining apps to a fresh IIS 6 machine and either leave the legacy apps running on IIS 5 or deploy a second IIS 6 machine running in IIS 5 isolation mode.

Switching Modes

You can also switch between the two application isolation modes of IIS 6, but this can have certain effects. For example, if you switch from IIS 5 isolation mode to worker process isolation mode, all of your isolated out-of-process web applications will be moved into a single application pool (the default application pool) that is created when

IIS 6 is installed. You can then create additional application pools, however, and move your applications to these pools to increase reliability. Switching application isolation modes can be done using a simple check box on a property sheet that's accessed by the Internet Information Services console tool, as you'll see in Chapter 9. You can also switch application isolation modes from the command-line using ADSI as you'll see in Chapter 11.

ADDITIONAL FEATURES

You now have a pretty good idea of the big picture of IIS 6 architecture, especially the two different application isolation modes and how they operate. But there are a few more architectural features of IIS 6 we haven't discussed yet, and I'll close the chapter by discussing these briefly.

Logging

Earlier versions of IIS included the ability to log HTTP requests in various text-file formats including native IIS format, NCSA standard format, and W3C Extended format. Requests could also be logged directly to an ODBC-compliant database or logging could be handled by installing a custom logging module (usually implemented as COM components). IIS 6 includes all the same logging capabilities but implements them differently. In IIS 5, for example, logging of all types was handled by the core inetinfo.exe process. In IIS 6, however, different processes handle logging:

- IIS, NCSA, and W3C Extended logging are performed by the Kernel Mode HTTP Listener http.sys.
- ODBC and custom logging are performed by individual worker processes instanced by w3wp.exe.

The advantage of moving text-based logging to the kernel is not only better performance but also the elimination of concurrency issues where several applications try to write to the same log file simultaneously. Such concurrency leads to thread blocking and thus performance degradation. This has been eliminated in IIS 6 and is another reason the current version performs better than earlier ones. Concurrency is usually not an issue with ODBC logging, however, since the database applications to which such logs are written are typically designed to manage concurrent access themselves.

However, problems could arise if custom logging modules designed for earlier versions are used with IIS 6. These are overcome by the fact that when IIS 6 is configured for either ODBC or custom logging, it automatically disables its kernel mode caching. Furthermore, when using custom logging modules, you should not implement web gardens or overlapped recycling, and you should make sure that all applications belonging to the website to which you wish to log are configured as belonging to the same application pool.

Caching

I mentioned earlier that http.sys also maintains an in-memory kernel mode cache for both static and dynamic content retrieved from IIS. This kernel mode cache, called *URI response cache*, is intelligently implemented using advanced heuristics that determine which content is worth caching and which should be discarded. Items that can be returned from cache take advantage of the higher privilege level of the kernel mode http.sys process and essentially bypass IIS entirely. In other words, when http.sys receives an HTTP GET request for a cached item, it immediately returns the item without transitioning the processor to user mode. Everything takes place in kernel mode, which makes performance very fast for cached content.

Also, as I discussed earlier, http.sys caches incoming HTTP requests, routing them to kernel mode queues mapped to corresponding application pools. So http.sys implements two kinds of in-memory kernel mode caches, one for incoming HTTP requests (in the kernel mode queues) and one for outgoing HTTP responses (in the URI response cache). You can even modify the size of the kernel mode queues by editing the metabase, allowing you great flexibility in tuning IIS performance. The URI response cache does not have a caching policy implemented by http.sys, however. Instead, web application developers can define caching policy programmatically.

Caching is also implemented in another form in IIS 6, namely, with regard to Active Server Pages (ASP). When an ASP page is requested by a client, the scripting engine compiles the ASP code into an intermediate form called an ASP template. These templates are stored in an in-memory cache for reuse purposes, a feature that was supported by IIS 5. In fact, IIS 6 can cache up to 250 ASP templates in-memory, and this number can be modified by editing the metabase. What's also new in IIS 6 is that once this in-memory cache of templates becomes full, the oldest items are not simply dropped as they were in IIS 5. Instead they are persisted to disk, that is, cached offline for later use if required. This new feature can significantly improve the performance of ASP applications running on IIS 6 as compared to previous versions.

Large Memory Support

For memory-intensive applications like large database applications, the IIS 6 in-memory cache can be configured to utilize up to 64GB of physical memory. This feature is called Large Memory Support and greatly increases the scalability of IIS 6, making it a suitable platform for running even the most demanding mission-critical line-of-business web-based applications.

64-Bit Architecture

Finally, the code for IIS 6 in particular (and Windows Server 2003 in general) is compiled to run on both the standard 32-bit x86 processor platform and the newer 64-bit Itanium platform. The 64-bit version of IIS 6 has the same architecture as the 32-bit version described in this chapter.

> ## Challenge
>
> You plan on migrating your IIS 5 web applications to the new IIS 6 platform. You're not sure if these applications will run properly on IIS 6, so naturally you plan to install them on a testbed IIS 6 system first before moving them to a production system. When testing your applications, should you run IIS 6 in worker process isolation mode or IIS 5 isolation mode? What are the advantages of running IIS 6 in worker process isolation mode where possible? What sort of IIS 5 applications are likely to break when run on IIS 6? Are the enhancements in IIS 6 significant enough that you might consider rewriting code to ensure it runs in worker process isolation mode instead of using IIS 5 isolation mode?

CHECKLIST: UNDERSTANDING IIS 6 ARCHITECTURE

The following is a checklist of essential concepts associated with the architecture of IIS 6. Read each one and check them off after you're sure you understand the significance of the concept because future chapters will make frequent use of them as you learn how to perform various IIS administrative tasks:

- [ ] http.sys, the Kernel Mode HTTP Listener, is responsible for handling incoming HTTP requests.

- [ ] Kernel mode queuing allows HTTP requests to be queued until the appropriate worker process can handle them.

- [ ] The IIS Admin Service (inetinfo.exe) manages the FTP, SMTP, and NNTP Services but not HTTP.

- [ ] Web applications can no longer be hosted in-process within inetinfo.exe.

- [ ] The Web Administration Service (WAS), a new component of the WWW Publishing Service (W3SVC), is responsible for managing the health of worker processes and maintaining the metabase.

- [ ] Instances of W3SVC (and hence the WAS) run as a DLL within a host process called svchost.exe.

- [ ] Worker processes are implemented as instances of the executable w3wp.exe and can host ISAPI applications and filters, ASP applications, CGI applications, and static web content.

- [ ] Using processor affinity, a worker process can be assigned to a specific processor on a symmetric multiprocessing (SMP) machine.

- [ ] All applications running on IIS 6 run within application pools, which consist of one kernel mode http.sys request queue and one or more worker processes.

- [ ] An application pool can host one or more applications running within it.

☐ A web garden is an application pool served by multiple worker processes.

☐ Demand Start allows applications to be loaded on-demand into their application pool when the first HTTP request for the application is received.

☐ Idle Timeout allows a worker process to be shut down to save memory if the application using it has not been used for a period of time.

☐ Process recycling allows worker processes to be restarted periodically to support applications that have memory leaks or other problems.

☐ Orphaning allows IIS to kill hung worker processes and start new ones to replace them.

☐ Rapid fail protection lets an application pool be switched to out-of-service if it fails frequently.

☐ Worker process isolation mode is the mode supporting new IIS 6 features such as worker processes, application pools, web gardens, and so on.

☐ IIS 5 isolation mode is an alternative IIS 6 mode to ensure compatibility with legacy applications that will not run properly in worker process isolation mode.

PART II

Deployment

CHAPTER 3

Planning Deployment

Now that you've learned about the new features in IIS 6 and examined its new and improved architecture, the next step is to learn how to deploy IIS 6 (and hence Windows Server 2003) using various tools and in a variety of different situations. This chapter provides you with an overview of deployment methods and issues, beginning with the big picture of deploying Windows Server 2003 and then focusing in on deploying IIS 6, a component of Windows Server 2003. The chapter also summarizes the various planning issues that you should think through before installing or upgrading to IIS 6. Chapter 4, "Installing IIS 6," then continues along this vein by walking you through several examples of installing and upgrading to IIS 6 using some of the methods discussed here.

THE DEPLOYMENT PROCESS

The way you approach deploying Windows Server 2003 in your enterprise depends on the scope of the rollout you have planned. Are you simply installing a few new IIS 6 web servers to your existing Windows NT– or Windows 2000–based network? Or are you upgrading your existing IIS 4/5 web servers to IIS 6? Are you doing a general upgrade of all servers on your Windows NT– or Windows 2000–based network to Windows Server 2003? Will you be doing it in stages or in one fell swoop? Is your network security model based on workgroups or domains? Do you have Active Directory deployed, or do you plan to deploy it? Do you have Apache web servers you want to migrate to IIS 6? And so on and so forth.

Obviously I can't answer all these questions in a book specifically dealing with IIS 6; I can only touch on some of them briefly and point you to further sources of information where you can find answers to all your deployment questions. What I will cover in this chapter is the following:

- General issues relating to deploying Windows Server 2003
- Tools and methods for deploying Windows Server 2003
- General planning issues related to deploying Windows Server 2003
- Specific planning issues related to deploying IIS 6 machines

Deployment Process Overview

There are several ways of outlining the general steps in upgrading a network to a new OS or application. The simplest approach is to ask three questions:

1. Where are we now?
2. Where do we want to go tomorrow?
3. How do we get there?

The first question includes both your knowledge of the current state of your network and your business reasons for upgrading. The bottom line is that you must have convincing reasons for upgrading before you jump into the process. The second question deals with envisioning what kind of upgrade is required to meet your articulated business needs. The third question deals with coming up with a plan to get from now to where you want to be. Always develop a plan before you start the upgrade process—acting first without planning is usually disastrous.

From a practical point of view, a deployment plan usually has four steps:

1. Assess what kind of upgrade needs to be performed.
2. Design systems that will meet your upgrade needs.
3. Test your design against your expectations and business needs.
4. Roll out your production systems in appropriate stages and continue testing.

Here are some further random thoughts on the preceding steps:

- Use a team approach with clearly defined responsibilities.
- Develop a written plan with scheduled milestones and a signing-off procedure.
- Create a baseline for your existing network by taking a complete inventory of hardware, software, roles, permissions, and users.
- Create a test lab that mirrors your real company network in hardware, applications, and traffic load.
- Test for application compatibility as well as hardware compatibility.
- Document the results of your tests at each stage of the process.
- Choose deployment methods that best satisfy your needs and resources.
- Consider doing a pilot rollout before undertaking a more general rollout.
- Have a rollback plan at each step of the deployment process in case the unexpected happens.
- Expect the unexpected, it's going to happen anyway.
- Continue testing after your final rollout is complete.

For more information on deploying Windows Server 2003 in the enterprise, see the Windows Server 2003 Deployment Kit from Microsoft. You can find information about this and other resource kits at http://www.microsoft.com/reskit/ on Microsoft's website.

Microsoft Solutions Framework (MSF)

Another way of describing the planning deployment process is with the Microsoft Solutions Framework (MSF) developed by Microsoft (see Figure 3-1). This approach defines four steps in any general project management process:

1. **Envisioning**   Defining and approving the goals and limits of the project
2. **Planning**   Defining and approving the actual steps of the project
3. **Developing**   Building and testing the elements of the project
4. **Deploying**   Making the new services available to end users

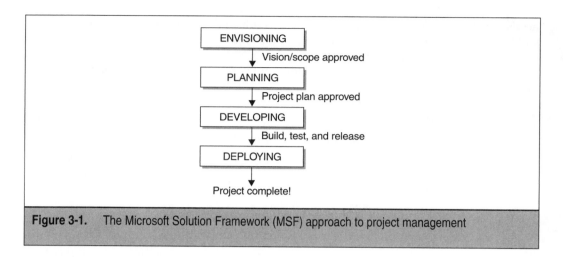

Figure 3-1.   The Microsoft Solution Framework (MSF) approach to project management

For more information about MSF see http://www.microsoft.com/business/services/mcsmsf.asp on Microsoft's website.

Domains vs. Workgroups

Except for small networks of only a few machines, most small business networks are domain based and have a single Windows NT domain (or a single Windows 2000 forest containing a single domain). Upgrading domains is more complicated than upgrading stand-alone machines and requires careful planning to ensure the migration goes smoothly. Because the focus of this book is IIS, it's beyond the scope of the book to cover domain migration in detail. Consult the Setup files in the \Docs folder on the product CD and the Getting Started guide for more details on how to migrate Windows NT and Windows 2000 domains and domain controllers to Windows Server 2003.

TIP   IIS can be installed on stand-alone servers (belonging to a workgroup), member servers (belonging to a domain), or domain controllers. Installing IIS on domain controllers is not recommended, however, as the overhead required by authentication processes on domain controllers is considerable and can affect performance of web applications running on IIS. Another reason not to install IIS on a domain controller is security, as this configuration can potentially expose your user account information should a vulnerability such as a buffer overflow occur in IIS.

Capacity Planning

Deploying IIS web servers effectively requires planning to ensure they will be able to meet the capacity requirements of users accessing them. Web server capacity planning is a complex subject that is sometimes more of an art than a science, and it involves planning adequate hardware requirements and identifying and resolving bottlenecks. An introduction to this subject is at http://www.microsoft.com/technet/prodtechnol/iis/plan/websize.asp on the Microsoft TechNet website.

DEPLOYMENT TOOLS AND METHODS

There are a number of methods for deploying Windows Server 2003 (and hence IIS 6) on your network. Some of these methods are simple (insert the product CD and reboot), while others are complex (using Microsoft Systems Management Server [SMS], for example). Some methods require manual intervention (such as installation from a network distribution point), while others are automated (such as disk imaging with Sysprep.exe and Sysprep.inf). To help you wade through the various concepts and terminologies involved, this section will first survey the various deployment tools you can use and then examine each deployment method in various degrees of detail. One could easily write a whole book on deploying Windows Server 2003, so what you will find here is an abbreviated tour.

Deployment Tools

I'll begin the tour with a brief overview of the tools and terminology associated with various manual and automated deployment methods outlined later in this chapter. If you're in a hurry, you can skip this section for now and refer back to it when reading the later sections "Manual Deployment Methods" and "Automated Deployment Methods."

Product CD

Besides using your Windows Server 2003 product CD for installing or upgrading systems, you should also keep this CD nearby in case you have problems booting your system. If key operating system files or the Registry becomes corrupt or bad drivers are loaded when new devices are installed, you may not be able to boot your system. In such a situation, you can boot your system directly from the product CD and use either the Recovery Console or Automated System Recovery to repair the problem. For information on how to troubleshoot startup problems using these and other tools, see the *Microsoft Windows Server 2003 Resource Kit* from Microsoft.

Cmdlines.txt

This file can be used to customize deployments using disk imaging, an automated deployment process described later in this chapter in the section "Automated Deployment Methods." When the Mini-Setup portion of the imaging process finishes, any commands in the Cmdlines.txt file are executed asynchronously prior to final system restart. To use Cmdlines.txt, you must specify it in the [Unattended] section of the Sysprep.inf file, and you must supply the Cmdlines.txt file for the target system either on a floppy disk or by copying it to the system's hard disk.

Distribution Point

Copying the contents of the product CD (or the contents of the I386 folder on the CD) to a shared folder on a network file server creates a distribution point to which machines to be upgraded or installed can connect and run Setup (or Winnt or Winnt32). This is discussed further in the section "Network Install"; see also the upcoming section "Setupmgr.exe."

Setup.exe

This file, located in the root directory of your product CD, is used to start the upgrade process for upgrading Windows NT 4 Server or Windows 2000 Server to Windows Server 2003. To run this program, you must be a member of the Administrators local group on your machine (or Domain Admins in a domain-based environment). After logging on to the local machine as Administrator, there are two ways you can manually start the upgrade process using Setup.exe:

- Insert the product CD into the system's CD-ROM drive. Autorun (if enabled) will launce Setup.exe automatically.

- Insert the product CD into a shared CD-ROM drive on a network file server (or copy the entire CD to a network share), connect to the network share by mapping a drive or entering the UNC path in the Run box, and double-click Setup.exe to start the upgrade.

When upgrading from Windows 2000, an alternative method of starting Setup.exe on a machine is to log on with your ordinary user account (not your Administrator account) and use the Runas command to start Setup.exe using your Administrator credentials. To do this, hold down the SHIFT key, right-click the Setup.exe file in Windows Explorer, and select Run As from the context menu. Enter the account, password, and domain of the credentials you want to use to run the program, and click OK. You can also use the runas command from the command line to run a program with alternate credentials; type **runas /?** at the command prompt for more info.

NOTE Setup.exe is used only for performing upgrades—to do a clean install, use either Winnt.exe or Winnt32.exe.

Setupmgr.exe

This tool, called Setup Manager, is included in the Deploy.cab file in the \Support\Tools folder on your product CD, and can be used to

- Create answer files on automated, unattended installations.

- Create a distribution point for network installs.

Setup Manager can be used to create answer files for several kinds of automated installations:

- Unattend.txt file for normal unattended installs

- Sysprep.inf for unattended installs using Sysprep and third-party disk imaging tools

- RIStndrd.sif for unattended installs using Remote Installation Services (RIS)

Changes in this new version of Setup Manager include encrypting administrator passwords for greater security; an improved interface; and eliminating context-sensitive Help, which is replaced with an improved .chm help file. For full instructions on how to use this tool, see the Microsoft Windows Corporate Deployment Tools User's Guide in the Deploy.chm file in the \Support\Tools folder on your product CD.

Sysprep.exe

The Microsoft Windows System Preparation tool (Sysprep) is used to prepare a system for duplication by disk imaging, an automated deployment process described later in this chapter. Sysprep is run on a master installation to ensure that each duplicated copy of the master's disk image is unique when distributed to target systems. Sysprep also ensures that the target systems start in a special setup mode called Mini-Setup when they are first booted after being imaged. Mini-Setup performs hardware detection and regenerates security identifiers (SIDs) to ensure the installed system is unique on the network. You can also automate the way Mini-Setup runs by customizing an .inf file called Sysprep.inf, described in the next section.

Sysprep can be run either as a GUI tool or from the command line. You can find Sysprep on your product CD or download the latest version from Microsoft's website.

Sysprep.inf

This text file is an answer file that can be used to automate how Mini-Setup runs when deploying systems using disk imaging, an automated deployment process described later in the section "Automated Deployment Methods." Sysprep.inf can be configured to respond to the prompts for user information during Mini-Setup, run scripts or commands when Mini-Setup is complete, and perform other tasks related to automating deployment by disk imaging.

Unattend.txt

This is an answer file used to automatically answer the prompts generated during normal Setup. By using Winnt.exe (or Winnt32.exe) with the appropriate switch and specifying the answer file, you can fully automate a normal Windows Server 2003 clean installation. For more information, see the section "Unattended Install" later in this chapter.

WinPE

This tool, Windows Preinstallation Environment, is specifically intended for use by original equipment manufacturers (OEMs) to enable them to preinstall Windows Server 2003 on new computers for customers. WinPE is essentially a bootable OS that provides you with limited functionality for performing certain preinstallation tasks (on legacy Windows NT systems, OEMs used to use MS-DOS for this same purpose). If you are an OEM, you can obtain the WinPE for Corporations toolkit from Microsoft. Some enterprise customers may also qualify for obtaining and using this kit, so contact Microsoft if you're interested.

Winnt.exe

This file is in the I386 folder on the product CD and can be used to perform a clean install of Windows Server 2003 on 16-bit MS-DOS and Windows 3.x systems. To perform a clean install on 32-bit Windows platforms, use Winnt32.exe instead, which is discussed next. As shown in Table 3-1, Winnt.exe has a number of command-line switches that can be used to automate installations and perform other tasks.

TIP   For more information on any of these switches, insert the product CD, switch to the I386 folder on it, and type **winnt /?** to see a Help listing.

Winnt32.exe

This file is in the I386 folder on the product CD and can be used to perform a clean install of Windows Server 2003 on 32-bit Windows platforms including Windows 9x/Me, Windows NT (requires Service Pack 5 or later), Windows 2000, and Windows XP. You can also use Winnt32.exe to upgrade from the Standard Edition of Windows Server 2003 to Enterprise Edition. To perform a clean install on 16-bit MS-DOS or Windows 3.x, use Winnt.exe instead, which is discussed in the preceding section. As shown in Table 3-2, Winnt32.exe has a number of command-line switches that can be used to automate installations and perform other tasks.

TIP   Some of these switches are not available when running Winnt32.exe on 64-bit Itanium systems. For more info on any of these switches, insert the product CD, switch to the I386 folder on it, and type **winnt32 /?** to see a Help listing.

Switch	Description
/s[:*sourcepath*]	Source location of installation files, must be a full path of form x:[*path*] or *server*\share[*path*]
/t[:*tempdrive*]	Tells Setup to put temporary files on specified drive and to install Windows on that drive
/u[:*answer file*]	Does an unattended installation using an answer file (requires /s)
/udf:*id* [,*UDF_file*]	Specifies an identifier (id) that Setup uses to specify a Uniqueness Database File (UDF) that modifies the answer file (see /u)
/r[:*folder*]	Specifies an optional folder to be installed (folder remains after Setup finishes)
/rx[:*folder*]	Specifies an optional folder to be copied (folder is deleted after Setup finishes)
/e	Specifies a command to be executed at the end of GUI-mode Setup
/a	Enables accessibility options

Table 3-1.   Optional Switches for Winnt.exe

Switch	Description
/checkupgradeonly	Does not perform an install, but simply checks your computer for upgrade compatibility with Windows Server 2003 (same as inserting product CD and selecting Check System Compatibility).
/cmd:*command*	Tells Setup to execute the specified command before final phase of Setup.
/cmdcons	Installs the Recovery Console as a startup option (this option can only be used after normal Setup is complete).
/copydir:i386*folder_name*	Creates the specified subfolder within the folder in which the operating system files are installed.
/copysource:*folder_name*	Creates an additional temporary subfolder within the folder in which the operating system files are installed.
/debug[*level*]:[*filename*]	Creates a debug log at the specified level.
/dudisable	Disables Dynamic Update from running during Setup.
/duprepare:*pathname*	Prepares an installation share to use with Dynamic Update files you downloaded from Windows Update.
/dushare:*pathname*	Specifies the share on which you previously downloaded Dynamic Update files and on which you previously ran /duprepare:*pathname*.
/emsport:{com1|com2|usebiossettings|off}	Enables/disables Emergency Management Services (EMS) during Setup and after the operating system has been installed.
/emsbaudrate:*baudrate*	Specifies baud rate for EMS when used with /emsport:com1 or /emsport:com2.
/m:*folder_name*	Tells Setup to copy replacement files from an alternate location.
/makelocalsource	Tells Setup to copy all installation source files to your local hard disk.
/noreboot	Tells Setup to not restart computer after file copy phase of Setup is finished.
/s:*sourcepath*	Specifies source location of installation files (to simultaneously copy files from multiple servers, use the /s:*sourcepath* option up to eight times).
/syspart:*drive_letter*	Lets you copy Setup startup files to a hard disk, mark the disk as active, and then install the disk into another computer; when you start that computer, it automatically begins the next phase of Setup (must also use /*tempdrive*).
/tempdrive:*drive_letter*	Tells Setup to put temporary files on specified partition.
/udf:*id* [,*UDB_file*]	Specifies an identifier (id) used by Setup to specify which Uniqueness Database (UDB) file modifies the answer file.
/unattend	Upgrades Windows NT 4 Server (with Service Pack 5 or later) or Windows 2000 Server in unattended Setup mode.
/unattend[*num*]:[*answer_file*]	Does a clean installation in unattended Setup mode using the specified answerfile.

Table 3-2. Optional Switches for Winnt32.exe

Manual Deployment Methods

Installing Windows Server manually is generally suitable for only small deployments of a dozen or so servers. This is mainly due to the length of time involved in performing each installation or upgrade. The manual deployment process is often referred to as *interactive setup* because it requires an administrator or operator to be present at the machine during the installation to interact with the various prompts generated by the setup program. There are four different ways to install or upgrade to Windows Server 2003 manually:

- Accessing your Windows Server 2003 CD from your existing OS
- Booting directly from your Windows Server 2003 CD
- Performing a network install from a shared distribution point containing the Windows Server 2003 source files
- Using a custom bootable CD you've created using WinPE

Let's examine each of these methods separately for installations and upgrades of x86-based systems (see your system manufacturer's documentation for installing or upgrading Itanium systems).

Upgrade Using Product CD

To upgrade using the product CD, insert the CD and follow the prompts. Of course, you must make sure your current OS supports upgrading to Windows Server 2003—see the section "Upgrade Paths" later in this chapter for more info.

Install Using Product CD

To do a clean install directly from the product CD on a system having no OS, simply configure your BIOS to boot from the CD-ROM drive, insert the CD, and follow the prompts. If your system has an existing OS, or if your BIOS doesn't support booting from CD-ROM, you have several options to choose from:

- If your system is running MS-DOS, first make sure you are using SMARTDrive to enable disk caching. Then insert the CD, type **d:** to switch to the CD-ROM drive, type **cd i386** to change to the I386 folder, and type **winnt** to run Winnt.exe and start the install.
- If your system is running Windows 3.*x*, again make sure that you are using SMARTDrive, and then open File Manager and navigate to the I386 folder on your CD-ROM drive. Double-click Winnt.exe to start the install.
- If your system is running Windows 9*x*/Me, Windows NT (requires Service Pack 5 or later), Windows 2000, or Windows XP, just insert the CD and follow the prompts.

Even if you have an existing OS on your system, if your BIOS supports booting from CD-ROM, you can simply insert the product CD and restart the computer to start the install. This is the easiest way of doing a clean install, and it requires only configuring the BIOS to boot from the CD-ROM before trying the C: drive.

Network Install

To perform an upgrade over the network, copy the contents of the product CD to a shared folder on a network file server. Then go to the system you want to upgrade, connect to the shared folder (called a *distribution point* because it distributes the product installation files to network clients that need them), and run Setup.exe (in the root directory of the product CD). Instead of copying the contents of the product CD to the file server, you can simply insert the CD into the file server's CD-ROM and share the CD-ROM drive. This alternate method will work fine if you are upgrading a single server; but if you are going to upgrade two or more servers at the same time, the method will suffer because of CD-ROM drive thrashing. For multiple simultaneous network installs, use a shared folder instead—or better yet, several distribution points on different file servers.

To perform a clean install over the network, follow the approach just described but run Winnt.exe or Winnt32.exe instead of Setup.exe. If the computer you are doing the install on is running MS-DOS or Windows 3.*x*, run Winnt.exe; if it's running Windows 9*x*/Me, Windows NT (with Service Pack 5 or later), Windows 2000, or Windows XP, run Winnt32.exe. See Tables 3-1 and 3-2 earlier in this chapter for a description of the optional switches you can use when running Winnt.exe and Winnt32.exe.

Custom Bootable CD

Using the Windows Preinstallation Environment (WinPE) tools available to OEMs and some enterprise volume licensing customers, you can create a bootable ISO image that contains the Windows Server 2003 installation files plus additional device drivers, scripts, and commands to run using Cmdlines.txt, and an unattend.txt file you specify. You can then burn this image onto a CD and use it to perform a custom manual installation of Windows Server 2003. For more information on how to use WinPE see the Microsoft Windows Corporate Deployment Tools User's Guide in the Deploy.chm file in the \Support\Tools folder on your product CD.

Automated Deployment Methods

Automated deployment of Windows Server 2003 is generally used only when there are large numbers of servers to be deployed, or when preconfigured servers need to be deployed in remote locations where IT staff lack the skills and training to handle other kinds of installation. This section looks briefly at some of the options for automated deployment. Full details on some of these methods are in the Microsoft Windows Corporate Users Deployment Tools Guide (in the Deploy.cab file in the \Support\Tools folder on the product CD) and in the Microsoft Windows Server 2003 Deployment Kit, available from Microsoft.

Unattended Install

Normal (manual) installation requires the user to answer various prompts during Setup, including accepting the EULA, specifying Regional Settings, and so on. You can automate this process by performing an unattended install of Windows Server 2003, an option available for clean installs only, not upgrades. To perform an unattended installation, you first create an answer file, a text file usually named unattend.txt that contains answers to Setup prompts and other information. You can create an unattend.txt file two ways:

- Using Setup Manager (Setupmgr.exe), a tool included in the Deploy.cab file in the \Support\Tools folder on your product CD.

- By copying the sample unattend.txt file from the \I386 folder on your product CD and modifying it as needed.

Once you've created your unattend.txt file, you can start an unattended installation by typing **winnt32.exe /unattend:unattend.txt** at the command line, assuming you've either inserted the product CD and changed to the I386 directory or you've connected to the I386 folder on your network distribution point. For more information about how to create and use answer files, see the documentation on Setup Manager in the Microsoft Windows Corporate Deployment Tools User's Guide in the Deploy.chm file in the \Support\Tools folder on your product CD.

Disk Imaging

This method of automated installation is sometimes called cloning and involves preconfiguring a system with Windows Server 2003 (and possibly other applications) installed on it, and then copying a bit-by-bit image of the installed system to other systems. The result is a series of identical installed systems that can quickly be deployed on the network. Disk imaging is supported by all editions of Windows Server 2003 and by Windows XP Professional. You can use this deployment method if you have a large number of similar systems (similar hardware and software) you want to quickly deploy. Note also that the imaging process is somewhat customizable—that is, the cloned systems don't always need to have exactly the same hardware.

To deploy Windows Server 2003 using disk imaging, you need two things:

- The Microsoft Windows System Preparation tool (Sysprep.exe), which was described earlier in the "Deployment Tools" section.

- A third-party disk imaging program like Norton Ghost from Symantec

The four-step process for deployment by disk imaging is as follows:

1. Install a master system that has the exact OS and application configuration you want to clone.

2. Run Sysprep on the master system to prepare its disk for being imaged.

3. Use a third-party disk imaging tool to create an image of the prepared system's disk.

4. Use the disk-imaging tool to copy the image to your target machines, either by burning the image on a CD or by storing it on a network distribution point and copying it across the network (requires a network boot disk for the target machine).

Some things to remember when considering disk imaging as a deployment method:

-   Disk imaging takes a lot of planning, so make sure you have enough installs to do to make it worth the effort.

-   The disk imaging process can be automated by using an answer file called Sysprep.inf, which was described in the "Deployment Tools" section earlier in this chapter.

-   You can only use this deployment approach when doing clean installs, not upgrades.

-   The master and target systems must have identical hardware abstraction layers (HALs).

-   Systems with plug-and-play (PnP) devices usually image well. Problems arise more often from legacy devices and mass storage controllers, and when imaging portable devices like CD-ROM and DVD-ROM drives. Imaging may also fail if the drive on the target machine has insufficient space for the image and for running the Mini-Setup process.

-   Domain controllers can't be deployed by this method. You must deploy them as stand-alone servers instead and then run Dcpromo.exe to make them domain controllers (or have Sysprep.inf run a script to do this when Mini-Setup finishes).

-   Systems where user-level permissions have been preconfigured can't be deployed by this method. You must deploy them first and then configure permissions afterward (or have Sysprep.inf run a script to do this when Mini-Setup finishes).

-   Your imaged system can be customized by running commands contained within the Cmdlines.txt file, provided you specify this in Sysprep.inf and supply a copy of Cmdlines.txt to the target machine (usually on a floppy). Commands in the Cmdlines.txt file are executed at the end of Mini-Setup just before final system reboot.

-   Certain components of Windows Server 2003 have to be configured after installation and therefore can't be deployed by imaging. Examples include Certificate Services, Cluster Service, files encrypted using the Encrypted File System (EFS), and applications that depend for their operation on Active Directory.

-   Third-party disk imaging tools have their own licensing requirements that must be adhered to, in addition to licensing requirements for Windows Server 2003 itself.

For more information on planning deployment by disk imaging, see the Microsoft Windows Server 2003 Deployment Guide from Microsoft and consult the documentation that accompanies your third-party disk imaging software.

NOTE   Sysprep has been improved in this version of Windows and can now successfully image servers running Windows Server 2003 that have IIS installed and configured on them.

RIS

Remote Installation Services (RIS) was first introduced in Windows 2000 Server as a tool for performing mass deployments of Windows 2000 Professional client machines. In Windows Server 2003, RIS now supports deployments of both server and client machines, so you can use RIS to deploy IIS 6 web servers if you have the time to learn how to use it and hardware that supports it (target machines must support remote booting using PXE ROMs or be started using special startup floppy disks). For more information on how to use RIS, see the Microsoft Windows Server 2003 Deployment Guide from Microsoft or consult Microsoft's website.

SMS

Finally, good old Microsoft Systems Management Server (SMS) can be used for upgrading Windows NT or Windows 2000 servers on your network to Windows Server 2003, as well as for distributing software updates and patches across your enterprise. SMS needs a whole book by itself to learn how to use it, so I won't go any further into it here. A good source for SMS information is http://www.myITforum.com, a popular site run by SMS guru Rod Trent.

GENERAL PLANNING ISSUES

In this section, we'll look at various general planning issues related to preparing to install or upgrade to Windows Server 2003. These issues are general in the sense that they apply whether you are preparing to deploy IIS web servers or other kinds of servers, such as remote access servers or file/print servers. After considering these general issues, I'll conclude the chapter with a look at some planning issues specifically related to deploying IIS web servers. The general issues we'll consider are as follows:

- Which product edition to deploy
- Whether to perform a clean install or an upgrade
- Hardware issues for successful deployment
- Performing backups in case you need to roll back an upgrade
- Issues related to networking
- Planning for security
- Licensing issues
- Windows Product Activation

Product Editions

An important up-front planning issue for your deployment is which edition of Windows Server 2003 to deploy. Several things figure into this decision:

- The hardware you plan to deploy on. Different editions have different hardware requirements, as described later in this chapter.

- The features available with each edition. If you want clustering, for example, you'll need to install Enterprise Edition. And if you want to deploy Active Directory, you can't do it on Web Edition.

- Your existing network configuration. If you're upgrading Windows NT or Windows 2000 servers, you need to consider which upgrade paths to Windows Server 2003 editions are possible and which are not. Upgrade paths are described later in this chapter in the section entitled "Upgrade Paths."

- Your business needs and budget. If you can get by with Standard Edition, you may want to do so—you can always upgrade to Enterprise Edition later.

If you need to review the capabilities of the various editions of Windows Server 2003, refer back to Chapter 1, "Introducing IIS 6." You can also find more information about the features of various editions at http://www.microsoft.com/windowsserver2003/ on Microsoft's website.

NOTE Web Edition, designed primarily for service providers running web hosting data centers, is available only through special Microsoft partner channels, not retail. To find a Microsoft partner channel for this product, see http://www.microsoft.com/serviceproviders/net/server.asp on Microsoft's website.

Installation vs. Upgrade

Let's move on to consider the pros and cons of doing clean installs vs. upgrades. Both have their advantages and disadvantages, and which method you select is an important part of the deployment planning process.

Why Do a Clean Install?

There are many good reasons for doing a clean install wherever possible instead of an upgrade. First off, your existing hardware may not meet the requirements for running Windows Server 2003, and it may be more costly to upgrade and maintain it than to switch to an entirely new system. This is especially an issue if you are running older Windows server software like Windows NT Server 3.51 (rare) or Windows NT Server 4 (common). Hardware running these platforms may be five years old or older, and hence

- Your BIOS may not fully support the newer Advanced Configuration and Power Interface (ACPI) 1.0b standard. Support for this standard enables Windows Server 2003 to support Hot Plug PCI, which lets you add, remove, or replace devices without needing to schedule downtime for the procedure.

- Your motherboard may include unneeded legacy ISA slots, limiting the number of PCI devices you can install. Newer motherboards usually include four or five PCI slots and a single shared ISA/PCI slot that you can use for either kind of device. Your motherboard also may have a slower PCI system bus such as PCI 2 or 2.1 instead of the newer PCI 2.2 or 2.3 (or the proposed PCI 3). And your motherboard certainly won't support new Windows Server 2003 features like hot add memory, which allows you to add more RAM while the system is running and without rebooting afterward; headless server operation, which lets you install and manage Windows Server 2003 on a machine that has no monitor, video card, keyboard, or mouse; and the new Human Interface Device (HID) specification for USB keyboards that include additional buttons to make common tasks easier.

- Your chipset may only support 512MB of RAM or less—or worse. For example, an Intel 430TX Pentium chipset supposedly supports 256MB of RAM, but in actuality it can cache only 64MB. The result is that if you run this chipset with more than 64MB RAM, performance can actually be *worse* than if you had only 64MB! Your chipset may also not allow your processor to be upgraded sufficiently to meet your needs. For example, a chipset that supports Pentium II CPUs will allow you to upgrade your processors to Pentium III CPUs but not to Pentium 4 CPUs.

In such cases, it's clear that older hardware can severely limit the performance of a system running Windows Server 2003 and may prevent many of the new hardware-related features of this operating system from functioning. So if you want maximum performance and want to take full advantage of the features of Windows Server 2003, it's often best to do a clean install on new hardware purchased from your vendor instead of trying to upgrade your existing hardware. This is especially true when moving from Windows NT 3.51 or 4 to Windows Server 2003—upgrading Windows 2000 Server systems is generally simpler as hardware that supports Windows 2000 will support most (but not all) features of Windows Server 2003. Clearly, upgrading servers is not like upgrading classic cars! After all, would you trade in a classic 1967 Mustang Shelby GT 500 for a BMW Z8 or Mercedes-Benz CL 600? I wish I could even dream about making that decision…

What if your existing server environment developed in a relatively unplanned fashion and you have a variety of different hardware platforms to manage from different vendors? If you're planning on upgrading everything to Windows Server 2003, then now's the time to start thinking about standardizing your hardware platform across your business. Standard hardware platforms (motherboard, chipset, BIOS, and so on) makes management of your servers easier, simplifies troubleshooting, and reduces cost by enabling you to stock fewer replacement parts. If you have the budget for it, buy the best hardware you can and stock up with parts to keep your server environment running continuously.

Another reason for installing instead of upgrading has to do with deploying new applications. If you're planning on deploying major new applications (ERP, CRM, database, ASP applications, whatever), then you should consider doing clean installs of

Windows Server 2003 instead of upgrading your earlier Windows NT or Windows 2000 servers to minimize incompatibility issues with existing applications. So it's not just new hardware that is a consideration as to whether to upgrade or install, but also new software.

Clean installs also often result in better OS and application performance than an upgrade. The reason for this is that NTFS drives tend to become fragmented after a time, and the disk defragmenter included with Windows Server 2003 doesn't completely defragment your drive (due to protected system sectors). By installing on a new system (or reformatting your existing system's drive) you may get a slight improvement in performance over upgrading—and even a slight performance increase can be significant in high-transaction scenarios such as e-commerce websites. This issue is particularly important if you previously upgraded your system, for example, from Windows NT 4 to Windows 2000, and now are considering upgrading it again.

Another disk-related reason for doing a clean install is that it gives you a chance to repartition your drives to better meet your requirements. Of course, Windows 2000 dynamic disks can be resized without reformatting, but see the section "Disk Partitions," later in the chapter, for important info regarding upgrading dynamic disks.

Why Upgrade?

I've talked about why you might want to do a clean install of Windows Server 2003; now I'll talk a bit about why you might want to upgrade instead. The major reason for performing an upgrade instead of a clean install is to maintain the existing configuration settings of your operating system and applications. The second reason companies sometimes upgrade is because it can be faster than doing a clean install, especially if you have lots of applications running on your server, since a clean install would also mean reinstalling (and reconfiguring) all your applications. The final reason companies sometimes prefer upgrading is because it's cheaper—you don't need to go out and buy new hardware.

An issue to consider is the scope of your deployment. Are you just migrating a few web servers from IIS 4 or 5 to IIS 6, or are you migrating your whole network infrastructure from Windows NT or Windows 2000 to Windows Server 2003? The latter is more complicated, especially the NT case, which requires a good understanding of the process for migrating Windows NT security models to Active Directory forests, domains, and organizational units. That kind of mass deployment is beyond the scope of this book, and you should use the *Windows Server 2003 Deployment Resource Kit* as your final guide in making such deployment decisions.

One more thing to consider—the operating system you're upgrading from. If your servers are currently running Windows 2000 Server, upgrading to Windows Server 2003 should be a snap in most cases, and this makes upgrading a viable alternative to doing a clean install. On the other hand, if you're running Windows NT Server 4, you'll likely want to do a clean install, not an upgrade (because of previously discussed hardware considerations). Nevertheless, for the sake of completeness, I'll discuss every possible upgrade path next.

Upgrade Paths

If you're considering upgrading your existing servers to Windows Server 2003, you need to know which upgrade paths are possible. These upgrade paths depend on the edition of Windows Server 2003 under consideration: Standard Edition, Enterprise Edition, Datacenter Edition, or Web Edition. Let's look at the various upgrade paths for each edition separately.

- **Standard Edition**   You can upgrade to this edition of Windows Server 2003 from the following platforms:
  - Windows NT Server 4 (requires Service Pack 5 or later)
  - Windows NT Server 4, Terminal Edition (requires Service Pack 5 or later)
  - Windows 2000 Server

Note that you can't upgrade from Windows NT Server 3.51 to Windows Server 2003. Instead, you need to first upgrade from Windows NT Server 3.51 to Windows NT 4, apply Service Pack 5 or later, and then upgrade to Windows Server 2003. Of course, if anyone reading this is still running Windows NT Server 3.51 on your servers, you'll probably want to keep running that wonderful OS for the next 50 years or so…

- **Enterprise Edition**   You can upgrade to this edition from the following platforms:
  - Windows NT Server 4 (requires Service Pack 5 or later)
  - Windows NT Server 4, Terminal Edition (requires Service Pack 5 or later)
  - Windows NT Server 4, Enterprise Edition (requires Service Pack 5 or later)
  - Windows 2000 Server
  - Windows 2000 Advanced Server
  - Windows Server 2003, Standard Edition

Note that you can't upgrade from Windows NT Server 4, Enterprise Edition, to Windows Server 2003, Standard Edition, only to Windows Server 2003, Enterprise Edition (or Datacenter Edition). Note also that you can also upgrade from Windows Server 2003, Standard Edition, to Windows Server 2003, Enterprise Edition.

- **Web Edition**   You cannot upgrade to this edition of Windows Server 2003 from any earlier operating system. The reason is fairly obvious: Windows Server 2003, Web Edition, is a specialized version of the new OS designed mainly for running on blade server hardware. Because no previous Microsoft Windows operating system was specifically designed for such a purpose, there is no upgrade path to follow—you have to perform a clean install.

- **Datacenter Edition**   Contact your OEM if you are one of the lucky ones who can afford to run Windows 2000 Server, Datacenter Edition, and you want to find out about how to upgrade to Windows Server 2003, Datacenter Edition.

I'll conclude by summarizing the upgrade paths again in Table 3-3. Note that S = Standard Edition and E = Enterprise Edition. I left out Web Edition (because it requires a clean install) and Datacenter Edition (because of its specialized nature). This table omits some of the finer points just discussed.

Hardware Issues

This section describes various hardware issues to consider prior to installing or upgrading your system to Windows Server 2003. In addition to what's discussed here, you should also check the release notes and other information on your Setup CD. These may include

- **Readme1st.txt**   Last-minute preinstallation notes that may apply to your hardware configuration
- **Release notes (Relnotes.htm)**   Postinstallation notes, but you should read them prior to installation anyway.
- **Setup notes**   Special instructions on performing clean installations and upgrades (pretty much the same as what's in the Getting Started guide).

BIOS

The first thing you should do before performing a clean install or upgrade is to make sure your system BIOS has been updated to its latest revision. This is important to ensure that installation proceeds smoothly and full support for ACPI 1.0b is provided for your machine. Visit the website for your system BIOS manufacturer for help on upgrading your flash BIOS. BIOS is used on x86-based platforms only; 64-bit Itanium

Current OS	S	E
Windows NT Server 3.51	Upgrade to NT 4 first	
Windows NT Server 4	√	√
Windows NT Server 4, Terminal Edition	√	√
Windows NT Server 4, Enterprise Edition		√
Windows 2000 Server	√	√
Windows 2000 Advanced Server		√
Windows Server 2003, Standard Edition		√

Table 3-3.   Possible Upgrade Paths to Standard and Enterprise Editions of Windows Server 2003

platforms use an Extensible Firmware Interface instead. You can view your current system BIOS information by pressing DEL or sometimes ESC during the initial text portion of the boot process.

Drivers

Another important task to perform prior to starting your install or upgrade is to make sure you have the latest versions of device drivers from manufacturers. This is particularly important for:

- Any non-PnP devices you have in your system (though it might be better to get rid of these first).

- Mass storage devices like SCSI, RAID, or Fibre Channel (especially if any of these is your primary storage device for your system/boot partition).

- Custom Hardware Abstraction Layer (HAL) files for certain OEM systems.

Make sure you have the latest drivers on hand for all your devices, in case the Windows Update site doesn't have them available for downloading by Dynamic Update. It's particularly important to have copies on hand (on floppies) of any mass storage (SCSI) drivers and HAL files as these may be required to complete Setup. To use mass storage device drivers during Setup, press F6 when prompted to do so. To use a HAL file during Setup, press F5 instead when you are prompted to press F6.

Using Winmsd to Inventory Hardware

If you have non-PnP devices on your system, it's also a good idea to do a system inventory to record configuration settings for such devices. You can use WinMSD for this purpose by typing **winmsd** at the command prompt. On Windows 2000 platforms, this command opens the System Information console (part of Computer Management) and allows you to save your hardware/software configuration info as a text file or Msinfo.Document (.nfo) file (the .nfo file is preferred). On Windows NT 4 platforms, this command runs Windows NT Diagnostics, which can also be started from the Administrative Tools menu and lets you either save your information to a text file or print it out directly.

TIP The updated version of WinMSD on Windows 2000 is really MSinfo32.exe, which is in the folder Program Files\Common Files\Microsoft Shared\MSInfo. When you type **winmsd** at the command line, this simply invokes a stub that executes msinfo32.exe instead. Note, however, that the folder in which msinfo32 is located is not in the default system path, so when you want to run WinMSD from a command prompt (or using Start | Run), it's easiest to type **winmsd**—typing **msinfo32** won't work.

Check Event Logs

An important step to take prior to starting your upgrade is to check your System log in the Event Viewer for any hardware-related events. Look for event messages that might indicate problems with hardware devices and their drivers, and consider updating drivers or even replacing these devices before upgrading.

You might also consider checking Device Manager when upgrading Windows 2000 servers to see if you have any obvious device conflicts such as two devices sharing an IRQ or memory address setting—although, if you've been running your server with disabled hardware for some time, you might want to have your brain examined, too!

Checking System Compatibility

Before you upgrade a Windows NT 4 Server or Windows 2000 Server system to Windows Server 2003, it's important to check that your current hardware configuration is supported by the Windows Server 2003. You can do this by performing a preinstallation compatibility check using the Setup CD. Simply insert the CD into your CD-ROM drive and, when the display screen comes up, select the option for Checking System Compatibility. This will test your hardware for compatibility with the new OS without actually starting the upgrade process. For example, if you try this on a machine running Windows 2000 Professional, you will receive a message that this form of upgrade (from Windows 2000 Professional to Windows Server 2003) is not supported. You can save the results of your test as a text file for later review, which is useful if the process has detected device or driver incompatibilities. Another way of running the compatibility check is from the command line: simply open a command prompt, change to the i386 folder on your CD-ROM drive, and type **winnt32 /checkupgradeonly** to start the process. For more information on Winnt and Winnt32 switches, see Tables 3-1 and 3-2, earlier in this chapter.

If you elect not to perform a preinstallation compatibility test, the system compatibility test is automatically performed anyway when you begin the upgrade process. Note also that different editions of Windows Server 2003 may have different support for certain hardware, so running the compatibility test using the Setup CDs for different editions may give different results. Make sure you use the correct Setup CD when testing a system for hardware compatibility!

Dynamic Update

If you have Internet connectivity on a system you plan to upgrade to Windows Server 2003, you can make use of a feature called Dynamic Update when you run Setup. Dynamic Update lets the system automatically download the latest Setup files and device drivers from the Windows Update website. Microsoft recommends using Dynamic Update whenever possible to ensure your upgrade runs smoothly and successfully. All updated drivers and files on the Windows Update site have been extensively tested, and no personal information is collected or sent to the site during the Dynamic Update process (the process does query your system concerning its configuration, but this information is not saved or sent to Microsoft).

You can even use Dynamic Update with unattended (automatic) installations of Windows Server 2003. For information on how to do this, see the *Windows Server 2003 Deployment Kit* from Microsoft.

Hardware Requirements

The minimum hardware requirements for running Windows Server 2003 depend on the edition selected. Table 3-4 summarizes the minimum requirements to install and run each edition, but real-word systems should comply with the stronger recommended requirements in the next section because systems meeting only minimum requirements will run too slowly for any practical use. The abbreviations used in the table are S = Standard Edition, E = Enterprise Edition, D = Datacenter Edition, and W = Web Edition. Note that the figures shown in the table are for x86-based platforms. 64-bit Itanium platforms may have different hardware requirements; consult the Microsoft website for the latest information. Note also that Datacenter Edition requires an SMP machine with a minimum of 8 CPUs (see the upcoming section "Multiprocessor Support").

If you are performing a network install (running Setup across a network connection to a shared distribution point) or if you are upgrading a FAT or FAT32 partition to NTFS during Setup, you should allow an additional 0.5GB of free disk space on your server.

As far as video and network card minimum requirements are concerned, VGA is supported but SVGA (800×600) is recommended. Some features of fancy video cards are not supported by Windows Server 2003—for some reason Microsoft decided that servers aren't used for playing games, so video driver support for Windows Server 2003 is pretty minimal as far as many vendors are concerned. Check the Hardware Compatibility List (HCL) on the Windows Hardware Driver Quality (WHDQ) website at http://www.microsoft.com/hwdq/hcl/ for more info about supported video cards (also read the earlier section "Checking System Compatibility"). When in doubt, you can try installing the Windows XP driver for a video card to get better results, but this is not supported and could cause hardware instability. Note also that Terminal Services, which is installed by default on Windows Server 2003, can cause problems with higher resolution displays and features for some video cards, especially those that have TV tuners and play DVD movies. Watching TV or playing DVD movies on your server would be a bit strange, don't you think?

I'll talk about supported network cards later in this chapter in the section "NIC Compatibility." As far as other fancy hardware is concerned, Microsoft has taken the stance that servers should be used as servers, and this can impact the use of certain hardware. For example, if you have a sound card installed on a machine and install Windows Server 2003, you might find that your sound doesn't work. This is because the Windows Audio Service is disabled by default on Windows Server 2003 because, according to Microsoft, why would you want a sound card on a server anyway? A

Requirement	S	E	W	D
CPU speed	133MHz	133MHz	133MHz	400MHz
RAM	128MB	128MB	128MB	512MB
Disk space	1.5GB	1.5GB	1.5GB	1.5GB

Table 3-4.   Minimum Hardware Requirements for Windows Server 2003 Editions

similar problem can occur when you try to use USB digital cameras with Windows Server 2003 because the Windows Imaging Service is also disabled by default. Remember Microsoft's promise to provide Windows Server 2003 in a locked-down configuration out of the box for improved security? Still another example is that IR (infrared) is not supported by Windows Server 2003, which may cause issues for running the product on a laptop—but then why would you want to run it on a laptop? Except perhaps if you were a Microsoft spokesperson wanting to demonstrate features of the product on a TechNet Tour!

Be aware that some of the drivers for hardware support in Windows 2000 Server have been deliberately removed from Windows Server 2003, again with the idea that servers are servers and shouldn't be used for fancy stuff like watching TV, burning CDs, scanning photos, running a multifunction printer/copier/fax machine, or synchronizing your PDA (if you want to do any of this kind of stuff, use a Windows XP machine instead!). Another reason Microsoft dropped support for many peripherals and drivers was to streamline and improve the performance of Windows Server 2003, which is hard to argue against. The key is to check the compatibility of your hardware before upgrading your all-in-one server-cum-fancy-peripheral setup to Windows Server 2003.

TIP You can also run Windows Server 2003 without a monitor, keyboard, or mouse on supported hardware. This kind of operation is called *headless operation*, and it is even possible to perform automated installs on headless servers. For more information on this new feature of Windows Server 2003, refer to the chapter on Emergency Management Services (EMS) in the Windows Server 2003 Resource Kit.

Hardware Recommendations

As mentioned previously, running Windows Server 2003 on systems that satisfy only minimum hardware requirements is not advisable for production systems. Instead, make sure that your production systems meet at *least* the hardware recommendations shown in Table 3-5. In most cases, you will want to exceed these hardware recommendations to ensure applications on your servers run free of bottlenecks. The best way of doing this is usually by adding more RAM—though for processor-bound applications, adding additional CPUs is another option. Note again that these figures are for x86-based systems. For hardware recommendations for Itanium systems, see Microsoft's website.

Recommendation	S	E	W	D
CPU speed	550MHz	733MHz	550MHz	773MHz
RAM	256MB	256MB	256MB	1GB
Disk space	1.5GB	1.5GB	1.5GB	1.5GB

Table 3-5. Recommended Hardware Requirements for Windows Server 2003 Editions

Edition	Maximum RAM
Standard	4GB
Enterprise	32GB
Web	2GB
Datacenter	64GB

Table 3-6. Maximum RAM for Windows Server 2003 Editions

Each edition also has a maximum amount of RAM it can support. These maximums are shown in Table 3-6. On certain OEM systems, it may be possible for these limits to be exceeded. Note also that the figures in Table 3-7 are for x86-based systems only; Itanium systems generally have higher limits (see Microsoft's website for Itanium recommendations and maximum RAM). Also, if you want to install more than 4GB of RAM on a machine running Enterprise or Datacenter Edition, first make sure that your hardware platform (motherboard, chipset, BIOS, and so on) allows this by checking the HCL on the WHDQ website. Also, remember that network installs require additional free disk space, as discussed in the preceding section. It's really a good idea to allow yourself extra free disk space (3–4GB should be sufficient) for installing Windows Server 2003. Even more free disk space may be required if you are upgrading a domain controller from Windows NT 4 Server to Windows Server 2003, due to the process of migrating accounts from the SAM database to Active Directory. Finally, the amount of free disk space you need depends on the amount of RAM you have installed, as the paging file is set by default to be 1.5 times the size of RAM. For example, if you are installing Windows Server 2003 on a system running 4GB of RAM, you should allow an additional 6GB of free disk space so Setup can complete properly!

Multiprocessor Support

Different editions of Windows Server 2003 support different numbers of CPUs on symmetric multiprocessing (SMP) hardware platforms. Table 3-7 shows the SMP support for each edition of the product. Datacenter Edition can only be installed on SMP systems with a minimum of 8 CPUs.

Edition	Number of CPUs
Standard	1 to 4
Enterprise	1 to 8
Web	1 or 2
Datacenter	8 to 32

Table 3-7. Multiprocessor Support for Windows Server 2003 Editions

Windows 2000 Server Edition	Maximum # CPUs	Windows Server 2003 Edition	Maximum # CPUs
Server	4	Standard	4
Advanced Server	8	Enterprise	8
Datacenter Server	32	Datacenter	32

Table 3-8.   Maximum Number of CPUs for Windows 2000 Server and Windows .NET Server 2003 Compared

Table 3-8 compares the SMP support for Windows 2000 Server editions and Windows Server 2003 editions. Note that this information applies to x86-based systems only. For information on the hardware requirements of Itanium systems, contact your OEM supplier.

Disk Partitions

The important thing to remember is *back up all your drives before modifying the partition scheme on your system*! If you're upgrading a Windows NT machine to Windows Server 2003, make sure you review your disk partitioning scheme before starting the upgrade. If your existing boot and system partitions are too small, you may not be able to perform the upgrade and may need to do a clean install instead. Also, if your existing boot and system partitions are FAT, you should consider converting them to NTFS before upgrading (see the next section, "File System").

If you're upgrading a Windows 2000 machine to Windows Server 2003, what you can do concerning your partition scheme depends on whether you have basic or dynamic disks. Basic disks are traditional disks, as in Windows NT, and they can be partitioned into partitions of fixed sizes (up to four partitions per disk) that can then be formatted using FAT, FAT32, or NTFS. Dynamic disks are disks that have been converted to dynamic using Disk Management, and they can be partitioned into volumes that can be formatted using NTFS and then dynamically resized without losing data. Also, to implement RAID technologies like mirroring or stripe sets in Windows 2000, you must use dynamic disks. If you want to upgrade a Windows 2000 system that has dynamic disks to Windows Server 2003, you should have no problem doing so (although you should check the Help and Support Center for certain restrictions on installing or upgrading systems with dynamic disks). However, if you want to perform a clean install of Windows Server 2003 on a drive on a Windows 2000 (or Windows XP) system that was converted directly to dynamic without any partitions created on it, you must revert the disk to basic first (back up your data!) before doing the install.

The bottom line is, if you're upgrading, you can't change your partition scheme during Setup (though after the upgrade is complete you can modify your partition scheme using Disk Management). If you're performing a clean install, however, Setup gives you the option of deleting existing partitions and creating new ones. This is one good reason clean installs are generally preferred over upgrades.

File System

You should use NTFS for all your drives for maximum security. The only possible reason for wanting to use a FAT drive on your server would be if you wanted to support multibooting to some earlier operating system like Windows 98 or Me—but this is a pretty silly option for a production machine on a business network, so I won't even discuss it here. You should use NTFS for all partitions on clean installations and convert all FAT or FAT32 partitions to NTFS prior to, after, or during upgrading (to convert from FAT to NFTS you can use the **convert** tool from the command line). Better yet, back up FAT/FAT32 partitions, reformat as NTFS, and restore the data to avoid the degree of fragmentation that occurs when converting partitions from FAT/FAT32 to NFTS.

NOTE   The Web Edition of Windows Server 2003 *only* supports NTFS volumes.

SECURITY ALERT   Some Itanium systems require a small FAT partition of around 100MB to enable the operating system to be loaded—don't delete this partition!

RAID

As shown in Table 3-9, both Windows NT Server 4 and Windows 2000 Server support various fault-tolerant disk technologies based on RAID technologies. Different names are used for these technologies on the two platforms, and implementing RAID on Windows 2000 requires that basic disks first be converted to dynamic disks. In addition to the RAID levels listed in Table 3-9, Windows NT also supports volume sets (called *spanned volumes* in Windows 2000), a technology that lets you combine multiple free areas on different disks together into a single logical volume.

RAID level	Windows NT	Windows 2000
0	Stripe set	Striped volume
1	Mirror set	Mirrored volume
5	Stripe set with parity	RAID-5 volume

Table 3-9.   RAID Levels for Windows NT and Windows 2000

If you plan to upgrade a Windows NT 4 server that has a stripe set, mirror set, or stripe set with parity to Windows Server 2003, you need to perform some preliminary steps before running Setup, specifically,

- If you have a mirror set, you must break the mirror before upgrading. After the upgrade is complete, you can convert the disks to dynamic disks and create a new mirrored volume using Disk Management.

- If you have a volume set, stripe set, or stripe set with parity, you must delete the set before upgrading. After the upgrade is complete, you can convert the disks to dynamic disks and create a new spanned volume, striped volume, or RAID-5 volume using Disk Management.

Of course, before you perform any of these actions, make sure you perform a backup so that none of your data will be lost!

TIP   If you neglect these steps and upgrade anyway, your mirror sets, volume sets, stripe sets, and stripe sets with parity created under Windows NT will be inaccessible under Windows Server 2003. If you open Disk Management to try to view these volumes, they will show up as Failed volumes that have drive letters but cannot be accessed by the file system. All is not lost, however—there is a command-line utility called Ftonline in the \Support\Tools folder on the product CD that may let you recover the data on these failed volumes and back it up to good volumes. Once you've recovered the data, delete the failed volumes in Disk Management, convert your drives to dynamic disks, and create new fault-tolerant volumes as desired.

Compressed Drives

Don't install Windows Server 2003 on a compressed drive unless it was compressed using the compression feature of NTFS. For example, if you have a system whose drive was compressed using DriveSpace or DoubleSpace (legacy MS-DOS and Windows 9x compression technologies), uncompress it using these tools first before running Setup for Windows Server 2003.

Clustering

Upgrading a cluster running Windows NT 4 Server, Enterprise Edition, or Windows 2000 Advanced Server to Windows Server 2003, Enterprise Edition, is a complex procedure and beyond the scope of this book. See the Setup text files in the \Docs folder on your product CD for more information on how to perform these actions.

UPS

If you have a UPS device connected to your server, make sure you physically disconnect it before starting the upgrade process. The reason for this is that Setup checks for devices connected to serial ports, and a connection UPS device can cause problems with the hardware-detection process.

Backups

In addition to anticipating the various hardware issues just discussed, it's important to back up your data prior to starting an upgrade. What data you actually back up depends on your drive configuration and server's role, but at the very least you should perform a complete backup of the following:

- System partition
- Boot partition
- System State information

Often the system and boot partitions may be the same partition (usually the C: drive). System State information consists of the Registry, system boot files, any files under Windows File Protection, COM+ Class Registration database, and performance counter configuration information; and for domain controllers, also Active Directory, SYSVOL, and the DNS database.

You should regularly perform a full backup of these items along with any other important data, either to tape or to a network file server. Burn yourself a CD copy also. Be prepared!

SECURITY ALERT   New to Windows Server 2003 is Automated System Recovery, an advanced feature of the Backup administrative tool that lets you periodically make a complete backup of all data necessary to quickly restore your boot and system partitions in the event of catastrophic hard disk failure.

Network

You should consider a few planning issues related to network connectivity before beginning your deployment of Windows Server 2003, to ensure your clean install or upgrade goes successfully.

NIC Compatibility

A major consideration if you are planning to upgrade an older system to Windows Server 2003 is that Microsoft has removed support for many older network interface cards (NICs) in Windows Server 2003, especially in Enterprise Edition, which has stricter hardware requirements and less legacy hardware support than other editions of Windows Server 2003—so don't expect that old NE2000-compatible NIC to work! In fact, support for many for 10Mbps Ethernet cards has been removed from this platform, probably because most servers today have 100 Mbps or 1 Gbps connections to network backbones. Again, make sure you run the System Compatibility Check from your product CD prior to upgrading to ensure older hardware will support Windows Server 2003.

Internet Connectivity

As discussed earlier in the section "Checking System Compatibility," it's a good idea to have live Internet connectivity for your server when upgrading from Windows NT or Windows 2000 to Windows Server 2003. This allows Setup to automatically connect to the Windows Update website and use Dynamic Update to download new Setup files or updated devices drivers for your hardware. This may not be an option in some enterprise environments, however, because corporate firewalls may prevent such connections—Windows Update may not be desirable from a security or management perspective. To satisfy the needs of its corporate customers for something more manageable than traditional Windows Update, Microsoft originally developed a Corporate version of Windows Update for Windows 2000 that allowed IT admins to manage the downloading of updates and patches and how they were applied to servers on the company's network. This system has now been retired, and Microsoft has replaced it with the Microsoft Software Update Service (SUS), which simplifies the process of keeping your Windows-based computers up-to-date. Using SUS, administrators can quickly and reliably deploy software patches and updates to machines running Windows 2000 Server or Professional, Windows XP Professional, and Windows Server 2003.

The way it works is that you install an SUS server on your network, and this server automatically downloads critical updates from Microsoft and informs the administrator of their presence. The administrator can then test the updates by installing them manually on selected machines and can then schedule when these updates will be applied and to which machines. Updates are sent from the SUS server to machines on the network using HTTP at the scheduled time, and the whole process is managed by a web-based administration tool on the SUS server. For more information about SUS, see http://www.microsoft.com/windows2000/windowsupdate/sus/ on Microsoft's website.

Choosing a Computer Name

When performing a new installation, you need to specify a computer name for your system. Computer names must be unique within a domain or workgroup, so make sure you choose a different name for each computer on your network. Setup will suggest a name for your computer, but these randomly specified names are hard to remember and go against the whole idea of computer names in the first place—friendly alphanumeric names that are easier to remember than cryptic IP addresses. The maximum length you can specify for a computer name is 63 bytes, but you should generally restrict computer names to 15 bytes or less because legacy systems running Windows NT or earlier versions of Windows can only recognize the first 15 bytes of computer names (if you gave your new Windows Server the name REALLYSUPERNEWMACHINE, legacy Windows clients on your network would see it as REALLYSUPERNEWM instead).

Most large companies have devised special rules for naming their computers. For example, a computer in the Marketing Department might have the name MK12, indicating machine number 12 in that department. Another approach is to use the geographical location in the computer name—for example, BLDG5FL4NUM166 would be machine number 166 on the fourth floor of Building 5. Sometimes large companies append the vendor serial number to the name of each computer to simplify their asset management; for example, DESK11924235S35 might be the name for a desktop computer with the serial number 11924235S35. The idea behind friendly names is not just to make them easier to remember, but more functional than IP addresses, which if assigned by a DHCP server are nonpermanent and can change with time.

TIP   Try to use only DNS-standard characters in your computer name, that is, letters A–Z (case doesn't matter), digits 0–9, and the dash (-) character. Note that you cannot use only numbers for a computer name.

IP Addressing

Servers should generally have static IP addresses, but you can also create DHCP reservations to ensure they receive a specific IP address from a DHCP server. The method you use depends on how many servers you have to manage on your network. IIS machines may need several IP addresses assigned to them if they are hosting multiple websites for different departments or companies, so make sure you plan your addressing scheme well before deploying your web servers.

TIP   If you choose to assign an IP address to your machine using DHCP but there is no DHCP server available on the network during Setup (or if network communications fail and prevent your machine from contacting the DHCP server), your server will automatically assign itself a randomly chosen IP address from the range 169.254.0.1 through 169.254.255.254 using the Automatic Private IP Addressing (APIPA) feature of Windows Server 2003. If this is the case, you will be unable to communicate with your machine over the network after Setup is complete. To check if this is what happened, open a command prompt on the machine and type **ipconfig**, and see if APIPA assigned an address from the range above. Once the DHCP server can be contacted, type **ipconfig /release** to release the address assigned by APIPA and **ipconfig /renew** to obtain a proper address from the DHCP server.

Role

Another network-related issue is planning the role you will assign to your new server. After installing Windows Server 2003 and logging on for the first time, you are presented with the Manager, Your Server screen, which lets you add new roles to your server and manage existing ones. Possible roles include

- File server
- Print server
- Web application (IIS + ASP.NET) server
- Mail (POP3) server
- Terminal server

- Remote access/VPN server
- WINS server
- DHCP server
- DNS server
- Domain controller
- Streaming media server

Adding the web application role to your server allows you to install IIS on your machine, something we'll discuss further in this chapter in the section "Installing IIS."

Security

Planning for security is another important part of the deployment planning process. The following sections deal briefly with security issues related to Windows Server 2003 in general—security issues related specifically to IIS 6 will be covered in a later chapter of this book.

Administrator Password

During a clean install, you'll be prompted to specify a password for the default Administrator account on the machine. If you choose a password with too few characters, you'll be prompted to enter a more complex one. Strong passwords should have at least 7 characters and contain a mixture of upper- and lowercase letters, numbers, and special symbols like * or $. Of course, if you make a password too complex, you may have to write it down to remember it—just don't put it on a sticky note under your keyboard! In Windows Server 2003, passwords can be up to 127 characters long. A good way of creating a complex password that's easy to remember is to use the first letter of each word in a line from a song and append a string of numbers to the end, for example, the line "Winter, spring, summer, or fall, all you have to do is call" (from Carole King's "You've Got a Friend") would give a password like WssfAyhtdic4321. Mind you, you might want to choose a more obscure song to create your password!

SECURITY ALERT   You can further secure your Administrator account by renaming it. You should rename the Guest account also, and leave it disabled. You can rename these accounts manually or use Group Policy; see article Q320053 in the Knowledge Base on the Microsoft Product Support Services (PSS) site at http://support.microsoft.com for more details.

Physical Security

It's important to ensure that your servers are physically secure during clean installs or upgrades because they can be vulnerable to attack during the Setup process. For example, an unsupervised install could allow a malicious user to interrupt the text-mode portion of Setup and copy files to the server or perform some other action. One way of preventing this is to do all server installs in a "clean room" that only administrators can access, and then move servers to their proper network locations afterward. This may not be feasible in an enterprise environment, but security should always be on your mind when deploying new systems or upgrading existing ones.

Licensing

Licensing is another planning issue to consider when upgrading to or installing Windows Server 2003. The two licensing modes supported by this platform are

- **Per Server licensing**   This mode requires that you specify how many clients can simultaneously access your server for accessing server services (such as file and print, remote access, and terminal services) that are controlled by licensing requirements. Per Server licensing is usually used only when you have a small network with a single server on it.

- **Per Seat licensing**   This mode requires that each client machine on your network be assigned a separate Client Access License (CAL) that lets it access as many servers as it requires. For networks with two or more servers, this is the preferred licensing mode.

Licensing is a complex issue. In most cases, you won't only be deploying IIS 6 web servers, you'll also be migrating large parts of your network to Windows Server 2003, so you'll need to plan your licensing strategy well prior to starting your deployment. Each Windows Server 2003 machine on your network requires a server license. In addition, each client that needs authenticated access to your servers or access to Windows Server 2003 services running on your servers needs a CAL. Authenticated users are users who either use Windows Server 2003 authentication methods or whose credentials are stored in Active Directory. If your users need to be authenticated by websites running on IIS 6, then you have two possible ways of licensing them to do so (licensing policies change frequently, so check this information on Microsoft's licensing site at www.microsoft.com/licensing to be sure). These two methods are to do one of the following:

- Purchase sufficient CALs (either Per Seat or Per Server type) to enable your users to legally access IIS 6 websites using Windows Server 2003 authentication.

- Purchase a special Internet Connector License for each web server. This license allows an unlimited number of users authenticated access to websites on your server. For IIS server farms, each server in the farm requires an Internet Connector License.

If your IIS 6 websites are only going to be accessed by anonymous users (no Windows Server 2003 authentication), then no licenses are required. Anonymous access is often used for public Internet websites, but authenticated access is usually required for internal (intranet) sites, so the type of IIS deployment you are planning determines whether you need additional licenses or not. If you do need authentication for an external website, you may be able to save money by reducing your licensing costs and using a third-party authentication tool or having authentication performed by a UNIX or Linux machine instead of using Active Directory and Windows Server 2003 authentication methods.

Large companies generally have special agreements called *volume licensing* that save them money over small companies that buy additional licenses separate from their product CDs, but a full discussion of volume licensing options is beyond the scope of this book. For further information on licensing Microsoft products, contact your VAR or see www.microsoft.com/licensing for details. Whatever you do, make sure you're properly licensed, or you might find law enforcement officials at your company's door some day!

Windows Product Activation

If you installed or upgraded to Windows Server 2003 using commercially purchased individual media (product CD), you must activate your software after installing it. Microsoft included *Windows Product Activation (WPA)* in Windows Server 2003 to thwart the ever-increasing software piracy occurring in the industry. Despite the inconvenience of using it, I support them in their efforts—it's not about Microsoft getting richer, it's about being legal and protecting a whole software industry from rampant piracy, something that affects our whole economy and ultimately our jobs as IT professionals.

When Setup is finished and you log on to your machine, you will be prompted to activate immediately. If you have a live Internet connection, this is a simple process that takes only a few seconds, and no personal information is sent to Microsoft (product activation is secure and uses SSL for communicating between your machine and Microsoft's secure WPA servers). When you activate Windows, your product key is associated with a random hash of the specific hardware configuration you've installed Windows on (activation ignores other software you may have installed on your machine—the process is not snooping to discover pirated software on your system, it's just ensuring that you use your Windows Server 2003 product CD on only a single system as the EULA requires). After activating your system, if you then try to install the same copy of Windows (using the same product CD) on a different system, you won't be allowed to activate it, because Microsoft keeps a database of associations between customer product keys and activated systems. Similarly, if someone steals your product CD (or you burn a copy for a friend), they won't be able to activate it after installing it. Microsoft keeps a random one-way hash (not the raw information) of your hardware configuration along with your product key on its WPA servers. Microsoft does not keep a record of your computer's hardware configuration on the servers—they don't know what hardware you're using, and they don't care. They're not snooping, they just want to enforce your product's EULA, which essentially says, "You buy one copy of the product, you can install it on one machine." For more information about what WPA is and what it isn't, see http://www.microsoft.com/piracy/basics/activation/ on Microsoft's website.

If you don't have a live Internet connection, you can also activate by telephoning Microsoft and following the steps displayed on your screen. If you choose not to activate immediately after Setup, you have a grace period (30 days) in which you can choose to activate. Once this period expires, you can still log on but you will only be able to use the Active Windows Wizard.

If you change your hardware configuration significantly, you may be required to reactivate your system to prove to Microsoft that you haven't gone and installed Windows on another system. Reactivation is only required when multiple significant changes have been made simultaneously to your hardware, and it's usually done by phone. This is the only potential hassle with product activation, and it's one of the main reasons people griped about activation when Microsoft first introduced it: when you have accumulated a certain number of product changes within a given time period, you are required to phone Microsoft to reactivate. These changes are counted different ways depending on what kind of hardware you are adding or replacing. For example, changing a video card once counts as a change, but changing it a second time doesn't. Replacing a hard drive counts as a change, but adding an additional drive doesn't. And adding RAM counts as a change, but adding more RAM doesn't. If you reach a certain number of changes within the 120-day period after you install or upgrade your system to Windows Server 2003, you have to reactivate. If you haven't reached the limit after 120 days, your system baseline is reset to its new hardware configuration and you start with zero changes again.

TIP   If you make a major change like upgrading the motherboard of your machine and find you have to reactivate Windows but can't do so, it may be that your BIOS clock is set incorrectly. If this is the case, set the clock, reboot, and try reactivating again.

Volume Licensing

Volume licensing customers, that is, enterprise customers who purchase large numbers of licenses directly from Microsoft or through their VAR, don't have the hassles of product activation that smaller customers buying individual CD media have. Also, special customers like MSDN subscribers and Microsoft-approved educational institutions also may have different activation requirements.

NOTE   Product activation is not the same as product registration, which is an optional post-installation procedure for providing Microsoft with personal and contact information that enables them to send you product updates and special offers.

IIS PLANNING ISSUES

I'll end this chapter by discussing a few matters connected specifically with installing IIS 6 once you've upgraded to or installed Windows Server 2003 on a system. Most of the deployment planning and work has to do with deploying the underlying Windows Server 2003 operating system; but because this is a book about IIS, you need to get that component up and running, too.

Installing IIS

As an extra security feature, when you install Windows Server 2003 Standard, Enterprise, or Datacenter Edition on a machine, IIS 6 is not automatically installed by default—you have to manually install it after Setup is finished in order to turn your machine into a web server. Obviously this is not the case with Web Edition, which installs IIS 6 by default because this is the main function of that edition!

If you have performed a clean install of Standard, Enterprise, or Datacenter Edition, there are two ways you can manually install IIS 6 after Setup is complete:

- Use the Manage Your Server Wizard that appears when you first log on as Administrator after installing Windows Server 2003 on your machine. In the Adding Roles To Your Server section, select Add Or Remove A Role to start the Configure Your Server Wizard. Then follow the prompts to install the Application Server (IIS or ASP.NET) role, select or deselect optional components for that role (ASP.NET is selected by default), and complete the wizard.

- Use the Start menu to select Control Panel | Add/Remove Programs | Add/ Remove Windows Components | Application Server. Click the Details button and select the components you want to install.

The second approach is a little more customizable than the first, but in most cases the Manage Your Server Wizard will suffice.

If you are doing an automated install, you can use the unattend.txt file to include IIS in the components to be installed. Similarly, if you are using Sysprep, you can install IIS 6 on your master system and then clone target systems using third-party disk imaging software. But if you are upgrading an existing IIS 4 (Windows NT) or IIS 5 (Windows 2000) web server to Windows Server 2003, you won't need to install IIS 6 afterward because IIS 4/5 will automatically be upgraded to IIS 6.

Installing ASP.NET

You need to install ASP.NET components on your web server only if you plan to develop and run dynamic web applications, not just static HTML content, on your server. In most cases, you'll want to do this of course, and I'll talk more about configuring applications in Chapter 8, "Creating and Configuring Applications."

Installing FrontPage Server Extensions

If you plan to have users develop and manage content on your web server using Microsoft FrontPage, you'll need to install the FrontPage Server Extensions after installing IIS. We'll look at using FrontPage Server Extensions in Chapter 16, "Publishing with IIS."

Sample Web Applications

Previous versions of IIS automatically installed sample scripts and web applications for you to play with and learn from. For security reasons (to harden the system), version 6 of IIS does not do this. You can, however, install sample scripts manually if you choose to, but doing this doesn't create a Scripts virtual directory under the default website as it did in earlier versions of IIS—this is another security improvement in version 6.

Web Service Extensions (WSE)

IIS 6 automatically installs in locked-down mode. To get things like ASP.NET applications to work properly, you have to selectively unlock various settings using the Web Service Extensions (WSE) node within the IIS console tree. We'll examine this matter in detail when we look at IIS security in Chapter 10, "Securing IIS," but be aware that configuring security settings on your web servers is a deployment planning issue you need to consider ahead of time.

Application Isolation Mode

Depending on whether you need to ensure compatibility with applications developed for IIS 5 or ensure the greatest degree of application reliability, you need to plan and decide which application isolation mode to run your IIS web server in: worker process isolation mode or IIS 5 isolation mode. During the deployment planning process, you should test your existing web applications to see if they will work properly in worker process isolation mode, which is the preferred operation mode that takes advantage of the new IIS 6 architecture. If you perform a clean install of Windows Server 2003 and install the IIS 6 component, your web server is automatically running in worker process isolation mode. If you upgraded your system from IIS 4 (Windows NT) or IIS 5 (Windows 2000), then it's running in IIS 5 isolation mode. You can, of course, change the mode if your deployment requires this; the procedure for doing so is outlined in Chapter 8, "Creating and Configuring Applications."

CHALLENGE

You have a medium-size business that has a network with a dozen servers and several hundred workstations. Your servers are running Windows 2000 Server and you want to take advantage of the new features of Windows Server 2003, particularly the increased stability and reliability of version 6 of IIS, which you see as advantageous for your company intranet. What edition of Windows Server 2003 would you upgrade your Windows 2000 Server machines to and why? What hardware considerations might be important in planning your upgrade? What budget considerations are important to your decision? What deployment method would you use and why?

CHECKLIST: DEPLOYMENT CHECKLIST

Important steps to take in planning a clean installation include:

☐ Reading the Release Notes on the product CD

☐ Selecting a licensing mode

☐ Deciding on a partition scheme

☐ Selecting the installation partition and choosing its file system

☐ Assigning a computer name and IP addressing scheme

Important steps to take in planning an upgrade include:

☐ Reading the Release Notes on the product CD

☐ Backing up your data, including the boot and system partitions and System State information

☐ Checking the System log in the Event Viewer for hardware-related issues

☐ Using the product CD to check the system's hardware compatibility for upgrading

☐ Reviewing your partition scheme and modifying it if necessary

☐ Breaking mirror sets and deleting volume sets, stripe sets, and stripe sets with parity (Windows NT 4 only)

☐ Applying Service Pack 5 or later (Windows NT 4 only)

☐ Disconnecting your UPS device if you have one

CHAPTER 4

Installing IIS 6

In the previous chapter we looked at planning issues related to deploying IIS 6 (and hence Windows Server 2003) in the enterprise. In this chapter I will walk you through several examples of deploying IIS 6 to give you an idea of the different approaches you can use. The specific methods we will look at include

- Performing a clean install directly from the product CD

- Performing a clean install from a network distribution point by booting the target machine with a network boot disk

- Performing an unattended clean install with a distribution point and answer file created using Setup Manager

- Upgrading from IIS 4 (Windows NT Server 4) to IIS 6

- Upgrading from IIS 5 (Windows 2000 Server) to IIS 6

In each of these walkthroughs, I will describe the steps involved and examine the results of the installation. For upgrades, I will also compare the IIS configuration before and after the installation.

CLEAN INSTALL FROM PRODUCT CD

Let's start with the simplest scenario, a clean install of Windows Server 2003 Standard Edition directly from the product CD (installing Enterprise Edition works exactly the same way). Begin by configuring the system BIOS on your machine to boot first from CD-ROM. Usually you do this by pressing DEL (or some other key) during startup to allow you to access your system's CMOS Setup utility, and then change the Boot Sequence accordingly. We'll install Standard Edition on a machine with no operating system—all existing partitions can be removed using a handy little tool called Delpart.exe, a DOS-based utility for wiping NTFS partitions from drives. Delpart was included in the Windows NT 3.1 Resource Kit and is an unsupported utility, but it usually works well. Wiping a machine with Delpart is simple: just copy Delpart.exe to an MS-DOS 6.22 boot disk, boot from the floppy, and use Delpart to remove all your NTFS partitions and save the changes to your partition table. Then use FDISK to confirm that your partitions have been deleted.

You can get Delpart from Microsoft's FTP site: just open the URL ftp://ftp .microsoft.com/bussys/winnt/winnt-public/reskit/nt31/i386/ in your browser window and download RESKIT.EXE, the Windows NT 3.1 Resource Kit. Install this kit on a machine and copy Delpart.exe to your DOS boot disk.

NOTE   You can also find Delpart at various other sites on the Internet, but don't confuse it with the Trojan Horse virus of the same name! Better to get the original file from Microsoft's FTP site than risk your machine getting contaminated with a Trojan!

Clean installation from the product CD on a wiped machine is simple to begin—just insert the CD and turn the power on. What follows is almost identical to what you've experienced installing Windows NT, Windows 2000, or Windows XP, so I'll review it only briefly here (refer back to Chapter 3, "Planning Deployment," for planning issues related to the Setup process). The first part of Setup is the blue screen Text Mode portion. If you have drivers for mass storage devices (SCSI drives) to install, press F6 when prompted to do so. After the Setup files have been loaded, follow the prompts for setting up Windows by pressing F8 to accept the EULA and pressing the appropriate key sequence to create a system/boot partition and format it using NTFS. Once the partition is formatted, files are copied to the installation folders, the system reboots, and the GUI Mode portion of Setup begins. After devices have been detected, you'll be presented with a series of prompts for specifying regional and language options, personalization info (name and organization), product key, licensing mode, computer name (accept the suggested name it randomly generates), administrator password (you'll be prompted to create a strong password), and date/time settings. After answering these prompts, networking components will be installed and you'll be prompted to select either Typical or Custom network settings. Typical uses DHCP to obtain TCP/IP settings for your machine (if a DHCP server is unavailable, Automatic Private IP Addressing [APIPA] will be used instead), while Custom can be used to add or remove networking components and assign static IP address settings. Next, specify whether your machine will belong to a workgroup or a domain. At that point, installation continues until Setup is finished, the system reboots, and you're presented with the logon screen.

Installing IIS

When the installation is complete and you log on as Administrator, you'll be presented with the Manage Your Server Wizard (see Figure 4-1). Before you use the wizard, you may also be prompted to modify your display settings and asked if you want Windows to automatically correct your screen resolution and color depth settings to more suitable values (800×600 at 32-bit depth is recommended). You'll also be prompted by a system tray message to activate your newly installed operating system. Windows Product Activation (WPA) was explained in Chapter 3; you should activate your copy of Windows before the grace period expires by clicking the key icon in the system tray.

Once your display settings are optimized, you can use the Manage Your Server Wizard to install IIS 6, which in Windows Server 2003 is *not* installed by default. Afterward, you can confirm which IIS components are installed this way by selecting Control Panel | Add Or Remove Programs | Add/Remove Windows Components | Application Server | Details | Internet Information Services (IIS). You can also manually install the IIS components you desire using this Control Panel utility if you desire, but the more intuitive method is to use the Manage Your Server Wizard. To do this, in the wizard, click Add Or Remove A Role to start the Configure Your Server Wizard (see

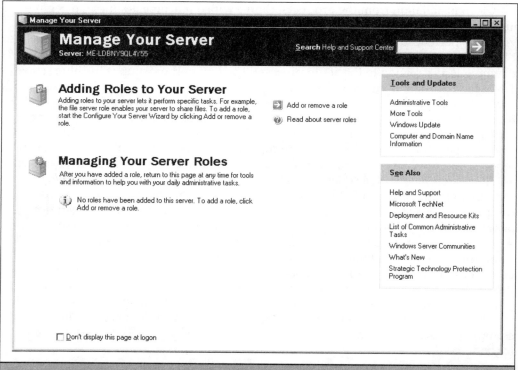

Figure 4-1. The Manage Your Server Wizard starts automatically after you install Standard or Enterprise Edition of Windows Server 2003.

Figure 4-2) and ensure that all your networking hardware is functioning properly. You may need your product CD for configuring certain roles, so make sure you have this handy (or ensure you have access to the product source files on a shared network distribution point).

Continuing with the wizard, click Next and wait while the operating system tests the network connections configured on the machine. After a short time, the next screen of the wizard presents you with the options of either configuring the first server for your network or creating a custom configuration. The first option is designed for organizations deploying a new Windows Server 2003–based network and will make the server the first domain controller on your network, installing Active Directory, DNS, and DHCP if required. Because you want to install IIS on your new server, choose the second option to perform a custom configuration of your system (see Figure 4-3).

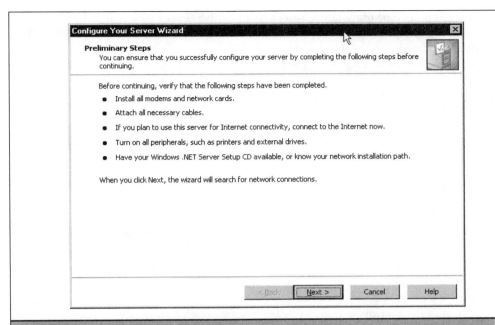

Figure 4-2.   Using the Configure Your Server Wizard to add a new role for your server

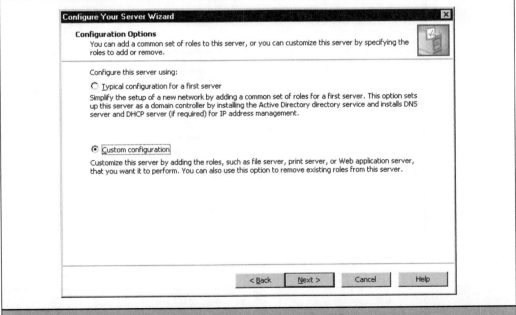

Figure 4-3.   Selecting the Custom Configuration option to install IIS components on your server

On the next screen of the wizard, select Application Server (IIS, ASP.NET) as the role you want to install on your server (see Figure 4-4). This will install IIS, ASP.NET, and related components to allow you to use your machine for hosting web and FTP sites. Note that by default your server will be configured to serve static HTML content only, and you'll have to use the Web Service Extension (WSE) node in the IIS console later to open it up for running dynamic content if this is your intention (we'll look at WES in Chapter 10).

The next screen of the wizard lets you select which additional Application Server components you want to install in addition to the core IIS components (see Figure 4-5). Optional components you can choose include

- **FrontPage Server Extensions**   Lets you publish content created on client machines using Microsoft FrontPage or Microsoft Visual Studio to your IIS machine.

- **Microsoft Data Engine (MSDE)**   Lets you host small (2GB data and five concurrent users) SQL databases on your IIS machine (no user interface to this component is provided; however, you could install Microsoft Access for this purpose).

- **ASP.NET**   Lets you host XML Web Services (.aspx code) on your IIS machine (selected by default).

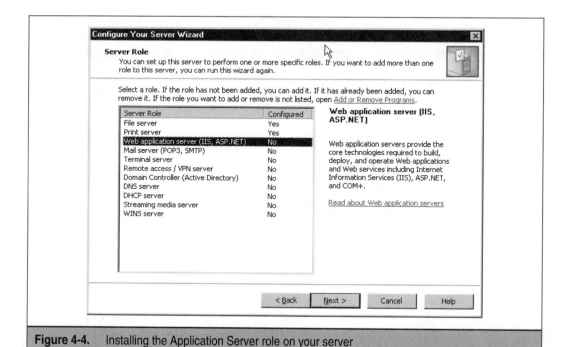

Figure 4-4.   Installing the Application Server role on your server

ASP.NET

ASP.NET is a separate component from Active Server Pages (ASP) and can be installed separately or together with ASP. Web applications written in ASP have pages with the extension .asp, while ASP.NET pages use .aspx to emphasize the XML nature of web services written for ASP.NET. Code written for ASP can easily be migrated to ASP.NET to take advantage of the new features of ASP.NET, which include support for VB.NET, C#, and JScript.NET and enhanced performance over traditional ASP. If you don't need ASP.NET at this time on your IIS machine, deselect it when adding the Application Server role to your server, as you can easily add it later by reconfiguring the role.

The final screen of the wizard displays a summary of the components that will be installed on your machine (see Figure 4-6). Review this list of components and, if necessary, go back in the wizard to add Or remove the components you desire. Note that you can also use the Add or Remove Programs utility in Control Panel later to make a more granular selection for adding or removing Application Server components. Clicking Next will start the Windows Components Wizard, and you'll be prompted to insert the product CD or specify the location of your installation files.

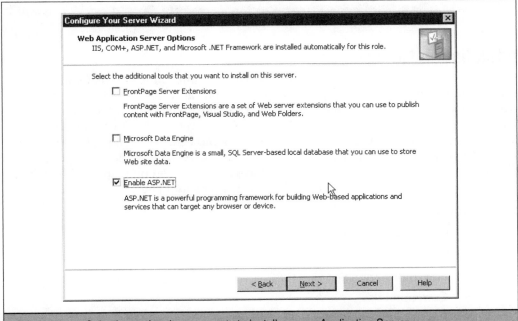

Figure 4-5.   Selecting optional components to install on your Application Server

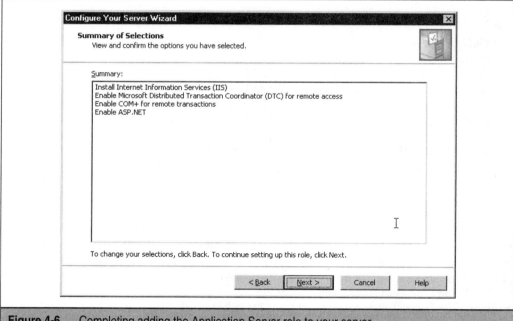

Figure 4-6.   Completing adding the Application Server role to your server

Postinstallation Notes

Once IIS is installed, a final wizard screen will appear informing you that your server is now running in the role of Application Server. You can verify your installation (or troubleshoot if a problem occurs) by viewing Configure Your Server.log, a text file located in the C:\WINDOWS\Debug folder. You'll be returned to the Manage Your Server Wizard, and the Application Server role should be listed along with any other roles you've installed on your server. You can also use Add Or Remove Programs in Control Panel to verify which components have been installed on your machine. The list of installed components under Application Server should be

- ASP.NET
- Enable network COM+ access
- Enable network DTC access
- Internet Information Services (IIS)
  - Common Files
  - Internet Information Services Manager
  - World Wide Web Service
- Application Server Console

You can use Add Or Remove Programs to install additional components for your Application Server, such as Active Server Pages or File Transfer Protocol (FTP) Service.

Now take a moment to open Internet Services Manager from Administrative Tools and see the configuration of your IIS machine (see Figure 4-7). Internet Services Manager is the Microsoft Management Console (MMC) used for managing IIS and will be covered in detail in the next chapter "Administering Standard/Enterprise Edition." Note in the console tree in the left pane of Figure 4-7 that installing version 6 of IIS does not install any sample website content as it did in versions 4 and 5 on the Windows NT and Windows 2000 platforms. In fact, IIS 6 only includes a default website with no content in it except an Under Construction page called iisstart.htm (you can view this page by right-clicking Default Web Site and selecting Browse). The other nodes in this console tree, Application Pools and Web Service Extensions, are discussed later in Chapter 10.

NOTE   The subdirectory located under the Default Web Site node is created when you install ASP.NET together with IIS. If you deselected ASP.NET when adding the Application Server role, this subdirectory will not be present in Internet Services Manager.

NOTE   If you install the IIS 6 component of Windows Server 2003 and discover that users can't connect to sites running on IIS, check to see if you enabled the Internet Connection Firewall (ICF) component on your server prior to installing IIS: select Start | Control Panel | Network Connections | Local Area Connection | Properties and click the Advanced button. If the check box under Internet Connection Firewall is selected, you have the ICF component enabled. You need to configure it to allow web clients to access IIS: select Settings | Services, select the Web Server (HTTP) check box, and specify the name or IP address of the IIS machine you want to allow clients to access.

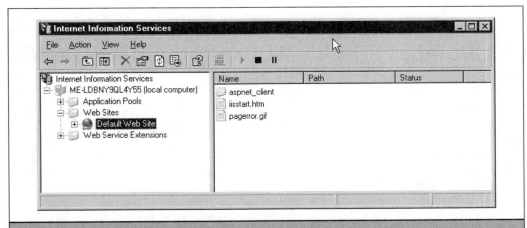

Figure 4-7.   IIS configuration displayed in Internet Services Manager console

SECURITY ALERT!   If you select the Web Service Extensions (WSE) node in the IIS console, when you add the Application Server role to Standard (and Enterprise) Edition using the default options presented, ASP.NET is allowed, while Active Server Pages and other service extensions are prohibited. This means that ASP.NET is installed and enabled so that .aspx applications will run, but ASP is not installed nor enabled. ASP applications will therefore not run unless you first install the ASP component from Control Panel and then enable ASP by setting its service extension to Allowed. This is another example of the improved security in this new version of IIS, whereby features like ASP are locked down by default and must be unlocked to use them.

Directory Structure

Installing IIS on a Windows Server 2003 machine also creates several new directories in your file system:

- **\Inetpub\wwwroot**   Contains an under construction page for your default website and represents the home directory for this site
- **\Inetpub\AdminScripts**   Contains several useful scripts for performing IIS administration from the command line or in batch mode
- **\Windows\Help\IISHelp**   Contains various IIS help docs and the \common directory that contains HTTP error message .htm pages, which you can customize (most IIS help docs are in \Windows\Help)
- **\Windows\System32\InetSrv**   Contains various IIS executables and component DLLs together with assorted scripts for performing IIS administration from the command line or in batch mode
- **\Windows\System32\InetSrv\History**   Contains metabase history files
- **\Windows\System32\InetSrv\MetaBack**   Contains metabase backups

CLEAN INSTALL FROM NETWORK DISTRIBUTION POINT

For your second installation, you'll create a shared network distribution point containing the source files for Windows Server 2003 Web Edition. Then you'll perform a clean install of Web Edition onto a machine that has no preinstalled operating system on it. You'll do this by creating a network boot disk that will enable you to boot your target machine from a floppy, connect to the distribution point, and run Winnt32.exe to perform your install. Creating and configuring a network boot disk is an exercise in walking down memory lane—specifically, DOS Avenue (and NT Boulevard as well)— but it's fun, and it's a useful skill to know.

Creating a Distribution Point

Begin by creating a shared distribution point for installing Windows Server 2003 Web Edition over the network. The simplest way to do this is to insert the product CD for this edition in the CD-ROM of a file server, copy the \I386 folder and its contents to the server's hard drive, and share the folder using the default share name I386. For this walkthrough, I'm using a Windows 2000 Professional test machine called SNOOPY as my file server, a stand-alone machine belonging to a workgroup called WORKGROUP. The UNC path that my network boot disk will need to connect to in order to access the installation source files will be \\SNOOPY\I386. The machine name and network path you are using will probably be different, so adjust the UNC path accordingly.

Creating a Network Boot Disk

Now it's time to create your network boot disk so you can boot your target machine with it, connect to \\SNOOPY\I386 (or whatever), download the Setup files, and perform the installation. Network boot disks are tricky—setting them up requires some knowledge of MS-DOS. However, most sysadmins have some working knowledge of this old workhorse operating system. Network boot disks are often used for performing unattended installations, and most third-party disk imaging applications include a network boot disk. If you don't have such software, don't despair—you can use the Windows NT Server 4 operating system to create a network boot disk. If you have a Windows NT 4 server on your network, you simply use Administrative Tools | Network Client Administrator | Make Network Installation Startup Disk and specify the necessary information to create the disk, as you'll see in a moment.

But what if you don't have an NT server handy on your network? Unfortunately, Windows 2000 Server does *not* include a utility for creating a network boot disk. But if you have a Windows NT Server 4 product CD handy, you can extract the necessary files from the CD and use them on a Windows 2000 system to create your boot disk. Let's try this approach. First, you'll need a bootable MS-DOS system disk for your network boot disk. To create such a disk, insert an MS-DOS boot disk (every sysadmin has a few dozen of these kicking around) into your Windows 2000 workstation, reboot, and type **FORMAT A: /S** at the MS-DOS prompt (make sure your boot disk is write-protected first). You'll be prompted to insert the disk you want to make bootable, so insert a blank floppy and press ENTER. Remove the formatted system disk and label it Network Boot Disk or something similar. Now reboot your workstation to Windows 2000 and do the following:

1. Use Windows Explorer to create the folder C:\Ncadmin.
2. Create a subfolder called \Clients within your \Ncadmin folder.
3. Insert the Windows NT 4 Server product CD into your CD-ROM drive (the R: drive in my example).

4. Copy the files Ncadmin.cn_, Ncadmin.ex_, and Ncadmin.hl_ from the \I386 folder of your NT Server product CD to your C:\Ncadmin folder.

5. Open a command prompt and switch to your C:\Ncadmin folder.

6. Type **expand -r ncadmin.*** at the command prompt to extract the files needed.

7. Leave the NT product CD in the R: drive.

Now type **ncadmin** at the command prompt to run Ncadmin.exe and start Network Client Administrator on your Windows 2000 machine (see Figure 4-8).

Select the Make Network Installation Startup Disk option and click Continue. The path should be R:\Clients; if it isn't, change it. Select the Share Files option and click OK (see Figure 4-9). You can remove this share after you have finished running Network Client Administrator on your machine.

Select the Network Client v3 For MS-DOS And Windows option and specify the network card installed on your target machine (the machine on which you plan to install Windows Server 2003). This is the only tricky part, because what if your network card is new and not supported by Windows NT 4? In this case, the workaround is usually to install the closest card you can and then modify the .ini files on your network boot disk accordingly. My own target machine in this example has a 3Com905C-TX network card in it. Luckily, I found a helpful document on 3Com's support website detailing how to create network startup disks for machines with 3c90x network cards (Doc# 06296 on www.support.3com.com). Following these instructions, I specified 3Com EtherLink III as my network card in the Target Workstation Configuration screen (see Figure 4-10) and clicked OK.

TIP   If your target machine has a network card from a different manufacturer, you should be able to modify the procedure used here once you've determined the name of the DOS driver on your card's driver CD.

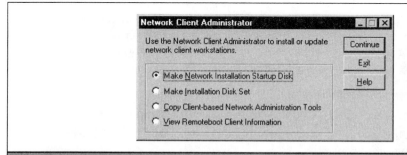

Figure 4-8.   Running the Network Client Administrator program

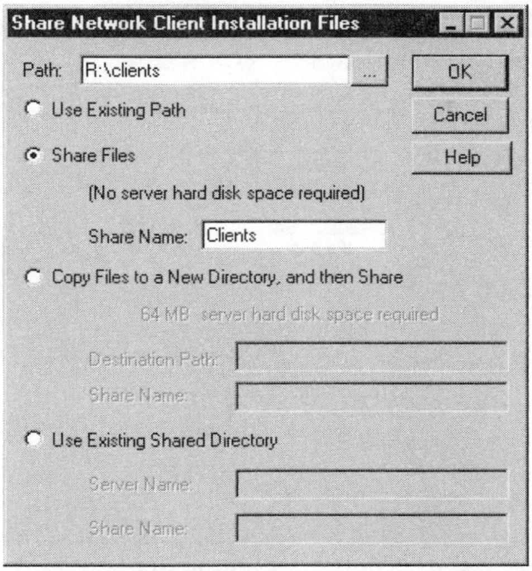

Figure 4-9.   Specifying the path to the network installation files

The Network Startup Disk Configuration screen appears next (see Figure 4-11). Here you need to specify a computer name for your target machine (anything will do, as long as it's unique to the network and will only be used temporarily), the domain to which the file server with your distribution point belongs (I left this blank because

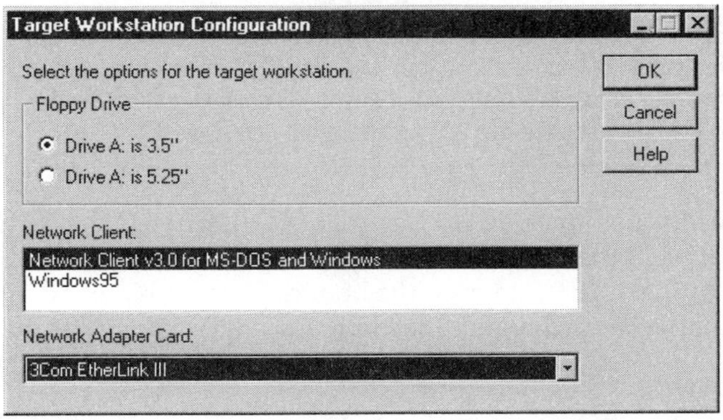

Figure 4-10.   Specifying the type of network boot disk and network adapter in the target machine

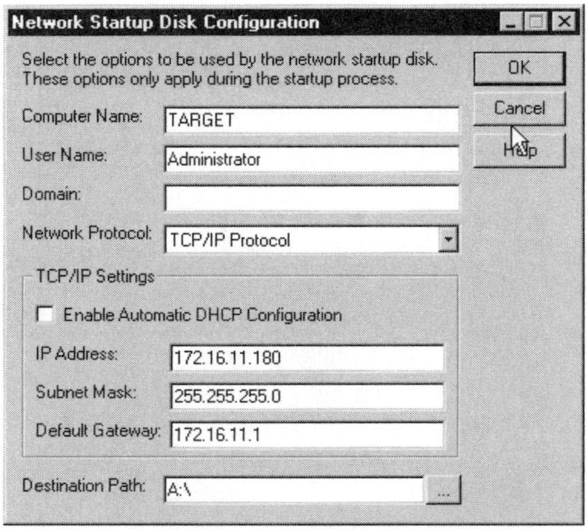

Figure 4-11. Configuring the network startup disk

SNOOPY is a stand-alone machine), a username for connecting to the distribution files (Administrator, in the example), and an IP address setting for your boot disk (again, anything will do as long as its unique to the network). Leave the destination path as the A: drive, where the boot disk will be created, insert your bootable floppy in your A: drive, and click OK twice. Close the Network Client Administrator program when finished.

 SECURITY ALERT! Actually, using your Administrator account to connect from your target machine to your distribution point isn't such a good idea because the network boot disk sends the account credentials across your network in plain text. If anyone is sniffing your network, your security could be badly compromised. I just used this account here out of laziness!

Now you have to customize your network boot disk to use the correct network card driver (you'll need the driver CD handy for your network card). First, open the SYSTEM.INI file in the \NET folder on the boot disk using Notepad. Since I'm using a 3Com905C TX network card on my machine, I need to change the line

```
netcard=elnk3.dos
```

so that it reads

```
netcard=el90x.dos
```

and save the changes. Then I need to open the PROTOCOL.INI file in the same folder and change the line

```
DRIVERNAME=ELNK3$
```

to read

```
DRIVERNAME=el90x$
```

and save the changes. Of course, your own system probably has a different network card, so change the preceding steps according to your own hardware configuration. Returning to my own system, I now insert the driver CD for my network card into my CD-ROM and use Windows Explorer to copy the file EL90X.DO_ to the \NET folder on my floppy. Next, I'll open a command prompt, switch to A:\NET as my current directory, and type **expand EL90X.DO_ EL90X.DOS** to expand the DOS driver for my card onto my network boot disk (adjust the steps in the preceding procedure according to the name of the DOS driver for your own network card).

You're almost finished. You still need to modify the autoexec.bat file on the network boot disk so it will connect to the shared distribution I386 point on SNOOPY (or whatever your distribution server is named) and run Winnt.exe, the 16-bit Setup program for installing Windows Server 2003. In autoexec.bat, change

```
net use z: \\SNOOPY\Clients
```

to

```
net use z: \\SNOOPY\I386
```

and change

```
z:\msclient\netsetup setup.exe /$
```

to

```
z:\winnt.exe /s:\\SNOOPY\I386
```

> **NOTE**   If you can't see the autoexec.bat file in the root directory when the network boot floppy is in the A: drive, start Windows Explorer and select Tools | Folder Options | View, and disable the option Hide Protected Operating System Files. This will make autoexec.bat visible. Right-click it and select Edit to open it in Notepad.

Next, you need to add the MS-DOS disk caching utility SmartDrive to your network boot disk; otherwise, Setup will take forever to copy files to your target machine (it's too bad that Windows NT's Network Client Administrator program doesn't automatically add SmartDrive to the boot disk it creates). If you have a machine with MS-DOS 6.22 installed on it, you could simply copy the file SMARTDRV.EXE from the machine to my network boot disk, but let's assume you don't. Not to worry, just dig out the three MS-DOS 6.22 installation floppies gathering dust in the bottom drawer of your filing cabinet (System Administrator's Rule #1: Never throw out *anything*!!). Copy the file SMARTDRV.EX_ from Disk 2 your my MS-DOS boot disk, boot your workstation using the boot disk, type **EXPAND SMARTERV.EX_ SMARTDRV.EXE** at the DOS prompt, and then use the COPY command to copy the expanded file SMARTDRV.EXE from your MS-DOS boot disk to the root of my network boot disk. Then you need to add the line

```
smartdrive.exe
```

to the beginning of the autoexec.bat file on your network boot disk so that SmartDrive will run and disk caching will be enabled when you boot the target machine using your network boot disk.

One final step—when Setup runs on your target machine, it needs to be able to copy the temporary Setup files to the machine's hard drive. To make this possible, you need to ensure that there is a formatted partition on the machine's hard drive. To do this, boot the target machine using your MS-DOS boot disk, use the FDISK command to create a primary partition of maximum size (2047KB) and mark it active, and then type **FORMAT C:** to format the new partition using the FAT file system.

Installing Web Edition

You're now prepared to install Windows Server 2003 Web Edition over the network. Insert your network boot disk into the target machine, turn it on, and when prompted supply the password for the Administrator account on the file server where the shared distribution point is located. Once the network boot disk connects to this distribution point, the blue screen Text Mode portion of Setup for Windows Server 2003 will begin. Installation files will be copied to the target machine's hard drive, and you're on your way. Don't forget to remove the network boot disk from A: drive when prompted to restart the system!

Once restarted, you can specify that the C: partition should be converted to NTFS (fortunately, the 2047 size of this partition is sufficient to allow this maneuver, since it's essential for security reasons that Windows Server 2003 be installed on an NTFS partition). After two more reboots, the GUI mode portion of Setup begins. All you need to do from here is respond to the Setup prompts as in the preceding section of this chapter (the GUI mode portion of Setup for Web Edition is identical to that for Standard Edition described earlier).

Postinstallation Notes

When you first log on to Web Edition, Internet Explorer starts up and presents you with a logon screen for the Web Interface For Server Administration tool (see Figure 4-12). This tool is a secure website for administering IIS using a web browser, and there is a shortcut in the Startup folder that causes this tool to open whenever you log on to Web

Figure 4-12.   Logon screen for Web Interface For Server Administration

Edition. The shortcut invokes the VBScript file SecureLaunch.vbs located in \System32\ ServerAppliance, which constructs a URL of the form https://*machine_name:port*, where

- https:// indicates that the connection between the browser and Administration website is secure because it is encrypted using SSL.

- *machine_name* is the name of the local machine (you can also use *localhost* or the machine's IP address or fully qualified domain name).

- *port* is the SSL port for the Administration website (value is 8098).

In the example installation, a machine name would be randomly generated, perhaps something like ME-LDBNY9QL4Y55, in which case the URL that is opened would be https:// ME-LDBNY9QL4Y55:8098. The extra logon screen in Figure 4-12 is there because the Administration website is configured to use Basic Authentication, which works through firewalls and thus allows administrators to manage their Web Edition machines remotely from any location over the Internet. Because Basic Authentication passes user credentials across the network in clear text, however, SSL is needed to ensure that the process of administering such servers is secure.

To open Web Interface For Server Administration, enter user credentials with Administrator privileges and click OK. Internet Explorer will access the Administration website using SSL and the interface will appear (see Figure 4-13). If a Warning status message appears under the server name at the top of the screen, click the message to open the status page for the tool and view any warning or informational status messages present. For example, you may be prompted to install a new certificate on the server because the SSL certificate that is preinstalled on the server is only intended for sustaining

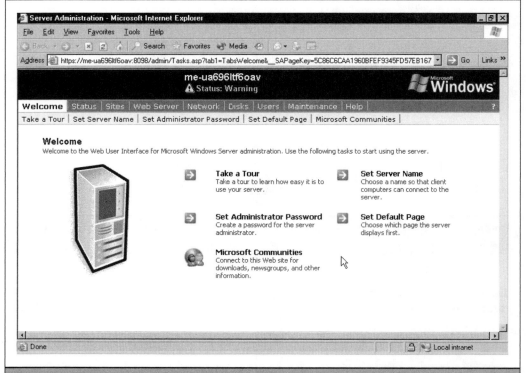

Figure 4-13. The initial screen of the Web Interface For Server Administration site

Web Services For Server Administration

While the Internet Services Manager console is the standard way of administering IIS machines, this tool is designed mainly to work across a company network. To administer IIS from a machine beyond the company network (for example, a remote user with a laptop connected to the Internet), use the Web Services For Server Administration tool instead. This tool is installed by default in Web Edition and starts each time the user logs on. On Standard and Enterprise Editions the tool is not installed by default, but you can install it afterward by using Control Panel | Add Or Remove Programs | Add/Remove Windows Components | Web Administration Server | Details | Internet Information Services (IIS) | Details | World Wide Web Service | Details | select Server Administration (HTML). The component then appears in Add/Remove Windows Components as Server Administration Tools.

an initial connection with it. If this happens, you should obtain your own unique SSL certificate from a certificate authority you trust and install it on your server for greater security.

 SECURITY ALERT! If you select the Remember My Password check box on the logon screen for Web Interface For Server Administration, the next time you log on to Windows your credentials will have been automatically entered into the logon screen, but you still have to click OK!

TIP If you accidentally close the Web Interface For Server Administration browser window, you can open it again from Administrative Tools (or you can log off and log on again to open it automatically). You don't have to type the URL out to access it—unless you're trying to access it from a remote machine, which is the whole intention of the tool anyway!

Web Interface For Server Administration is more than just a browser-based version of the IIS console. In addition to being able to create and manage websites with it, you can also manage local users and groups and volumes and disk quotas and perform other tasks suitable for an all-in-one interface to a web server appliance like a machine running Windows Server 2003 Web Edition. We'll look more at the Web Services For Server Administration tool in Chapter 6, and we will discuss SSL in more detail in Chapter 10. For now, let's finish our postinstallation tour of Web Edition by opening the IIS console from Administrative Tools and examine the installed IIS components and their configuration (see Figure 4-14). Note that there are two websites listed in the console tree, Default Web Site and Administration. Note that Default Web Site has only static content in it—a single Under Construction page called iisstart.htm. I mentioned earlier that the dynamic sample websites of earlier versions of IIS have been removed

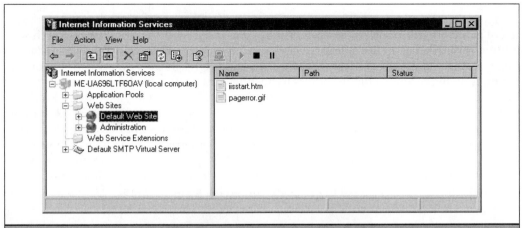

Figure 4-14. Initial configuration of Web Edition as viewed in IIS console

from version 6 for increased security. Notice also the Administration site, an ASP application that runs the Web Interface For Server Administration tool. Finally, note that the SMTP Service is automatically installed with Web Edition.

 SECURITY ALERT!   Recall from the previous walkthrough that the Active Server Pages (ASP) component of IIS is not installed by default when you add the Application Server role to Standard or Enterprise Edition. With Web Edition, however, this component must be installed for the Web Interface For Server Administration tool to work because the tool is implemented as an ASP application. You can verify that ASP is installed on Web Edition by selecting the Web Service Extensions node in the IIS console and verifying that Active Server Pages is marked Allowed (other installed extensions are marked Prohibited, which means they are installed but need to be enabled before they can be used).

For a full view of which IIS components are installed by default in Web Edition, go to Add Or Remove Programs in Control Panel. You'll see the following components are installed under Web Administration Server:

- Enable network COM+ access
- Internet Information Services (IIS)
  - Common Files
  - Internet Information Services Manager
  - SMTP Service
  - World Wide Web Service
  - Active Server Pages
  - Server Administration (HTML)
  - World Wide Web Service

Note that if you use Add Or Remove Programs in Control Panel to view the complete list of available components for Web Edition, you'll see why Microsoft positions this edition for niche use in the enterprise and service provider markets. Web Edition lacks major features like Active Directory and RRAS and is envisioned primarily for either running on high-density blade servers in hosting data centers for Internet service providers (ISPs) and application service providers (ASPs) or serving as front-end IIS web servers running on repurposed PCs in enterprise or e-commerce web farms. Web Edition saves service providers and enterprises money in both of these scenarios. Because Web Edition is designed to prevent running certain types of enterprise-level applications on it (such as directory services, database, and messaging applications), it can only be used for hosting static content and dynamic applications developed with technologies like ASP and Cold Fusion whose databases are run on back-end servers.

UNATTENDED CLEAN INSTALL

For the third installation, you're going to perform a clean install of Enterprise Edition using the standard unattended installation method. First you'll install the support tool Setup Manager on the previously installed Standard Server machine. You'll use this tool to create an answer file and shared distribution point on the server. Then you'll use a modified version of your previously created network boot disk to boot a wiped machine, connect to the distribution point, and perform a completely unattended installation.

Microsoft Windows Corporate Deployment Tools

The \Support\Tools folder on the Windows Server 2003 product CD contains a number of goodies, including Deploy.cab, a Windows cabinet file that contains various tools and documentation for automated deployment of Windows Server 2003 including

- **Setupmgr.exe**   An application called Setup Manager that is used for creating answer files and distribution points for automated installation of Windows Server 2003

- **Deploy.chm**   A Windows Help file containing the Microsoft Windows Corporate Deployment Tools User Guide, with documentation on how to use Setup Manager, Sysprep, and other automated deployment tools

- **Ref.chm**   The Microsoft Windows Preinstallation Reference, with documentation of the various types of answer files you can create with Setup Manager

To use these tools, extract them from the cabinet file by copying them to the hard drive on the file server you plan to use for hosting the shared distribution point. Microsoft sometimes calls this machine the technician computer, while the machine you want to automatically deploy Windows on is the target or destination computer.

Running Setup Manager

Double-click the extracted Setupmgr.exe file to start Setup Manager on your technician computer (see Figure 4-15). This opens a wizard screen that walks you through the process of preparing for automated deployment. You'll use the wizard now to create an answer file called unattend.txt that will allow you to perform a fully automated installation of Enterprise Edition using the following parameters:

- Computer name: MACBETH

- Workgroup: WORKGROUP

- IP address: 172.16.11.175

- Subnet Mask: 255.255.255.0

Figure 4-15.   Using Setup Manager to prepare for automated deployment

- Default Gateway: 172.16.11.1
- Time Zone: Central Time

and so forth.

I won't show all the screens of the Setup Manager wizard here. Instead, I'll walk you through the steps you would perform to prepare for the installation. First, make sure your Enterprise Edition product CD is in the CD-ROM drive of the technician machine, and then select the following options on each screen of the wizard:

1. New Or Existing Answer File: select Create New.

2. Type Of Setup: select Unattended Setup (other options are Sysprep and RIS).

3. Product: select Windows .NET Enterprise Server.

4. User Interaction: select Fully Automated (the other four options have various degrees of user interaction during Setup).

5. Distribution Share: select Create A New Distribution Share.

6. Location Of Setup Files: select On The CD.

7. Distribution Share Location: accept the defaults of C:\windist as the distribution share location and Windist as the share name.

8. License Agreement: select the check box to accept the license agreement.

NOTE The listed pages of the wizard vary depending on what selections you make as you move through it. The preceding steps are typical for creating an answer file for fully automated unattended Setup.

The initial wizard screen disappears and the main Setup Manager window is displayed (see Figure 4-16). The wizard now walks you through the process of specifying answers to Setup prompts for creating the answer file.

9. Name And Organization: Fill in your own name and company (I'll use Mitch Tulloch and MyBigCompany for purposes of illustration).

10. Display Settings: leave as Windows Default.

11. Time Zone: Specify your time zone (I'll choose Central Time).

12. Product Key: enter your 25-character product key.

13. Licensing Mode: leave at Per Server, Max 5 Connections.

14. Computer Names: add the name for the target computer here (I'll use MACBETH). Note that you can enter multiple computer names here, and then use .udf files in conjunction with unattend.txt for installing multiple machines using a single answer file—see the Corporate Deployment Guide on your Windows Server 2003 product CD for more information.

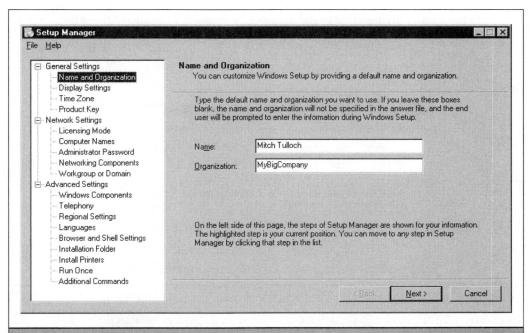

Figure 4-16. Using Setup Manager to create an answer file

15. Administrator Password: enter your Administrator password and select the option to encrypt the password in the answer file (for extra security in case your answer file is lost or stolen).

16. Network Components: select the Custom option and specify the IP address, subnet mask, default gateway, and DNS server addresses as previously indicated.

17. Workgroup Or Domain: leave as WORKGROUP because you're deploying a stand-alone server.

18. Windows Components: Select the World Wide Web Service to install IIS.

19. Telephony: leave unspecified.

20. Regional Settings: select English (United States).

21. Languages: leave settings as they are.

22. Browser and Shell Settings: leave settings as they are.

23. Installation Folder: leave as A Folder Named Windows.

24. Install Printers: leave unspecified.

25. Run Once: leave unspecified.

26. Additional Commands: leave unspecified.

27. Click Finish, and a screen appears prompting you for the name and location to save your newly created answer file (see Figure 4-17). The default is to create a file named unattend.txt in the distribution folder C:\windist. Accept the defaults by clicking OK, and Setup Manager will begin copying the Enterprise Edition source files to the distribution folder. This will take a few minutes.

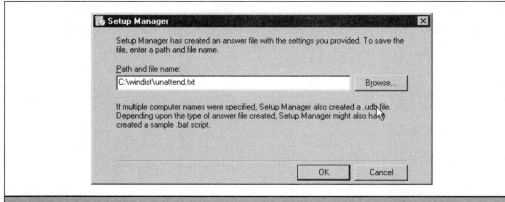

Figure 4-17. Specifying a name and location for your newly created answer file

Results of Running Setup Manager

When Setup Manager has finished running, your distribution point and answer point are ready for use. Here's what the answer file unattend.txt from my own walkthrough looks like (yours will differ slightly depending on the choices you made in the preceding walkthrough):

```
;SetupMgrTag
[Data]
    AutoPartition=1
    MsDosInitiated="0"
    UnattendedInstall="Yes"

[Unattended]
    UnattendMode=FullUnattended
    OemSkipEula=Yes
    OemPreinstall=Yes
    TargetPath=\WINDOWS

[GuiUnattended]

AdminPassword=4bac4743f2c462e0944e2df489a880e45f19da0790b6ebe30cf4eed547c5d972
    EncryptedAdminPassword=Yes
    AutoLogon=No
    AutoLogonCount=1
    OEMSkipRegional=1
    TimeZone=20
    OemSkipWelcome=1

[UserData]
    ProductKey=DWYG2-CYP93-QKYJ4-49QMQ-WF66M
    FullName="Mitch Tulloch"
    OrgName="MyBigCompany"
    ComputerName=Macbeth

[LicenseFilePrintData]
    AutoMode=PerServer
    AutoUsers=5

[RegionalSettings]
    LanguageGroup=1
    Language=00000409

[SetupMgr]
    DistFolder=C:\windist
    DistShare=windist

[Components]
    accessopt=On
```

```
        calc=On
        charmap=On
        clipbook=On
        deskpaper=On
        templates=On
        mousepoint=On
        paint=On
        freecell=Off
        hearts=Off
        zonegames=Off
        minesweeper=Off
        solitaire=Off
        spider=Off
        indexsrv_system=On
        msnexplr=Off
        certsrv=Off
        certsrv_client=Off
        certsrv_server=Off
        iis_www=On
        iis_ftp=Off
        iis_smtp=Off
        iis_smtp_docs=Off
        iis_nntp=Off
        iis_nntp_docs=Off
        reminst=Off
        rstorage=Off
        TerminalServer=Off
        wms=Off
        wms_admin_asp=Off
        wms_admin_mmc=Off
        wms_server=Off
        chat=On
        dialer=On
        hypertrm=On
        cdplayer=On
        mplay=On
        media_clips=On
        media_utopia=On
        rec=On
        vol=On

[Identification]
        JoinWorkgroup=WORKGROUP

[Networking]
        InstallDefaultComponents=No

[NetAdapters]
        Adapter1=params.Adapter1
```

```
[params.Adapter1]
    INFID=*

[NetClients]
    MS_MSClient=params.MS_MSClient

[NetServices]
    MS_SERVER=params.MS_SERVER

[NetProtocols]
    MS_TCPIP=params.MS_TCPIP

[params.MS_TCPIP]
    DNS=No
    UseDomainNameDevolution=No
    EnableLMHosts=Yes
    AdapterSections=params.MS_TCPIP.Adapter1

[params.MS_TCPIP.Adapter1]
    SpecificTo=Adapter1
    DHCP=No
    IPAddress=172.16.11.175
    SubnetMask=255.255.255.0
    DefaultGateway=172.16.11.1
    DNSServerSearchOrder=205.200.16.65,205.200.16.69
    WINS=No
    NetBIOSOptions=0
```

Note that in the walkthrough, Setup Manager also created a batch file called unattend.bat that you can view to learn more about how to use your answer file. Here are the contents of unattend.bat:

```
@rem SetupMgrTag
@echo off

rem
rem This is a SAMPLE batch script generated by Setup Manager.
rem If this script is moved from the location where it was generated, it may
have to be modified.
rem

set AnswerFile=.\unattend.txt
set SetupFiles=\\ME-LDBNY9QL4Y55\windist\I386

\\ME-LDBNY9QL4Y55\windist\I386\winnt32 /s:%SetupFiles% /unattend:%AnswerFile%
```

Now you need to modify your network boot disk to use your answer file for unattended Setup.

> **TIP**   There are a number of new answer file options for controlling how unattended installation of IIS 6 components can be performed on Windows Server 2003. You can find out more about these options in the Internet Information Services (IIS) help docs in the Help and Support Center. You can then use the Sysocmgr.exe utility together with your IIS answer file to perform a separate unattended installation of IIS after completing your installation of Windows Server 2003.

Preparing Network Boot Disk

You'll simply modify the network boot disk you created earlier in this chapter to enable unattended installation using the answer file. There are several ways of doing this, but perhaps the simplest is to copy the answer file (unattend.txt) to the root of the boot disk. Then use Notepad to open autoexec.bat on the boot disk and change

```
net use z: \\SNOOPY\I386
```

to

```
net use z: \\ME-LDBNY9QL4Y55\windist
```

so that the Z: drive is mapped to the folder in our shared distribution point that contains the Setup program winnt.exe. Then you need to replace the line

```
z:\winnt.exe /s:\\SNOOPY\I386
```

with

```
z:\I386\winnt.exe /s:z:\I386 /u:unattend.txt
```

and save the changes. Note that your computer names are probably different so adjust the preceding steps accordingly. You're ready for automated Setup!

Performing an Unattended Installation

Insert the network boot disk, start the machine, and watch it connect to the distribution point, copy files, and install Windows Server 2003 without any intervention on your part!

The only issue with this method is that if you prepared the target machine's hard drive the way the previous walkthrough was performed, the result is that Windows Server 2003 is installed on a 2GB FAT partition instead of NTFS. This is not a big issue, since you can run convert c: /fs:ntfs from the command line afterwards to schedule your boot partition to be converted from FAT to NTFS at the next system reboot. The new version of the Convert utility included with Windows Server 2003 is smart enough to apply a security template during the conversion process so that the resulting NTFS file and folder permissions are identical, as if Windows had been originally installed on NTFS instead. Then you can convert your disk to dynamic and extend the C: volume to any size desired. The downside of this approach is that the converted disk is somewhat more fragmented than if you had formatted it as NTFS during the Text Mode portion of Setup as in a manual install. Another way around this problem if you are an enterprise customer is to obtain the Windows Preinstallation Environment (WinPE) kit from your Microsoft representative. Using the WinPE CD, you can boot directly from the CD, create partitions, and format them using NTFS to prepare your disk for unattended Setup. Or you can use a third-party tool like PartitionMagic from PowerQuest to create your partitions and format your drives using NTFS. You can also use Remote Installation Services (RIS) for performing automated installs, but that topic is beyond the scope of this book.

Postinstallation Notes

The results of this installation are pretty much the same as the results of installing Standard Edition earlier in this chapter. The only website visible in the IIS console is the Default Web Site, and if you go into Control Panel and use Add Or Remove Programs, you'll see that the following components of IIS have been installed under Application Server:

- Enable network COM+ access
- Internet Information Services (IIS)
  - Common Files
  - Internet Information Services Manager
  - World Wide Web Service

Note that neither Active Server Pages nor ASP.NET have been installed, but you can easily install them now using Add/Remove Windows Components.

UPGRADING FROM IIS 4

Having considered various methods for performing clean installs, it's time to move on to upgrading to IIS 6 from earlier versions of IIS. You'll begin with upgrading a stand-alone IIS 4 (Windows NT Server 4 with NT 4 Option Pack) machine to IIS 6 (Windows Server 2003). This is likely to be a common scenario in enterprises that decided to postpone migrating their Windows NT 4 networks to Windows 2000 because of the complexity of Active Directory and fears concerning the stability and reliability of Windows 2000. Experience has shown that such fears were unfounded, since Windows 2000 turned out to be a stable and reliable operating system. Nevertheless, many enterprises decided to take a wait-and-see attitude when Windows 2000 first came out, considering that if their existing Windows NT network worked fine, there was no compelling business reason for replacing it. Instead, these enterprises decided to wait until the bugs were shaken out of Windows 2000, and many decided to postpone their network migrations until the next version of Windows came out, which turned out to be Windows Server 2003.

Preinstallation Notes

Let's begin by reviewing the preinstallation configuration of the machine you're going to upgrade. After the upgrade is finished, we'll examine the postinstallation configuration and compare it for significant changes.

The IIS 4 machine I am using for this example is a stand-alone server named BORIS belonging to a workgroup named WORKGROUP (if you have an IIS 4 machine available, you can try following along; but your configuration is likely to differ in some points, so I've tried to make this example illustrative rather than prescriptive). The operating system is Windows NT Server 4 with Service Pack 6A and the Windows NT 4 Option Pack installed (the Option Pack was installed to upgrade from IIS 3 to IIS 4). The machine has three IP addresses assigned to it:

- 172.16.11.150

- 172.16.11.151

- 172.16.11.152

There are three IP addresses because there are three websites running on the machine (see Figure 4-18):

- **Default Web Site**   This site contains the sample applications included with IIS 4 and responds to any unassigned IP addresses on the machine. IIS 4 included a collection of sample applications that demonstrated how the then-new Active Server Pages (ASP) technology and scripting technologies like VBScript and JScript could be used to create dynamic web applications. The root of the Default Web Site defines the starting point of an application called Default Application, which together with the other sample applications and scripts runs in-process, which means they run in the same memory space as the default IIS process called inetinfo.exe (if necessary, you can review the architectures of IIS 4, 5, and 6 in Chapter 2, "IIS 6 Architecture").

- **AppOne**   This website contains a custom ASP application and responds to the IP address 172.16.11.151. The root of the AppOne website defines the starting point of an application called First App, and the home directory (where the application's .asp files and other content are located) is the folder C:\app1 on the local machine. Because this application is relatively untested, it has been configured to run in a separate memory space using the process isolation feature of IIS 4 (see Figure 4-19). This way, if AppOne fails, it won't bring down other applications running on the server.

- **AppTwo**   This website contains another custom ASP application and responds to the IP address 172.16.11.152. The starting point of the application is called Second App and the home directory is C:\app2. This application is also configured to run using process isolation.

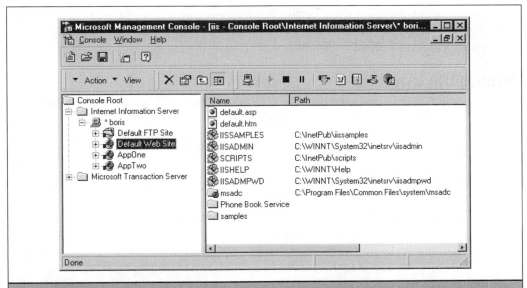

Figure 4-18. The IIS 4 machine is hosting three websites, as shown here in the Internet Services Manager console.

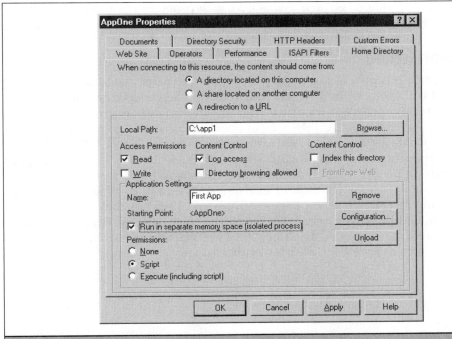

Figure 4-19. The AppOne site contains an application called First App that is configured to run out-of-process using process isolation.

To summarize, there are three applications running on the IIS 4 machine, one in-process and two out-of-process. We'll check later and see how these apps are running when the upgrade is complete.

Performing the Upgrade

Let's upgrade this IIS 4 machine directly to Windows Server 2003 Standard Edition from the product CD. The steps for doing this are as follows:

1. Insert the Windows Server 2003 Standard Edition product CD into the CD-ROM drive.

2. Select the Check System Compatibility option to make sure the hardware configuration will support the upgrade.

3. If the compatibility check goes OK, select Install Windows Server 2003 Standard Edition to start the upgrade process.

4. When the Welcome To Windows Setup screen appears, leave the Installation Type as Upgrade (Recommended) and click Next (see Figure 4-20). Note that you can instead choose to do a clean install by selecting the appropriate option here.

5. Accept the License Agreement, enter the product key, and wait while files are copied, the machine reboots a couple of times, and the installation finishes. It may take a while, so go pour yourself a cup of coffee—in fact, upgrades take longer than clean installs, so have a sandwich, too.

Postinstallation Notes

When the upgrade is complete and you log on as Administrator, the Manage Your Server Wizard will open, telling you that your Windows Server 2003 is running in the Application Server role (it may also be running in the File Server role). To get a better idea of which IIS and ASP.NET components are installed on the upgraded machine, go to Control Panel, select Add Or Remove Programs, select Add/Remove Windows Components, select Application Server, and click Details. Note that ASP.NET is not installed and neither is the Application Server Console MMC tool. Now select Internet Information Services (IIS), click Details, select World Wide Web Service, click Details, and note that Active Server Pages (ASP) is installed. You may want to uninstall components you won't need (such as the Internet Database Connector, which is installed because you upgraded the sample IIS 4 website) and install other components you may need, such as FrontPage 2002 Server Extensions.

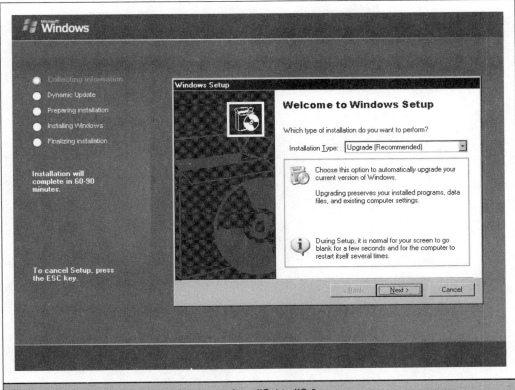

Figure 4-20.   Starting the upgrade process from IIS 4 to IIS 6

Next, let's look at what IIS 6 isolation mode the newly upgraded server is running in. Open the Internet Information Services (IIS) console from Administrative Tools, expand the console tree in the left pane, right-click the Web Sites node, and select Properties. Switch to the Service tab of the Web Sites Properties sheet and note that your server is running in IIS 5 Isolation Mode (see Figure 4-21). This is to be expected, as this Isolation Mode is designed to support compatibility with legacy IIS 4/5 applications.

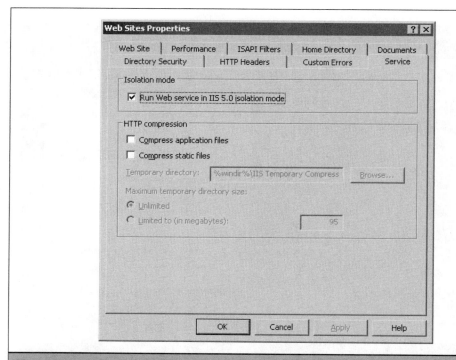

Figure 4-21. An upgraded IIS 4 web server runs in IIS 5 Compatibility mode.

NOTE You may have noticed that the Application Pools node is missing for your IIS server in the IIS Manager console tree. In your previous clean installs, this mode was always present; but when you upgrade to IIS 6 from IIS 4 or 5, this node is missing. This is because upgrading always leaves the server in IIS 5 Isolation Mode, and application pools aren't supported in this IIS 6 Isolation Mode, they're only supported when IIS 6 runs in Worker Process Isolation Mode. If you change the Isolation Mode from IIS 5 Isolation Mode to Worker Process Isolation Mode, the Application Pools node will magically appear.

Remember that on the original IIS 4 server, the Default Web Site ran in-process together with inetinfo.exe while the two custom applications ran out-of-process in isolated memory spaces. Let's look at how these three sites are configured to run once the server has been upgraded to IIS 6. In the IIS console, open the properties sheet for the Default Web Site and select the Home Directory tab (see Figure 4-22). As expected, the Default Web Site is running under Low (IIS Process) application protection, that is, in the same memory space as the WWW Service and inetinfo.exe.

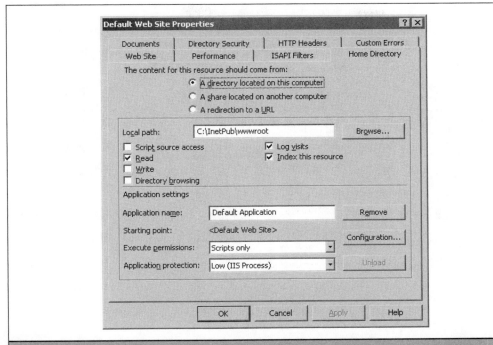

Figure 4-22. An application running in-process on IIS 4 runs with Low (IIS process) application protection in IIS 5 compatibility mode on IIS 6.

Now let's look at what happened to the custom applications on the upgraded server. Open the properties sheet for AppOne and select the Home Directory tab (see Figure 4-23). As expected, the application is running under High (Isolated) application protection, just as it was before the upgrade. Note also that the application name, application starting point, and permissions are the same as they were previously.

At this point you should test your applications to make sure they still run properly (they do), and consider testing the applications under worker process isolation mode to take advantage of the new and improved architecture of IIS 6. We'll look at configuring applications to run in different isolation modes later in Chapter 8, "Creating and Configuring Applications."

Finally, note that if the sample content from earlier versions was installed, this content will also be present in the Default Web Site when you upgrade to version 6 of IIS. Sample content in IIS 4 and 5 includes things like Ad Rotator, Content Linker, Page Counter, and so on. You may want to delete this content from your upgraded server for security reasons. If you need any of this content afterward, you can find copies of it in the IIS 6 Resource Kit.

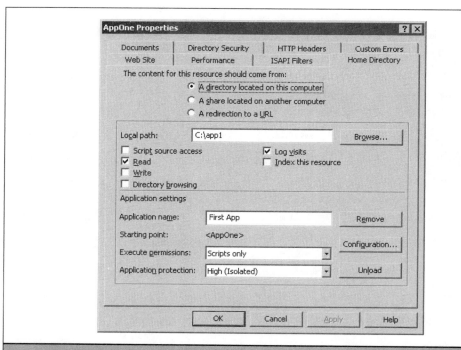

Figure 4-23. An application running out-of-process on IIS 4 runs with High (Isolated) application protection in IIS 5 compatibility mode on IIS 6.

UPGRADING FROM IIS 5

Our final walkthrough is upgrading an IIS 5 (Windows 2000 Server) machine to IIS 6 (Windows Server 2003). It will be interesting to compare the results afterward with those from the previous walkthrough (upgrading IIS 4 to IIS 6).

Preinstallation Notes

This walkthrough will upgrade an IIS 5 machine named ROMEO that belongs to a workgroup named WORKGROUP. The operating system is Windows 2000 Server, and just like in the previous walkthrough, the machine has three IP addresses assigned to it:

- 172.16.11.155
- 172.16.11.156
- 172.16.11.157

ROMEO is hosting four websites (see Figure 4-24): the Default Web Site with its sample applications, the Administration Web Site that enables browser-based administration

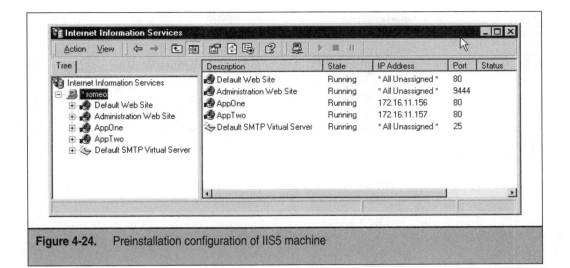

Figure 4-24. Preinstallation configuration of IIS5 machine

of IIS, and two custom ASP applications named AppOne and AppTwo (there is also a Default SMTP Virtual Server node in the IIS console tree because the SMTP Service is installed by default on Windows 2000 Server). These custom applications are the same ones used in the previous walkthrough, and their IP addresses and application name settings are configured as follows:

- AppOne: 172.16.11.156 with application name First App
- AppTwo: 172.16.11.157 with application name Second App

The main difference this time (to make things more interesting) is the level of application protection assigned to each of the applications:

- The Default Web Site and Administration Web Site are both running with Medium (Pooled) application protection (this is their default setting).
- AppOne is running with Low (IIS Process) application protection.
- AppTwo is running with High (Isolated) application protection.

This difference from the previous walkthrough is possible because of the different architectures of IIS 5 and IIS 4.

Performing the Upgrade

The steps for upgrading this IIS 5 machine directly to Windows .NET Standard Server from the product CD are identical to those outlined in the previous walkthrough, so I won't bother repeating them here. The only difference in the process is that when the System Compatibility Check runs, it tells you that Setup has detected the IIS World Wide Web Publishing Service (WWW Service, or W3SVC) running on the machine and that it will be disabled during the upgrade for security reasons. When the upgrade process is complete, you'll have to re-enable the service to get your websites up and running again. If, however, you previously downloaded the IIS 5 Lockdown Wizard from Microsoft's website and installed it on the machine, the WWW Service will not be disabled during the upgrade process. Also, the process for upgrading IIS 5 will take somewhat longer than for upgrading IIS 4.

Note that disabling W3SVC during upgrades is the default behavior and has been included for security reasons because websites may be vulnerable to attack while being upgraded and before final permissions have been reviewed. There are several ways to disable this feature however, including

- Adding the key HKLM\SYSTEM\CurrentControlSet\Services\W3SVC\RetainW3SVCStatus to the Registry and assigning this key any non-null value

- Including the line DisableWebServiceOnUpgrade = false in the unattended installation file

Postinstallation Notes

Once you log on to the upgraded machine, open the IIS console and you will see that all the websites are in a Stopped condition. To fix this, you need to do two things:

1. Open the Computer Management console in Administrative Tools, select the Services node under Services And Applications, and double-click the World Wide Web Publishing Service to open its properties sheet (see Figure 4-25). Note that the Startup Type setting for the service is Disabled; change this to Automatic and click Apply. Then click the Start button to start the service and click OK to close the properties sheet.

2. Go back to the IIS console and right-click each website and select Start from the shortcut menu.

Once the websites are running, open their properties sheets and confirm that the server is running in IIS 5 Isolation Mode as expected and that the application protection level for each of the four websites is unchanged from before.

NOTE The old Administration Web Site of IIS 5 is still present on the upgraded IIS 6 server, but it no longer works. You need to install the new Remote Administration (HTML) component of IIS 6 using Add Or Remove Programs to perform browser-based administration of your IIS 6 server.

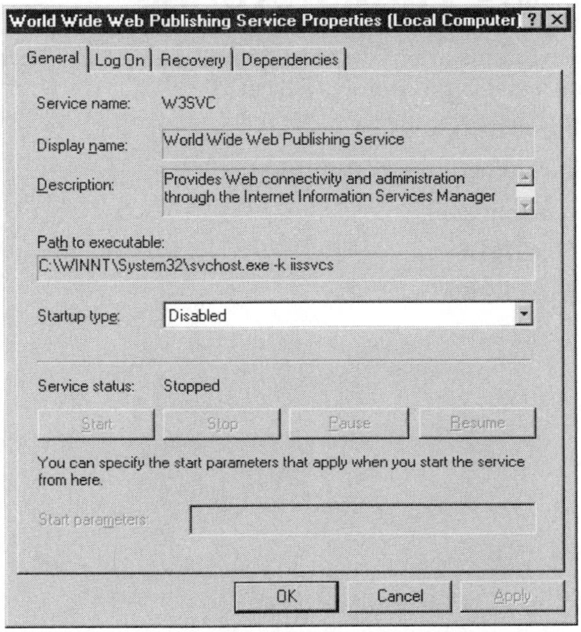

Figure 4-25. Properties of World Wide Web Publishing Service

CHALLENGE

You have an IIS 4 machine running several ASP applications in-process for a company intranet and want to migrate these applications to IIS 6. The machine is a dual-processor Pentium II 400 with 256MB RAM and uses disk-striping with parity (RAID 5). Should you upgrade the machine to Windows Server 2003 Standard Server, or should you perform a clean install on a more-powerful machine and then migrate the apps? If you decide to upgrade, what hardware considerations are important? What installation method would you choose: manual or unattended? Why? What new features of IIS 6 may enable your applications to run more reliably than they did before?

CHECKLIST: INSTALLATION METHODS

Check off the following items after you have gained experience performing the indicated method for installing Windows Server 2003:

☐ Clean install from product CD

☐ Clean install from network distribution point

☐ Unattended clean install

☐ Upgrading from IIS 4

☐ Upgrading from IIS 5

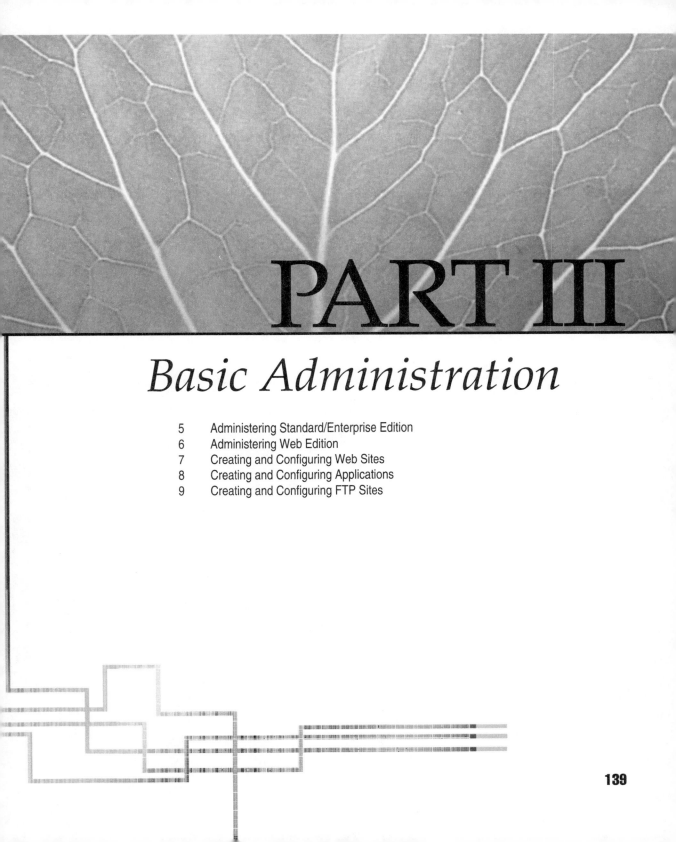

PART III

Basic Administration

CHAPTER 5

Administering Standard/Enterprise Edition

N ow that we've examined the new architecture of IIS 6 and learned how to deploy it, we'll move on and start looking at how to administer this exciting new platform. This chapter will provide an overview of the tools for administering IIS on Standard and Enterprise Edition; we'll defer looking at administering Web Edition until the next chapter, "Administering Web Edition." The focus in these two chapters will be on administration using the GUI, while command-line administration will be covered in Chapter 11, "Working from the Command Line."

Whether you plan to have a few or hundreds of machines running IIS 6, you need to be able to administer these machines. Ideally, you'd like to be able to do this remotely and from a single, centralized location, such as the desk in your administrator's office. It turns out this is possible, but there are a few hurdles you need to overcome along the way, and that's what this chapter is all about.

ADMINISTRATION METHODS

Microsoft has provided an abundance of tools and methods for administering IIS 6 and other aspects of Windows Server 2003. These include

- Microsoft Management Console (MMC) tools (.msc files) that can be used over a LAN or WAN connection to administer most aspects of Windows Server 2003. These are available in the Administrative Tools program group and can be customized as desired.

- The Windows Server 2003 Administration Tools Pack, which allows you to install *all* MMC administrative tools on Windows .NET member servers and *some* on Windows XP Professional machines.

- Remote Desktop, the latest incarnation of Terminal Services and installed by default in Windows Server 2003. Using Remote Desktop, you can connect to a remote IIS 6 machine and manage it as if you were sitting at its local console.

- Remote Desktop Web Connection, which allows you to access the Remote Desktop feature using Internet Explorer and lets you manage your IIS 6 machines over the Internet from anywhere in the world.

- Remote Administration (HTML), the latest incarnation of the IIS Administration website that allows you to manage IIS using Internet Explorer (this is installed by default in Web Edition).

In addition to these GUI methods for managing Windows Server 2003 machines, there are command-line tools for managing them, including a collection of VBScript scripts in \System32 for managing various aspects of IIS 6, the ADSUTIL.VBS script in the \Inetpub\Adminscripts folder for editing the metabase, various Windows commands, and Telnet. The rest of this chapter deals with the GUI administration methods just listed.

IIS MANAGER

The first tool for administering IIS we'll look at is IIS Manager, an MMC console that is installed in the Administrative Tools program group when IIS is installed on Windows Server 2003. IIS Manager is a GUI tool that lets you manage FTP, SMTP, NNTP, or websites; configure Application Pools; lock down or unlock various IIS features; and so on. You can use IIS Manager to administer any number of IIS machines locally at the console or remotely over a LAN or even WAN connection (IIS Manager usually works through proxy servers). IIS Manager provides administrators with access to a wide range of IIS configuration settings including performance, security, quality of service, maintenance, and content management functions. You can use it to manually perform almost any IIS administration task (for automating sequences of administration tasks you need to use scripting).

NOTE   IIS Manager was called Internet Services Manager (ISM) in previous versions of IIS.

Starting IIS Manager

You can start IIS Manager a lot of different ways:

- Select Start | Administrative Tools | Internet Information Services (IIS) Manager.
- Select Start | Run, type **inetmgr**, and click OK.
- Select Start | Run, type **%SystemRoot%\System32\inetsrv\iis.msc**, and click OK. Open a command prompt, change to %SystemRoot%\System32\inetsrv as your current directory, and type **inetmrg** or **iis.msc**.

SECURITY ALERT   Like other Windows 2000 administrative tools, you must be a member of the Administrators group to use IIS Manager. You can also run IIS Manager when logged on with ordinary user credentials by using the runas command. For example, from the command line you would type **runas /user:administrator_accountname "mmc %systemroot%\system32\inetsrv\iis.msc"** to open IIS Manager on your machine (provided you are doing this either from a machine running Windows Server 2003 or a workstation with the Windows .NET Administration Tools Pack installed on it).

Console Tree

Like any MMC console, the IIS Manager window is divided into a left pane showing the console tree containing manageable objects and a right pane showing details about the current object selected in the left pane (see Figure 5-1). When IIS is added

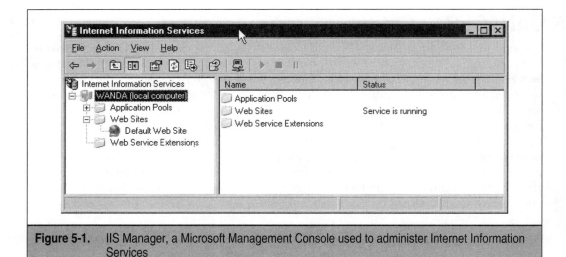

Figure 5-1. IIS Manager, a Microsoft Management Console used to administer Internet Information Services

to a clean install of Windows Server 2003, the result is three nodes in the console tree of IIS Manager:

- **Application Pools** Lets you assign worker processes to applications and configure worker process identity, health, recycling, and performance settings. We'll talk more about application pools in Chapters 8, "Creating and Configuring Applications," and in Chapter 12, "Performance Tuning and Monitoring."

- **Web Sites** Lets you create and configure websites and virtual directories for hosting content or running dynamic applications on your server. We'll discuss this more in Chapter 7, "Creating and Configuring Websites," and in Chapter 8.

- **Web Service Extensions (WSE)** Lets you lock down or unlock specific security features for IIS, such as whether or not ASP, ASP.NET, CGI, or ISAPI components are enabled (these are all initially in a locked-down state and must be unlocked in order to function). We'll examine IIS security in detail in Chapter 10, "Securing IIS."

 SECURITY ALERT The IIS Lockdown Wizard, available as a downloadable add-on for IIS 4 and 5, has been replaced in IIS 6 with Web Service Extensions (WSE), a more granular tool for configuring IIS security.

Properties Sheets

Most nodes in the console tree have configurable settings, which you view and modify by right-clicking the node and selecting Properties from the task menu. For example, the properties sheet for the Web Sites node has nine tabs of settings you can modify (see Figure 5-2), which we will look at in detail in Chapter 7 and later chapters.

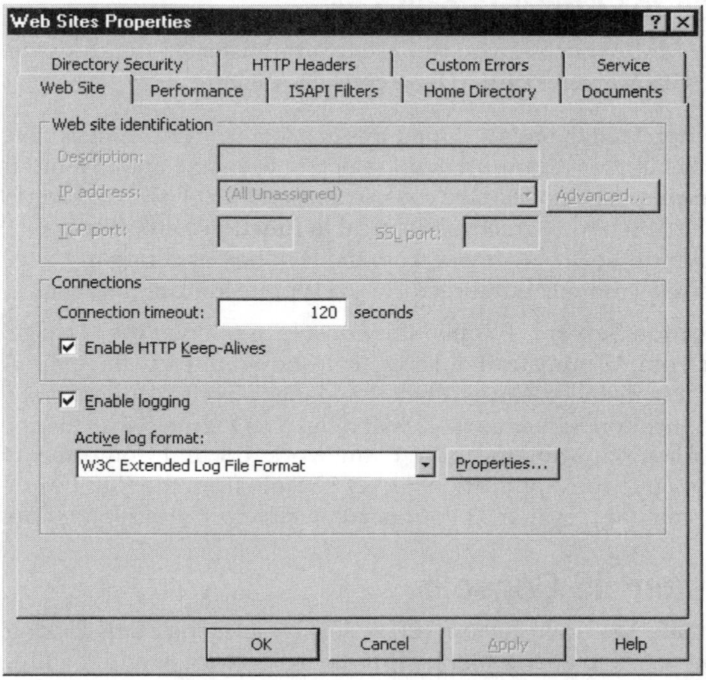

Figure 5-2.   IIS Manager uses properties sheets for configuring IIS settings.

Task Menus

Various administrative tasks can be performed by right-clicking nodes in the console tree and selecting different options from the task menu. For example, right-clicking the root Internet Information Services node or local computer node lets you connect to another IIS machine to manage it. The local computer node also lets you back up or restore IIS configuration info, restart IIS, save configuration changes to disk, browse the home page of the default website, change the view options for the right-hand details pane, export the contents of the details pane to a text file, or open online Help to read the IIS documentation. We'll be looking at some of these task menu options later in this chapter in the section "Basic Administration Tasks."

Other Consoles for Administering IIS

There are other MMC consoles you can use to administer IIS that provide the same functionality as IIS Manager does. These consoles include

- **Computer Management** Open this console from Administrative Tools (or by right-clicking My Computer and selecting Manage) and expand the Services And Applications node in the console tree, and you'll see the Internet Information Services (IIS) node, which is identical in function to IIS Manager. You can also start Computer Management from the Run box or command line by making \System32 your current directory and typing **compmgmt.msc**.

- **Application Server** To open this console, first open the Manage Your Server screen from Administrative Tools. You should already have the Application Server role installed, so just click the Manage Your Application Server link and the Application Server console will open (see Figure 5-3). This console includes nodes for configuring the .NET Framework, IIS, and Component Services. You can also open the Application Server console from the Run box or command line by making \System32 your current directory and typing **appsrv.msc**.

Creating a Custom IIS Console

You can also create your own custom IIS console by selecting Start, clicking Run, typing **mmc**, and clicking OK to open a blank MMC console. Now, to add the IIS snap-in, select File | Add/Remove Snap-In | Add | Internet Information Services (IIS) | Add | Close, and then click OK. Then save your console with a friendly name and the extension .msc in Administrative tools or some other location (such as a network share that only

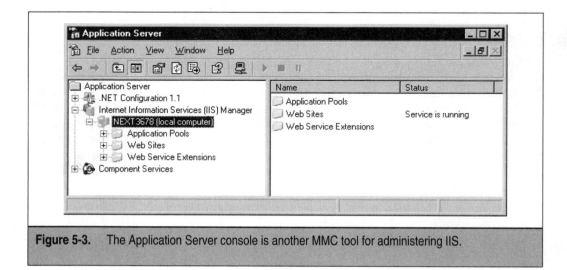

Figure 5-3. The Application Server console is another MMC tool for administering IIS.

Administrators can access). You can even e-mail this .msc file to another Administrator so they can use it on their machine.

Basic Administration Tasks

Let's take a look now at some of the basic administration tasks you can perform using IIS Manager. I'll focus on general tasks relating to the IIS machines themselves—more specific tasks relating to creating and configuring websites, managing applications, performance tuning, and maintenance will be covered in later chapters.

Connecting to IIS

To use IIS Manager to administer a machine running IIS, you first have to connect to that machine. This can be done two ways:

- Right-click the root Internet Information Services node and select Connect.
- Right-clock the node for any connected IIS machine and select Connect.

For example, if you open IIS Manager on a machine called NEXT3678 and follow one of these procedures, the Connect To Computer dialog box appears (see Figure 5-4).

In the Computer Name box, either type the name of the computer you want to connect to if you know it, or click Browse to find it on your network. The name you enter here depends on the name resolution method you are using on your network. It can be a fully qualified domain name (FQDN) if you are using DNS, or a NetBIOS name if you are using WINS. You can also enter the IP address of the target computer if you know it. If necessary, you may need to enter suitable credentials for logging on to the target machine, for example, if it belongs to a different domain.

Clicking Browse brings up the Select Computer dialog box, which lets you specify a different location for the computer you want to connect to (Figure 5-5). In this example,

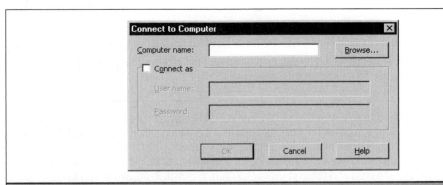

Figure 5-4. To use IIS Manager, first connect to the computer you want to manage.

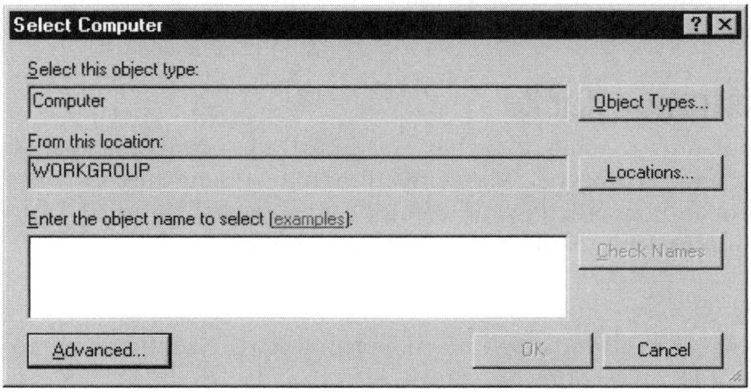

Figure 5-5.   Specifying the IIS machine you want to connect to with IIS Manager

I have several machines running IIS that belong to a workgroup named WORKGROUP. If I entered WANDA as the name of the computer I wanted to connect to and clicked Check Names, the response would be WORKGROUP\WANDA, indicating that machine WANDA was positively identified as belonging to workgroup WORKGROUP.

What if you can't remember the name of the machine you want to connect to? In that case, click Advanced to expand the Select Computer box to allow you to query your network (or Active Directory, if it is installed) to find the computer you want. Once you've found the name of the target machine, click OK to return to the Connect To Computer dialog box and then click OK again to connect to the machine.

Once your console tree of IIS Manager includes a second node (for WANDA in the example in Figure 5-6), you can connect to other IIS machines to administer them as well. You can also remove machines from the console tree by right-clicking them and selecting Disconnect.

NOTE   You can use IIS Manager to connect to and manage machines running IIS 4, 5, 5.1, and 6. You can't use IIS Manager to administer IIS 3 machines.

TIP   If you can't connect to a remote IIS machine using IIS Manager, it may be that the Internet Connection Firewall (ICF) component of Windows Server 2003 was installed and enabled on that machine prior to installing IIS on the machine. In this case, you need to either remove the ICF component or configure ICF to allow clients running IIS Manager to access the machine. See the ICF documentation in the Help and Support Center for more information on configuring ICF.

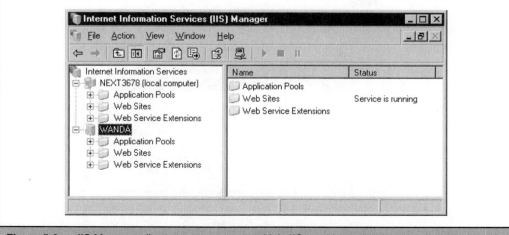

Figure 5-6. IIS Manager allows you to manage multiple IIS machines concurrently.

Backup/Restore Configuration

When you right-click a node for a connected IIS machine in the console tree, the All Tasks option in the task menu gives you three choices. The first of these is Backup/ Restore Configuration, which can be used to create a backup of the metabase on your machine. The metabase contains configuration information about the FTP and websites, and their virtual directories and files being hosted on your IIS machine. You'll learn more about that in Chapter 14, "Working with the Metabase." For now, I'll show you how to back up two files on your IIS machine, the metabase (metabase.xml) and the metabase schema (mbschema.xml).

 SECURITY ALERT   Not all IIS configuration settings are stored in the metabase. A small but significant portion of it is stored in the Registry, and the Backup/Restore Configuration option I discuss here backs up only the metabase, not the Registry. Because of this, this option isn't meant as a replacement for a full backup of operating system files and system state information, which you should do regularly as part of your disaster recovery plan.

To manually back up the metabase using IIS Manager, right-click the IIS server whose configuration you want to back up. Select All Tasks | Backup/Restore Configuration to display the Configuration Backup/Restore dialog box (see Figure 5-7). This dialog box displays all the previously created backups, including the initial configuration backup (see the "Initial Configuration Backup" sidebar later in the chapter) and

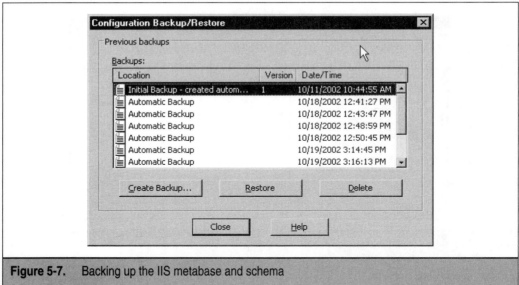

Figure 5-7. Backing up the IIS metabase and schema

various other automatic backups created by IIS. For example, when you reboot your server, IIS automatically makes several backups of the metabase; and when you create a new website, a metabase backup is automatically performed a short time later.

Now click Create Backup and type a name for your configuration backup (see Figure 5-8). You can optionally enter a password to secure your backup. The advantage of doing this is that a password-protected backup can be restored to a different IIS machine if necessary, while a backup not protected with a password can be restored only on the machine on which the backup was created.

Your new backup should show up in the list on the Configuration Backup/Restore dialog box, along with a version number. These version numbers start from zero and increment for each backup given the same name. For example, in Figure 5-8, the name given to the configuration backup is NewBackup and the version number assigned is zero. If you performed a second backup and gave it the same name, it would be version number 1 (if you gave the backup a different name, versioning would start from zero for that name).

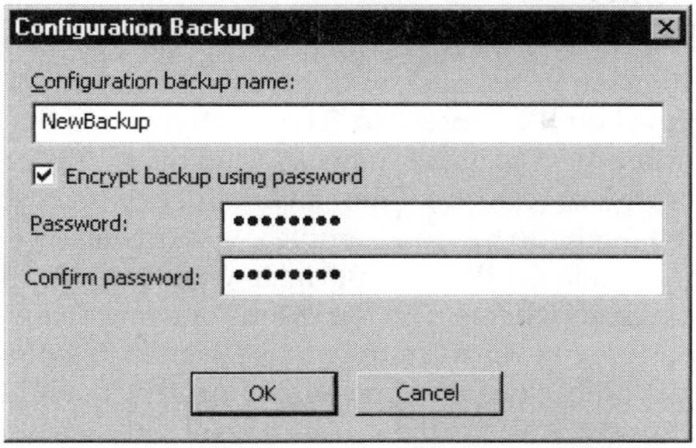

Figure 5-8. Creating a password-protected backup that is machine independent

The actual backup files are located in the folder %Systemroot%\System32\ inetserv\MetaBack and are identified by the following file extensions:

- .md0 for the metabase backup file
- .sc0 for the metabase schema backup file

We'll look more at backing up and restoring the metabase in Chapter 13, "Maintenance and Troubleshooting," and in Chapter 14.

Finally, in IIS 6 you can even back up portions of the metabase corresponding to the configuration for individual websites, FTP sites, or application pools, something we'll examine further in Chapter 7.

TIP It's a good idea to make a password-protected backup of your IIS configuration every time you make a significant change to your IIS machine, such as creating a new website or configuring quality-of-service settings. This way, you can restore your configuration to another IIS machine should the metabase on the first one become corrupt.

Initial Configuration Backup

As a safety precaution, an initial backup of metabase configuration settings is made automatically when IIS is installed. This configuration backup is stored in the folder %SystemRoot%\System32\inetsrv\MetaBack, and its purpose is to provide you with a way of restoring IIS in an emergency to its state immediately after installation. You might do this for example if your metabase became hopelessly corrupt. This allows you to get IIS working again without uninstalling and then reinstalling its various components. The file extensions for the initial configuration backup are .md1 and .sc1, and version number 1 is assigned to the backup. In addition, this initial configuration backup is *not* password protected, and therefore can only be used on the machine it was created on. As a result, it's a good idea to make an additional password-protected configuration backup immediately after installing and configuring IIS on a machine. This allows you to restore the configuration to a different system if IIS stops working on your original machine.

Restart IIS

If things seriously go wrong with IIS, you can restart IIS to try and get your sites and applications working again. This is a last-ditch solution, however, as restarting IIS has some negative consequences:

- Any data being held in memory by IIS applications is lost.
- Any users connected to IIS have their sessions terminated.
- Any sites or applications still running are unavailable until restart is complete.

IIS may have various services running depending on which components have been installed. Table 5-1 lists the various Windows Server 2003 services that support IIS, the

Name of Service	Component DLL	Host Process
WWW Service	iisw3adm.dll	svchost.exe
FTP Service	ftpsvc.dll	inetinfo.exe
SMTP Service	smtpsvc.dll	inetinfo.exe
NNTP Service	nntpsvc.dll	inetinfo.exe
IIS Admin Service	iisadmin.dll	inetinfo.exe

Table 5-1. IIS Services and Their Component DLLs and Host Processes

component DLL used to implement each service, and the host process within which the DLL runs.

NOTE   Before restarting IIS, make sure you back up your IIS configuration information as described in the preceding section to ensure against loss of important configuration data on the machine.

Stopping and starting IIS services is usually done differently from other Windows Server 2003 services, which are generally started and stopped using the Services node in Computer Management (though you can use this method with IIS also). To restart IIS, right-click the server you want to manage in IIS Manager and select All Tasks | Restart IIS. A dialog box will appear offering you several restart options including

- Restart IIS
- Restart Server
- Stop IIS
- Start IIS

The last two options give you more control over the restart process. When you select Stop IIS, the operating system attempts to perform a smooth shutdown of IIS services and allots up to 5 minutes (300 seconds) for shutdown to finish (if this time is exceeded, a forced shutdown of these services occurs). Alternatively, you can click End Now to force a shutdown of IIS immediately if needed, but the smooth shutdown approach usually takes only a few seconds to complete. Afterward, a red X will appear over the Web Sites node in IIS Manager to indicate IIS is stopped. You can then restart IIS by selecting All Tasks | Restart IIS and choosing the Start IIS option. Alternatively, you can start IIS by starting any individual website on your machine (though this leaves all other websites stopped).

If you select the Restart Server option, you are given five minutes to save your work and close any open files or running applications before reboot occurs, and you can't stop the shutdown process.

TIP   If you make configuration changes for a site or application and the changes don't seem to take effect immediately, try restarting IIS. See also the upcoming section "Save Configuration to Disk."

NOTE   You can also restart the IIS Admin Service from the command line using the IISReset command and the World Wide Web Publishing Service (WWW Service) using the Net Start command.

Automatic Restart

Windows Server 2003 automatically restarts services like IIS under certain conditions, for example,

- When the IIS Admin Service (inetinfo.exe) abnormally terminates
- When an IIS DLL running within inetinfo.exe abnormally terminates
- When the WWW Service or its host process svchost.exe abnormally terminates

If you want to disable this automatic restart feature, open Computer Management, select the Services node, and open the properties sheet for the IIS Admin Service. Select the Recovery tab and note that this service is configured to run the **iisreset /start** command should the service terminate unexpectedly (see Figure 5-9). To disable automatic restart, change the list box settings for First Failure, Second Failure, and Subsequent Failures from Run A Program to Take No Action and click OK.

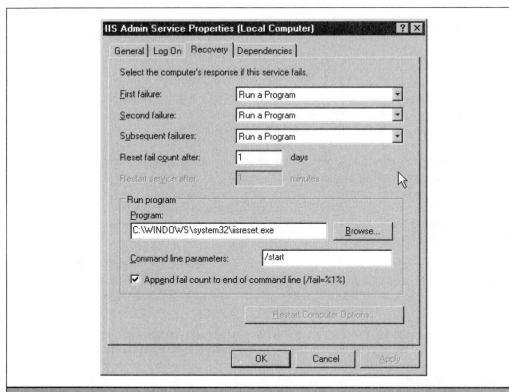

Figure 5-9.   Configuring the automatic restart feature of the IIS Admin service

---

NOTE   You can similarly disable automatic restart for the WWW Service.

Save Configuration To Disk

If you made changes to the configuration of IIS or sites and applications running on it, you can force them to be written to the metabase immediately by selecting All Tasks | Save Configuration To Disk. Whenever you make a change to IIS and it doesn't seem to take effect, try this approach and see if it helps. Note that you can also perform this action from the command line using a script.

Server Properties

If you right-click an IIS server node in IIS Manager and select Properties, the properties sheet for that server opens (see Figure 5-10). Changes made here affect your entire IIS machine, and you may be prompted to restart IIS after you make changes to this properties sheet. Let's examine the settings you can modify here.

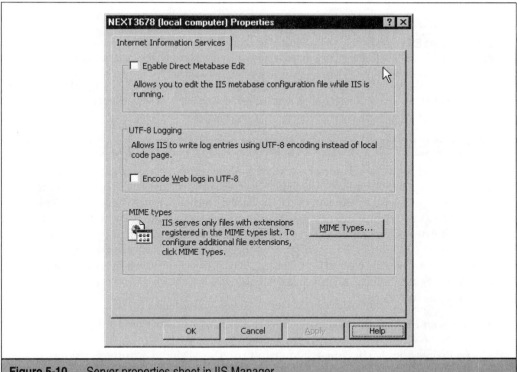

Figure 5-10.   Server properties sheet in IIS Manager

Enable Direct Metabase Edit

Enabling this check box allows you to directly edit the XML metabase while IIS is running using a text editing tool like Notepad.

UTF-8 Logging

IIS usually writes its log files using the local character set (typically ASCII). By enabling this feature, IIS will write its log in UTF-8 instead. UTF-8 is an ASCII-preserving encoding method that is part of the Unicode 3 standard and is described in RFC 2279.

MIME Types

Here you can define and modify the global MIME map for IIS, which defines which kinds of file types (based on file extensions) that IIS can serve to requesting HTTP clients. You'll see later that you can also define a MIME map at the level of individual websites and virtual directories, but any changes made here affect all sites and directories running on your machine (if you make a change that conflicts with a lower level, you are prompted whether to override the lower setting and have it inherit the setting made here). I'll defer discussion of MIME maps until Chapter 7, when I talk about administering websites.

 SECURITY ALERT There is one significant change to MIME maps between this version and earlier versions of IIS. In IIS 5, if a client requested a file having an extension that had no corresponding MIME type associated with it in the MIME map, the file would be served to the client using the application/octet-stream MIME type. In IIS 6, however, if a client requests a file type that has no MIME type defined on the server, the request is rejected and a 404.3 error is served to the client instead.

WINDOWS SERVER 2003 ADMINISTRATION TOOLS PACK

IIS Manager and many other administrative tools are available on machines running Windows Server 2003, enabling you to administer servers anywhere on your network. In many cases however, servers are kept in locked rooms to ensure their physical security, and it's an inconvenience for an administrator to have to go to the server room to configure or restart a server. A preferable way of administering IIS machines and other servers is to install administrative tools on a workstation sitting in the administrator's office, and Windows Server 2003 allows you to do this by installing the Windows Server 2003 Administration Tools Pack on your workstation. There are several caveats, however:

- You *can't* install the Windows Server 2003 Administration Tools Pack on *any* Windows 2000 computer, regardless of whether it's Server, Advanced Server, or Professional. This means you can't use the MMC to administer Windows Server 2003 machines from a Windows 2000 computer, which is unfortunate (but probably part of Microsoft's marketing strategy for nudging users toward the new platform). If you want to administer Windows Server 2003 machines from Windows 2000 computers, you need to use Remote Desktop Connection (Terminal Services Administration) instead. However, this is only a workaround because TSA is not a practical solution for performing concurrent administration tasks on a number of servers—multiple TSA sessions consume a lot more overhead than using a single MMC console does.

- You *can* install the Windows Server 2003 Administration Tools Pack on a Windows XP Professional workstation (providing it has Windows XP Service Pack 1 installed), but it *doesn't* give you a complete set of MMC consoles for administering your Windows Server 2003. In particular, the IIS Manager console is missing and so is the Internet Information Services snap-in, so you *can't* administer IIS 6 servers from an administrator workstation running Windows XP. Service Pack 2 for Windows XP is expected to solve this problem and allow the complete slate of Windows Server 2003 administrative consoles to be installed on Windows XP workstations; but until this service pack is released, you'll have to use Remote Desktop Connection (RDC) to manage IIS 6 machines from a Windows XP desktop.

The only solution at present to this dilemma is for administrators to install a Windows Server 2003 *member server* in their office as an administrator workstation (a domain controller has too much overhead), and then install the Windows Server 2003 Administration Tools Pack on this machine. The reason you have to go the extra step of installing the Administration Tools Pack on your member server is that by default the only administrative consoles installed on a server are those needed for managing the services installed on that server. For example, if you have a member server that doesn't have the DNS service installed on it, the DNS console will not be installed in the Administrative Tools program group. Also, the DNS snap-in will not be available on the machine, so you won't be able to create a new MMC console for managing DNS servers either. The reason this snap-in is not installed on the member server is because it requires the DLL dnsmgr.dll in \System32 to function, and this DLL is not installed on a member server unless you install the DNS service on that server. However, by installing the Administration Tools Pack on your Windows Server 2003 member server, you install all the administrative DLLs and snap-ins, and you get *all* of the administrative consoles installed in the Administrative Tools program group. This allows you to manage *any* Windows Server 2003 from the member server in your office.

So let's do it. To install the Windows Server 2003 Administration Tools Pack on a Windows Server 2003 member server, log on to that machine using the local Administrator account (or use the runas command), insert the Windows Server 2003 product CD, and browse the \I386 folder on the CD to locate the file adminpak .msi. This is a Windows Installer Package that can be installed by right-clicking it and selecting Install (alternatively, you could switch to the \I386 directory from the command line and type **adminpak.msi** to start the installation). The Windows Server 2003 Administration Tools Pack Setup Wizard then leads you through the process of installing the Windows Server 2003 tools on your machine. If you select Start | Administrative Tools, you should see the complete slate of administrative consoles installed on your machine, and you will be able to administer *any* aspect of *all* Windows Server 2003 machines on your network from the member server in your office.

TIP It's a good idea to install adminpak.msi on all the Windows Server 2003 machines on your network. That way you can manage any aspect of any server from any server on your network.

NOTE The Administration Tools Packs for Windows 2000 Server and Windows Server 2003 are incompatible and can only be used for managing machines running their own platform. For more information, see the Help and Support Center on Windows Server 2003.

NEXT STEPS IN ADMINISTERING IIS

If you plan to continue working with IIS Manager as your main tool for administering IIS 6, your next steps will probably be something like this:

- Unlock the features of IIS needed to enable your websites and applications to run properly. To do this, you will need to use the Web Service Extensions (WSE) node in your IIS Manager console tree, and this is covered in Chapter 10, "Securing IIS."

- Create and configure websites and applications on your server (see Chapter 7, "Creating and Configuring Websites," and also Chapter 8, "Creating and Configuring Applications").

- Create and configure FTP, SMTP, and NNTP sites on your server (see Chapter 9, "Creating and Configuring FTP Sites," and Chapter 15, "SMTP and NNTP").

- Monitor, tune, maintain, and troubleshoot IIS (covered in Chapter 12, "Performance Tuning and Monitoring," and Chapter 13, "Maintenance and Troubleshooting").

Before we look at these procedures in detail, however, let's look at some other methods of remotely administering IIS 6 machines on your network.

REMOTE DESKTOP

Another way of remotely administering IIS machines is to use the Remote Desktop feature of Windows Server 2003. On the earlier Windows 2000 Server platform, an optional Terminal Services component could be installed, turning your machine into a terminal server (TS). In Windows 2000, you could configure your TS to run in one of two possible modes:

- **Remote Administration**   This mode allowed you to remotely manage your TS from any Windows computer running the appropriate Terminal Services client. Remote Administration mode supported up to two concurrent connections from TS clients.

- **Application Server**   This mode enabled your Terminal Services clients to run Windows applications directly on the TS, offloading some of the processing power and disk space needed on client computers and allowing you to deploy "thin clients" on your network.

Things are different, however, in Windows Server 2003. The new Remote Desktop feature of Windows Server 2003 corresponds to the earlier Remote Administration mode for Terminal Services in Windows 2000 Server, and you don't need to install Remote Desktop on your Windows Server 2003 because it's installed automatically by default—you just have to enable it. Once Remote Desktop is enabled on your .NET Server, you can connect to it from any other Windows Server 2003 on your network (or from any computer having Remote Desktop Connection client software installed on it) and administer your server as if you were sitting at its local console.

NOTE   If you want to use your Windows Server 2003 machine as a real TS for running applications for clients, however, you still need to install the Terminal Services component of Windows Server 2003 to do so.

Components of Remote Desktop

The Remote Desktop (RD) feature of Windows Server 2003 has two components, which are both installed by default during Setup (they cannot be deselected). These components are

- **Remote Desktop for Administration (RDA)**   This is the server-side component of RD and allows client computers to connect to your server to remotely manage the desktop. RDA depends on Terminal Services, a Windows Server 2003 service, as do other features like Remote Assistance (which lets you invite a remote user to take control of your machine to try to fix a problem) and Terminal Services (the full TS component that allows clients to run applications remotely). Note that while Terminal Services *the service* is installed and started by default on Windows Server 2003 machines, Terminal Services *the component* (for turning your machine into a terminal server) is not installed by default!

- **Remote Desktop Connection (RDC)**   This is the client-side component of RD and enables client computers to connect to *one* Windows Server 2003 machine to manage it by accessing its desktop remotely.

In addition, there is a Remote Desktops MMC console that functions as another client-side component of RD and enables you to simultaneously connect to *multiple*

Windows Server 2003 machines and remotely manage them from a single console window. You can also add the Remote Desktops snap-in to a blank MMC console to create your own custom console for administering Windows Server 2003 remotely.

TIP Windows XP includes a desktop version of Remote Desktop for Administration, but it's called Remote Desktop on that platform.

Enabling Remote Desktop

The first thing you need to do if you want to remotely manage an IIS 6 server using Remote Desktop is to enable RDA on the server. This is straightforward—just open the System utility in Control Panel on your IIS 6 machine, switch to the Remote tab, and select the check box that says Allow Users To Connect Remotely To This Computer (see Figure 5-11). When you do this, you will be warned that you cannot use RD to log

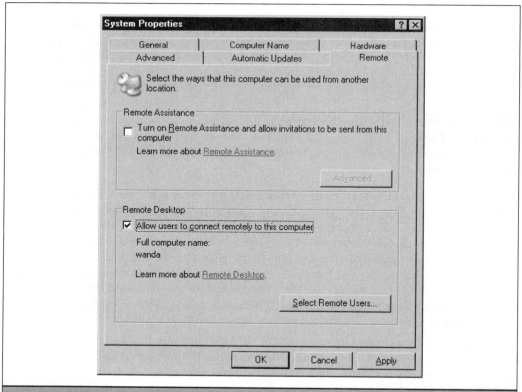

Figure 5-11. Enabling Remote Desktop on a Windows Server 2003 machine

on to a remote machine if your password is blank, and that if you have a firewall you need the RDP port (normally 3389) open to connect to the remote machine. Click OK to close the System utility, and your IIS 6 machine is ready for remote administration!

If you like, you can click Select Remote Users to specify accounts for users allowed to remotely manage this machine. You can also add your own user account and other user accounts to the Remote Desktop Users group on the local machine. To do this, open Computer Management and select the Local Users And Groups node in the console tree. Adding yourself to the Remote Desktop Users group has the effect that you no longer need to log on when you connect to your server remotely using Remote Desktop Connection. If you decide to do this, be sure to add your regular user account to this group, not your Administrator account. Otherwise, you will have to log on to your client computer using your Administrator account, which is not recommended as a security best practice.

Using Remote Desktop Connection

Now go to your client machine and connect to your IIS 6 server, and remotely manage it using Remote Desktop Connection. Start with the simplest case, where the client machine is another computer running Windows Server 2003. Just click Start and select All Programs | Accessories | Communications | and Remote Desktop Connection to open the Remote Desktop Connection dialog box, and type the name (DNS or NetBIOS) or IP address of the computer you want to remotely manage (see Figure 5-12). To configure your connection settings, click Options and modify the settings for connection speed, color depth, and so on. Click Connect when you're ready to connect to the remote machine.

At this point you may have to enter your credentials to log on to the remote machine, unless you have configured the connection option for automatic logon with your username and password (or added your user account to the Remote Desktop Users group on the remote machine).

Figure 5-12.   Using Remote Desktop Connection to log on to a remote server using Terminal Services

After you log on, you are presented with the desktop on the remote machine, and you can manage it as if you were sitting in front of its local console. A connection bar is displayed at the top of the screen, indicating that you are viewing the desktop of a remote machine and displaying the name of the remote machine. The resize buttons on the connection bar also allow you to switch between window mode and full-screen mode for managing the remote server (the default is full-screen mode). With window mode, you can also perform tasks on your local computer while managing the remote machine.

Now it's time to remotely administer your IIS machine. Click Start | Administrative Tools | Internet Information Services (IIS) to open the IIS Manager console on the remote machine (see Figure 5-13). If the mouse pointer movement seems jerky, that's because your keyboard, mouse, and monitor commands are being sent over the network to the remote machine using Remote Desktop Protocol (RDP), the underlying protocol behind Terminal Services and Remote Desktop. The overhead of this protocol, the latency of TCP/IP connections, and the speed of your network all affect RDP and result in a responsiveness somewhat less than what you would get if you were sitting at the local console of the remote machine.

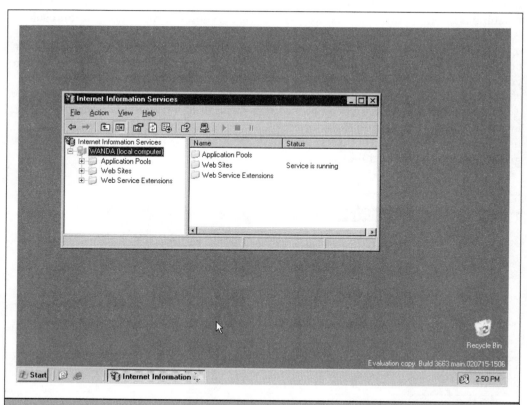

Figure 5-13.   Using IIS Manager within a full-screen Remote Desktop session

Now see if it works. Open the properties sheet for the IIS machine and make a change to its configuration, such as enabling the check box for Direct Metabase Edit. Close the property sheet to apply the change and log off your Remote Desktop session by selecting Start | Windows Security | Log Off | Log Off (if you click the Close gadget on the connection bar or RD session window, you will be disconnected, but any applications you opened will continue to run). The connection bar will disappear and you will be looking at your local computer's desktop again. Now go to the IIS 6 machine and log on to the local console. Start IIS Manager and confirm that the configuration change you made during your Remote Desktop session has in fact been made.

NOTE   You can also use Remote Desktop Connection to remotely administer Windows 2000 Server computers that have Terminal Services installed and are running in Remote Administration mode.

Using the Remote Desktops Console

An alternative way of connecting to an IIS 6 machine using RD is using the Remote Desktops console in Administrative Tools (or by installing the Remote Desktops snap-in in a blank MMC console). Just open this console, right-click the Remote Desktops node, and select Add New Connection (see Figure 5-14). Then specify the

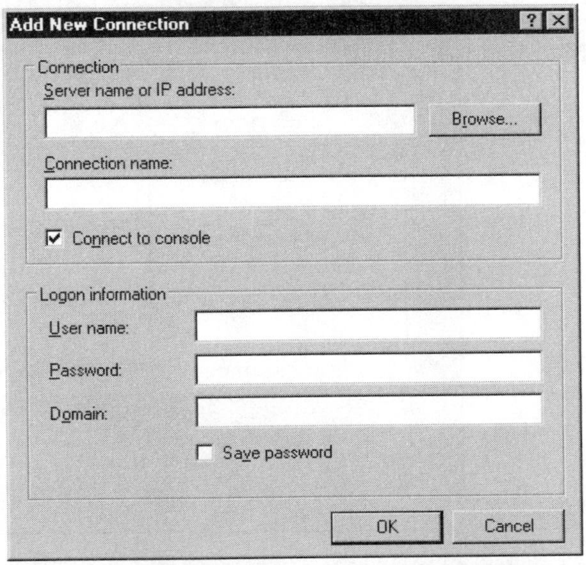

Figure 5-14.   Adding a new connection to the Remote Desktops console

name or IP address of the remote computer you want to administer, a friendly name to remember the connection, and the credentials to use to connect, and click OK.

Now expand the Remote Desktops node in the console tree, select the new connection you created, and watch as the console logs on to Terminal Services on the remote machine and displays its desktop within the right-side details pane of the console (see Figure 5-15). Note that the desktop of the remote machine is compressed in this view, and some Start menu items may be difficult to access unless you use smaller icons in the menu. The advantage of performing remote administration this way is that you can connect to several machines remotely using a single console tool (Remote Desktop Connection only supports one remote connection). The disadvantage is that you have a bit less space on the remote desktop to perform administration tasks (although you can configure the details pane to display differently).

TIP To log off from your remote connection, right-click the connection in the console tree and select Disconnect. To configure the connection and its display properties, right-click it and select Properties.

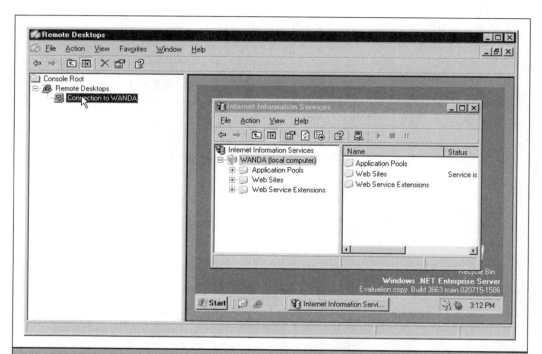

Figure 5-15. Using the Remote Desktops console to administer a remote IIS machine using Terminal Services

> **NOTE** You can also use the Remote Desktops console of Windows Server 2003 to remotely administer Windows 2000 Server computers that have Terminal Services installed and running in Remote Administration mode.

Other Remote Desktop Clients

Remote Desktop Connection is automatically installed on Windows XP Professional machines, and this allows you to use Terminal Services to remotely administer any Windows .NET Server anywhere on your network. Just go to a Windows XP workstation, click Start and All Programs | Accessories | Communications | Remote Desktop Connection to open the Remote Desktop Connection dialog box, and type the name of the computer you want to remotely manage and continue as discussed previously.

You can also install Remote Desktop Connection on any Windows 95, Windows 98, Windows NT 4, and Windows 2000 machine from any machine running Windows Server 2003. Just go to your .NET Server and share the %SystemRoot%\System32\Clients\ Tsclient folder using the share name Tsclient to make the Terminal Services client available to your 32-bit Windows machines. Then go to your 32-bit Windows computer, log on as Administrator, click Start, and select Run. Type **computer_name\tsclient\ win32\setup.exe**, where **computer_name** is the name of the Windows Server 2003 machines on which you share the \Tsclient folder. Then follow the prompts to install Remote Desktop Connection and access it as for XP.

REMOTE DESKTOP WEB CONNECTION

Another Terminal Services client included with Windows Server 2003 (but not installed by default) is Remote Desktop Web Connection, an ActiveX control that lets you access your Windows Server 2003 machine across the Internet using Internet Explorer (version 5 or later). The Remote Desktop client described in the previous sections must first be locally installed on a Windows computer before you can use it to connect to a remote server. Furthermore, the Remote Desktop client is intended for use within a company's network—that is, within the intranet, not across the Internet (you can use Remote Desktop Connection across a LAN, a WAN link, a modem connection, or a VPN connection). The advantages of using the Remote Desktop Web Connection client are that it can be used across the Internet from any machine anywhere that is running Internet Explorer, and you don't have to install any additional software on that machine before using it.

But before you can use Remote Desktop Web Connection, you first have to install it on the IIS 6 machine you want to remotely administer. To do this, select Control Panel | open Add Or Remove Programs | select Add/Remove Windows Components | select Application Server | click Details | select Internet Information Services | click Details | select World Wide Web Service | click Details, and select the Remote Desktop Web Connection check box. Completing this procedure creates a new virtual directory called tsweb within the default website (see Figure 5-16). This virtual directory contains a

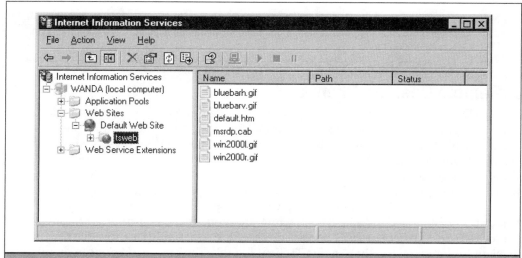

Figure 5-16.   The Tsweb virtual directory supports remote administration through the ActiveX-based remote Desktop Web Connection feature.

default.htm page that a remote browser can access to download and install the ActiveX control for Remote Desktop Web Connection (found within a cabinet file) to administer the server remotely using a browser.

To remotely administer an IIS 6 machine on which the Remote Desktop Web Connection has been installed (you must have enabled the Remote Desktop feature on the Remote tab of the System utility in Control Panel as well), simply open Internet Explorer and type the URL **http://computer_name/tsweb**, where **computer_name** is the name (DNS on the Internet, NetBIOS on an intranet) or IP address of the IIS 6 machine. The default.htm page will open up and a dialog box will prompt you to install the Remote Desktop ActiveX Control on your local machine. Click Yes and wait until Done appears in the status bar of your browser, and then enter the name of the IIS 6 machine you want to connect to and remotely administer (see Figure 5-17).

TIP   The \tsweb\default.htm page can even be customized; for example, you could brand it with your company logo and a privacy policy.

Once you've entered your credentials and logged on, you'll be presented with a full-screen Remote Desktop session just as with Remote Desktop Connection—provided you selected Full Screen from the list box on the /tsweb/default.htm page. You can

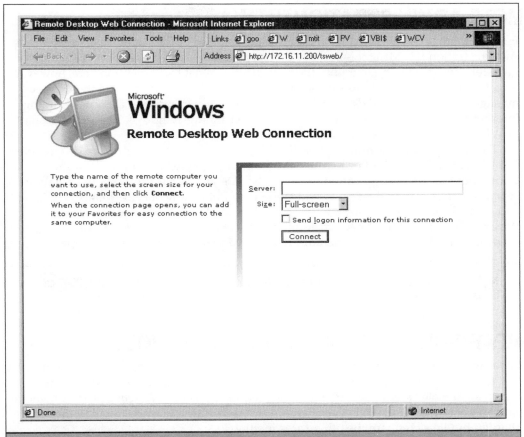

Figure 5-17.   Using Internet Explorer to remotely administer an IIS machine using Remote Desktop Web Connection

also select other screen sizes, such a 640×480 or 800×600 to display the remote desktop within a browser window. This is very cool: you can administer your IIS 6 servers from a Windows XP computer at an Internet cafe in Tahiti——provided the cafe has a fast enough Internet connection!

TIP   You only need to install the Remote Desktop Web Connection component on *one* of your Windows Server 2003 machines on your network because when you open the \tsweb\default.htm page, you can specify a different server's name to remotely manage.

REMOTE ADMINISTRATION (HTML)

Finally, another GUI method for remote administration of IIS machines is the Remote Administration (HTML) tool. Because this tool is installed by default on Web Edition, I'll defer a full discussion of it until the next chapter. What I will mention here, however, is that you can also install this tool on Standard or Enterprise Edition and then remotely manage your IIS 6 machines over the Internet from any Windows computer running Internet Explorer 5 or higher, such as a machine running Windows 2000 Professional or Windows XP Professional.

To install Remote Administration (HTML) on Standard or Enterprise Edition, select Control Panel | open Add or Remove Programs | select Add/Remove Windows Components | select Application Server | click Details | select Internet Information Services | click Details | select World Wide Web Publishing Service | click Details | and select Remote Administration (HTML). This starts the Windows Components Wizard, and when it has finished, you can connect to your IIS machine from a remote workstation using a browser and administer it. More on that in the next chapter.

NOTE   The version of Remote Administration (HTML) included with Windows Server 2003 can only be used for administering IIS 6 machines, not servers running earlier versions of IIS.

COMPARISON OF ADMINISTRATION METHODS

So far we've looked at four methods for administering IIS 6 machines, both remotely and from the local console: IIS Manager (MMC console), Remote Desktop (Terminal Services), Remote Desktop Web Connection (Terminal Services Web control), and Remote Administration (HTML). I'll cover Remote Administration in more detail in the next chapter, but let's compare the other three methods:

- IIS Manager is most useful on an intranet (internal company network) and has the advantage of being able to administer *down-level* servers as well, including IIS 4, 5, and 5.1. If you work mainly within an enterprise environment and have a mixed network of current and down-level versions of IIS machines, the IIS Manager console is probably your best tool for IIS administration.

- Remote Desktop is particularly useful for managing IIS machines in remote branch offices where no sysadmin is present. It supports up-level administration, allowing you to manage your IIS 6 machines using a Terminal Services client running on Windows .NET Server, Windows XP, Windows 2000, Windows NT 4, or Windows 98. This provides a great deal of flexibility for administrators who work with a variety of Windows desktop platforms in their enterprise.

- Remote Desktop Web Connection is essential for administrators who travel and need to be able to access and manage their IIS machines from anywhere using a computer running Internet Explorer.

Whatever your situation as an IIS administrator, there's a tool available to meet your administration needs!

Challenge

Your enterprise plans to deploy IIS 6 servers for a corporate intranet that will be used by branch offices and mobile employees. Larger branch offices are connected to company headquarters using dedicated T-1 and fractional T-1 connections, while smaller offices and mobile users use dial-up Virtual Private Network (VPN). You are the IIS administrator for your company, but you plan to delegate administration portions of the intranet to department heads at various branch offices and to senior mobile sales professionals. What tools for administering IIS will you provide these individuals with? What preliminary configuration steps will you have to perform on your network, firewalls, and IIS machines in order for these tools to work? What methods do you prefer yourself as administrator for managing your IIS machines, and why? How will the release of Service Pack 2 for Windows XP make your life easier?

CHECKLIST: IIS ADMINISTRATION TOOLS AND TASKS

Check off each of the IIS administration tools in this list as you gain familiarity with their deployment, configuration, and use:

- ☐ IIS Manager console
- ☐ Application Server console
- ☐ Computer Management console
- ☐ Custom MMC console with Internet Information Services snap-in
- ☐ Windows Server 2003 Administration Tools Pack
- ☐ Remote Desktop Connection
- ☐ Remote Desktop Web Connection
- ☐ Remote Administration (HTML)

Check off each of the following general IIS administration tasks as you become familiar with performing them using the IIS Manager console:

- ☐ Connecting to a remote IIS machine
- ☐ Backing up the metabase and schema
- ☐ Restarting IIS
- ☐ Enabling/disabling automatic restart of the IIS Admin service
- ☐ Saving IIS configuration changes to disk
- ☐ Enabling direct metabase edit

☐ Enabling UTF-8 logging

☐ Viewing and modifying the global MIME map

☐ Installing IIS Manager on a Windows .NET member server not running IIS

☐ Enabling Remote Desktop on a Windows .NET Server

☐ Installing the Remote Desktop Web Connection component on an IIS machine

☐ Installing the Remote Administration (HTML) component on an IIS machine

CHAPTER 6

Administering
Web Edition

In the previous chapter, we looked at the various tools and methods you can use to manage Standard and Enterprise Editions of Windows Server 2003. In this chapter I'll focus on Web Edition, the edition specially designed for web application hosting on "blade" servers running in service provider data centers. A blade is a complete computer built on a card or module; and by housing multiple blades in a single rack-mountable chassis, service providers can save valuable rack space in their data centers. In particular, we'll look at the Web Interface for Server Administration (WISA), an Active Server Pages application running on IIS 6 that allows administrators to remotely manage many aspects of their IIS machines remotely using Internet Explorer. You'll also see how Telnet can be used to remotely administer IIS machines using a command-line interface, though I'll defer a full discussion of command-line administration until Chapter 11, "Working from the Command Line."

ADMINISTRATION METHODS

You saw in Chapter 1 that Web Edition is in many ways a "light" version of Windows Server 2003. For instance, although a Web Server machine can be part of a domain, you can't install Active Directory on a machine running Web Edition, so a Web Server machine can't assume the role of domain controller for your network. However, you can administer Active Directory from a Web Server machine by opening a blank MMC console and adding the appropriate snap-ins (if you're missing any snap-ins, you can install the Windows Server 2003 Administration Tools Pack on the machine to install the necessary DLLs).

TIP   While machines running Web Edition can belong to a domain, the usual configuration in an ISP or ASP web-hosting data center is to configure them as belonging to a workgroup and assign the local Administrator account to a user that owns each collocated server.

As far as IIS 6 administration is concerned, Web Edition supports all the methods available for Standard and Enterprise Edition, as described in the preceding chapter. In other words, you can administer a Web Server machine using the IIS Manager console by enabling the Remote Desktop feature and connecting to it using Remote Desktop Connection, by installing the Remote Desktop Web Connection component so you can manage it using Terminal Services over HTTP, and so on. The main differences between Web Edition and the other editions regarding IIS are as follows:

- IIS installs by default on Web Edition. On Standard and Enterprise Editions you have to manually add the Application Server role using the Manage Your Server Wizard. This wizard is not available (nor needed) on Web Edition because the only role it is intended for is hosting websites.

- Web Edition installs the Remote Administration (HTML) component of the World Wide Web service by default. This creates an Administration website for IIS that enables you to securely manage the server using Internet Explorer over an SSL connection. Toward the end of the preceding chapter, you learned that

Remote Administration (HTML) could also be installed on the Standard and Enterprise editions—but it isn't installed by default on those editions as it is on Web Edition.

SECURITY ALERT   For Remote Administration (HTML) to function, Web Edition also installs the Active Server Pages (ASP) component of IIS by default. If you open IIS Manager on Web Server and select the Web Service Extensions node, you will see that ASP is enabled (in an Allowed state as opposed to a Prohibited state).

The rest of this chapter focuses on administering Web Edition using this Remote Administration (HTML) component. We will also look briefly at using Telnet to administer Web Server, as this is a commonly used tool for command-line administration of remote servers.

WEB INTERFACE FOR SERVER ADMINISTRATION

When you install Web Edition on a machine and log on to Windows, Internet Explorer tries to connect to the Administration website on the IIS machine. The Administration website is configured to require Basic Authentication secured by Secure Sockets Layer (SSL) encryption, and this is what generates the additional logon screen that appears (see Figure 6-1).

TIP   If you select the Remember My Password check box, the next time you log on to Windows, this second logon screen will appear prepopulated with your username and password—all you need to do is click OK. Of course, this can be a security risk if you left your administrative workstation unlocked!

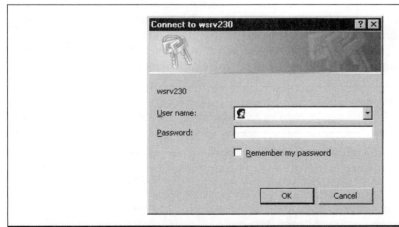

Figure 6-1.   Logging on to the Web Interface for Server Administration (WISA)

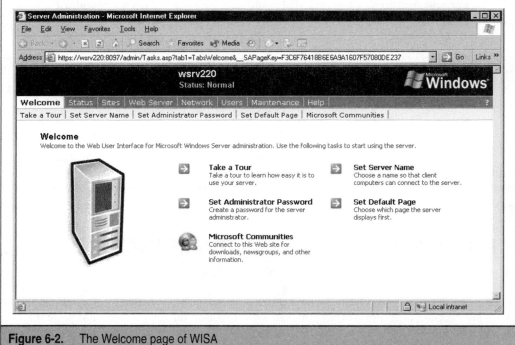

Figure 6-2.   The Welcome page of WISA

When you enter your administrator credentials and click OK, your credentials are encrypted using SSL and are submitted to the Administration website for authentication. Once authenticated, the logon screen disappears and the Welcome page of the Administration website appears (see Figure 6-2). As viewed in the browser, this site is known as the Web User Interface for Microsoft Windows Server Administration, or Web Interface for Server Administration (WISA) for short. In other words, whether I call it the Administration website, the Remote Administration (HTML) component of IIS, or the Web Interface for Server Administration (WISA), I'm talking about one and the same thing.

SECURITY ALERT   The Administrator account must *not* have a null password if you are going to use WISA to manage IIS (this is also the case for administering IIS using Remote Desktop).

WISA is configured to start automatically each time you log on to Windows (there's a shortcut to a script that starts it in the Startup programs group). You can also open WISA several other ways on the local machine:

- Select Start | choose All Programs | select Administrative Tools | and select Web Interface for Remote Administration.

- Select Start and choose Run; then type **%SystemRoot\System32\ ServerAppliance\SecureLaunch.vbs** and click OK.

- From the command line, change to the %SystemRoot\System32\ServerAppliance directory and type **securelaunch.vbs**.

- Open Windows Explorer and navigate to the %SystemRoot\System32\ ServerAppliance folder and double-click SecureLaunch.vbs.

You can also open WISA on the local machine using any of the following URLs:

- http://127.0.0.1:8098

- http://localhost:8098

- http://*computer_name*:8098 where *computer_name* is the name (NetBIOS or DNS) of the local machine

- http://*IP_address*:8098 where *IP_address* is any IP address not specifically assigned to a website on the local machine (There may be multiple IP addresses assigned if the server hosts multiple websites, and the Administration website is configured to respond to all unassigned IP addresses on the machine.)

For example, you could click Start | Run, type **http://localhost:8098,** and click OK to open Internet Explorer; then connect to the Administration website, enter your credentials, and access the WISA Welcome screen.

NOTE The %SystemRoot\System32\ServerAppliance directory contains the various DLLs and .asp pages that make Remote Administration (HTML) work. In particular, the %SystemRoot\System32\ServerAppliance\web directory contains the .asp pages of the Administration website, as you can determine by opening the properties sheet for the Administration website in IIS Manager and selecting the Home Directory tab.

A couple of tips on using WISA:

- Don't forget to use https:// instead of http:// when opening WISA, since the Administration website only works with SSL (8099 is the non-SSL TCP port for the site, but accessing it using that port doesn't do anything).

- When opening WISA for administering a *remote* Web Edition machine over a network or Internet connection, use http://*computer_name*:8098 or http://*IP_address*:8098.

Let's now take a look at the various pages of the WISA interface, which include the Welcome, Status, Sites, Web Server, Network, Users, Maintenance, and Help pages.

NOTE Don't forget to activate your copy of Web Edition after you first log on, unless you are an enterprise or volume licensing customer that is not required to activate.

For greater security, you may want to restrict which computers are allowed to connect to the Administrator website and use WISA to manage IIS. To do this, open the IIS Manager console on the machine, right-click the Administration website and select Properties and then the Directory Security tab. Click Edit under IP Address And Domain Name Restrictions, select Denied Access, and click Add. Then specify which computer (single IP address), group of computers (IP network ID plus subnet mask), or domain name you want to allow access to the Administration website. (You can also do this remotely using the Remote Desktop option on WISA's Maintenance page, as described in the section "Maintenance Page," later in this chapter)

SECURITY ALERT   If you leave your WISA browser window open for an extended period of time without using it, the SSL connection to the Administration website will time out for security reasons, and you will have to reopen the WISA shortcut or URL again.

Welcome Page

Let's begin by examining the layout of the WISA interface (refer back to Figure 6-2). At the top of each page is the status area, which displays the name of the server and its current status. This page can be customized to include a company logo, privacy policy, or other information if desired. If you click the status information, it will take you to the status page, which I'll discuss in a moment. Beneath the status area are two navigation bars: a primary one you can use to select different types of administrative tasks such as managing users or network settings, and a secondary one whose options vary depending on which primary task you select. Beneath the navigation bars is the main content area, which contains web elements that let you select a particular task or perform the task you've selected.

The task options on the Welcome page are

- **Take A Tour**   Opens a Help window that has information on working with WISA.

- **Set Server Name**   Lets you change the name of the server, add a DNS suffix that is appended to the server name to create a fully qualified domain name (FQDN), and specify whether the server is to belong to a workgroup or domain. Any changes you perform here will be reflected in the more common GUI tools for managing Windows Server 2003. For example, changing the server name causes the change to be reflected on the Computer Name tab of the System utility in Control Panel, and adding a DNS suffix causes this suffix to appear on the DNS tab of the Advanced TCP/IP Settings properties sheet of your Local Area Connection. Some changes, like changing the server name, require that the server be rebooted before they take effect, and WISA will prompt you in this regard.

- **Set Administrator Password**   Lets you change the password for your *local* Administrator account on the server. You must be logged on with the local Administrator account to change its password using this method. To change the password for domain accounts, use the Active Directory Users And Computers console and connect to a domain controller on your network.

- **Set Default Page**   Lets you specify either the Welcome or Status page as the default page that appears when you open WISA.

- **Microsoft Communities**   Opens the Windows Server Community home page on Microsoft's website. This page has links to downloads, newsgroups, events, and so on, that might be of interest to users of Microsoft Windows server products.

Status Page

If you select the Status page link (or click the Status message at the top), you'll open WISA's Status page where you'll find alerts (if there are any) and other status information about web server. The Status message at the top displays Normal, Information, Warning, or Critical, depending on the current state of your system, and the Status page provides you with more details. When you first log on to your server, you will find several alerts prompting you to change the server name (which is a good idea if you let Setup randomly assign your machine a name), change the administrator password (if necessary to make it more secure), and install a new server certificate to replace the default one installed during Setup (to provide secure SSL communications with the Administration website). If you click any of these alerts, additional information will be displayed underneath. Clicking the Clear Message link will clear the alert without addressing the issue that generated it. To resolve the issue, select the appropriate nav function on the WISA screen, such as changing the computer name or admin password.

Interestingly enough, the server certificate issue can't be resolved using WISA. Instead, you have to open the IIS Manager console, open the properties sheet for the Administration website, select the Directory Security tab, and click Server Certificates to start the Web Server Certificate Wizard. We'll look at this later in Chapter 10 when we talk about securing IIS. For now let's just clear all the alerts so that Status: Normal appears in green in the Status area, and move on to the next page.

Sites Page

The Sites page displays all the websites installed on your server, and can be used to pause, stop, and start them. You can also click Create to create a new website from scratch (we'll look at this in the next chapter, "Creating and Configuring Websites"), Delete to remove a site, and Modify to change the settings for the site. You cannot pause, stop, start, delete, or modify the Administration website because to do so could interfere with the operation of the WISA interface. Nor can you modify the configuration of the Default Web Site using this tool (Microsoft expects that you will leave this site unchanged and create new websites instead as needed). You can, however, change the port number of the Administration website, as you'll see when you get to the Network page. Finally, if you have a large number of websites configured on the machine, you can use the Search feature to find a site based on its description, IP address, TCP port number, host header name, or status. I'll talk more about what determines the identity of a website in the next chapter.

Web Server Page

The Web Server page lets you manage various aspects of web and FTP sites on your server. We'll look at them in detail because there are a few tricky issues to explain.

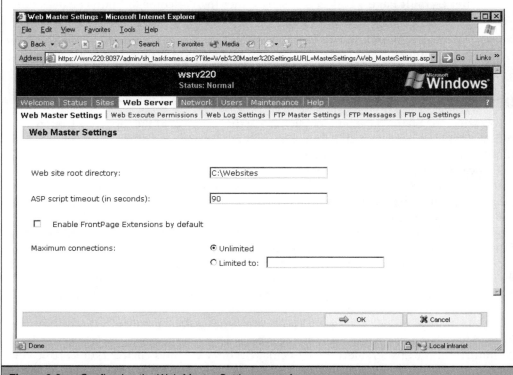

Figure 6-3. Configuring the Web Master Settings page for your remote server

Web Master Settings

The Web Master Settings page lets you configure master settings for all websites on your machine (see Figure 6-3). These settings include

- Specifying the Web Site Root Directory, which is where content for new websites is located. The default location is C:\Websites*site_name*, where *site_name* is the name you use to describe the site. The first time you create a new website on the machine, the C:\Websites directory and a subdirectory under it is automatically created and assigned as home directory. If the site name is Sales, for example, the home directory created for the site will be C:\Websites\Sales. If you change C:\Websites to something else on the Web Master Settings page, home directories for existing sites will be unchanged, but all future websites you create will have home directories in the new location.

- Specifying the ASP Script Timeout (in Seconds), which is a timeout value for Active Server Pages applications in the website. The default timeout is 90 seconds. If you change the value here, it changes for all websites on your machine, both existing ones and new ones you create (including the Default and Administration websites).

- Specifying whether to Enable FrontPage Extensions By Default for all *new* websites you create on the machine. You still have to manually configure FrontPage Extensions on *existing* websites using the Modify button on the Sites page. You must first install the FrontPage component of IIS using Add Or Remove Programs in Control Panel, and then enable FrontPage Extensions globally on the Web Master Settings page (so that new sites will have these extensions enabled by default), and manually enable them for each existing site you create on your server using the Modify button on the Sites page. If you enable FrontPage extensions on this page but haven't installed the FrontPage 2003 Server Extensions component, you won't receive any warning message here. I'll talk more about configuring FrontPage extensions in the next chapter.

- Specifying the Maximum Connections, which means limiting the number of web client connections to each site to a specified value. This allows you to manage bandwidth more efficiently. I'll discuss configuring website settings in the next chapter; connection limiting is covered in Chapter 12, "Performance Tuning and Monitoring."

Web Log Settings and Web Execute Permissions

The Web Log Settings page lets you configure logging options for all websites on your machine, including the logging format and time between logs. Website logging is a useful feature for troubleshooting HTTP connections; I'll discuss it more in the next chapter.

The Web Execute Permissions page lets you specify whether scripts and executables should be allowed to run for each website. The possible options you can choose for Default Execute Permissions are

- None
- Scripts only
- Scripts and Executables

What you do is first choose one of the preceding options for your Default Execute Permissions and then select either

- **Apply To All Websites That Use The Default Value**   This option applies your Default Execute Permissions setting to any *new* websites you create on the server (it has no effect on *existing* sites).

- **Apply To All Websites (Override Individual Settings)**   This option applies your Default Execute Permissions setting to all existing websites *and* any new ones you create. It has no effect, however, on the Default and Administration websites.

I'll talk more about Execute permissions in Chapter 8, "Creating and Configuring Applications," and also in Chapter 10.

FTP Settings

The three options for configuring FTP work only if you have already installed the FTP component of IIS using Add Or Remove Programs in Control Panel. The options are

- **FTP Master Settings**   This includes enabling FTP for content uploading, specifying a directory listing style, and specifying maximum connections and connection timeout values. Selecting the Enabling FTP For Content Uploading option will stop the Default FTP site and create a new FTP site called Web Site Content, whose root directory is C:\Web Site Content FTP Root. Selecting any of the other options applies the selected setting to all FTP sites on the server.

- **FTP Messages**   This lets you specify welcome, exit, and maximum connection messages for FTP users.

- **FTP Log Settings**   This lets you configure logging options for all FTP sites on your machine, including the logging format and time between logs. FTP site logging is a useful feature for troubleshooting FTP connections.

Network Page

The options on the Network page let you perform a variety of tasks, including

- **Identification**   Performs the same tasks as the Set Server Name option discussed in the earlier "Welcome Page" section.

- **Global Settings**   Lets you configure the various TCP/IP settings that you usually configure using the Advanced TCP/IP Settings properties sheet for Local Area Connection. The settings you can configure here include specifying additional DNS suffixes, modifying the HOSTS and LMHOSTS file, and related tasks.

- **Interfaces**   Lets you rename and configure network interfaces on your server. For each interface, you can modify the IP address, subnet mask, or default gateway; change from static to dynamic addressing; add additional IP or default gateway addresses; specify a metric; and specify DNS and WINS server addresses.

- **Administrator**   Performs the same tasks as the Set Administrator Password discussed in the "Welcome Page" section.

- **Administration Web Site**   Lets you specify the IP address and port to which a browser must connect to access the Administration Web Site and use the WISA. By default, the Administrator Web Site is configured to respond to any IP address on the server and to port 8098 for secure (SSL) access. For example, if the server's network interface has five IP addresses assigned, you can use any of these addresses in the URL https://IP_address:8098 to open the WISA interface. If you prefer, you can specify a single IP address for opening WISA while the remaining addresses are used as identifiers for other websites hosted on the server. If you change the secure port on this page, you will immediately be required to log on again to WISA using the new port. There is also an additional port configured for nonsecure access to the Administration Web Site (TCP port 8099); but because SSL is required for running WISA, it doesn't really do anything.

- **Telnet**   Lets you enable and start the Telnet service on your machine, making it a Telnet server that supports up to two concurrent connections from Telnet clients. Telnet is another tool you can use for remotely administering IIS machines, and is discussed later in this chapter in the section entitled "Using Telnet."

Users Page

The Users page lets you create, delete, configure, and manage local user accounts and groups on the server. For user accounts, you can perform common tasks like disabling accounts, changing passwords, and creating home directories; for groups, you can add or remove members to the group. In short, you can perform many of the tasks usually performed using Local Users And Groups in the Computer Management console.

Maintenance Page

The Maintenance page lets you perform common configuration and maintenance tasks for your server. These include setting the date and time, shutting down or restarting the server (you can also schedule a shutdown to occur at a specific time), and changing language settings. If you schedule a shutdown or restart and change your mind, you can cancel it by selecting Maintenance | Shutdown | Scheduled Shutdown | No Scheduled Shutdown Or Alert. Note that if you select Maintenance | Shutdown, click the scheduled alert listed under Showdown Related Alerts, and then select Clear Message, the alert is cleared but the event remains scheduled!

On this page you can also select

- **Logs**   Lets you view, clear, display, or download Application, Security, System, and Web Administration logs. The first three logs are normally viewed using Event Viewer, while the web logs are generated by IIS for troubleshooting various issues (web logs are discussed in the next chapter). For Event logs, you can also view the details (verbose mode) of each event you select, and you can download Event logs in three formats: .evt for viewing in Event Viewer, and .log or .csv for importing into Excel and other programs.

- **Set Alert E-Mail**   Lets you enable or disable having the system send e-mail messages to administrators when alerts are generated (see Figure 6-4). This requires that the SMTP service be running on your IIS machine (which it is by default in Web Edition). To configure this feature, select the types of alerts (critical, warning, and/or informational) to send by e-mail, the e-mail address of the administrator, and the IP address or FQDN of the SMTP server to use for forwarding the mail. Click the Test button to see if it works; and if it does, click OK to save the changes. In a normal Internet environment, you may not need to configure anything else to make this feature work (providing your ISP's

SMTP host is configured to receive e-mail from your network's DNS domain). If you're using Exchange Server as your Internet SMTP host, however, you will need to ask your Exchange administrator for the name of the SMTP gateway to use.

- **Remote Desktop Connection** Lets you download and install the Remote Desktop ActiveX Control so you can connect to your server using Remote Desktop Web Connection and perform administrative tasks as if you were sitting right at the server's local console. However, you must first enable the Remote Desktop feature on the server by using the Remote tab of the System utility in Control Panel—and you can't perform this step using WISA! I covered Remote Desktop in the previous chapter, "Administering Standard/Enterprise Edition," so I won't go into it further here.

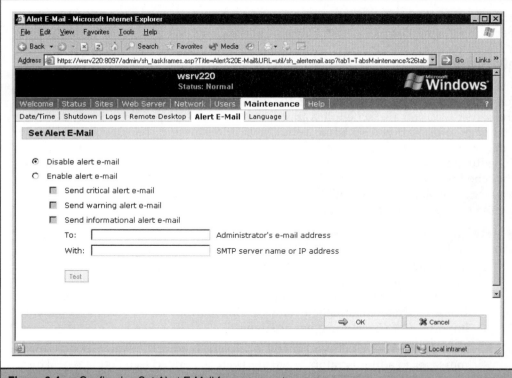

Figure 6-4. Configuring Set Alert E-Mail for your remote server

The Verdict on Remote Administration (HTML)

WISA is not just an IIS administration tool but also a web browser interface for managing general aspects of remote servers. WISA not only lets you create and configure websites but also lets you manage user accounts, modify network settings, rename your server, and so on. These are common general server administration tasks, and WISA lets you perform them remotely from anywhere in the world using a web browser as your interface. This is cool, but only a limited number of tasks can be directly performed using WISA. For example, you can create new local user accounts and change their password or create home directories for them, but you can't configure a user profile or logon script for these accounts. Also, you can't configure startup settings for network services, share folders, manage devices, or run System Monitor. In fact, WISA's deficiencies are emphasized by the fact that the Maintenance page includes an option for opening a Remote Desktop Connection to the server so that you can perform tasks that WISA itself cannot be used for!

What's the point then? Using the MMC or Remote Desktop, you can do *anything* an administrator needs to do to manage a server, and Remote Desktop Web Connection even lets you do this using a web browser. WISA seems to be a holdover from an earlier Microsoft initiative to "webify" every aspect of remote administration, and it is really no longer required because it is made obsolete by Remote Desktop Web Connection. About the only advantage of WISA over other administrative tools is that it provides a simplified interface for performing some common web server administration tasks. For this reason, you might be tempted as administrator to allow subordinates to use WISA for managing certain aspects of departmental web servers. Remember, however, that to use WISA you must be a member of the local Administrators group, and this gives you the inherent ability to do *anything* on the server (even though the interface itself limits you to certain predefined tasks).

Another problem I have with WISA is that it's generally slower and more cumbersome than using the MMC or Remote Desktop. In addition, you can only use WISA for administering IIS 6 machines, not machines running earlier versions of IIS. I've covered WISA here because it's an integral part of IIS 6 on the Windows Server 2003 platform, but whether you finally decide to use it or not is your choice!

USING TELNET

Earlier in this chapter you saw how WISA can be used to enable the Telnet service on your machine, turning it into a Telnet server supporting two concurrent connections from Telnet clients. Telnet is commonly used in the UNIX world for remotely administering machines by running character mode applications on them from a remote Telnet client. With Windows 2000 Server, Microsoft began to include a Telnet service or daemon with their Windows server operating systems, thus providing yet another avenue for remotely administering Windows servers, including Windows Server 2003.

Once the Telnet service has been enabled on the IIS machine using the Network page of WISA, you can connect to it from any other machine by using a Telnet client. On Windows 2000 and Windows Server 2003, the Telnet client is integrated into the command line; you start it by typing **telnet** *server_name*, where *server_name* is the name (NetBIOS or DNS) of the remote IIS machine (or its IP address). Alternatively, you can also simply type **telnet** to start the Telnet client and then type **open** *server_name* to establish a connection with the server. (Type **help** to see other Telnet commands.) After you specify the name or IP address of the remote server, Telnet will prompt you for administrator credentials, which are securely passed over the network using NTLM authentication.

Once you're logged on, you have a command-prompt window running on the remote machine (see Figure 6-5), something you can also do with Remote Desktop if you prefer (provided Remote Desktop is enabled on the IIS machine). Using Telnet, you can run executables and scripts on the remote machine from the command prompt. You can even remotely administer the Telnet service on the web server by typing **tlntadmn** in your Telnet window. To end a Telnet session, type **exit** or **quit**. I'll discuss command-line administration of IIS 6 more thoroughly in Chapter 11.

TIP You can also enable the Telnet service using the Services node in Computer Management. Just open the properties sheet for this service, change the Startup value to Automatic, and start the service.

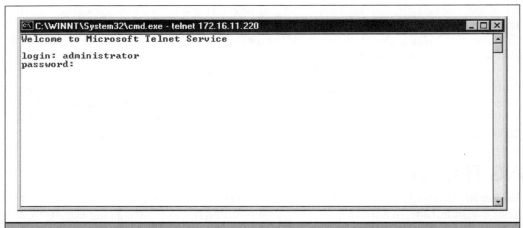

Figure 6-5. Starting a Telnet session with the remote server

> ### CHALLENGE
>
> You are an Application Service Provider (ASP) and web hosting company and you plan to deploy Web Edition on blade servers in your data center. For some clients, you will simply be collocating IIS servers for them and they will manage their servers themselves. Other servers may host web applications from multiple clients on the same machine. What administration tool(s) will you use for managing these servers and for enabling clients to manage their sites and applications? What are the advantages and disadvantages of using the Web Interface for Remote Administration (WISA) for these purposes?

CHECKLIST: USING WISA

Check off each of the administrative tasks once you become familiar with how to perform them using the Web Interface for Server Administration (WISA):

☐ Open URL in Internet Explorer to connect to a remote machine, and open the web interface for administering that machine.

☐ Change the name of the server and add a DNS suffix.

☐ Change the local Administrator password on the server.

☐ View the status of the server.

☐ View or modify the configuration of websites on the server.

☐ Modify the Master Settings for all web and FTP sites on the server.

☐ Configure logging options for web and FTP sites.

☐ Configure web execute permissions for applications running on the server.

☐ Specify FTP welcome, exit, and maximum connection messages.

☐ Configure TCP/IP settings such as IP address and default gateway, DNS and WINS settings, HOSTS and LMHOSTS files, and so on.

☐ Change the SSL port for accessing the Administration Web Site.

☐ Enable the Telnet service on the remote server.

☐ Create and modify settings for local user and group accounts on the server.

☐ View and download Event Viewer and Web Administration logs from the server.

☐ Configure the alert e-mail service on the server.

☐ Open a Remote Desktop Web Connection to the server.

CHAPTER 7

Creating and Configuring Websites

I n the previous two chapters, we examined the various tools that can be used to administer IIS 6 machines. In this chapter, we'll look at how to create and configure websites on these machines. Specifically, we'll look at basic website configuration and how to create and use virtual directories for hosting site content. Configuration settings related to security, performance, and content publishing will be covered later in Chapter 10, "Securing IIS"; Chapter 12, "Performance Tuning and Monitoring"; and Chapter 16, "Publishing with IIS."

CONFIGURING THE DEFAULT WEB SITE

Let's begin by looking at the Default Web Site that is created automatically when IIS 6 is installed on a Windows Server 2003 machine (see Figure 7-1). The Default Web Site in IIS 6 contains only a static "under construction" page called iisstart.htm in its home directory C:\Inetpub\wwwroot. If you right-click this site in IIS Manager and select Browse, Internet Explorer will open and display this page. Selecting the Default Web Site node in the console tree of IIS Manager displays some details about this site in the left-hand details pane. For example, the Default Web Site has a site identifier of 1, its state is Running, its IP address is All Unassigned, its port number is 80, and so on. Site identifiers are numbers automatically assigned by IIS when you create websites, and each new website you create has an identifier assigned that is incremented by one over the last created site.

If you want to start publishing content on your web server immediately, you can simply copy your HTML files to the \wwwroot directory, and your site will be up and running. Users can then access this site by using any of the following URLs:

- http://*server_name*, where *server_name* is the NetBIOS name of your IIS machine. This method usually works only on an intranet, that is, within a corporate network. It won't work across the public Internet unless you're running your IIS machine on a home network using a cable modem, in which case other users in your neighborhood may be able to access it this way.

- http://*IP_address* where *IP_address* is the IP address of your IIS machine. This method will work in an Internet environment if your IIS machine is sitting on the perimeter network and has a globally unique IP address assigned to it by your ISP. It can also work from the Internet if your firewall's Network Address Translation (NAT) filter is configured to forward incoming HTTP requests to your IIS machine when it is behind your firewall.

Of course, if you really want users to be able to access your website from the Internet, you should register a DNS name for the IP address of the Default Web Site on your IIS machine. Users will then be able to access the site using the URL http://*domain_name*, where *domain_name* is something like www.mycompanyname.com. For more information on registering DNS names, see the Internet Corporation for Assigned Names and Numbers (ICANN) website (www.icann.org) or contact your company's ISP.

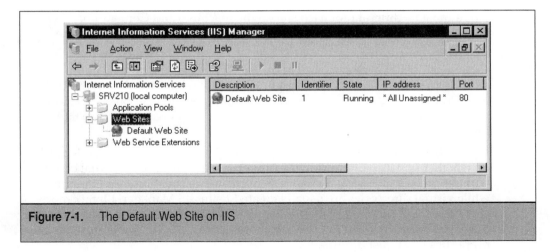

Figure 7-1. The Default Web Site on IIS

Once you've decided to use the Default Web Site on your IIS machine for hosting content, you can further configure the site using properties sheets in IIS Manager. Of course, you don't have to use the Default Web Site if you don't want to. In fact, you can delete it without any harm and create new sites—it's up to you.

NOTE If you delete the Default Web Site and then create a new site with the same name and identical properties, the new site will have a different site identifier randomly assigned to it.

Using IIS Properties Sheets

An important thing to know about IIS properties sheets is that they exist at different levels, with those lower down inheriting their settings from (or overriding the settings of, if you select that option) those higher up. There are five different levels of IIS properties sheets that can be used to configure website settings:

- *server_name* **Properties** Where *server_name* is the name of the IIS machine. You saw this sheet in Chapter 5, "Administering Standard/Enterprise Edition," (see Figure 5-10 in that chapter). It has only one tab, Internet Information Services, on which you can configure global MIME types, enable direct metabase editing, and enable UTF-8 logging. Of these settings, only MIME types can be configured at lower levels; I'll discuss this shortly.

- **Web Sites Properties** You saw this sheet also in Chapter 5 (see Figure 5-2). It has nine tabs that can be used to configure global settings for all websites on the IIS machine. Any changes made on this sheet are inherited by all sites and virtual directories on the machine. As shown on Figure 5-2, certain configuration settings are grayed because these settings are specific to individual websites. Examples of such unique settings include Web Site Identity on the Web Sites tab (it must be different for each site on the machine) and Content Location on the Home Directory tab (it's usually different for each site on the machine).

- *web_site_name* **Properties**   Where *web_site_name* is the name of a particular website on the IIS machine (see Figure 7-2 for the properties sheet of the Default Web Site). This sheet has eight tabs, all of which are also on the Web Sites Properties sheet just described (it's lacking the nine tab called Service), and any settings configured here override those configured at the Web Site Properties level above it.

- **Directory (or Virtual Directory) Properties**   The name of this sheet depends on whether you are configuring the properties of a physical or virtual directory within a website. Physical directories are created using Windows Explorer, while virtual directories are usually created using IIS Manager; I'll talk more about their difference later in this chapter. Either way, this properties sheet has five tabs that correspond to five similar ones at the *web_site_name* and Web Site properties levels just discussed.

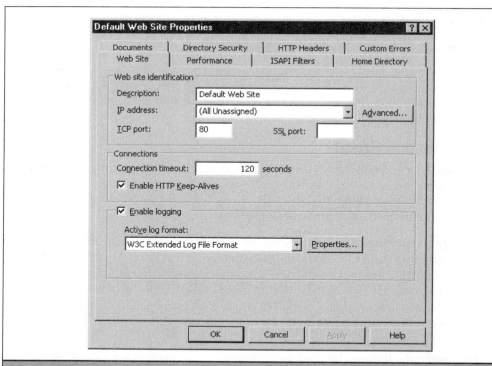

Figure 7-2.   Properties sheet for the Default Web Site, showing the Web Site tab

Tab	Web Sites Level	*web_site* Level	Directory Level	File Level
Web Site	√	√		
Performance	√	√		
ISAPI Filters	√	√		
Home Directory	√	√	√	√
Documents	√	√	√	√
Directory Security	√	√	√	√
HTTP Headers	√	√	√	√
Custom Errors	√	√	√	√
Service	√	√	√	√

[1]This tab is called Directory for physical directories and Virtual Directory for virtual directories.
[2]This tab is called File at the File level.
[3]This tab is called File Security at the File level.

Table 7-1. IIS Properties Sheets Tabs of Different Levels

- *file_name* **Properties** Where *file_name* is the name of the file; for example, iisstart.htm Properties would be the name of the properties sheet for the file iisstart.htm in the home directory of the Default Web Site.

To help you get the big picture of configuring websites and their directories and files, Table 7-1 shows which tabs appear on the properties sheets for each configuration level just described.

Inheritance and Override

The following walkthrough demonstrates how inheritance and override of properties sheet settings work with IIS. Open the properties sheet for the Default Web Site, select the HTTP Headers tab, and verify that the content expiration feature is disabled (unchecked). Close this properties sheet and open the one for the Web Sites node, which is one level above the properties for individual web sites. Select the HTTP Headers tab and click the check box to enable content expiration globally for all websites on IIS. Close this properties sheet to apply the changes, and then open the Default Web Site Properties again and verify the change has been applied to this specific website. Close the Default Web Site Properties and open the properties sheet for the iisstart.htm file in this site's home directory. Switch to the HTTP Headers tab of the iisstart.htm Properties and verify again that individual files have inherited this setting.

Now clear the check box on the HTTP Headers tab of iisstart.htm Properties to disable content expiration for this specific file and override the global setting made earlier at the Web Site level. Click OK to apply the changes and close the sheet. Open the Default Web Site Properties, switch to the HTTP Headers tab, and clear the check box here as well. Click OK to apply the changes, and notice that this time an Inheritance Overrides dialog box appears (see Figure 7-3). This didn't appear when you made the change at the file level because there are no child nodes beneath the file level. Now you are making a change at the website, and the site contains a file (iisstart.htm) that has previously had this setting changed, so IIS asks you whether you want to apply these changes to child nodes beneath the selected level and override the changes made previously. Select the iisstart.htm file within this dialog box (or click the Select All button to cause all child nodes to inherit the change), and close the box to apply the changes.

NOTE   The Inheritance Overrides dialog box *only* appears when the action you are about to perform might override *similar* settings that have been previously configured at a *lower* level. In other words, it only appears when a conflict in settings occurs. For example, say you changed the content expiration setting on a virtual directory within a website. If you then changed a different setting at the site level, such as defining a custom HTTP header, the Inheritance Overrides dialog box will not appear because the custom HTTP header settings were not previously changed at the directory level—the dialog box will only appear if you try to change the same setting (content expiration) at the higher level that was previously changed at the lower level.

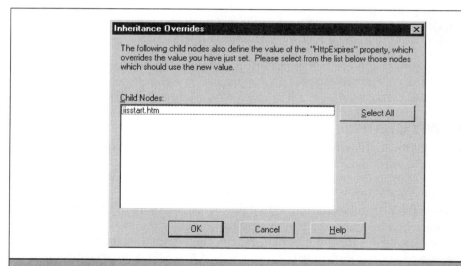

Figure 7-3.   The Inheritance Overrides dialog box tells you when you are about to overwrite previously configured IIS settings.

Default Web Site Identity

Let's now examine some of the basic configuration settings at the individual website level. I won't cover everything about configuring websites in this chapter; I'll defer discussing application, performance, and publishing settings later in Chapters 8, 10, and 16, where they can be covered in a more consistent fashion.

We'll begin by looking at the Web Site tab of the Default Web Site Properties sheet (see Figure 7-2 again). Every website you create using IIS has to have a website identity. In this case, the Description (name) specified for the site is Default Web Site, the IP Address is (All Unassigned), and the TCP port is 80. Changing the description here changes the name displayed for the site in IIS Manager but has no effect on how users access the site using their web browsers. In other words, the Description field is simply a friendly name for the site as displayed in IIS Manager. The Web Site Identification specified here is different from the *site identifier* discussed previously, which is generated automatically by IIS when the site is created and cannot be changed here.

The interesting thing about the identity of the Default Web Site is that its IP address is (All Unassigned). To understand this, consider that IIS is designed to host multiple websites, and often each site will have its own assigned IP address. Say you had five IP addresses ranging from 172.16.11.15 through 172.16.11.19, bound to the IIS machine's network card (I'll use addresses from the private class B address space 172.16.0.0–172.31.255.255 because I'm working in an intranet environment). Now say you create two new websites on the machine and assign the address 172.16.11.15 to site A and 172.16.11.16 to site B. The following list shows what happens when you try to open different URLs using Internet Explorer on a computer on our network:

- http://172.16.11.15 opens home page for site A.
- http://172.16.11.16 opens home page for site B.
- http://172.16.11.17 through 172.16.11.19 opens the home page (or under construction page) for Default Web Site.

Thus, (All Unassigned) means that when you try to open a URL with any IP address bound to your IIS machine's NIC, but which is not specifically assigned to another website on the machine, the Default Web Site is opened in the browser window. I'll talk more about website identities later in this chapter in the "Creating Websites" section. I'll defer a discussion of connections settings until Chapter 12 and website logging until Chapter 13. First, I'll delve a little deeper into this idea of a *default* website.

NOTE   If you have multiple IP addresses and multiple websites on your IIS machine and try to open the URL http://*server_name*, where *server_name* is your machine's NetBIOS name, you will open the website that has been assigned the *first* IP address in the IP address drop-down list on the Website tab.

Why Have a Default Website?

By the way, only one website on your machine can have All Unassigned as its IP address on the Web Site tab of its properties sheet. Whatever the actual name (description) of that site, by assigning it this address it *becomes* the default website on the machine. However, you don't *have* to have a website with this setting on your machine, and if you like, you can assign the Default Web Site a specific IP address from the drop-down list of addresses. The whole idea is that this All Unassigned option lets you have your machine serve up a specific default site whenever a user tries to open a URL with an IP address bound to the machine's network adapter but not specifically assigned to a website on the machine. This is particularly useful in a public web-hosting environment at an ISP. For example, say you have 100 IP addresses on your IIS machine and it hosts 50 websites with 50 of these addresses. You can create a home page for your fifty-first site, the Default Web Site, and have that page display your ISP company logo, a suggestion like "This space available for web hosting," and your pricing scheme for hosting. Then if a user tries browsing all the IP addresses of your machine in sequence (yes, there are people who actually like to do this), half the time they will see the page showing your logo and pricing message.

Another use for this feature is to make the home page of your Default Web Site say something like, "There's a problem with your site, please contact your ISP administrator." Say you're a customer that owns one of the 50 websites created on the IIS machine, and say your website stops for some reason (maybe the administrator stopped it to make some changes and forgot to restart it). Now when your customers try to access your stopped site, the home page for the Default Web Site will be displayed instead. Soon they'll be phoning you and asking you what the problem is, and you'll know to contact your ISP to find out if your site is stopped.

What if you don't have a website on your server that has All Unassigned as its IP address? When users try to open URLs containing IP addresses that are bound to the machine but not assigned to specific sites, they will get a simple message saying "Bad Request (Invalid Hostname)" in their browser window. Not very informative, is it? Perhaps you can come up with some other creative scenarios in which there might be a default website on your machine that has All Unassigned for its IP address setting!

Location of Content

Switch to the Home Directory tab of the Default Web Site Properties (Figure 7-4). As you can see, there are three possible locations for a website's content: local directory, network share, or redirection.

Local Directory

If you select the A Directory Located On This Computer option, your home directory will be a directory on the IIS machine itself. By default, the Default Web Site is assigned the home directory C:\Inetpub\wwwroot on the local machine, but you can change this to a different directory by clicking the Browse button on the Home Directory tab. Locating content on the local machine provides best performance in most cases.

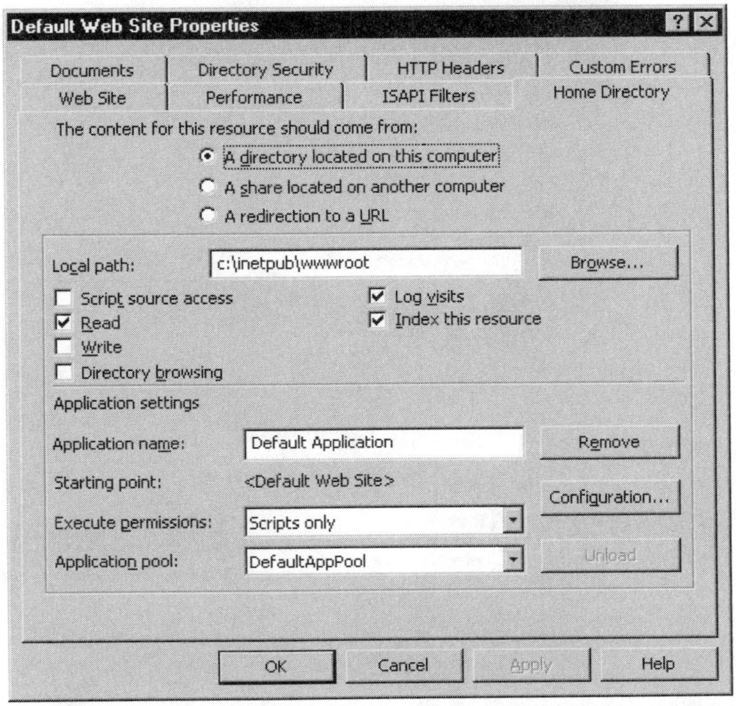

Figure 7-4.   The Home Directory tab of the Default Web Site Properties sheet

---

TIP   To change the location of content on your local server, you can either move the content of the \wwwroot directory to a new folder on your machine or rename the \wwwroot directory directly. Be sure to stop your website before you specify a new location for the content associated with its home directory. You will learn how to pause, stop, resume, and restart a website later in this chapter in the section "Stopping, Pausing, and Starting Sites."

NOTE   You can also change the location of your site's home directory by editing the metabase, something you'll learn about later in Chapter 14, "Working with the Metabase."

Network Share

If you select the A Share Located On Another Computer option (see Figure 7-5), your home directory will be a shared folder on another machine. It may often be desirable or

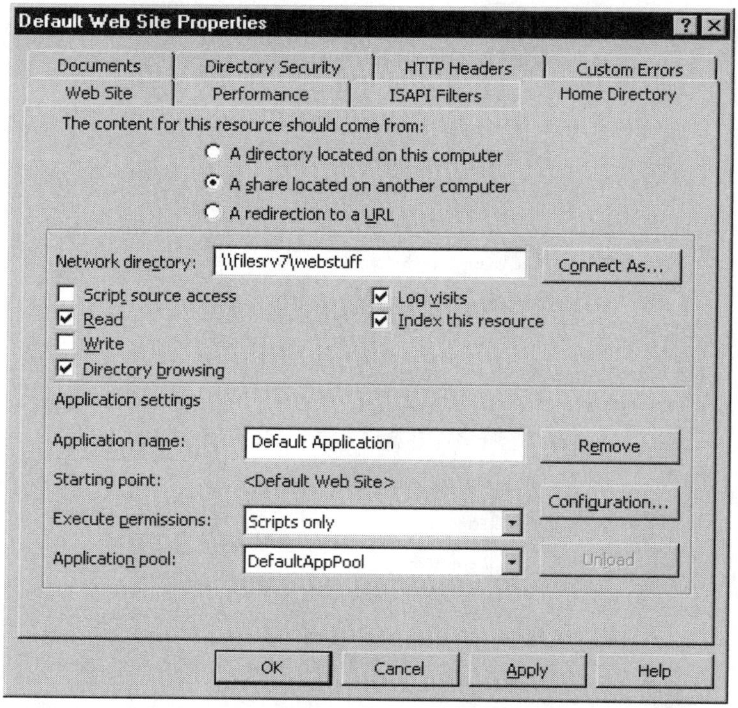

Figure 7-5.   Specifying a remote home directory for the Default Web Site

convenient to create and store web content on a different machine—for example, a file server on your network. In this case, you can point IIS to the network share as the home directory for your website. If you select this option and specify a share (using a UNC pathname such as *server_name**share_name*), the default setting is for the connection to use the credentials of the logged-on user (the user trying to access the content) for purposes of accessing the share. Alternatively, you can also enter other credentials for accessing this share. For these credentials, do *not* use an account belonging to the local Administrators group or Domain Admins group because this may constitute a security risk and allow clients access to server operations. Instead, create an ordinary user account and make sure the shared folder permissions grant this account sufficient permissions for IIS to access the content using the account. You can also do this by granting the appropriate permissions to the Users Or Domain Users group to which this user account belongs, or by granting these permissions to the Everyone built-in group.

If you are working in a domain environment, you can select a specific domain account for connecting your IIS machine to the remote network share by clicking the Connect As button, deselecting the Always Use The Authenticated User's Credentials When Validating Access To The Network Directory check box (see Figure 7-6), and clicking the Browse button to search Active Directory for the domain account you want to use. If you are working in a workgroup scenario, it's a little trickier: first use Local Users And Groups in Computer Management to create *identical* local user accounts (identical names and passwords) on both the IIS machine and file server, and then deselect the check box shown in Figure 7-6 and enter the username and password for the account (you will be prompted to confirm the password). If you try to use a local user account on the file server but don't have an identical local account on the IIS machine, you may be able to initially connect to the share in IIS Manager, but when you try to browse the website you will get an HTTP 500 Internal Server Error message. Make sure the local user account you create is a member of the Users local group but not the Administrators group, and the account is configured so that the password is complex (it can't be guessed) and does not expire.

Redirection

An alternative to locating your website content on the local IIS machine or a share on a network file server is to use *redirection*, which allows you to point your home directory to a file or folder on another website, even one located elsewhere on the Internet. Redirection is often used temporarily when content is being moved or reorganized on a site, or it can be used permanently when a business changes its name or becomes a subsidiary of another business. Because redirection is more of a publishing issue than a basic administration one, we'll discuss it in detail in Chapter 16, Publishing With IIS.

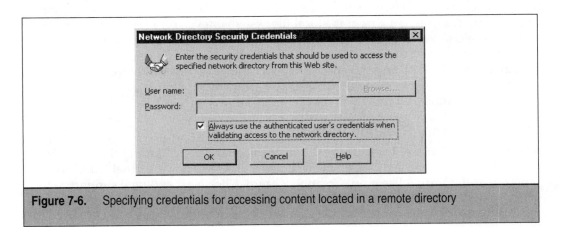

Figure 7-6. Specifying credentials for accessing content located in a remote directory

Creating Virtual Directories

Once you've decided on the location for the home directory of your website, you can create additional directories for hosting other portions of your site's content. IIS gives you a great deal of flexibility in how to do this, and you can use either physical or virtual directories, as I'll describe next.

Physical vs. Virtual Directories

A *physical directory* is simply a subdirectory of your home directory. For example, say you've decided to use the Default Web Site on your server for hosting your company's intranet site. The default home directory for this site is C:\Inetpub\wwwroot, and users can access the home page Default.htm for this site by using the URL http://snoopy where SNOOPY is the name of your IIS machine (or they could use the server's IP address or DNS name if DNS is configured). Say you want to create two subsections for the intranet, one for Sales and one for Support, and you want employees to be able to access these sections using http://snoopy/sales and http://snoopy/support. First, create a physical directory for the Sales Department as follows: right-click the Default Web Site in the console tree in IIS Manager and select Explore. This displays the contents of the home directory \wwwroot using a Windows Explorer window for the details pane. Now right-click an empty spot in the details pane and select New | Folder, and then type **sales** for the name of the folder and press ENTER. Press F5 to refresh the console and expand the Default Web Site node to display the new subfolder \wwwroot\sales you've created. To test this, copy the iisstart.htm page from the home directory into the Sales subdirectory and then click Start | Run and type **http://localhost/sales**. Note that the Sales directory appears in your browser window as expected.

There's another way to do this using virtual instead of physical directories. A *virtual directory* behaves as if it were simply a subdirectory of the home directory, but in fact it is located in a different part of the local file system or even on a remote file server somewhere else on the network. Continuing the previous example, you could create a virtual directory called Support that allows users to access the Support portion of the intranet using the URL http://snoopy/support. However, instead of this department's content being located in the folder C:\Inetpub\wwwroot\support as expected, it's actually in C:\other. I'll show you how to do this now.

Virtual Directory Creation Wizard

Use Windows Explorer to create the C:\other folder and copy iisstart.htm into it. Now go to IIS Manager, right-click Default Web Site and select New | Virtual Directory. This opens the Virtual Directory Creation Wizard. Click Next and type **support** as the alias for the virtual directory you are going to create (see Figure 7-7). The alias of a virtual directory is the name that will be used to identify the directory in URL used to access it, and since you want to access this directory using http://snoopy/support, you'd use Support as the alias for the directory.

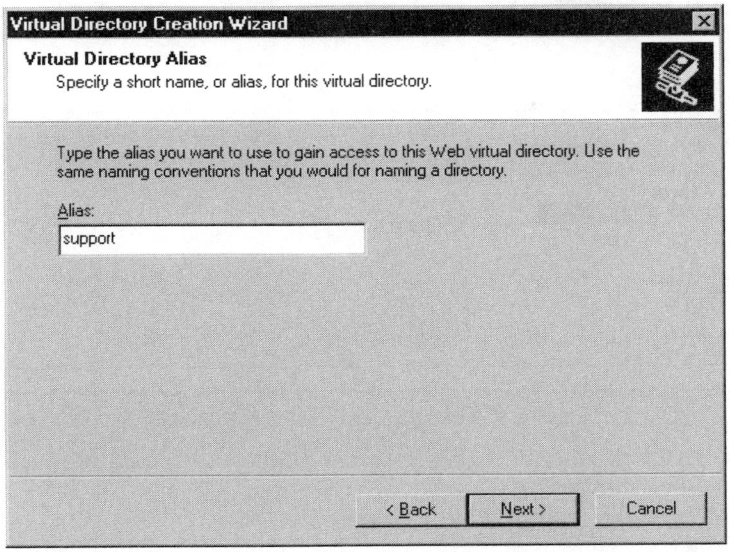

Virtual Directory Creation Wizard

Virtual Directory Alias
Specify a short name, or alias, for this virtual directory.

Type the alias you want to use to gain access to this Web virtual directory. Use the same naming conventions that you would for naming a directory.

Alias:

support

< Back   Next >   Cancel

Figure 7-7.   Specifying an alias for a new virtual directory

Click Next and specify the path to the directory as C:\other, or click Browse to locate this folder. Click Next and specify the IIS permissions for this directory, which by default are to allow Read And Run Scripts and to deny anything else. (I'll talk about permissions in detail in Chapter 10, so just accept the defaults for now.) Click Next and then Finish to complete the wizard and create the new Support virtual directory within the Default Web Site. Then click Start | Run and type **http://localhost/support**; the Support virtual directory opens up in your browser window as expected. Now select the Default Web Site in the console tree and note that virtual directories are displayed differently from physical ones in two ways: they have a different icon (the gear icon) and display the corresponding physical directory C:\other to which the alias is mapped (see Figure 7-8).

SECURITY ALERT   Using virtual directories instead of physical ones has a security aspect as well, since it means users won't be able to guess where the content they are viewing is actually being stored. Another advantage of virtual over physical directories is that they make it easier for you to relocate your content when required, even if it means moving content to a different server.

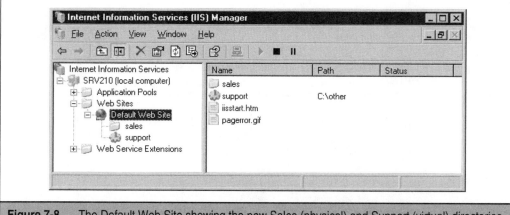

Figure 7-8. The Default Web Site showing the new Sales (physical) and Support (virtual) directories

NOTE Note that deleting a physical directory deletes your content as well, while deleting a virtual directory in IIS Manager simply removes the alias but has no effect on the content directory it was mapped to.

Local vs. Remote Virtual Directories

Virtual directories may be either local or remote—in other words, an alias can map to either a folder on the local file system or a UNC path to a network share on some file server. Creating a remote virtual directory is almost the same as making a local one—simply start the Virtual Directory Creation Wizard; and when asked to specify the location of the website content directory, type the UNC path to the network share and then specify credentials for accessing this share (similar to credentials for accessing a remote home directory, as described earlier in this chapter). Alternatively, you can create a local virtual directory first and then open its properties sheet, select the Virtual Directory tab, and specify that the content for this directory will come from a share located on another computer.

Web Sharing

Another way of creating a virtual directory is to use the Web Sharing feature of Windows Explorer. Simply right-click the physical folder in Windows Explorer for which you want to create an alias and select Properties, and then select the Web Sharing tab. To use this tab to create a new virtual directory, follow this procedure:

1. Select the website within which the virtual directory is to be created using the Share On drop-down box.

2. Select the Share This Folder option to open the Edit Alias dialog box (Figure 7-9).

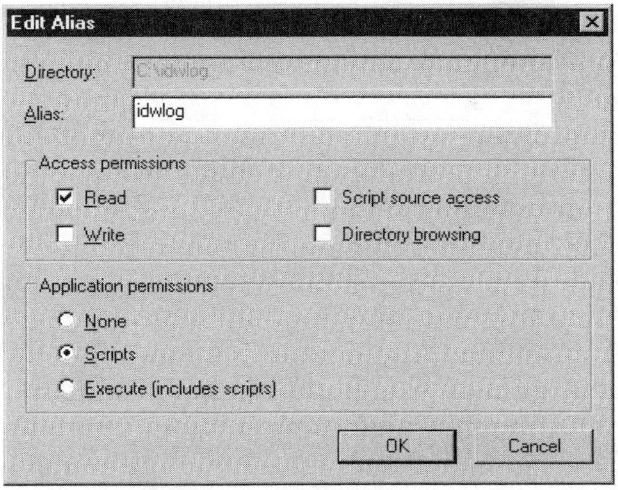

Figure 7-9.   Creating a virtual directory using Web Sharing

3. Specify an alias for the virtual directory (or accept the default alias, which is the same as the name of the physical directory it maps to).

4. Select the default permissions or modify them as desired.

5. Click OK to create the virtual directory.

Now go to IIS Manager and refresh the console to verify that the virtual directory was indeed created.

TIP   Using Web Sharing, you can easily create multiple aliases for a directory and then assign each alias to a different website.

Importing a Configuration File

You can create a virtual directory by importing a configuration file, which is an XML file containing a portion of the metabase describing the configuration of the virtual directory. You could create such a configuration file by hand—if you were bold (or crazy) enough—but it's more likely you would export a virtual directory configuration file from another IIS server and import it into your own server, for example, when migrating virtual directories from one site to another or from one server to another. Try this:

1. Open IIS Manager, right-click a virtual directory you created earlier, and select All Tasks | Save Configuration To A File to open the Save Configuration To a File dialog box (see Figure 7-10).

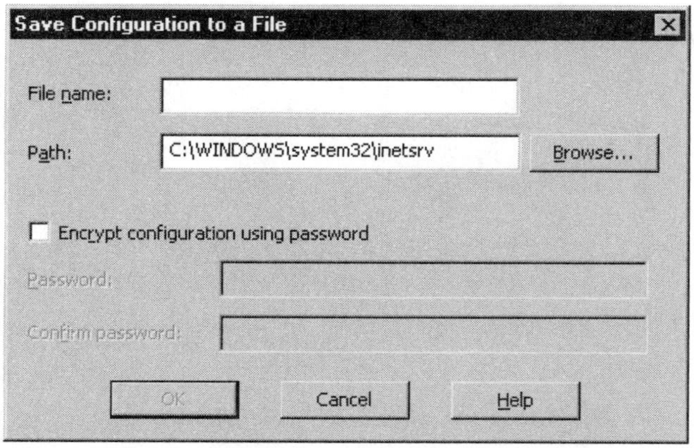

Figure 7-10. Saving the configuration of a virtual directory to an XML file

2. Specify a name for the configuration file, the folder in which to save the file, and optional password for encrypting the file.

3. Click OK to save the configuration file (you can open it in Notepad to view its contents).

4. Right-click the virtual directory, and select Delete to remove it from your site (this deletes the alias only, not the content).

5. Right-click the Default Web Site and select New | Virtual Directory (From File) to open the Import Configuration dialog box, and browse to locate the saved configuration file you created earlier.

6. Click the Read File button, and the alias of the virtual directory will be read from the configuration file and displayed in the dialog box.

7. Select the name of the virtual directory under Location, and click OK to import the configuration and re-create the virtual directory.

You should now again see the virtual directory you previously deleted in IIS Manager!

NOTE You'll learn more about the new XML metabase and how to work with it in Chapter 14.

TIP You can also create virtual directories from the command line using the iisvdir.vbs script included with IIS 6. We'll look at command-line administration of IIS in Chapter 11.

Default Document

When you try to open a nonspecific URL like http://snoopy or http://snoopy/sales, one that doesn't explicitly specify the name of the exact file that should be opened, IIS responds to the browser by sending it the default document for the site or directory. Typical names for default documents include

- Default.htm
- Default.asp
- index.htm

The Default Web Site includes a special default document called iisstart.htm that displays an "under construction" page when viewed in a browser. But how does IIS know which file is the default document for a given site or directory? The answer is on the Documents tab of the properties sheet for the site or directory. For example, the Documents tab for the Default Web Site properties sheet shows several possible names for default documents (see Figure 7-11). When a nonspecific URL is used to access this

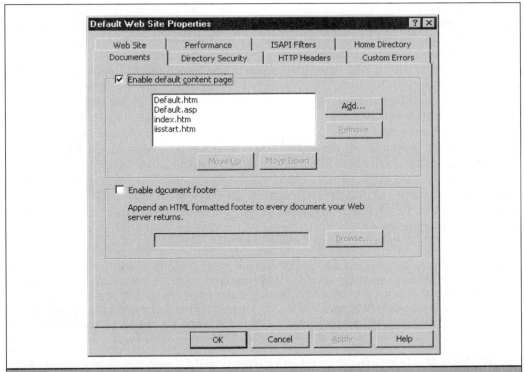

Figure 7-11.   Specifying default documents for the Default Web Site

site, IIS begins at the top of the list and searches for a file in the home directory having one of the names listed. You can rearrange the order of these default documents so that IIS searches for them in a different order, and you can add additional names for default documents or remove unneeded ones.

If you deselect the Enable Default Content Page check box, IIS won't look for a default document, and it will respond to nonspecific URL requests with an HTTP 403 Forbidden message unless you also enable directory browsing on the Home Directory tab. (Directory browsing is not usually recommended, however, because it exposes the contents of your directory to users if there is no default document in the directory.) Note that you can specify default documents separately for the site's home directory and for each virtual directory within the site.

MIME Types

I mentioned MIME types in Chapter 5, and now's the time to talk about them detail. On the HTTP Headers tab of the Default Web Site properties sheet, there is a button called MIME Types that you can use to register additional MIME types for this website, that is, in addition to the default MIME types defined globally at the server level for all sites on IIS. MIME stands for Multipurpose Internet Mail Exchange and is used to specify which types of files IIS will serve to browser clients in response to HTTP GET requests. To understand MIME types better, try the following exercise: Create a simple HTML page named test.xyz and place it in the \wwwroot directory, which is the home directory for the Default Web Site on your machine. Open Internet Explorer and try to open the URL http://localhost/test.xyz and see what happens. You should get an HTTP 404 Error—File or directory not found. This is because the file extension .xyz is unknown to IIS—that is, it has no associated MIME type registered for it. To verify this fact, right-click the *server_name* node in IIS Manager and select Properties to open the properties sheet for the IIS server (see Figure 5-10 again in Chapter 5). Click the MIME Types button to open the MIME Types box showing global MIME mappings defined by default on IIS (see Figure 7-12). Now if you scroll through this list, you can verify that there is no longer any registered mapping for the .xyz extension. In other words, when IIS receives a URL requesting a file of type .xyz, it simply doesn't know what to do with it, so it generates a 404.3 error.

NOTE   In the previous version of IIS, if a client requested a file having an extension with no registered MIME type associated with it, the MIME type defaulted to application/octet-stream and the server prompted the user to download the file using a dialog box. The fact that version 6 of IIS no longer does this is a security improvement to reject improper client requests. Creating a wildcard MIME mapping, as described next, essentially has the effect of disabling this new IIS 6 security feature.

TIP   You only have to restart IIS after changing MIME types if you want your changes to take effect immediately. Otherwise, the server will cause the changes to take effect when the worker processes recycle.

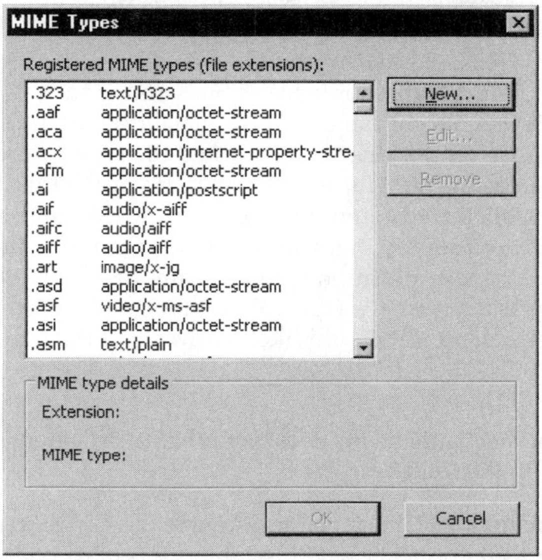

Figure 7-12.   The list of global MIME mappings that are registered by default

Let's say that for some weird reason you want your IIS machine to recognize and serve .xyz files as standard HTML files. To see how to do this, scroll down the list of registered MIME types in the global MIME Types dialog box and note that the MIME type for .htm files, which is the normal extension for HTML files, is text/html. To define a new MIME type at the global level that applies to all sites running on the IIS machine, click the New button and type **xyz** in the Extension field and **text/html** in the MIME Type field (see Figure 7-13). Click OK, and the new MIME type should appear in the

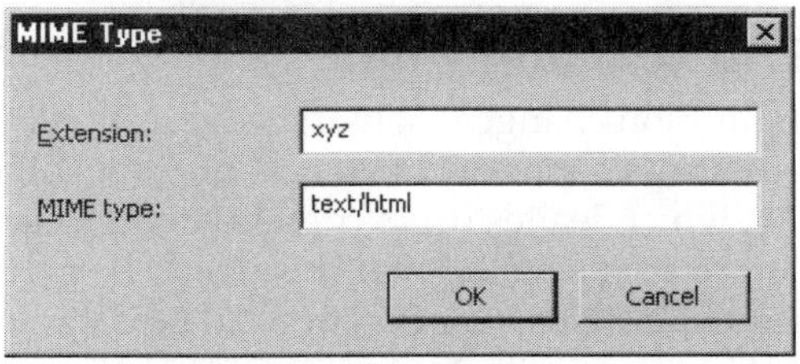

Figure 7-13.   Creating a new MIME type mapping

list. Right-click the *server_name* node and select Restart IIS to update the server's internal list of MIME types, and then try opening the URL http://localhost/test.xyz. It should display the HTML page as expected.

You can also define MIME types for the Web Sites node and at the level of individual websites or directories on your machine, and the usual rules of inheritance and override apply. You can configure IIS to serve any requested file type by creating a wildcard MIME type that has an asterisk (*) for its extension. If you do this and specify text/html as the MIME type, any file extension not in the global MIME map will be interpreted by IIS as an HTML file and served that way to clients. Or, if you map the wildcard extension to the MIME type application/octet-stream, IIS will treat any file extension not in the MIME map as a binary file (IIS will first try to interpret it as HTML, and if it can't do so, will ask the client if it would like to download the file).

Under the Hood

IIS has three different mechanisms for deciding what to do when clients request files, and they are applied in the following order:

- **Special extensions** File extensions like .exe or .dll are treated as ISAPI extensions or CGI applications. This behavior is hard-coded into IIS and cannot be changed.

- **Scriptmap entries** File extensions that match a scriptmap entry are processed by the ISAPI extension or CGI application indicated in the scriptmap. The IIS scriptmap specifies which script processor is used for executing a given script type (for example, .asp for Active Server Pages). You can view or modify scriptmap settings on the Home Directory tab of a website's properties sheet (or the Virtual Directory of a virtual directory's properties sheet). Scriptmap settings are in the IIS metabase in a series of lines starting with ScriptMaps and can be modified by editing the metabase (see Chapter 14 for more info).

- **MIME types** All other file extensions are passed to the internal MIME map and are served by IIS using the HTTP protocol, except that for the application/octet-stream MIME type, the client is prompted to download the file instead.

Stopping, Pausing, and Starting Sites

Before you make a configuration change to a live site, you should stop the site. Stopping a website disconnects any users connected to it and prevents others from accessing it. You can also pause a site, which leaves users presently connected to the site unaffected while preventing others from accessing the site. This would be preferable in an e-commerce scenario where you want to allow user transactions to be completed to avoid causing problems for users and losing business. In this case, pause the site for a short period of time until all users disconnect, and then stop the site, make your configuration changes, and start the site again.

To stop, pause, resume, and start a website on IIS, right-click the site in IIS Manager and select Stop, Pause, or Start (selecting Pause twice resumes a paused site).

NOTE   If you stop a website and then restart IIS using the method described in Chapter 5, the website will still be in a stopped state afterward and must be restarted using the method just described.

TIP   You can also stop, pause, and start websites from the command line, which I'll cover in Chapter 11.

Saving Site Configuration

I already mentioned that you can save the configuration of an individual virtual directory as an XML file and then use this to move the virtual directory to another site or IIS machine. The same goes with entire websites—you can save their configuration as a file and import it back into the same server or a different one. Let's try this with the Default Web Site:

1. Right-click the Default Web Site, and select All Tasks | Save Configuration To A File.

2. Right-click the Default Web Site and select Delete to remove it from your server. This deletes only the alias for the virtual server for the site—the C:\Inetpub\wwwroot content directory is unaffected by this action.

3. Right-click the Web Sites node in the console tree and select New | Web Site (From File)

4. Browse to find the configuration file you saved earlier, and click the Read File button to verify its integrity.

5. Select Default Web Site as the configuration you wish to import.

6. Click OK to import the configuration and re-create the Default Web Site again.

7. Restart the Default Web Site (importing a website configuration from a file leaves the new site in a stopped condition).

Other Configuration Tasks

Here are a few more administration tasks you can perform on the Default Web Site by right-clicking its node in IIS Manager:

- **Explore**   Switches the details pane to Windows Explorer view—but only while that node is still selected in the console tree!

- **Open**   Opens a separate Explorer window displaying the contents of the home directory C:\Inetpub\wwwroot.

- **Permissions**   Lets you configure the NTFS permissions of the home directory.

- **Browse**   Switches the details pane to Internet Explorer view—again, only while that node is still selected in the console tree.

- **Rename**   Same effect as changing the Description field on the Web Site tab of the Default Web Site Properties sheet.

You can list all the websites on your server by selecting the Web Sites node in IIS Manager. This will display the identifier, IP address, port number, status, and other attributes of each site.

CREATING WEB SITES

Let's move on and look at how to create additional websites on your IIS machine. IIS supports hosting a limitless number of websites on a single machine—the real limit being the hardware that supports the platform, because hosting too many sites on a given machine will eventually affect performance. Let's assume that you've already created some directories on the machine (or on a network file server) as home directories for the sites you are going to create, and that you've assigned some additional IP addresses to the machine for those sites requiring their own separate IP address. How do you go about creating a new website on IIS? The answer is another wizard!

Web Site Creation Wizard

You can create a new website on an IIS machine using the Web Site Creation Wizard (see Figure 7-14). Just right-click the Web Sites node in IIS Manager and select New | Web Site to start the wizard (or import a site configuration file, as discussed earlier). Then follow these steps, clicking Next when appropriate:

1. Specify a description (name) for the website. This name is not used by users for accessing the site, it is simply used to identify the site in IIS Manager.

2. Specify an IP address, port number, and/or host header name to identify the site to users (more about this in a moment).

3. Specify the path to the home directory for the site and whether anonymous users will be allowed to access the site. If the site will be used as a public Internet site, leave anonymous access enabled; if it's used as a corporate intranet site, deselect this option and configure the appropriate authentication method you desire later (IIS authentication methods will be covered in Chapter 10).

4. Specify suitable website access permissions for your site (the default is to allow Read And Run Scripts and deny everything else).

5. Click Finish to create the new site (it is started automatically).

Figure 7-14. The Web Site Creation Wizard

NOTE You can also create new websites from the command line using the iisweb.vbs script, which we'll look at later in Chapter 11.

Try opening your new website by right-clicking it in IIS Manager and selecting Browse. If you can't open it, check to see that you have the proper default document configured for the site and that the home directory is correct. If you get an authentication dialog box appearing asking for your credentials before you can browse the site, check to make sure that anonymous access is enabled using the Directory Security tab, and check the NTFS permissions for your site's home directory to ensure that Everyone or some other suitable group or built-in identity is granted at least Read permissions on the home directory. For more information about troubleshooting IIS, see Chapter 13.

Web Site Identity

One thing I glossed over is how to identify websites to users when you are hosting multiple sites on a single IIS machine. Web Site Identity is configured on the Web Site tab of the site's properties sheet (see Figure 7-2 again) and is determined by three kinds of attributes: IP address, port number, and host header name. Two different websites hosted on the same IIS machine must differ in their identities by *at least one* of these three attributes. Let's look at each of these attributes separately and discuss the pros and cons of using them for identifying websites.

Multiple IP Addresses

First, you can identify each website on your machine using a separate IP address. This scenario is typically used in a public web hosting environment at an ISP or ASP and ensures that any web browser (including very old ones) can access each site. The method can also be used in a corporate (intranet) environment, provided the administrator obtains a sufficient quantity of globally unique IP addresses from the company's ISP to enable the site to be accessed by mobile or remote users over the Internet. Finally, this method should be used when hosting secure websites that use SSL, since host header names (the other popular method for identifying websites) don't work in this scenario.

So in this method, each website is uniquely identified to users by assigning them a different IP address, while the TCP port numbers are left at 80, and no host header names are created. The Default Web Site (if you have one) should be assigned the IP address All Unassigned and you should ensure you have enough IP addresses bound to your server's network card to go around.

NOTE   There's also a performance issue associated with having too many websites identified by unique IP addresses on a single machine; see Chapter 12 for more information.

Nonstandard Port Numbers

Normally, the TCP port number for a website is left at its default value of port 80 (or port 443 if you have SSL enabled on your site). You can uniquely identify a website on your machine by giving it a different port number. The only problem with this is that for users to access your site, they need to know the port number if it is something different from 80 (or 443 for SSL).

For example, I could create two websites on a server named SNOOPY and assign both sites the same IP address. Let's say I call one site Sales and assign it TCP port number 80, while the other is called Support and is assigned port number 8080. To access the Sales site, users would use the URL http://snoopy; while to access the Support site, they would have to type **http://snoopy:8080**. As in this example, whenever a nonstandard TCP port number is used by a site, the URL to access the site must explicitly indicate this port number using the syntax http://*server_name:port_number*.

Clearly, this is not a popular solution for identifying websites, and it is generally only used for "secret" websites like the Administration Web Site (see Chapter 6) and other websites created by geeks for geeks.

NOTE   If you choose to identify a site by its port number, be sure to choose a number greater than 1023 because those below this number are well-known ports assigned to other network services. You don't want to interfere with the operation of these services, or problems might result.

Host Header Names

This method is the main alternative to using separate IP addresses for each website and allows multiple sites on a single IIS machine to use the same IP address and port number. There are several considerations, however, when using this method:

- It doesn't work with SSL, so you can't use host header names to identify e-commerce sites or other secure sites.

- Users will no longer be able to use IP addresses to access sites on your machine.

- It requires that you configure a name resolution service on your network and register these host header names with this service.

- It only works with client browsers that are HTTP/1.1 compliant, meaning that users must have Internet Explorer 3 or higher (or Netscape Navigator 3 or higher).

The advantages of using host header names often outweigh the disadvantages, however. Specifically, host header names do the following:

- Conserve valuable globally unique IP addresses

- Provide better performance than using multiple IP addresses when servers host large numbers of sites

Host header names include the DNS name of the requested site in the HTTP header of the request when an HTTP/1.1-compliant browser issues an HTTP GET request to a website running on an IIS machine. The IIS machine then parses this header to find the name of the site requested and returns the content from the site that has the host header name that matches the included DNS name. For example, if the client is trying to download the home page of the Sales website that has the host header name www.mtit.com, the HTTP header in the GET request includes this DNS name. Of course, this means you must be using DNS on your network as a name resolution method, but this is standard both on the Internet and in an intranet environment where Windows Server 2003 is running—at least if Active Directory is deployed.

On a small network, an alternative to registering your host header names with your DNS name servers is to create a HOSTS file and copy this to the %SystemRoot%\ System32\drivers\etc folder on all your Windows NT/2000/XP/.NET machines and map all of the host header names to the single IP address of the IIS machine. You can also use host header names with NetBIOS (WINS or LMHOSTS) as your name resolution system if working in an intranet environment.

TIP   It's generally not a good idea to assign host header names to the Default Web Site because it can cause problems with certain applications that make use of this site. One example is Microsoft Proxy Server, the precursor of Microsoft Internet Security and Acceleration (ISA) Server. Another example is SharePoint Portal Server, which experiences problems if you create host header names for the Default Web Site.

Testing the Different Methods

Let's do a short walkthrough to illustrate the different methods for specifying website identity. I'm running an IIS 6 machine called SNOOPY and have three IP addresses bound to the network adapter:

- 172.16.11.210
- 172.16.11.211
- 172.16 11.212

TIP   Always assign static IP addresses to your IIS machine; never use DHCP or problems may result.

The Default Web Site has All Unassigned as its IP address, port 80 (the default), and no host header names configured. Using IIS Manager, I'll first create a Sales website with the following identity:

- IP address 172.16.11.210
- Port 80
- No host header names

The home directory for the Sales website (and for the other sites I will create) is C:\Sales, which contains a copy of the iisstart.htm file from C:\Inetpub\wwwroot, renamed as default.htm and edited using Notepad to add <H1>Sales</H1> after the <BODY>tag. (I'm assuming you know a little HTML if you're working with IIS.)

Now I create another website called Support and give it the following identity:

- IP address 172.16.11.210
- Port 9009
- No host header names

I use C:\Support for the home directory.

Next, I create another website called HR website and give it the following identity:

- IP address 172.16.11.211
- Port 80
- Single host header name hr.mtit.com

Then I create another website called Management website and give it the following identity:

- IP address 172.16.11.211
- Port 80
- Two host header names mgmt.mtit.com and exec.mtit.com

The Web Site Creation Wizard lets you assign only a single host header name to the site you create, but you can add additional host header names later by clicking the Advanced button on the Web Site tab of your website's properties sheet (see Figure 7-2 again). This opens the Advanced Web Site Identification dialog box, where you can click Add to add additional host header names (or more generally, additional website identities) to the selected site (see Figure 7-15).

The identities of the different sites on SNOOPY so far are summarized in Table 7-2.

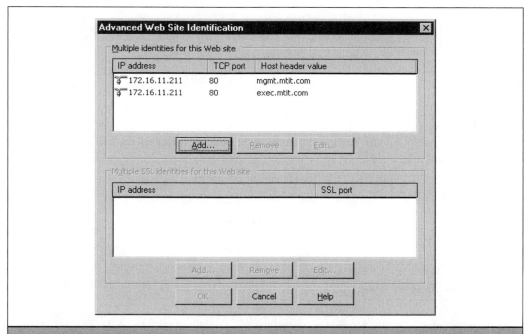

Figure 7-15.   Configuring multiple host header names for a site

Website	IP Address	TCP Port	Host Header Names
Default	(All Unassigned)	80	None
Sales	172.16.11.210	80	None
Support	172.16.11.210	9009	None
HR	172.16.11.211	80	hr.mtit.com
Management	172.16.11.211	80	mgmt.mtit.com exec.mtit.com

Table 7-2.   Final Configuration of Websites on IIS Server SNOOPY

Before I test my configuration, I'll configure name resolution to support my host header names by opening the HOSTS file in the C:\Windows\System32\drivers\etc folder on SNOOPY and adding the following lines to the end of the file:

```
172.16.11.211          hr.mtit.com

172.16.11.211          mgmt.mtit.com

172.16.11.211          exec.mtit.com
```

Now when I open Internet Explorer on SNOOPY and browse various URLs, I get the results shown in Table 7-3.

Look over Table 7-3 carefully, and make sure you understand the reason for each result.

URL	Result
http://snoopy	Sales website (since first IP address is 172.16.11.210)
http://172.16.11.210	Sales website
http://172.16.11.211	Default Web Site
http://172.16.11.212	Default Web Site
http://172.16.11.210:9009	Support website
http://hr.mtit.com	HR website
http://mgmt.mtit.com	Management website
http://exec.mtit.com	Management website

Table 7-3.   Results of Trying to Open Various URLs for Sites on SNOOPY

> **TIP** What will happen if you stop the Sales website and try to open the URL http://snoopy or http://172.16.11.210? Remember why it's good to have a Default Web Site on your IIS machine!

Other Configuration Tasks

In this chapter, we've only looked at the Web Site, Home Directory, Documents, and HTTP Headers tabs on website properties sheets, and even for these tabs we haven't covered every single configuration setting available. In later chapters, we'll look at the purpose of the remaining website configuration settings, but here's a quick guide to where each tab is covered in case you want to flip ahead:

- **Web Site**   More in Chapter 12
- **Performance**   Chapter 12
- **ISAPI Filters**   Chapter 8
- **Home Directory**   More in Chapters 8, 10, and 12
- **Documents**   More in Chapter 16
- **Directory Security**   Chapter 10
- **HTTP Headers**   More in Chapter 16
- **Custom Errors**   Chapter 13

Web Interface for Server Administration

Creating and configuring websites on IIS 6 wouldn't be complete without mentioning again the Web Interface for Administration (WISA), the Administration Web site that is installed by default on Web Edition (and was previously covered in Chapter 6). You can use this interface to create new websites on IIS machines, but you can only configure a basic subset of website properties with it. Personally, I don't find this tool very useful; so for the rest of this book, I plan to ignore it.

Challenge

You plan to use your IIS server to host multiple websites for both your company's intranet and for its public Internet presence. What method(s) would you use for establishing a unique website identity for each site on your machine? Why would you choose these methods? What additional configuration might you have to perform on your network or at your ISP to ensure that users will be able to access your sites properly?

CHECKLIST: ADMINISTERING WEBSITES WITH IIS MANAGER

Check off each of the following website administration tasks after you learn how to perform them using IIS Manager:

- ☐ Configuring IIS properties sheets at various levels, including inheritance and override of settings
- ☐ Configuring a Default Web Site to serve special content when other sites are not specified or available
- ☐ Creating a new website on your server using the Web Site Creation Wizard
- ☐ Specifying a local or remote home directory for a website
- ☐ Saving a website's settings to an XML configuration file
- ☐ Creating a new website by importing an XML configuration file
- ☐ Creating a local or remote virtual directory within a website using the Web Site Creation Wizard
- ☐ Creating a virtual directory by importing an XML configuration file
- ☐ Creating a virtual directory using Web Sharing
- ☐ Saving a virtual directory's settings to an XML configuration file
- ☐ Specifying a default document for a website or directory
- ☐ Configuring MIME mappings at global, site, and directory levels
- ☐ Stopping, pausing, and restarting a website

CHAPTER 8

Creating and Configuring Applications

In the previous chapter, we looked at how to create and configure basic websites on IIS 6. But IIS is more than just a web hosting platform, it's an application server that supports a variety of application architectures, including ASP, ASP.NET, ISAPI, and legacy CGI. We'll begin this chapter by examining these different types of dynamic applications and then look at how to create and configure applications to run on IIS.

TYPES OF IIS APPLICATIONS

IIS 6 supports a variety of application architectures to provide both flexibility in application development and compatibility with earlier IIS platforms and non-Microsoft web server platforms. The four main types of applications that can run on IIS 6 are ASP, ASP.NET, ISAPI, and CGI.

ASP

ASP stands for Active Server Pages and was developed by Microsoft for version 3 of IIS, which was part of the Windows NT 4 Server platform. ASP is a server-side scripting environment that can be used to create dynamic and interactive web applications. ASP pages usually have the file extension .asp and are generally written using Visual Basic Scripting Edition (VBScript) or JScript, two scripting languages developed by Microsoft specifically for the ASP environment (VBScript is an offshoot of Visual Basic [VB], while JScript is Microsoft's equivalent of Netscape's JavaScript language). However, the ASP model can be extended to use scripts written in other languages such as Perl, which is commonly used on UNIX platform web servers like Apache.

The way ASP works is that a client (web browser) begins by requesting an .asp page from a website or virtual directory on IIS. When the server receives the HTTP request, it passes the request to the ASP script interpreter, an ISAPI extension called asp.dll. This interpreter then processes the script and generates an HTML response for the client and/or performs some other action such as calling a COM component in order to write a record to a database.

ASP was originally developed by Microsoft as an alternative to the slower CGI script-processing architecture common on UNIX platforms and the more complex ISAPI model Microsoft developed for IIS 2 (more about these two architectures in a moment).

ASP Example

Writing ASP applications is easy if you have basic knowledge of HTML and previous experience with either VB or JavaScript. Here's a simple ASP application that displays the date and time when the client runs the application:

```
<HTML>
<BODY>
<H1>Welcome to ASP!</H1>
```

```
<P>This page was last refreshed on <%= Now() %><P>
</BODY>
</HTML>
```

Note that the executed script is contained between the delimiters <% and %> and is embedded within a standard HTML page. No scripting language has been explicitly declared for this ASP page, so ASP assumes the default scripting language (VBScript) has been used.

To run the preceding application, create it using Notepad, save it as the filename Default.asp, and copy it to the home directory of the Default Web Site on your IIS machine (you'll do this later in this chapter).

What's New in ASP for IIS 6

ASP has been steadily improved since version 3 of IIS, with new features being added to speed up and simplify the development process and make ASP applications more powerful. Some of these new features of ASP in IIS 6 include

- Greater reliability by detecting hung ASP threads and fixing them by recycling the worker process that hosts the instance of asp.dll associated with the thread.

- Improved error handling that lets you trap errors and display them in custom error message .asp files.

- Improved performance by automatically spawning additional threads when required, including a self-tuning feature that automatically reduces the number of threads should the server become processor-bound.

- Improved performance for scriptless .asp pages that contain only HTML and no script content (in earlier versions you had to name these pages as .htm for best performance).

- Better security through encoding ASP scripts so that they appear on both server and client side as unreadable ASCII characters.

There are also a few changes to ASP in IIS 6 that you need to watch out for if you are developing ASP applications for that platform:

- ASP is disabled by default on IIS 6 and must first be enabled before your applications will run.

- ASP will not support parent paths unless the metabase is configured to allow it to do so (this prevents various kinds of hacking attacks).

- There are some changes in how the global.asa file handles the security context for the execution of events.

For more information about these changes, see the ASP documentation for IIS.

Where to Learn More

ASP is a popular platform for developing web applications for IIS, and it's been around for a few years now, so there are lots of good sites where you can learn how to use it. Here are a few of my favorites:

- www.learnasp.com
- www.asp101.com
- www.15seconds.com
- www.aspin.com
- www.asp-help.com

Most of these sites are now emphasizing the new ASP.NET platform that is included with IIS 6, and you may need to drill down to find "classic ASP" material on them. Of course, IIS 6 still supports ASP for backward compatibility and more easily migrating legacy ASP applications to the new platform; but for new applications, you might consider developing them using ASP.NET, which I'll discuss next.

ASP.NET

ASP.NET is a brand new programming model from Microsoft for developing dynamic web applications for IIS 6. ASP.NET is more than just a new version of ASP. It incorporates important features of Microsoft's new .NET Framework, such as the common language runtime (CLR), which allows ASP.NET applications to make use of inheritance, type safety, versioning, and language interoperability, and enabling ASP.NET applications to be more robust, scalable, and reliable than legacy ASP applications. ASP.NET also supports the latest web standards such as Extensible Markup Language (XML) and Simple Object Access Protocol (SOAP), which makes ASP.NET an ideal platform for developing enterprise-class web services.

ASP.NET supports many more programming languages than ASP (more than 25 at time of writing), making it a much more flexible development environment. Among the languages ASP.NET natively supports are VB.NET, JScript.NET, and C#. ASP.NET recognizes most ASP code, too, which makes it relatively easy to migrate legacy ASP applications to the ASP.NET platform. ASP also supports COM+, the latest version of Microsoft's architecture for developing distributed applications.

In addition to these improvements, ASP.NET simplifies the process of building applications by providing server controls for displaying data, validating, user input, and other common tasks. These controls generate HTML code that works with any web browser and enable ASP.NET applications to be written faster and with less code than legacy ASP applications. Using Visual Studio.NET, you can rapidly build and deploy ASP.NET applications with the same ease with which you can create VB applications. For example, you can visually design a Web Form by dragging and dropping controls onto the page and double-clicking them to configure their parameters. This is indeed cool.

Other advantages of ASP.NET over ASP include:

- **Easier deployment**   Simply copy your ASP.NET files to your web server. You don't even need to restart the server to get your application up and running.

- **Better performance**   ASP.NET runs as compiled code, it's not interpreted like ASP. This can significantly improve the performance of your web applications.

- **Flexible caching**   ASP.NET can cache entire pages or portions of pages as needed to increase application responsiveness.

- **Better internationalization**   ASP.NET uses Unicode (UTF-8) internally for representing request/response data.

- **Easier debugging**   ASP.NET includes a tracking feature that makes it easier to debug faulty applications.

- **Easier configurability**   ASP.NET configuration settings are stored in text files and formatted in XML for easy editing.

- **Web farm session state**   ASP.NET lets multiple IIS servers in a web farm share session state information for a single application, making IIS more scalable.

- **Improved crash protection**   ASP.NET automatically detects memory leaks and deadlocks and tries to recover from them with no intervention needed.

- **Support for .NET Framework**   This support includes .NET class library, Web Forms, and XML Web Services.

ASP.NET Example

Creating a simple ASP.NET application is just as easy as writing one with ASP. Here's a simple ASP.NET application that displays the date and time when the client runs the application:

```
<HTML>
<BODY>
<H1>Welcome to ASP.NET!</H1>
<P> This page was last refreshed on <%
Response.Write(DateTime.Now.ToString()) %><P>
</BODY>
</HTML>
```

Again, the VBScript code that is executed is contained between the delimiters <% and %> and is embedded within a standard HTML page. To run the preceding application, create it using Notepad, save it with the filename Default.aspx (note the new .aspx extension for ASP.NET pages), and copy it to the home directory of the Default Web Site on your IIS machine. Of course, ASP.NET first has to be installed and enabled! I'll walk you through this process later in the chapter in the section entitled "Working with ASP.NET."

NOTE The files within an ASP.NET application can have a variety of extensions including .htm for plain HTML files, .aspx for Web Forms pages, .ascx for Web Forms user controls, .asmx for XML Web Services, .config for application configuration files, .dll for compiled assemblies saved as project DLLs using Visual Studio.NET, and so on. DLLs for ASP.NET applications generally go in the \bin subdirectory of your website's home directory, while other files can be located in local or remote virtual directories.

Of course, there's a lot more to ASP.NET than this simple example illustrates. I could talk next about using the global.asax file for adding event handling logic to your application, or discuss how to manage application state using various methods, or explain the purpose of the machine.config and web.config files. But this is not a book on how to develop ASP.NET applications—our focus is on how to configure them to run on IIS 6.

NOTE You can run ASP and ASP.NET applications side by side on the same IIS 6 server. This gives you the flexibility to support older apps written for earlier versions of IIS while migrating them to ASP.NET and testing them.

ISAPI

Internet Server Application Programming Interface (ISAPI) was created by Microsoft as a replacement for the CGI processing model popular on UNIX web server platforms. ISAPI really represents two kinds of routines:

- **ISAPI applications** These can be called from any web page to perform dynamic and interactive functions like accessing a database or validating a form. Another name for these is *ISAPI extensions*, because ISAPI can *extend* the functionality of IIS beyond serving static HTML and do things similar to what ASP applications do (only faster). ISAPI applications can be written in several different languages but are usually written in C++ for best execution performance. ISAPI applications can be configured at either the web site or virtual directory level, so a single web site may have multiple ISAPI applications running in different directories performing different application-related tasks when they are called.

- **ISAPI filters** These are used to preprocess and post-process HTTP requests and perform actions such as compressing or encrypting information, performing redirection, monitoring security, and so on. ISAPI filters are always written in C++, as they usually examine *all* incoming traffic for your site and so have to be built for speed. ISAPI filters are always configured at the web site level—you can't configure an ISAPI filter for a virtual directory within a site.

The main advantage of ISAPI over CGI is that it avoids the performance penalty incurred by CGI, which spawns a new process each time code is run. However, the problem with the ISAPI model is that you need C++ or similar high-level programming knowledge to develop ISAPI applications and filters, while CGI apps are commonly written using Perl or some other interpreted scripting language. Because of the development cost of writing C++ code, Microsoft developed the simpler ASP model described earlier that is more widely used than ISAPI.

We'll look briefly at several aspects of configuring ISAPI extensions and installing ISAPI filters on IIS later in this chapter in the section entitled "Working with ISAPI."

NOTE Because IIS 6 supports wildcard script mappings, which are discussed in the section "Working with ISAPI," you can now use ISAPI extensions anywhere ISAPI filters were used in previous versions of IIS. ISAPI extensions can be executed asynchronously (while ISAPI filters can only be executed synchronously), so Microsoft recommends that ISAPI filters no longer be used with IIS 6 and that you replace them with suitable ISAPI extensions wherever possible.

CGI

The Common Gateway Interface (CGI) is a programming model originally developed for web servers running on the UNIX platform. CGI programs are typically either scripts written in Perl, Python, or some other scripting language, or executables written in C or C++. On UNIX web servers, these programs are usually placed in the \cgi-bin directory on your web server and called from web pages for performing tasks such as processing input from forms or writing a record to a database. IIS supports CGI mainly to simplify the process of migrating applications from UNIX to IIS; for most purposes today, ASP is used for developing applications for IIS.

We'll look briefly at how to install and configure CGI applications on IIS later in the section "Working with CGI."

NOTE The term *Web Server Extension* refers to any feature of IIS that extends its capability beyond serving static HTML content. In this context, ASP, ASP.NET, ISAPI, and CGI all represent examples of different Web Server Extensions on IIS. ASP and ASP.NET are themselves implemented as ISAPI extensions on IIS.

PREPARING IIS FOR HOSTING APPLICATIONS

Before you can run your dynamic web applications on IIS 6, you have to perform certain tasks to prepare your server:

- Decide which isolation mode to run your server in, and change modes if necessary.

- Use the Web Service Extensions node in IIS Manager to enable the appropriate extensions for running your applications.

Isolation Modes

As discussed in Chapter 2, IIS 6 has an adjustable architecture that can run in either of two modes:

- **Worker process isolation mode**   This mode uses the new IIS 6 architecture that isolates key portions of the World Wide Web Publishing Service (W3SVC) from the main IIS process inetinfo.exe, thus preventing a faulty website from bringing down other sites running on the server. Worker process isolation mode makes IIS more reliable by letting you isolate web applications into separate application pools and providing health-monitoring and worker process—recycling support. This mode also provides enhanced security by running worker processes using the Network Service account, a built-in identity that has fewer access rights than the Local System account used by IIS 5 isolation mode, described next. Scalability and performance are also enhanced through the use of web gardens and processor affinity.

- **IIS 5 isolation mode**   This mode uses the same architecture as the earlier IIS 5 platform and allows applications to run in one of three levels of application protection: Low (IIS Process), Medium (Pooled), or High (Isolated). This mode does not support any of the new IIS 6 features such as web gardens, processor affinity, health monitoring, or worker process recycling that are available when IIS 6 is running in worker process isolation mode.

NOTE   IIS 6 can only run in one mode at a time—you can't run some applications in worker process isolation mode and others in IIS 5 isolation mode on the same server.

Default Mode for Install/Upgrade

As discussed in Chapter 3, the mode your IIS 6 machine is running in by default depends on whether you performed a clean install or upgraded from an earlier version of IIS. Specifically, IIS 6 will run by default in worker process isolation mode if you performed a clean install of Windows Server 2003 and configured the server to run in application server role. If you upgraded your server from IIS 5 (Windows 2000 Server) or IIS 4 (Windows NT 4 Server with Option Pack), however, IIS 6 will run by default in IIS 5 isolation mode.

Changing Modes

Regardless of the mode your server is currently running in, you can change it to the other mode by following these steps:

1. Open the properties sheet for the Web Sites node in IIS Manager and select the Services tab (see Figure 8-1).

2. Select the Isolation Mode check box to switch to IIS 5 isolation mode (or deselect it to switch to worker process isolation mode) and click OK to apply the change.

3. Click Yes to restart IIS so the mode change will take effect.

SECURITY ALERT You must have Administrator credentials to change the mode of your IIS 6 machine.

TIP A quick way to tell which mode your server is running in is to examine the console tree in IIS Manager. If there is an Application Pools node under your *servername* node, you are running in worker process isolation mode. If there is no Application Pools node, then you are running in IIS 5 isolation mode where application pools are not part of the IIS architecture.

Which Mode to Use

Deciding which mode to use is simple: try running your application in worker process isolation mode, and if there are no problems, leave your server running in this mode. This allows you to take advantage of the performance, reliability, scalability, and security enhancements in the new architecture of IIS 6.

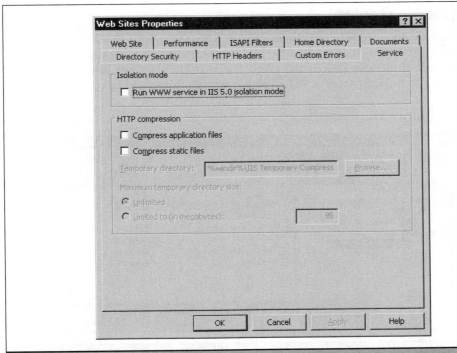

Figure 8-1. Changing the isolation mode using the Services tab of Web Sites Properties

If your applications won't run properly in worker process isolation mode, switch to IIS 5 isolation mode using the procedure just outlined. Examples of applications that may need to run in IIS 5 isolation mode include legacy applications developed for earlier versions of IIS, especially the following:

- ISAPI applications that were designed to be loaded by multiple processes that run concurrently, often called multi-instance ISAPIs

- ASP applications that were designed to persist session state information in-process

- Applications that were specifically designed to run within the inetinfo.exe process or within a dllhost.exe environment

- Applications that were specifically designed to farm out requests to other worker processes

- Applications that require read raw data filters

NOTE From this point forward in this chapter, we will assume that your IIS 6 machine is running in worker process isolation mode unless otherwise specified.

Enabling Dynamic Content

In addition to selecting an isolation mode, the other step you need to take before you can run your applications on IIS is to enable dynamic content on the server. This is done using the Web Service Extensions (WSE) node in IIS Manager (see Figure 8-2), which has a similar function to the IIS lockdown wizard that could be downloaded and

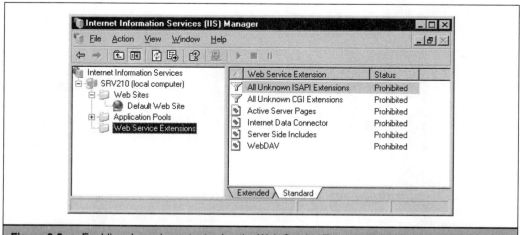

Figure 8-2. Enabling dynamic content using the Web Service Extensions (WSE) node

installed on IIS 5. I'll discuss WSE in more detail in Chapter 10 when we look at IIS security, but for now I'll just note that IIS 6 is installed in a locked-down state that can only serve static HTML content. To serve dynamic content, you selectively enable the extensions you want using WSE, as outlined in later sections of this chapter.

WORKING WITH ASP.NET

The rest of this chapter looks in detail at installing and configuring different types of web applications on IIS. We'll begin by looking at ASP.NET applications and how to install and configure them on IIS.

NOTE   ASP.NET applications can also work when IIS is configured to run in IIS 5 isolation mode, but ASP.NET works differently in this case. Specifically, when IIS is running in worker process isolation mode, ASP.NET uses the same worker process architecture used by IIS, including support for recycling, health monitoring, and so on. When IIS is running in IIS 5 isolation mode, ASP.NET uses its own process model where ASP.NET configuration settings are defined in the XML configuration file machine.config, which is contained in the directory SystemRoot%\Microsoft.NET\Framework\<*version*>\CONFIG, where <*version*> is the version of the .NET Framework installed on the machine. There are some exceptions to this, however; see the ASP.NET documentation for more info.

Installing ASP.NET

If you refer back to Figure 8-2, you'll notice that ASP.NET is not listed in the Web Service Extension column of the details pane. This is because in my particular configuration of Windows Server 2003, Enterprise Edition, I added the Application Server role but did not install ASP.NET as part of that role. The first thing I must do if I want to run ASP.NET applications (such as the sample application earlier in this chapter) is install ASP.NET on my IIS machine: To do this, open Add Or Remove Programs, select Add/ Remove Windows Components, choose Application Server, click the Details button, select ASP.NET, and click OK. Once this is finished, press F5 to refresh IIS Manager, and the WSE node should show ASP.NET in its list of extensions.

TIP   If ASP.NET shows up as an extension in WSE but has the status Prohibited, it means the ASP.NET component of IIS is installed on the server but it is not yet enabled. In this case, right-click the ASP.NET extension of WSE and select Allow to enable ASP.NET applications to run on your server.

Using the Default Application

Let's see if you can get the sample ASP.NET application I described earlier in this chapter to work on IIS. The simplest way to do this is to use the Default Web Site that is created when IIS is installed and which has C:\Inetpub\wwwroot as its home directory. Start by copying the default.aspx page you created to this directory. Now let's look at your Default Web site in IIS Manager (see Figure 8-3).

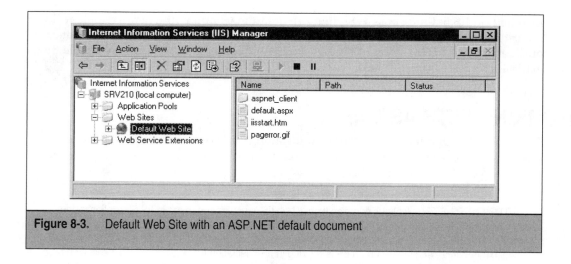

Figure 8-3. Default Web Site with an ASP.NET default document

Notice that there is a subdirectory called aspnet_client in your Default Web Site. This directory is automatically created to allow ASP.NET to take advantage of the client-side script processing features of .NET Framework server controls. This is a developers' topic and is beyond the scope of this book, so I won't discuss it further here.

Now right-click the Default Web Site and select Browse. You might expect the sample ASP.NET application to run at this point, displaying the message "This page was last refreshed on [date] [time]"; but instead, the "under construction" message from your iisstart.htm page is displayed. This is likely a problem with the default document order, so open the Default Web Site Properties sheet and select the Documents tab (see Figure 8-4).

Note that installing and enabling ASP.NET adds Default.aspx to your list of default documents, but unfortunately it's at the bottom of the list. The solution is to either move it to the top of the list or delete any other default documents, such as iisstart.htm, from the site's home directory. In this example, keep iisstart.htm and move Default.aspx to the top of the default documents list.

Right-click the Default Web Site again and select Browse. This time, the sample ASP.NET application should run and display the expected message in the details pane (see Figure 8-5).

Application Pools

Before you look at creating other ASP.NET applications on your machine, let's pause for a moment and discuss application pools, a feature of IIS when it is running in worker process isolation mode. An *application pool* is basically a logical representation of the worker process(es) that service an ASP.NET application running on IIS. By default, each application pool has a single worker process (w3wp.exe) associated with

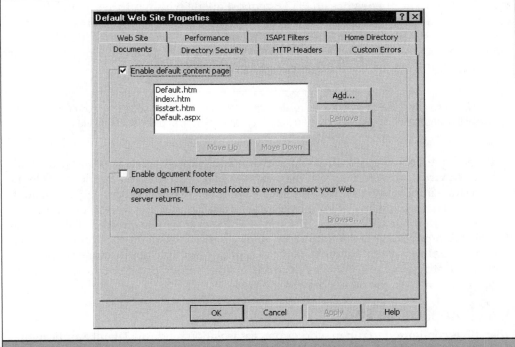

Figure 8-4. Changing the default document order

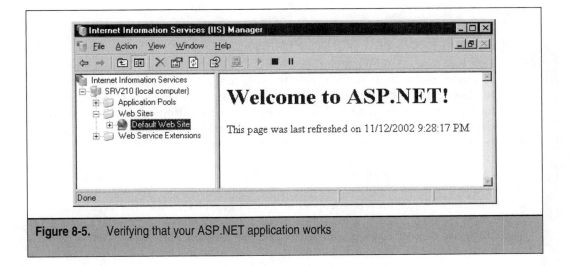

Figure 8-5. Verifying that your ASP.NET application works

it, and each worker process has an HTTP request queue within http.sys associated with it. When a client (web browser) tries to open the Default.aspx page in your Default Web Site, http.sys places the request in the queue for the Default Application Pool (the application pool associated with the Default Web Site) until the worker process for that pool can pull the request from the queue and generate a response.

NOTE A common way to describe the relationship between application pools and worker processes is to say that application pools are separated from each other by worker process boundaries.

If you have several applications running on your server (corresponding to several websites or virtual directories), you may want to place each of your applications in its own separate application pool so they each have their own worker process associated with them. That way, if any of your applications fail, none of the worker processes associated with other applications running on the server will be affected. This feature of application pools is thus integral to the ability of IIS 6 to isolate applications from each other for improved reliability. You can also run multiple applications within a given application pool to conserve resources on your server; but if you do and one of the applications fails, the others may be affected.

Default Application Pool

When IIS is configured to run in worker process isolation mode, a Default Application Pool called DefaultAppPool is created under the Application Pools node in IIS Manager (see Figure 8-6). This pool contains the Default Application, which is automatically created for the Default Web Site when IIS is installed.

Application Pools and Worker Processes

There are two cases in which an application pool may have more than one worker process associated with it. The first is when you create a web garden, a feature of IIS that allows you to have multiple worker processes service a given application pool for improved performance. The other is if the application pool is configured for overlapped recycling to occur, in which case when the worker process is recycled, there will briefly be two worker processes (the one being terminated and the new one generated to take its place) associated with the same pool. In both cases, an application within the pool may experience what is called multi-instancing, that is, multiple instances of the application running concurrently. This can cause problems if the application is not specifically designed to handle this situation. Older ISAPI extensions and ASP applications are particularly vulnerable to this issue and may require recoding (or running in IIS 5 isolation mode). Alternatively, you can avoid using a web garden for your application, or you can disable overlapped recycling for the pool. Web gardens and worker process recycling are covered in more detail in Chapter 12.

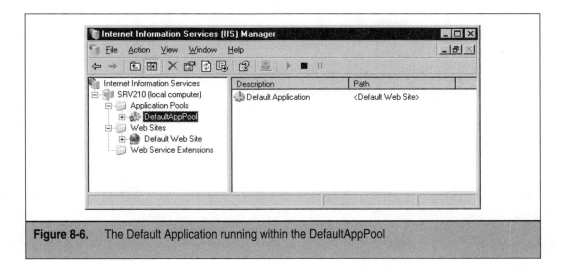

Figure 8-6.   The Default Application running within the DefaultAppPool

Right-clicking the DefaultAppPool allows you to perform a number of administrative tasks on it, including:

- **Manually stopping and starting the pool**   When an application pool is manually stopped by an administrator, all applications associated with it are rendered unavailable to clients and a "service unavailable" message is displayed in the browser window until the pool is started again. Application pools may also suddenly stop for other reasons, such as configuration errors where nonexistent identities are used as a security context for running the pool or the initiation of the rapid-fail protection feature of IIS. Stopping an application pool is not the same as stopping the website containing the application.

- **Manually recycling the worker process(es) associated with the pool**   Recycling is an IIS 6 feature that lets you periodically restart worker processes associated with the pool; it is typically used when running flaky applications that have a tendency to crash over time. Recycling is discussed in more detail in Chapter 12.

- **Saving configuration to a file**   This saves the configuration of the application pool to an XML file that can then be imported into another server.

- **Opening the properties sheet for the pool**   This allows you to configure recycling, performance, health, and identity settings for the pool. I'll discuss configuring application pools in Chapters 10 and 12.

Creating Application Pools

Let's create a second application pool on your server so you can experiment with moving applications between pools. Right-click the Application Pools node and select New | Application Pool to open the Add New Application Pool dialog box (see Figure 8-7).

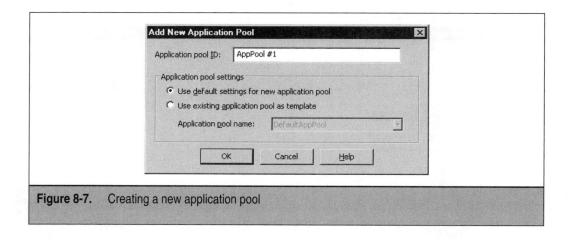

Figure 8-7. Creating a new application pool

Type a friendly name for the pool (**AppPool #1** is suggested) that will only be used in IIS Manager, and specify whether to use the default settings for the new pool or copy its configuration settings from a pool you specify (for this example, use the former option).

You should now have two pools (DefaultAppPool and AppPool #1) displayed under the Application Pools node in the console tree. At this point, the DefaultAppPool has an application (the Default Application) running in it, while AppPool #1 has no application running in it.

TIP Even if you only have one website (the Default Web Site) running on your server, you may want to create a second application pool in addition to the DefaultAppPool. The reason is that if you are modifying your ASP.NET application, you can run both the existing and modified versions simultaneously, each assigned to its own pool, to simplify testing your modifications. In other words, you will be using application pools to isolate different versions of your application from each other.

Assigning Applications to Application Pools

Now let's move the Default Application from the DefaultAppPool to AppPool #1 by *assigning* the Default Application to AppPool #1:

1. Right-click the Default Web Site (which contains the Default Application) and select Properties to open its properties sheet.

2. Switch to the Home Directory tab and select AppPool #1 from the Application Pool list box.

3. Click OK to apply the change, and close the properties sheet.

Notice now that the Default Application in IIS Manager has moved from the DefaultAppPool to AppPool #1 (see Figure 8-8).

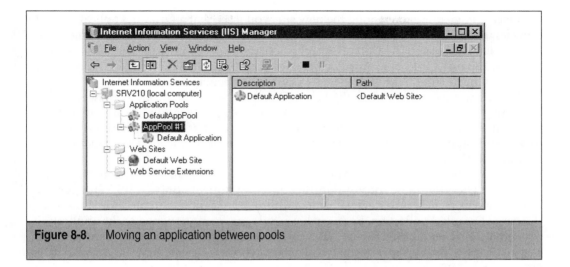

Figure 8-8.   Moving an application between pools

NOTE   You can't delete an application pool if there are still applications assigned to it. You must first move the applications to other pools and then delete the pool.

Creating Applications

Now let's create a few more ASP.NET applications on your server and experiment with configuring these applications. For simplicity, I'll explain how to edit the Default.aspx file in C:\Inetpub\wwwroot to display the heading "Welcome to ASP.NET #####", where ##### is the friendly name of the website that will host your new application. Then you'll create a content folder to contain the modified page and make this folder the home directory of the website or virtual directory that contains your application. Specifically, go ahead and create the following directories:

- C:\webstuff\appone which contains Default.aspx where ##### = Site One
- C:\webstuff\apptwo which contains Default.aspx where ##### = Site Two

and so on as necessary.

Creating a Root-Level Application

To create a new root-level application on IIS, first create a new website using the methods outlined in Chapter 7. For this example, use the Web Site Creation Wizard to create a new site called Site One and assign it one of the several IP addresses bound to your server's network card. This ensures the site has a unique identity so it can start properly. As the home directory for your new site, choose the folder \appone described earlier.

Once you've finished creating the new site, you'll see that a Default Application node appears under the DefaultAppPool node in the console tree (see Figure 8-9). Remember that earlier you moved the Default Application associated with your Default Web Site from the DefaultAppPool to AppPool #1. Notice also that this new node is associated with Site One, not the Default Web Site. Why has this new node appeared?

The answer can be found on the Home Directory tab of the properties sheet for the newly created Site One (see Figure 8-10). Your new application has an application name, an application starting point, and specific execute permissions, and it is assigned to a specific application pool. Let's examine each of these application settings for our new application.

First, the application name for your new application is Default Application. Application Name is a friendly name for your application that appears only in IIS Manager. By default, when you create a new website on IIS, an application is created for it and given the name Default Application. Because this is the same name assigned to the application created for the Default Web Site, it is somewhat confusing—you now have two separate applications with the same name but different content directories. To eliminate this confusion, rename your new application something different, such as App One. Before you do this, however, let's continue to look at the application settings for your application.

The starting point for your new application is <Site One>. This is the name of the node in the IIS metabase that contains the configuration settings for your application, and the name of the website you created is used to generate this name.

The Execute Permissions is set by default as Scripts Only. This setting lets ASP.NET pages run but not executable code such as .exe files. This is a safety feature to ensure hostile code won't run on the server. However, you can select Scripts and Executables if you want to allow any code (compiled or scripted) to run in the directory, or you can select None if you want to allow only static HTML to be served from this directory.

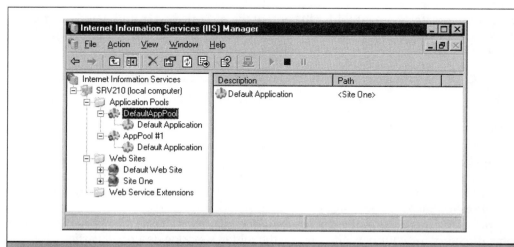

Figure 8-9. Are there now two Default Applications?

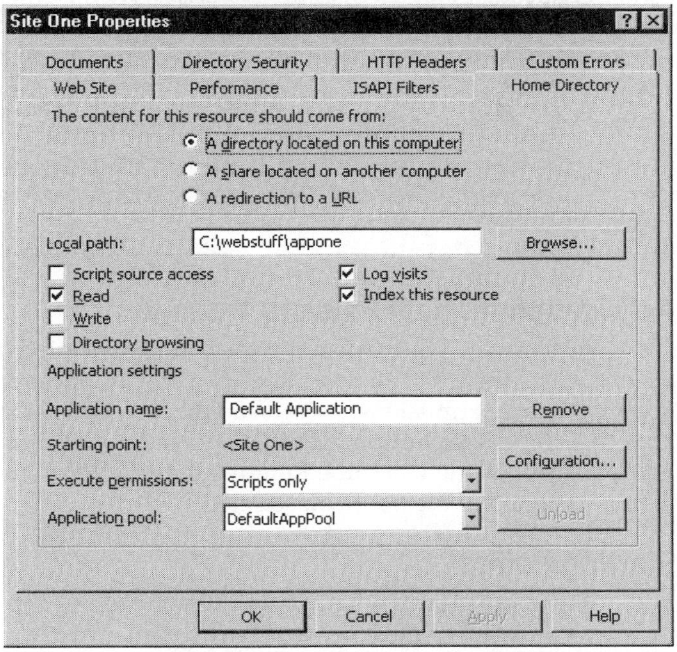

Figure 8-10. Defining an application using an application name and starting point

Finally, the application pool to which the new application is assigned is the DefaultAppPool. This is done automatically for every new root application you create on IIS, but as I mentioned earlier, you can move your application to a separate pool to isolate it if you want to.

Renaming an Application

You can rename your new application simply by overtyping a new name in the Application Name field on the Home Directory tab and clicking Apply (see Figure 8-10 again). Try changing its name from Default Application to App One, and note that the node under the DefaultAppPool also changes from Default Application to App One, which is a little easier to follow.

Removing an Application

Let's say you changed your mind and don't want to host an ASP.NET application in your new website named Site One (perhaps you just want to serve static HTML from the site instead). To remove your App One application, click the Remove button on the Home Directory tab (shown in Figure 8-10). The result of this action is that the application name field goes blank and the starting point changes to <No Application Defined>. IIS takes some time to flush the configuration changes to the metabase, so App One may still be displayed for a while under DefaultAppPool in IIS Manager, even if you press F5 to refresh the console.

NOTE   Instead of disappearing entirely from the DefaultAppPool, a new node called ROOT may appear that appears to be mapped to <Site One>. This appears to indicate that there is a website on the server that has no application configured for it.

Creating an Application from an Existing Website

You still have a new website called Site One but there is no application defined for the site, so let's create one. Click the Create button, specify a new application name such as New App One, specify execute permissions, select an application pool for the application, and click OK. Note that the Create button is only displayed if you first remove the existing default Application Name using the Remove Button. Verify in IIS Manager that the application is assigned to the pool you selected.

Application Starting Points

I should pause and define more clearly what we mean by the term "application." In IIS lingo, an *application* is a collection of files contained in a given virtual directory (and usually its subdirectories) and that can be executed using an applicable web service extension like ASP or ASP.NET. For example, on an IIS machine, the Default Web Site might contain the virtual (or physical) directories \sales, \service, \support and \support\legacy. All of these subdirectories are usually part of the same application: the root application called Default Application. On the other hand, you could select one of these subdirectories—\support, for example—and remove the Default Application from the Directory tab of its properties sheet, and then create a new application for the directory. At this point, any subdirectories beneath the \support directory (such as \legacy) would be part of the new application and would no longer belong to the Default Application. So another way of defining an application on IIS is as a contiguous subtree of folders whose root folder is the application starting point, where none of the lower nodes have their own starting points defined but instead share the same starting point as the root folder. More briefly, every file and directory beneath the starting point directory of a website is part of the same application until another starting point directory is found.

TIP   If you remove the application starting point from a subdirectory (either virtual or physical) of a site's home directory, clients will not be able to start the application by opening files in this subdirectory (or in directories beneath it). Note that removing an application starting point does not remove the content itself from the associated directory.

Applications and Virtual Directories

I should point out an important difference between physical and virtual directories as far as IIS applications are concerned. If you create a physical subdirectory within the home directory of a website on which an application is defined, the physical directory has the same name, starting point, execute permissions, and application pool as the root application defined for the parent website. If you create a *virtual* subdirectory within the home directory of the site, however, a *new* application name is assigned to the virtual directory (by default, IIS uses the virtual directory name for the application name). For example, if you create a virtual directory called \Sales in Site One described previously, and you open the properties sheet for this virtual directory, on the Virtual Directory tab the application name will be listed as Sales and the application starting point as <Site One>\Sales. The execute permissions and application pool settings are inherited from the parent application, however. If you want your new virtual directory to be part of the parent application (website root application) instead of being a separate application, click Remote on the Virtual Directory tab. When you do this, the icon for the virtual directory's node in IIS Manager changes from a gear icon (signifying a separate application) to a folder icon with a small world attached to it (signifying it is part of the parent website, which has a large world icon).

Unloading Applications

If an application is started by a client request, it is loaded into memory for execution. You can manually unload your application from memory by clicking the Unload button on the Home Directory tab of the application's associated website. However, you can only perform an unload from the application's home directory, not from any subdirectory beneath it.

Configuring Applications

Once you've created a new application on IIS, you need to configure it. To configure an ASP.NET application, click the Configuration button on the Home Directory tab of the website on which the application is defined. This opens the Application Configuration screen (see Figure 8-11), which has three tabs: Mappings, Options, and Debugging. We'll examine each of these and the settings they contain. But first, note that application settings can be configured at three levels:

- **Web Sites level**   These settings are global for all sites on the server.
- **Website level**   Each site is configured separately.
- **Virtual directory level**   For virtual directories within a particular website.

There are a few differences when configuring application settings at these different levels:

- The option for caching ISAPI applications cannot be configured at the virtual directory level. Instead, this level inherits the value for this setting from its parent website. Caching ISAPI applications is discussed in Chapters 12 and 13.

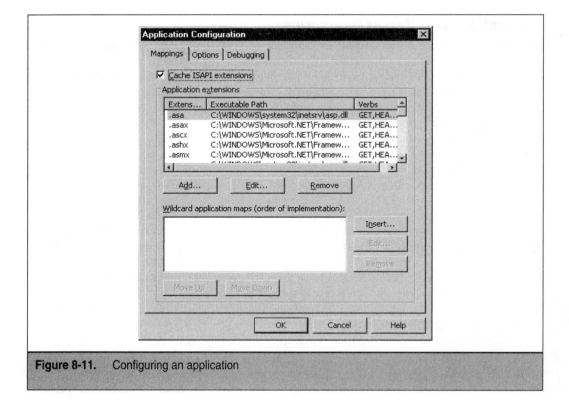

Figure 8-11. Configuring an application

- The Web Sites level has a fourth tab called ASP Caching that enables and configures the caching of compiled ASP templates on IIS. This feature is covered in Chapter 12 when we discuss IIS performance.

- You can programmatically override virtual directory or website application settings for each individual ASP.NET page within a virtual directory or website.

NOTE Physical subdirectories within a website configured as an application do not have configurable application settings—only virtual directories do.

Application Configuration: Mappings

This tab is used to associate specific filename extensions to the associated ISAPI or CGI program used to execute these files, a process called *application mapping*. IIS 6 comes with a set of predefined application mappings that associate various file extensions with the different ISAPI extensions, as shown in Table 8-1.

You can add, remove, or modify any of these application mappings by specifying a different ISAPI DLL for executing files having that extension, specifying which HTTP verbs like GET or POST should be passed to the DLL for processing (other verbs will

ISAPI Extension	Associated File Extensions
asp.dll	.asa, .asp, .cdx, .cer
aspnet_isapi.dll	.asax, .ascx, .ashx, .asmx, .aspx, .axd, .cs, .csproj, .licx, .rem, .resources, .resx, .soap, .vb, .vbproj, .vsdisco, .webinfo
httpobdc.dll	.idc
ssinc.dll	.shtm, .shtml, .stm

Table 8-1. Default File Extensions Defined for Different ISAPI Extensions

not be passed), and whether you want to allow the application to run in a directory without execute permissions. You can also create your own custom application mappings by associating specific file extensions with a specific ISAPI DLL. For example, I could map the file extension .mitch to asp.dll and save all my ASP pages with this extension. (I don't know why I would do this—vanity probably!)

Of course, a more common use for application mappings is to configure IIS to use new scripting languages other than the default VBScript and JScript. For example, Perl is a scripting language that is commonly used for developing CGI scripts to run on UNIX web servers. If you obtained a Perl engine or script interpreter (typically perl.exe) from some third-party vendor, you could configure IIS to process Perl scripts (text files with the file extension .pl) using this engine as follows:

1. Open the properties sheet for the website where the Perl script will run and switch to the Home Directory tab.

2. Click the Configuration button to display the Mappings tab of the Application Configuration screen (see Figure 8-11 again).

3. Click Add and browse to where the Perl engine is located, typically \Perl\bin or something similar.

4. Specify .pl as the file extension to be mapped to the engine.

5. Specify which verbs should be passed to the engine when processing HTTP requests (typically GET or POST).

6. Select the Script Engine check box to allow the Perl engine to execute, and click OK. Note that if you leave this check box unselected, you will have to specify Scripts And Executables as execute permissions on the web site where your Perl application resides; but if you select the check box, then you can use the Scripts Only permissions instead, which is safer.

Of course, the steps may differ slightly depending on the instructions that come with your third-party script engine.

TIP The Verbs field on the Mappings tab indicates which HTTP verbs are allowed. In earlier versions of IIS, this field was named Exclusions and indicated which verbs were prohibited.

NOTE For information on configuring wildcard application mappings, see the section "Working with ISAPI," later in this chapter.

Application Configuration: Options

The Options tab of the Application Configuration screen lets you configure certain functional and performance aspects of running ASP.NET applications on IIS (see Figure 8-12). For example, Session Timeout lets you persist session state information for your application and allows you to configure how long this information will be persisted before it is discarded. Persisting session state information is important in multipage ASP.NET applications such as online order forms to prevent users from having to re-enter information during their session. By default, session state is enabled with a timeout of 20 minutes.

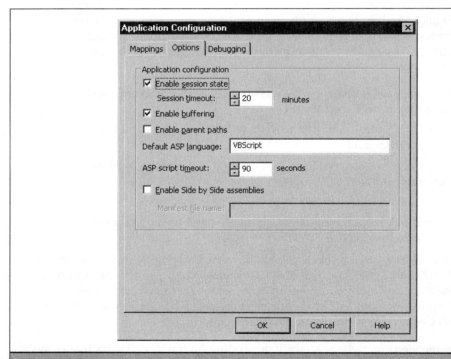

Figure 8-12. Configuring application options

ActivePerl

You can obtain Perl for Windows from Active State (www.activestate.com). When Windows Server 2003 is released, Active State will probably have a version of their ActivePerl product that runs on this platform. The latest beta version of ActivePerl installs as a Windows Installer Package (.msi file) and automatically configures Perl to run on IIS by creating .pl and .plx file extensions and mapping them to perl.exe (for CGI execution) and perlis.dll (for ISAPI execution). The nice thing about ActivePerl is that it comes in both CGI and ISAPI varieties, and you can choose which form to use for interpreting your scripts. Once you install ActivePerl on IIS you can test it using the sample script found in Knowledge Base article Q245225 on the Microsoft Product Support Services (PSS) website at support.microsoft.com. Don't forget to enable the appropriate CGI and ISAPI extensions for your Perl engine using WSE, or your Perl scripts won't work!

Another setting you can configure on this tab is the default scripting language used for the ASP.NET application. This is the scripting language assumed for .aspx pages when no language is explicitly declared within the page; it is VBScript by default. If you do not wish to use VBScript, you must manually type the default scripting language you prefer in this field (JScript is the main alternative to VBScript on IIS).

Another setting on this tab is ASP Script Timeout, which lets you specify in seconds how long IIS lets a script run before terminating it. The timeout value can range from 1 second upward, with a default setting of 90 seconds. A shorter timeout value will reduce wasted IIS resources but may interfere with distributed applications when the network is slow.

As for the remaining settings on this page, I'll cover enabling parent paths in Chapter 10 when we deal with IIS security, and buffering in Chapter 12 when we discuss performance issues.

NOTE When a script is terminated by IIS, an event is written to the Event Log. See Chapter 13 for information about IIS events in the Event Log.

Application Configuration: Debugging

The Debugging tab lets you enable client- and server-side debugging for your ASP.NET applications and configure custom error messages for script errors that may occur. I'll talk about application debugging more in Chapter 13 when we look at maintaining and troubleshooting IIS.

WORKING WITH ASP

The good news is that everything we've discussed so far about creating and configuring ASP.NET applications on IIS 6 also applies to ASP applications! The only real difference is that you must enable ASP instead of ASP.NET using the Web Service Extensions (WSE) node in IIS Manager—and of course your .asp pages must comply with the ASP programming model.

WORKING WITH ISAPI

An important thing to configure for ISAPI extensions running on your server, whether these are default extensions included with IIS (like asp.dll, the ASP script engine) or custom DLLs you develop or obtain from a third-party vendor (like Active State's perlis.dll Perl script engine), is enabling caching of ISAPI extensions. However, since this is a performance issue, we'll talk about it later in Chapter 12, when we discuss IIS performance tuning and monitoring.

The other issue with ISAPI extensions is that before they will work on IIS they need to be enabled using the Web Service Extensions (WSE) node of IIS Manager (refer back to Figure 8-2). If your ISAPI extension isn't listed on the WSE screen, you can either add it manually or allow all ISAPI extensions to execute—I'll discuss the difference in Chapter 10.

ISAPI Filters

ISAPI filters are another matter. You can install and configure these using the ISAPI Filters tab on the properties sheet for either the Web Sites node (global filters) or for individual websites (site filters). For example, if you have enabled ASP.NET using WSE, an ISAPI filter called aspnet_filter.dll is listed on the ISAPI Filters tab of the Web Sites Properties sheet (see Figure 8-13). Note that this filter does not appear on the ISAPI Filters tab of any individual website properties sheet—filters defined at the global level appear only on the Web Sites Properties sheet.

Using the interface on this tab, you can add, remove, edit, and change the processing order of ISAPI filters on your site or server. If you have multiple ISAPI filters installed and registered for the same web server event, filters with high priority are called before filters with low priority, and filters with the same priority are processed in sequence with global filters executing before site filters.

NOTE   When you add, remove, or modify a global filter, you must restart IIS before it will load and run (see Chapter 5 on how to restart IIS). This extra step is not required for site filters, however, which are automatically loaded when you add them to the site properties.

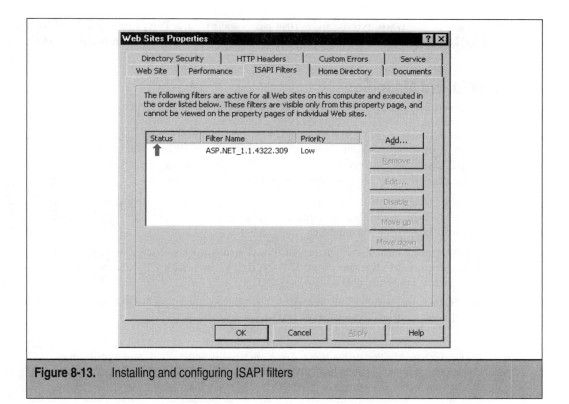

Figure 8-13. Installing and configuring ISAPI filters

Wildcard Application Mappings

Instead of using ISAPI filters to preprocess HTTP requests, IIS 6 allows ISAPI extensions to perform this task by configuring wildcard application mappings. This is advantageous over using ISAPI filters for several reasons:

- ISAPI filters can only be configured at the global or site level, not at the virtual directory level.

- ISAPI filters execute synchronously and are therefore not suitable for long-running processing operations such as certain forms of encryption, distributed authentication over slow WAN links, processing complex business logic to validate orders or transactions, and so on.

- ISAPI filters can only parse information in HTTP headers and cannot be used to process information contained in the body of an HTTP request.

The alternative to using ISAPI filters is to create an ISAPI extension that performs the same job and then create a wildcard mapping so that every HTTP GET request for a file, regardless of the file's extension, is first processed by the ISAPI extension before being sent to the script engine or interpreter that executes the application running on the site.

Adding Wildcard Mappings

To add a wildcard application mapping to a site, server, or virtual directory, perform the following steps:

1. Open the properties sheet—for a virtual directory within a site, a specific website, or the global Web Sites node in IIS Manager—and switch to the Virtual Directory or Home Directory tab as appropriate.

2. Click the Configuration button to open the Application Configuration screen, select the Mappings tab, and click Insert to open the Add/Edit Application Extension Mapping dialog box.

3. Type the path to the ISAPI filter you want to assign a wildcard mapping to, or browse to locate the file on your hard drive, and click OK to verify the file exists. You'll return to the Mappings tab.

4. If you have several wildcard mappings created, you can move them up or down in the list to put their execution in the order you prefer.

TIP   If the Configuration button on the Virtual Directory tab is dimmed out, it means your virtual directory is not an application starting point and therefore can't be configured. Go instead to the properties sheet for the parent website of the directory and make the changes there.

WORKING WITH CGI

Last and definitely least, you can also install and configure CGI applications (whether scripts or executables) on IIS 6, although this is not recommended due to the performance overhead involved. About the only time you'd want to use this feature is if you have legacy UNIX apps that you can recompile for the Windows platform but don't have the time or resources to rewrite as ISAPI extensions or ASP/ASP.NET applications. Here are a few tips on how to deploy CGI apps on IIS:

- Put all your CGI apps for a given site in a separate subdirectory. The usual name for such a directory on UNIX platforms is \cgi-bin—but you don't have to use this name, you can use anything you like. The point is that it's safer to segregate your CGI scripts and executables from your static HTML content, especially if you have executable (.exe) CGI apps and not just scripts.

- If your CGI apps are executables (.exe), give the \cgi-bin directory Scripts And Executables as their execute permission on the Directory tab of the \cgi-bin properties sheet. If your apps are scripts (for example, .pl for Perl scripts), instead give the \cgi-bin directory Scripts Only permission and make sure you have installed and properly configured the necessary script engine (for example, perl.exe) and set up the appropriate application mappings, making sure that you select the Script Engine check box on the Application Extension Mapping dialog box for the CGI extension you're using (such as .pl).

- Don't forget to enable your CGI extensions using WSE if you want your CGI applications to run. You can do this either by manually adding the appropriate extension to the WSE screen or by allowing all CGI extensions to run—I'll discuss the difference in Chapter 10.

CHALLENGE

You plan to deploy an e-commerce application on IIS that will accept orders and process them. Which application architecture would you use to develop your application: ASP, ASP.NET, ISAPI, or CGI? Explain the reasons behind your choice. Would you run IIS in worker process isolation mode or IIS 5 isolation mode? What is the advantage of the mode you would choose? What special features of IIS 6 would make this a better platform for deploying your app than earlier versions of IIS?

CHECKLIST: ADMINISTERING APPLICATIONS

Check off each task relating to administering applications on IIS 6 as you become familiar with how to perform it:

- ☐ Switching IIS between worker process isolation mode and IIS 5 isolation mode
- ☐ Enabling dynamic content on IIS using the Web Service Extensions (WSE) node in IIS Manager
- ☐ Using the Default Application to deploy an ASP or ASP.NET application
- ☐ Creating application pools and assigning applications to different pools
- ☐ Creating a root-level application
- ☐ Creating a virtual directory–level application
- ☐ Unloading an application from memory
- ☐ Configuring an application at the server, site, and virtual directory level
- ☐ Displaying and modifying application mappings
- ☐ Creating a new application mapping
- ☐ Configuring session timeouts, the default scripting language, and script timeouts for ASP or ASP.NET applications
- ☐ Installing and configuring the execution order of ISAPI filters
- ☐ Creating wildcard application mappings
- ☐ Configuring CGI applications to run on IIS

CHAPTER 9

Creating and Configuring FTP Sites

IS 6 is more than just a platform for hosting websites and applications—it can also be used as an FTP server to provide users with a place to upload and download their files across a corporate intranet or over the Internet. In this chapter, we'll look at how to create and configure FTP sites and cover the new features of FTP in IIS 6.

INSTALLING THE FTP SERVICE

Before you can use IIS as an FTP server, you first have to install the File Transfer Protocol (FTP) Service component of IIS because it is *not* included in a default installation of IIS 6. Installing the FTP Service is simple: open Control Panel and select Add/Remove Programs, choose Add/Remove Windows Components, select Application Server, click Details, select Internet Information Services (IIS), choose File Transfer Protocol (FTP) Service, and click OK. You may be prompted for the Windows Server 2003 installation files, so have your product CD-ROM or installation distribution point handy.

TIP Make sure to perform the preceding steps when your IIS machine is not under use because users may lose connections to websites running on IIS while the FTP Service is being installed. If you have IIS Manager running when you install FTP, the console will lose its connection to the server and you'll have to reconnect or reopen the console to begin managing your FTP sites.

FTP Features in IIS 6

Before you start working with FTP Service, you should know about the changes and improvements to it in IIS 6:

- **FTP User Isolation**   This is new to IIS 6 and is a way of setting up FTP for large service providers like ISPs and ASPs. It allows users to use FTP to upload content to home directories on an IIS 6 FTP server. Each user's home directory is actually a subdirectory of a single FTP site running on the server, but the nice thing is that to each user, their home directory behaves as if it's the root or top-level directory of the FTP server. This way, users cannot go higher in the directory tree than their home directory, and therefore cannot view or modify content in each other's home directories. We'll look at how to implement this feature later in this chapter in the section entitled "Using FTP User Isolation."

- **Server-to-Server FTP Transfer**   This advanced feature lets a user transfer files between two remote FTP servers. It's been around since IIS 4 but is configured differently now, and we'll look at how to perform this later in this chapter in the section entitled "Using Server-to-Server FTP Transfer."

- **FTP Restart**   This feature is new to IIS 6 and allows users to resume interrupted file transfers without having to start over from the beginning. It's an especially useful feature for sites where the files being transferred are large, such as medical images or multimedia files. For this to work, however, the FTP client used must support this feature, and unfortunately the Windows command-line FTP client doesn't support FTP Restart.

- **Active/Passive FTP connections**   IIS 6 supports both types of RCF-compliant FTP connection modes: Active (also called Standard or PORT) and Passive (or PASV). This flexibility helps you perform file transfers through firewalls and proxy servers, provided you configure their port settings correctly. As far as Microsoft FTP clients are concerned, the command-line version of FTP supports only active transfers, while Internet Explorer version 5.5 or later supports both modes (earlier versions of IE support only passive transfers). You can change the FTP connection mode in IE by selecting Tools | Internet Options, clicking Advanced, and selecting the Enable Folder View for FTP Sites check box to configure IE to operate as a standard mode FTP client. To switch to passive mode, clear the Enable Folder View for FTP Sites check box and select the Use Passive FTP check box.

CONFIGURING THE DEFAULT FTP SITE

Once you've installed the FTP Service, it's easy to start using it because IIS automatically creates a Default FTP Site. Users can immediately use this to upload or download content (see Figure 9-1). Configuring the Default FTP Site is even simpler than configuring the Default Web Site (see Chapter 7, "Creating and Configuring Websites"), since FTP sites have fewer configuration options than websites do. And, like the WWW Service on IIS, the FTP Service can be configured using properties sheets at several levels, though for FTP there are fewer levels than WWW:

- **FTP Sites level**   By right-clicking the FTP Sites node in IIS Manager and selecting Properties, you can open the FTP Sites properties sheet, which allows you to configure settings globally for all FTP sites running on your server.

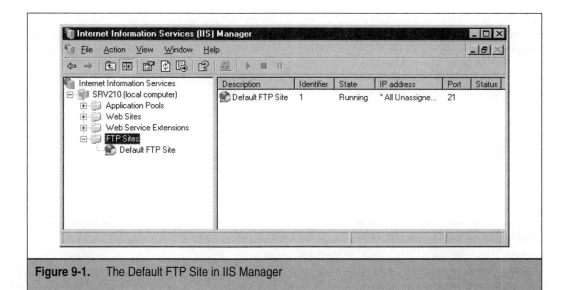

Figure 9-1.   The Default FTP Site in IIS Manager

- **FTP Site level** The properties sheet for individual FTP sites like the Default FTP Site lets you configure settings specifically for that site alone.

- **Virtual Directory level** The properties sheet for a virtual directory within an FTP site lets you configure settings specifically for that directory alone.

NOTE While the WWW Service lets you configure settings at the file level for individual web pages, this is not the case for the FTP Services. In fact, neither files nor physical directories are displayed when you select an FTP site in IIS Manager; only FTP sites and virtual directories are displayed and can be configured.

Just as we did for websites in Chapter 7, we'll first look at the big picture of how to configure FTP sites and their directories and files. Table 9-1 shows which tabs appear on the properties sheets for each configuration level just described.

NOTE Like the WWW Service, when you configure FTP settings at higher levels, they are inherited at lower levels; and if you configure settings at lower levels, they override settings at higher levels. Also, if you change a lower-level setting and then try to change the same setting at a higher level, you are prompted to choose whether your higher-level change should overwrite the previously changed lower-level one.

Location of Content

Let's begin our look at configuring the Default FTP Site by examining the location for storing its content. By default, the home directory for the Default FTP Site is C:\ Inetpub\ftproot, but it can be modified using the Home Directory tab of the Default FTP Site properties sheet (Figure 9-2).

Like websites (covered in Chapter 7), FTP sites can use either a local directory or a network share for the location of their home directory. If a network share is selected, it must be specified as a UNC path, and credentials must be specified for accessing the

Name of Tab	FTP Sites Level	FTP Site Level	Virtual Directory Level
FTP Site	√	√	
Security Accounts	√	√	
Messages	√	√	
Home Directory	√	√	√*
Directory Security	√	√	√

*This tab is called Virtual Directory for virtual directories.

Table 9-1. Tabs on IIS Properties Sheets of Different Levels (FTP)

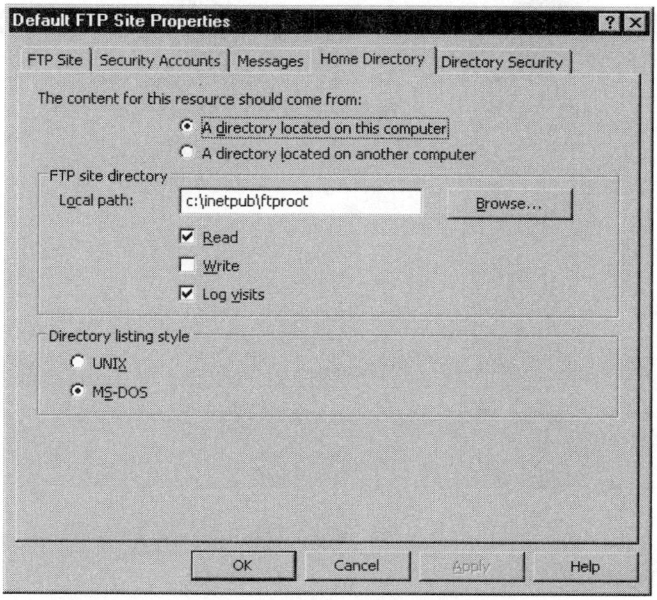

Figure 9-2.   Specifying the content location for the Default FTP Site

share. These credentials can be either a specific user account (local or domain user, depending on whether the server is part of a workgroup or domain), or you can use the credentials of the authenticated user (the user running the FTP client and accessing the FTP site on IIS).

> **TIP**   You can also change the home directory of an FTP site by editing the metabase, as you'll see in Chapter 14, "Working with the Metabase."

Take a moment to test your Default FTP Site by creating a text file called test.txt that contains the sentence, "The quick brown fox…" and placing it in the folder C:\ Inetpub\ftproot. Now, start Internet Explorer on your IIS machine and open the URL ftp://localhost. The test.txt file should be displayed in the browser window (Figure 9-3).

> **TIP**   When you select the Default FTP Site in IIS Manager, the file test.txt isn't displayed in the right pane of the console. However, if you right-click the Default FTP Site and select Browse or Explorer, you can see that the file is indeed there.

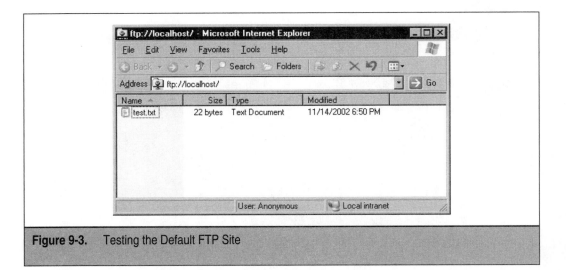

Figure 9-3. Testing the Default FTP Site

Virtual Directories

To make files available to your users for download from the Default FTP Site, simply use Windows Explorer to copy them (or use xcopy from the command line) from wherever the files are currently located to C:\Inetpub\ftproot, the home directory of the Default FTP Site. Alternatively, if the files you want to make available to users are stored in a different directory on the server or on a file server somewhere on your network, you can create a virtual directory within the Default FTP Site and map the alias of this virtual directory to the physical directory or network share where the files are currently stored.

You should be familiar with virtual directories from Chapter 7, so try the following walkthrough. Create a folder C:\moreftp on your IIS machine and create a text file moretest.txt in this directory (this file can contain the sentence "…jumps over…," if you like). Now right-click the Default FTP Site and select New | Virtual Directory to start the Virtual Directory Creation Wizard. Go through the wizard. Specify More for the directory's alias and C:\moreftp as the physical directory represented by this alias, and leave the directory permissions set at their default Read setting. When the wizard is finished, the new virtual directory is displayed in IIS Manager as expected (Figure 9-4).

Accessing Virtual Directories

Now here's a difference between browsing FTP and websites: when you open the URL ftp://localhost on your machine again after creating the /more virtual directory in the preceding, the contents of your FTP site will still appear to be the same as before (see Figure 9-3 again). Virtual directories don't show up when browsing an FTP site with Internet Explorer, so users won't be aware of the virtual directory unless you tell them

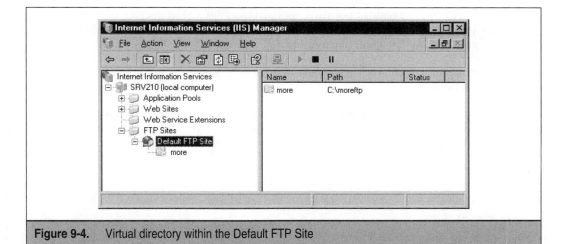

Figure 9-4.   Virtual directory within the Default FTP Site

about it! Once they know about the virtual directory, however, they can display its contents by opening the appropriate URL (on the local IIS machine, this would be ftp://localhost/more).

The same is true for any other FTP client, including the command-line FTP client included in all versions of Windows. Here's an example of a command-line session on the FTP server with a play-by-play commentary of what's going on:

```
C:\>ftp
ftp> open localhost
Connected to localhost.
220 Microsoft FTP Service
User (localhost:(none)): anonymous
331 Anonymous access allowed, send identity (e-mail name) as password.
Password:
230 Anonymous user logged in.
```

You're now logged on to the Default FTP Site as an anonymous user. Now do a directory listing of the FTP site's home directory using the list (ls) command and see what you find to download:

```
ftp> ls
200 PORT command successful.
150 Opening ASCII mode data connection for file list.
test.txt
226 Transfer complete.
ftp: 10 bytes received in 0.00Seconds 10000.00Kbytes/sec.
```

Notice that your old file test.txt is sitting there in the root FTP directory of the site, but the /more virtual directory isn't displayed. It's there, though, and you can switch to this directory by using the change directory (cd) command:

```
ftp> cd more
250 CWD command successful.
```

You're in the /more virtual directory now (as you'd expect of a virtual directory, it appears like a subdirectory of the FTP site's root directory), so see what's in this directory:

```
ftp> ls
200 PORT command successful.
150 Opening ASCII mode data connection for file list.
moretext.txt
226 Transfer complete.
ftp: 14 bytes received in 0.00Seconds 14000.00Kbytes/sec.
```

There's the moretext.txt file! Grab it and download it to your local system's current directory C:\, and then do a dir to verify the download worked after you log off from the Default FTP Site and end your FTP client session:

```
ftp> get moretext.txt
200 PORT command successful.
150 Opening ASCII mode data connection for moretext.txt(17 bytes).
226 Transfer complete.
ftp: 17 bytes received in 0.00Seconds 17000.00Kbytes/sec.
ftp> close
221
ftp> quit

C:\>dir m*
 Volume in drive C has no label.
 Volume Serial Number is 5CA7-A222

 Directory of C:\

11/04/2002  11:38 PM    <DIR>          management
11/14/2002  06:55 PM    <DIR>          moreftp
11/14/2002  07:15 PM                17 moretext.txt
              1 File(s)             17 bytes
              2 Dir(s)   4,075,888,640 bytes free

C:\>
```

Accessing Physical Subdirectories

You've seen how virtual directories work in FTP sites, but how about physical directories? Let's now use Windows Explorer to create the subdirectory C:\Inetpub\ftproot\less, and then create a text file called lesstest.txt that says "…the lazy dog…" within the \less directory. Now switch to IIS Manager again and press F5 to refresh the view of the Default FTP Site's contents. Notice that it still looks exactly like Figure 9-4—in other words, virtual directories of FTP sites are displayed in IIS Manager but physical subdirectories of an FTP site's home directory are *not* displayed!

TIP However, if you right-click the FTP site and select Browse or Explorer, physical subdirectories and files *are* displayed in the details pane—but virtual subdirectories are not!!

Now open the URL http://localhost again using IE, and this time notice that the folder \less shows up in the directory listing of the Default FTP Site's home directory (Figure 9-5). Double-click the \less directory to view the directory's contents and read or download the file in it. Now, here's a question for you: what if you ran through the same command-line FTP session you did previously? Would the \less directory show up when you did the first ls of the root directory's contents?

Other Configuration Tasks

Once you've decided on the location of the root or home directory for the Default FTP Site, there are a few other configuration tasks you can perform for the site. Some of these are performed using the properties sheet for the Default FTP Site, while others

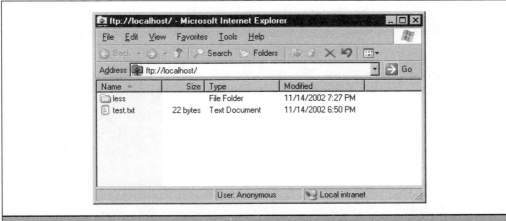

Figure 9-5. Physical directories are displayed in FTP client directory listings.

are performed by right-clicking the node for the site in IIS Manager. We'll take a look at some of these tasks here, but I'll defer a discussion of FTP settings relating to security, performance, and maintenance until Chapter 10, "Securing IIS," Chapter 12, "Performance Tuning and Maintenance," and Chapter 13, "Maintenance and Troubleshooting."

Default FTP Site Identity

By modifying the Description field on the FTP Site tab, you can give the site a different "friendly name" than Default FTP Site. Note, however, that this name is only displayed in IIS Manager and is not used for anything else. For the IP address and port settings, as you'd expect, the Default FTP Site has (All Unassigned) as its IP address, and the meaning of this is the same as it was for the Default Web Site as explained in Chapter 7. I'll talk more about FTP site identity later in this chapter when we discuss how to create additional FTP sites on your server in the section entitled "Creating Additional FTP Sites."

Directory Listing Style

On the Home Directory tab (refer back to Figure 9-2 again) you can choose between two different directory listing styles: UNIX and MS-DOS. The choice you make here determines the format in which results are displayed when your FTP client issues a list (ls) command. If you have mostly Windows clients accessing your site, leave the setting as MS-DOS, which is the default.

FTP Messages

On the Messages tab (see Figure 9-6), you can specify messages that will be sent to your FTP clients under certain conditions:

- **Banner** This message appears when the user tries to access the site but before the user logs on (if anonymous users are allowed to access the site, the banner message will not be displayed).

- **Welcome** This message appears immediately after the user logs on to the site.

- **Exit** This message appears after the user logs off the site.

- **Maximum Connections** This message is displayed when a user tries to access an FTP site that already has the maximum number of users connected to it.

Here's a transcript of a command-line FTP session showing how these four messages might work. To make the Maximum Connections message appear, I configured the FTP Site Connections setting on the FTP Site tab to limit the number of client connections to the site to only one connection.

```
C:\>ftp
ftp> open localhost
Connected to localhost.
220-Microsoft FTP Service
220 YOU ARE ABOUT TO ENTER MY SITE...
```

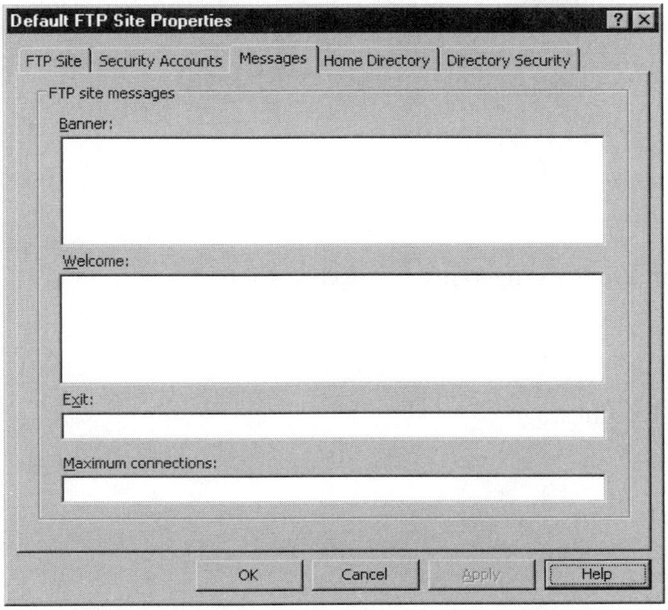

Figure 9-6. Specifying FTP messages

There's the Banner message showing up.

```
User (localhost:(none)): anonymous
331 Anonymous access allowed, send identity (e-mail name) as password.
Password:
230-YOU MADE IT IN, CONGRATULATIONS!
```

And there's the Welcome message.

```
230 Anonymous user logged in.
ftp> !
```

The ! (exclamation mark) command temporarily breaks out of the FTP command-line session back to the Windows command interpreter, which gives me the opportunity of trying to open another FTP session with the server.

```
Microsoft Windows [Version 5.2.3678]
(C) Copyright 1985-2002 Microsoft Corp.

C:\>ftp
ftp> open localhost
```

```
Connected to localhost.
421 SORRY, I'VE GOT FRIENDS OVER RIGHT NOW.
```

There's the Maximum Connections message as expected.

```
Connection closed by remote host.
ftp> quit
```

```
C:\>exit
```

The exit command returns me to my first FTP session.

```
ftp> close
221 THANKS FOR DROPPING BY!
```

And there's the Exit message.

```
ftp> quit
```

```
C:\>
```

Other Tasks

You can stop and start (or pause and resume) FTP sites using IIS Manager. You can also save the metabase configuration of a site to an XML file and import it into a different site or server. These functions work the same way websites do, as we discussed in Chapter 7.

CREATING ADDITIONAL FTP SITES

Just as you can create multiple websites on an IIS machine, you can also create multiple FTP sites if the need arises. FTP sites are created by right-clicking the FTP Sites node in IIS Manager and selecting New | FTP Site, which starts the FTP Site Creation Wizard. After specifying a friendly name to display in IIS Manager for your new site, the next screen asks you to specify IP address and port settings for the site (see Figure 9-7).

Let's pause for a moment and talk about FTP site identity. In Chapter 7, you saw that websites are identified by three parameters (IP address, port number, and host header name) and that two websites running on the same machine must differ in at least one of these parameters (otherwise one of them won't start). FTP sites are simpler, however, and are only identified by two parameters: IP address and port number (host header names are not part of the FTP specification). The usual approach if you want to host multiple FTP sites on a single server is to assign each site a different IP address and leave all their port numbers set to the default port 21. This way, clients can connect to the sites without needing to include the port number in their URLs. Because the Default FTP Site already has All Unassigned as its IP address setting, change the IP address for this new site to one of the IP addresses assigned to your server and click Next to continue the wizard.

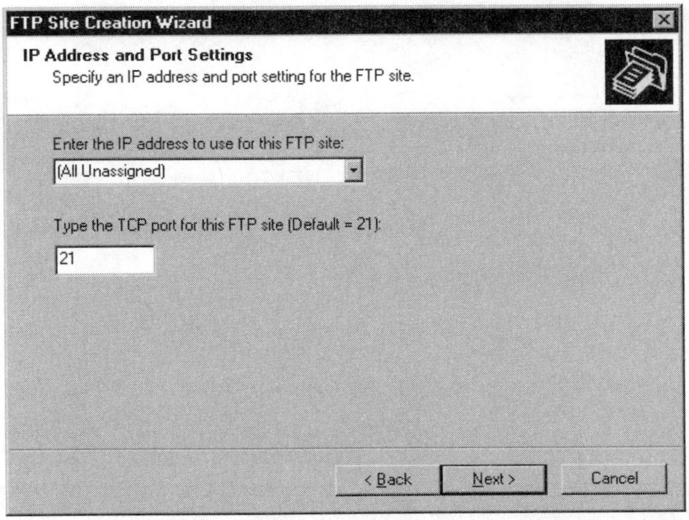

Figure 9-7. Specifying IP address and port settings for a new FTP site

---

NOTE If you do want to identify a new FTP site using a different port number than the default port 21, choose a port number above 1023 so you don't conflict with any of the well-known port numbers for recognized network services.

The next screen of the wizard asks you if you want to configure the new FTP User Isolation feature of IIS 6 for this new FTP site. We'll cover this topic later in this chapter, so for now select the default option Do Not Isolate Users, and click Next to continue.

The next screen asks you to specify the location of your new site's home directory. Click Browse and choose a folder on your local file system or create a new folder if desired. You cannot enter a UNC path to a network share here, but you can configure this option later once the site is created if you want to.

The final screen of the wizard asks you to specify FTP Site Access Permissions, with the default being read-only. I'll talk more about FTP permissions when I cover IIS security in Chapter 10. Once the wizard is finished, your new FTP site will be displayed under the FTP Sites node in IIS Manager (see Figure 9-8).

NOTE You can also create FTP sites and virtual directories beneath them from the command line using administrative scripts included with IIS 6. We'll cover this later in Chapter 11, "Working from the Command-Line," when we discuss command-line administration of IIS.

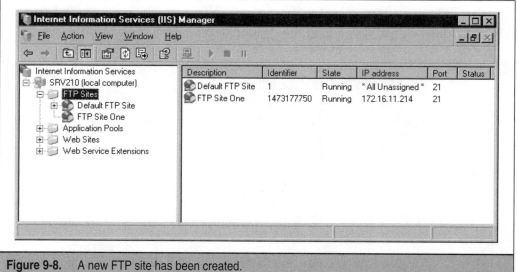

Figure 9-8. A new FTP site has been created.

USING FTP USER ISOLATION

I explained the new FTP User Isolation feature of IIS 6 earlier in this chapter, so let's try it out here and see how it works. Create another new FTP site on your server. This time, when you get to the FTP User Isolation screen of the wizard, pause and examine the options presented (see Figure 9-9):

- **Do Not Isolate Users**   If you choose this option, you will create a traditional FTP site where all users have the same level of access to the root directory and all subdirectories under it. If you create individual subdirectories for each user under root (/), then users will be able to snoop around and examine the contents of each other's directories. This option is fine if the site is a public one that is mainly used for downloading files, but it certainly won't work in an ISP environment when users are uploading content to their websites using FTP!

- **Isolate Users**   This option means that users are first authenticated against local or domain accounts (depending on whether your FTP server is part of a workgroup or a domain) and then granted access to their home directories once successfully authenticated. Home directories for users must be directly beneath a folder called LocalUser that itself is directly beneath the root directory for the FTP site, and the name of each user's home directory must match their associated username. Once this directory structure is in place, IIS enforces FTP user isolation, and each user will see their subdirectory as the root directory of the FTP server, with the result that they won't be able to access each other's home directories.

- **Isolate Users Using Active Directory**   This is essentially the same as the previous option except that domain accounts are authenticated against a container in Active Directory rather than Active Directory as a whole. This improves the performance of FTP User Isolation considerably when large numbers of home directories have been created for your FTP site.

TIP   If you enable FTP User Isolation for an FTP site, you can allow all users to access a public directory in the site by creating a virtual directory for this purpose.

Let's test this feature in a simple workgroup setting. First, create the following local user accounts on a stand-alone IIS machine using Local Users And Groups in Computer Management:

- Bob Smith (username bsmith)
- Ted Jones (username tjones)
- Alice B. Toklas (username atoklas)

Now create the directory structure on your IIS machine as shown in Table 9-2.

In addition to the physical directories outlined in Table 9-2, create a virtual directory for your FTP site, giving it the alias /shared and mapping it to the folder C:\shared on the server (the folder contains a file named shared.txt).

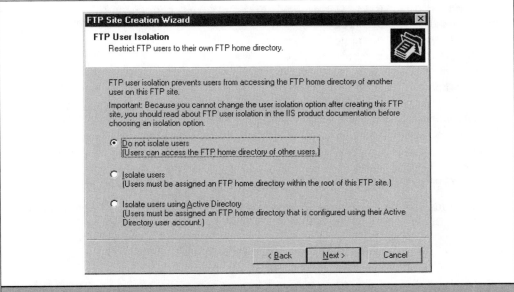

Figure 9-9.   Enabling FTP User Isolation for a new FTP site

Directory	Description
C:\ftpstuff	Home directory for FTP site on which FTP User Isolation is enabled.
C:\ftpstuff\LocalUser	This directory must be created to contain user directories.
C:\ftpstuff\LocalUser\bsmith	Home directory for user Bob Smith, contains the file bob.txt.
C:\ftpstuff\LocalUser\tjones	Home directory for user Ted Jones, contains the file ted.txt.
C:\ftpstuff\LocalUser\atoklas	Home directory for user Alice B. Toklas, contains the file alice.txt.
C:\ftpstuff\LocalUser\Public	Home directory for anonymous users, contains the file pub.txt.

Table 9-2. Directory Structure for Implementing FTP User Isolation

If FTP User Isolation works, then

- Bob should be able to access his home directory and /shared.
- Ted should be able to access his home directory and /shared.
- Alice should be able to access his home directory and /shared.
- Anonymous users should be able to access the Public directory and /shared.

I tested this in the following FTP session:

```
C:\>ftp 172.16.11.210
Connected to 172.16.11.210.
220 Microsoft FTP Service
User (172.16.11.210:(none)): bsmith
331 Password required for bsmith.
Password:
230 User bsmith logged in.
ftp> ls
200 PORT command successful.
150 Opening ASCII mode data connection for file list.
bob.txt
226 Transfer complete.
ftp: 9 bytes received in 0.00Seconds 9000.00Kbytes/sec.
```

Bob is obviously in his own home directory, so let's see if he can move upward to the LocalUser directory to view the contents of other users' home directories:

```
ftp> cd ..
250 CWD command successful.
ftp> ls
```

```
200 PORT command successful.
150 Opening ASCII mode data connection for file list.
bob.txt
226 Transfer complete.
ftp: 9 bytes received in 0.00Seconds 9000.00Kbytes/sec.
```

It didn't work. Bob is still in his home directory. Clearly, users' home directories are isolated from each other on this FTP site. Bob should be able to change to the /shared virtual directory. Let's see if he can do so:

```
ftp> cd shared
250 CWD command successful.
ftp> ls
200 PORT command successful.
150 Opening ASCII mode data connection for file list.
shared.txt
226 Transfer complete.
ftp: 12 bytes received in 0.00Seconds 12000.00Kbytes/sec.
```

That worked. Let's break out of Bob's FTP session and start another session, this time for an anonymous user:

```
ftp> !
Microsoft Windows [Version 5.2.3678]
(C) Copyright 1985-2002 Microsoft Corp.

C:\>ftp 172.16.11.210
Connected to 172.16.11.210.
220 Microsoft FTP Service
User (172.16.11.210:(none)): anonymous
331 Anonymous access allowed, send identity (e-mail name) as password.
Password:
230 Anonymous user logged in.
ftp> ls
200 PORT command successful.
150 Opening ASCII mode data connection for file list.
pub.txt
226 Transfer complete.
ftp: 9 bytes received in 0.00Seconds 9000.00Kbytes/sec.
```

As expected, anonymous users find themselves in the Public directory as their home directory. Further testing shows that anonymous users are restricted to this Public directory, except they can also access the /shared virtual directory.

Pretty cool!

USING SERVER-TO-SERVER FTP TRANSFER

Another new feature of IIS 6 is that you can actually control the transfer of files between two FTP servers from another computer, typically an administrator's workstation. Before I explain this, I should note that for security reasons (FTP passes all credentials in clear text), you shouldn't perform this task when the transfer must take place over an Internet connection.

To illustrate this, I have two FTP servers set up, both with Default FTP Sites configured on them as follows:

- Server A has IP address 172.16.11.210.
- Server B has IP address 172.16.11.220.

Furthermore, files are going to be transferred from Server A to Server B. Specifically, a file named test.txt resides in the home directory on Server A, and your job will be to transfer it to Server B using an FTP session initiated on Workstation C. First, you have to change a Registry setting on each server to enable the transfer to be performed. On Server A, open Registry Editor and find the following key:

```
HKLM\System\CurrentControlSet\Services\MSFTPSVC\Parameters
```

Create a DWORD value named EnableDataConnTo3rdIP with a data value of 1. Then go to Server B and create a DWORD value named EnablePasvConnFrom3rdIP in the same location and give it the same data value of 1. Finally, open IIS Manager on Server B, switch to the Home Directory tab, and enable Write permission so files can be uploaded to the server.

You're ready—switch to Workstation C and let's do some rather esoteric FTP work. Open up two command prompts, one for an FTP session with Server A and another for an FTP session with Server B. For simplicity, I've combined the two sessions here to show the order in which commands need to be issued, and the session with Server B is in italics:

```
C:\>ftp 172.16.11.210
Connected to 172.16.11.210.
220 Microsoft FTP Service
User (172.16.11.210:(none)): anonymous
331 Anonymous access allowed, send identity (e-mail name) as password.
Password:
230 Anonymous user logged in.
```

Session A (the session with Server A) has been established. Note that I have anonymous authentication enabled on my FTP servers, so I can actually perform the whole transfer as an anonymous user—not very secure; but I'm not covering IIS security until Chapter 10, so we won't worry about it for now.

```
c:\>ftp 172.16.11.220
Connected to 172.16.11.220.
220 Microsoft FTP Service
User (172.16.11.220:(none)): anonymous
331 Anonymous access allowed, send identity (e-mail name) as password.
Password:
230 Anonymous user logged in.
```

Session B has now been established.

```
ftp> literal pasv
227 Entering Passive Mode (172,16,11,220,15,118).
```

This command requests that Server B open a data port and wait for a connection (instead of initiating one upon receipt of a transfer command). The numbers in brackets represent the IP address and listening data port of Server B. I now need to open this same port from Server A:

```
ftp> literal port 172,16,11,220,15,118
200 PORT command successful.
```

This command tells Server A what data port Server B is listening on.

```
ftp> literal retr test.txt
150 Opening ASCII mode data connection for test.txt (22 bytes).
```

This begins the file transfer from Server A to Server B.

```
ftp> literal stor test.bin
125 Data connection already open; Transfer starting.
```

This tells Server B to accept the file transfer being initiated by Server A.

```
ftp> literal stat
226 Transfer complete.
```

This checks the status of the file transfer, and you can see that it has been completed. If I now right-click the Default FTP Site on Server B and select Browse, I can see that the file test.txt has indeed been transferred.

NOTE   For more information about literal, pasv, port, retr, stor, stat, and other esoteric FTP commands, see RFC 959 on the RFC Editor at www.rfc-editor.org.

CHALLENGE

You are a small ISP and plan to use IIS 6 as the web hosting platform for your customers. Users will be assigned home directories and will be able to FTP their web pages to these directories to create personal websites. What feature of FTP on IIS 6 simplifies your job? What kind of directory structure will you plan for your web and FTP site directories? What URL would a user open to access their personal website?

CHECKLIST: ADMINISTERING FTP SITES

Check off each of the following FTP administration tasks once you have learned how to perform them on a test IIS 6 system:

- ☐ Install the FTP service on an IIS machine.
- ☐ Configure the home directory of the Default FTP Site as either a local folder or a network share.
- ☐ Create physical and virtual directories within the Default FTP Site and access them using the Windows command-line FTP client.
- ☐ Create additional FTP sites on your server and assign them unique site identities.
- ☐ Configure the directory listing style appropriate for the FTP clients accessing your FTP server.
- ☐ Configure FTP banner, welcome, exit, and maximum connections messages.
- ☐ Stop, start, pause, and resume FTP sites and save their configuration to an XML file.
- ☐ Implement FTP User Isolation to give each user a private home directory.
- ☐ Perform a file transfer between two FTP servers from a workstation.

PART IV

*Advanced
Administration*

CHAPTER 10

Securing IIS

Now that you've learned how to perform basic IIS administration tasks such as creating and configuring websites, FTP sites, and applications, it's time to dig deeper into the platform and learn about more advanced administration topics including securing IIS, working from the command line, performance monitoring and tuning, working with the metabase, and so on. We'll begin by looking at how to secure IIS, focusing especially on websites hosting both static and dynamic content. And where better to start than the topic of permissions!

PERMISSIONS

Permissions form the foundation of securing any application or operating system platform. When referring to IIS, however, you have to be careful because there are two sets of permissions you must deal with:

- **NTFS permissions**   These are file system permissions that control who is able to access a file or folder and what level of access they have.
- **Web permissions**   These are special permissions that determine whether a web or FTP client can read files on an IIS website's home or virtual directory, write to the directory, browse the directory, and so on.

These permissions work differently, and we'll begin by examining how they operate and then look at what happens when you combine them together. But first I should note that there may be one other type of permissions used with IIS: shared folder permissions. These come into play when a website's home directory or a virtual directory has its content located in a shared folder on a network file server, and IIS maps the site name or directory alias to the share using its UNC path (see Chapter 7, "Creating and Configuring Websites," for information on how to do this). I'll discuss shared folder permissions briefly after I cover the other two types of permissions, NTFS and IIS.

NTFS Permissions

NTFS permissions are the bedrock of IIS security (and Windows Server 2003 security as well). Understanding NTFS permissions is therefore an essential prerequisite to being able to securely host static content and applications on your web server. I'll briefly review how NTFS permissions work and give some tips on using them to secure IIS. To make things more interesting, let's work with a concrete example and use C:\Inetpub\wwwroot, the home directory of the Default Web Site.

NTFS Permissions on \wwwroot

Open Windows Explorer, find the C:\Inetpub\wwwroot directory, right-click it to open its properties sheet, and select the Security tab (Figure 10-1). This displays the NTFS permissions configured on the \wwwroot directory. If you select each security principal (user or group account) in turn, you'll see that each of them has a unique

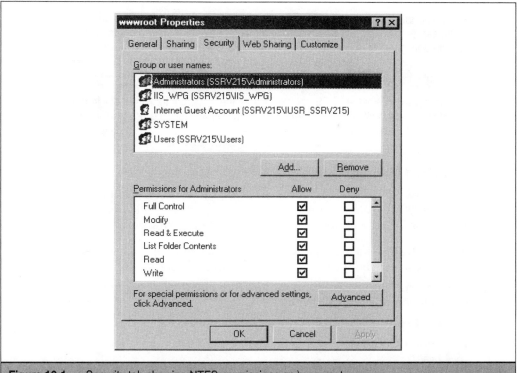

Figure 10-1. Security tab showing NTFS permissions on \wwwroot

set of permissions assigned to them as defined in Table 10-1. The settings in this table represent the access control list (ACL) configured for the \wwwroot file system object.

Security Principal	Full Control	Modify	Read & Execute	List Folder Contents	Read	Write
Administrators	Allow	Allow	Allow	Allow	Allow	Allow
IIS_WPG			Allow	Allow	Allow	
Internet Guest Account					Deny	
SYSTEM	Allow	Allow	Allow	Allow	Allow	Allow
Users			Allow	Allow	Allow	

Table 10-1. Default Permissions for \wwwroot

> **NOTE** The permissions for \wwwroot in Table 10-1 are the same whether the IIS machine is a standalone server (belongs to a workgroup) or a member server (part of a domain). The meaning of these permissions may differ however, for example, the Internet Guest Account is a local user account in a workgroup scenario and a domain user account when Active Directory is being used.

> **TIP** You can also access the NTFS permissions for the \wwwroot folder directly from IIS Manager by right-clicking the Default Web Site and selecting Permissions. This also works for virtual directories but not with individual files.

NTFS Standard Permissions

There are about two dozen NTFS permissions you can configure, but to simplify things Windows Server 2003 groups these into overlapping subsets called NTFS standard permissions. As listed in Table 10-1, there are six standard permissions you can configure:

- **Full Control**   Lets users add, modify, delete, and move files and their properties, and change permissions on files and subdirectories.
- **Modify**   Lets users view and modify files and their properties, and add or delete files to/from a directory.
- **Read & Execute**   Lets users run scripts and executable files.
- **List Folder Contents**   Lets users view the contents of a directory.
- **Read**   Lets users view files and their properties.
- **Write**   Lets users write files and their properties.

Note that some of these standard permissions appear as if they are incompatible with one another, as you will quickly find out if you try to configure them for a file or folder. The reason for this is not that the various standard permissions are incompatible but that as cumulative rather than atomic permissions they overlap somewhat. For example, create a New Folder on your desktop and open the Security tab of its properties sheet. Click Add and type **Users** to add the Users group to the folder's ACL, and note that by default the following permissions are allowed:

- Read & Execute
- List Folder Contents
- Read

Now try to clear only the Read & Execute check box, and note that the Read check box automatically clears also—as it must, because Read & Execute includes Read. Then select Allow Under Full Control, and note that all of the check boxes are automatically allowed. Here are some additional important things to note about NTFS permissions:

- NTFS permissions are only available on NTFS volumes. You should *always* keep your web or FTP site content stored on NTFS volumes, *never* on FAT or FAT32 volumes!

- NTFS permissions apply only to the security principal (user or group) they are granted to and only for the specific file system object (volume, folder, or file) they are applied to (unless they are inherited from above). For example, permissions assigned to the Administrators group for \wwwroot affect only members of that group and only for the \wwwroot folder.

- NTFS permissions secure files and folders for websites, FTP sites, local console access, and network access using UNC paths. In other words, NTFS permissions are a feature of the operating system and secure file system objects against *any* form of access, and not just for browsers accessing IIS websites.

- List Folder Contents applies to folders only, not files. In other words, there are six NTFS standard permissions you can use for folders and five for files.

- If you want more granular control over how users access your files and folders, you can configure NTFS special permissions by clicking the Advanced button in Figure 10-1. Note that NTFS special permissions can get quite complicated, however, and using them properly requires a good understanding of how NTFS works in Windows Server 2003 and is beyond the scope of this book.

- NTFS permissions can be either allowed or denied. For example, the Deny Write permission configured on the Internet Guest Account is a security measure that prevents anonymous users from being able to write to websites using WebDAV or some other method. Normally, however, Deny permissions are not recommended and configuring appropriate Allow permissions should suffice.

- If you create a web page within \wwwroot, the new page inherits the NTFS permissions of its parent directory \wwwroot.

- If you copy web content to \wwwroot from a folder on the same NTFS volume, the content inherits the NTFS permissions of \wwwroot. The same goes if you copy the content from a folder on a different NTFS volume.

- If you move web content to \wwwroot from a folder on the same NTFS volume, the content retains the NTFS permissions of its original folder. But if you move the content from a folder on a different NTFS volume, the content inherits the NTFS permissions of \wwwroot.

The last two items in the preceding list are import to remember if you are going to be moving content around on your web server using xcopy or some other method.

Security Principals

I mentioned security principals in the previous section, and what this term means is a Windows Server 2003 object that has a security identifier (SID) associated with it.

Typically, this means user accounts and groups, but it can also mean computer accounts if you are using Active Directory. In an intranet scenario, for example, you could configure NTFS permissions for individual computer accounts (or global groups containing computer accounts) in order to control access to IIS content based on which workstation a user is using.

In any case, let's look at the various security principals that have NTFS permissions configured for \wwwroot:

- **Administrators**   A local group in a workgroup scenario (or domain local group in an Active Directory scenario) for system administrators. Note that users of this group have full control over \wwwroot, and this is generally good practice and should not be changed, as it allows administrators to fix things should anything go wrong with the directory's permissions or content.

- **IIS_WPG**   This local (or domain local) group is new to IIS 6 and grants the necessary privileges required by user accounts used as process identities for worker processes servicing application pools. I'll discuss this in more detail later in the section "Configuring Application Pool Identities."

- **Internet Guest Account**   This local (or domain) user account has the name IUSR_*computername* where *computername* is the name of the local IIS machine. This account impersonates anonymous users to allow them access to web content on IIS when anonymous access is configured for the site (see the section "Anonymous Access" for more on this topic). The IUSR_*computername* account has a randomly generated password associated with it; and, generally, you should not try to change the password for this account because it might cause the metabase to get out of sync with Active Directory, resulting in content access problems that are difficult to troubleshoot. You can, however, create additional Internet Guest Accounts, and you can assign each site on your IIS machine a different such account, but this is not common practice.

- **SYSTEM**   This is a special identity or built-in group created by Windows Server 2003 and should always have full control of your web content directory.

- **Users**   This local (or domain local) group contains ordinary network users. By default, this group is assigned Read and Read & Execute permissions so that when ordinary users are properly authenticated using Integrated Windows Authentication (or some other method), they can view static content or execute scripts to generate dynamic content on the IIS machine.

NOTE   In IIS 6, the IUSR_*computername* account no longer requires the Log On Locally right, which makes this account more secure than in previous versions of IIS.

NTFS Permissions in IIS 5

For administrators familiar with IIS 5 on Windows 2000, you'll have noticed by now that the NTFS permissions on \wwwroot have significantly changed in this version. On IIS 5 the permissions on \wwwroot were as follows:

- Administrators: Full Control
- Everyone: Read & Execute
- SYSTEM: Full Control

Note the security improvements in IIS 6 over this old scheme:

- The Everyone special identity has been removed from the ACL for \wwwroot
- The Internet Guest Account has Write permission explicitly denied for \wwwroot.

Effective Permissions

Permissions problems can be tricky to troubleshoot, but fortunately Windows Server 2003 includes a new feature that lets you easily view the effective permissions assigned to a security principle for a file system object. Try this out: on the Security tab for \wwwroot properties, click Advanced and select the Effective Permissions tab (Figure 10-2).

Now click Select to open the Select User Or Group dialog box. Click Advanced, then Find Now, and scroll to select the IUSR_*computername* account. Click OK twice to return to the Effective Permissions tab and view the effective permissions for the Internet Guest Account. These permissions are

- Traverse Folder/Execute File
- List Folder/Read Data
- Read Attributes
- Read Extended Attributes
- Read Permissions

A little exploration will show that these are the same permissions assigned for \wwwroot to the Users group: Read & Execute permissions.

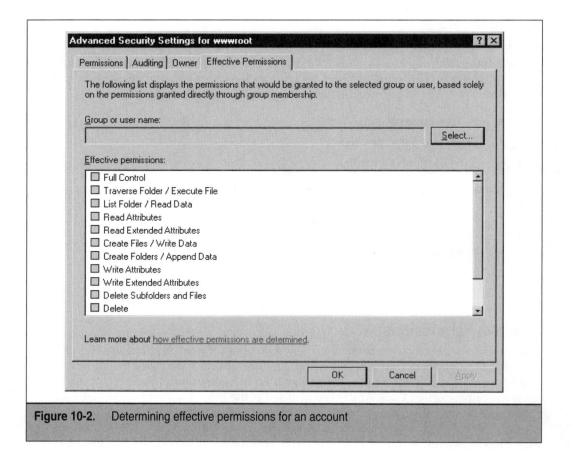

Figure 10-2. Determining effective permissions for an account

NTFS Permissions for New Websites

We've looked at NTFS permissions for the Default Web Site, but what about for new websites you create on your IIS machine? Try this: using IIS Manager, right-click the Web Sites node and select New | Web Site, and follow the prompts accepting the defaults. Be sure to assign the site an IP address; leaving it as All Unassigned will conflict with the Default Web Site, and the new site won't start. When asked where the home directory should be located, click Browse, select C: drive, click Make Folder, and create a folder named \stuff for the new site's home directory. Finish the wizard, and open the properties sheet for C:\stuff and view the Security tab. Here's what you find:

- Administrators have Full Control.
- Creator Owner has Special Permissions.
- System has Full Control.
- Users have Read & Execute.

Click Advanced to view the permissions in more detail, and you will see that most of them are inherited from the root directory of the C: drive. A few things to note:

- The Internet Guest Account does not have permissions explicitly assigned to it, but this is not really necessary because the account only impersonates anonymous users.

- The NTFS permissions on \stuff are the same regardless of what settings you select or deselect when running the Web Site Creation Wizard. For example, if you deselect the Allow Anonymous Access To This Site check box, the final NTFS permissions are the same, and only the web permissions change for the site. (We'll look at web permissions in the next section of this chapter.)

You might be wondering how anonymous users will be able to access content on your new website, as IUSR_*computername* is not listed on the Security tab as it was for the Default Web Site. The answer is that IUSR_*computername* is considered by Windows Server 2003 as belonging to the Authenticated Users built-in group. Authenticated Users is one of many special groups (or special identities) whose membership is controlled by the operating system and cannot be changed by administrators. And since Authenticated Users rolls up into the Users group, the permissions for Users are inherited by IUSR_*computername*, which gives anonymous users access to anything members of the Users group can access on your site.

If, on the other hand, you want *only* anonymous users to be able to access your site, you can remove the permissions allowed to Users and add IUSR_*computername* to your ACL. Then assign IUSR_*computername* suitable permissions such as Read or Read & Execute, depending on the type of content your site contains. By explicitly granting permissions to IUSR_*computername*, you grant anonymous users access to your site.

NOTE   If you create a new virtual directory within the Default Web Site, the NTFS permissions assigned to it by the Virtual Directory Wizard are the same as for a new website as just described.

Web Permissions

Another kind of permissions you need to be familiar with when securing content on IIS sites is web permissions (sometimes referred to as "IIS access permission" or "IIS permissions"). To configure web permissions for the Default Web Site, open the properties sheet for this site in IIS Manager and select the Home Directory tab (Figure 10-3).

There's nothing on this Home Directory tab that says "web permissions," but they're right there in the middle of the screen:

- **Read**   Lets users view or download files in the directory. You will almost always want to leave this checked so people can visit your site! An exception might be when you are making modifications to your site directly on a production server.

- **Write**   Lets users upload or modify files in the directory. This is needed, for example, when a user wants to upload files to the server using WebDAV, something we'll discuss in Chapter 16, "Publishing with IIS."

- **Directory Browsing**   Allows a directory listing to be returned to users when they browse a site that has no home page (no default document defined or present). Most of the time you will leave this cleared to prevent users from nosing around.

- **Script Source Access**   Selecting this in conjunction with Read lets users view the source code of ASP pages; in conjunction with Write, it enables them to modify ASP pages on your server. Not a good idea! Select this option only on development servers on isolated testbed networks when debugging ASP apps you are developing.

NOTE   If both the Read and Write check boxes are cleared, the Script Source Access check box will be unavailable.

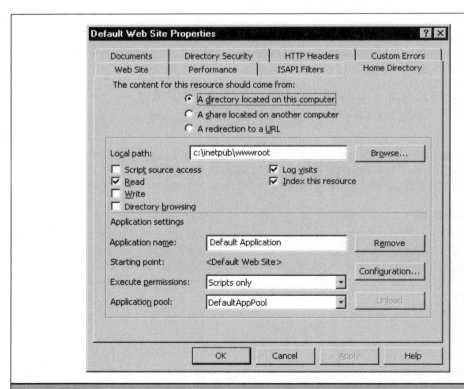

Figure 10-3.   Configuring web permissions for the Default Web Site

There are two other settings here that are sometimes also considered web permissions because of their proximity on this properties sheet to the preceding settings:

- **Log Visits**   Turns on logging for the site, provided logging is actually enabled on the Web Site tab. While logging visits to your site can indeed be a security issue because you can use web logs to discover malicious traffic patterns, it's not really a permissions issue, so I'll defer a discussion of this feature until Chapter 12, "Performance Tuning and Monitoring."

- **Index This Resource**   Causes the Content Indexing Service to create a full-text index of the site's content. You typically use this if you plan to include a search engine on your site; it has nothing to do with security or permissions.

Finally, note the Execute Permissions list box near the bottom of the Home Directory tab. This list relates to application permissions, which I'll talk about in the "Configuring Execute Permissions" section.

NOTE   "Web permissions" is somewhat of a misnomer, since Read and Write permissions, as well as Log Visits, are also available on the Home Directory tab of FTP site properties sheets.

Working with Web Permissions

Web permissions can be assigned at four levels. Remember, as stated in Chapter 7, you can configure IIS properties sheets at multiple levels. Web permissions can be configured for:

- **All websites using the Home Directory tab on the properties sheet for the Web Sites node**   The default web permissions at this level have none of the check boxes selected. Changes made here are inherited by all websites on the machine.

- **A particular website using the Home Directory tab on the properties sheet for that site**   The default web permissions for a site depend on the settings you select when running the Web Site Creation Wizard. For example, if you clear the default option of allowing Read permission when running the wizard, the check box for Read permission will be cleared on the Home Directory tab. Changes made at this level are inherited by all files and virtual directories in the site.

- **A particular directory (or virtual directory) using the Directory (or Virtual Directory) tab on the properties sheet for that directory (or virtual directory)**   The default web permissions for a virtual directory also depend on the choices you make when running the Virtual Directory Creating Wizard, while those for a directory inherit the settings of the parent (home) directory. Changes made at the directory (or virtual directory) level are inherited by all files within the directory (or virtual directory).

- **A particular file within a virtual directory using the File tab on the properties sheet for that file**

NOTE The first three levels of web permissions can also be configured for FTP sites.

How Web and NTFS Permissions Differ

Why are there two sets of permissions for securing websites? And what's the difference between the NTFS Read permission and the Read permission on the Home Directory tab for a site? All the difference in the world! Here's how they work under the hood:

- **NTFS permissions** When a user tries to access a web page located on an NTFS volume, an access token is first created using the user's SID. The token is then passed to the server, which compares the SID in the token to the SIDs in the ACL for the page. If a match is found, the user is granted the level of access specified in the ACL; and if no match is found, the user is denied access to the page.

- **Web permissions** When a user tries to access a web page on an IIS site, the user's browser issues an HTTP request with headers containing an HTTP verb that specifies the type of request being made. For example, an HTTP GET request is a request to read the page. For IIS to respond to such a request, it must have the Read web permission assigned to the page (that is, to the directory in which the page resides). Likewise, WebDAV uses HTTP LOCK and HTTP PROPFIND requests to publish content to your web server, and for this to work you must have Read, Write, and Directory Browsing web permissions enabled.

In conclusion, NTFS permissions are a characteristic of the Windows file system and are enforced by the operating system, while web permissions are a characteristic of HTTP and are enforced by IIS. There are other differences as well, the most important being that NTFS permissions apply *only* to the specific users and groups for which they are configured. For example, Users has Read & Execute permission, while Administrators has Full Control. If you want different groups of users to have different levels of access to your site's content, use NTFS permissions to achieve this. By contrast, web permissions apply equally to *all* users and groups for the site on which they are configured.

Combining NTFS and Web Permissions

What happens if your site's home directory has Read web permission but lacks Read NTFS permission for users needing to access it? Or what happens if the reverse is the case, and the directory has Read NTFS permission but lacks Read web permission? In both cases, users will not be able to access the site. Try this as an exercise: create a local user called Test with password "password" on your stand-alone server running IIS. Now open the properties sheet for the Default Web Site, switch to the Directory

Security tab, click Edit under Authentication And Access Control, and clear the check box to disable anonymous access. (I'll talk about IIS authentication methods in the upcoming section "Authentication.") Go to another machine on your network and type the URL for the Default Web Site on your IIS machine (usually http://*iismachinename* will do, where *iismachinename* is the NetBIOS or DNS name or IP address of your IIS machine). You should get an authentication dialog box, so enter the username and password for user Test to view the iisstart.htm "under construction" page.

Now remove the Read web permission for the site on the Home Directory tab of its properties sheet. Refresh the page on your client machine's browser, and you should see the message "HTTP Error 403.2—Forbidden: Read access is denied." Re-enable the Read web permission on the server, right-click the Default Web Site, and select Permissions to access the ACL for \wwwroot. Click Add, type Test, click Check Names, and click OK to add Test to the ACL for \wwwroot. Note that, by default, Test has Read & Execute permissions assigned (since Test belongs to the Users group which has these permissions). Override this by clicking the check box to Deny Read permission, and save the changes.

Now go back to your client machine and refresh your browser. This time the logon box will ask you three times for Test's credentials before finally returning the message "HTTP Error 401.3—Unauthorized: Access is denied due to an ACL set on the requested resource." Go back and remove Test from the ACL for the \wwwroot, and re-enable anonymous access for the Default Web Site.

What do you think happens if NTFS permissions for a site's home directory are Read and Write while its web permission is only Read? Or what if both Read and Write web permissions are enabled while NTFS is only Read? In both cases, users will only be able to read content on the site, not write to it. The general rule is if web and NTFS permissions differ, the more restrictive of the two applies. This is not to say web permissions replace NTFS permissions, they augment them by adding an additional layer of security on top of NTFS—modifying one has no effect on the other. The more important of the two types of permissions, however, is NTFS, which has much greater flexibility and granularity for securing file system resources including IIS content.

NOTE When a client tries to access a site, IIS first checks to see if web permissions will allow the requested level of access. If the answer is yes, IIS checks to see if NTFS permissions will allow access. I'll talk more about the order in which IIS processes security requests in the upcoming section "Putting It All Together."

Shared Folder Permissions

As if things weren't confusing enough, there's one more type of permission you may sometimes have to deal with in IIS: shared folder permissions. The only time these become important is when your website content is located on a different server from your IIS machine, such as on a network file server. In this case, as you saw previously in Chapter 7, you need to specify the UNC path on the Home Directory tab of your site's properties sheet so it points to the shared folder where the site's content resides.

This consideration also applies to FTP sites, as discussed previously in Chapter 9, "Creating and Configuring FTP Sites."

Fortunately, shared folder permissions are simpler than NTFS permissions, as they have only three possible settings:

- Read
- Change
- Full Control

In most cases, Read will suffice; but if Change or Full Control is required for applications to work, make sure your NTFS permissions are configured properly to prevent unauthorized access.

SECURITY ALERT   Never use an administrator account as credentials for accessing content stored on remote network shares. This goes for websites, FTP sites, and virtual directories. The usual setting is to use the default, that is, the authenticated user's credentials are used for accessing the site. Alternatively, specify some non-administrator account if required for accessing the share.

AUTHENTICATION

When users try to access web or FTP sites on IIS, they are "authenticated" to determine whether they should be allowed access to the content on the site. Authentication complements permissions as an essential part of securing any web or FTP site: it specifies *who* can access the site. Once users are authenticated for site access, permissions then determine *which* resources on the site they can access and *what* actions they can perform on those resources (view, modify, delete, upload, and so on).

IIS 6 offers a number of ways to authenticate users, including:

- Anonymous access
- Integrated Windows Authentication
- Digest Authentication
- Basic Authentication
- .NET Passport Authentication

All five of these authentication methods are available for websites on IIS, while only anonymous access and Basic Authentication are available for FTP sites.

TIP   FTP is inherently insecure because both the authentication process and data transfer occur in unencrypted form, so anyone sniffing the network can read your data and discover your password. If you must use FTP for transferring sensitive files over the Internet, consider using it over a tunneled connection using Point-to-Point Tunneling Protocol (PPTP) or IPSec protocol. A good alternative to FTP for secure file transfer is WebDAV, which can use SSL and is discussed in Chapter 16.

Configuring Authentication Methods

For websites, authentication methods can be configured at four levels:

- For the Web Sites node, with the Directory Security tab
- For an individual website such as the Default Web Site, with the Directory Security tab (Figure 10-4)
- For a virtual directory, with the Directory Security tab
- For an individual file, with the File Security tab

All five authentication methods are available for each of these levels. If you wanted to, you could make a site available to anonymous users but restrict access to a virtual directory within the site using Integrated Windows Authentication and control access to a single page within the site using .NET Passport—but this would make things this complicated!

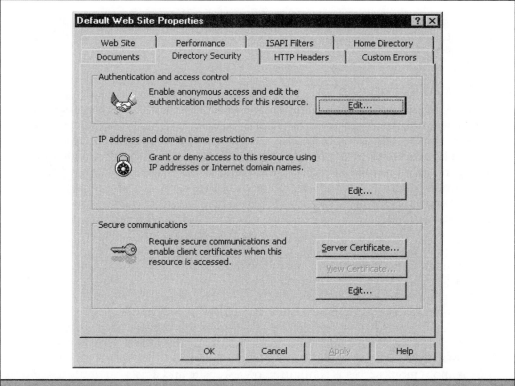

Figure 10-4.   Directory Security tab for Default Web Site

The usual website properties inheritance applies to configuring authentication methods. For example, if you enable Basic Authentication for a website and create a virtual directory within that site, it will automatically have Basic Authentication enabled as well, as will any individual pages within the site. You can override inheritance by configuring different authentication methods for files within directories or directories within sites.

One quirk to note concerning website property inheritance is that if you create a new website using the Web Site Creation Wizard, the authentication methods enabled for this new site will always be anonymous access and Integrated Windows Authentication, regardless of what authentication methods are configured on the Web Sites node. (If you change the authentication methods for the Web Sites node in the console tree, the change will be propagated to all websites on the machine.)

For FTP sites, authentication can only be configured at two levels:

- For the FTP Sites node, with the Security Accounts tab
- For an individual FTP site such as the Default FTP Site, with the Security Accounts tab

This means virtual directories and individual files within FTP sites cannot be secured with authentication; only the sites themselves (or all sites using the FTP Sites node) can be.

Anonymous Access

Anonymous access is designed to allow anonymous users (that is, everyone) access to content on a site. Anonymous access is intended mainly for public sites hosted on web servers directly connected to the Internet. For example, if your company wants to put up a public website with support information for your products, then anonymous access is perfect for this because it allows customers to access the site without any visible authentication process (that is, without needing to enter a userid and password). Anonymous access is therefore suitable for sites where security is not an issue—security from the perspective of *who* can access your site, that is; even with anonymous access, you still need NTFS and web permissions to control what visitors can *do* once they've gained access to your site!

Anonymous access is enabled by default on the Default Web Site and Default FTP Site. When you create a new website using the Web Site Creation Wizard, you can deselect the Allow Anonymous Access To This Site check box when running the wizard to create a new website that has Integrated Windows Authentication as its only authentication method. When you create a new FTP site using the FTP Site Creation Wizard, however, you don't have the option of disabling anonymous access but can do this after the site has been created if required.

When anonymous access is configured on a website and a user attempts to connect to your site, IIS assigns the Internet Guest Account (IUSR_*computername*) to the connection and uses this account as the security context for granting access to secured resources on

IIS 6 Administration

Blueprints

Table of Contents

Map of Properties sheets for configuring
Default Web Site and Default Application Pool

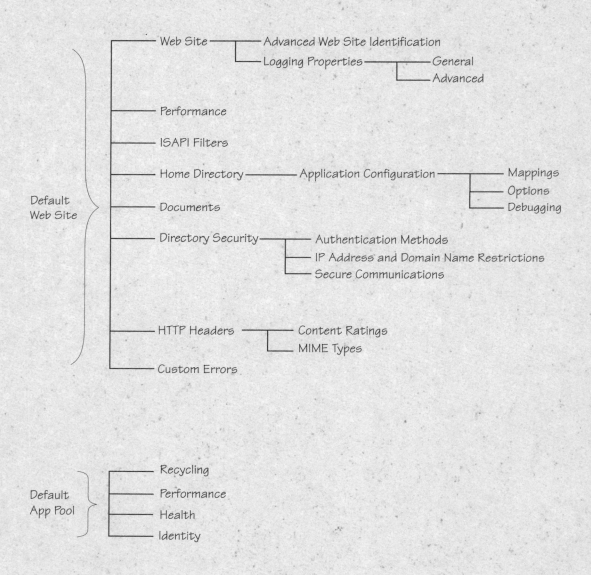

How IIS security allows or denies a client connection

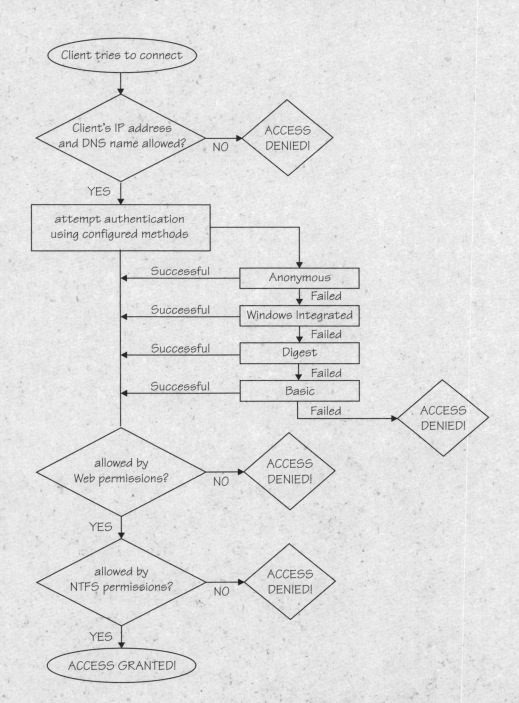

IIS 6 Architecture 1: Worker Process Isolation Mode

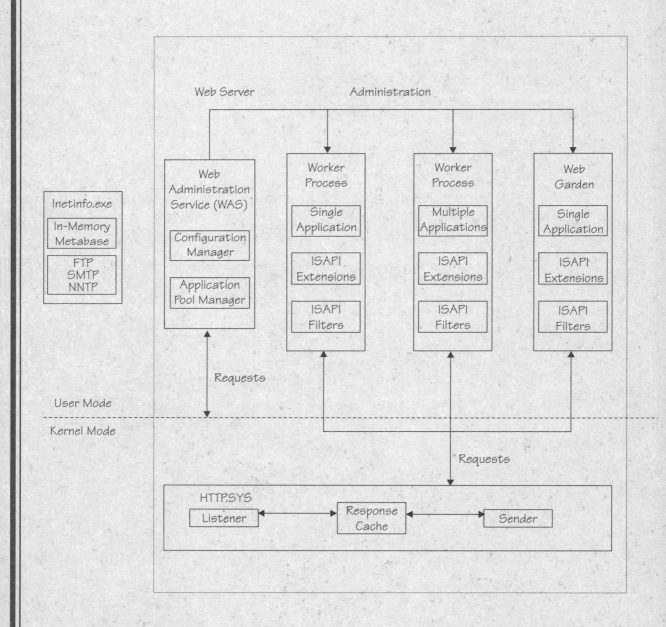

IIS 6 Architecture 2: IIS 5 Isolation Mode

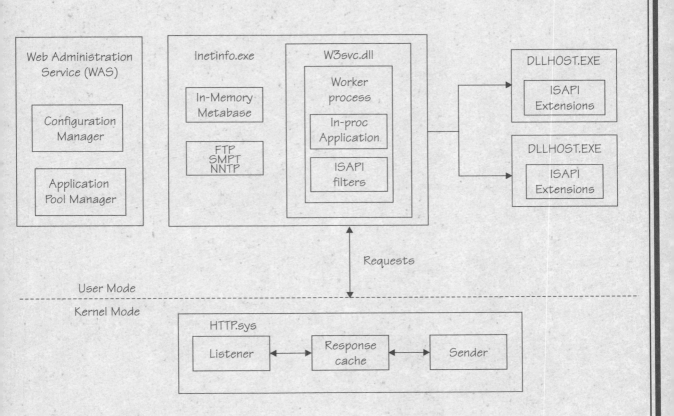

Evolution of Internet
Information Services (IIS)

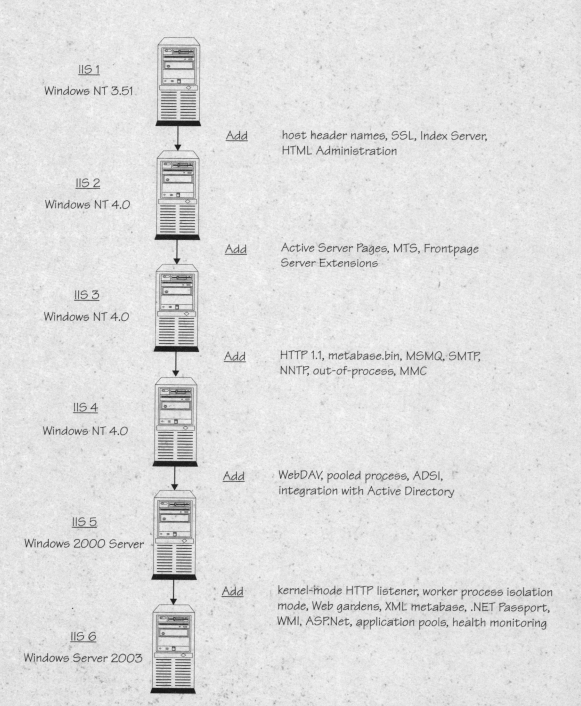

IIS 1

Windows NT 3.51

Add — host header names, SSL, Index Server, HTML Administration

IIS 2

Windows NT 4.0

Add — Active Server Pages, MTS, Frontpage Server Extensions

IIS 3

Windows NT 4.0

Add — HTTP 1.1, metabase.bin, MSMQ, SMTP, NNTP, out-of-process, MMC

IIS 4

Windows NT 4.0

Add — WebDAV, pooled process, ADSI, integration with Active Directory

IIS 5

Windows 2000 Server

Add — kernel-mode HTTP listener, worker process isolation mode, Web gardens, XML metabase, .NET Passport, WMI, ASP.Net, application pools, health monitoring

IIS 6

Windows Server 2003

Tools for administering IIS 6

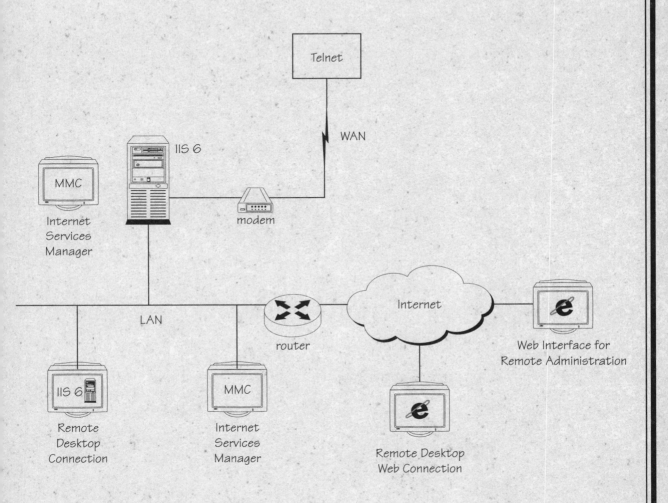

Telnet

WAN

IIS 6

MMC

Internet
Services
Manager

modem

LAN

router

Internet

IIS 6

Remote
Desktop
Connection

MMC

Internet
Services
Manager

Remote Desktop
Web Connection

Web Interface for
Remote Administration

Location of metabase keys and map
of hierarchical metabase namespace

Metabase Keys	Metabase Namespace
<?xml version ="1.0"?>	.
<configuration>	/
<MBProperty>	/LM
IIS_Global	/LM/IISADMIN
IIS_ROOT	/LM/IISADMIN/EXTENSIONS
IIsComputer	/LM/IISADMIN/EXTENSIONS/DCOMCLSIDS
IIsConfigObject	/LM/IISADMIN/PROPERTYREGISTRATION
IIsConfigObject...	/LM/Logging
IIsLogModules	/LM/Logging/Custom Logging
IIsCustomLogModule	/LM/Logging/Custom Logging/Date
IIsCustomLogModule...	/LM/Logging/Custom Logging/Extended Properties
IIsLogModule	/LM/Logging/Custom Logging/Time
IIsLogModule...	/LM/Logging/Microsoft IIS Log File Format
IIsMimeMap	/LM/Logging/NCSA Common Log File Format
IIsWebService	/LM/Logging/ODBC Logging
IIsWebServer	/LM/Logging/W3C Extended Log File Format
IIsFilters	/LM/MimeMap
IIsCertMapper	/LM/W3SVC
IIsWebVirtualDir	/LM/W3SVC/1
IIsWebServer	/LM/W3SVC/1/Filters
IIsFilters	/LM/W3SVC/1/IIsCertMapper
IIsWebVirtualDir	/LM/W3SVC/1/ROOT
IIsApplicationPools	/LM/W3SVC/388907640
IIsApplicationPool	/LM/W3SVC/388907640/filters
IIsFilters	/LM/W3SVC/388907640/root
IIsFilter	/LM/W3SVC/AppPools
IIsCompressionScheme	/LM/W3SVC/AppPools/DefaultAppPool
IIsCompressionScheme	/LM/W3SVC/Filters
IIsCompressionSchemes	/LM/W3SVC/Filters/Compression
IIsWebInfo	/LM/W3SVC/Filters/Compression/deflate
IIsConfigObject	/LM/W3SVC/Filters/Compression/gzip
IIsWebServer	/LM/W3SVC/Filters/Compression/Parameters
IIsWebVirtualDir	/LM/W3SVC/Info
IIsWebServer	/LM/W3SVC/Info/Templates
IIsWebVirtualDir	/LM/W3SVC/Info/Templates/Public Web Site
</MBProperty>	/LM/W3SVC/Info/Templates/Public Web Site/Root
</configuration>	/LM/W3SVC/Info/Templates/Secure Web Site
	/LM/W3SVC/Info/Templates/Secure Web Site/Root

the site. IUSR_*computername* is a member of the Guests group and its level of access to resources is determined by this membership.

SECURITY ALERT   Do not make the Internet Guest Account a member of any other group than Guests, and do not change the rights on guests or grant it permissions on any of your network resources, as this can constitute a weakness in your network security.

Enabling Anonymous Access for Websites

To enable anonymous access to a website (or virtual directory or file within a site), click the Edit button in the Authentication and Access Control section on the Directory Security (or File Security) tab (see Figure 10-4 again). Clicking this button opens the Authentication Methods dialog box (Figure 10-5).

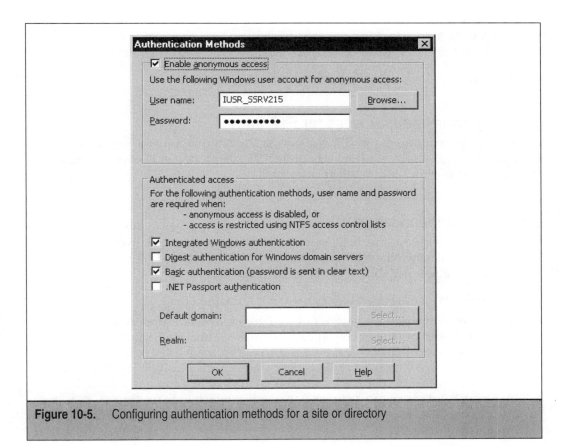

Figure 10-5.   Configuring authentication methods for a site or directory

As mentioned previously, the Default Web Site has anonymous access and Integrated Windows Authentication enabled by default. When a user tries to connect to this site, IIS first tries to authenticate the user using anonymous access. If anonymous access fails, then the Integrated Windows Authentication method is tried (if you have additional authentication methods configured, see the "Order of Authentication" sidebar for more information). About the only way anonymous access can fail is if you try to change the password of the IUSR_*computername* account, which you can do using this dialog box (the box is mainly intended for selecting a different account to use as your Internet Guest Account).

Testing anonymous access to a site such as the Default Web Site is simple. Just open the Authentication Methods dialog box and clear every check box except Enable Anonymous Access. Then, from a separate machine, log on as a network user and open a URL containing the IP address of your IIS machine. You should see the default Under Construction page in your browser and should not be presented with any authentication dialog box.

 SECURITY ALERT!   What if you disable all authentication methods for a site by clearing all check boxes on its Authentication Methods dialog box? Browsers trying to access the site will receive the message "HTTP Error 401.2—Unauthorized: Access is denied due to server configuration." This is a good clue that your site has an authentication configuration problem.

Enabling Anonymous Access for FTP Sites

Enabling anonymous access on FTP sites works a little differently for websites. Here you use the Security Accounts tab of the FTP site properties sheet to configure authentication methods for the site (Figure 10-6).

Order of Authentication

If you have multiple authentication methods configured on an IIS website, virtual directory, or file, then the following rules can determine the order in which these methods are attempted during the authentication process:

1. If anonymous access is configured, it is attempted first.

2. If anonymous access fails, is not configured, or is not supported by the client, then other authentication methods are attempted, starting with the most secure method (Windows Integrated Authentication), followed by progressively weaker methods (first Digest Authentication and then Basic Authentication). Each enabled method is then attempted until the client and server can agree on a method, at which time the user's credentials are checked and the client is either authenticated or denied access to the site.

3. If .NET Passport Authentication is selected, no other methods are available.

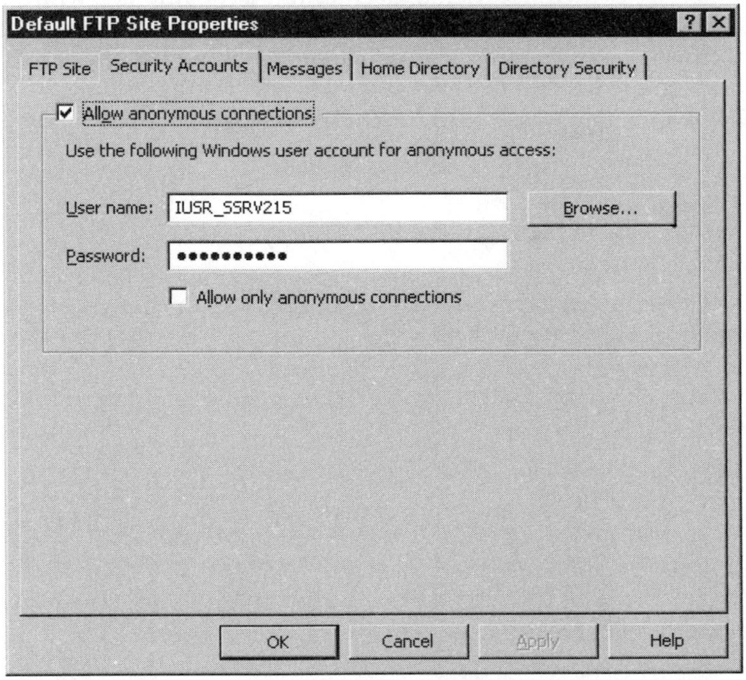

Figure 10-6. Configuring FTP site authentication

For the Default FTP Site, you can see that anonymous access is enabled because the Allow Anonymous Connections check box is selected. What's not immediately plain from this is that Basic Authentication is also enabled by default. If you also select the Allow Only Anonymous Connections check box, however, you turn off Basic Authentication, and the site allows *only* anonymous access—that is, users' credentials will not be checked.

You can test anonymous access for FTP sites by selecting the second check box on the Security Accounts tab of the Default FTP Site. For testing purposes, create a file called welcome.txt in the C:\Inetpub\ftproot directory, the home directory of the Default FTP Site. From another machine, open a command prompt and use the ftp command to connect to the site and display a list of files in the root directory.

Here's an example of an FTP session. User John Smith connects to an FTP server with address 172.16.11.215 and tries to enter his own credentials (userid and password), which are either stored in Active Directory (in a domain scenario) or on the IIS machine (in a workgroup scenario). Because the server is configured to only allow anonymous access,

John's credentials are denied. He then tries entering "anonymous" (without the quotes) as his userid, and the server responds by saying that he should enter his e-mail address as his password (this is not required—you can enter anything for your anonymous password). John enters his e-mail address, and access is granted to the FTP site. (Note that when you enter a password, no characters are displayed on the screen.)

```
C:\>ftp
ftp> open 172.16.11.215
Connected to 172.16.11.215.
220 Microsoft FTP Service
User (172.16.11.215:(none)): jsmith
331 Password required for johnsmith.
Password:
530 User johnsmith cannot log in.
Login failed.
ftp> user
Username anonymous
331 Anonymous access allowed, send identity (e-mail name) as password.
Password:
230 Anonymous user logged in.
ftp> ls
200 PORT command successful.
150 Opening ASCII mode data connection for file list.
welcome.txt
226 Transfer complete.
ftp: 13 bytes received in 0.01Seconds 1.30Kbytes/sec.
ftp> quit
221
C:\>
```

You can also test anonymous FTP access by opening the URL ftp://172.16.11.215 (or whatever your machine's IP address is). The browser should display a Notepad icon for the welcome.txt file. Right-click the file and select Copy To Folder to download the file to your machine.

Integrated Windows Authentication

Integrated Windows Authentication is the normal method for authenticating users when they try to log on to a Windows Server 2003 computer or network. Integrated Windows Authentication is an evolution of the original NTLM authentication scheme developed by Microsoft for its early LAN Manager server product. It was renamed Windows NT Challenge/Response authentication for Windows NT, and then renamed again as Integrated Windows Authentication for Windows 2000. On the Windows 2000 and Windows 2003 platforms, Integrated Windows Authentication represents two separate authentication methods:

- **NTLMv2**   The direct successor to the challenge/response NTLM authentication method. This method is used when IIS machines are part of a workgroup or on Windows Server 2003 networks that still have some legacy Windows NT domain controllers present.

- **Kerberos**   An industry-standard, ticket-based authentication method. This method is used when IIS machines are part of a domain and there are no legacy Windows NT domain controllers present.

Integrated Windows Authentication is the most secure way to authenticate users attempting to connect to IIS. Users' passwords are not transmitted in any way, shape, or form across the network connection, so if intruders are trying to sniff passwords using a packet sniffer, they're out of luck. If you want to provide users with secure access to your IIS websites, for example to provide remote users access to your company intranet, this is often the best way to go. There are two caveats to observe, however:

- Integrated Windows Authentication requires Internet Explorer 3.01 or later, so legacy Windows clients may be out of luck.

- Integrated Windows Authentication sometimes doesn't work through firewalls or proxy servers, so your intranet web server may need to be located somewhere on your perimeter network instead of completely behind the company firewall. More specifically, NTLM has problems with proxy servers and Kerberos has difficulties with firewalls. A workaround for this problem can be achieved by having clients access your web server using a tunneled connection, for example using Point-to-Point Tunneling Protocol (PPTP). This works because tunnels can be proxied and firewall ports can also be opened to let them through. This kind of approach is often used by companies to allow remote clients to securely access a company intranet.

Integrated Windows Authentication in a Workgroup Scenario

It's easy to test Integrated Windows Authentication in a workgroup scenario where you have a stand-alone IIS machine. Start by opening Computer Management on your IIS machine and use Local Users And Groups to create a test user like John Smith, as just discussed (you might use userid=jsmith and password=password). Then go to a separate machine, log on as Administrator, and try to open the URL for the Default Web Site on your IIS machine. The result is a Connect To dialog box requesting the credentials of a valid user account on the IIS machine (Figure 10-7). Enter the credentials for John Smith in this dialog box and click OK, and you can access the home page of the site.

A couple of things to note concerning Integrated Windows Authentication:

- You can explicitly specify a local user account on the IIS machine in the Connect To dialog box by typing it in the form *computername\userid*, where *computername* is the NetBIOS or DNS name or IP address of the IIS machine, and *userid* is the username of the user account you are trying to authenticate.

Figure 10-7. Logging on to a site using Integrated Windows Authentication

- If you make a mistake entering your credentials, you get two more tries before your authentication attempt is rejected.

- If your credentials are finally rejected, the error message returned is "HTTP Error 401.1—Unauthorized: Access is denied due to invalid credentials."

Integrated Windows Authentication in a Domain Scenario

Integrated Windows Authentication is more often used in a domain scenario, where Active Directory controls access to network resources and to a corporate intranet site running on IIS. To test this, you'll need two machines, a domain controller and a standalone machine belonging to a workgroup. Let's say your domain name is mtit.local and you've created a test user called Mary Jones using Active Directory Users And Computers. Mary Jones will therefore be a member of the Users group in this domain and will typically have a logon name like mjones@mtit.local. Now install IIS on your domain controller (not really a good idea from a security standpoint, but this is only a test), and configure the Default Web Site to use Integrated Windows Authentication only by disabling anonymous access. Go to the stand-alone machine and try to open a URL for the domain controller running IIS. The Connect To dialog box should appear, so enter Mary's credentials (her userid mjones@mtit.local and her password, whatever it is), and you should be authenticated using Integrated Windows Authentication.

Now join the second machine to the domain by opening the System utility in Control Panel, selecting the Computer Name tab, clicking Change, selecting Domain, and typing **mtit.local** (or your own domain name if your have a different test network).

Make sure your second machine points to the domain controller as its primary DNS server, and click OK to join the domain. Enter the credentials of a domain administrator account to complete the process and reboot your machine, and your second machine is part of the domain.

When the machine restarts, this time log on as domain user Mary Jones by typing **mjones@mtit.local** in the User Name box. Open Internet Explorer and try to open the URL for the Default Web Site on your domain controller running IIS. This time you shouldn't have to specify your credentials, since when Integrated Windows Authentication is being used, the browser first tries to automatically use the credentials of the currently logged-on user (Mary Jones) and pass these to IIS for authentication.

If you get a dialog box in the preceding example, it's probably because you used your IIS machine's IP address or DNS name in the URL you opened. If this is the case, IIS assumes that the client is connecting over an Internet connection and for extra security generates the logon box. In an intranet scenario however, where Integrated Windows Authentication is usually used, you can use the server name in the URL (For example, http://snoopy) and you should not see the logon box because the credentials of the currently logged on user will be passed silently to IIS for authentication. An alternative to this is to change the security zone settings for Internet Explorer to allow logon information to be passed silently to IIS, which lets you use an IP address or DNS name in the URL, so you won't see a logon box.

Digest Authentication

Digest Authentication is similar to Basic Authentication (which I will discuss soon) but is more secure because it employs a challenge/response mechanism and transmits user credentials across a network using an encrypted MD5 hash. However, Digest Authentication has some requirements you need to meet if you plan to use it:

- Client computers must be using Internet Explorer version 5 or higher as their web browser.

- Both your users and your IIS machine must be members of (or trusted by) the same domain.

- You must be using Active Directory with either Windows 2000 or Windows 2003 domain controllers and have domain user accounts for your users.

- If your IIS machine is running in worker process isolation mode, it must be using the LocalSystem account as its identity.

NOTE   If your domain controllers are running Windows 2000 while your IIS machine is running Windows Server 2003, you must enable subauthentication by installing and configuring a component called iissuba.dll on your IIS 6 machine (see IIS online help for information on how to do this).

Advanced Digest Authentication

IIS 6 also supports a variant of Digest Authentication called Advanced Digest Authentication that is more secure because it securely stores user passwords on domain controllers as MD5 hashes instead of using plaintext. To use Advanced Digest Authentication, both your domain controllers and IIS machines must be running Windows Server 2003, and the UseDigestSSP metabase property must be True. Some IIS docs say that to use Digest Authentication, your users must also have the Store Password Using Reversible Encryption setting enabled on the Accounts tab of their properties sheet. Actually; this setting is enabled by default in Active Directory on Windows Server 2003, so when you enable Digest Authentication on IIS 6, you are really enabling Advanced Digest Authentication.

Testing Digest Authentication

You can test Digest Authentication using the setup from the preceding example if you have your network configured similarly. Open the Authentication Methods dialog box on the domain controller running IIS, select Digest Authentication, and deselect any other authentication methods that you had previously selected. Click the Realm button, and you'll see a list of domains you can choose to authenticate from. Select your own domain from the list.

Now go to another machine belonging to the domain, log on as a domain user account—you did with Mary Jones in the preceding example, and try to open the Default Web Site on the IIS machine. This time you should get an Enter Network Password dialog box (Figure 10-8). Type your credentials and you should be able to access the site.

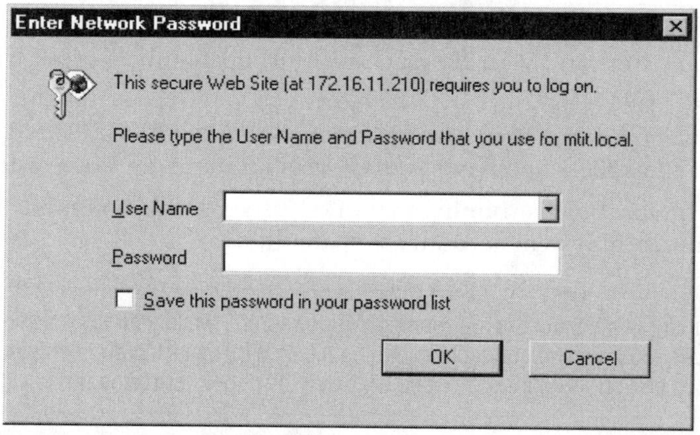

Figure 10-8. Logging on to a site using Digest Authentication

Basic Authentication

Basic Authentication is the weakest form of authentication available on IIS and should only be used when all other forms of authentication fail. The main advantage of Basic Authentication is that it is an Internet standard that works with any browser client. Another advantage of Basic Authentication is that it can work through a proxy server, while Integrated Windows Authentication cannot.

The main disadvantage of Basic Authentication is that it transmits your credentials across the network connection in plaintext (actually, your credentials are Base64 encoded, but this is trivial to decode into plaintext). As a result, any intruder sniffing your network can read your userid and password when you use Basic Authentication. Another disadvantage is that Basic Authentication caches user tokens for 15 minutes, and an attacker who cracks your system during this time interval will be able to read your credentials. However, you can disable such caching in the Registry—see the IIS help files for information.

Basic Authentication is generally not a good idea for authenticating users to your IIS websites, though it's the only authentication method that works with every browser client (because Basic Authentication is part of the HTTP 1.0 standard). We'll look at it briefly, particularly because it is the only authenticated access method for FTP sites. However, if you do use this authentication method, *never* use administrator credentials when accessing your website. If these credentials are stolen, your network is toast. If you *do* have to use Basic Authentication for your website and you are concerned about users submitting their credentials insecurely, then use SSL to encrypt the authentication session.

NOTE   In previous versions of IIS, Basic Authentication required that you grant users the Log On Locally right on your IIS machine for this authentication method to work, which constituted an additional security hazard. In IIS 6, however, this right is no longer required.

Enabling Basic Authentication for Web Sites

To enable Basic Authentication, select the check box for this option on the Authentication Methods dialog box. Then click the Select button beside the Default Domain text box, and choose a domain to which users will be authenticated (if you're running IIS on a stand-alone machine belonging to a workgroup, this step is not necessary). Note that if you leave Default Domain blank, IIS uses its own domain as the Default Domain for authenticating users, it doesn't use the domain of the users' machines. Don't bother specifying a realm, as this feature doesn't really do anything for Basic Authentication—it displays the configured realm in the logon box on the client.

To test this setup, go to another machine and try to open the site using Internet Explorer. You'll be presented with a Connect To dialog box similar to that for Integrated Windows Authentication. Enter the credentials of a local user on the IIS machine (for a workgroup scenario) or a domain user in Active Directory (in a domain scenario), and you should be able to access the site. If necessary, configure the local security policy on your IIS machine to allow the users you want to access your site the right to log on locally. Like Integrated Windows Authentication, Basic Authentication gives you three authentication tries before generating an error.

Enabling Basic Authentication for FTP Sites

Basic Authentication is already enabled by default for FTP sites. If you want to *disable* it, select the Allow Only Anonymous Connections on the Security Accounts tab of your FTP site's properties sheet. This will leave anonymous access the only method for accessing your site. If you want to configure your FTP site to use *only* Basic Authentication, clear the Allow Anonymous Connections check box. This makes it look like there are no authentication methods configured for the site, but in fact Basic Authentication will be used even though there is nothing in the GUI to indicate this.

You can test Basic Authentication for FTP sites using the command-line FTP client of Windows Server 2003 or Windows XP.

.NET Passport Authentication

Another method IIS can use for authenticating users is.NET Passport, a single sign-on (SSO) web services technology developed by Microsoft. With this type of authentication, each user's credentials must be associated with a unique Passport account stored on central Passport servers managed by Microsoft and connected to the Internet. This association is made using the e-mail address of the user, so in a way a user's e-mail address is their Passport. Then when a user tries to access an IIS website that has been configured to use Passport Authentication, IIS forwards the user's Passport information to the Passport servers that authenticate the user on behalf of IIS.

Associating a User Account with a Passport

To test Passport Authentication on IIS, you first need to associate your user account with Passport. For simplicity, this example will test Passport Authentication on a stand-alone IIS machine belonging to a workgroup and will not use SSL (for information about using SSL, see the later section "Using SSL to Secure IIS").

Start by using Local Users And Groups in Computer Management to create a local user account jsmith for ordinary user John Smith. To use Passport, you need an e-mail account, so open Internet Explorer and create a free e-mail account using a service like Yahoo! (www.yahoo.com) for user John Smith. You could also use a Passport-enabled e-mail service like MSN or Hotmail, but I want to keep this example as general as possible, so use some other service instead.

Now log on to your IIS machine using account jsmith, and open the URL www.passport.com to go to Microsoft's .NET Passport site. Click the image or link that says Register For Your Free .NET Passport Today to open the Member Services Registration page. Type the e-mail address for John Smith, specify a password to protect your new Passport account, read the NDA, and click I Agree to continue. Once your registration is complete, click Continue to return to the main Passport page. You've now created a Passport account for John Smith.

You still have to verify who you say you are to the Passport servers, so, still logged on as jsmith, open your mailbox for your free mail service and check your mail. There should be a message waiting for you from Passport. Read it and click the link asking you to verify that you really want to register with Passport. This will open a new browser window and take you to a page on the Passport site that asks you to verify your e-mail address. Click Continue, and the .NET Passport Wizard appears (Figure 10-9).

This wizard guides you through the process of associating your newly created Passport account with the currently logged-on user account (jsmith). Follow the steps of the wizard by specifying your e-mail address again and entering your Passport password, making sure that the Save My .NET Passport Information in the My Windows User Account check box is selected (Figure 10-10). When you reach the You're Done! page, a message should state that your user account has been associated with your Passport e-mail address. Click Finish, close your browser window, and log off as John Smith.

Configuring Passport on the Server

Now configure your IIS machine to require Passport Authentication from users. Log on as Administrator and configure the Default Web Site to use Passport Authentication as follows:

1. Open IIS Manager, right-click the Default Web Site, and select Properties.

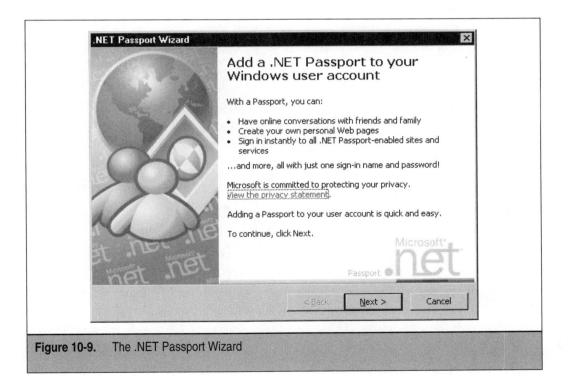

Figure 10-9. The .NET Passport Wizard

2. Select the Directory Security tab, and click the Edit button under Authentication and Access Control.

3. Select the .NET Passport check box and clear all other check boxes; then close the Authentication Methods sheet.

4. Click OK to close the Default Web Site properties sheet and apply the changes.

This enables Passport Authentication on your IIS machine, but, by default, Passport is configured to require an SSL server certificate. You can change this by editing the Registry. Open the Registry Editor (regedt32.exe) and find the following Registry key:

```
HKLM\Software\Microsoft\Passport\SecureLevel
```

By default, this REG_DWORD key has the hexadecimal value A, or decimal value 10, which means that an SSL server certificate is required on the server. Change this value to zero and close Registry Editor. This will cause your IIS machine to use its default encryption key for Passport Authentication instead of a server certificate that you would obtain and install in a normal production environment.

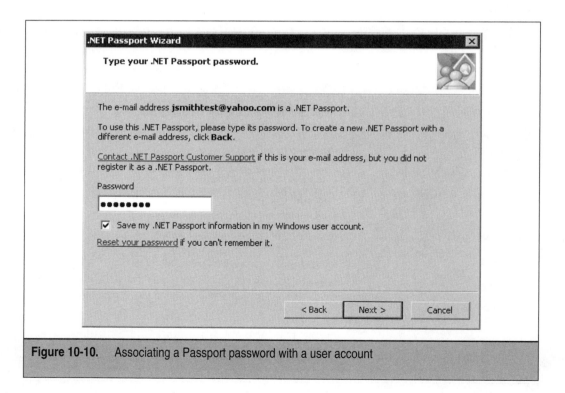

Figure 10-10.   Associating a Passport password with a user account

Testing Passport Authentication

Now log off as Administrator and log on again as John Smith. To display the home page of the Default Web Site, open the URL http://localhost in Internet Explorer. A Passport Authentication dialog box will appear, displaying the e-mail address for the Passport account associated with your local user account (Figure 10-11). Type your Passport password, click OK, and your browser will open the home page of your Default Web Site.

Developing Passport-Authenticated Websites

I've only scratched the surface of using Passport to authenticate users against IIS. In a real-world environment there will be at least two other stages in the development of your sites, the preproduction (PREP) and final production stages. For these stages you will have to do things such as:

- Use the Passport Manager Administration Utility (msppcnfg.exe) on your IIS machine to configure a site ID and other Passport settings.

- Obtain a server certificate for your website to establish its identity when communicating with Microsoft's Passport servers.

- Register your website with Microsoft's Passport site by completing the necessary forms and agreements.

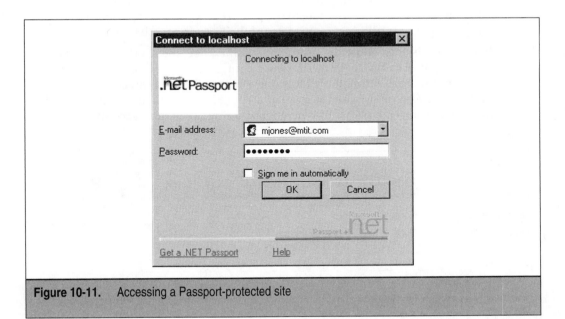

Figure 10-11. Accessing a Passport-protected site

For more information on these and related procedures regarding implementing Passport on your sites, see IIS online help, the MSDN site (msdn.microsoft.com), and the Passport site (www.passport.com).

Summary of Authentication Methods

The authentication methods are summarized in Table 10-2 for easy comparison. This will be helpful in deciding which authentication methods to enable when creating IIS websites for various purposes.

Combining Authentication and Permissions

I've covered two aspects of IIS security: authentication and permissions. Which is applied first? The answer is simple: users must be authenticated to a site before permissions can be applied to control their access to the site. Putting it all together, here's how IIS authenticates clients:

1. The user is first authenticated and granted an access token. If anonymous access is enabled, this is used. Otherwise, other methods are used, starting from the most secure and working downward. If .NET Passport Authentication is configured, however, only this method is used.

2. The web permissions configured for the site are then applied to determine what level of access the user has to the page requested. Web permissions are applied equally to all users, regardless of their group membership.

3. If web permissions allow the user access to the page, the user's access token is then compared to the NTFS permissions configured for the page, and these NTFS permissions ultimately determine whether the user can access the page or not; they also determine the level of access granted. NTFS permissions take the user's group membership when determining access into account as well.

Feature	Anonymous Access	Integrated Windows Authentication	Digest Authentication	Basic Authentication	.NET Passport Authentication
Level of security	None	High	Medium	Low	High
Password transmission	None	Kerberos ticket or NTLM hash	MD5 hash	Base64	SSL
Supported Clients	All	IE 2 or higher	IE 5 or higher	All	All
Through proxy server	Yes	No	Yes	Yes	Yes

Table 10-2.   Summary of IIS 6 Authentication Methods

There's one more level of security that IIS can use: IP address and domain name restrictions.

IP ADDRESS AND DOMAIN NAME RESTRICTIONS

IIS can also allow or deny users access to all sites, a particular site, a virtual directory, or even a file, all based on the identity of the computer that the user is using. This identity can be specified either as the machine's IP address or as its DNS domain name (if it has one). Using this method you can block a single computer, a group of computers on a TCP/IP subnet, or even all computers from a given DNS domain from accessing sites or portions of sites on your IIS machine. To use this feature, select the Directory Security (or File Security) tab on the properties sheet for your site, directory, or file, and click the Edit button under IP Address and Domain Name Restrictions to open the dialog box with the same name (Figure 10-12).

Note that, by default, all client computers are allowed access to your site, file, or directory. You can now proceed to define specific rules to lock out access from specific computers, networks, or domains. Alternatively, you can deny access to everyone and then allow access for specific computers, networks, or domains. As an example, say your IIS machine has IP address 172.16.11.215, and for test purposes you want to block access to all clients on the local subnet having network ID 172.16.11.0 and subnet mask 255.255.255.0. To lock this network out, click Add to open the Deny Access dialog box,

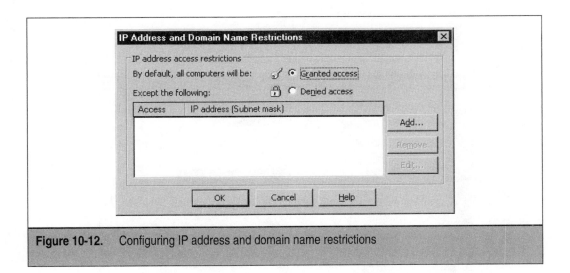

Figure 10-12.   Configuring IP address and domain name restrictions

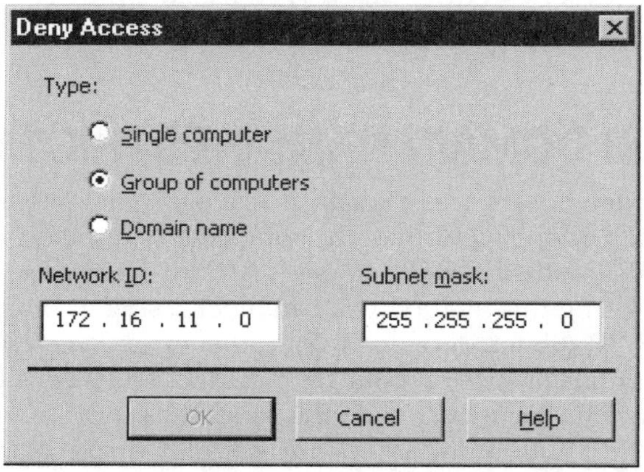

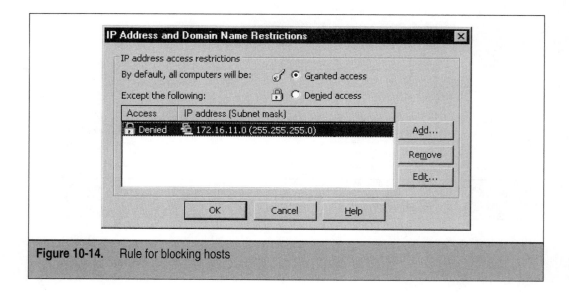

Figure 10-13. Locking out a subnet of hosts

select Group of Computers, and enter the network ID and subnet mask in the fields provided (Figure 10-13).

Click OK to return to the IP Address and Domain Name Restrictions box, and notice that you now have a rule created to lock out clients on the local network (Figure 10-14).

Figure 10-14. Rule for blocking hosts

Click OK and then Apply to apply your rule. To test whether it works, go to another machine such as 172.16.11.210 on the local subnet and try opening the Default Web Site. You should get the following error message: "HTTP Error 403.6—Forbidden: IP address of the client has been rejected."

NOTE   IP address restrictions can also be configured for FTP sites using the Directory Security tab on the properties sheet for your FTP site. The main difference between how this feature is implemented for FTP and websites is that FTP site restrictions can only be based on computer or subnet, not on DNS domain.

When would you use IP address and domain name restrictions for securing IIS? I can only think of two scenarios where this might be useful:

- If your web server is experiencing attack from a specific computer, network, or domain on the Internet, you can use this feature to block all access to your server from the attacker. Remember though that you may be blocking out legitimate clients if the attacking computer is a compromised system.

- If you are using your web server strictly for corporate intranet use and therefore know exactly which IP addresses legitimate client computer will have, you can allow access to only those IP addresses. Of course, IP addresses can be spoofed, so this may give you a false sense of security. Note that if you use this approach and allow specific computers, networks, or domains to access your site, there is an implicit Deny All in place here—all clients are denied access unless specifically allowed.

In other words, this IIS security feature is not all that useful. Firewalls are much better at doing this sort of thing than IIS!

NOTE   You should generally try to avoid the domain option when using this feature; that is, don't allow or deny access to your site based on the client's DNS domain. Enabling this feature would mean that IIS would have to perform a reverse DNS lookup each time a client tried to connect. This takes time and consumes additional system resources and can severely impact your web server's performance.

Putting It All Together

You now have enough info to put together the entire four-step process IIS uses to secure sites, directories, and files:

1. IP address and domain restrictions are used first to allow or deny access.
2. The user is authenticated next using the configured authentication methods.
3. Web permissions are next applied to determine the level of access the user has for the resource, regardless of the user's group membership.

4. NTFS permissions are applied last to more granularly control the level of access the user has for the resource based on group membership.

That's the security model for IIS, and it applies to both static (HTML) and dynamic (ASP, ASP.NET, CGI, or ISAPI) content. But for dynamic applications, there's another level of security that IIS uses in addition to these: application security.

APPLICATION SECURITY

In Chapter 8, "Creating and Configuring Applications," you learned how to create applications on IIS, define application starting points, create application pools, and move applications to different pools. But if you plan to use IIS for hosting dynamic web applications, there are additional steps you need to take to allow your applications to run securely. These steps include:

- Enabling Web Service Extensions (WSE) to allow different types of applications to run in general.

- Configuring execute permissions to allow applications in specific sites and virtual directories to run with the proper permissions level.

- Configuring application pool identities to manage how worker processes that host applications will run.

Configuring Web Service Extensions (WSE)

A great improvement in IIS 6 over earlier versions is that IIS installs in a locked-down mode where only static content can be served to clients. To use IIS for running dynamic web applications, the first thing you have to do is unlock IIS to allow it to serve clients the types of applications you plan to run. To accomplish this, you use the Web Service Extensions (WSE) feature in the IIS Manager console tree. Figure 10-15 shows WSE in Standard view, which displays which Web Service Extensions are allowed and which are prohibited—note that by default all of them are prohibited from running, so any dynamic content currently on the server will not run unless the appropriate extension is allowed.

NOTE If ASP or ASP.NET are not visible in the details pane when the WSE node is selected, these components of IIS have not been installed on the machine. Use Add Or Remove Programs to install the missing Application Server components and then allow the extensions you need to run your applications.

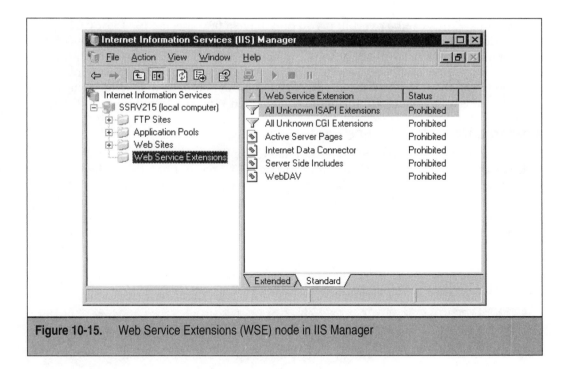

Figure 10-15.   Web Service Extensions (WSE) node in IIS Manager

Allowing a Web Service Extension

Let's say you've copied an ASP application to the root directory of your website and you want users to be able to use it. All you have to do is enable the extension for ASP by right-clicking it and selecting Allow. If you change your mind later and no longer want to run ASP applications on your server, just right-click ASP again and select Prohibit. Then if a user tries to run your ASP page, an "HTTP Error 404—File Not Found" message will be returned.

Allowing ISAPI and CGI Extensions

The standard view of WSE gives you two options for allowing ISAPI or CGI applications to run on IIS:

- **Allow Unknown ISAPI Extensions**   Lets *all* ISAPI extensions run on the server.
- **Allow Unknown CGI Extensions**   Lets *all* CGI extensions run on the server.

Obviously, this can be overkill if you only have a few specific ISAPI or CGI applications you want to run on the server, and it can constitute a security risk if someone uploads a risky ISAPI or CGI application to your server. As a result, IIS lets you create your own Web Service Extensions and specify which applications are allowed to call them. To do this, you must switch from Standard to Extended view using the tabs at the bottom of the details pane when WSE is selected (Figure 10-16).

Adding a New Web Service Extension

You can add a new Web Service Extension using the first hyperlink in Extended view. This has the effect of registering the appropriate HTTP request handler to the list of Web Service Extensions on the server. Click the hyperlink to open the New Web Service Extension dialog box, type a friendly name for your extension to identify it in IIS Manager, and select the EXEs (for CGI) or DLLs (for ISAPI) required for the new extension to work. Table 10-3 shows the DLLs for the request handlers of common application types.

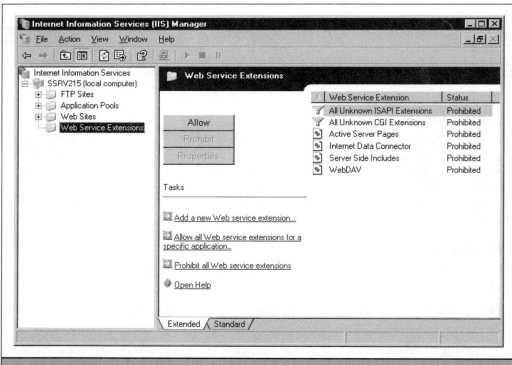

Figure 10-16. WSE Extended view

Application Type	HTTP Request Handler DLL
Active Server Pages	C:\WINDOWS\system32\inetsrv\asp.dll
Internet Data Connector	C:\WINDOWS\system32\inetsrv\httpodbc.dll
Server Side Includes	C:\WINDOWS\system32\inetsrv\ssinc.dll
WebDAV	C:\WINDOWS\system32\inetsrv\httpext.dll

Table 10-3.   HTTP Request Handler DLLs for Common Types of Applications

Allowing All Web Service Extensions Necessary for an Application

You can also allow all necessary Web Service Extensions for a specific application to run by selecting the second hyperlink when Extended view is selected for WSE. Just click the link, select the application from the drop-down box, and click OK. This is useful if you have copied a complex application to IIS that uses many dynamic features such as ASP, ISAPI, CGI, and so on. In one step, you can allow all the extensions necessary for the application to run.

Disable All Web Service Extensions

Extended view also allows you to disable *all* dynamic content on IIS in one easy step by clicking the third hyperlink in the details pane.

TIP   The three hyperlinks in Extended view that I just discussed are not present in Standard view, but, by right-clicking the WSE node in the console tree, you can perform any of these actions in Standard view.

Configuring Execute Permissions

Once you've enabled the proper Web Service Extensions to allow your application to run on IIS, you still need to configure permissions for it to run properly. These application permissions are different from the NTFS or web permissions discussed earlier in this chapter, though those still apply for the files (ASP, DLL, EXE, and so on) that constitute your application. Application permissions are commonly called *execute permissions* and are configured on the Home Directory (or Virtual Directory) tab where the root of your application is located (depending on whether the application root is the site's home directory or a subdirectory). Using the Execute Permissions drop-down box on this tab, you can set the execute permissions for your application to three possible settings (Figure 10-17):

- **None**   Dynamic applications won't run and IIS will only serve static HTML to clients.

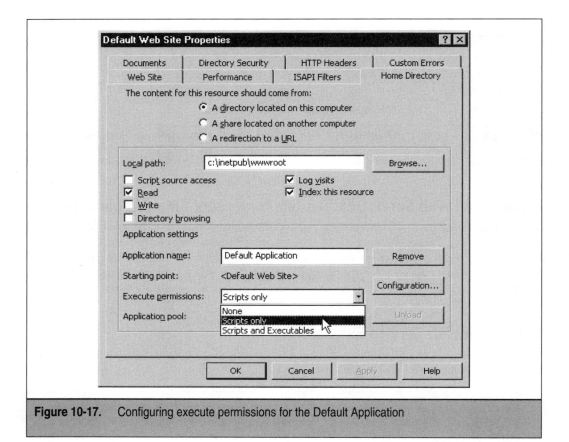

Figure 10-17. Configuring execute permissions for the Default Application

- **Scripts Only**   Only scripts (such as VBS or PERL) can run in this application, while executables (EXE files) won't be allowed to run.
- **Scripts and Executables**   Both scripts and executables can run.

Configuring Application Pool Identities

You may recall from our earlier discussion in Chapter 2, "IIS 6 Architecture," that application pooling is a new feature of IIS 6 that allows you to group together (or isolate) applications into separate pools that can each be serviced by one or more worker processes. All applications within a pool share the same worker process, and by configuring Web Gardens you can have multiple worker processes servicing the same application pool. Each worker process is an instance of w3wp.exe and runs in the context of a special user account called an *application pool identity*. The worker process servicing the pool uses this account as its process identity, and this account can be assigned to either an existing account or a custom account you create.

IIS creates new worker processes when they're needed; and when a new worker process is created by the Web Administration Service (WAS), the built-in service account Network Service is assigned by default as its application pool identity (it's called a service account because it's used only by the operating system as a process identity for running network services). This doesn't mean, however, that an application within the pool runs with that identity. When the application receives a client request to process, the thread that processes the requests *impersonates* the identity of the process token associated with the client for its process identity. For example, if an application receives and accepts a request from an anonymous user, the client's process token is associated with the IUSR_*computername* account and it is *this* account, not Network Service, that is matched against the ACL of files the application needs to access.

What's the point of having application pool identities then? The reason is that the application must still run within a security context even when no user requests are received.

Selecting an Application Pool Identity

The guiding principle in choosing an application pool identity is to select one with just enough privileges to allow your application to run properly. If you assign an account to your worker process that has too high a level of privileges, the application may be able to do things it wasn't designed to do. Also, if your application has faulty code and is compromised by an intruder, the intruder may be able to use your application pool identity to elevate his or her privileges and compromise your network.

When choosing an application pool identity, you can select from several built-in service accounts used by Windows Server 2003:

- **Network Service**   An account that has very few privileges. It can act as any computer on the network, has no password, and goes by the internal name of NT AUTHORITY\NetworkService. The account is a member of the Everyone and Authenticated Users built-in groups, so if ACLs grant access for these groups to any object, Local Service has the same level of access.

- **Local Service**   The same privileges as Network Service, but this only presents anonymous credentials over a network connection—in other words, it can only access resources on the local computer, not on remote ones. The account has no password and goes by the internal name of NT AUTHORITY\LocalService. This account also is a member of the Everyone and Authenticated Users built-in groups; so if ACLs grant access for these groups to any object, then Local Service has the same level of access.

- **Local System**   Very powerful with a lot of privileges. It can act as any computer on the network, has no password, and goes by the internal name of \LocalSystem. Any process that runs in the context of this account has the same level of privileges as the Service Control Manager (SCM), the portion of the operating system than manages network services running on the machine.

Of these three accounts, the one with the lowest level of privileges and greatest flexibility is Network Service, and this is usually the best choice and the account IIS uses by default. When this account is used and an intruder gains control of your application, the level of privileges gained is so low that the intruder can hardly do anything on your server (they can't even list directories or read files). The worst of these to select is Local System, as this account has considerable privileges on the machine. An attacker elevating their privileges to this level would be able to do almost anything. For example, if you have an application pool configured to use the Local System account as its process identity and your application opens a command prompt window to run a batch file for some reason, an attacker could press CTRL+C on the machine, terminate the batch file, and have access to a command prompt window running with Local System privileges, which basically lets him or her do anything. Interestingly enough, in IIS 5, applications ran by default using the Local System process identity!

Remember that application pools and worker processes apply only when IIS 6 is running in worker process isolation mode. If your server is running in IIS 5 isolation mode, applications running in common memory with inetinfo.exe using low isolation mode will execute using the Local System process identity, just as they did in IIS 5! Likewise, applications running in medium or high isolation mode will execute using IWAM_*computername* as their process identity, also as they did in IIS 5. When you're migrating IIS 5 applications to IIS 6, make sure to recode your applications as necessary to enable them to run in worker process isolation mode using a safe identity like Network Service.

NOTE   For those of you geeky enough to be interested in such things, Network Services has only 3 privileges assigned to it compared to 22 for Local System!

Configuring a Custom Application Pool Identity

If you don't want to use one of the built-in service accounts, you can create your own user account and assign it as the application pool identity for the worker process servicing your pool. For this to work, however, your account must be granted certain privileges. This is easily done by making your account a member of the built-in IIS_WPG group. This is a local group when IIS is running in a workgroup environment, and a domain local group when Active Directory is being used. The three service accounts discussed in the preceding section (Network Service, Local System, and Local Service) are by default all members of this group, as is the built-in IWAM_*computername* account used to launch applications out-of-process on IIS. If you create a custom account and configure it as the process identity for your pool but don't make your account a member of

IIS_WPG, the worker processes associated with your pool won't be able to start and your application will fail.

Why would you want to create custom process identities for your different application pools? For enhanced security! Creating separate pools for applications increases *reliability* because if one application fails it won't bring down the others. Likewise, creating a custom application pool identity for each pool increases *security* because if one application is compromised it won't compromise others on the same server. In both cases, the effect is to better isolate applications from each other, which is a big concern for service providers hosting websites for multiple companies on a single machine. On the other hand, it's still important to code your applications properly: a poorly written ISAPI application is still a Win32 DLL that can consume excessive CPU resources, fill up your hard disk with useless files, and do lots of other harmful things that can affect the performance of all web applications running on your IIS machine.

Configuring a custom process identity for an application pool is simple: First, create a local user account (for a stand-alone IIS machine) or domain user account (if Active Directory is involved) that will be specifically used for this purpose. Be sure to assign the account a complex password. Then add the account you created to the IIS_WPG built-in group to grant it the necessary privileges to be able to instantiate worker processes. Now right-click an application pool (such as the Default Application Pool) in IIS Manager and select Properties to open the properties sheet for the pool, and switch to the Identity tab (Figure 10-18).

TIP You can configure the same process identity for all your application pools by selecting the Application Pools node in the console tree and performing the same procedure as the preceding. Unfortunately, the GUI doesn't allow you to change their properties simultaneously using CTRL+click— it's one or all, no in between.

By default, the Predefined option is selected. Use the drop-down menu to select any of the three predefined service accounts just described. To configure a different account as the process identity for worker processes servicing this pool, choose the Configurable option instead. By default, IIS suggests using the IWAM_*computername* account as a process identity. This is because if you've migrated legacy IIS 5 applications to your IIS 6 machine those applications may need this account as their process identity if they originally ran on IIS 5 using medium or high application isolation. However, you can also click Browse and select the user account you specially created for this purpose, or choose any local or domain user account as your process identity (provided it belongs to the IIS_WPG group).

NOTE If you create a user account for a custom application pool identity, there should be no spaces in the name of this account.

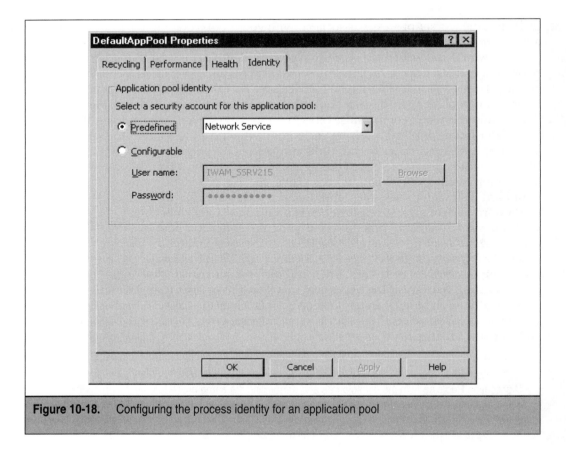

Figure 10-18. Configuring the process identity for an application pool

Verifying Application Pool Identity

Here's a simple way to check that your application is really running under its configured process identity. Create a simple ASP application or use the one you created earlier in Chapter 8, and copy it to the \wwwroot directory, the home directory of the Default Web Site. Make sure ASP is enabled using the WES node, and check the Default Application Pool to verify that the process identity is NETWORK SERVICE. Now right-click the Default Web Site in IIS Manager, and select Browse to run the application. Open Task Manager by right-clicking the taskbar at the bottom of your screen, select the Process tab, and find w3wp.exe in the Image Name column. This executable represents the executable for the worker process servicing your application pool. In the User Name column beside it, you should see NETWORK SERVICE (Figure 10-19). Try creating a custom user account and assigning it as the process identity for your pool, and repeat the experiment to verify that the process is actually running under this identity.

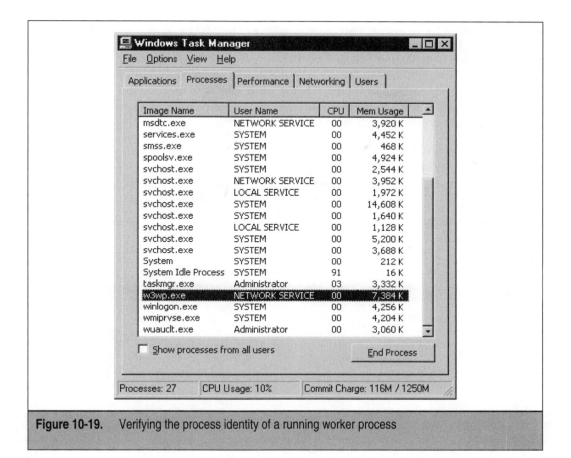

Figure 10-19.   Verifying the process identity of a running worker process

Other Application Security Issues

There are two more security issues relating to applications running on IIS 6: parent paths and ASP security.

Parent Paths

Parent paths is an ASP feature that allows you to use path statements such as "..\" for upward file access relative to the current directory. Parent paths were enabled by default for ASP on IIS 5, but this constituted a security hazard because server-side includes that used the ".." notation could enable an intruder to gain access past the root of the application to the root of the Windows file system to wreak havoc. This is especially hazardous if you give the parent directory execute permission because, if an intruder can gain access to a script in that directory, they can execute any program in that directory.

As a result of these issues, parent paths are not enabled by default in IIS 6 as they were in IIS 5. Because this may affect existing ASP applications you try to port from the old platform, the option of enabling parent paths in IIS 6 is there to ensure that you can make your old apps run properly once you migrate them to the new system. To avoid a security hazard, however, a better approach is to recode your old apps so they don't need that feature anymore. If you need to enable parent paths to get your old app working on IIS 6, here's how to do it:

1. Find the root node of your application in IIS Manager and right-click it to open its properties sheet.

2. Select the Home Directory (or Virtual Directory) tab, and click the Configuration button to open the Application Configuration box.

3. Switch to the Options tab and select the Enable Parent Paths check box (Figure 10-20).

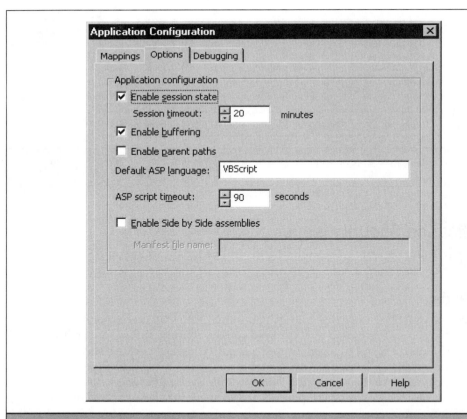

Figure 10-20. Enabling parent paths for an application

ASP Security

It's obvious but sometimes forgotten that applications running on IIS are secure only if *both* IIS and the application code itself are secure! Writing secure code for ASP or ASP.NET applications is beyond the scope of this book, but here are a few tips you can pass on to your developer:

- Don't hard code administrator account names and passwords in ASP pages or scripts.

- Don't store sensitive information in hidden input fields on your web pages or in cookies.

- Don't code decision branches into your application based on input from HTTP request headers, as these headers can be forged.

- Always validate form input before letting your application process it.

- Watch out for buffer overflows produced by bad coding practices.

- Use SSL to encrypt session cookies to prevent your applications from being hijacked.

- Port your ASP application to ASP.NET if you want to use URL authorization to secure your URL space.

USING SSL TO SECURE IIS

Websites running on IIS can also be secured using an extra layer of security called *Secure Sockets Layer (SSL)*, an encryption technology first developed by Netscape. SSL uses public key cryptography to establish an encrypted session key to ensure that communication between a web server and client is private and not open to eavesdropping. To use SSL on IIS, you need to obtain a *digital certificate* from a *certificate authority (CA)* and install it on your server as a server certificate. This certificate both encrypts communications and guarantees the identity of the server to the client, ensuring trust so that the client is willing to submit sensitive information such as user credentials, credit card info, and so on. Commercial certificate authorities from which you can purchase server certificates for your web server include these companies:

- Verisign (www.verisign.com)
- GeoTrust (www.geotrust.com)
- GlobalSign (www.globalsign.com)
- Thawte (www.thawte.com)
- IT Institute (www.wholesaleurl.com)

Prices and services differ for these sites, and some of them, such as Verisign, offer free trial offers. Purchasing a server certificate from a public CA like Verisign is important if you plan to use SSL to run e-commerce applications on your IIS machine, because browsers like Internet Explorer have root certificates from many of these companies preinstalled. This allows users to use their browser to connect to SSL-enabled sites and be sure that their communications are private, so they can confidently submit their credit card or bank account information to purchase products and services or make other financial transactions.

SSL can also ensure secure communication between remote employees and company intranets in an intranet environment. In this case, an alternative to purchasing server certificates from public CAs is to set up your own internal CA on your company network. Microsoft provides such a tool for the Windows Server 2003 platform—Certificate Services, an optional component you can install using Add Or Remove Programs. Using Certificate Services, you can set up different types of CAs on your network and manage them yourself, including

- **Enterprise CA**   This type of CA is integrated into Active Directory and is the most common type in enterprise environments to provide secure intranet access.

- **Stand-alone CA**   This type of CA does not use Active Directory and is therefore less manageable, but can be used for either Internet or intranet scenarios.

You can also create a *chain* of CAs within your enterprise if it is large or geographically dispersed. These chains start with root CAs whose trust is assumed rather than guaranteed by some other CA, followed by subordinate CAs whose trust is derived from the root. For root CAs, you can use either Certificate Services itself or some other public CA, which gives you considerable flexibility in how you establish your CA chain of trust.

Requesting and Installing a Server Certificate

For this example, I'll assume that you've first installed Certificate Services on a domain controller in your network as an Enterprise Root CA using Add Or Remove Programs in Control Panel. (This installation is performed with a wizard, so I won't go into it here; a full treatment of Certificate Services is beyond the scope of this book.)

To request and install a server certificate on your IIS machine, use the Web Server Certificate Wizard (Figure 10-21). You'll request a certificate for the Default Web Site and later enable SSL on this site for secure communications. To do this, follow these steps:

1. Open IIS Manager, right-click the Default Web Site, and select Properties.

2. Switch to the Directory Security tab and click the Server Certificate button to start the wizard.

3. Click Next.

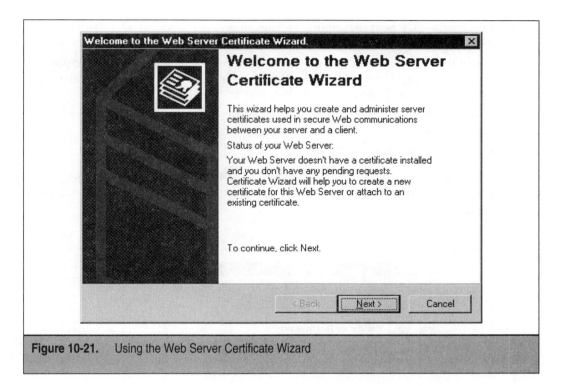

Figure 10-21. Using the Web Server Certificate Wizard

4. Select the option Create a New Certificate and click Next.

5. Select the option Send the Request Immediately to an Online Certificate Authority and click Next.

6. Type a descriptive name for the new certificate, specify a bit length, and click Next. The bit length is 1024 bits by default. Increasing this makes communications more secure but also slower (SSL usually adds a performance hit of more than a factor of 10 when enabled on web servers).

7. Type the name of your organization (company) and organizational unit (division or department), and click Next.

8. Type the common name of your site, which is typically the NetBIOS name of the IIS machine in an intranet environment or the DNS name for an Internet site, and click Next.

9. Select your country code and type the full name of your state and city, and click Next.

10. Specify the TCP port for secure SSL communications, which by default is port 443, and click Next.

11. Select the CA from your enterprise network from which you want to request and obtain your server certificate (the DNS name of the domain controller on which Certificate Services is installed) and click Next.

12. Review the information you've entered on the next screen, and if you're satisfied click Next to request and install the certificate.

13. Click Finish to complete the wizard.

You can now view your newly installed server certificate by clicking the View Certificate button on the Directory Security tab of the Default Web Site properties sheet (Figure 10-22).

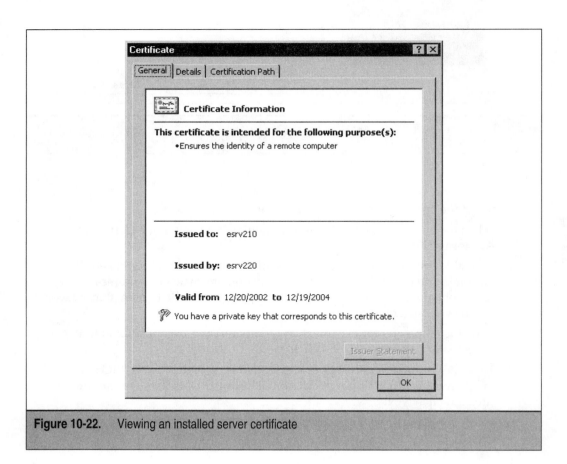

Figure 10-22. Viewing an installed server certificate

Enabling SSL

Now that you've installed a server certificate from your CA on your Default Web Site, you can enable SSL on the server:

1. Return to the Directory Security tab of the Default Web Site properties sheet, and click the Edit button under Secure Communications.

2. In the Secure Communications box, select Require Secure Channel (SSL) (Figure 10-23).

3. Click OK and then Apply.

SSL is now enabled on the server! By default, you've configured SSL to use whatever encryption level the client supports and to ignore any client certificates installed on the client. Client certificates verify the identity of the client to the server, a process that is usually unnecessary in commercial transactions with public e-commerce sites (they

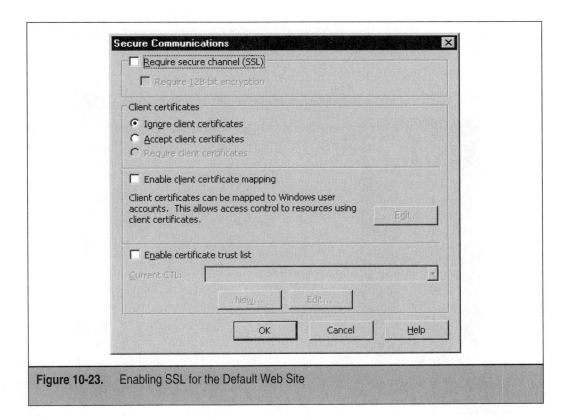

Figure 10-23. Enabling SSL for the Default Web Site

don't care who you are, they just want your money), but they can ensure the identity of the client to the server in corporate intranet scenarios.

Testing the Server Certificate

Now you can test this new server certificate on the machine on which you've installed it:

1. Open Internet Explorer on your IIS machine and try to open the URL https:// localhost to securely access the Default Web Site. The "s" in "https://" tells the server that the client wants to use SSL for the connection.

2. Next, a Security Alert box appears indicating a problem with the certificate on the server. The reason for this is that the client (Internet Explorer) does not recognize the server certificate as issued by a trusted CA. For the client to trust the certificate, it needs to install a copy of the certificate as a trusted root certificate in its own certificate store. To do this, click View Certificate and then Install to start the Certificate Import Wizard (Figure 10-24).

3. Click Next twice and then Finish, accepting the defaults and closing the wizard. You should see a message that the import was successful. Click OK twice to return to the Security Alert box.

Figure 10-24. Using the Certificate Import Wizard

4. Click Yes to accept the certificate, and you should be able to access your Default Web Site using SSL.

Managing the Server Certificate

You can perform various administrative housekeeping tasks for your server certificate by returning to the Directory Security tab and clicking the Server Certificate button again. This restarts the Web Server Certificate Wizard, and, when you click Next, you are presented with a number of management options, including

- Renewing the current certificate, which you should do before it expires to ensure your clients can continue to communicate securely with your site

- Removing or replacing the current certificate if it expires or you no longer need SSL for your site

- Exporting the current certificate if you want to make a copy you can store elsewhere

- Copying or moving the current certificate if you want to move it to a different site or server

ADDITIONAL STEPS FOR SECURING IIS

I'll end this chapter with a potpourri of additional tips and recommendations on securing IIS, including where you can find some additional resources for keeping up to date on IIS security issues.

Worker Process Isolation Mode

I already mentioned this in passing in this chapter, but I'll repeat and emphasize it again here: wherever possible, make sure you run your IIS machine in worker process isolation mode, not IIS 5 isolation mode. Worker process isolation mode offers greater reliability and security than IIS 5 isolation mode because it causes your application pools to use Network Service as their process identity, a system account with very few privileges. In contrast, when your server is running in IIS 5 isolation mode, all in-process applications run by default using Local System as their process identity, an account with very high privileges. Refer back to Chapter 8 to find out how to switch modes in IIS.

Virtual Directories

Virtual directories, discussed in Chapter 7, enhance IIS security because they help prevent intruders from guessing where your content is physically located on your machine, or on which other remote machine your content resides. The aliases used by virtual directories hide the true location of your content from your users and discourage URL snooping, which is when users take a deep-linked URL and gradually chop portions of it off trying to find directories where content might be hidden. Use virtual directories instead of physical ones wherever possible.

IIS Logging

Logging traffic to your IIS sites and reviewing these logs periodically is another important aspect of web server security, but, because IIS logging is also important as a maintenance and troubleshooting issue, I've deferred a discussion of this topic until Chapter 13, "Maintenance and Troubleshooting."

CGI Parameters

IIS 6 strengthens security for running CGI applications by preventing certain special characters from being used in URLs passed to CGI applications. These forbidden characters are

```
|  (  ,  ;  %  <  >
```

Before you port legacy CGI applications to IIS 6, make sure that your input strings do not require any of these characters, or the port won't work.

General Operating System Security

Last but not least in importance, don't forget that securing IIS is really just a part of the overall process of securing the Windows Server 2003 operating system itself. Familiarity with securing the underlying platform is essential if you want your web servers to be hardened against attack. Obviously, a full treatment of Windows Server 2003 security is well beyond the scope of this book, but you should be sure that you fully understand these features:

- Active Directory, how it works and how it is secured
- Group Policy, including local and domain security policies and their settings
- Security templates and the Security Configuration and Analysis console
- File system auditing on NTFS volumes
- Which network services are essential and which can be safely disabled
- TCP/IP port filtering, IPSec policies, and Internet Firewall settings

Also, be sure to install the latest hotfixes, security rollups, and services packs as they become available for the Windows Server 2003 platform. Check out Microsoft's main website at www.microsoft.com, as well as Microsoft Product Support Services (PSS) at support.microsoft.com, for the latest security bulletins, tutorials, and tools for managing hotfixes and rollups to ensure you have the latest information on how to secure both IIS in particular and Windows Server 2003 in general. Because this chapter was written while the product was in RC2 stage, some of the tools and procedures on these sites are still subject to change, but some of those you should keep an eye on include:

- **Microsoft Baseline Security Analyzer**   This tool lets administrators use either a GUI interface or the command line to perform security scans of local or remote systems and determine what needs to be done to make them more secure. This tool is currently only available for Windows 2000 Server but should soon be updated for Windows Server 2003. It includes the Microsoft Network Security Hotfix Checker utility (HFNetChk), a tool that checks for missing security updates and service packs for the operating system; optional components like IIS; and other Microsoft server applications.

- **URLScan**   This is a downloadable add-on first made available for IIS 5. It screens incoming HTTP requests and compares them to a ruleset you can create to block requests that might have malformed URL that intruders can use to try to compromise IIS. While IIS 6 fully supports URLScan, you can now use the WSE node in IIS Manager to block requests to specific code without having to look at a file extension in a URL; in some ways, this is simpler than using URLScan and replaces some of its functionality. The main feature that URLScan has that isn't explicitly built into IIS is the ability to deny access based on URL character sequences. If you do download and use URLScan, just make sure it is the latest version and is compatible with IIS 6.

- **URLAUTH**   This is a new feature of Windows Server 2003 that works together with the new Authorization Manager component to provide role-based security in addition to traditional ACL-based NTFS security. URLAUTH is implemented as an ISAPI filter and can reduce the attack surface on your web server, but it's still being developed at this stage and will likely be released as an add-on after Windows Server 2003 is released.

- **HisecWeb**   This is a security template for Windows 2000 Server that can be used with the Security Configuration and Analysis console to lock down underlying operating system security for IIS 5 web servers. It's likely that Microsoft will update this template for Windows Server 2003 and IIS 6, so keep an eye out for it on Microsoft's website.

- **Windows Update**   Windows Server 2003 includes an Automatic Updates Setup Wizard that lets you configure your server to download and install new security patches and fixes from Microsoft automatically or according to a schedule you define. For enterprise customers that don't want their machines to automatically retrieve software updates from the Internet using Windows Update, the Windows Server 2003 platform also includes a new Software Update Service (SUS) that lets administrators securely download updates to a central server on their network and then distribute them to servers across the network automatically.

Challenge

You plan to use IIS for secure intranet access for your corporate users in an enterprise environment that uses Active Directory. Access for both local and remote clients is needed, and you want the highest level of security for your intranet, which will contain sensitive web applications developed using Active Server Pages technology. Which permissions will you assign to your content resources to ensure high security? Which authentication method(s) will you choose to implement? Will you use IP address and domain name restrictions? Why or why not? How will you configure your ASP applications to run securely on your server? Will you employ SSL to ensure encrypted communications between clients and servers? Why or why not? What other steps would you take to secure your web servers and their underlying operating system?

CHECKLIST: SECURING IIS

Check off each IIS or Windows Server 2003 security feature or concept once you have become familiar with its operation, use, and configuration.

- ☐ NTFS standard permissions
- ☐ NTFS special permissions
- ☐ Effective permissions
- ☐ Shared folder permissions
- ☐ Web permissions
- ☐ Security principals
- ☐ Built-in special identities
- ☐ Service accounts
- ☐ IUSR_computername
- ☐ IWAM_computername
- ☐ IIS_WPG
- ☐ Anonymous access
- ☐ Basic Authentication
- ☐ Digest Authentication
- ☐ Windows Integrated Authentication
- ☐ .NET Passport Authentication
- ☐ FTP site security
- ☐ IP address and domain name restrictions

- ☐ Four-step IIS security model
- ☐ Web Service Extensions (WSE)
- ☐ Execute permissions
- ☐ Application pool identity
- ☐ Network Service account
- ☐ Local System account
- ☐ Parent paths
- ☐ ASP security
- ☐ Secure Sockets Layer (SSL)
- ☐ Server certificates

CHAPTER 11

Working from the Command-Line

Significantly enhanced in IIS 6 specifically (and Windows Server 2003 in general) is the ability to manage a server from the command line. By including many new Windows commands and administration scripts, Microsoft has made it easier for administrators to remotely manage their servers, perform batch operations, and schedule tasks to occur during off-peak hours.

This chapter focuses on the tools and methods for administering IIS 6 machines from the command line. No background in programming or scripting is assumed because as you'll see, Microsoft has included a number of useful scripts with IIS 6 that can be used to perform common administrative tasks.

METHODS FOR COMMAND-LINE ADMINISTRATION

There are four types of commands that can be used to administer IIS from the command line:

- **IISReset**   A command-line utility for starting and stopping IIS.

- **Windows Management Instrumentation (WMI)**   A scripting interface for managing virtually any aspect of Windows Server 2003.

- **Active Directory Services Interface (ADSI)**   An API for scripted management of Active Directory that can be used to manage certain aspects of IIS.

- **Miscellaneous commands**   These include standard Windows commands and Support Tools utilities, some of which are applicable to administering IIS.

Let's look at each of these in a bit more detail.

IISReset

Near the top of an administrator's list of useful IIS command-line utilities is IISReset, a tool that has been around since IIS 5 and can be used to stop and restart IIS or reboot the server from the command line. Alternatively, you can restart IIS using IIS Manager, as discussed earlier in Chapter 5, "Administering Standard/Enterprise Edition," or using the Web Interface for Server Administration (WISA) tool, as discussed in Chapter 6, "Administering Web Server Edition." In fact, both these GUI methods actually use the IISReset.exe command-line utility for stopping and starting IIS, so if this utility is missing or permissions prevent it from being used, the GUI methods of restarting IIS won't work either!

A typical reason for restarting IIS is dealing with application instability in ASP or ASP.NET applications running on your IIS machines. Particularly during the development stage, such applications often have bugs that generate resource leaks or other nasty conditions, and restarting IIS periodically is an easy way of ensuring these leaks don't get out of hand or of recovering IIS when an application suddenly fails. Another name for this kind of condition is "accumulated instability," that is, when the application runs long enough it becomes sufficiently stable to start affecting the overall stability of the underlying operating system, eventually causing the system to become unresponsive (hang) or even crash (blue screen of death). In such an environment, IISReset can be a lifesaver and can be used to nightly stop and start IIS or even reboot the server.

Of course, with IIS 6 part of this instability issue for buggy ASP applications is solved by using application pool recycling, which is enabled by default. But this doesn't always solve all such instability problems, and restarting IIS or rebooting the server is sometimes the only way to ensure a buggy application will keep working or to quickly recover when it fails. And with the rapid pace of development these days, when applications are developed, tested, and released in weeks instead of months or years, the occurrence of bugs causing instabilities is much more prevalent than in the good old mainframe days. As you'll see in the later section "Using IISReset," in which we discuss the syntax of this command, you can even use the Windows Task Scheduler to run IISReset periodically; for example, each night at midnight, when terminating user connections is likely to have the least impact.

NOTE   It would be nice if Microsoft had included a separate command-line tool that could be used to manually recycle a specific application pool on IIS, but unfortunately this is not the case. If enough admins ask for it however, you can probably expect such a utility to be included with IIS 7!

Another reason for restarting IIS is that certain configuration changes you make on IIS don't take effect until you restart IIS. Examples of such configuration changes include:

- Changing the IIS isolation mode (IIS restarts automatically).
- Modifying a Registry entry relating to global IIS configuration (these are found under HKLM\Software\Microsoft\InetMgr\Parameters).
- Manually restoring the metabase from a metabase history file. This may be necessary if the metabase is corrupt and cannot be enumerated by IIS Manager and as a result you can't use IIS Manager to restore the metabase directly.
- Manually enabling metabase edit-while-running from the command line by modifying the EnableEditWhileRunning property in the metabase instead of using the properties sheet for the server node in IIS Manager. Enabling edit-while-running (also called direct metabase edit) allows you to make changes later to the metabase without having to stop IIS first.

An important thing to consider here regarding restarting IIS is that when changes are made to the metabase they occur in memory and are not immediately written to disk. Instead, the in-memory metabase is copied to disk every five minutes, or once 50 metabase edits have accumulated. So if you restart IIS while metabase edits are pending in memory, these edits will be lost. The same problem can also occur when you modify the metabase indirectly using the IIS Manager, that is, changes are written to memory first and later written to disk, and if you restart IIS before the changes have been written to disk, they may be lost. Because of this, it's a good idea to flush the IIS memory cache (which contains the in-memory metabase) to disk before stopping or restarting IIS. This can be done either from the command line using the iiscnfg.vbs /save command, as described in Chapter 13, "Maintenance and Troubleshooting," or by right-clicking the server node in IIS Manager and selecting All Tasks | Backup/Restore Configuration, as described earlier in Chapter 5. An alternative approach after making configuration changes to IIS is to simply wait at least five minutes before restarting IIS to ensure that all in-memory metabase changes have been written to disk first.

WMI

Windows Management Instrumentation (WMI) is Microsoft's implementation of Web-Based Enterprise Management (WBEM), an industry initiative to establish standard methods for accessing and manipulating management information for systems and network devices. WBEM (and hence WMI) is based on the Common Information Model (CIM), a set of schema for describing management information for systems and network devices that was developed by the Distributed Management Task Force (DMTF), the same group that developed WBEM.

The implementation of WMI on Windows Server 2003 includes a new IIS WMI Provider. Using VBScript or JScript, you can use this provider to write WMI scripts to perform common IIS administration tasks such as creating websites and virtual directories, enabling and disabling web service extensions, exporting and importing portions of the metabase, or just about anything else you want to do—WMI goes way beyond just IIS and allows you to manage virtually any aspect of Windows computers.

To make life easy for the busy IIS admin, Microsoft has included a number of sample admin scripts for you that use WMI right out of the box. These are found in the \Windows\System32 directory and include:

- **iisapp.vbs**   Lists web applications running on an IIS machine
- **iisback.vbs**   Backs up, restores, lists, and deletes IIS configurations
- **iisCnfg.vbs**   Exports and imports IIS configurations as XML files, copies configurations, and saves configurations to disk
- **iisext.vbs**   Enables and lists applications; adds and removes application dependencies; enables, disables, and lists web service extensions; and adds, removes, enables, disables, and lists web service extension files
- **iisFtp.vbs**   Creates, deletes, starts, stops, and lists FTP sites and configures Active Directory user isolation for FTP sites
- **iisFtpdr.vbs**   Creates and deletes virtual directories within FTP sites and displays the virtual directories within a given root
- **iisvdir.vbs**   Creates and deletes virtual directories within websites and displays the virtual directories within a given root
- **iisweb.vbs**   Creates, deletes, starts, stops, and lists websites

We'll look at many of these scripts in more detail later in this chapter, starting with the section "Managing Websites." However, I'll defer coverage of two of them (iisback.vbs and iiscnfg.vbs) until Chapter 13 where discussion of them is more appropriate.

NOTE   Anything you can do using these WMI admin scripts included with IIS 6 can of course also be done using IIS Manager. The advantage of the scripted approach is that you can schedule administrative tasks and perform bulk operations such as deleting multiple websites simultaneously, which can speed common administrative tasks on IIS machines that host large numbers of sites.

ADSI

Active Directory Services Interface (ADSI) is Microsoft's directory service model for Windows Server 2003. ADSI is implemented as a set of COM interfaces that can be scripted to access and manipulate Active Directory objects for management purposes. Windows Server 2003 includes an IIS ADSI Provider that allows programmatic or scripted administration of IIS properties, allowing you to display and configure settings for websites, virtual directories, applications, and more.

Microsoft touted ADSI as the way to go for command-line administration in IIS 5, but with the IIS WMI Provider included in IIS 6 they are now de-emphasizing ADSI and instead recommending WMI as the preferred method due to its richer query support and standards-based implementation.

CAUTION   Custom ADSI scripts designed for managing IIS 5 may not work with IIS 6 due to ADSI 2 methods included with Windows Server 2003. Be sure to test your old admin scripts carefully before using them in an IIS 6 production environment. Also, if your existing ADSI scripts have functionality relating to applications, you will need to modify them to enable them to work with application pools.

Other Commands

A number of Windows commands such as net start and net stop can be used to manage certain aspects of IIS, and there are additional commands in the Support Tools folder on the Windows Server 2003 CD-ROM that are also applicable to IIS. I'll cover some of these later in the section "Windows Commands and Support Tools."

RUNNING REMOTE COMMANDS

You can administer IIS from the command line two ways: locally or from a remote machine. To administer IIS locally, log on interactively to the machine's console, open a command-prompt window, and type the command you want to run. For example, say you want to restart your IIS machine using the iisreset command. To do this, log on to the machine's console using an account with administrator privileges, open a command prompt, and type **iisreset**. The result of doing this is shown in Figure 11-1. Note that to use IISReset your user account must be one of the following:

- A member of the Administrators group on the IIS machine (such as the default Administrator account created during installation).
- A member of the Domain Admins group (if IIS is deployed in a domain instead of a workgroup scenario).

What if you want to do this remotely instead? Most admins prefer to do their work using an administrator workstation in their office instead of going to the server room to log on locally to a server. If your administrator console is a Windows Server 2003 machine, simply open a command prompt, and type **iisreset** *computername* where *computername* is the IP address, NetBIOS name, or DNS name of your IIS machine. The type of name you use will depend on what name resolution method you are working with and whether your IIS and administrator machines are on the same LAN or connected via the Internet. If this doesn't work and you get a message like the one in Figure 11-2, then you probably aren't using the right credentials to perform the action. In a domain scenario this shouldn't be a problem since the Administrator account is a member of the Domain Admins group. In a workgroup scenario this problem may occur if the local Administrator accounts on your administrator and IIS machines have different passwords, and the simple workaround in a workgroup scenario is to make sure all your IIS machines and your administrator machine have the same passwords for their Administrator account.

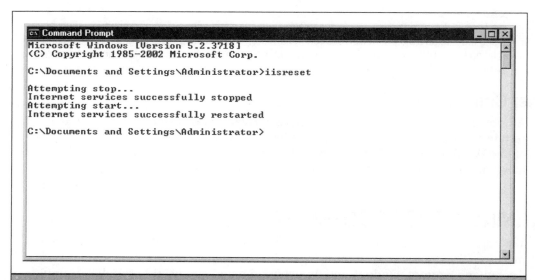

Figure 11-1. Running IISReset on the local machine as Administrator

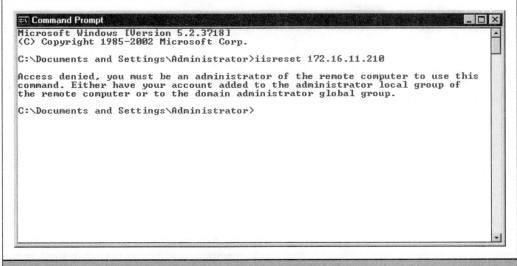

Figure 11-2. Message when IISReset is run with the wrong credentials

What if you are logged onto your administrator machine using ordinary user credentials instead of the Administrator account? After all, best practices suggest you use your Administrator account only when performing administrative tasks. Wherever possible, you should use your ordinary user account for daily use such as checking mail and browsing the Web. In this case (or if the Administrator accounts on the two machines have different passwords), you can use the runas command or secondary logon to run IISReset using Administrator credentials while logged on as a different user. Figure 11-3 shows an example of using runas to run the iisreset command as Administrator while logged on as user JSmith. The example here is a workgroup scenario—in a domain-based network you would use administrator@*domainname* (or *domainname*\administrator) as credentials instead of just administrator. Note that Figure 11-3 doesn't show the second command-prompt window that pops up to execute the iisreset command and closes immediately afterwards.

What if your administrator workstation is a Windows 2000 or Windows XP machine? In the case of Windows 2000, you have a problem, because the version of IISReset included with that platform is different from the one on IIS 6. If you're using Windows XP, as I mentioned in a previous chapter, even if you have the Admin Tools Pack for Windows Server 2003 installed on a Windows XP machine, you still don't have a full set of administrative tools and capabilities for administering Windows Server 2003 machines, and until Service Pack 2 for XP comes out, this situation is not likely to be rectified. If you plan to roll out Windows Server 2003 immediately on your network, your best option is to use a Windows Server 2003 machine as your administrator console.

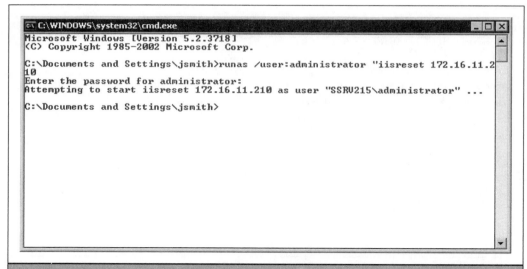

Figure 11-3.   Using secondary logon to run IISReset

Of course, there are a couple of ways around this issue. You could use Remote Desktop to connect to your IIS machine and run IISReset as if you were at the machine's local console. Or you could enable the Telnet Server service on your IIS machine and do the same using Telnet. We looked in detail at Remote Desktop in Chapter 5, so let's look at Telnet now.

Using Telnet

Let's walk through an example of using Telnet to run IISReset on a remote IIS machine, whose IP address we'll assume is 172.16.11.215 and which belongs to a workgroup, not a domain. First, you must enable the Telnet Server service on the IIS machine, which by default is set to Disabled. To enable it, log on to the machine as Administrator and click Start | Administrative Tools | Services to open the Services console. Scroll down the right pane and double-click Telnet to open the properties sheet for the Telnet Server service (Figure 11-4).

Change the Startup Type from Disabled to Automatic, click Apply, and then click Start to start the Telnet Server services on your machine. Once the service starts, close the properties sheet and verify the service is listed as running in the Services console.

Now go to another machine, open a command prompt, and start the Telnet client. The steps differ slightly depending on whether you are using Windows 2000, Windows XP, or Windows Server 2003 as your second machine; the following steps

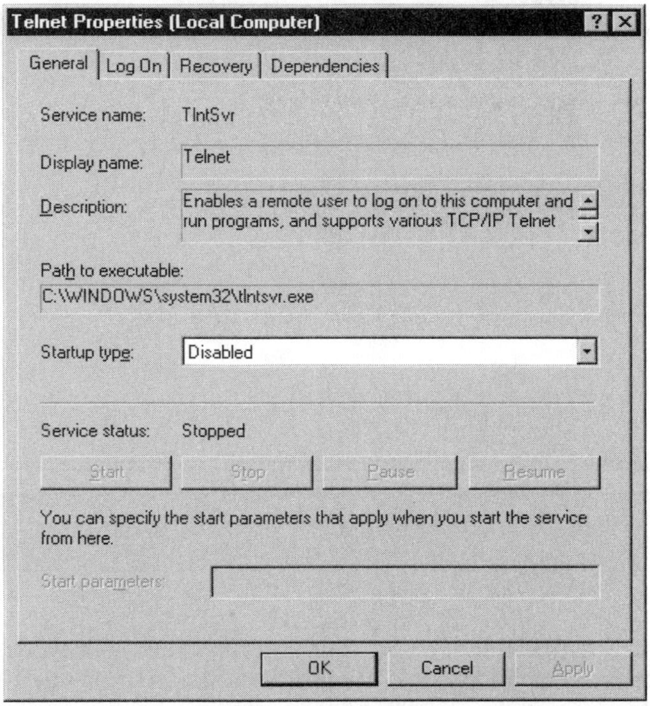

Figure 11-4.   Configuring the Telnet Server service

are for Windows Server 2003. To start the Telnet client on this platform, type **telnet** at the command prompt (Figure 11-5).

After pressing ENTER, the Telnet client starts and runs in session mode (Figure 11-6). The Telnet client in Windows Server 2003 (and in Windows 2000 and Windows XP) has two modes of operation:

- **Session mode**   This mode allows you to open and close connections to remote hosts (Telnet servers), set terminal options, and close the Telnet client when you have finished with it.

- **Command mode**   If you open a connection to a Telnet server while in session mode, the Telnet client automatically switches to command mode. In this mode, you can interactively run character-based applications on the remote host, which is what you want to do—you want to run IISReset on the remote IIS machine.

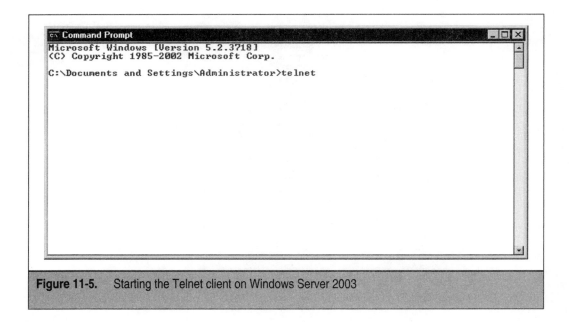

Figure 11-5. Starting the Telnet client on Windows Server 2003

To display the possible Telnet commands you can use in session mode, type **help** (or **h** or **?**). The open command is used to open a session, so type **open 172.16.11.215**

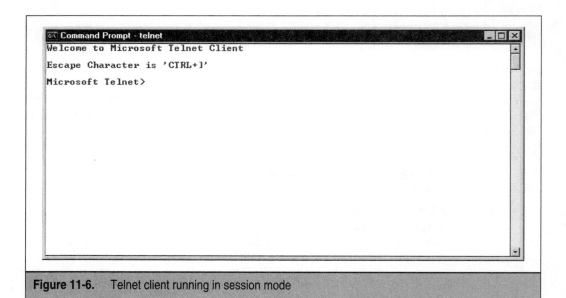

Figure 11-6. Telnet client running in session mode

and press ENTER to try to open a session with the Telnet Server service on your IIS machine. The client responds by warning you that your password is being sent over an insecure communications channel and prompts you with Y/N for whether to continue. Press Y and then ENTER, and the client connects with the Telnet server on the IIS machine and switches from session to command mode. You are now looking at a command-prompt window running interactively on the remote machine (Figure 11-7).

At this point, you can simply type **iisreset**, and the command will execute on the IIS server, causing it to restart. If you need to switch back to command mode to change the session options, press the escape character combination CTRL+], configure your options, and press ENTER to return to command mode. To leave command mode, type **exit**; to quit session mode and close your Telnet client, type **quit**.

There's obviously a lot more to how Telnet is implemented on the Windows Server 2003 platform that we could talk about, but that's all beyond the scope of this book. Consult any good book on general Windows Server 2003 administration for more information on this topic.

Telnet vs. Remote Desktop

Which is better for performing command-line administration of IIS 6, Telnet or Remote Desktop? Admins with a Unix background that are familiar with Telnet might prefer this tool instead of Remote Desktop, and an advantage of Telnet is that you can administer IIS from even a Unix or Linux machine. But security is an important issue regarding Telnet—if you enable the Telnet Server service on an IIS machine, you are potentially opening a door for malicious users to try to hack your system. Also, while

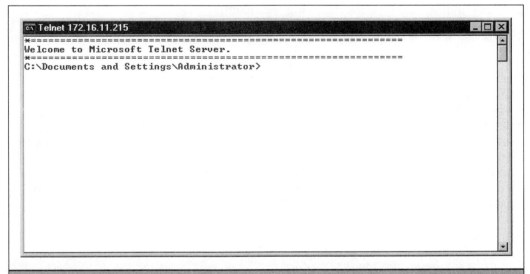

Figure 11-7.   Telnet client connected to an IIS machine and running in command mode

a Telnet authentication session might be encrypted, all other data exchanged between Telnet clients and servers is passed unencrypted over your network, so if anyone is listening using a sniffer, they can follow all the details of your administration session. Remote Desktop by contrast is configured to encrypt all communication by default and is therefore more secure. So, while Telnet is a great idea in principle for remote administration of IIS 6 machines using the command line, in practice, you've got to be very careful if you plan on using it.

Running Scripts

Before I leave this topic of how to remotely run commands for administering IIS 6 machines, let's talk about running scripts. So far you've seen how to remotely run a character-mode command like iisreset and that you can do this three ways:

- Run the command on a machine where the executable is present and using the name of the remote machine. For example, by typing **iisreset** *servername* while logged on as Administrator to another Windows Server 2003 machine.
- Run the command on the remote machine by using Remote Desktop.
- Run the command on the remote machine by using Telnet.

Is there any difference if you want to run a script on the remote machine instead? Let's test this using the iisweb.vbs script, which I'll discuss in more detail in the section "Managing Websites." You'll run this script on a remote machine to try to stop the Default Web Site on 172.16.11.215.

First, go to a different machine running Windows Server 2003, open a command-prompt window, and type the following command:

```
iisweb /stop "Default Web Site" /s 172.16.11.215
```

The syntax of this command says, "Use the iisweb.vbs script to stop the Default Web Site on the server named 172.16.11.215." If a pop-up message appears saying, "This script does not work with Wscript," click OK. A dialog box will then appear saying, "Would you like to register CScript as your default host for VBScript?"; click Yes. This will configure CSript.exe (which runs scripts as console-based processes) instead of WScript.exe (which runs them as Windows-based processes) as the default host for running scripts written using VBScript. These two utilities are part of the Windows Script Host (WSH) model used by Windows Server 2003 for running scripts. By default, scripts run using WScript, which assumes they have a GUI interface. You need to change that so you can run them from the command line. If you don't make CScript your default host, you'll have to type the following to stop the Default Web Site on the remote machine, which is a bit more work.

```
cscript.exe C:\Windows\System32\iisweb.vbs /stop "Default Web Site" /s
172.16.11.215
```

Making CScript the default host for VBScripts simplifies typing your commands for administering IIS, so choose that route. Returning to the first command, enter it, and the script will use WMI to connect to your remote machine and stop the Default Web Site (Figure 11-8). After the script is finished, log on to the IIS machine, open IIS Manager, and verify the site is stopped.

NOTE If you're wondering what W3SVC/1 means in the previous session, 1 is the ID number of the Default Web Site in IIS Manager, so W3SVC/1 means "website with ID number 1" on the IIS machine.

Running Scripts with Telnet or Remote Desktop

If you're going to use Telnet or Remote Desktop to run the script on the remote machine, the syntax is even easier:

```
iisweb /stop "Default Web Site"
```

This time you can leave out the name of the server on which to run the script because you are actually running the script interactively on the target machine. Couldn't be easier!

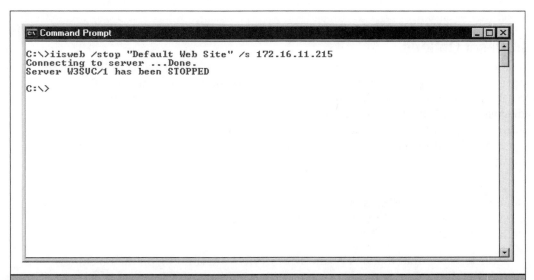

Figure 11-8. Stopping a website on a remote machine using the iisweb.vbs script

MANAGING SERVICES

Now that I've covered the types of commands and ways of running them, I'll discuss in detail how to use each command for remotely administering IIS 6 machines. I'll start with the general task of administering services essential to running IIS.

Using IISReset

As discussed previously, IISReset is your first line of defense for recovering and maintaining buggy applications that application pool recycling fails to protect against. As you've seen, in its simplest usage, typing **iisreset** at the command line on a console session causes all IIS services on the local machine to stop and then start. Exactly the same thing can be done using the GUI by right-clicking the IIS server node in IIS Manager and selecting All Tasks | Restart IIS (in fact, the GUI method uses IISReset to accomplish this task). Note that neither of these approaches cause the HTTP Listener (http.sys) to restart, and neither do they affect any non-IIS Internet services running on the machine, such as the POP3 mail service. As I mentioned previously, IISReset should be a last ditch option only, because stopping IIS terminates any existing connections from Internet clients, causing users frustration and possible data loss. Also, unless you save your configuration to disk first, using IISReset to restart IIS may result in recent metabase changes being lost. Nevertheless, and particularly in a development environment, IISReset is a common method for recovering resource-leaking ASP applications and preventing "accumulated instability" from bringing down your machine.

IISReset Options

You can do more with IISReset than just restart IIS. Let's take a look at the various options for running this command and try each one out. For simplicity, run this command on the IIS machine itself, although most of the options (with an exception I'll shortly discuss) work from a remote machine also, as long as you include the name or IP address of your target IIS machine in the command syntax.

First of all, the /status switch displays which IIS services are currently running on the machine:

```
C:\>iisreset /status
Status for World Wide Web Publishing Service ( W3SVC ) : Running
Status for FTP Publishing Service ( MSFtpsvc ) : Running
Status for HTTP SSL ( HTTPFilter ) : Running
```

This tells you that the WWW and FTP services are running on the machine, along with HTTP Filter, a user-mode process used to implement SSL encryption on IIS. This HTTP Filter component is hosted within the lsass.exe process when IIS is configured to run in worker process isolation mode, and within the inetinfo.exe process when IIS is running in IIS 5 isolation mode. You can verify that these services are running by opening Services in Administrative Tools. By examining the Dependencies tab of each service, you can discover what other services they depend on and what services depend on them (Figure 11-9). For example, all three of the services displayed in the previous command-line session depend upon the IISAdmin service, which the iisreset /status command does not display as running. The WWW service also depends on the HTTP SSL service, which is the name displayed in the Services console for the HTTP Filter component.

If you want to simply stop all IIS services as opposed to restarting (stopping and then starting) them, use the /stop switch:

```
C:\>iisreset /stop
Attempting stop...
Internet services successfully stopped
```

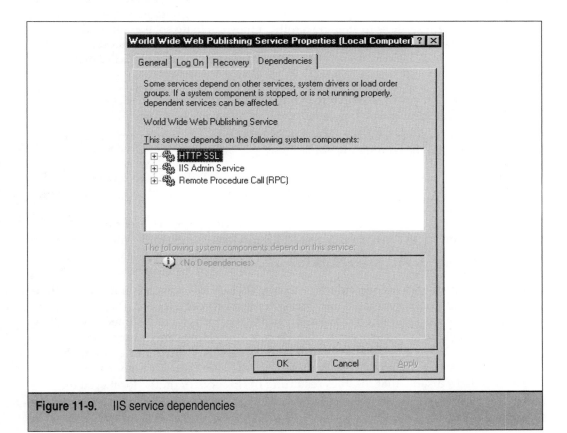

Figure 11-9.   IIS service dependencies

Now if you check the status of IIS you can verify that the services have been stopped:

```
C:\>iisreset /status
Status for World Wide Web Publishing Service ( W3SVC ) : Stopped
Status for FTP Publishing Service ( MSFtpsvc ) : Stopped
Status for HTTP SSL ( HTTPFilter ) : Stopped
```

To start the stopped services, use the /start switch:

```
C:\>iisreset /start
Attempting start...
Internet services successfully started
```

Of course, you can verify that the services have started using /status as before. An issue to consider is what happens if it takes a long time for IIS services to stop gracefully (as opposed to terminate abruptly with possible data loss)? By default, iisreset /stop waits 60 seconds for services to stop gracefully. If they fail to do so, it assumes there is a problem with the server and forces the services to stop abruptly, while iisreset /restart waits only 20 seconds before forcing termination of services. You can modify this process two ways:

- Use the /timeout:val switch to explicitly specify how long in seconds the command should wait before stopping or restarting services.

- Use the /noforce switch to indicate that if services cannot be gracefully shut down, then the command should abort.

Another administrative action you can perform with IISReset is to reboot your IIS machine using the /reboot switch (Figure 11-10). This gives you 20 seconds before the server automatically reboots.

You can also use the /rebootonerror switch to force a reboot to occur if an error occurs when you try to start, stop, or restart IIS services. For example, the command

```
iisreset /stop /rebootonerror /timeout:1
```

will give the command one second to try to stop IIS services, which is not enough time, so an error condition is generated and /rebootonerror forces a reboot.

Finally, a concern you might have as an administrator is what if someone else uses IISReset remotely to stop services on your IIS machine? How can you prevent them from doing this? Of course, that individual would need Administrator credentials to accomplish this, but credentials can be stolen, so Microsoft added another switch to IISReset called /disable that disables restarting of IIS services on the local system:

```
C:\>iisreset /disable
Access to IIS restart API disabled to this computer
C:\>iisreset /restart
Attempting stop...
Restart attempt failed.
Restarting of Internet Services has been disabled.
```

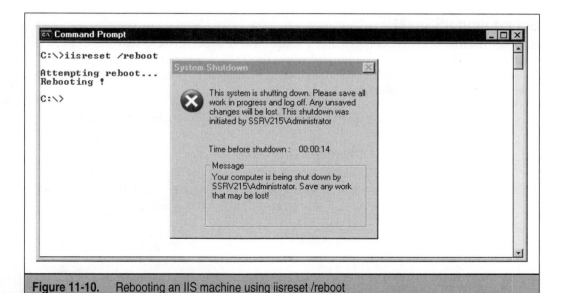

Figure 11-10. Rebooting an IIS machine using iisreset /reboot

They also provided another switch that you can use to enable the command if it's disabled:

```
C:\>iisreset /enable
Restarting of Internet Services has been enabled.
```

How does that make things more secure? Couldn't an attacker simply enable the command if they found it disabled on a machine? The key is that the /disable and /enable switches only work if you run them interactively (locally) on the IIS machine. For example, if you run iisreset /disable on an IIS machine 172.16.11.215 and then try to stop the services from a remote machine, the command fails to stop the services:

```
C:\>iisreset 172.16.11.215 /stop
Attempting stop...
Stop attempt failed.
Restarting of Internet Services has been disabled.
```

NOTE If you run iisreset *computername* /disable from a remote machine to disable services on an IIS machine named *computername*, the response says that "Restarting of Internet services has been disabled," but this is not correct—try iisreset *computername* /restart next and you'll see that it works!

Scheduling IISReset

Another useful approach you can take to administering IIS services with IISReset is to schedule operation of this command using the Task Scheduler of Windows Server 2003. For example, to schedule IIS to restart according to a predefined schedule or interval of time, follow these steps:

1. Click Start | Settings, open Control Panel, select Scheduled Tasks, and choose Add Scheduled Task.
2. Click Next to run the Scheduled Task Wizard and be presented with a list of common Windows programs whose operation you might wish to schedule.
3. Because IISReset is not in the displayed list of programs, click Browse, navigate to the \Windows\System32 folder, and double-click IISReset.exe to select it (Figure 11-11).
4. Type a friendly name for the task ("iisreset" is suggested), select a schedule condition, and click Next.
5. Specify the Administrator credentials for running the command and click Next.
6. Select the check box to further configure advanced properties for the task and click Finish.
7. On the Task tab of the properties sheet for the task, in the Run box, add any optional switches you require at the end of the command string and click OK.

To test this out, try creating a scheduled task that will stop IIS services the next time you log on to your IIS machine. Then log off and log on again and open IIS Manager. You should see the Web Sites and FTP Sites disabled with red circles containing an X. If this is not the case, make sure you didn't run iisreset /disable previously on the machine!

TIP You can also schedule tasks from the command line using the new Schtasks.exe command of Windows Server 2003, which replaces the At.exe command of earlier versions (though it's still present for down-level compatibility reasons). To find out more about Schtasks.exe, open the Help and Support Center on your Windows Server 2003 machine.

Using net Commands

You can also stop, start, and pause other IIS services using the net commands, part of the general Windows commands on Windows Server 2003. For example, to stop only the WWW service but leave the IIS Admin service running, use net stop as follows:

```
C:\>net stop w3svc
The World Wide Web Publishing Service service is stopping.
The World Wide Web Publishing Service service was stopped successfully.
```

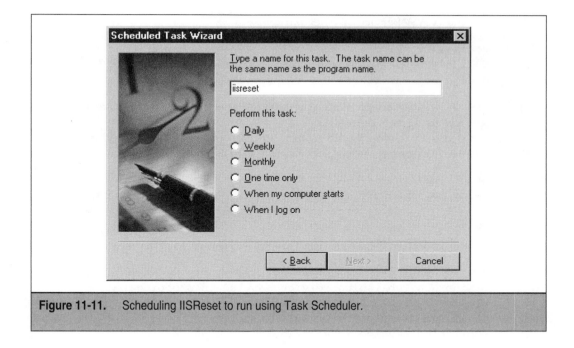

Figure 11-11. Scheduling IISReset to run using Task Scheduler.

Now if you open IIS Manager, you'll see a red circle with an X on it over the Web Sites node, indicating that all websites on the machine are stopped (Figure 11-12).

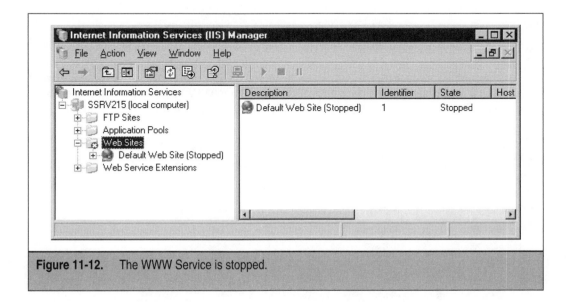

Figure 11-12. The WWW Service is stopped.

To restart the WWW Service, use net start:

```
C:\>net start w3svc
The World Wide Web Publishing Service service is starting.
The World Wide Web Publishing Service service was started successfully.
```

Table 11-1 shows the service name you need to use when you want to stop, start, or pause IIS services using net commands.

Note that if you try to stop the IIS Admin service, you will be prompted whether to continue because it stops dependent services like WWW and FTP as well:

```
C:\>net stop iisadmin
The following services are dependent on the IIS Admin Service service.
Stopping the IIS Admin Service service will also stop these services.
   World Wide Web Publishing Service
   FTP Publishing Service
   HTTP SSL
Do you want to continue this operation? (Y/N) [N]: y
The World Wide Web Publishing Service service is stopping.
The World Wide Web Publishing Service service was stopped successfully.
The FTP Publishing Service service is stopping.
The FTP Publishing Service service was stopped successfully.
The HTTP SSL service is stopping.
The HTTP SSL service was stopped successfully.
The IIS Admin Service service is stopping.
The IIS Admin Service service was stopped successfully.
```

If you want to stop the IIS Admin service without having to respond to the prompt, use this:

```
net stop /y iisadmin
```

Unfortunately, restarting IIS Admin using net start iisadmin only starts the IIS Admin service alone and doesn't start dependent services like WWW or FTP. To restart all the IIS services, use iisreset /start. You can verify that this worked with iisreset /status.

Service	Name for net Commands
IIS Admin service	iisadmin
WWW service	w3svc
FTP service	msftpsvc
SMTP service	smtpsvc
NNTP service	nntpsvc

Table 11-1. Service Names for net Commands

MANAGING WEBSITES

Let's move on now and look at managing IIS using the command-line WMI scripts included in the \System32 directory of your IIS machine. We'll start by looking at the iisweb.vbs script, which you can use to create, delete, start, stop, pause, and query websites from the command line, either while logged on interactively to the local IIS machine or from a remote machine as discussed in the section "Running Scripts" earlier in this chapter. I'll break these tasks down into several groups and walk you through them using command-line sessions.

For the purpose of the walkthroughs in this section and those following, first make sure your IIS machine has five IP addresses assigned to the local area connection. In the following examples these addresses are 172.16.11.215 through 172.16.11.219, but if you have different addresses assigned you can easily modify the procedures. Make sure also that:

- Your IIS machine is running in worker process isolation mode.
- The only website present is the Default Web Site.
- The FTP service is installed and the only FTP site present is the Default FTP Site.
- The only application pool present is the DefaultAppPool, and the only application this contains is the Default Application.

Finally, leave IIS Manager open so you can refresh it by pressing F5 to verify the results after you run each of the following admin script examples. If F5 doesn't refresh IIS Manager, try closing and reopening the console.

NOTE   All the WMI admin scripts included with IIS 6 require Administrator credentials for running them and only work on machines running version 6 of IIS.

Creating Websites

Creating a website using iisweb.vbs is simple. Let's say you want to create a new website called Accounting that has an IP address of 172.16.11.216 and C:\finance as its home directory, but that this directory does not yet exist on the server. Here's a command-line session showing how to do this from a command-prompt window opened on the IIS machine (you're either logged on interactively to the IIS machine or connected to it using Remote Desktop or Telnet):

```
C:\>iisweb /create C:\finance Accounting /i 172.16.11.216
Connecting to server ...Done.
Server        = SSRV215
Site Name     = Accounting
Metabase Path = W3SVC/376238833
IP            = 172.16.11.216
Host          = NOT SPECIFIED
```

```
Port          = 80
Root          = C:\finance
Status        = STARTED
```

Let's analyze this, first by looking at the syntax of the command, which is something like this:

```
iisweb /create Path SiteName /i IPAddress
```

Taking this apart, you see that:

- *Path* is the physical location of the home directory for the new site. Note that if this directory doesn't exist on the IIS machine, the script creates it.

- *SiteName* is the friendly or descriptive name of the new site for display in IIS Manager. If your site name has spaces in it, enclose the site name in quotation marks.

- The /i switch must be followed by the IP address you want to assign to the site. If you omit this switch, IIS will make All Unassigned the IP address for the new site, and this will conflict with the settings of the existing Default Web Site and the new site will not be able to start.

Looking at the output of the iisweb /create command in the preceding session, note that your new site is

- Located on an IIS machine named SSRV215

- Has the friendly name Accounting, as expected

- Has the metabase path W3SVC/376238833, which indicates that it is a website (the W3SVC part) with an internal ID number 376238833 (see Figure 11-13)

- Has IP address 172.16.11.216, as expected

- Has no host header name assigned to it

- Listens on port 80, the standard HTTP port number

- Has C:\finance as its home (root) directory, as expected

- Is started and running on the IIS machine

Now let's create another site on the machine, this time making the home directory C:\HR, the site name Human Resources, and the IP address 172.16.11.217. Because the HR department wants to keep this site under wraps, you'll assign it a nonstandard port number such as 8050 (anything above 1023 will do so that it will not conflict with well-known port assignments). You'll also assign the site a host header of hr.mtit.com. And because the site has no content in it yet, you need to make sure the new site is stopped and not started after it is created. Finally, instead of running iisweb on the machine itself, run it from another Windows Server 2003 machine on the network.

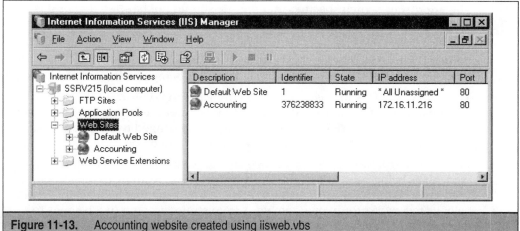

Figure 11-13. Accounting website created using iisweb.vbs

Let's say the machine you're running it on is part of the mtit.com domain, but the IIS machine is a stand-alone machine on the DMZ of your network. You'll need the right credentials to create the site on your IIS machine, so use the local Administrator account on that machine (or SSRV215\Administrator because the name of the machine is SSRV215) and also the password. Here's the syntax to accomplish all this and the results that are displayed when the script runs:

```
C:\>iisweb /create C:\HR "Human Resources" /b 8050 /i 172.16.11.217 /d
hr.mtit.com /dontstart /s 172.16.11.215 /u SSRV215\Administrator /p
pa$$w0rd
Connecting to server ...Done.
Server        = 172.16.11.215
Site Name     = Human Resources
Metabase Path = W3SVC/1525757177
IP            = 172.16.11.217
Host          = hr.mtit.com
Port          = 8050
Root          = C:\HR
Status        = STOPPED
```

Here are the new elements of the syntax of iisweb that are being used in this command:

- The /b 8050 option causes the new site to listen on port 8050.
- The /d hr.mtit.com option assigns the host header name hr.mtit.com to the new site.

- The /dontstart switch specifies that the site should not be started after it is created.

- The /s 172.16.11.215 option indicates that the script should be run on the remote IIS machine having this IP address (or you could use SSRV215 for its name here instead, or its DNS name if DNS is being used).

- The /u SSRV215\Administrator option indicates that you want to run the script using the credentials of the local Administrator account on the stand-alone IIS machine named SSRV215. If the IIS machine belonged to a domain like mtit.com, you would use /u MTIT\Administrator here instead.

- The /p pa$$w0rd option is used to specify the password of the Administrator credentials being used to perform the command. The Administrator account used must be the local Administrator account on the remote IIS machine (if it belongs to a workgroup) or a domain Administrator account (if it belongs to a domain). You could also use an account that has been delegated the appropriate authority.

CAUTION   These scripts send Administrator credentials unencrypted over the network, so only use them to manage IIS machines located on your LAN. Do not use them for managing IIS machines over the Internet unless you are running them using Remote Desktop, which encrypts all communications.

The output of the script suggests it ran successfully, but, to make sure, open the properties sheet for the site in IIS Manager and make sure the settings are as expected; then trying starting the site and see if it works. If you can't start the site, something was wrong with your script that resulted in a faulty configuration for the site—try deleting it and creating it again.

By the way, now that you know how to use this script to connect to a remote IIS machine and run it on that machine, I'll keep things simple for the remaining examples by running them locally on the IIS machine. Once you understand the /s and /u and /p switches and how they work, you'll see how any of these scripts can be run remotely.

A few more things to note when creating websites using this script:

- *Path* must always precede *SiteName* in the command's syntax.

- The home directory for the new site must be local to the IIS machine. You can't specify a network share using a UNC path when you use this script. If you need to give your new site a remote home directory, you must change the location afterward with IIS Manager.

- It's possible for two websites to have the same friendly name in IIS Manager, so in theory you could use the script to create another site called Default Web Site if you like. But internally (in the metabase), the two sites are described using their unique site IDs so IIS won't get confused about which is which.

- All other properties of your newly created site are inherited from the properties of the Web Sites node above it (see the console tree in IIS Manager). You can customize your new site by modifying its properties afterward using IIS Manager.

Starting, Stopping, and Pausing Websites

You can also use iisweb to start, stop, and pause websites on your machine. Pausing a site prevents new client connections from being formed but doesn't break off existing connections the way stopping does. Here's how to stop and then start the Accounting website created earlier:

```
C:\>iisweb /stop Accounting
Connecting to server ...Done.
Server W3SVC/376238833 has been STOPPED
C:\>iisweb /start W3SVC/376238833
Connecting to server ...Done.
Server W3SVC/376238833 has been STARTED
```

Notice that you can use either the friendly name or metabase ID of the site you want to stop or start.

Now try pausing both the Accounting and Human Resources websites and then continue (unpause) them by starting them again:

```
C:\>iisweb /pause Accounting "Human Resources"
Connecting to server ...Done.
Server W3SVC/376238833 has been PAUSED
Server W3SVC/1525757177 has been PAUSED
C:\>iisweb /start accounting "human resources"
Connecting to server ...Done.
Server W3SVC/376238833 has been CONTINUED
Server W3SVC/1525757177 has been CONTINUED
```

Note from this example that:

- You can specify multiple names of sites for starting, stopping, or pausing them.
- The names of sites are not case specific (accounting is the same as Accounting).

You might think that iisweb /pause would pause *all* websites on the machine, but unfortunately this is not the case. However, as you saw earlier, you can always stop all websites by using iisreset /stop to stop the WWW service.

Querying Websites

To display all the websites on our IIS machine:

```
C:\>iisweb /query
Connecting to server ...Done.
```

```
Site Name (Metabase Path)                        Status  IP              Port  Host
================================================================================
Default Web Site (W3SVC/1)                        STARTED ALL              80   N/A
Accounting (W3SVC/376238833)                      STARTED 172.16.11.216    80   N/A
Human Resources (W3SVC/1525757177)                STARTED 172.16.11.217    8050 hr.mtit.com
```

Note that the name, metabase ID, status, IP address, port, and host header name(s) are displayed for all sites on your server. You could also query for information about one or more sites instead of all of them:

```
C:\>iisweb /query "Default Web Site" w3svc/1525757177
Connecting to server ...Done.
Site Name (Metabase Path)                        Status  IP              Port  Host
================================================================================
Default Web Site (W3SVC/1)                        STARTED ALL              80   N/A
Human Resources (W3SVC/1525757177)                STARTED 172.16.11.217    8050 hr.mtit.com
```

Deleting Websites

Finally, delete your Human Resources website since you don't need it anymore:

```
C:\>iisweb /delete "Human Resources"
Connecting to server ...Done.
Server W3SVC/1525757177 has been deleted
```

Use IIS Manager to verify that the site is gone, or use iisweb /query to list the remaining sites. You can delete multiple websites at the same time by naming them in succession.

NOTE   Deleting a website does *not* delete its associated home directory.

MANAGING VIRTUAL DIRECTORIES

A lot of what you learned in the preceding section applies to many of the other admin scripts included with IIS 6 (particularly the /s, /u, and /p switches, which can be used with any of the scripts to run them from a remote Windows Server 2003 machine), so we'll move more quickly through the remaining scripts. Next, we'll look at how to create, delete, and query virtual directories.

Creating Virtual Directories

For these examples, you'll work with the Accounting website with a home directory of C:\finance that you created earlier. Start by creating a virtual directory with an alias of "budget" that maps to the physical directory C:\planning:

```
C:\>iisvdir /create Accounting budget C:\planning
Connecting to server ...Done.
Virtual Path  = Accounting/ROOT/budget
ROOT          = C:\planning
Metabase Path = W3SVC/376238833/ROOT/budget
```

The output should be easy to understand now after what you learned in the preceding section. Open IIS Manager and verify that the virtual directory exists and has the settings you expected (Figure 11-14).

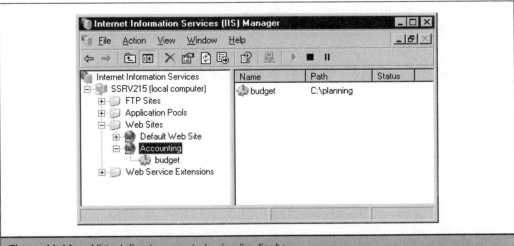

Figure 11-14.   Virtual directory created using iisvdir.vbs

Invisible Virtual Directories

Something you need to watch out for when creating virtual directories (with either iisvdir.vbs or IIS Manager) is invisible virtual directories. This happens when the alias for a virtual directory is identical to a physical subdirectory within the website root folder. For example, say your website home directory is C:\Inetpub\wwwroot, as it is for the Default Web Site, and you create a *physical* subdirectory \test under \wwwroot. If users want to access the default.htm file located in this directory, they can open the URL http://*servername*/test on the client machine. But what if you now create a *virtual* directory within your site and give it the alias "test" and map this to a folder called C:\stuff. Now you have a problem, because when a user tries to open the same URL http://servername/test, IIS will assume you want the contents of the virtual directory and will return the default.htm file from C:\stuff. The result is that once you create your test virtual directory, users can no longer access the files in the physical \test directory! Watch out for this!

Now create another virtual directory, this time within the existing virtual directory called budget that you just created. The new virtual directory should have the alias 2003 and be mapped to C:\planning\2003 as its content location:

```
C:\>iisvdir /create Accounting/budget 2003 C:\planning\2003
Connecting to server ...Done.
Virtual Path  = Accounting/ROOT/budget/2003
ROOT          = C:\planning\2003
Metabase Path = W3SVC/376238833/ROOT/budget/2003
```

Verify in IIS Manager that a new 2003 virtual directory exists below "budget" in the console tree. Easy as pie!

Querying Virtual Directories

Just as you can use iisweb.vbs to display the websites on your machine, you can use iisvdir.vbs to display the virtual directories within a website:

```
C:\>iisvdir /query Accounting
Connecting to server ...Done.
Alias                          Physical Root
========================================================================
/budget                        C:\planning
```

Note that running /query against a website does not recursively list all virtual directories on the machine, but only those beneath the root. To display virtual directories within virtual directories, try this:

```
C:\>iisvdir /query Accounting\budget
Connecting to server ...Done.
Alias                             Physical Root
==============================================================================
/2003                            C:\planning\2003
```

And if you try to go even deeper, here's what happens:

```
C:\>iisvdir /query Accounting\budget\2003
Connecting to server ...Done.
No virtual sub-directories available.
```

Deleting Virtual Directories

Now delete the 2003 virtual directory you created earlier:

```
C:\>iisvdir /delete Accounting\budget\2003
Connecting to server ...Done.
Web directory Accounting/ROOT/budget/2003 has been DELETED
```

Now confirm that 2003 has been deleted:

```
C:\>iisvdir /query Accounting\budget
Connecting to server ...Done.
No virtual sub-directories available.
```

Like websites, deleting a virtual directory does not delete its associated content directory.

MANAGING FTP SITES AND VIRTUAL DIRECTORIES

Managing FTP sites and their virtual directories is almost identical to managing websites and their virtual directories as discussed in the preceding section. The main difference is that you use different scripts:

- The iisftp.vbs script creates, deletes, starts, stops, and pauses FTP sites.
- The iisftpdr.vbs script creates, deletes, and queries FTP virtual directories.

The syntax is so similar that I won't go into it here. The only real difference is that the iisftp.vbs script can also be used for configuring your FTP site to run in user isolation mode either as Local or Active Directory user isolation. For example, to create a new

FTP site called "Company FTP Site" with root directory C:\employees and IP address 172.16.11.215, and that is configured to run using Local isolation mode, do this:

```
C:\>iisftp /create C:\employees "Company FTP Site" /i 172.16.11.216 /
isolation Local
Connecting to server ...Done.
Server       = SSRV215
Site Name    = Company FTP Site
Metabase Path = MSFTPSVC/1465812683
IP           = 172.16.11.216
Port         = 21
Root         = C:\employees
IsoMode      = Local
Status       = STARTED
```

To create an FTP site configured to run in Active Directory isolation mode, simply replace "Local" with "Active Directory" in the preceding command.

MANAGING APPLICATIONS AND WEB SERVICE EXTENSIONS

You can also manage applications and web service extensions from the command line using two admin scripts provided with IIS 6:

- The isapp.vbs script reports the process identifiers (PIDs) of worker processes (instances of W3pwp.exe) that are currently serving a specified application pool.

- The iisext.vbs script enables, disables, or lists web service extensions; adds or removes application dependencies; enables or lists applications; and adds, removes, enables, disables, or lists individual files (DLLs or EXEs) needed by web service extensions.

This is pretty deep stuff, but a few examples will make things clear.

NOTE Remember that web service extensions are ISAPI files (DLLs) or CGI executables (EXEs) that extend the functionality of IIS and enable it to serve different kinds of dynamic content or perform special actions.

Listing Web Service Extensions

To list the IDs of all web service extensions defined on the machine, do this:

```
C:\>iisext /listext
Connecting to server ...Done.
```

```
SSINC
ASP
HTTPODBC
WEBDAV
```

These extensions are all defined as entries under the WebSvcExtRestrictionList property in the metabase (we'll look at the metabase in detail in Chapter 14, "Working with the Metabase"). The output of the command shows that Server Side Includes, Active Server Pages, Internet Data Connector, and WebDAV are all defined extensions on the machine (Figure 11-15). Note that this list shows what extensions are defined regardless of whether they are enabled or not.

Listing Files Associated with Web Service Extensions

To list the actual files (DLLs or EXEs) associated with these extensions, do this:

```
C:\>iisext /listfile
Connecting to server ...Done.
Status / Extension Path
───────────────────────────

0    *.dll
0    *.exe
0    C:\WINDOWS\system32\inetsrv\ssinc.dll
1    C:\WINDOWS\system32\inetsrv\asp.dll
0    C:\WINDOWS\system32\inetsrv\httpodbc.dll
0    C:\WINDOWS\system32\inetsrv\httpext.dll
```

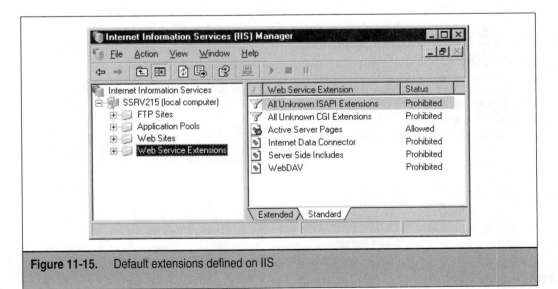

Figure 11-15.   Default extensions defined on IIS

Note that this matches the information specified in Table 10-3 of Chapter 10, "Securing IIS." The "1" at the start of the fourth line indicates that the asp.dll (Active Server Pages) extension is currently enabled on the server while the other extensions are disabled.

Enabling a Web Service Extension File

To enable the WebDAV (httpext.dll) extension, do this:

```
C:\>iisext /enfile C:\windows\system32\inetsrv\httpext.dll
Connecting to server ...Done.
Enabling extension file complete.

C:\>iisext /listfile
Connecting to server ...Done.
Status / Extension Path
_____

0  *.dll
0  *.exe
0  C:\WINDOWS\system32\inetsrv\ssinc.dll
1  C:\WINDOWS\system32\inetsrv\asp.dll
0  C:\WINDOWS\system32\inetsrv\httpodbc.dll
1  C:\WINDOWS\system32\inetsrv\httpext.dll
```

This also verifies that the extension is enabled by running iisext /listfile again. You can similarly disable an extension using iisext /disfile and remove the extension entirely by removing the association with its DLL or EXE using iisext /rmfile.

Add a New Extension

To add a new file as a web service extension, do this:

```
C:\>iisext /addfile C:\windows\system32\blah.dll 0 Blah 1 "Extension
for bored developers"
Connecting to server ...Done.
Adding extension file complete.

C:\>iisext /listext
Connecting to server ...Done.
SSINC
ASP
HTTPODBC
WEBDAV
Blah
```

```
C:\>iisext /listfile
Connecting to server ...Done.
Status / Extension Path
_____
0   *.dll
0   *.exe
0   C:\WINDOWS\system32\inetsrv\ssinc.dll
1   C:\WINDOWS\system32\inetsrv\asp.dll
0   C:\WINDOWS\system32\inetsrv\httpodbc.dll
1   C:\WINDOWS\system32\inetsrv\httpext.dll
0   C:\WINDOWS\system32\blah.dll
```

The iisext /addfile command has the following syntax:

- C:\windows\system32\blah.dll specifies the DLL associated with the new extension.
- The first number (0) indicates that the extension when created will be left disabled (using 1 instead will enable it).
- "Blah" is the ID associated with the extension and will be displayed in IIS Manager when the Web Service Extensions (WSE) node is selected.
- The second number (1) indicates that the extension can be removed afterward if desired (using 0 instead prevents this).
- The string at the end is a short description of the extension, which also appears in IIS Manager

Running the preceding iisweb /listext command verifies that the extension has been defined, and running iisweb /listfile verifies the association with the DLL and that the extension is disabled.

Enabling a Web Service Extension

This is basically the same as enabling a web service extension file discussed previously, but is a little easier to do:

```
C:\>iisext /enext Blah
Connecting to server ...Done.
Enabling extension complete.

C:\>iisext /listfile
Connecting to server ...Done.
Status / Extension Path
_____
0   *.dll
0   *.exe
```

```
0   C:\WINDOWS\system32\inetsrv\ssinc.dll
1   C:\WINDOWS\system32\inetsrv\asp.dll
0   C:\WINDOWS\system32\inetsrv\httpodbc.dll
1   C:\WINDOWS\system32\inetsrv\httpext.dll
1   C:\windows\system32\blah.dll
```

Here you can simply specify the ID ("Blah" in the example) of the extension you want to enable, which is easier than using iisweb /enfile and specifying the path to the DLL. Similarly, you can disable an extension using iisext /disext. Once again, you can verify that the extension is enabled by using iisext /listfile as in the previous session.

Managing Application Dependencies

The ApplicationDependencies list in the metabase manages the web service extensions that your web applications depend on. To display the contents of this list, do this:

```
C:\>iisext /listapp
Connecting to server ...Done.
Active Server Pages
Internet Data Connector
Server Side Includes
WebDAV
```

To make the Accounting application dependent upon the Blah web service extension:

```
C:\>iisext /addep Accounting Blah
Connecting to server ...Done.
Adding dependency complete.
```

To remove this dependency, use iisext /rmdep; to enable an application, use iisext /enapp.

Listing Running Applications

You can use the iisapp script to list all running web applications, showing their process identity (PID) and the application pool they are assigned to. In order to make this more interesting, do the following: create a new application pool called AccountingAppPool and assign your Accounting website to this pool. Then add a simple ASP application to the home directory of both the Default Web Site and your Accounting website, open these applications in a browser (using http://172.16.11.215 and http://172.16.11.216), and do the following:

```
C:\>iisapp
W3WP.exe PID: 3224    AppPoolId: DefaultAppPool
W3WP.exe PID: 2844    AppPoolId: AccountingAppPool
```

Note that each application pool is serviced by a different worker process. If you have a lot of applications running on your machine and know the PID of the one you want to check on, do this:

```
C:\>iisapp /p 2844
W3WP.exe PID: 2844    AppPoolId: AccountingAppPool
```

ADSUTIL

I'll be brief here: WMI is in and ADSI is out, as far as managing IIS is concerned. Well, not completely—ADSI is still fully supported by IIS 6, but Microsoft has indicated that WMI is the wave of the future; so, after using the scripts in the preceding sections, you might want to read the short tutorial about how to write WMI scripts in the IIS online help file. But if you've worked extensively with IIS version 5, you're probably already familiar with Adsutil.vbs, a script that uses ADSI to manipulate IIS configuration info. If not, you can read about Adsutil in IIS online help, but I won't go into it any further here.

WINDOWS COMMANDS AND SUPPORT TOOLS

To finish off, there are a few standard Windows commands that are sometimes useful for managing certain aspects of IIS. For example, I talked earlier in this chapter about using the net start and net stop commands to start and stop IIS services. Other net commands are also useful at times:

- **net localgroup**   Adds a user account to the IIS_WPG group, to which accounts used as application pool identities must belong.
- **cacls**   Captures a list of all NTFS permissions on your server, which can help you troubleshoot if things go wrong.
- **convlog**   Converts IIS log files to NCSA format.

Furthermore, certain resource kit utilities may also be useful:

- **auditpol**   Modifies audit policies from the command line.
- **secedit**   Manages security templates on the system.
- **showmbrs**   Displays members of security groups that have permissions on directories and files.

Also included in the \Support\Tools folder of your Windows Server 2003 CD-ROM is httpcfg.exe, a command-line tool that lets you configure the IP Listen List of http.sys, which is the IIS 6 alternative to socket pooling in IIS 5.

Challenge

You are an admin who has a strong Unix background, and you want to be able to manage your IIS machines remotely from the command line as much as possible. What kind of tasks can you perform this way? What tasks will require access to the GUI instead? Why might it be worthwhile for you to take the time to learn how WMI works and how to write scripts using Visual Basic Scripting Edition?

NOTE There is another admin script included with IIS 6 that I haven't talked about yet: rgroup.vbs, which is located in \System32\Inetsrv and is used to create and delete newsgroups from the command line. I'll cover NNTP in Chapter 15, "SMTP and NNTP."

CHECKLIST: COMMAND-LINE ADMINISTRATION

Check off each of the administration tasks below after you learn how to perform them from the command line:

- ☐ Run commands remotely from another Windows Server 2003 machine.
- ☐ Run commands remotely using Remote Desktop.
- ☐ Run commands remotely using Telnet.
- ☐ Stop, start, and restart IIS using IISReset.
- ☐ Stop, pause, and start IIS services using net commands.
- ☐ Disable remote restarting or rebooting of IIS.
- ☐ Schedule commands using Task Scheduler.
- ☐ Manage websites using iisweb.vbs.
- ☐ Manage website virtual directories using iisvdir.vbs.
- ☐ Manage FTP sites using iisftp.vbs.
- ☐ Manage FTP virtual directories using iisftpdr.vbs.
- ☐ Manage web service extensions and application dependences using iisext.vbs.
- ☐ Display application info using iisapp.vbs.

CHAPTER 12

Performance Tuning
and Monitoring

I t's one thing to deploy applications on an IIS machine, and it's another to make sure your applications and server perform well from the user's perspective. The topic of performance tuning is an important one in a fast-paced world where users will move on if a page is not returned a few seconds after clicking it, and where they will abandon a purchase if an online credit card returns an HTTP error code. This chapter looks in detail at how to tune IIS servers, sites, and applications to ensure that response time and throughput are sufficient to meet the needs of potential users. It also looks briefly at the subject of performance monitoring in general and how to monitor IIS machines using tools included with Windows Server 2003.

TUNING IIS

I'll begin by focusing on tuning IIS itself to ensure that web applications run on it with the best possible levels of scalability, reliability, and performance. Of course, bad application coding can nullify many of the performance gains from any actions you take tuning IIS; so later in this chapter, in the section titled "Additional Server Tuning Tips," I'll discuss performance issues relating to specific types of applications such as ASP, ASP.NET, ISAPI, and CGI. First, however, I'll focus more generally on how to tune IIS for the widest possible range of applications to run well.

Choosing an Isolation Mode

Tuning IIS for maximum performance, reliability, and security starts with a simple decision: will you be running your server in worker process isolation mode or IIS 5 isolation mode? To ensure the highest level of performance and best security, you need to configure your servers to run in worker process isolation mode so they can take full advantage of the new architectural features of IIS 6, including:

- Using application pools and worker processes with their associated tuning features of recycling, idle timeout, request queue limits, CPU monitoring, processor affinity, web gardens, health monitoring, rapid-fail protection, startup and shutdown time limits, and queue length limits.

- Using ASP.NET as an application development platform with its associated benefits of XML integration, improved performance, broader programming language support, and faster development using Web Forms.

To change the isolation mode in which your IIS machine runs, use IIS Manager to open the properties sheet for the Web Sites node and select the Services tab (Figure 12-1). The default mode for your server depends on whether you have upgraded from a previous version of IIS or performed a fresh install, as discussed previously in Chapter 8, "Creating and Configuring Applications."

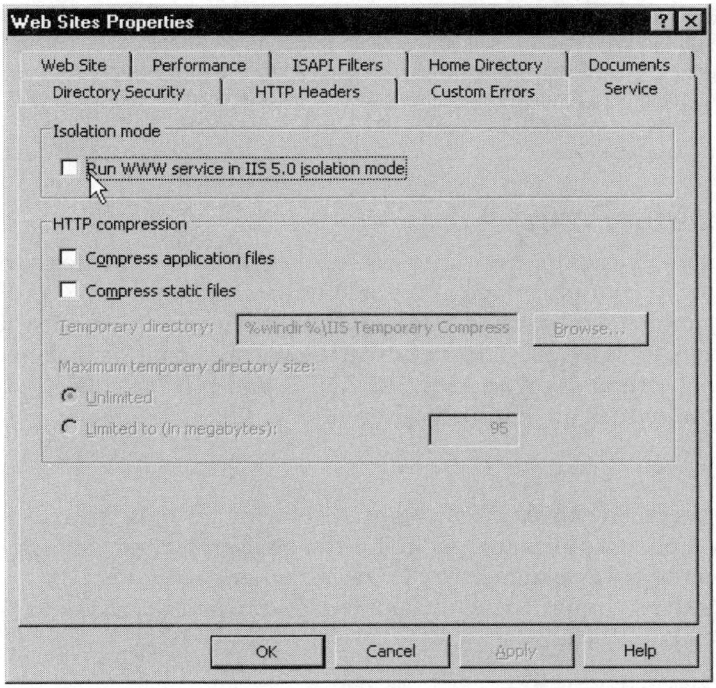

Figure 12-1.   Configuring isolation mode

If you are running your server in IIS 5 isolation mode, you should be aware that running applications with an application isolation setting of High (Isolated) incurs an additional performance penalty due to the RPC mechanism used by COM. When using this mode, configure your applications to run as either Medium (Pooled) or Low (IIS Process) isolation wherever possible, with the former being preferable from a reliability standpoint.

Regardless of which isolation mode you choose for running your IIS machine, you can still take advantage of quality of service tuning features such as HTTP keep-alives, HTTP Compression, limiting connections, connection timeouts, bandwidth throttling, and CPU monitoring. You can also enhance the performance of IIS by editing various metabase parameters and Registry settings, though some of these are not available when running in IIS 5 isolation mode.

> **TIP**   You can't run IIS 6 in both isolation modes simultaneously; so if some of your legacy applications require that you run them in IIS 5 isolation mode to work properly, consider setting up an additional IIS 6 machine running in IIS 5 isolation mode that is used specifically for hosting such legacy apps. Then configure your main IIS 6 machine to run in worker process isolation mode and use it for your newer applications.

Tuning Application Pools

Assuming that you've configured your server to run in worker process isolation mode, let's look at how to take advantage of the architectural enhancements of this new mode to tune IIS for optimal performance. I discussed these new features of IIS 6 in Chapter 2, "IIS 6 Architecture"; now you'll learn how to enable and configure them. Note that application pool settings apply to ASP, ASP.NET, and ISAPI applications but not to CGI applications, which are handled differently by IIS.

Recycling

Worker process recycling increases reliability by allowing IIS to periodically restart worker processes servicing an application pool. This can be useful when web applications are buggy and hang or fail due to memory leaks and other conditions.

Recycling can be configured in different ways. Specifically, a worker process (w3wp.exe) can be recycled:

- Manually, using IIS Manager.

- After a specified number of minutes of inactivity have elapsed. This setting is enabled by default and set to 1740 minutes or 29 hours.

- After the worker process has handled a specified number of requests. The default value if this setting is enabled is 35,000 connections.

- At one or more specific times during the day, for example at 2:00 A.M. during a nightly maintenance window. The default value if this setting is enabled is the current server time.

- Once the utilization of virtual memory by the worker process reaches a specified threshold level. The default value if this setting is enabled is 500MB.

- Once the utilization of privately allocated system physical memory by the worker process reaches a specified threshold level. The default value if this setting is enabled is 192MB.

- Programmatically by coding an ISAPI application within the application pool to declare itself unhealthy to the WWW Service by using HSE_REQ_REPORT_ UNHEALTHY, a new ServerSupportFunction for ISAPI extensions supported by IIS 6.

TIP If you configure recycling to occur at specific times of the day and you change the system clock settings, manually recycle worker processes once to ensure that automated recycling will occur at the correct times afterward.

By default, IIS 6 is configured to recycle worker processes based on the second criteria, that is, after the worker process has been inactive for a certain period of time (Figure 12-2). The settings on this properties sheet can be configured at two different levels:

- **Application Pools** By right-clicking the Application Pools node in IIS Manager and selecting Properties, you can configure all worker processes in all application pools to recycle according to the same criteria.
- **Specific Application Pool** By right-clicking a specific application pool such as the DefaultAppPool and selecting Properties, you can configure all worker processes associated with that specific pool to recycle the same way.

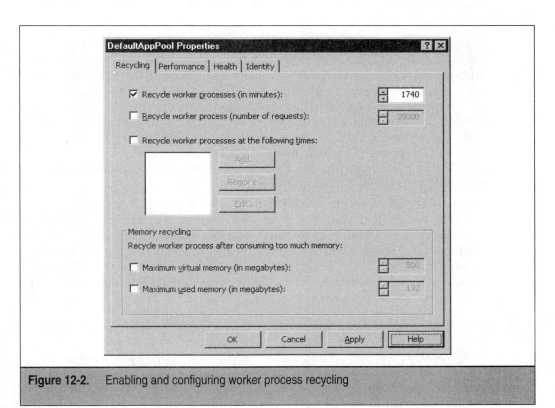

Figure 12-2. Enabling and configuring worker process recycling

Note that application pools inherit their recycling settings (and all other settings) from the parent Application Pools node, although you can override these settings for each pool. As usual, you must be a member of the Administrators group on the local machine (or a member of Domains Admins in a domain scenario) to perform these tasks.

To manually recycle worker processes for a specific application pool, right-click the pool and select Recycle. You cannot recycle all application pools simultaneously using IIS Manager; you have to recycle each pool separately.

TIP   If your IIS machine serves only static HTML pages, you can disable worker processing for all application pools. If you are serving dynamic content that has been thoroughly debugged and tested, you can also disable recycling, although you may want to leave it enabled just in case undetected bugs manifest themselves. After all, users are the best beta testers for finding bugs! If it can be broken, a user will somehow break it!

Looking at things from an internal or architectural perspective, there are two basic ways that recycling can occur:

- **Overlapped recycling**   IIS starts up a new worker process while leaving the old one to drain its HTTP request queue of current requests (terminating the worker process does not terminate the associated request queue, as these request queues are managed by Http.sys within the TCP/IP stack and not by IIS). Once the request queue is drained, the old worker process has nothing to do and gracefully shuts itself down. If the old process does not shut down within a specific time interval, however, IIS will force it to terminate and shift the remaining contents of the request queue to the new process. Either way, because the new process starts before the old one finishes, there is never any interruption in service and users will be unaware of anything strange happening.

- **Nonoverlapped recycling**   Under certain workload conditions, IIS may forcefully terminate the old worker process and then start a new one to replace it. A condition where this might occur is if there are insufficient memory or CPU resources for IIS to create a new worker process unless it kills the old one first. Another condition where this might occur is when a worker process becomes blocked and can't function properly, with the result that IIS terminates it and starts a new one to replace it.

If you have multiple worker processes servicing a given application pool and you configure the pool to recycle after a specific interval of time (or after a specific number of requests have been processed), IIS staggers the recycling of these processes so they aren't all recycled at the same time. This is because recycling a worker process generates momentary system overhead, and recycling multiple processes simultaneously could therefore cause the server to incur a brief but noticeable performance hit.

When might you want to configure recycling for worker processes? Which conditions might you configure to trigger recycling? Here are a few scenarios:

- Your ASP, ASP.NET, or ISAPI applications have bugs in them and it's not feasible for you to fix them at present. For example, if your application has difficulty running for an extended period of time and tends to hang or crash after running for a while, consider configuring recycling based on time interval or number of requests. You might also consider configuring recycling at a specific time each day during off-peak hours.

- Your applications have memory leaks or cause the memory heap to become fragmented with time. If the problem is a memory leak, configure recycling to occur based on allocated memory growing above a specified size. If the problem is excessive fragmentation of the memory heap, configure recycling to occur based on virtual memory size becoming too large.

- If your IIS machine is experiencing intermittent problems of an undetermined nature, try configuring recycling based on time interval, number of requests, or at specific times of the day. If this fixes the problems, you may have buggy applications.

- As administrator you've noticed that an application within an application pool has failed for some undetermined reason. If this is the only time this has happened to the application, consider recycling the pool containing the application as opposed to restarting IIS and interrupting all applications running on the server. In particular, if you were using IISReset previously to keep your applications running normally, try using recycling instead.

TIP Of course, the best solution to buggy applications is to get rid of the bugs! One way an IIS admin can help is to become part of the development team to advise developers on issues such as memory and network resource limitations that might affect how their applications run within the company infrastructure.

Idle Timeout

Idle timeout allows IIS to shut down worker processes that aren't doing anything. When a web application receives its first HTTP request, a worker process is started up to service the pool where the application resides (unless a worker process is already running for this purpose). When an application stops receiving requests, having this worker process continue to run idly is unnecessary and wasteful of resources, so, by default, IIS spins down a worker process after a period of inactivity. By default, this occurs after 20 minutes of inactivity, but you can configure a longer or shorter time (or disable idle timeout entirely) using the Performance tab of the application pool (Figure 12-3).

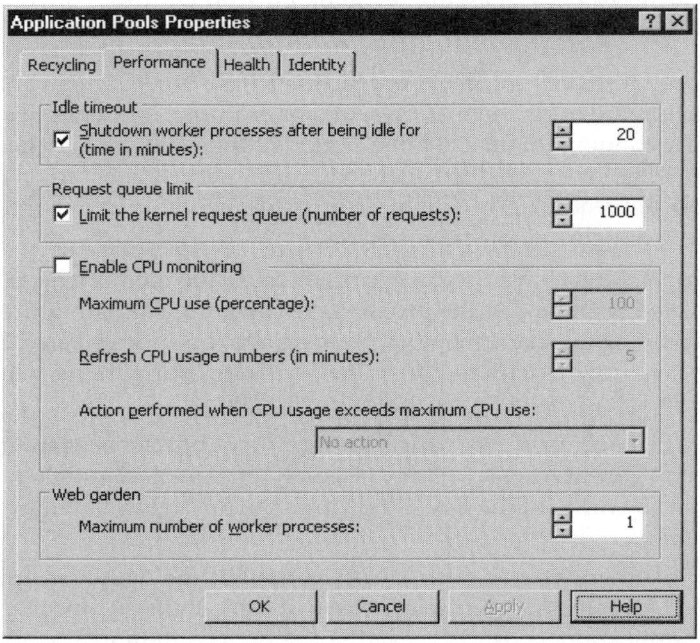

Figure 12-3.   Enabling and configuring idle timeout

Or, as mentioned previously, you can configure this setting for *all* application pools by using the properties sheet of the Application Pools node.

When is this idle timeout feature helpful for enhancing web server performance? Here are a few scenarios:

- If your server is low on system resources (few CPUs, small memory), idle timeout lets you conserve valuable resources to ensure the availability of applications running on your server.

- If your server is under heavy load from client requests, idle timeout lets you better manage your system resources. In this case, you may want to reduce the idle timeout setting from its default value of 20 minutes to ensure that idle worker processes are terminated quickly to release system resources.

- If you have an application that is frequently in an idle state for some reason, this feature can again free up system resources.

On the other hand, setting idle timeout too aggressively low can create its own set of problems. For example, idle timeouts should not be set lower than the idle session termination interval for ASP or ASP.NET sessions, or user connections could be terminated during a session, resulting in data loss and user frustration. Also, since spinning up a worker process briefly involves extra utilization of resources, setting idle timeout too low could result in more system resources being utilized instead of less—sort of like switching a fluorescent light on and off frequently (a fluorescent light uses much more electricity when it is being started up, a process that typically takes a couple of seconds, than when it is running steadily). Like most server performance issues, balance is the key here.

Request Queue Limits

Another setting you can configure on the Performance tab (refer to Figure 12-3) is the request queue limit. A request queue is a kernel-mode queue used by Http.sys to queue and forward HTTP requests to the associated application pool. By default, IIS is configured to monitor the number of requests in these queues and to limit them to 1000 requests per queue. If the queue becomes full and more requests come in, IIS rejects these additional requests and immediately returns an "HTTP 503—Service Unavailable" response to the client.

If the request queue grows too large, the server's performance will seem sluggish from the client's perspective. Limiting the queue prevents that. You can enable or disable the request queue limit for all applications within an application pool, and you can increase or decrease the limit for the number of requests to be queued.

CPU Monitoring

Another setting you can configure on the Performance tab is CPU monitoring. By enabling this feature (it is disabled by default), you can track the CPU usage for worker processes associated with an application pool, specifying how often CPU usage is to be measured and the maximum usage allowed (Figure 12-4). Should usage exceed the maximum level specified, you can configure IIS to perform one of the following actions:

- **No action**   The worker process is allowed to continue, but an error event is written to the event log recording the occurrence.

- **Shutdown**   All worker processes associated with the pool are shut down, gracefully if possible and forcefully if necessary. Then the application pool itself resets and new worker processes are started up.

TIP   Don't set the maximum CPU usage value too low, or the pool may be reset often and impact server performance. Also, don't set the refresh interval too low, as this will generate extra overhead on your server.

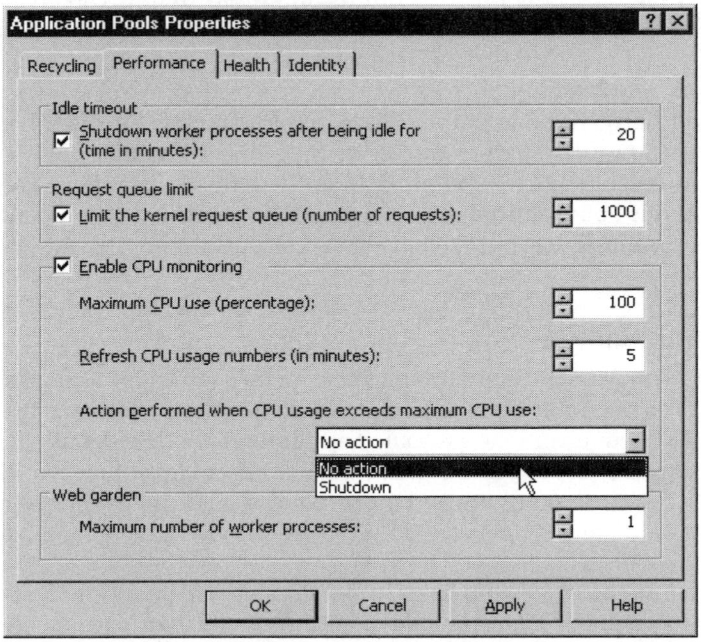

Figure 12-4. Enabling and configuring CPU monitoring

Web Gardens

Web gardens is a feature of IIS 6 that lets multiple worker processes service a single application pool. This enhances performance several ways:

- If one worker process for the pool stops responding for some reason, the others can take up the load.

- When several worker processes are servicing an application pool, new TCP connections are assigned on a round-robin basis to each worker process. This results in reduced resource contention and smoothing out the workload by distributing it equally among the worker processes.

Enabling a web garden is simple: just increase the setting for maximum number of worker processes from one to the value you desire on the Performance tab (refer to Figure 12-4). A value of one here means web gardens is disabled for the pool.

Health Monitoring

Another performance-related feature of worker processes is health monitoring. This involves the WWW Service "pinging" worker processes periodically to ensure they are still running properly. If a worker process responds to a ping, it is assumed to be healthy. If it doesn't respond, it is assumed to be sick—that is, to be hung or to lack sufficient thread resources to be able to respond.

This ping is a system message sent from the WWW Service to the worker process. The WWW Service also maintains a communications channel with each worker process, and, if this channel is dropped, it has the same effect as a response not being returned from a ping.

If a worker process is determined to be sick, IIS can take one of two actions:

- Terminate it and start a new worker process to replace it—in other words, recycle the worker process. This occurs regardless of whether recycling is configured on the Recycling tab of the pool's properties sheet.

- Release it (leave it running but not servicing IIS requests), start a new worker process to replace it, and run a preconfigured action configured by the Administrator, for example, starting a debugger and attaching it to the orphaned worker process. To enable releasing of sick worker processes, you must edit the metabase and change the OrphanWorkerProcess property to true. To configure the action to occur for the orphaned process, modify the OrphanActionExe property.

In both cases, an event is also written to the event log to leave a record of the problem. By default, IIS is configured to terminate unhealthy worker processes and not release them. This is usually recommended, since allowing worker process to be released could result in large numbers of orphaned worker processes running on your machine and consuming valuable system resources. You can change how IIS handles sick worker processes by modifying the metabase. See Chapter 14, "Working with the Metabase," for more information on metabase settings and how to modify the metabase.

You can enable pinging of worker processes and specify the time interval between pings using the Health tab of the properties sheet for an application pool (Figure 12-5). By default, pinging is enabled and occurs every 30 seconds after the last response was received from the pinged worker process. This default ping interval is usually suitable for most cases. The ping timeout value (the time that the WWW Service waits for a response before declaring the worker process unhealthy) is configured in the metabase as 90 seconds and can be changed by editing the metabase.

Rapid-Fail Protection

IIS also has a feature that allows it to detect when multiple worker processes servicing an application pool are unhealthy. This feature is called *rapid-fail protection,* and it lets

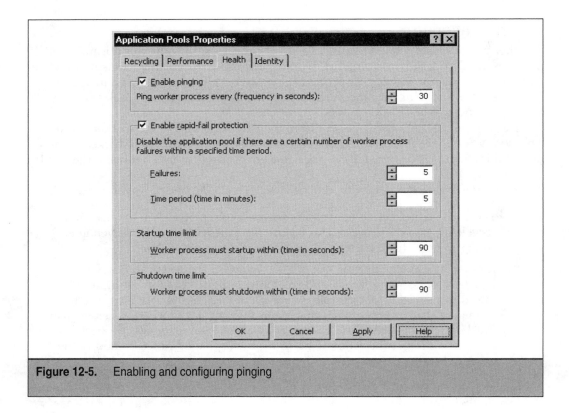

Figure 12-5. Enabling and configuring pinging

you specify a maximum number of consecutive failures of worker processes to occur within a specified interval of time. If these conditions are exceeded (the default is five failed worker processes within five minutes), IIS stops the application pool serviced by these processes, taking it offline until an Administrator can determine the cause. Until the pool is brought online again, users trying to access applications within the pool will receive "HTTP 503—Service Unavailable" errors.

To enable and configure rapid-fail protection settings, use the Health tab (refer to Figure 12-5), either for an individual application pool or for all pools using the Application Pools node in IIS Manager.

NOTE Other reasons an application pool might stop include a nonexistent identity being configured on the Identity tab for the pool, a job object reaching its time limit, or an Administrator manually stopping the pool using IIS Manager.

Startup and Shutdown Time Limits

These limits, found on the Health tab, refer specifically to unhealthy worker processes. If the WWW Service pings a worker process and the process fails to respond, the process is assumed to be sick and is marked for termination. The worker process is then given the time specified by the shutdown limit to gracefully shut itself down, but, if this time has elapsed and the process is still running, it is forcefully terminated. It's best to tune this setting relative to your server workload to ensure graceful shutdowns. The startup value specifies the time interval within which a new worker process should be started to replace the sick one, and this startup time should generally be less than or equal to the shutdown time. The default value for both time intervals is 90 seconds.

Processor Affinity

A final feature relating to worker process performance is processor affinity, which lets you establish an affinity (association or connection) between a worker process and a specific CPU on an SMP machine. This can increase performance by utilizing CPU caches more effectively, because when a thread moves from one CPU to another the first CPU's cache must be flushed. By establishing affinity between worker processes and CPUs, such cache flushes can be eliminated, reducing overhead and freeing up processing resources.

The down side of using this feature is that it may prevent threads from migrating to the least busy CPU if that CPU is bound to a specific worker process. As with all performance tuning settings, you should test this one after enabling it to see if it helps or hurts. To enable processor affinity, configure the SMPProcessorAfffinityMask property in the metabase.

Quality of Service

In addition to tuning application pools, you can tune IIS performance by enabling and configuring the various quality of service (QoS) features of IIS. These QoS features include:

- **HTTP keep-Alives**   Reusing TCP connections for multiple HTTP requests.
- **HTTP compression**   Making more effective use of bandwidth for HTTP sessions.
- **Limiting connections**   Restricting the number of simultaneous connections.
- **Connection timeouts**   Reclaiming system resources by closing idle connections.
- **Bandwidth throttling**   Ensuring that clients can access other services on your web server.

Let's look at each of these different features and how to use them to enhance IIS performance.

HTTP Keep-Alives

The original HTTP 1.0 specification was inefficient because each time an HTTP request was made, a TCP session was established and then torn down. That meant that a page with four embedded images would require five client TCP connections, each requiring a three-step TCP session acknowledgement and a two-step session termination, adding to the session overhead.

The HTTP 1.1 specification improves on this considerably and allows multiple HTTP requests to be pipelined into a single TCP connection. It also provides a feature known as HTTP keep-alives, which allows you to keep TCP connections between client and web server open for a period of time in case further HTTP requests are made. Using keep-alives has a significant positive impact on web server performance, and you can enable or disable this feature as follows:

1. In IIS Manager, right-click the Web Sites node and select Properties.

2. Switch to the Web Site tab and select or clear the Enable HTTP Keep-Alives check box (Figure 12-6).

3. Click Apply and then OK.

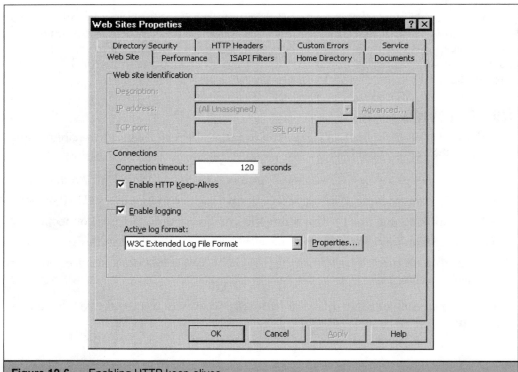

Figure 12-6. Enabling HTTP keep-alives

This procedure will enable keep-alives for all websites running on your IIS machine, but you can also enable or disable keep-alives for individual websites by using the Web Site tab of a website's properties sheet. Note that keep-alives are enabled by default on IIS, and you should generally leave it this way. The Connection Timeout setting determines the length of time that keep-alives keep TCP connections alive, 120 seconds by default.

NOTE   Disabling keep-alives will prevent client access to websites configured for anonymous access or Integrated Windows Authentication. Only Basic Authentication will allow clients to access websites where keep-alives are disabled.

HTTP Compression

If your connection bandwidth is limited or your websites generate large amounts of content, you can utilize your bandwidth more efficiently by enabling HTTP Compression on IIS. This feature allows IIS to compress static HTML files and/or dynamic response content, but it comes at a price: higher CPU utilization to compress the files. Like all performance tuning actions, the trick is to try enabling this feature and see if it improves performance or makes it worse by monitoring performance for a while and comparing it to your previously established baseline. Furthermore, this feature only works with clients that support it, which means any web browser developed after 1998:

- Internet Explorer 4 or higher (version 5 or higher on Macintosh platforms)
- Netscape Navigator 4.5 or higher (earlier versions support it but are buggy)
- Opera 5 or higher

NOTE   HTTP Compression is a feature of the HTTP 1.1 specification, where it is known as "content encoding."

HTTP Compression has more of a performance hit for dynamic content than static because when static HTML files are compressed the results are cached so they can be reused when the file is requested again. Dynamic content, however, must be compressed each time it is requested, which requires additional processing, so don't enable HTTP Compression if your web server CPU utilization is already in the high zone, for example, if your %ProcessorTime counter averages around 80 percent or more.

To enable HTTP Compression for all websites on your machine, do the following:

1. Right-click the Web Sites node in IIS Manager and select Properties.
2. Select the Service tab.
3. Select the Compress Application Files check box to compress dynamic content if desired.
4. Select the Compress Static Files check box to compress static HTML files if desired (Figure 12-7).

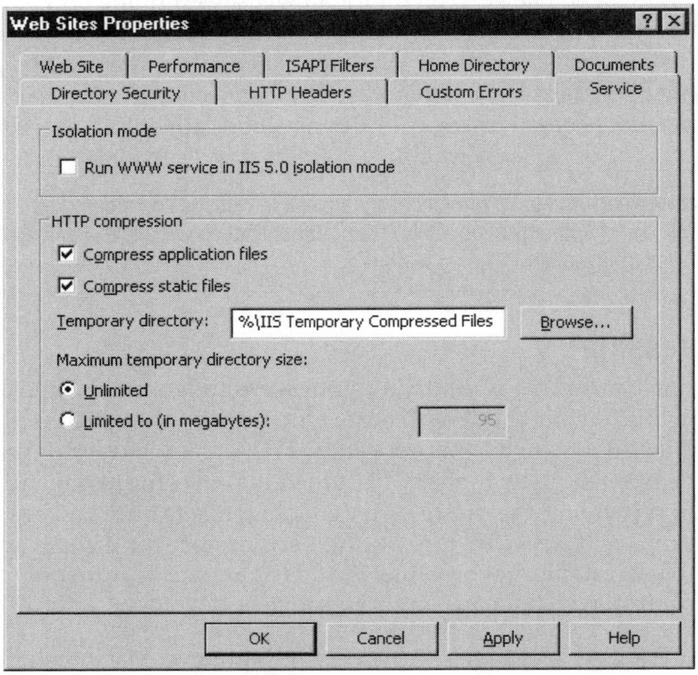

Figure 12-7.   Enabling and configuring HTTP Compression

If you enable compression of static files, you can also configure the directory where compressed files will be cached. In addition, you can specify the maximum amount of files in megabytes that can be cached or leave this setting as Unlimited to allow unlimited caching. Note that HTTP Compression can only be configured globally at the Web Sites level and not for individual websites on your IIS machine.

SECURITY ALERT   If you enable static content compression, make sure the temporary directory is located on an NTFS volume and that it is not shared.

Limiting Connections

If you have other important network services running on your IIS machine, for example, using it as a file server or e-mail server, then you may need to limit the number of simultaneous connections that IIS will allow to enable clients to access these other services. This is called *limiting connections* and is configured on

- The Performance tab on a properties sheet for a website (Figure 12-8).

- The FTP Site tab on the properties sheet for an FTP site.

It can also be configured globally for all websites using the Web Sites node in IIS Manager and for all FTP sites using the FTP Sites node.

There are some things you need to consider when configuring these settings:

- The default setting is Unlimited, which means that IIS does not try to limit the number of incoming connections it accepts. If IIS is not able to handle all incoming connections, this setting may result in users finding the server slow or unresponsive.

- If a specific connection limit is configured (the suggested value is a maximum of 1000 incoming connections for websites), then when this limit is exceeded, the server will return an "HTTP 403.9 Forbidden—Too Many Users" message to clients exceeding the limit. This may be preferable to the default Unlimited setting because at least the users will know why the web server is not responding to their requests.

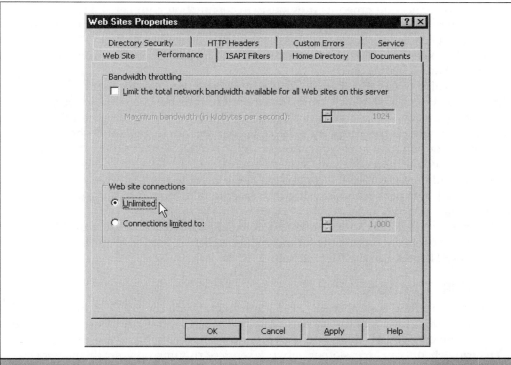

Figure 12-8.   Configuring website connections limit

- The default connection limit for FTP sites is different: it is set to 100,000 connections by default, not to Unlimited as it is for websites.

- If you have connection limits configured differently for individual websites (or FTP sites) and at the global Web Sites (or FTP Sites) level, note that IIS checks the global limits first before checking the site-level limits for this setting.

- Limiting connections is also useful for dealing with denial-of-service (DoS) attacks against your web or FTP server, as these attacks are designed to overload your machine with large numbers of forged connection attempts. Although firewalls and IDS devices really form the front wall against such attacks, this is another good reason for not using the default Unlimited value for this setting.

- To determine what specific connection limit you should configure for your server, monitor the Current Connections, Maximum Connections, and Total Connection Attempts counters for the WWW and FTP services for a period of time using System Monitor. Performance counters and System Monitor are discussed in the section "How to Monitor Performance."

Connection Timeouts

I mentioned connection timeouts previously in conjunction with HTTP keep-alives. Connection timeouts allow networking subsystem resources to be reclaimed when connections become idle and are no longer needed. To enable connection timeouts, enable HTTP keep-alives as previously discussed, and specify a value using the list box (the default is 120 seconds).

You can also tweak this feature further by editing the Registry to modify the MinFileBytesPerSec key, which limits the amount of time the client has to receive a response to its request (see the section "Registry Tuning Tips" for more information). The default value for this property is 240 bytes per second. In general, it should not be set lower or you may open your server to a form of DoS attack where the attacker establishes a connection with your server, requests a large file such as downloading an image, and then throttles the connection at the client to some unreasonably slow rate such as 1 byte per second, causing the server to take forever to serve just one file to one client.

Connection timeouts can be configured at the global level for websites or FTP sites. To configure connection timeouts for individual websites, use the Web Site tab; for individual FTP sites, use the FTP Site tab.

Bandwidth Throttling

Bandwidth throttling is another IIS QoS feature and lets you control how much network bandwidth your individual websites use and how much bandwidth IIS uses as a whole. Like limiting connections discussed above, bandwidth throttling can be a useful way of ensuring clients can access other network services running on your IIS machine.

Bandwidth throttling is enabled and configured on the Performance tab (refer to Figure 12-8), and the suggested setting is 1024 kilobytes/second. This value can then be increased or decreased based on your studies of performance counters related to network traffic on your server. In general, you should consider throttling bandwidth if your machine utilizes more than 50 percent of available network bandwidth.

Unlike other features, global bandwidth throttling settings do *not* override those configured for individual websites. Instead, global bandwidth throttling settings affect the bandwidth used by all websites on the machine that are *not* configured for bandwidth throttling. Note also that global throttling *only* affects websites and not FTP sites or other IIS services like SMTP or NNTP.

NOTE Apparently this feature never worked properly in earlier versions of IIS, even though it was there in the GUI. Let's hope it now works properly in version 6!

Registry Tuning Tips

While most IIS configuration settings are stored in the metabase, there are some important settings related to performance stored in the Windows registry. Of course, be careful when editing the Registry because you can wreck your server and may not be able to recover it short of a fresh install. We'll look briefly at some settings that can have an impact on the performance of IIS. Note that when you change any of these settings you usually need to restart IIS for the change to take effect.

The following are some Registry settings that can be used to globally tune IIS performance. Usually, if you cannot find the key on your own IIS machine, it means the default value is being used. To change this to some other value, first create the key on your machine.

FTP Connection Monitoring

I should briefly mention FTP site monitoring, a feature that lets you display information concerning current sessions between FTP clients and your site, including the identity of the connected user, when the user established the connection, and how long the connection has been active. To display the FTP User Sessions box showing this information, click the Current Sessions button on the FTP Sites tab of the properties sheet for your site (Figure 12-9).

Note that anonymous connections using Internet Explorer as your FTP client show up here as IEUser@ in the Connected Users column, while anonymous connections from other clients like the Windows command-line FTP client show up as the user's e-mail address (or whatever the user types as their password when connecting). Authenticated clients will show up showing the username of the connected user. Note that you can also use the FTP User Sessions box to disconnect one or more users by selecting them and clicking Disconnect, or you can disconnect all users by clicking Disconnect All. To get the most recent statistics, click the Refresh button.

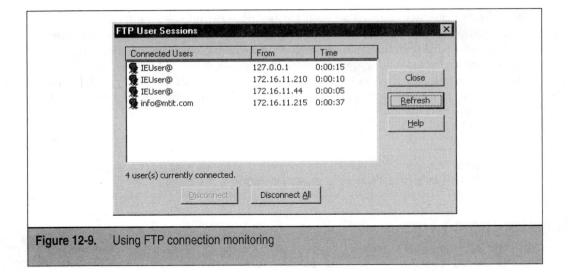

Figure 12-9. Using FTP connection monitoring

First, here are some keys under HKLM\SYSTEM\CurrentControlSet\Services\
Inetinfo\Parameters that relate to Inetinfo.exe and hence affect IIS as a whole:

- **CacheSecurityDescriptor** The default value of 1 enables caching of security descriptors for file objects, which speeds retrieval of cached content when some other authentication method than anonymous is being used.

- **CheckCertRevocation** The default value of 0 disables checking client certificates for evocation. Changing this to 1 to enable revocation checking can have a terrible impact on your server's performance and should only be used in an intranet situation where the feature is required.

- **DisableMemoryCache** Setting this key to 0 enables static file caching on your IIS machine, so leave it set to this value on production servers.

- **ListenBackLog** Specifies the maximum number of active connections that should be held in the queue to await attention from the server. The default value is 25, but this can be increased up to 50 for improved performance when the server is under heavy load.

- **MacCachedFileSize** Controls the maximum size of files that can be cached and is 256KB by default. If your server has files in its content directories larger than this setting, these files will not be cached. You may need to increase this setting if your server is used for serving up large files such as images or video clips to clients.

- **MaxPoolThreads**   Controls how many pool threads can be created for each processor, not counting threads used by ISAPI applications. The default value is 4 and this should generally not be set to higher than 20. If you are running more than four CGI applications on your server (IIS only supports four concurrent GGI applications by default), then increase this value to improve performance.

- **MemCacheSize**   Specifies the size in megabytes of the file cache. If this key does not exist, then IIS controls the cache size dynamically, adjusting it every 60 seconds and using no more than half of the available physical memory on the machine. You might specify a lower setting if you have other important network services running on your machine, or specify a higher setting if your machine is a large, dedicated web server.

- **MinFileBytesPerSec**   Discussed earlier in the section called "Connection Timeouts," this key can range from 1 to 8192 and has a default value of 240. It can be adjusted to help protect against certain kinds of DoS attacks against your web server.

- **ObjectCacheTTL**   The default value of 30 seconds specifies how long objects are held in the static file cache before being phased out. If your web server is serving predominantly dynamic content or if system memory is in short supply, you can lower this value to enhance performance and prevent system memory from being used for caching objects. If you set the value to 0xFFFFFFFF, it disables the cache scavenger and lets cached objects stay in the cache until they are overwritten. If your server is serving mainly static content or has tons of available system memory, consider disabling the cache scavenger optimal utilization of memory or raising the value to several minutes for improved performance.

One Registry setting under HKLM\SYSTEM\CurrentControlSet\Services\ASP\Parameters relates specifically to Active Server Pages applications:

- **DisableLazyContentPropagation**   When you update your IIS machine with a large amount of content in one fell swoop, the default value of 0 propagates content using lazy propagation, so the web server is not overwhelmed and brought to a standstill. You should leave this setting to its default value of 0 for production machines, but, on development machines, you can change it to 1 to give priority to updating your content.

A Registry setting under HKLM\SYSTEM\CurrentControlSet\Services\W3SVC\Parameters relates to the WWW Service:

- **UploadReadAhead**   Specifies the amount of request data that IIS will accept from a client before passing control to the requested application, which is then responsible for accepting the remainder of the request data. If you have lots of RAM on your server, you can try increasing this upward from its default value of 48KB to see if performance improves.

A couple of settings under HKLM\SYSTEM\CurrentControlSet\Services\HTTP\ Parameters relate to the operation of the HTTP Listener (Http.sys) and hence also affect IIS as a whole:

- **UriMaxCacheMegabyteCount**   The default value of 0 lets Http.sys use its own heuristic to determine how much memory should be used for its cache, but you can specify any value up to 0xFFFFFFFF hexadecimal to tune the performance of Http.sys.

- **UriScavengerPeriod**   The default value of 120 specifies the interval in seconds between times when the URI cache scavenger runs to flush (remove) stale entries. The valid range is from 10 to 0xFFFFFFFF.

TIP   There are additional Registry settings you can configure to control certain aspects of the WWW and FTP services on IIS. See the Registry Reference in the IIS Help file for more information.

Metabase Tuning Tips

Although I am deferring a full treatment of the XML metabase until Chapter 14, there are some metabase properties that can specifically affect performance, especially for ASP, ASP.NET, and ISAPI applications, so let's look at some of these here. Note that when you change any of these settings, you usually need to restart IIS for the change to take effect. Here are some metabase properties followed by a description of how they can be tweaked to tune IIS:

- **AppAllowDebugging**   ASP debugging should only be enabled on development servers because it causes IIS application threads to become serialized—that is, each application can execute only one thread at a time. On production servers, make sure this property is set to False, or application performance will degrade.

- **AspBufferingOn**   Make sure this is set to True on production servers to ensure application output is saved in the output buffer before flushing to clients. If it's set to False, applications stream their output directly to clients, which may seem to improve performance for the first client but it won't for subsequent ones. When developing applications, you may want to turn buffering off for testing purposes.

- **AspQueueConnectionTestTime**   Sometimes users who are impatient keep submitting the same request from their browser over and over again, wondering why the web server doesn't respond. Often such users then abandon their requests before the server responds and move on to another site, leaving multiple unfulfilled requests waiting in the queue for that application's pool. By setting the value for this property to something small like 3 seconds, you can force the server to check if the client is still connected before starting execution of the requested application and wasting your server's time.

- **AspScriptEngineCacheMax**   By increasing the value of this property, you can increase the number of scripting engines ASP can cache in memory from its default setting of 125 to some large value. This should generally only be done for large, complex sites with thousands of pages.

- **AspScriptFileCacheSize**   Closely related to the previous property, this specifies how many precompiled ASP templates can be cached on your machine. Caching ASP templates dramatically increases performance of ASP applications, and possible settings here include –1 for caching all requested script files, 0 for disabling ASP caching, and any numerical value for specifying a maximum number of cached templates. Disabling ASP caching has a terrible impact on performance, so only configure a zero value for this property in a development environment, not on production servers. For servers that have sites with only a small number of frequently requested ASP pages, you can set this property to a small value to free up more system memory.

- **CacheISAPI**   Setting this property to True causes ISAPI extensions to be cached in memory after use and kept there until the server is stopped. Setting it to False causes the extension to be unloaded from memory once it is no longer required. Caching ISAPI extensions in memory can improve performance, so set it to True for production servers.

Additional Server Tuning Tips

I'll conclude this section with a few additional tuning tips, in no particular order, to help you get the most out of your IIS machine.

Add RAM

In general, the quickest, easiest, and cheapest way of improving the performance of your IIS machine is to add more RAM and rely on the self-tuning capability of IIS to get the most out of the additional memory.

Maximize Data Throughput Setting

Adding more RAM is not enough—you also need to make sure your server is configured to use it wisely. Although an IIS machine is really an application server, when you perform a clean install of Windows Server 2003, the resulting server configures itself by default for best performance as a file server instead, even if you install the additional IIS components on your machine. To change this and get the most out of IIS, do the following:

1. Click Start | Control Panel, select Network Connections, and open Local Area Connection.

2. On the Local Area Connection Status box, select the General tab, and click the Properties button.

3. On the Local Area Connection properties sheet, select File and Print Sharing for Microsoft Networks and click Properties.

4. Note that the default setting on the File and Print Sharing for Microsoft Networks Properties sheet is Maximize Data Throughput for File Sharing (Figure 12-10). Change this to Maximize Data Throughput for Network Applications and click OK.

Your IIS machine is now configured as an application server, which should give better performance than the default file server setting. This setting provides

- Support for a larger amount of physical memory
- Improved SMP scalability on multiprocessor machines
- Better support for distributed applications that employ their own memory caching
- Improved networking performance

Note, however, that if your IIS machine is serving only static content, the performance gains from changing this setting will be minimal.

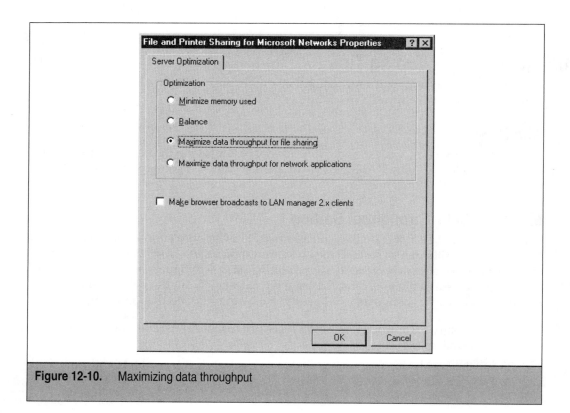

Figure 12-10. Maximizing data throughput

Use RAID 0

By employing disk striping without parity you can get the maximum performance from your hard disk subsystem, but if you really want to gain the most from this be sure to use a hardware RAID system instead of the software RAID included with Windows Server 2003. Using software RAID places additional demands on your processor subsystem, whereas hardware RAID offloads these demands to the RAID unit instead.

Defragment Regularly

Windows Server 2003 does a better job of defragmenting NTFS drives than the earlier Windows 2000 Server platform did, so be sure to take advantage of this by defragmenting your server's drives regularly to ensure optimal performance of your disk subsystem.

Paging File

Configuring a fixed (but generously large) paging file size will ensure your paging file doesn't become fragmented, and distributing your paging file across multiple drives (each with their own controllers) can also significantly improve performance of your hard disk subsystem.

Add a Processor

Using an SMP-capable motherboard allows you to add an additional CPU when needed to increase the processing power of your machine and help avoid bottlenecks; it also takes advantage of the new processor affinity feature of IIS 6 discussed earlier in this chapter.

Avoid CGI

Port your old CGI applications to ASP or ASP.NET (or to ISAPI for even better performance) to avoid the performance penalty incurred using the older CGI program execution model.

Avoid ISAPI Filters

The new wildcard mapping feature of IIS 6 lets you use ISAPI extensions where previously you might have used ISAPI filters. The result will generally be improved performance, so avoid ISAPI filters wherever possible, or rewrite them to work as extensions. Another alternative to consider is porting ISAPI applications to HTTP modules using .NET programming tools.

Avoid FTP User Isolation

Although the new FTP user isolation feature is a great idea, performance of your server can suffer when you create hundreds of user directories with this method, especially if you are using local authentication instead of Active Directory. If you must use FTP user isolation, make sure you set up a separate IIS machine as your FTP server and keep your websites on a different machine.

Avoid Remote Virtual Directories

For best performance when using virtual directories to store website content, keep your virtual directories on your local IIS machine instead of having them map to a share on a remote network server.

Avoid Footers on Web Pages

Adding document footers using the Documents tab of your website's properties sheet can incur a significant performance hit on your server, especially if the site is heavily used. If you must use document footers, make sure you store them on the local machine as HTML snippets, not whole HTML pages, and use them only for static pages, not dynamic ones. I'll discuss document footers in more detail in Chapter 16, "Publishing with IIS."

Avoid Too Much Logging

If you configure IIS to log website traffic, remember that logging consumes processor, memory, and disk resources. If you are using IIS in a service provider scenario and are hosting hundreds or even thousands of sites on a single box and you *must* log traffic for your sites, consider using the new *centralized binary logging* feature of IIS 6, which logs traffic to multiple sites in raw format to a single log file. Centralized binary logging is a global property of IIS that must either be used for all sites or none and is enabled as follows:

1. Click Start, choose Run, **type cscript.exe adsutil.vbs SET W3SVC/ CentralBinaryLoggingEnabled true**, and click OK.

2. Stop and start the WWW Service by typing **net stop W3SVC** followed by **net start W3SVC**.

Raw log files will now be created by IIS using the extension *.ibl for Internet Binary Log. To read these logs, you can use the parsing tool included with the IIS 6 Resource Kit or create your own using the IIS 6 SDK available from msdn.microsoft.com.

Avoid Remote Logging

This version of IIS allows you to write log files to a remote network share specified using a UNC path. While this seems like a great idea because it lets you centralize your log files for several IIS machines, in reality it's not so good because remote logging is slower than storing log files on the local machine. The issue is not really IIS but network latency at work; so, if your file server is on the same network segment, the performance hit might be minimal, but test this before implementing remote logging in a production environment.

Another issue to consider is that remote logging transmits ASCII log files over the network in clear text, which constitutes a security hazard. The way around this is to encrypt communications between IIS and the file server using IPSec, but this adds another performance hit, since encryption is a processor-intensive task.

Avoid ODBC Logging

If you enable ODBC logging on IIS, kernel-mode caching is disabled resulting in degraded performance, so it's usually best to avoid using ODBC logging and use W3C Extended logging instead. If you *must* use ODBC logging on IIS, make sure you don't use the SA account for logging to Microsoft SQL Server as this constitutes a security risk.

Avoid Using Custom Logging Modules

The same issue that degrades performance when ODBC logging is used affects custom logging modules: IIS disables kernel-mode caching when a COM-based logging module is installed. So avoid using custom logging if at all possible on IIS.

Disable Indexing

By default, IIS enables content indexing for all web sites. If your sites have large amounts of content but won't be implementing user search pages, save CPU cycles by disabling: clear the Index This Resource check box on the Home Directory tab of the property sheet for your website.

Using Host Headers

If you are an ISP and plan to use IIS for hosting hundreds or even thousands of sites per machine, you may have decided to use host headers to reduce the number of IP addresses each server will need. If so, don't be concerned about the possible performance penalty of using host headers, as there doesn't seem to be any significant impact of using them on IIS.

Use Clustering

For high-end web servers such as those used for e-commerce sites, using Windows clustering and network load balancing (NLB) to set up a web farm ensures the highest level of reliability for sites running on IIS. For an explanation of how to use these features, see any good book on general Windows Server 2003 administration. An alternative to NLB is to use third-party load-balancing tools such as Cisco's Content Services Switch or F5's BigIP Load Balancer, which are both excellent alternatives to Microsoft's NLB.

TUNING APPLICATIONS

I've already discussed some Registry settings and metabase properties that can be modified to tune the performance of ASP, ASP.NET, and ISAPI applications on IIS 6. But there are also a couple of things you can do with IIS Manager to tune web applications performance on IIS.

ISAPI Caching

When an application processes a client request, ASP compiles the application script into a template that is then cached in memory in case a client requests the script again. ASP templates are stored as an intermediate byte code that can be executed faster than a script, an IIS 6 feature that significantly improves ASP performance over earlier versions.

You enable ASP caching for an application by first enabling caching of ISAPI extensions for that application, since ASP itself is implemented as an ISAPI extension (asp.dll) on IIS. To enable ISAPI caching do the following:

1. Open the properties sheet for the website containing the application and select the Home Directory tab.

2. If the application has no name, create it by clicking the Create button.

3. Click the Configuration button to open the Application Configuration properties sheet for your application.

4. On the Mappings tab, make sure Cache ISAPI Extensions is checked, which it is by default (Figure 12-11).

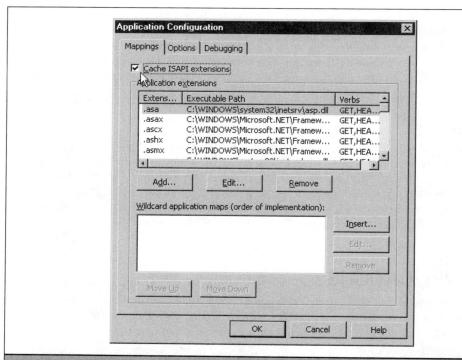

Figure 12-11.   Enabling caching of ISAPI applications

Recall that by default ASP caches 250 templates in memory, with additional templates being cached to disk. If the server is under heavy load, and you need more templates in memory, change the AspScriptFileCacheSize setting in the metabase, as discussed in the earlier section "Metabase Tuning Tips."

ASP Buffering

ASP buffering causes output from ASP applications to be buffered (that is, collected or accumulated) in memory before sending it to the client. This can improve performance for certain types of ASP applications. Configure this setting with the Options tab of the Application Configurations properties sheet discussed in the preceding section (Figure 12-12). ASP buffering is enabled by default and can also be configured by editing the AspBufferingOn metabase property as discussed in the earlier section "Metabase Tuning Tips."

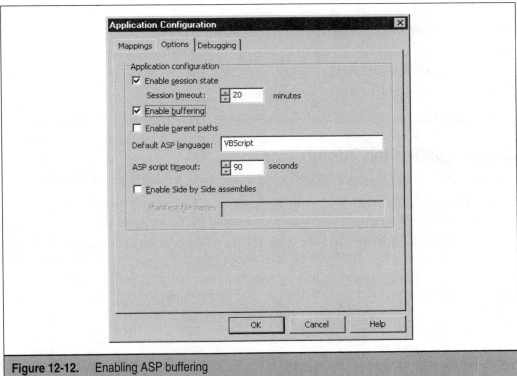

Figure 12-12.   Enabling ASP buffering

Writing High-Performance Applications

To ensure that dynamic applications run with the highest possible performance on IIS, in addition to everything I've already talked about, you still need to code your applications efficiently. ISAPI applications run the fastest because they are coded using a high-level programming language such as C or C++, but that means they are also difficult to develop. ASP is the most common development platform for web applications running on IIS, but ASP.NET provides certain enhancements over ASP that make it preferable for developing scalable, high-performance web applications. Here is a brief potpourri of tips for tuning ASP.NET applications for maximum performance:

- Disable Session State if you don't plan to use it, and store your application session data out-of-process when deploying web gardens and web farms.

- Perform all input validation on the client to reduce the number of round trips needed to the server.

- Use stored procedures instead of ad hoc queries when accessing data on back-end SQL servers.

- Trap exceptions instead of using them to direct program flow.

- Use Option Strict in VBScript code to ensure type-safe coding.

- Always leave caching turned on.

- Be sparing in your use of server controls.

For more ASP.NET programming tips, see Microsoft's website http://gotdotnet.com.

Additional Application Tuning Tips

Finally, here are a few more miscellaneous tips for tuning applications running on IIS 6:

- Where possible within your applications, use static HTML files. They are faster than ASP or ISAPI and use less memory and processor resources.

- Configure expire headers for static HTML files and image files so the client will cache these. (See Chapter 16 for how to enable and configure content expiration.)

- Use SSL sparingly and only for pages that require it: the performance hit for implementing SSL encryption is heavy, and extensive CPU resources are required.

- Recode ASP scripts longer than 100 lines as COM+ components for huge improvements in performance.

PERFORMANCE MONITORING

So far in this chapter, I've talked about how to tune IIS by using IIS Manager properties sheets, editing the Registry, and modifying various metabase properties. Unfortunately, performance tuning is more an art than a science, and changing such settings arbitrarily can sometimes end up making things worse instead of better. The solution is to carefully monitor the performance of your server to see what effect such changes have. I'll conclude this chapter by looking at performance monitoring and how to do it, focusing particularly on monitoring the performance of IIS 6 machines.

Tools for Performance Monitoring

The main tools for performance monitoring on the Windows Server 2003 platform are two MMC snap-ins:

- **System Monitor**   Previously known as Performance Monitor on the Windows NT platform, this tool can be used to monitor different aspects of your server's performance by collecting real-time data and displaying it graphically in the form of charts, generating reports, and generating alerts when specified conditions arise.

- **Performance Logs and Alerts**   This tool can be used for collecting performance information and saving it in logs that can be displayed and analyzed afterwards using System Monitor or exported to a spreadsheet or database program for analysis and reporting.

To make life simple for the administrator, Windows Server 2003 combines both of these snap-ins into a single MMC console called Performance that can be found in the Administrative Tools program group (Figure 12-13). Windows Server 2003 also includes a command-line tool called logman that can be used in conjunction with Performance Logs and Alerts to trace IIS and kernel events for advanced performance tuning. For general help regarding the syntax of using this tool, open a command-prompt and type **logman /?** to view the various options for running it.

TIP   Other options for monitoring IIS include third-party SNMP monitoring applications and Microsoft Operations Manager (MOM). Monitoring servers is really a subject of its own; I cover only tools provided with Windows Server 2003 in this chapter.

Other Windows Server 2003 tools that can be useful in certain aspects of performance monitoring include:

- **Task Manager**   Can be used to display various system activity in real time. Task Manager can display names of applications that are currently running, memory and CPU usage of active processes, who is currently logged on to the server, and various memory and networking usage statistics.

- **Network Monitor**   Mainly used for troubleshooting problems with network connections and services, but can also be used to monitor network utilization statistics.

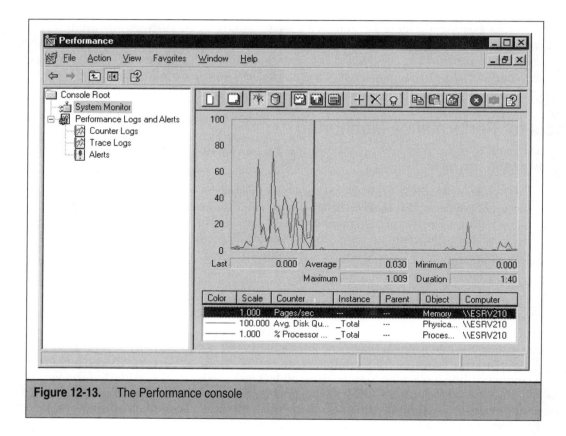

Figure 12-13. The Performance console

- **Web Application Stress Tool (WAST)** You can download this tool from the Microsoft website; it simulates the effect of multiple web browsers simultaneously connecting to IIS to download content or run applications, and it can be configured to simulate various loads so you can see how your web server behaves under them and then tune it accordingly.

How to Monitor Performance

To use the Performance console to monitor the performance of an IIS machine, start by setting up a controlled environment or testbed network on which you can expose your server and its applications to predictable loads and measure its response. Using WAST is a good way to generate such loads, and Performance should be your main tool for collecting and analyzing the resulting data. To use Performance, you have to add the performance counters you want to measure; I'll talk about which counters are useful to collect for tuning IIS machines in a moment.

Analyzing your server under predictable loads will likely expose *bottlenecks*, which are limitations in the hardware/software configuration that affect performance. Bottlenecks can result from hardware (insufficient memory or processing power, slow disk subsystem, or inadequate network connection) or software (applications, middleware, or back-end databases). Once you've identified possible bottlenecks, try to eliminate them by modifying hardware (adding more RAM, adding another processor, using a faster network adapter, or using RAID), tweaking software (recoding applications more efficiently, or using a faster database program), or tuning IIS performance using the procedures outlined previously in this chapter (changing properties sheet settings in IIS Manager, editing the Registry, and modifying metabase properties). Be aware that fixing a bottleneck in one area can sometimes create a bottleneck in another area or expose another bottleneck that was previously hidden by the first one.

The trick to performance tuning is to *modify one setting or property at a time* and then use Performance to observe the effect to see if performance improves or degrades. There's no particular order to what you should try, just be systematic in how you do this, and don't expect to ever get it perfect. Performance tuning is often a win/lose situation where improving things in one area can make them worse in another. In general, a good approach is to tweak hardware first, for example, adding more RAM is often the single most important action you can perform for boosting a server's performance. If your server is using SSL, adding another processor can also significantly boost performance, as SSL encryption is a very processor-intensive activity. But don't think hardware will solve all your problems, as one bad Registry or metabase setting (such as disabling caching) can have a tremendous negative impact on IIS performance.

Once your server has been thoroughly tuned in a controlled environment and your applications have been thoroughly debugged, move the server from the development stage to production and connect it to your real live network. Continue collecting performance data periodically, especially during heavy load times, to establish a baseline of your server's normal operation. Once you've established your baseline, you can continue tuning your server and comparing the results to it.

Another reason for continuing to collect performance data over the long haul is to monitor usage pattern changes. For example, as your website becomes popular, usage will rise and your web server's performance may start to suffer. At this point, you are using Performance as a tool for capacity planning to determine when you should upgrade your hardware or software to meet changing demands. Performance monitoring and capacity planning should continue on a regular basis throughout the life of your server so you can anticipate issues before they arise and adjust your configuration accordingly so that users always experience satisfactory response and throughput.

Important Performance Counters

There are hundreds of performance counters you can collect for Windows Server 2003 in general and IIS 6 specifically, so I can't cover all of them here. Instead, I'll summarize some of the more common and useful counters for monitoring performance of IIS machines, including general counters related to system resources and specific counters related to IIS services. For more information on available IIS counters, see the Performance Counters Reference in IIS Help.

General Counters

When monitoring any aspect of Windows Server 2003 (including IIS), you should always collect counters for the four system resources: memory, processor, disk, and network. Some of the more useful counters for these resources are shown in Table 12-1, along with comments relating to what values are acceptable for IIS and what values may indicate a bottleneck. Note that the disk counters may refer to either a logical or physical disk, depending on which object you select. Counters are expressed as *object:counter*, for example Memory:Available Bytes.

Object	Counter	Comment
Memory	Available Bytes	Keep greater than 20MB.
	Cache Bytes	If this starts to decrease, IIS may be running out of memory.
	Committed Bytes	Keep less than 75 percent of physical memory.
	Pages/sec	Keep low (under 20); if it's high (over 80), you need more RAM.
	Page Faults/sec	Too many hard page faults can degrade performance. Compensate by adding more RAM.
	Pool Nonpaged Bytes	If slowly rising over time, your application may have a memory leak.
Processor	% Processor Time	If higher (over 80) for sustained period but disk and network utilization are low, there may be a processor bottleneck.
Disk	% Disk time	Keep as low as possible.
	Avg. Disk Bytes/Transfer	Should be as high as possible
	Avg. Disk Queue Length	Should be 4 or less.
Network	Bytes Total/sec	Compare to bandwidth of network card to see if network connection is the bottleneck.
System	Context Switches/sec	Should be low with respect to System: System Calls/sec counter.
	Processor Queue Length	If 2 or more for sustained period, there may be a processor bottleneck.
Paging File	% Usage	Make sure paging file is at least twice the size of physical memory. If this counter is high, consider using disk striping.

Table 12-1.   General Performance Counters Useful for Monitoring IIS

Object	Counter	Comment
WWW Service	Bytes Total/Sec	Should be as high as possible.
	File Cache %	Shows how often IIS is finding requested files in the cache; if low, consider redesigning application to improve cache hit rate.
	File Cache Hits	Should be as high as possible if you have static content, but may be low if Kernel: URI Cache Hits % counter is high.
	ISAPI Extension	If this drops under heavy load, your application may be a bottleneck and may need to be redesigned.

Table 12-2.   Useful Performance Counters for Monitoring the WWW Service

TIP   When logging performance data, put your log files on a separate drive because the logging process itself has a performance impact on the machine.

WWW Service Counters

Table 12-2 lists some counters to watch that specifically relate to the WWW Service.

ASP Counters

Table 12-3 lists some counters to watch that specifically relate to ASP.

Object	Counter	Comment
Active Server Pages	Request Wait Time	Should be low, but response as perceived by users is often more a result of network latency.
	Requests Queued	Keep low. If greater than metabase property AspRequestQueueMax, additional connection attempts receive an "HTTP 500—Server Too Busy" error.
	Requests/Sec	If low under heavy server load, your application may be a bottleneck.

Table 12-3.   Useful Performance Counters for Monitoring ASP

You have an IIS 6 machine that you plan to use to host two web applications, one a large and complex ASP application that will be used as your company intranet site, which will have lots of static content, and the other an ISAPI application that will be used for online provisioning against a back-end database, which must have high availability. How would you configure IIS for maximum performance of these two applications? What isolation mode would you use? Would you assign them to the same or different application pools? What QoS features would you use to ensure high availability for your ISAPI application? What metabase properties might you modify to tune the performance of your ASP application? What other general steps might you take to tune the performance of your server? How would you plan to monitor your server's performance to ensure that it performs properly in a production environment?

CHECKLIST: PERFORMANCE TUNING

Check off the following steps for tuning your server's performance as you become familiar with how to perform them:

- ☐ Enabling worker process isolation mode.
- ☐ Enabling worker process isolation.
- ☐ Manually recycling a worker process.
- ☐ Scheduling the recycling of a worker process.
- ☐ Configuring idle timeout.
- ☐ Setting Http.sys request queue limits.
- ☐ Enabling CPU monitoring.
- ☐ Using web gardens.
- ☐ Enabling health monitoring.
- ☐ Enabling orphaning of unhealthy worker processes
- ☐ Enabling rapid-fail protection.
- ☐ Configuring worker process startup and shutdown time limits.
- ☐ Using processor affinity.
- ☐ Enabling HTTP keep-alives.
- ☐ Enabling HTTP Compression.
- ☐ Limiting connections to your site or server.

- ☐ Configuring connection timeouts.
- ☐ Using bandwidth throttling.
- ☐ Using FTP connection monitoring.
- ☐ Tuning performance by editing the Registry.
- ☐ Tuning performance by editing the metabase.
- ☐ Adding more memory or another processor to increase performance.
- ☐ Changing the maximize data throughput setting.
- ☐ Using RAID disk striping to improve performance.
- ☐ Defragmenting drives regularly.
- ☐ Choosing the best type of application for optimum performance.
- ☐ Using local virtual directories only.
- ☐ Disabling indexing and page footers.
- ☐ Using clustering.

CHAPTER 13

Maintenance and Troubleshooting

Maintaining and troubleshooting IIS web servers requires detailed understanding of HTTP error messages, IIS logging, event lots, and other aspects of Windows Server 2003. This chapter covers these topics and also provides tips on troubleshooting different aspects of IIS operation.

HTTP ERROR MESSAGES

HTTP error messages are a subset of more general messages called *HTTP status codes*. These status codes are returned in the response headers when a web browser requests a page from a web server, and every HTTP response includes one of these status codes whether the request is successful or not. Before we look at HTTP error codes, how they can be customized in IIS, and how they can be used for troubleshooting purposes, let's first look at these status codes.

HTTP Status Codes

HTTP status codes are defined in the HTTP/1.1 specification, which is defined in RFC 2616. Full details of these codes can be found on the World Wide Web Consortium website at www.w3c.org; what follows here is only a brief summary.

HTTP status codes are three-digit numbers that are divided into five classes as shown in Table 13-1.

The following are a few examples of actual HTTP status codes for these different classes:

- **200 OK**   The client request has succeeded and contains the information requested by the client. For example, a web page is returned from the web server in response to an HTTP GET request by a client browser.

- **301 Moved Permanently**   The URL for this page has moved permanently, and the client is being automatically redirected to the new location.

- **403 Forbidden**   The server refuses to fulfill the request. This typically happens because the client cannot be authenticated by the server or has insufficient permissions to access the requested page.

- **500 Internal Server Error**   An unexpected condition has occurred on the server and it cannot fulfill the client's request.

Viewing HTTP Status Codes

HTTP status codes are returned to the client by the server with every response sent, but they are normally only seen on the client when an error occurs, either on the client side (4xx error) or server side (5xx error). However, you can display the status code for any response by using Telnet as your client and entering the client's HTTP headers manually. This makes Telnet a good tool for troubleshooting unusual problems with web servers, but it requires a good understanding of the syntax of HTTP headers.

Code	Class	Description
1xx	Informational	Used for experimental purposes only. Not used by real-world web servers.
2xx	Successful	Client request was successfully received and understood.
3xx	Redirection	Client needs to take further action to fulfill the request.
4xx	Client Error	An error has occurred at the client.
5xx	Server Error	An error has occurred at the server.

Table 13-1.   Categories of HTTP Status Codes

As an example, let's use Telnet to request the home page default.asp of an ASP application for the Default Web Site of an IIS server that has an IP address of 172.16.11.210. If you need to review how to use the Telnet client on the Windows Server 2003 platform, turn back to Chapter 11, "Working from the Command Line."

Start by opening a command prompt on another Windows machine on your network. Type **telnet** and press ENTER to start the Telnet client. When using Telnet to send HTTP headers directly to the web server, it will help if you turn on Local Echo so that you can see the headers you type. To do this at the Telnet prompt, type **set LOCAL_ECHO** and press ENTER.

Now open a connection to the web server on port 80 by typing **open 172.16.11.210 80** and pressing ENTER. The command-prompt window should go blank once the connection has been established with the web server because the web server is now waiting for you to enter your HTTP request.

Now type the following:

```
GET /default.asp HTTP/1.1
Accept: */*
User-Agent: Mozilla/4.0
Host: 172.16.11.210
```

Note the blank line at the end—this is important because it indicates to the server that your HTTP request is finished and can now be processed. The lines of this request are interpreted as follows:

- **Line 1**   The client is requesting the file default.asp located in the root directory of the requested web (host). The client also informs the server that it supports version 1.1 of the HTTP protocol.

- **Line 2**   The client will accept any MIME types from the server. If the client wanted to be more specific, it could provide a list of MIME types it can understand, such as text/html, image/gif, and so on, but */* is easier to use here unless you're troubleshooting MIME-type issues.

- **Line 3** The client is compatible with the Mozilla/4.0 web browser standard. Version 4 and higher of Internet Explorer comply with this standard. You could be more specific and add information indicating exactly what version of IE the client is using, but that's superfluous unless you're troubleshooting version-related client problems.

- **Line 4** The client is requesting the website listening at 172.16.11.210, which in this example is the Default Web Site on the IIS machine.

- **Line 5** The blank line at the end signals to the client that all the headers of the HTTP request have been submitted, and the server should now attempt to process the request.

Here's a typical response from the server:

```
HTTP/1.1 200 OK
Date: Wed, 15 Jan 2003 21:08:38 GMT
Server: Microsoft-IIS/6.0
X-Powered-By: ASP.NET
Content-Length: 277
Content-Type: text/html
Set-Cookie: ASPSESSIONIDQSQRBBAR=MIANHFOCCKHOOIMJDPINGBLC; path=/
Cache-control: private

<html>
<head>
<meta http-equiv="Content-Type" content="text/html; charset=windows-1252">
<title>My First ASP Page</title>
</head>
<body>
Hello World! The current date and time are:  1/15/2003 3:08:38 PM.<BR>The result
 of our calculation is:  210
</body>
</html>

Connection to host lost.
Press any key to continue...
```

Note the status code of 200 in the first line of the response generated by the server. This indicates that the request was successful and is being fulfilled by the server in the remaining lines of the response. The lines beginning <html> are the HTML code for the requested file, which are generated dynamically by the ASP application.

Notice also that at the end of the response the server terminates the TCP connection with the client. You can instead keep the connection open at the end by adding the following line to your request headers immediately after the Host line:

```
Connection: Keep-Alive
```

Wfetch.exe

Another useful tool for troubleshooting HTTP connections is Wfetch.exe, which can be used to display the headers in HTTP Request and HTTP Response packets sent between web browsers and web servers. Wfetch.exe can be downloaded for free from Microsoft's website. Its operation is explained in Knowledge Base article 284285 on the Microsoft Product Support Services (PSS) website at support .microsoft.com.

This takes advantage of the support for HTTP 1.1 Keep-Alives by IIS 6 and makes communications between the client and server more efficient by reducing the overhead of creating and tearing down TCP sessions for each request.

One more example, this time of a bad request and the resulting response:

```
GET /default.asp HTTP/1.1
Accept: */*
User-Agent: Mozilla/4.0

HTTP/1.1 400 Bad Request
Content-Type: text/html
Date: Wed, 15 Jan 2003 21:39:48 GMT
Connection: close
Content-Length: 39

<h1>Bad Request (Invalid Hostname)</h1>
```

This time you left out the header specifying the name or IP address of the host (website) where the requested page resides, and the web server responds with an "HTTP 400—Bad Request" status code. IIS also returns additional information indicating that the problem was an Invalid Hostname, which is helpful.

> **TIP** You can find more about HTTP headers in the HTTP/1.1 specification referred to at the beginning of this section. Another useful tool is Network Monitor, an optional component of Windows Server 2003 that can be used for capturing HTTP traffic and studying it.

Common HTTP Error Messages

It's important to have a thorough knowledge of HTTP error messages and their status codes for troubleshooting problems with IIS, so I'll summarize some of the more common ones you will encounter. First, client (4xx) errors:

- **400 Bad Request** The server can't understand the request, usually because the syntax of the URL is wrong.

- **401 Unauthorized**   The request requires authorization of the user's credentials, and the credentials offered are not accepted.

- **403 Forbidden**   The server refuses to fulfill the client's request for various reasons, even though the client's credentials may have been successfully authenticated.

- **404 Not Found**   The server doesn't have the requested file or it's located in a directory path that the client has not specified properly.

- **405 Method Not Allowed**   The client issued an HTTP GET request for a file that requires an HTTP POST request, or something similar.

- **406 Not Acceptable**   The client has sent the server a list of supported MIME types in the request headers, but the file requested is of a type not supported by the client and won't be sent.

- **407 Proxy Authentication Required**   Similar to 401 Unauthorized, but indicates the client must first authenticate itself with the proxy server before the web server can respond.

- **410 Gone**   The requested file is no longer present on the server, and the server has no knowledge of where it now resides. (If the server knew its new location, it could automatically redirect the client to the new location using a 301 or 307 status code in its response.)

The list of common server (5xx) errors is smaller:

- **500 Internal Server Error**   Something has gone wrong on the server (this message can mean a lot of different things).

- **501 Not Implemented**   The client is requesting the server use an HTTP method that it currently does not have implemented.

- **502 Bad Gateway**   The server is acting as a gateway for another server upstream from it, and the upstream server has sent an invalid response.

- **503 Service Unavailable**   The client is requesting a service that the server is currently unable to provide.

Substatus Error Codes

Many HTTP 4xx and 5xx status codes aren't very informative. For example, 500 Internal Server Error doesn't tell the client anything at all about why the server didn't return the desired response. To make it easier to troubleshoot connection problems between web browsers and IIS, Microsoft has extended the industry-standard HTTP status codes with a more granular set of proprietary *substatus* error codes. For example,

```
500.13 Internet Server Error - Server Too Busy
```

indicates that the server is too busy to respond to the client's request, because of bandwidth throttling, connection limits, or some other condition.

Table 13-2 shows a comprehensive list of HTTP error messages with substatus codes that are used by the IIS 6 platform.

Status Code	Substatus Code	Default Error Message
400	None	Bad Request
401	1	Unauthorized—Logon failed
	2	Unauthorized—Logon failed due to server configuration
	3	Unauthorized—Unauthorized due to ACL on resource
	4	Unauthorized—Authorization failed by filter
	5	Unauthorized—Authorization failed by ISAPI/CGI app
	7	Unauthorized—Denied due to URL Authorization policy
403	1	Forbidden—Execute access denied
	2	Forbidden—Read access denied
	3	Forbidden—Write access denied
	4	Forbidden—SSL required
	5	Forbidden—SSL 128 required
	6	Forbidden—IP address rejected
	7	Forbidden—Client certificate required
	8	Forbidden—Site access denied
	9	Forbidden—Too many users
	10	Forbidden—Invalid configuration
	11	Forbidden—Password change
	12	Forbidden—Mapper access denied
	13	Forbidden—Client certificate revoked
	14	Forbidden—Directory listing denied
	15	Forbidden—Client Access Licenses exceeded
	16	Forbidden—Client certificate untrusted or ill-formed
	17	Forbidden—Client certificate has expired or is not yet valid
	18	Forbidden—Cannot execute request from this application pool
	19	Forbidden—CGI access denied
	20	Forbidden—Passport login failed
404	None	Not Found
	2	Not Found—Denied due to Lockdown Policy
	3	Not Found—Denied due to MIMEMAP Policy
405	None	Method Not Allowed
406	None	Not Acceptable

Table 13-2.   IIS Default HTTP Errors Showing Substatus Codes

Status Code	Substatus Code	Default Error Message
407	None	Proxy Authentication Required
412	None	Precondition Failed
414	None	Request—URI too long
415	None	Unsupported Media Type
500	None	Internal Server Error
	12	Internal Server Error—Application restarting
	13	Internal Server Error—Server too busy
	15	Internal Server Error—Direct requests for GLOBAL.ASA forbidden
	16	Internal Server Error—UNC access error
	17	Internal Server Error—URL Authorization store not found
	18	Internal Server Error—URL Authorization store cannot be opened
	19	Internal Server Error—Bad file metadata
	100	Internal Server Error—ASP error
501	None	Not Implemented
502	None	Bad Gateway
503	None	Service Unavailable

Table 13-2. IIS Default HTTP Errors Showing Substatus Codes *(continued)*

Custom HTTP Error Messages

In its default out-of-the-box configuration, IIS returns only the following default HTTP errors:

- 403;14 Forbidden—Directory listing denied
- 500 Internal Server Error
- 500;100 Internal Server Error—ASP error
- 501 Not Implemented
- 502 Bad Gateway

For all other HTTP errors, IIS returns a *custom* error message instead of the default messages shown in Table 13-2. These custom error messages have two advantages over the default ones:

- They are more informative and often provide tips on what might have gone wrong and how to troubleshoot the problem.
- They can be customized by the IIS administrator, for example, by adding a company logo and Help Desk phone number for users to contact.

To customize HTTP error messages in IIS, right-click the Web Sites node in IIS Manager and select Properties. Then select the Custom Errors tab (Figure 13-1).

The Custom Errors tab displays a list of HTTP errors used by IIS. By default, most of these are custom error messages that are implemented as HTML pages stored in the \Windows\Help\IISHelp\Common directory. By editing these HTML files with Notepad (if you know HTML) or Microsoft FrontPage (or some similar editor), you can customize them to meet the needs of your organization.

NOTE   The location of custom error message files has changed from IIS 5 to this new version of IIS.

If you prefer that default (HTTP/1.1 standard) error messages are returned to users instead of the "friendly" custom ones used by IIS, you can configure IIS to do this by selecting an error message from the list on the Custom Errors tab and clicking the Default button. This will cause IIS to send the default message for that error condition instead of the more detailed custom one. If you wish your server to return only default HTTP error messages, hold down the SHIFT key, select *all* of the message from the list, and click Default.

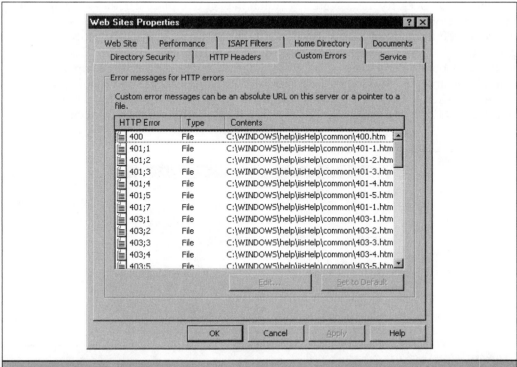

Figure 13-1.   The Custom Errors tab

Another option for error messages is to redirect the user to a URL pointing to a different site or server when an error condition arises. To do this, select an error message from the list and click Edit. This opens the Edit Custom Error Properties for the particular error message you've selected (Figure 13-2).

By using the Message Type list box on this properties sheet you can select any of three ways for implementing this error message:

- **Default**   Uses the standard HTTP/1.1 error message, short and terse.
- **File**   Uses a custom error message implemented by an HTML file.
- **URL**   Redirects to a URL where the error message resides.

NOTE   Configuring the Custom Errors tab obeys the usual IIS feature of inheritance of properties sheets settings. In other words, configuring this at the Web Sites level causes the configuration to be inherited by all websites, virtual directories, and files under it. You can configure Custom Errors at the global (Web Sites), site, directory, and file level.

Examples of Custom and Default Messages

To see how the user will experience the difference between friendly HTTP error messages and the default ones, try this. Create a default.htm page and place it in the home directory of a website on your IIS machine. Open the URL for the site (for example, using its IP address) in Internet Explorer to verify that the page displays properly. Now open the properties sheet for the default.htm page in IIS Manager, select the File tab, clear the Read check box to deny Read access to the page, and click Apply. Try to open the page again in IE, and you should get the custom 403.2 error message shown in Figure 13-3.

Now switch to the Custom Errors tab of the properties sheet for the default.htm file, select the 403.2 error message in the list box, click Default to change from custom to

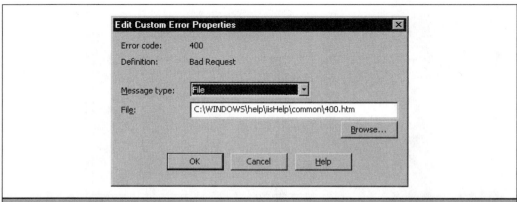

Figure 13-2.   Edit Custom Error Properties box

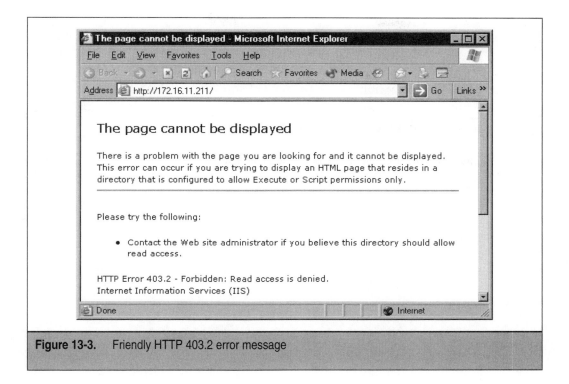

Figure 13-3.   Friendly HTTP 403.2 error message

default message for this error, and click Apply. Refresh your browser window, and you will now get the considerably less verbose error message shown in Figure 13-4.

Custom HTTP Error Messages In Detail

Some of the error messages shown in Table 13-2 are fairly self-explanatory, but others are somewhat obscure, and it's not always clear what steps could be taken to troubleshoot the condition that produced them. To help you use IIS friendly error messages for troubleshooting purposes, the following subsections summarize the important content displayed by each of these messages. This information is not included in the Help file for IIS, so it's useful to include it here. A couple of things to note about this reference section:

- The first error listed is the generic "The page cannot be displayed" error that can appear when IIS is misconfigured in certain ways or when Internet Explorer tries to access a site that doesn't exist. This error is *not* accompanied by an HTTP status code.

- In addition to the text of the various IIS custom errors listed in these sections, I've added "Additional Troubleshooting Tips" at the end of some of these subsections to help you determine what might have generated the error.

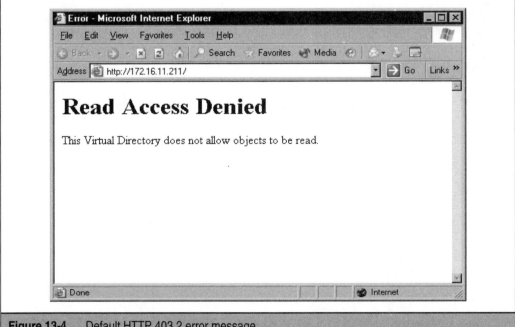

Figure 13-4.   Default HTTP 403.2 error message

IIS sometimes returns generic error messages (messages without substatus codes) when it responds to certain error conditions. For example, when a client tries to access a file that has a file extension that is not in the MIME map for the web server, you would expect a 404.3 Not Found—Denied due to MIMEMAP Policy error to be returned to the client, but instead IIS returns a standard 404 Not Found error. This is a security measure to reduce the attack surface on the web server by preventing malicious users from gaining knowledge about the server's configuration from detailed error messages.

So what use are custom error messages if they are sometimes (as in the case of 404.2 and 404.3, for example) replaced by generic ones instead? The answer is that when IIS returns an HTTP error message to the client, it also logs the error in the web logs for the site (if web logging is enabled and W3C Extended Logging is being used), and substatus codes like 404.3 are included in these logs to provide administrators with full details about such events. I'll talk about web logging in the section "Web Logging."

The Page Cannot Be Displayed

The page you are looking for is currently unavailable.

Please try the following:

- Click the Refresh button, or try again later.
- If you typed the page address in the Address bar, make sure that it is spelled correctly.

- To check your connection settings, click the Tools menu, and then click Internet Options. On the Connections tab, click Settings. The settings should match those provided by your local area network (LAN) administrator or Internet service provider (ISP).

- If your Network Administrator has enabled it, Microsoft Windows can examine your network and automatically discover network connection settings. If you would like Windows to try and discover them, click Detect Network Settings.

- Some sites require 128-bit connection security. Click the Help menu and then click About Internet Explorer to determine what strength security you have installed.

- If you are trying to reach a secure site, make sure your Security settings can support it. Click the Tools menu, and then click Internet Options. On the Advanced tab, scroll to the Security section and check settings for SSL 2.0, SSL 3.0, TLS 1.0, PCT 1.0.

- Click the Back button to try another link.

Cannot Find Server or DNS Error

Additional Troubleshooting Tips:

- This error typically occurs when the client spells the domain name of the website incorrectly in the requested URL.

- This error can also occur when the port number of the website has been changed from its standard setting of port 80 to some nonstandard port number, and the client, being unaware of this change, tries to access the site using the default port number (which it always does when the URL contains no explicit port number).

- This error can also occur if the website has been paused or stopped for maintenance by the administrator.

400 Bad Request

The page that you are looking for might have been removed, had its name changed, had its content expired, or be temporarily unavailable.

Please try the following:

- Make sure that the website address displayed in the Address bar of your browser is spelled and formatted correctly.

- If you reached this page by clicking a link, contact the website administrator to alert them that the link is incorrectly formatted.

- Click the Back button or open the home page for this website and look for other links to the information that you want.

HTTP Error 400—Request is badly formed.

Additional Troubleshooting Tips

- When this request is returned, a simple "Bad Requests (explanation)" page is returned to the client instead of the friendly (custom) HTTP error message configured for IIS for this error.

- Usually this is caused by a problem with the client. Web browsers like Internet Explorer can often detect a problem with URL syntax and automatically fix it before submitting the request to the web server, and problems with mistyped URLs usually result in "404 File Not Found" errors instead of a 400 error. However, if you use Telnet as a client for troubleshooting IIS and don't type the HTTP headers exactly as required, 400 errors will result.

- On some web servers, using spaces in URLs can generate 400 errors, but Internet Explorer automatically substitutes "%20" for spaces typed in URLs and 404 errors generally result.

- This error can also result when the Default Web Site has its IP address changed from All Unassigned to an address that is not the address shown on the TCP/IP properties sheet, but is instead one of the additional addresses shown on the IP Settings tab of the Advanced TCP/IP properties sheet. This means, of course, that the IIS machine has multiple IP addresses assigned to it. The error returned in this case is "Bad Request (Invalid Hostname)."

401 You Are Not Authorized to View This Page

You do not have permission to view this directory or page using the credentials that you supplied.

Please try the following:

- Contact the website administrator if you believe you should be able to view this directory or page.

- Click the Refresh button to try again with different credentials.

HTTP Error 401—Unauthorized: Access is denied due to invalid credentials.

Additional Troubleshooting Tips

- This message will also be returned if the credentials submitted are for a nonexistent user account.

- If mappings are configured between .NET Passports and user accounts in Active Directory, this error will be returned if a mapping fails.

401.1 You Are Not Authorized to View This Page

Same as the preceding 401 error.

401.2 You Are Not Authorized to View This Page

You do not have permission to view this directory or page using the credentials that you supplied because your web browser is sending a WWW-Authenticate header field that the web server is not configured to accept.

Please try the following:

- Contact the website administrator if you believe you should be able to view this directory or page.

- Click the Refresh button to try again with different credentials.

HTTP Error 401.2—Unauthorized: Access is denied due to server configuration.

Additional Troubleshooting Tips

- This error occurs when trying to access a remote virtual directory with the wrong credentials. It only works for authentication schemes that support delegation of credentials for authentication. Integrated Windows Authentication does not support such delegation.

- This error will also be returned if *no* authentication methods are configured for the site being accessed.

401.3 You Are Not Authorized to View This Page

You do not have permission to view this directory or page due to the access control list (ACL) that is configured for this resource on the web server.

Please try the following:

- Contact the website administrator if you believe you should be able to view this directory or page.

- Click the Refresh button to try again with different credentials.

HTTP Error 401.3—Unauthorized: Access is denied due to an ACL set on the requested resource.

Additional Troubleshooting Tips

- This error usually means NTFS permissions are set incorrectly on the requested file.

401.4 You Are Not Authorized to View This Page

You might not have permission to view this directory or page using the credentials that you supplied. The web server has a filter installed to verify users connecting to the server and it failed to authenticate your credentials.

Please try the following:

- Contact the website administrator if you believe you should be able to view this directory or page.

- Click the Refresh button to try again with different credentials.

HTTP Error 401.4—Unauthorized: Authorization failed by filter installed on the web server.

401.5 You Are Not Authorized to View This Page

The URL you attempted to reach has an ISAPI or CGI application installed that verifies user credentials before proceeding. This application cannot verify your credentials.

Please try the following:

- Contact the website administrator if you believe you should be able to view this directory or page.

- Click the Refresh button to try again with different credentials.

HTTP Error 401.5—Unauthorized: Authorization failed by an ISAPI/CGI application.

401.6 You Are Not Authorized to View This Page

The credentials that you supplied for this URL cannot be verified at this time because the authorization scope associated with the URL cannot be found on the web server.

Please try the following:

- Contact the website administrator if you believe you should be able to view this directory or page.

- Click the Refresh button to try again with different credentials.

HTTP Error 401.6—Unauthorized: URL authorization scope was not found on the server.

401.7 You Are Not Authorized to View This Page

You do not have permission to view this directory or page due to the URL Authorization policy set on the web server.

Please try the following:

- Contact the website administrator if you believe you should be able to view this directory or page.

- Click the Refresh button to try again with different credentials.

HTTP Error 401.7—Unauthorized: Access denied by URL authorization policy on the web server.

403 You Are Not Authorized to View This Page

You do not have permission to view this directory or page using the credentials that you supplied.

Please try the following:

- Contact the website administrator if you believe you should be able to view this directory or page.

- Click the Refresh button to try again with different credentials.

HTTP Error 403—Forbidden: Access is denied.

Additional troubleshooting tips

- This error will be returned if a client tries to directly access ASP.NET configuration files such as machine.config. This is to prevent users from accessing sensitive information stored within these files.

- This error will also occur if there are no authentication methods configured for a site.

403.1 The page cannot be displayed

You have attempted to execute a CGI, ISAPI, or other executable program from a directory that does not allow programs to be executed.

Please try the following:

- Contact the website administrator if you believe this directory should allow execute access.

HTTP Error 403.1—Forbidden: Execute access is denied.

Additional Troubleshooting Tips

- Check the Execute Permissions on the Home Directory tab for your site to make sure they are configured properly. CGI and ISAPI applications generally require this property set to Scripts and Executables, while ASP applications need it set to Scripts Only instead.

403.2 The Page Cannot Be Displayed

There is a problem with the page you are looking for and it cannot be displayed. This error can occur if you are trying to display an HTML page that resides in a directory that is configured to allow Execute or Script permissions only.

Please try the following:

- Contact the website administrator if you believe this directory should allow Read access.

HTTP Error 403.2—Forbidden: Read access is denied.

Additional Troubleshooting Tips

- Check the Home Directory tab for the website to make sure Read permission is enabled. Also, if necessary, check the Virtual Directory tab for a file within a virtual directory and the File tab for the file itself for the same setting, in case web permissions were configured at a lower level, overriding site level settings.

403.3 The Page Cannot Be Saved

There is a problem saving the page to the website. This error can occur if you attempt to upload a file or modify a file in a directory that does not allow Write access.
Please try the following:

- Contact the website administrator if you believe this directory should allow Write access.

HTTP Error 403.3—Forbidden: Write access is denied.

Additional Troubleshooting Tips

- This error can occur when using WebDAV or FrontPage to upload pages to a site if permissions are set incorrectly for the site.
- It can also occur when trying to upload files to FTP sites when Write permission is disabled for the site.

403.4 The Page Must Be Viewed over a Secure Channel

The page you are trying to access is secured with Secure Sockets Layer (SSL).
Please try the following:

- Type https:// at the beginning of the address you are attempting to reach and press ENTER.

HTTP Error 403.4—Forbidden: SSL is required to view this resource.

403.5 The Page Must Be Viewed with a High-Security Web Browser

The resource you are trying to access is secured with a 128-bit version of Secure Sockets Layer (SSL). In order to view this resource, you need a browser that supports this version of SSL.
Please try the following:

- Contact the website administrator if your web browser does support 128-bit encryption, or if you believe you should be able to view this directory or page.
- Upgrade your web browser to a version that supports 128-bit encryption.

HTTP Error 403.5—Forbidden: SSL 128 is required to view this resource.

403.6 You Are Not Authorized to View This Page

The web server you are attempting to reach has a list of IP addresses that are not allowed to access the website, and the IP address of your browsing computer is on this list.
Please try the following:

- Contact the website administrator if you believe you should be able to view this directory or page.

HTTP Error 403.6—Forbidden: IP address of the client has been rejected.

Additional Troubleshooting Tips

- Check the IP Address and Domain Name Restrictions list on the Directory Security tab for the site to make sure the client's IP address is not blocked from accessing the site.

403.7 The Page Requires a Client Certificate

The page you are attempting to access requires your browser to have a Secure Sockets Layer (SSL) client certificate that the web server will recognize. The client certificate is used for identifying you as a valid user of the resource.
Please try the following:

- Contact the website administrator if you believe you should be able to view this directory or page without a client certificate, or to obtain a client certificate.

- If you already have a client certificate, use your web browser's security features to ensure that your client certificate is installed properly. (Some web browsers refer to client certificates as browser or personal certificates.)

HTTP Error 403.7—Forbidden: SSL client certificate is required.

403.8 You Are Not Authorized to View This Page

The web server you are attempting to reach has a list of DNS names that are not allowed to access this website, and the DNS name of your browsing computer is on this list.
Please try the following:

- Contact the website administrator if you believe you should be able to view this directory or page.

HTTP Error 403.8—Forbidden: DNS name of the client is rejected.

Additional Troubleshooting Tips   Check the IP Address and Domain Name Restrictions list on the Directory Security tab for the site to make sure the client's DNS domain name is not blocked from accessing the site.

403.9 The Page Cannot Be Displayed

The web server is too busy to process your request at this time.
Please try the following:

- Click the Refresh button, or try again later.

HTTP Error 403.9—Forbidden: Too many clients are trying to connect to the
Web server.

Additional Troubleshooting Tips   This error will be returned if Connection Limits has
been enabled and configured globally for the web server, and the configured limit
has been exceeded by the client's request. This will occur regardless of the Connection
Limits configured for individual sites on the server.

403.10 You Are Not Authorized to View This Page

You have attempted to execute a CGI, ISAPI, or other executable program from
a directory that does not allow programs to be executed.
Please try the following:

- Contact the website administrator if you believe this directory should allow
  execute access.

HTTP Error 403.10—Forbidden: Web server is configured to deny Execute access.

403.11 You Are Not Authorized to View This Page

You do not have permission to view this directory or page using the credentials that you
supplied.
Please try the following:

- Contact the website administrator if you believe you should be able
  to view this directory or page.
- Click the Refresh button to try again with different credentials.

HTTP Error 403.11—Forbidden: Password has been changed.

403.12 The Requested Page Requires a Valid SSL Client Certificate

The account to which your client certificate is mapped on the web server has been
denied access to this website. A Secure Sockets Layer (SSL) client certificate is used
for identifying you as a valid user of the resource.
Please try the following:

- Contact the website administrator to establish client certificate permissions.

- If you already have a valid client certificate, use your web browser's security features to ensure that your client certificate is installed properly. (Some web browsers refer to client certificates as browser or personal certificates.)

- Change your client certificate and click the Refresh button, if appropriate.

HTTP Error 403.12—Forbidden: Client certificate is denied access by the server certificate mapper.

403.13 The Page Requires a Valid SSL Client Certificate

Your client certificate was revoked, or the revocation status could not be determined. A Secure Sockets Layer (SSL) client certificate is used for identifying you as a valid user of the resource.
Please try the following:

- Contact the website administrator to establish client certificate permissions or to obtain a new certificate.

HTTP Error 403.13—Forbidden: Client certificate has been revoked on the web server.

403.14 Directory Listing Is Denied

The web server is configured not to display a list of the contents of this directory.
Please try the following:

- Contact the website administrator if you believe this directory should allow browsers to display a list of its contents.

HTTP Error 403.14—Forbidden: Directory listing denied.

Additional Troubleshooting Tips   This error commonly occurs when there is no default document and the Directory Browsing setting has not been enabled on the Home Directory tab for the site. If you enable Directory Browsing, you must also enable Read web permission on the same tab or a "403.2 Forbidden—Read Access Is Denied" error will be returned.

403.15 The Page Cannot Be Displayed

There are too many people accessing the website at this time. The web server has exceeded its Client Access License limit.
Please try the following:

- Click the Refresh button, or try again later.

HTTP Error 403.15—Forbidden: Client access licenses have exceeded limits on the Web server.

403.16 The Page Requires a Valid SSL Client Certificate

Your client certificate is untrusted or invalid. A Secure Sockets Layer (SSL) client certificate is used for identifying you as a valid user of the resource.

Please try the following:

- Contact the site administrator to establish client certificate permissions.
- If you already have a valid client certificate, use your web browser's security features to ensure that your client certificate is installed properly. (Some web browsers refer to client certificates as browser or personal certificates.)
- Change your client certificate and click the Refresh button, if appropriate.

HTTP Error 403.16—Forbidden: Client certificate is ill-formed or is not trusted by the Web server.

403.17 The Page Requires a Valid SSL Client Certificate

Your client certificate has expired or is not yet valid. A Secure Sockets Layer (SSL) client certificate is used for identifying you as a valid user of the resource.

Please try the following:

- Contact the site administrator to establish client certificate permissions.
- If you already have a valid client certificate, use your web browser's security features to ensure that your client certificate is installed properly. (Some web browsers refer to client certificates as browser or personal certificates.)
- Change your client certificate and click the Refresh button, if appropriate.

HTTP Error 403.17—Forbidden: Client certificate has expired or is not yet valid.

403.18 Cannot Execute Request from the Current Application Pool

The specified request cannot be executed in the application pool that is configured for this resource on the web server.

Please try the following:

- Contact the website administrator if you believe you should be able to view this directory or page.

HTTP Error 403.18—Forbidden: Cannot execute requested URL in the current application pool.

403.19 Cannot Execute CGI Applications in the Current Application Pool on the Web Server

The configured user for this application pool does not have sufficient privileges to execute CGI applications.

Please try the following:

- Contact the website administrator if you believe you should be able to execute CGI applications.

HTTP Error 403.19—Forbidden: Cannot execute CGIs for the client in this application pool.

403.20 Passport Login Failed

The Passport logon server returned an error to the website during logon.
Please try the following:

- Contact the website administrator if you believe you should be able to view this directory or page.
- Click the Refresh button to try to login again via Passport.

HTTP Error 403.20—Forbidden: Passport logon failed.

404 The Page Cannot Be Found

The page you are looking for might have been removed, had its name changed, or is temporarily unavailable.
Please try the following:

- Make sure that the website address displayed in the address bar of your browser is spelled and formatted correctly.
- If you reached this page by clicking a link, contact the website administrator to alert them that the link is incorrectly formatted.
- Click the Back button to try another link.

HTTP Error 404—File or directory not found.

404.1 The Website Cannot Be Found

The website you are trying to access has an IP address that is configured not to accept requests that specify a port number.
Please try the following:

- Make sure that the website address displayed in the address bar of your browser is spelled and formatted correctly.
- If you reached this page by clicking a link, contact the website administrator to alert them that the link is incorrectly formatted.
- Click the Back button to try another link.

HTTP Error 404.1—File or directory not found: website not accessible on the requested port.

Additional Troubleshooting Tips

- This error is returned only when the IIS machine has multiple IP addresses and the client is requesting a URL for an IP address that is not used by IIS. For example, if the machine has addresses 172.16.11.210 and 172.16.11.211 and the Default Web Site is specifically assigned the first address and is the only website on the machine, then a request for the URL http://172.16.11.211 will return a 404.1 error. The client receives a generic 404 error in this case; but if W3C Extended Logging is configured on the server, a 404.1 event will be logged accordingly.

404.2 The Page Cannot Be Found

The page you are requesting cannot be served due to the web service extensions that are configured on the web server.

Please try the following:

- Contact the website administrator to alert them that they have not enabled the necessary web service extensions.

HTTP Error 404.2—File or directory not found: Lockdown policy prevents this request.

Additional Troubleshooting Tips

- This error commonly occurs when the necessary web service extensions have not been enabled for a web application. This includes ASP, ASP.NET, ISAPI, and CGI apps. It can also occur if a client tries to access an application that uses server-side includes, tries to upload files using WebDAV, or tries to manage content on a site using FrontPage Extensions if these features have not been enabled on the server.

- If you have a CGI app and have enabled web service extensions for them (or for "all unknown CGI extensions") but have not assigned the user account under which the CGI app runs the proper rights, this error will be returned. To assign an account for CGI the proper rights, make it a member of the IIS_WPG group on the server and assign it the "adjust memory quotas for a process" and "replace a process level token" user rights.

- If you have an application extension that is not mapped in IIS, client requests for this application will return this error. To map an application extension for an application, open the properties sheet for the website where the application resides, select the Home Directory tab, click Configuration, select the Mappings tab, and click Add. Refer back to Chapter 8, "Creating and Configuring Applications," for more information.

404.3 The Page Cannot Be Found

The page you are requesting cannot be served due to the Multipurpose Internet Mail Extensions (MIME) map policy that is configured on the web server. The page you requested has a filename extension that is not recognized, and is therefore not allowed.

Please try the following:

- Contact the website administrator to alert them that they have not enabled the necessary file extensions through their MIME map policy.

HTTP Error 404.3—File or directory not found: MIME map policy prevents this request.

Additional Troubleshooting Tips

- This error typically occurs when a client tries to request a static file whose filename extension is not defined in the MIME map for the site or server. Adding a wildcard MIME map will prevent these errors from happening, but this is not recommended for security reasons.

405 The Page Cannot Be Displayed

The page you are looking for cannot be displayed because an invalid method (HTTP verb) was used to attempt access.

Please try the following:

- Contact the website administrator if you believe that this request should be allowed.

- Make sure that the website address displayed in the address bar of your browser is spelled and formatted correctly.

HTTP Error 405—The HTTP verb used to access this page is not allowed.

406 The Resource Cannot Be Displayed

The page you are looking for cannot be opened by your browser because it has a filename extension that your browser does not accept.

Please try the following:

- Change the Multipurpose Internet Mail Extensions (MIME) or security settings of your browser to accept the filename extension of the requested page. Your browser might currently be configured in a highly secure mode that protects your computer. Please read the Help for your browser before changing any settings.

HTTP Error 406—Client browser does not accept the MIME type of the requested page.

407 Proxy Authentication Required

You must be authenticated by a proxy server before the web server can execute your request.
Please try the following:

- Log on to your proxy server and try again.
- Contact the proxy server administrator if you believe you should be able to view this directory or page.

HTTP Error 407—Initial proxy authentication required by the web server.

410 The Page Does Not Exist

The page you are looking for has been removed.
Please try the following:

- Navigate to the home page for this website and look for links to the information that you want.

HTTP Error 410—File has been removed.

412 The Page Cannot Be Displayed

The request was not completed due to preconditions that are set in the request header. Preconditions prevent the requested method from being applied to a resource other than the one intended. An example of a precondition is testing for expired content in the page cache of the client.
Please try the following:

- Navigate to the home page for this website and look for links to the information that you want.
- Use your web browser's tools to delete cached pages and then click the Refresh button to try again.

HTTP Error 412—Precondition failed.

414 The Page Cannot Be Displayed

The web server is refusing to service the request because the requested URL address is too long. This condition might occur if the client has encountered a redirection problem (for example, a redirected URL prefix that points to a suffix of itself), or the client has improperly converted a POST request to a GET request with long query information, or the web server is under attack by the client.
Please try the following:

- Contact the website administrator to inform them that this error has occurred for this URL address.

- Make sure that the website address displayed in the address bar of your browser is spelled and formatted correctly.

HTTP Error 414—The Request-URI is too large.

415 The Page Cannot Be Returned

The web server cannot service the request because the requested file is in a format that the server is configured not to download.
Please try the following:

- Contact the website administrator to inform them that this error has occurred for this file type.

HTTP 415—Unsupported Media Type.

500 The Page Cannot Be Displayed

There is a problem with the page you are looking for, and it cannot be displayed.
Please try the following:

- Contact the website administrator to inform them that this error has occurred for this URL address.

HTTP Error 500—Internal server error.

Additional Troubleshooting Tips

- This error does *not* necessarily indicate that the worker process servicing the application pool where the application resides has become unhealthy.

500.11 The Page Cannot Be Displayed

The request cannot be processed because the website is shutting down.
Please try the following:

- Click the Refresh button, or try again later.
- If this error persists, contact the website administrator to inform them that this error continues to occur for this URL address.

HTTP Error 500.11—Server error: Application is shutting down on the Web server.

500.12 The Page Cannot Be Displayed

The request cannot be processed while the website is restarting.
Please try the following:

- Click the Refresh button, or try again later.
- If this error persists, contact the website administrator to inform them that this error continues to occur for this URL address.

HTTP Error 500.12—Server error: Application is busy restarting on the Web server.

500.13 The Page Cannot Be Displayed

The request cannot be processed at this time. The amount of traffic exceeds the website's configured capacity.

Please try the following:

- Click the Refresh button, or try again later.

- If this error persists, contact the website administrator to inform them that this error continues to occur for this URL address.

HTTP Error 500.13—Server error: Web server is too busy.

Additional Troubleshooting Tips

- This error will be returned if the client requests an ASP page but the queue is full (that is, the number of concurrent ASP requests exceeds the value defined in the metabase property AspRequestQueueMax). It can also occur if the number of concurrent ASP sessions with the server exceeds the value defined in the metabase property AspSessionMax.

500.14 The Page Cannot Be Displayed

The request cannot be processed due to application configuration errors on the web server.

Please try the following:

- Contact the website administrator to inform them that this error has occurred for this URL address.

HTTP Error 500.14—Server error: Invalid application configuration on the server.

500.15 The Page Cannot Be Displayed

GLOBAL.ASA is a special file that cannot be accessed directly by your browser.

Please try the following:

- In the Address bar of your browser, delete "global.asa" from the end of URL address, and press ENTER.

- If a link from another web page brought you to this page, contact the administrator of that website to inform them which page has the link.

HTTP Error 500.15—Server error: Direct requests for GLOBAL.ASA are not allowed.

500.16 The Page Cannot Be Displayed

The page you are requesting cannot be accessed due to UNC authorization settings that are configured incorrectly on the web server.

Please try the following:

- Contact the website administrator to inform them that this error has occurred for this URL address.

HTTP Error 500.16—Server error: UNC authorization credentials incorrect.

Additional Troubleshooting Tips

- This error can occur if the client is trying to access a site whose directory is mapped to a remote share using a UNC path. It generally has to do with the credentials used to access the share and typically occurs when the user account is correct but the password is wrong.

500.17 The Page Cannot Be Displayed

The URL Authorization store for the page you requested cannot be found on the web server, therefore your credentials cannot be verified.
Please try the following:

- Contact the website administrator to inform them that this error has occurred for this URL address.

HTTP Error 500.17—Server error: URL authorization store cannot be found.

500.18 The Page Cannot Be Displayed

The URL Authorization store for the page you requested cannot be opened on the web server, therefore your credentials cannot be verified.
Please try the following:

- Contact the website administrator to inform them that this error has occurred for this URL address.

HTTP Error 500.18—Server error: URL authorization store cannot be opened.

500.19 The Page Cannot Be Displayed

The requested page cannot be accessed because the related configuration data for the page is invalid in the metabase on the web server.
Please try the following:

- Contact the website administrator to inform them that this error has occurred for this URL address.

HTTP Error 500.19—Server error: Data for this file is configured improperly in the metabase.

500.100 The Page Cannot Be Displayed

There is a problem with the page you are trying to reach and it cannot be displayed.

Please try the following:

- Contact the website administrator to let them know that this error has occurred for this URL address.

HTTP 500.100—Internal server error: ASP error.

Technical Information (for support personnel)

- Error Type: *text_generated_here*
- Browser Type: *text_generated_here*
- Page: *text_generated_here*
- Time: *text_generated_here*

NOTE   500.100 errors are generated dynamically when ASP applications fail and include additional technical information as shown to help the developer troubleshoot what went wrong.

---

501 The Page Cannot Be Displayed

The page you are looking for cannot be displayed because a header value in the request does not match certain configuration settings on the web server. For example, a request header might specify a POST to a static file that cannot be posted to, or specify a Transfer-Encoding value that cannot make use of compression.
Please try the following:

- Contact the website administrator to inform them that this error has occurred for this URL address.

Error 501—Method not implemented on the Web server.

502 The Page Cannot Be Displayed

There is a problem with the page you are looking for, and it cannot be displayed. When the web server (while acting as a gateway or proxy) contacted the upstream content server, it received an invalid response from the content server.
Please try the following:

- Log on to your proxy server and try again.
- Contact the website administrator to inform them that this error has occurred for this URL address.

HTTP Error 502—Web server received an invalid response while acting as a gateway or proxy server.

HTTP Error 503 Service Unavailable

Another error that IIS might return on occasion is the HTTP 503 Service Unavailable error, which will be returned if the incoming client request exceeds the size of the application pool queue length. You can configure the queue length by right-clicking the Application Pools node and selecting Properties, choosing the Performance tab, selecting the check box to enable limiting the kernel request queue, and using the up and down arrows to specify the maximum number of queued requests to be permitted. If you clear the check box for limiting the kernel request queue, this error will never be returned, but then too many requests for applications in the pool may cause IIS to run out of memory.

Note that there is no way of customizing HTTP 503 errors in IIS 6; they are generated automatically by the server and provide no further information concerning what caused them. They are often related to problems with application pools, however; and in addition to the preceding scenario, they can be returned when an application pool is manually stopped by an administrator or automatically stopped and taken out of service because of rapid-fail protection being enabled.

Another situation where this error can be returned is if the maximum number of website connections has been limited to some value on the Performance tab instead of the default Unlimited Connections setting being used. If a client tries to access the site when the maximum number of connections has already been established with the server, a Service Unavailable message will be returned.

Finally, this error can be returned if a client tries to access the site while IIS is being restarted by the administrator. However, if IIS is still running but the requested website has been stopped or paused, a generic "Page Cannot Be Displayed" error message will be returned instead.

WEB LOGGING

Another useful feature of IIS for troubleshooting problems with client connections to IIS is web logging, also called website logging or IIS logging. This feature lets you log the activity of users connecting to your sites in log files that can be viewed and analyzed to look for traffic patterns. Using these logs you can

- Determine which sites on your server or portions of your sites are most heavily viewed, and configure IIS quality of service (QoS) settings to optimize performance accordingly. You can also use logging information to more effectively target users with marketing information.

- Detect trends such as growth patterns in user visits and plan how to upgrade the hardware and software on your IIS machine to accommodate such growth in the future.

- Detect unusual traffic patterns that can indicate problems with the operation of your IIS machine or attempts by malicious users to hack into your sites. For example, repeated log entries showing failed authentication events can indicate an attacker probing your site.

Other good reasons for enabling logging on your IIS machines include the following:

- While IIS generates errors, warning, and informational events in the event logs, often additional information is logged in the web logs concerning these events. It's a good idea to review your web logs whenever you find an IIS event in the System or Application logs using Event Viewer. For more information about IIS and event logs, see the later section "IIS and Event Logs."

- Even when IIS is configured to generate friendly (custom) HTTP error messages using the Custom Errors tab on IIS Manager properties sheets, IIS will sometimes return only standard HTTP error codes with no substatus codes attached to help troubleshoot the problem. If web logging is enabled, however, and the W3C Extended Format is configured, substatus codes are always recorded in the web logs when IIS generates HTTP errors. This helps administrators who can review the web logs to gain more insight into the causes of HTTP errors.

NOTE   In earlier versions of IIS, web logs were managed by the IIS Admin Service service. In IIS 6, web logging using W3C Extended, IIS, and NCSA formats is handled by the HTTP Listener (Http.sys) for better performance and to avoid concurrency issues. Web logging using ODBC, however, is managed by the worker process (w3wp.exe) associated with the site.

Enabling and Configuring Web Logging

Like other IIS properties, web logging can be enabled and configured at various levels, and settings at higher levels are inherited by lower levels in the usual way. You can enable web logging (turn it on) at two levels:

- **Web Sites level**   Enabling web logging at this level turns it on for all websites on the IIS machine.

- **Individual websites level**   You can also enable web logging on a per-website level.

Once web logging has been enabled for a site or for all sites, you can configure which specific home directories, virtual directories, subdirectories, and files should have their access logged.

Let's say, for example, that you want to log access to only the default.asp page within the home directory of the Default Web Site, and not for files in any other sites on your server. There are three steps you need to take to make this happen:

1. Open the properties sheet for the Default Web Site and select the Enable Logging check box on the Web Site tab to enable web logging for this particular site (Figure 13-5). This turns on web logging, but no logs are created unless specific directories and files have been marked for logging within the site (see step 3). However, *all* directories and files are marked by default for logging in IIS, so it's really a matter of specifying which directories and files you *don't* want to log access to.

2. On the same Web Site tab, select the log file format you want your web logs to be recorded in using the Active Log Format list box. You can click Properties to further configure it by specifying where your log files will be stored and various other settings that depend upon the particular format you've selected. I'll talk more about logging formats soon in the section "Log File Formats."

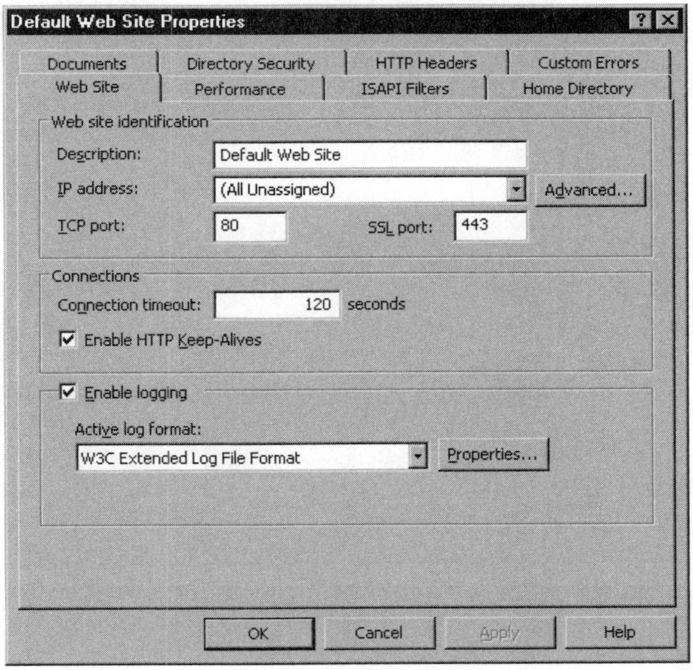

Default Web Site Properties   ? ✕

| Documents | Directory Security | HTTP Headers | Custom Errors |
| Web Site | Performance | ISAPI Filters | Home Directory |

Web site identification

Description: Default Web Site

IP address: (All Unassigned) ▾   Advanced...

TCP port: 80   SSL port: 443

Connections

Connection timeout: 120 seconds

☑ Enable HTTP Keep-Alives

☑ Enable logging

Active log format:

W3C Extended Log File Format ▾   Properties...

OK   Cancel   Apply   Help

Figure 13-5. Enabling logging for the Default Web Site

3. Finally, you need to mark which directories and files you want to log. If you want to log access to everything (physical and virtual subdirectories and files) in your website, switch to the Home Directory tab and make sure the Log Visits check box is selected. Similarly, to log access to files in a virtual directory, use the Virtual Directory tab on the properties sheet for the virtual directory. To log one specific file, use the File tab on the properties sheet for the file. In the example, you only want to log access to the file default.asp; so open the properties sheet for the Default Web Site, select the Home Directory tab, clear the Log Visits check box, and click OK. This leaves all files and directories in the site *unmarked* for logging (no logging will occur). Now open the properties sheet for default.asp and select the check box for Log Visits on the File tab to mark this file for logging of client connection attempts (Figure 13-6). Click OK to apply the setting.

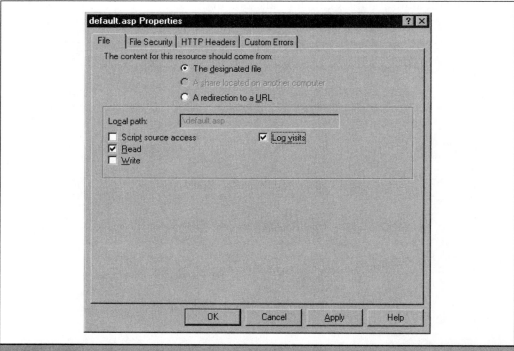

Figure 13-6.   Marking the default.asp page for logging

Log File Formats

There are five different logging formats that can be chosen for web logs:

- **W3C Extended Lot File format**   This is a customizable format developed by the World Wide Web Consortium (W3C) that allows you to select which properties you want to write to your logs. By default, IIS selects this format for web logging, and all logging is done in ASCII unless UTF-8 logging is enabled on the IIS machine (see the upcoming "UTF-8 Logging" sidebar).

- **IIS Log File format**   This is a fixed format that cannot be customized and was developed by Microsoft for early versions of IIS. Although this format records more information than the NCSA format, the IIS log file format is rarely used nowadays, having been superceded by the more powerful and flexible W3C Extended format.

- **NCSA Log File Format**   This fixed format cannot be customized and was developed by the National Center for Supercomputing Applications (NCSA) for Mosaic. An advantage of this format is that it is used by the widest range of web server products, but W3C Extended format is more powerful and flexible and is preferred by most IIS shops.

- **ODBC Logging format**   This lets IIS log connection attempts to an ODBC-compliant database like Microsoft SQL Server. A major disadvantage of ODBC logging is that enabling it disables kernel-mode caching in IIS, which can significantly degrade IIS server performance. As a result, ODBC logging is not recommended in most circumstances.

- **Centralized Binary Logging format**   This is new to version 6 of IIS and allows multiple websites to write to a single log file using a binary format. Centralized binary logging is particularly useful in a web hosting environment where an ISP is hosting hundreds of websites on a single IIS machine and it would consume too much system resources and degrade performance if individual web logs were used for each website. See IIS Help for information on how to use Adsutil.vbs to enable and configure centralized binary logging.

NOTE   While all five log file formats can be used for logging visits to websites, only three of them (W3C Extended, ODBC, and IIS formats) can be used for logging visits to FTP sites on IIS.

In addition to the preceding logging methods included with IIS, you can also develop your own custom logging modules using COM and use them for logging website visits. Unfortunately, using custom logging modules disables kernel-mode caching in IIS and thus degrades performance of your server; so unless there is some compelling reason for using this approach, it's best avoided.

> ## UTF-8 Logging
>
> A new feature of version 6 of IIS is support for writing web log files using UTF-8 (a type of Unicode character encoding) instead of the traditional ASCII character encoding that uses the local character set on the machine. The advantage of UTF-8 logging is that you can write data in non-European character sets to the web logs. To enable UTF-8 logging, right-click the *server_name* node in IIS Manager, select Properties, and select the check box labeled Encode Web Logs In UTF-8. Two things to note about UTF-8 logging are that it is a global setting that is turned on or off for all web logging, and it cannot be used for logging visits to FTP sites.

Using W3C Extended Logging

Unless you are working in a web hosting environment where centralized binary logging could be advantageous, the best choice for web logging is W3C Extended format. Because of this, I'll focus on the details of how to configure and interpret logs created using this format.

Try the following walkthrough. Enable logging for the Default Web Site on your IIS machine, and use Windows Explorer to navigate to the \Windows\System32\LogFiles folder where IIS web logs are stored by default. There should be no files present in the folder.

Now open the URL http://localhost on your IIS machine and view the default document for the Default Web Site. In the \LogFiles folder in Windows Explorer, you should see a text file appear with a name something like ex030116.log, where

- ex stands for W3C Extended format
- 03 are the last two digits of the current year
- 01 is the current month
- 16 is today's date

The name of your log file will be different, of course. Try opening the file—it will probably be blank because IIS first creates the web log file and then, a short time later, writes the first entry to it, so wait a few seconds and open the file again and you should see something like this:

```
#Software: Microsoft Internet Information Services 6.0
#Version: 1.0
#Date: 2003-01-16 23:16:46
#Fields: date time s-ip cs-method cs-uri-stem cs-uri-query s-port cs-
username c-ip cs(User-Agent) sc-status sc-substatus sc-win32-status
2003-01-16 23:16:46 127.0.0.1 GET /Default.asp—80—127.0.0.1
Mozilla/4.0+(compatible;+MSIE+6.0;+Windows+NT+5.2;+.NET+CLR+1.1.4322) 200 0 0
```

The first three lines identify the log, while the fourth line (beginning with #Fields) displays the names of the different properties that are logged. The fifth line (beginning with 2003-01-06) displays the log information for the visit that occurred when you opened http://localhost on the IIS machine. Because the lines are long and wrap in the log text in the text, and because fields are separated by spaces instead of commas or tabs, it's difficult to read and interpret the text. To make it more understandable, I've reformatted the last two lines (fields header and record of first visit) as Table 13-3.

TIP   A useful property you should always log for troubleshooting purposes is sc-substatus, which logs substatus codes (such as 404.3) for HTTP error messages.

Field Definitions for W3C Extended Logs

To better enable you to read and interpret W3C Extended logs such as the sample file just shown, here is a quick reference to the various fields and what they mean. Note that the different prefixes have specific meanings, for example:

- **s-**   The action occurs on the server
- **c-**   The action occurs on the client
- **cs-**   A client-to-server action (a request)
- **sc-**   A server-to-client action (a response)

Table 13-4 shows the various fields and their meaning for W3C Extended logging.

Log Field	Sample Value	Interpretation
date	2003-01-16	Today
time	23:16:46	A few minutes ago
s-ip	127.0.0.1	The Default Web Site on localhost
cs-method	GET	HTTP GET request for default document
cs-uri-stem	/Default.asp	Default document
cs-uri-query	-	No data
s-port	80	Standard TCP port for HTTP
cs-username	-	No data
c-ip	127.0.0.1	Client browser is also on localhost
cs(User-Agent)	Mozilla/4.0+(etc)	Type of web browser used
sc-status	200	HTTP 200 status code indicates request was successful
sc-substatus	0	0 indicates no HTTP substatus code was logged
sc-win32-status	0	Used by Microsoft Windows

Table 13-3.   Sample Record for W3C Extended Log File

Field	Appears As	Description
Date	date	Date activity occurred
Time	time	Time activity occurred
Client IP Address	c-ip	IP address of client accessing server
User Name	cs-username	Name of authenticated user (anonymous users indicated by dash)
Service Name	s-sitename	Internet service and instance number accessed
Server Name	s-computername	Name of server
Server IP Address	s-ip	IP address of server
Server Port	s-port	Port number used
Method	cs-method	HTTP verb used in client request
URI Stem	cs-uri-stem	File accessed
URI Query	cs-uri-query	Query performed by client
Protocol Status	sc-status	Status of action in HTTP or FTP terms
Win32® Status	sc-win32-status	Status of the action in terms used by Microsoft Windows
Bytes Sent	sc-bytes	Number of bytes sent by server to client
Bytes Received	cs-bytes	Number of bytes received by server from client
Time Taken	time-taken	Time duration (milliseconds) consumed by action
Protocol Version	cs-version	Protocol version used by client
Host	cs-host	Contents of host header
User Agent	cs(User-Agent)	Web browser used by client
Cookie	cs(Cookie)	Content of cookie sent or received (if any)
Referrer	cs(Referer)	Last site visited by user if redirected

Table 13-4.   Summary of Field Definitions for W3C Extended Log File Format

Scheduling W3C Extended Logging

To configure when your W3C web logs will be created and what information will be written to them, click Properties on the Web Sites tab of your website to open Logging Properties. The General tab on this properties sheet (Figure 13-7) is used for configuring the following aspects of logging:

- **New Log Schedule**   Indicates the condition under which new log files are created. This can be hourly, daily, weekly, monthly, or when the current log reaches a specified size, or you can keep on logging to the same file and let it grow as big as you want. Daily is the default option, and it creates a new log file when the first visit occurs after midnight. On high-volume sites, you might choose the Hourly option, but don't choose Unlimited File Size unless you've got terabytes of disk space available on your machine! Log files are named differently depending on the new log schedule you select, and these naming conventions are summarized in Table 13-5.

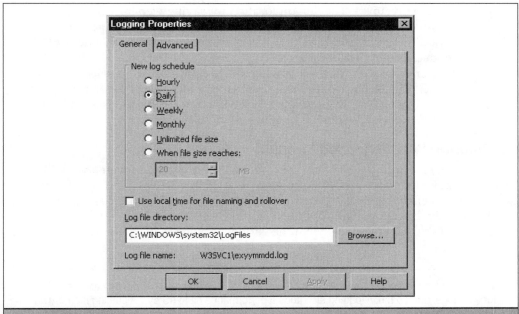

Figure 13-7.   Specifying a new log schedule and log file directory

- **Use Local Time for File Naming and Rollover**   I just noted that the Daily option creates new log files at midnight, but for W3C Extended logging this means midnight Coordinated Universal Time (UTC), which is essentially midnight Greenwich Mean Time (GMT). You can cause IIS to create new log files at midnight local time by selecting this option, but even if you do so the visit times recorded in the log file will be UTC times. To see how to convert the times in your log files to your local time zone, see the section "Converting Log Formats" later in this chapter.

New Log Schedule	Pattern for Log Filename
Hourly	exyymmddhh.log
Daily	exyymmdd.log
Weekly	exyymmww.log
Monthly	exyymm.log
Unlimited	extend#.log
Specified size	extend#.log

Table 13-5.   Naming Conventions for W3C Extended Log Files

- **Log File Directory**   The default location for saving web logs is within a subdirectory of the \Windows\System32\LogFiles folder. The name of the subdirectory depends on the log file format you've chosen, and for W3C Extended format the subfolder is \W3SVC*site_id*, where *site_id* is the website identifier displayed for the site when the Web Sites node is selected in IIS Manager. The Default Web Site is assigned the identifier 1 (one) so the actual location where W3C Extended log files will be stored for the Default Web Site is the \Windows\System32\LogFiles\W3SVC1 folder.

Configuring W3C Extended Logging

In addition to scheduling when new log files will be created and where they will be saved, you can also configure what properties are saved in these files for each record generated by a client connection attempt. To configure which properties to log, use the Advanced tab on Logging Properties (Figure 13-8).

Refer to Table 13-4 to review what the various properties mean for W3C Extended logging.

TIP   Don't log too many properties in your web logs. Not only do you need adequate disk space for your logs, but too much logging also adds a performance hit to IIS by consuming memory and processor resources. Log only what you need, and only for the sites or portions of sites (virtual directories, physical directories, and files) that you are most concerned about for reasons of security or performance or for gathering statistics.

Securing Web Logs

You can better protect your web logs from intruders by moving them to a different directory than the default directory IIS uses to store them, which is the \Windows\System32\LogFiles folder. To change the location of W3C Extended, IIS, or NCSA log

Remote Logging

While earlier versions of IIS required the log file directory be located on the local machine, version 6 lets you log to a shared folder on a file server on your network. To do this, type the UNC path to the share in the Log File Directory textbox (shown in Figure 13-7). This new approach has the advantage of allowing you to centralize the backup of log files from multiple IIS machines to a single file server, but because of the performance penalty incurred it is generally not recommended. If you do decide to employ remote logging for your IIS machines, Microsoft suggests you consider using IPSec for the connection between your web and file server, as anyone sniffing your network can read your log files because they are being sent as plain text.

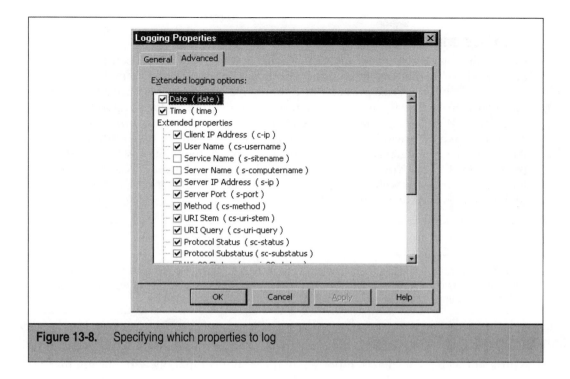

Figure 13-8.   Specifying which properties to log

files, click the Properties button on the Web Site tab of your site's properties sheet and specify a new Log File Directory in the text box (refer to Figure 13-7).

To secure your new log file folder, make sure you assign appropriate ACLs to it as follows:

- **Administrators**   Full Control
- **IIS_WPG group**   Full Control
- **SYSTEM**   Full Control

Managing Web Logs

To delete web logs, first stop the website the logs are associated with, and then delete them using Windows Explorer. If you don't stop the website, you may not be able to delete the files due to a sharing violation.

To review web logs like W3C Extended logs that are written in ASCII format, open them using a text editor like Notepad or import them into a spreadsheet or database program for analysis. If you've selected the Hourly or Daily new log option and you have too many log files to review, use the copy command to combine multiple text files into a single large file. Type **copy /?** at the command line for information on how to append multiple files.

Analysis and Reporting Tools

Generating logs is one thing, analyzing them another. Notepad is useful for a quick peek at log files that have small amounts of information in them, but web servers running in service provider or e-commerce environments need something more powerful for analyzing and generating reports from IIS logs. A good tool to look at is WebTrends Analysis Suite from NetIQ (www.netiq.com), which is powerful but a bit pricey. At the other end of the spectrum are free utilities like Analog (www.analog.cx) and inexpensive tools like Active LogView from SoftCab (www.softcab.com). You can also download the free Log Parser 2.0 command-line tool from Microsoft's website (www.microsoft.com) and perform SQL-like queries on IIS log files and display the results.

NOTE   If IIS runs out of disk space and can't add records to the log file, IIS will automatically shut down and an event will be recorded in the Application log of Event Viewer. When more disk space is added (for example, by extending the volume), IIS starts and logging resumes.

Converting Log Formats

The different web log formats supported by IIS are not compatible with one another. For example, while both NCSA and W3C Extended logging record dates using four-digit year format, IIS logging records dates earlier than 1999 as two-digit years, and four-digit years thereafter. Furthermore, IIS log file format separates fields using commas, but NCSA and W3C Extended formats use spaces as separators instead. Another difference is that while W3C Extended records event times using UTC (coordinated universal time, sometimes called Greenwich Mean Time or GMT), the IIS and NCSA formats employ local time instead.

To help you compare web logs generated using different log file formats, Windows Server 2003 includes the utility convlog.exe in \Windows\System32 that can be used to convert log files that use W3C Extended or IIS log file formats to standard NCSA format. The conversion process automatically performs a time zone offset (using an offset you specify) in order to change the times in the log from UTC to local time, making them easier to read and interpret. In addition, this utility can be used to replace IP addresses in log files with DNS domain names associated with them. For syntax on how to use this tool, type **convlog /?** at the command line or see IIS Help.

IIS AND EVENT LOGS

IIS also generates error, warning, and informational events that can be displayed using Event Viewer. Whenever a problem occurs with IIS, it's a good idea to review the System and Application logs in Event Viewer to see if there is any useful information there that can be used for troubleshooting purposes. Events can be logged for IIS services like the WWW Service or FTP Service, for ASP or ASP.NET applications, and so on.

The list of possible events IIS can generate is long; for a detailed list, see the Events Reference in IIS Help. Here I'll just mention a few tips regarding IIS events in the event logs.

Logging ASP Events

There are two metabase properties that can be used to configure how logging of ASP errors occurs in the Application log. AspLogErrorRequests controls whether unsuccessful client requests for ASP pages are logged to the event logs, while AspErrorsToNTLog controls whether such errors are logged to the web logs. Table 13-6 shows how configuring these two properties affects logging of ASP errors to event and web logs.

You can also completely disable logging of ASP errors using the DontLog and LogType metabase properties.

Eventquery.vbs

Windows Server 2003 includes an admin script called eventquery.vbs that can be used to list events of specified types from the command line. The output from running this script can be formatted as a table, list, or comma-separated (*.csv) file for importing into a spreadsheet or database for further analysis. For more information, see the command-line reference in the Help and Support Center.

AspLogErrorRequests	AspErrorsToNTLog	Result
True	True	All ASP errors are logged to Application log and also to the web logs.
True	False	Some common ASP errors are logged to Application log but not to the web logs.
False	True	All ASP errors are logged to the web logs.
False	False	Some common ASP errors are logged to the web logs.

Table 13-6. Configuring How ASP Errors are Logged

MORE TROUBLESHOOTING TIPS

I'll end this chapter with a potpourri of tips for troubleshooting various aspects of IIS. These are in no particular order, it's just useful stuff you need to know. As you work with IIS, you'll probably be able to add to this list, so I left some blank template sections at the end for you so you can do this.

Can't Access Site

Obviously, a lot of different conditions can prevent users from accessing a site on your IIS machine. The first thing you can do is try pinging its IP address to see if it's there or not. Then try pinging its NetBIOS name if the server is on the intranet, or its DNS name if it's on the Internet. Pinging its DNS name successfully also depends on whether DNS is configured properly, so you may need to test your DNS servers with nslookup as well.

If you still can't access your site, check the server to see if the location of the home directory is specified properly. Check the Directory Security tab to see if authentication is configured correctly and to see whether there are any IP address or domain name restrictions configured. Check the web permissions and execute permissions on the Home Directory tab. Check the IP address, port, and host header settings assigned to the site. Check the NTFS permissions on the content directories and files. Make sure a default document is specified and is present in your root directory.

If all that fails but you get an HTTP error message, use the information in the section entitled "Custom HTTP Error Messages in Detail," previously in this chapter, to try to troubleshoot the problem based on the message you received from the web server.

If everything still seems OK, try restarting the website. If that fails, try restarting IIS. Try logging on to the machine itself and see if you can access the site. If you're connecting as an authenticated user, verify your credentials on the local machine (in a workgroup scenario) or in Active Directory (in a domain scenario). Make sure a domain controller is available on the network.

Another common reason clients cannot access websites or FTP sites is because of a misconfigured firewall or proxy server at the perimeter of your network. If internal clients can access the site but external ones can't, check the configuration of your firewall or proxy server. If that doesn't reveal anything, check your DNS configuration.

Don't forget that Windows Server 2003 has its own built-in Internet Connection Firewall, To see if this is causing the problem, open the properties sheet for the local area connection, select the Advanced tab, and view the settings.

Some Users Can't Access FTP Site

If some users can access your FTP site and others can't, it may be a firewall configuration issue that allows standard (PORT) mode FTP clients to connect while denying connections to passive (PASV) mode clients. You can configure FTP on IIS 6 to support *both* PORT and PASV clients simultaneously: see Knowledge Base article 323446 on support.microsoft .com for more info. This problem can also occur if the client is behind a NAT device.

Logging Worker Process Recycling

You can use the LogEventOnRecycle metabase property to configure the WWW Service to log recycling events for worker processes in the Application log, which you can view later using Event Viewer. You can configure this property so that logging of such events happens according to time consumed, requests processed, scheduled recycles, and so on. See the Metabase Property Reference in IIS Help for detailed information of all metabase properties.

Can't Administer IIS Using Remote Desktop

Make sure that you don't have a blank password for the account you are using to connect to IIS using Remote Desktop. You could instead modify the Local Security Policy on your IIS machine to allow blank passwords, but this is not recommended for security reasons.

Host Header Issues

If you put a space in a host header name, the website will be unavailable to clients trying to connect to it. Another host header issue is that two websites running on the same IIS machine can't have the same host header name and port number while having different IP addresses (if you configure them this way, one of them won't start).

ASP Error Messages

By default, ASP is configured to send detailed error messages to clients when problems occur. You may want to disable this feature and send a generic error message instead, as detailed messages can sometimes provide malicious users with information they can use to hack your system. To configure this feature, open the properties sheet for the website of your application in IIS Manager, select the Home Directory tab, click the Configuration button, select the Debugging tab, select the check box for sending a standard text error message to the client, and type your message in the text box (Figure 13-9).

Anonymous Users Can't Run CGI Apps

If your CGI app resides in the \Windows\System32 directory or makes use of other executables such as cmd.exe located in that directory, your CGI app will fail for anonymous users unless you remove the Deny ACL for the IUSR_*computername* account for these executables. The purpose of this ACL is to prevent anonymous users from running cmd.exe and other dangerous executables found in \System32, so do this with caution!

Automatic Restart Disabled

If a flaky application kills your server and the server doesn't automatically restart, it may be that you've disabled the Automatic Restart feature of IIS. Automatic Restart is

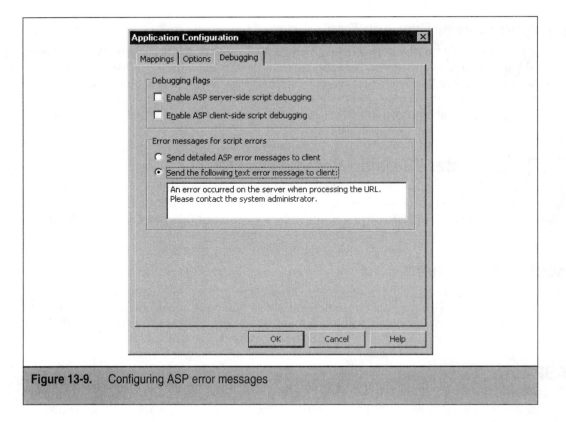

Figure 13-9. Configuring ASP error messages

a feature that enables the IIS Admin service to automatically start itself when it stops for some unexpected reason. Automatic Restart can be disabled two ways:

- Type **iisreset /disable** from the command line. See Chapter 11 for more information on the iisreset command.

- Use the Services console in Administrative Tools, and configure the Recovery tab options on the properties sheet for the service (either IIS Admin or WWW).

My Troubleshooting Tips

You can add your own troubleshooting tips for IIS 6 on the following pages as you discover them from further reading, hands-on use of the platform, and discussion with colleagues.

Problem:

_____

Try the following: _____
_____
_____
_____
_____
_____

Problem:

_____

Try the following: _____
_____
_____
_____
_____
_____

Problem:

_____

Try the following: _____
_____
_____
_____
_____
_____

Problem:

_____

Try the following: _____
_____
_____
_____
_____
_____

Problem:

_____

Try the following: _____
_____
_____
_____
_____

Problem:

_____

Try the following: _____
_____
_____
_____
_____

Problem:

_____

Try the following: _____
_____
_____
_____
_____

Problem:

_____

Try the following: _____
_____
_____
_____
_____

Problem:

_____

Try the following: _____

_____

_____

_____

_____

Problem:

_____

Try the following: _____

_____

_____

_____

_____

Problem:

_____

Try the following: _____

_____

_____

_____

_____

Problem:

_____

Try the following: _____

_____

_____

_____

_____

Problem:

_____

Try the following: _____

_____

_____

_____

_____

_____

CHALLENGE

Your challenge this time is to try to come up with additional tips and procedures for troubleshooting IIS 6 based on your discussions with colleagues, your reading of IIS and Windows Server 2003 documentation, and your experience with the platform. When you've come up with some additional tips, be sure to share them with your colleagues!

CHECKLIST: TROUBLESHOOTING TOOLS AND PROCEDURES

Check off each of the items below once you become familiar with the particular approach to troubleshooting IIS listed.

- ☐ Understanding standard HTTP status codes.
- ☐ Understanding Microsoft HTTP substatus codes for IIS.
- ☐ Using Telnet to troubleshoot HTTP connections.
- ☐ Understanding HTTP header syntax.
- ☐ Using Wfetch.exe.
- ☐ Customizing friendly HTTP error messages in IIS.
- ☐ Enabling web logging for a site or all sites.
- ☐ Marking a site, directory, or file for logging.
- ☐ Selecting a log file format.
- ☐ Enabling UTF-8 logging.
- ☐ Configuring a new log schedule.
- ☐ Configuring a log file directory.

☐ Interpreting W3C Extended log files.

☐ Configuring which properties to log in W3C Extended logging.

☐ Securing log files with ACLs.

☐ Viewing and deleting log files.

☐ Converting W3C Extended log files to NCSA Common format with convlog.exe.

☐ Reviewing Event logs for IIS errors, warnings, and informational events.

☐ Configuring logging of ASP events.

☐ Reviewing Event logs with eventquery.vbs.

☐ Troubleshooting site access problems.

☐ Logging worker process recycling.

☐ Troubleshooting host header problems.

☐ Configuring ASP error messages.

☐ Troubleshooting CGI issues.

☐ Enabling and disabling Automatic Restart.

CHAPTER 14

Working with the Metabase

T his chapter examines the metabase, the main repository for IIS configuration information. I'll begin with an overview of what the metabase is and how it works, and then analyze in detail a sample metabase from a clean install of Windows Server 2003 with IIS 6 installed. The concluding section deals with how to manage the metabase including backing up and restoring IIS configurations and exporting them to other servers.

OVERVIEW OF METABASE

IIS 4 introduced a hierarchical structure called the *metabase* for storing IIS configuration information. As an alternative to the Registry, the metabase provides enhanced performance because it can be loaded into memory where its settings can be accessed more quickly. Let's examine the structure and function of the metabase in IIS 6 and how it differs from previous versions.

Changes in IIS 6

The biggest change in IIS 6 is that the metabase is no longer saved in binary format as metabase.bin, but is instead formatted as a plain text file using the Extensible Markup Language (XML). This makes it possible to edit the metabase file using a text editor such as Notepad. IIS 6 also features *edit-while-running*, which lets you make changes manually (or programmatically using WMI or ADSI) to the metabase file without stopping IIS first. This helps you minimize downtime on your server when you need to make changes to IIS configuration using the metabase.

NOTE   Although the metabase files are plain text, they do not use ASCII, but instead use UTF-8, a Unicode-related character set. Notepad supports this format and can therefore be used to edit the metabase directly.

IIS 6 also includes a new *metabase history* feature that automatically saves backups of the metabase when changes are made to it. That way, if you goof by modifying the metabase so that IIS doesn't work properly, you can quickly revert to a previous working version of the metabase.

Another new feature of IIS 6 is the ability to export a machine-independent version of the metabase and then import it onto a different IIS 6 machine. This allows you to copy IIS configurations from one machine to another, something that previously required third-party tools. You can also create a template metabase and copy it to multiple IIS 6 machines to deploy multiple web servers with similar configurations. Or, you can export and import only a portion of the metabase, such as a specific website or virtual directory.

IIS 6 also includes a WMI provider for IIS that lets you programmatically edit the metabase using Windows Management Instrumentation (WMI). For backward compatibility, you can modify the metabase using Active Directory Services Interface (ADSI), if you prefer.

Finally, there are about 50 metabase properties that have been removed in version 6 of IIS, and more than 100 new ones added. This is important because it may mean some ADSI scripts written to programmatically modify the IIS 5 metabase may not work with IIS 6, and all such scripts should be carefully tested before using them on the new platform. For more information on metabase properties that were added or removed in IIS 6, see the IIS Help file.

XML Metabase

XML has made significant inroads in the last couple of years as a standard for web services, especially business-to-business (B2B) communications, and it was only a matter of time before it made inroads into Microsoft Windows in general, and IIS in particular (I wouldn't be surprised if the Registry itself was ported to XML in the next version of Windows). But why was this done for the IIS metabase?

Advantages of XML

One advantage of using industry-standard XML for the metabase instead of the previous proprietary binary format is that it allows administrators to view and modify the metabase using a simple text editor such as Notepad. But why would anyone even want to edit the metabase directly anyway? There are three reasons:

- Although IIS Manager is the main tool for configuring IIS, there are some advanced metabase properties that are not accessible from the GUI and can only be viewed and modified by editing the metabase, either manually or programmatically.

- In a service provider scenario where your IIS machine is hosting hundreds of websites, using IIS Manager will take forever. It can be much quicker to write a WMI script to simultaneously modify the appropriate metabase properties for multiple sites, and then use this script whenever it is needed.

- If you're administering IIS over a slow network connection such as a 56K remote access modem link, then it may be impractical to use IIS Manager due to the bandwidth required for this tool to respond adequately. Using Notepad to edit the metabase directly, however (or a WMI script to modify it programmatically), uses much less bandwidth than IIS, making it easier to configure IIS over a slow WAN link.

Because the metabase is now a plain text XML file, you can use tools like Windiff (included in the Windows Server 2003 Resource Kit) when the metabase becomes corrupted to find out what's wrong by comparing a bad version of the metabase with a saved good version. This makes it easier to repair the metabase when it becomes corrupted. Using XML also makes it easier to edit machine-independent information from the metabase to allow it to be restored on a different computer in the case of a critical failure of your IIS machine.

Another reason XML is superior to the old proprietary binary metabase format is that XML is an extensible language. This means you can now add your own custom properties to the metabase by extending the schema. See the section "The Metabase Schema File " later in this chapter for more information.

Finally, the new XML format helps make IIS 6 perform better than earlier versions of the platform. When IIS starts up, the XML metabase can be read and parsed faster than the old binary metabase used in IIS 4 and 5, partly because the XML metabase generally has a smaller footprint than the old binary version.

TIP   It's a good idea for IIS admins to learn some basic XML for two reasons: to better understand the structure and format of the metabase, and to know the difference between XML that is well-formed and valid and XML that is bad. This will allow you to more easily diagnose metabase corruption arising from bad XML. A good book to reference is *XML: The Complete Reference* by Heather Williamson from Osborne/McGraw-Hill.

Function

The function of the metabase is to provide a place for IIS to store most of its configuration information, that is, the various settings you can configure using properties sheets in IIS Manager, plus additional settings not accessible from the GUI. Note that I said *most* configuration information and not all. There are still a few IIS configuration settings that are stored in the Windows Registry and not in the metabase, and these can be found under the following Registry keys:

- HKLM\SOFTWARE\Microsoft\InetMgr\Parameters
- HKLM\SYSTEM\CurrentControlSet\Services\InetInfo\Parameters
- HKLM\SYSTEM\CurrentControlSet\Services\ASP\Parameters
- HKLM\SYSTEM\CurrentControlSet\Services\Http\Parameters\LogBufferSize
- HKLM\SYSTEM\CurrentControlSet\Services\W3SVC\Parameters
- HKLM\SYSTEM\CurrentControlSet\Services\MSFTPSVC\Parameters

For more information on these Registry keys and the values they can contain, see the Registry Reference in IIS Help.

Physical Structure

Let's now dig into the structure of the metabase so you can see how it's built and navigate your way around it when you need to change something. I'll also show you how IIS updates the metabase internally when changes have been made using either IIS Manager, a text editor, or a script. Finally, you'll look at how IIS maintains the metabase by automatically saving copies of it in the metabase history folder.

Metabase Files

While in previous versions of IIS there was only one metabase file, metabase.bin, in this version there are two files that together make up the metabase:

- **MetaBase.xml** This is a plain-text file formatted in XML that contains the actual configuration information for IIS organized in a hierarchical fashion.

- **MBSchema.xml** This is a plain-text file formatted in XML that contains the schema information for the MetaBase.xml file. The schema determines which IIS settings are stored in the metabase and enforces their data types. Administrators can also extend this schema to define custom metabase properties.

These two metabase files are stored in the \Windows\System32\Inetsrv folder with the following ACLs to control who can access or modify them:

- **Administrators** Full Control
- **SYSTEM** Full Control

NOTE While the new edit-while-running feature of IIS 6 allows you to edit the metabase directory, this applies only to the metabase configuration file MetaBase.xml. IIS 6 does not support editing the metabase schema file MBSchema.xml while IIS is running. To modify the MBSchema.xml file, you must use ADSI or Admin Base Objects (ABO) using a C++ program.

In-Memory Metabase

There's a third component to the metabase, and that's the in-memory metabase, which contains the latest versions of these two files in volatile RAM. When you boot up a Windows Server 2003 machine with IIS installed, an IIS component called the Metabase Storage Layer reads the files metabase.cml and MBSchema.xml from disk and converts them from XML to binary format. The storage layer then uses Admin Base Objects (ABO), a COM object that provides low-level interfaces for programmatic access, using high-level languages like C++ or C#, to write the metabase into a portion of RAM called the *IIS file cache*.

For best performance, IIS then uses the in-memory version of the metabase rather than the two files on disk. For example, when you use IIS Manager to make a configuration change to IIS, this change is first written to the in-memory metabase and then periodically flushed to disk to maintain a permanent record of the changes in case a power failure causes the contents of RAM to be lost. You can also force the in-memory metabase to be persisted to disk by manually stopping IIS with IIS Manager.

NOTE Just as there are two metabase files on disk, the in-memory metabase has two nodes, a configuration node corresponding to MetaBase.xml and a schema node corresponding to MBSchema.xml.

Operation

The IIS Admin service (inetinfo.exe) is responsible overall for managing metabase operations, including the Metabase Storage Layer and ABO just described. In addition, IIS Admin keeps track of any changes made to metabase files and ensures that the in-memory and on-disk versions of the metabase are periodically synchronized. Finally, IIS Admin is responsible for the operation of the metabase history feature that automatically saves backup copies of the metabase to record a history of changes to the metabase and allow administrators to revert to a previous working version of the metabase should corruption occur.

Automatic Flushing

Whenever changes are made to the in-memory metabase, typically by changing properties sheet settings with IIS Manager, these changes are *not* flushed immediately to disk. Instead, IIS waits 60 seconds to see if further changes will be made to the in-memory metabase. If none are forthcoming, the MetaBase.xml and MBSchema.xml files are overwritten by the contents of the in-memory metabase nodes, and a new history file pair is created with the major version number incremented by one.

If, however, more than 30 changes are made to the in-memory metabase before the 60 seconds are up, IIS postpones the overwrite for an additional 60 seconds. Such postponements can occur up to a maximum of five times until IIS finally forces flushing the modified files to disk. In other words, metabase flushing occurs a maximum of five minutes after IIS settings are changed using IIS Manager.

If edit-while-running is enabled, however, and the in-memory metabase nodes are modified programmatically using ADSI, these changes are immediately flushed to disk.

Saving to Disk

When you try to stop (or restart) IIS using IIS Manager, IIS first checks the in-memory metabase to see if any configuration changes have been made recently and not persisted to disk. If there are no changes pending, IIS stops as expected. If there are still changes pending, however, the contents of the in-memory metabase overwrite the MetaBase.xml and MBSchema.xml files on disk to ensure a permanent record of the changes, a new metabase history file is saved on disk for both the configuration and schema files, and finally, IIS stops (or restarts). Having IIS operate in this fashion allows administrators to shut down or restart IIS more quickly if no configuration changes have been recently made.

When IIS is started again (or a restart is continued), the Metabase Storage Layer reads the MetaBase.xml and MBSchema.xml files on disk, converts them to binary format, and uses ABO to write them to memory to re-create the two in-memory metabase nodes. If the metabase is corrupt, however, IIS won't be able to start. See the section "Example of Serious Metabase Corruption" for information on how metabase corruption can arise and how you can recover from it.

History Files

History files are versioned (time-stamped) copies of the metabase that are generated automatically by IIS. These files are saved in a directory called the *history folder* whose default location is

```
\Windows\System32\Inetsrv\History
```

Each versioned copy consists of a pair of files, one a copy of the current MetaBase.xml node in memory and the other of the MBSchema.xml node. These files can be viewed, modified, and deleted only by members of the Administrators group.

History files are created whenever configuration changes have occurred since the last time the in-memory metabase was flushed to disk. More exactly, whenever IIS flushes the in-memory metabase to disk, overwriting the MetaBase.xml and/or MBSchema.xml files, a new history file pair is also created, incrementing the major version number of these files by one.

History File Versioning

Each history file is uniquely identified by two versioning numbers:

- **Major version**   This number is incremented by one whenever the in-memory metabase is flushed to disk. This can happen several ways:

  - **By manually restarting IIS using IIS Manager**   In this situation a new history file is always created whether or not there are in-memory metabase updates waiting to be flushed to disk.

  - **By manually stopping IIS using IIS Manager or by typing** net stop iisadmin **at the command prompt**   In this situation also, a new history file is always created whether or not there are in-memory metabase updates waiting to be flushed to disk.

  - **By manually saving the IIS configuration to disk**   To do this, open IIS Manager, right-click the *servername* node, and select All Tasks and then Save Configuration To Disk. Note that this only creates a new history file when there are actually unsaved metabase updates in memory. For example, if you open IIS Manager and perform this operation, no history file will be created. But if you open IIS Manager, change a setting on a website or an FTP site, and then perform the operation, there are updates pending in-memory that need to be flushed to disk, so this time the operation will result in a new history file being created.

  - **By waiting until IIS automatically flushes pending in-memory metabase updates to disk**   This usually happens a few minutes after you make changes to IIS property sheets.

- **Minor version**   This number increments by one if the edit-while-running metabase feature is enabled and changes have been manually made to the metabase files on disk. Also, the minor version number is reset to zero whenever the major version number increments by one, that is, whenever the MetaBase.xml and MBSchema.xml files are flushed to disk.

The naming convention IIS uses for history files employs two version numbers, as follows:

- Metabase_*majorversion_minorversion*.xml are history files for the MetaBase.xml file.

- MBSchema_*majorversion_minorversion*.xml are history files for the MBSchema.xml file.

Figure 14-1 shows examples of such history files within the metabase history folder. Note that both the major and minor versioning numbers in history filenames are automatically left-padded with zeros by IIS to make ten-digit versioning numbers.

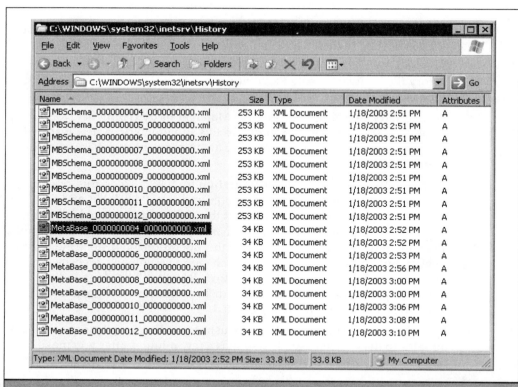

Figure 14-1.   Contents of the metabase history folder

Note also that for every MetaBase.xml history file, there is a corresponding MBSchema.xml history file because these history files are always created in pairs, even if only one of them has changed.

Versioning information for metabase history files is stored differently, depending on whether one refers to major or minor versioning. Major version numbers are stored within the metbase.xml file itself as the HistoryMajorVersionNumber property of the IIS_Global metabase node (I'll explain what this means in a moment). Minor version numbers are not stored in metbase.xml but are calculated by IIS dynamically by looking at the highest current minor version number of files in the history folder.

NOTE   Don't change the HistoryMajorVersionNumber of a metabase file by editing it directly or problems can result.

Configuring History Settings

The new metabase history feature of IIS 6 is enabled by default and should generally not be disabled, as this will make it more difficult to recover the metabase should corruption occur, either due to careless metabase editing or an attack on your server. If you do want to disable this feature, however, you can do so by adding the EnableHistory property to the /LM level of the metabase and setting the value of this property to 0.

Note that the EnableHistory property is not present in the metabase for a default installation of IIS. This is for performance, to keep the size of the metabase small. Specifically, if a property is not present in the metabase, IIS assumes that the property has its default value. Because the default value for the EnableHistory property is 1, this means by default the history feature is enabled. If you disable the history feature by adding the EnableHistory property to the metabase and assigning it the value 0, you have to either remove the property entirely or change its value to 1 to re-enable metabase history.

Another metabase property you can use to configure how the history feature behaves is MaxHistoryFiles, which determines how many history files for each of MetaBase.xml and MBSchema.xml are stored in the file before the oldest ones drop out. By default, this property is set to 10, which means when the eleventh history file is created, the first one is deleted. You can increase this value to save more versions of history files, but before you do this make sure you have sufficient disk space for this purpose. If your disk becomes full, IIS will not be able to create new history files and will automatically shut down until you free up disk space.

You'll look at how to restore the metabase from history files later in this chapter in the section entitled "Restoring from History Files."

Error Files

From time to time, you may find files within the history folder named as follows:

```
MetaBaseError_versionnumber.xml
```

Here, *versionnumber* is a ten-digit number starting from zero, incrementing by one each time, and left-padded with zeros, for example

```
MetaBaseError_0000000000.xml
MetaBaseError_0000000001.xml
MetaBaseError_0000000002.xml
```

and so on. These metabase error files are created whenever the MetaBase.xml file is edited directly using Notepad (this requires edit-while-running to be enabled) and the edit creates corruption in the file. This corruption might be a misspelled metabase property, a missing XML tag, a metabase file whose HistoryMajorVersionNumber has been changed and conflicts with the filename itself, and so on. It's a good idea, after making changes manually to the metabase using a text editor, to see if an error file has been created, which would indicate a problem with the changes you made to the file.

Logical Structure

Now that you've looked at the physical structure and operation of the metabase, let's examine its logical structure, that is, its nature as an XML document. It will help you follow this discussion if you already have some basic knowledge of XML. But I'll try to keep things simple enough that you can follow even if you don't know any XML.

> **NOTE**   You're going to spend a good part of the following sections learning about the logical structure of the metabase because you need to understand this subject well before you start manually editing your metabase and possibly corrupting it, causing your IIS machine to fail!

XML Terminology

Like any XML document, the Metabase.xml and MBSchema.xml files are hierarchically organized as a collection of *elements* defined by *tags*. These elements are defined by opening and closing tags, for example:

```
<IisComputer>stuff</IIsComputer>
```

where *stuff* may be additional elements or ordinary text (in the metabase it is always additional elements or nothing at all).

Elements can also contain additional information by defining *attributes* for these elements, for example:

```
<IisComputer Location ="/LM" EnableEditWhileRunning="0" EnableHistory="1"
MaxBandwidth="4294967295" MaxHistoryFiles="10"></IIsComputer>
```

This element contains five attributes with string values assigned to them. To make things easier to read, additional spaces, tabs, and carriage returns can be inserted without changing the meaning of the elements. For example:

```
<IIsComputer     Location ="/LM"
          EnableEditWhileRunning="0"
          EnableHistory="1"
          MaxBandwidth="4294967295"
          MaxHistoryFiles="10"

     >
</IIsComputer>
```

IIS employs such a "structured text" approach to make it easier for human eyes to read and modify the metabase using a text editor.

XML elements and attributes are case-sensitive, so be sure you type lower- and uppercase letters properly when you modify the metabase.

And that's about all you really need to know about XML to work with the XML metabase!

Metabase Terminology

Now let's look more specifically at XML terminology as it applies to the metabase. First of all, the two metabase files must begin with a standard XML declaration indicating that the files are XML documents. This declaration is the statement:

```
<?xml version ="1.0"?>
```

NOTE The XML 1.0 specification also requires a <!DOCTYPE> statement to identify the schema (if any) that is associated with an XML document. IIS metabase files do not contain this statement, however, and in this sense (and this sense only) they are not valid XML documents.

When you edit the metabase by hand, you can insert comments in the form of text separated by <!-- and --> tags, just as in HTML. These comments can document changes you have made so you can refer back later and understand what you did. However, insert these comments sparingly because they increase the size of the metabase—and don't place comments above the IIS_Global node.

Another terminology issue is that XML elements (pairs of tags) in the metabase represent something called *keys*. An example is the IIsComputer key discussed previously, which is represented in the metabase by the <IIsComputer> and </IIsComputer> start and end tags.

The name of a metabase key is usually referred to as the *KeyType* property for the key. For example, the key defined by the tag pair <IIsComputer></IIsComputer> has the value "IIsComputer" for its KeyType property.

NOTE   Another name for KeyType is Admin Base Object (ABO) class name.

Metabase keys are analogous to Registry keys in the Windows Registry and hold metabase configuration information in the form of attributes and their values. A good analogy is to think of a metabase key as a folder that can contain name/value pairs in the form of attributes. Metabase keys can also contain other metabase keys in hierarchical fashion, with their corresponding tags properly nested and not overlapping.

Each metabase key must contain a Location attribute that indicates the location of this key in the metabase. In other words, there are two ways in which the metabase is structured hierarchically:

- **Elements (expressed as pairs of tags)**   Can be nested to create a hierarchical structure of tags.

- **Keys (defined by names of elements)**   Can be assigned a hierarchical location using Location attributes (another name for key is *node*).

Note that these two methods of describing the structure of the metabase do *not* coincide, and it's the latter that really matters as far as the logical structure of the metabase is concerned.

Location Attributes

The true hierarchical structure of the metabase can only be understood if you grasp the meaning of Location attributes. Each metabase key contains a Location attribute that specifies where the key resides compared to other keys in the metabase. For example, in a default installation of IIS there is one website created, namely the Default Web Site. The metabase key for this website has the name IIsWebServer and is expressed in XML as the pair of tags <IIsWebServer> and </IIsWebServer>. By default, the name/value pair of the Location attribute for this key is

```
Location ="/LM/W3SVC/1"
```

This means that the IIsWebserver key is a child node of the IIsWebService key whose location is /LM/W3SVC, which is a child node of the IIsComputer key whose location is /LM, which is itself a child node of the IIsRoot key whose location is "/". In other words, you can represent the location of the metabase node (key) for the Default Web Site within the logical structure of the metabase in the following hierarchical fashion:

```
IIsRoot
    IIsComputer
        IIsWebService
            IIsWebserver
```

However, the corresponding elements for these keys are *not* organized hierarchically, but instead are organized linearly (all on the same level) as follows:

```
<IIsRoot>
...
<\IIsRoot>
...
<IIsComputer>
...
<\IIsComputer>
...
<IIsWebService>
...
<\IIsWebService>
...
<IIsWebserver>
...
<\IIsWebserver>
...
```

Properties

The term *property* is essentially synonymous with "attribute" when talking about the metabase. Properties specify the actual configuration information for IIS, and there are two different types of properties found in the metabase:

- **In-schema**   Attributes that have their data types and permitted values that are enforced by the metabase schema (the MBSchema.xml file). In other words, for every unique KeyType property, there is a corresponding portion of the schema that defines what types and values of attributes are permitted for the key defined by that KeyType.
- **Custom**   Attributes that can be used to override default settings for properties defined in the schema.

Here's an example from the metabase to illustrate the difference between these two types of properties:

```
<IIsComputer    Location ="/LM"
        EnableEditWhileRunning="0"
        EnableHistory="1"
        MaxBandwidth="4294967295"
        MaxHistoryFiles="10"
    >
</IIsComputer>
```

The preceding shows an in-schema metabase property with a KeyType of IIsComputer, a location of /LM, and four additional name/value attribute pairs containing general IIS configuration information about whether edit-while-running is enabled or disabled, whether the metabase history feature is enabled or disabled, and so on.

Now, here's an example of a custom metabase property:

```
<IIsConfigObject     Location ="/LM/IISADMIN/EXTENSIONS/DCOMCLSIDS"
     >
     <Custom
          Name="MD_IISADMIN_EXTENSIONS"
          ID="1028"
          Value="{61738644-F196-11D0-9953-00C04FD919C1}"
          Type="MULTISZ"
          UserType="IIS_MD_UT_SERVER"
          Attributes="NO_ATTRIBUTES"
     />
</IIsConfigObject>
```

Keys like the preceding that are named IIsConfigObject are special in IIS because they can contain any property and are not named using a KeyType value. Also, there can be multiple keys with the same name of IIsConfigObject within the metabase.

Because keys like IIsConfigObject can occur multiple times in the MetaBase.xml file, how are they distinguished from one another? By their Location attribute! In other words, metabase keys are uniquely defined by two things, their name (KeyType property) and location (Location attribute). While custom properties can have the same KeyType, no two properties (or keys or nodes) within the metabase can have the same Location attribute.

Another example like this is the IIsWebServer key, of which there will be more than one if you create additional websites on your IIS machine. The keys for different websites are also distinguished by their Location property, which is of the form

```
Location="/LM/W3SVC/siteID"
```

where *siteID* is the numerical identifier that IIS randomly generates for each site and that can be displayed by selecting the Web Sites node in IIS Manager.

Property Inheritance

A feature that helps keep the footprint (size) of the metabase to a minimum is *property inheritance*. This feature improves IIS performance by reducing the amount of cache memory required to hold the in-memory metabase and improving the time IIS needs to read and write configuration information to the metabase.

The way property inheritance works is simple: if a key is a child key of another key (based on the values of their Location attributes), then inheritable properties that are not explicitly set for the child key are inherited from the parent key. For example, if you use IIS Manager to configure the Web Sites node to enable HTTP Keep-Alives, then every website under this node will automatically inherit this setting. However, in the metabase, only the Web Sites node (represented by the IIsWebService property) actually has this HTTP Keep-Alives property explicitly defined in the form of the AllowKeepAlive attribute:

```
<IIsWebService       Location ="/LM/W3SVC"
          AllowKeepAlive="TRUE"
          AnonymousUserName="IUSR_ESRV220B"
...
</IIswebService>
```

For comparison, the AllowKeepAlive attribute is not even present in the IIsWebServer property, which represents the Default Web Site node in IIS Manager:

```
<IIsWebServer       Location ="/LM/W3SVC/1"
          AppPoolId="DefaultAppPool"
          DefaultDoc="Default.htm,Default.asp,index.htm,iisstart.htm"
          ServerBindings=":80:"
          ServerComment="Default Web Site"
          ServerSize="1"

     >
</IIsWebServer>
```

As you can see from the preceding, the IIsWebServer key has only six attributes specifying configuration information specific to the Default Web Site: the key's location in the metabase, the application pool to which the site is assigned, the default documents for the site (included because iisstart.htm is used for this site only), the TCP port number used for communication with HTTP clients, the friendly name for the site in IIS Manager, and a ServerSize attribute that is used internally to indicate that this is a medium-sized site that is configured to handle between 10,000 and 100,000 hits per day.

By comparison, the IIsWebService property has over 100 attributes contained within it. Property inheritance thus reduces the number of attributes needed by the Default Web Site (and other websites) from over a hundred to a mere handful. Of course, as soon as you start changing the configuration settings for the Default Web Site using IIS Manager, more attributes will start to appear in the IIsWebServer property to override the default settings of the IIsWebService property.

NOTE While IIS_Global is the highest-level key that can have properties (attributes) defined, no properties configured at this level can be inherited by the IIS_ROOT key beneath it. The IIS_ROOT key is the highest-level key that can have properties inherited by child keys below it.

THE METABASE CONFIGURATION FILE

Now that you understand the terminology associated with the XML metabase, let's move on and examine in detail the structure and contents of the metabase configuration file MetaBase.xml. We'll start by examining an actual metabase file from a freshly installed IIS machine. Remember, the MetaBase.xml file is the file that actually contains IIS configuration info—the other metabase file (MBSchema.xml) simply enforces what sort of XML content can be present in the MetaBase.xml file.

Analyzing a Sample MetaBase.xml File

The following pages show the contents of the MetaBase.xml file for a typical IIS 6 machine. I've added inline comments immediately after selected metabase features of interest.

```
<?xml version ="1.0"?>
```

The preceding statement is anXML declaration that must always be the first line of the MetaBase.xml file.

```
<configuration xmlns="urn:microsoft-catalog:XML_Metabase_V54_0">
```

The <configuration> element is the root (topmost) element of the file and contains all other XML elements in the file. At the end of this section, you'll see the corresponding </configuration> tag as the last line of the file.

```
<MBProperty>
```

The <MBProperty> element is always contained directly within the <configuration> element and designates the remaining content of the file as representing metabase properties. As expected, the second last line of the file is </MBProperty>.

```
<IIS_Global      Location ="."
          BINSchemaTimeStamp="248e296f33bfc201"
          ChangeNumber="443"
          HistoryMajorVersionNumber="6"
```

```
SessionKey="49634b62980000004c000000400000000102000001680000000a400005fd46cd3
50fbc84e276e6bee11e5a845fd4e693aca95464cd73f2101d96435108a51807205057ede3178
af325b6f6aa71f20955d8e13d800d0a1c0597a35e16c3d0043006169d38aaa99cefece9c6f9d
744bf653fe205035818dcc8a4dffe8441ec44aff7027a460229502ff6cca80a3ce83abdb07fe
b30a9128768904f38dc2c263c11d"
```

```
          XMLSchemaTimeStamp="a4c7356f33bfc201"
      >
</IIS_Global>
```

The IIS_Global key is the highest-level property in the metabase. Note that the location of this property is ".", which indicates the top of the metabase hierarchy. Don't edit any of the properties (attributes) for this node.

```
<IIS_ROOT       Location ="/"
```

```
AdminACL="49634462f0000000a4000000400000003b15b816894cdce9ee3d88e550da92f6d2
f3baf166bf973fc44300b048ddcb2f6c0bf739aea29375ad73f07d24a27bc9ffe2ae30ec615c
d08f8b8813ff2353ddb5a48b8c6bcaee802d2b2cfad22fc3563513639dc23e5c7dcc38710955
bed070ca3459b5d1d056d816b5c731532d7edaad3c8aea36a105537c4eb0771b9bf8bfc3d080
9f81ba6fd34d6c58b8e1becdf18aa94c32f3f07334c21f5f12fcaf40a8d48f9c5157d28e113a
8e843c15ac7ead7b865e3a21b25b24c95ac6a0f7c33fdefeab8a8f51c38fceb722c2db960982
eb87bde6e844aa3cd4e08e3d6e7ed821e93257c3e597eabb09"
```

```
    >
</IIS_ROOT>
```

The IIS_ROOT key is directly under the IIS_Global key and is thus a child key of IIS_Global. The location for the IIS_ROOT key is "/". Any properties IIS defines here (such as the previous AdminACL) apply generally to all aspects of IIS, including websites and FTP sites and NNTP and SMTP virtual servers. You generally don't define or edit any properties here either.

```
<IIsComputer     Location ="/LM"
         EnableEditWhileRunning="0"
         EnableHistory="1"
         MaxBandwidth="4294967295"
         MaxHistoryFiles="10"
    >
</IIsComputer>
```

The IIsComputer key is a child node of IIS_ROOT and similarly defines properties that apply to IIS as a whole. Here, for example, the maximum network bandwidth used by all IIS services is specified, as are settings for edit-while-running and metabase history. You can modify some of these properties here directly using edit-while-running.

The location of the IIsComputer node in the metabase hierarchy is "/LM" (which stands for Local Machine). All remaining keys have locations that are of the form "/LM/*stuff1*[/*stuff2*[. . .]]", where *stuff1* and *stuff2* represent, for example, W3SVC for the WWW Service, AppPools for application pools, and so on. Another way of describing this is to say that the Local Machine (LM) namespace is the parent location for all sites and services on the IIS machine. The general syntax for the Location attribute of a key is

```
/LM/service/site/ROOT/virtualdirectory/directory/file
```

but there are many exceptions to this, as in /LM/IISADMIN, /LM/MimeMap, and so on, as you'll see.

How can you understand the syntax of the property MaxBandwidth="4294967295" for the IIsComputer key? By looking up MaxBandwidth in the Metabase Reference in IIS Help. Here's a short excerpt from the discussion in Help of this property so you can get a flavor for what's found there:

The MaxBandwidth property specifies the maximum network bandwidth used for IIS. You can use this setting to help prevent overloading the network with IIS activity. This is not an inheritable property, but the value set at the machine level is globally available to all server instances. MaxBandWidth can be set individually, so that specific server instances are used instead of the global value, and can exceed the global setting established at the machine level.

The World Wide Web Publishing Service (WWW Service) must be restarted before changes to this property take effect.

The metabase represents unlimited as the DWORD value of 4294967295 (0xFFFFFFFF); however, VBScript represents unlimited in hexadecimal format as &HFFFFFFFF. Previous versions of IIS represented unlimited as -1.

```
<IIsConfigObject     Location ="/LM/IISADMIN"
    >
</IIsConfigObject>
```

The preceding IIsConfigObject key records any DCOM extensions to IIS.

```
<IIsConfigObject     Location ="/LM/IISADMIN/EXTENSIONS"
    >
</IIsConfigObject>
```

The preceding key is named IIsConfigObject like the one before it, but is distinguished by having a different Location attribute.

```
<IIsConfigObject        Location ="/LM/IISADMIN/EXTENSIONS/DCOMCLSIDS"
    >
    <Custom
        Name="MD_IISADMIN_EXTENSIONS"
        ID="1028"
        Value="{61738644-F196-11D0-9953-00C04FD919C1}"
        Type="MULTISZ"
        UserType="IIS_MD_UT_SERVER"
        Attributes="NO_ATTRIBUTES"
    />
</IIsConfigObject>
<IIsConfigObject        Location ="/LM/IISADMIN/PROPERTYREGISTRATION"
    >
    <Custom
        Name="MD_METADATA_ID_REGISTRATION"
        ID="1030"
```

```
        Value="0-65535;Microsoft Reserved
                65536-524288;Microsoft IIS Admin Objects Reserved"
        Type="MULTISZ"
        UserType="IIS_MD_UT_SERVER"
        Attributes="INHERIT"
    />
</IIsConfigObject>
```

You can see from the preceding that IIS can have many keys named IIsConfigObject!

```
<IIsLogModules      Location ="/LM/Logging"

AdminACL="49634462a00000005800000040000003b15b816894cdce95a3d88e584da92f6d2
f3baf166bf973fc4434cb04dddcb2f6c0bfb398ca29775ad70f07d24a27bc9cce2ae30cc6348
d007898813fe2253d895a48b895fc8ee802c2908fa5b2fc3531416639de23c5c7874cdc802d1
6f5faac05cafeba90944485c56bad32d7c36da2e0b7a2661dfecb6d0b431041e1b74fa75d5f5
6df4e802eeeffbafd80de2429a8e08b33e54108184"

    >
</IIsLogModules>
```

The preceding key with location "/LM/Logging" is used to configure general aspects of IIS logging. More logging-related keys follow:

```
<IIsCustomLogModule      Location ="/LM/Logging/Custom Logging"
        LogCustomPropertyServicesString="W3SVC
                MSFTPSVC
                SMTPSVC
                NNTPSVC"
    >
</IIsCustomLogModule>
```

The preceding key specifies which IIS services can use IIS logging.

```
<IIsCustomLogModule      Location ="/LM/Logging/Custom Logging/Date"
        LogCustomPropertyDataType="6"
        LogCustomPropertyHeader="date"
        LogCustomPropertyID="4013"
        LogCustomPropertyMask="1"
        LogCustomPropertyName="Date"
        LogCustomPropertyNodeID="1"
    >
</IIsCustomLogModule>
<IIsCustomLogModule      Location ="/LM/Logging/Custom Logging/Extended Properties"
        LogCustomPropertyDataType="6"
        LogCustomPropertyID="4013"
        LogCustomPropertyName="Extended Properties"
        LogCustomPropertyNodeID="3"
```

```
        >
</IIsCustomLogModule>
<IIsCustomLogModule     Location ="/LM/Logging/Custom Logging/Extended
Properties/Bytes Received"
        LogCustomPropertyDataType="3"
        LogCustomPropertyHeader="cs-bytes"
        LogCustomPropertyMask="8192"
        LogCustomPropertyName="Bytes Received"
        LogCustomPropertyNodeID="17"
    >
</IIsCustomLogModule>
```

Now we're into keys that define specific properties for the W3C Extended Log file format. The preceding key defines the Bytes Received property, which appears as the cs-bytes field in log files created using this log file format. Note how many keys have the same name (IisCustomLogModule) but different locations, and note the hierarchical value of the Location attribute. More keys follow, defining additional properties for this log file format.

```
<IIsCustomLogModule     Location ="/LM/Logging/Custom Logging/Extended Properties/
Bytes Sent"
        LogCustomPropertyDataType="3"
        LogCustomPropertyHeader="sc-bytes"
        LogCustomPropertyMask="4096"
        LogCustomPropertyName="Bytes Sent"
        LogCustomPropertyNodeID="16"
    >
</IIsCustomLogModule>
<IIsCustomLogModule     Location ="/LM/Logging/Custom Logging/Extended
Properties/Client IP Address"
        LogCustomPropertyDataType="6"
        LogCustomPropertyHeader="c-ip"
        LogCustomPropertyMask="4"
        LogCustomPropertyName="Client IP Address"
        LogCustomPropertyNodeID="5"
    >
</IIsCustomLogModule>
<IIsCustomLogModule     Location ="/LM/Logging/Custom Logging/Extended Properties/
Cookie"
        LogCustomPropertyDataType="6"
        LogCustomPropertyHeader="cs(Cookie)"
        LogCustomPropertyMask="131072"
        LogCustomPropertyName="Cookie"
        LogCustomPropertyNodeID="22"
    >
</IIsCustomLogModule>
<IIsCustomLogModule     Location ="/LM/Logging/Custom Logging/Extended Properties/
Host"
        LogCustomPropertyDataType="6"
```

```
            LogCustomPropertyHeader="cs-host"
            LogCustomPropertyMask="1048576"
            LogCustomPropertyName="Host"
            LogCustomPropertyNodeID="20"
     >
</IIsCustomLogModule>
<IIsCustomLogModule      Location ="/LM/Logging/Custom Logging/Extended
Properties/Method"
            LogCustomPropertyDataType="6"
            LogCustomPropertyHeader="cs-method"
            LogCustomPropertyMask="128"
            LogCustomPropertyName="Method"
            LogCustomPropertyNodeID="11"
     >
</IIsCustomLogModule>
<IIsCustomLogModule      Location ="/LM/Logging/Custom Logging/Extended Properties/
Protocol Status"
            LogCustomPropertyDataType="3"
            LogCustomPropertyHeader="sc-status"
            LogCustomPropertyMask="1024"
            LogCustomPropertyName="Protocol Status"
            LogCustomPropertyNodeID="14"
     >
</IIsCustomLogModule>
<IIsCustomLogModule      Location ="/LM/Logging/Custom Logging/Extended Properties/
Protocol Substatus"
            LogCustomPropertyDataType="3"
            LogCustomPropertyHeader="sc-substatus"
            LogCustomPropertyMask="2097152"
            LogCustomPropertyName="Protocol Substatus"
            LogCustomPropertyNodeID="32"
     >
</IIsCustomLogModule>
<IIsCustomLogModule      Location ="/LM/Logging/Custom Logging/Extended Properties/
Protocol Version"
            LogCustomPropertyDataType="6"
            LogCustomPropertyHeader="cs-version"
            LogCustomPropertyMask="524288"
            LogCustomPropertyName="Protocol Version"
            LogCustomPropertyNodeID="19"
     >
</IIsCustomLogModule>
<IIsCustomLogModule      Location ="/LM/Logging/Custom Logging/Extended Properties/
Referer"
            LogCustomPropertyDataType="6"
            LogCustomPropertyHeader="cs(Referer)"
            LogCustomPropertyMask="262144"
            LogCustomPropertyName="Referer"
            LogCustomPropertyNodeID="23"
```

```
        >
</IIsCustomLogModule>
<IIsCustomLogModule      Location ="/LM/Logging/Custom Logging/Extended Properties/
Server IP"
          LogCustomPropertyDataType="6"
          LogCustomPropertyHeader="s-ip"
          LogCustomPropertyMask="64"
          LogCustomPropertyName="Server IP Address"
          LogCustomPropertyNodeID="9"
      >
</IIsCustomLogModule>
<IIsCustomLogModule      Location ="/LM/Logging/Custom Logging/Extended Properties/
Server Name"
          LogCustomPropertyDataType="6"
          LogCustomPropertyHeader="s-computername"
          LogCustomPropertyMask="32"
          LogCustomPropertyName="Server Name"
          LogCustomPropertyNodeID="8"
      >
</IIsCustomLogModule>
<IIsCustomLogModule      Location ="/LM/Logging/Custom Logging/Extended Properties/
Server Port"
          LogCustomPropertyDataType="3"
          LogCustomPropertyHeader="s-port"
          LogCustomPropertyMask="32768"
          LogCustomPropertyName="Server Port"
          LogCustomPropertyNodeID="10"
      >
</IIsCustomLogModule>
<IIsCustomLogModule      Location ="/LM/Logging/Custom Logging/Extended Properties/
Service Name"
          LogCustomPropertyDataType="6"
          LogCustomPropertyHeader="s-sitename"
          LogCustomPropertyMask="16"
          LogCustomPropertyName="Service Name"
          LogCustomPropertyNodeID="7"
      >
</IIsCustomLogModule>
<IIsCustomLogModule      Location ="/LM/Logging/Custom Logging/Extended Properties/
Time Taken"
          LogCustomPropertyDataType="3"
          LogCustomPropertyHeader="time-taken"
          LogCustomPropertyMask="16384"
          LogCustomPropertyName="Time Taken"
          LogCustomPropertyNodeID="18"
      >
</IIsCustomLogModule>
<IIsCustomLogModule      Location ="/LM/Logging/Custom Logging/Extended Properties/
URI Query"
```

```
                LogCustomPropertyDataType="6"
                LogCustomPropertyHeader="cs-uri-query"
                LogCustomPropertyMask="512"
                LogCustomPropertyName="URI Query"
                LogCustomPropertyNodeID="13"
        >
</IIsCustomLogModule>
<IIsCustomLogModule      Location ="/LM/Logging/Custom Logging/Extended Properties/
URI Stem"
                LogCustomPropertyDataType="6"
                LogCustomPropertyHeader="cs-uri-stem"
                LogCustomPropertyMask="256"
                LogCustomPropertyName="URI Stem"
                LogCustomPropertyNodeID="12"
        >
</IIsCustomLogModule>
<IIsCustomLogModule      Location ="/LM/Logging/Custom Logging/Extended Properties/
User Agent"
                LogCustomPropertyDataType="6"
                LogCustomPropertyHeader="cs(User-Agent)"
                LogCustomPropertyMask="65536"
                LogCustomPropertyName="User Agent"
                LogCustomPropertyNodeID="21"
        >
</IIsCustomLogModule>
<IIsCustomLogModule      Location ="/LM/Logging/Custom Logging/Extended Properties/
User Name"
                LogCustomPropertyDataType="6"
                LogCustomPropertyHeader="cs-username"
                LogCustomPropertyMask="8"
                LogCustomPropertyName="User Name"
                LogCustomPropertyNodeID="6"
        >
</IIsCustomLogModule>
<IIsCustomLogModule      Location ="/LM/Logging/Custom Logging/Extended Properties/
Win32 Status"
                LogCustomPropertyDataType="3"
                LogCustomPropertyHeader="sc-win32-status"
                LogCustomPropertyMask="2048"
                LogCustomPropertyName="Win32 Status"
                LogCustomPropertyNodeID="15"
        >
</IIsCustomLogModule>
```

That's the end of keys defining properties for the W3C Extended Log file format!

```
<IIsCustomLogModule      Location ="/LM/Logging/Custom Logging/Time"
            LogCustomPropertyDataType="6"
            LogCustomPropertyHeader="time"
```

```
                  LogCustomPropertyID="4013"
                  LogCustomPropertyMask="2"
                  LogCustomPropertyName="Time"
                  LogCustomPropertyNodeID="2"
        >
</IIsCustomLogModule>
<IIsLogModule      Location ="/LM/Logging/Microsoft IIS Log File Format"
          LogModuleId="{FF160657-DE82-11CF-BC0A-00AA006111E0}"
          LogModuleUiId="{31DCAB87-BB3E-11d0-9299-00C04FB6678B}"
        >
```

The preceding is a key related to the Microsoft IIS Log file format, and the following two keys are for NCSA and ODBC logging:

```
</IIsLogModule>
<IIsLogModule      Location ="/LM/Logging/NCSA Common Log File Format"
          LogModuleId="{FF16065F-DE82-11CF-BC0A-00AA006111E0}"
          LogModuleUiId="{31DCAB85-BB3E-11d0-9299-00C04FB6678B}"
        >
</IIsLogModule>
<IIsLogModule      Location ="/LM/Logging/ODBC Logging"
          LogModuleId="{FF16065B-DE82-11CF-BC0A-00AA006111E0}"
          LogModuleUiId="{31DCAB86-BB3E-11d0-9299-00C04FB6678B}"
        >
</IIsLogModule>
```

Here's another key for the W3C Extended Log file format:

```
<IIsLogModule      Location ="/LM/Logging/W3C Extended Log File Format"
          LogModuleId="{FF160663-DE82-11CF-BC0A-00AA006111E0}"
          LogModuleUiId="{31DCAB88-BB3E-11d0-9299-00C04FB6678B}"
        >
</IIsLogModule>
```

That's the end of keys related to logging. There's really no reason for editing these keys directly. Instead, you should use IIS Manager for configuring all aspects of IIS logging.

Now let's move on to global MimeMap properties. The IIsMimeMap key that comes next is a long one that contains the various MIME associations defined globally for IIS. Changes made to the properties sheet of the *servername* node in IIS Manager (see Figure 14-5, later in this chapter) are saved under this key in the Registry.

```
<IIsMimeMap      Location ="/LM/MimeMap"
          MimeMap=".asx,video/x-ms-asf
             .xml,text/xml
             .tsv,text/tab-separated-values
```

```
.ra,audio/x-pn-realaudio
.sv4crc,application/x-sv4crc
.spc,application/x-pkcs7-certificates
.pmc,application/x-perfmon
.lit,application/x-ms-reader
.crd,application/x-mscardfile
.isp,application/x-internet-signup
.wmlsc,application/vnd.wap.wmlscriptc
.vst,application/vnd.visio
.ttf,application/octet-stream
.pfm,application/octet-stream
.csv,application/octet-stream
.aaf,application/octet-stream
.hta,application/hta
.323,text/h323
.mhtml,message/rfc822
.midi,audio/mid
.p7r,application/x-pkcs7-certreqresp
.mny,application/x-msmoney
.clp,application/x-msclip
.vsd,application/vnd.visio
.lpk,application/octet-stream
.bin,application/octet-stream
.x,application/directx
.wvx,video/x-ms-wvx
.vcf,text/x-vcard
.htc,text/x-component
.htt,text/webviewhtml
.h,text/plain
.mht,message/rfc822
.mid,audio/mid
.p7b,application/x-pkcs7-certificates
.gz,application/x-gzip
.dvi,application/x-dvi
.cpio,application/x-cpio
.vdx,application/vnd.visio
.xlm,application/vnd.ms-excel
.fdf,application/vnd.fdf
.setreg,application/set-registration-initiation
.eps,application/postscript
.p7s,application/pkcs7-signature
.toc,application/octet-stream
.mdp,application/octet-stream
.ics,application/octet-stream
```

```
.chm,application/octet-stream
.asi,application/octet-stream
.afm,application/octet-stream
.evy,application/envoy
.wmp,video/x-ms-wmp
.qt,video/quicktime
.mpv2,video/mpeg
.xslt,text/xml
.etx,text/x-setext
.png,image/png
.cod,image/cis-cod
.snd,audio/basic
.au,audio/basic
.man,application/x-troff-man
.qtl,application/x-quicktimeplayer
.pmw,application/x-perfmon
.class,application/x-java-applet
.iii,application/x-iphone
.csh,application/x-csh
.z,application/x-compress
.vtx,application/vnd.visio
.vsw,application/vnd.visio
.wps,application/vnd.ms-works
.ps,application/postscript
.p7c,application/pkcs7-mime
.thn,application/octet-stream
.dot,application/msword
.doc,application/msword
.sgml,text/sgml
.nws,message/rfc822
.pbm,image/x-portable-bitmap
.ief,image/ief
.wav,audio/wav
.texi,application/x-texinfo
.mvb,application/x-msmediaview
.hdf,application/x-hdf
.vsx,application/vnd.visio
.psm,application/octet-stream
.java,application/octet-stream
.eot,application/octet-stream
.jar,application/java-archive
.mpeg,video/mpeg
.map,text/plain
.uls,text/iuls
```

```
.rf,image/vnd.rn-realflash
.m3u,audio/x-mpegurl
.wma,audio/x-ms-wma
.aifc,audio/aiff
.mdb,application/x-msaccess
.stl,application/vnd.ms-pki.stl
.setpay,application/set-payment-initiation
.prm,application/octet-stream
.mix,application/octet-stream
.lzh,application/octet-stream
.hhk,application/octet-stream
.xaf,x-world/x-vrml
.flr,x-world/x-vrml
.IVF,video/x-ivf
.cnf,text/plain
.asm,text/plain
.tiff,image/tiff
.wax,audio/x-ms-wax
.ms,application/x-troff-ms
.tcl,application/x-tcl
.shar,application/x-shar
.sh,application/x-sh
.nc,application/x-netcdf
.hlp,application/winhlp
.oda,application/oda
.pfb,application/octet-stream
.fla,application/octet-stream
.wm,video/x-ms-wm
.rgb,image/x-rgb
.ppm,image/x-portable-pixmap
.ram,audio/x-pn-realaudio
.sit,application/x-stuffit
.dir,application/x-director
.mpp,application/vnd.ms-project
.xla,application/vnd.ms-excel
.ssm,application/streamingmedia
.axs,application/olescript
.ods,application/oleobject
.psp,application/octet-stream
.jpb,application/octet-stream
.wrz,x-world/x-vrml
.m1v,video/mpeg
.mno,text/xml
.cmx,image/x-cmx
```

```
.jpeg,image/jpeg
.dib,image/bmp
.rmi,audio/mid
.aiff,audio/aiff
.wmd,application/x-ms-wmd
.wri,application/x-mswrite
.pub,application/x-mspublisher
.ins,application/x-internet-signup
.wks,application/vnd.ms-works
.xls,application/vnd.ms-excel
.ai,application/postscript
.crl,application/pkix-crl
.qxd,application/octet-stream
.dwp,application/octet-stream
.xof,x-world/x-vrml
.wmv,video/x-ms-wmv
.nsc,video/x-ms-asf
.mpa,video/mpeg
.pnm,image/x-portable-anymap
.rpm,audio/x-pn-realaudio-plugin
.aif,audio/x-aiff
.me,application/x-troff-me
.pml,application/x-perfmon
.trm,application/x-msterminal
.m13,application/x-msmediaview
.js,application/x-javascript
.dxr,application/x-director
.xlt,application/vnd.ms-excel
.xlc,application/vnd.ms-excel
.p10,application/pkcs10
.smi,application/octet-stream
.sea,application/octet-stream
.hqx,application/mac-binhex40
.spl,application/futuresplash
.movie,video/x-sgi-movie
.lsf,video/x-la-asf
.txt,text/plain
.jfif,image/pjpeg
.jpe,image/jpeg
.zip,application/x-zip-compressed
.wmf,application/x-msmetafile
.m14,application/x-msmediaview
.latex,application/x-latex
.wcm,application/vnd.ms-works
```

```
.hhp,application/octet-stream
.aca,application/octet-stream
.jcz,application/liquidmotion
.wrl,x-world/x-vrml
.wmx,video/x-ms-wmx
.asr,video/x-ms-asf
.lsx,video/x-la-asf
.xsl,text/xml
.html,text/html
.tif,image/tiff
.der,application/x-x509-ca-cert
.pfx,application/x-pkcs12
.p12,application/x-pkcs12
.cur,application/octet-stream
.hdml,text/x-hdml
.htm,text/html
.xbm,image/x-xbitmap
.jpg,image/jpeg
.texinfo,application/x-texinfo
.xlw,application/vnd.ms-excel
.rm,application/vnd.rn-realmedia
.pdf,application/pdf
.rar,application/octet-stream
.psd,application/octet-stream
.inf,application/octet-stream
.emz,application/octet-stream
.dsp,application/octet-stream
.jck,application/liquidmotion
.mpe,video/mpeg
.mp2,video/mpeg
.sct,text/scriptlet
.ras,image/x-cmu-raster
.swf,application/x-shockwave-flash
.wmz,application/x-ms-wmz
.gtar,application/x-gtar
.dcr,application/x-director
.pps,application/vnd.ms-powerpoint
.p7m,application/pkcs7-mime
.ocx,application/octet-stream
.mov,video/quicktime
.wmls,text/vnd.wap.wmlscript
.cpp,text/plain
.c,text/plain
.bas,text/plain
```

```
.css,text/css
.art,image/x-jg
.mp3,audio/mpeg
.t,application/x-troff
.roff,application/x-troff
.tar,application/x-tar
.hhc,application/x-oleobject
.scd,application/x-msschedule
.pko,application/vnd.ms-pki.pko
.sst,application/vnd.ms-pki.certstore
.ppt,application/vnd.ms-powerpoint
.pcx,application/octet-stream
.msi,application/octet-stream
.exe,application/octet-stream
.asd,application/octet-stream
.fif,application/fractals
.mpg,video/mpeg
.vml,text/xml
.xdr,text/plain
.vcs,text/plain
.hxt,text/html
.eml,message/rfc822
.xpm,image/x-xpixmap
.ico,image/x-icon
.gif,image/gif
.dwf,drawing/x-dwf
.src,application/x-wais-source
.tr,application/x-troff
.pmr,application/x-perfmon
.pma,application/x-perfmon
.dll,application/x-msdownload
.bcpio,application/x-bcpio
.wmlc,application/vnd.wap.wmlc
.wdb,application/vnd.ms-works
.pot,application/vnd.ms-powerpoint
.rtf,application/rtf
.prf,application/pics-rules
.snp,application/octet-stream
.cab,application/octet-stream
.avi,video/x-msvideo
.asf,video/x-ms-asf
.dtd,text/xml
.wml,text/vnd.wap.wml
.vbs,text/vbscript
```

```
        .rtx,text/richtext
        .dlm,text/dlm
        .xwd,image/x-xwindowdump
        .pgm,image/x-portable-graymap
        .wbmp,image/vnd.wap.wbmp
        .bmp,image/bmp
        .crt,application/x-x509-ca-cert
        .ustar,application/x-ustar
        .tex,application/x-tex
        .sv4cpio,application/x-sv4cpio
        .tgz,application/x-compressed
        .cdf,application/x-cdf
        .vss,application/vnd.visio
        .cat,application/vnd.ms-pki.seccat
        .prx,application/octet-stream
        .pcz,application/octet-stream
        .acx,application/internet-property-stream"
    >
</IIsMimeMap>
```

Now we're coming to metabase keys you are more likely to want to configure using edit-while-running. The first is the IIsWebService key, which defines global configuration settings for the WWW service that apply to all websites running on IIS. Note the location of this node in the LM namespace.

Many of the properties contained in this key can be set in the GUI using the properties sheet for the Web Sites node. Remember, to find out what any of these properties represent (some you can guess from their names), refer to the Metabase Reference in IIS Help. I've noted a few interesting properties for this key in a couple of places in the following:

```
<IIsWebService      Location ="/LM/W3SVC"
        AllowKeepAlive="TRUE"
        AnonymousUserName="IUSR_ESRV220B"
        AnonymousUserPass="4963446270000000022000000400000003b15b816b84ce0694a3dd6e5a
1dae7f6ecf3eaf117bfaa3fe74333b07bdda92f6c0b000001000100fd8a74f690bdad557a484
49422cc55a3f187d9c4a7164865fd57d235b334d80e2464628b0379749d18387b3d30e27ee54
15ec7895fde3914f4b1cc0ea1ec62b2"
        AppAllowClientDebug="FALSE"
        AppAllowDebugging="FALSE"
        AppPoolId="DefaultAppPool"
        ApplicationDependencies="Active Server Pages;ASP
            Internet Data Connector;HTTPODBC
            Server Side Includes;SSINC
            WebDAV;WEBDAV"
```

```
AspAllowOutOfProcComponents="TRUE"
AspAllowSessionState="TRUE"
AspAppServiceFlags="0"
AspBufferingLimit="4194304"
AspBufferingOn="TRUE"
AspCalcLineNumber="TRUE"
AspCodepage="0"
AspDiskTemplateCacheDirectory="%windir%\system32\inetsrv\ASP
        Compiled Templates"
AspEnableApplicationRestart="TRUE"
AspEnableAspHtmlFallback="FALSE"
AspEnableChunkedEncoding="TRUE"
AspEnableParentPaths="FALSE"
AspEnableTypelibCache="TRUE"
AspErrorsToNTLog="FALSE"
AspExceptionCatchEnable="TRUE"
AspExecuteInMTA="0"
AspKeepSessionIDSecure="0"
AspLCID="2048"
AspLogErrorRequests="TRUE"
AspMaxDiskTemplateCacheFiles="2000"
AspMaxRequestEntityAllowed="204800"
AspProcessorThreadMax="25"
AspQueueConnectionTestTime="3"
AspQueueTimeout="4294967295"
AspRequestQueueMax="3000"
AspRunOnEndAnonymously="TRUE"
AspScriptEngineCacheMax="250"
AspScriptErrorMessage="An error occurred on the server when
        processing the URL.  Please contact the system administrator."
AspScriptErrorSentToBrowser="TRUE"
AspScriptFileCacheSize="500"
AspScriptLanguage="VBScript"
AspScriptTimeout="90"
AspSessionMax="4294967295"
AspSessionTimeout="20"
AspTrackThreadingModel="FALSE"
AuthChangeURL="/iisadmpwd/achg.asp"
AuthExpiredURL="/iisadmpwd/aexp.asp"
AuthExpiredUnsecureURL="/iisadmpwd/aexp3.asp"
AuthFlags="AuthAnonymous | AuthNTLM"
AuthNotifyPwdExpURL="/iisadmpwd/anot.asp"
AuthNotifyPwdExpUnsecureURL="/iisadmpwd/anot3.asp"
CGITimeout="300"
```

```
CacheISAPI="TRUE"
CentralBinaryLoggingEnabled="FALSE"
```

There's where centralized binary logging is enabled in IIS. There's no GUI element in IIS Manager to do this, you have to edit the metabase instead. You have to restart IIS to make this change take effect.

```
ConnectionTimeout="120"
ContentIndexed="TRUE"
DefaultDoc="Default.htm,Default.asp,index.htm"
```

Note the preceding format for multiple values for a property whose data type is STRING.

```
DirBrowseFlags="DirBrowseShowDate | DirBrowseShowTime |
DirBrowseShowSize | DirBrowseShowExtension | DirBrowseShowLongDate |
EnableDefaultDoc"
```

The preceding data type is DWORD, a 4-byte (32-bit) number. However, here it is used to define a series of 1-bit flags instead.

```
DownlevelAdminInstance="1"
```

The Metabase Reference in IIS Help says this about the preceding property: "The DownlevelAdminInstance indicates the server instance for remote administration clients." Doesn't tell you much, does it?

```
HttpErrors="400,*,FILE,C:\WINDOWS\help\iisHelp\common\400.htm
       401,1,FILE,C:\WINDOWS\help\iisHelp\common\401-1.htm
       401,2,FILE,C:\WINDOWS\help\iisHelp\common\401-2.htm
       401,3,FILE,C:\WINDOWS\help\iisHelp\common\401-3.htm
       401,4,FILE,C:\WINDOWS\help\iisHelp\common\401-4.htm
       401,5,FILE,C:\WINDOWS\help\iisHelp\common\401-5.htm
       401,7,FILE,C:\WINDOWS\help\iisHelp\common\401-1.htm
       403,1,FILE,C:\WINDOWS\help\iisHelp\common\403-1.htm
       403,2,FILE,C:\WINDOWS\help\iisHelp\common\403-2.htm
       403,3,FILE,C:\WINDOWS\help\iisHelp\common\403-3.htm
       403,4,FILE,C:\WINDOWS\help\iisHelp\common\403-4.htm
       403,5,FILE,C:\WINDOWS\help\iisHelp\common\403-5.htm
       403,6,FILE,C:\WINDOWS\help\iisHelp\common\403-6.htm
       403,7,FILE,C:\WINDOWS\help\iisHelp\common\403-7.htm
       403,8,FILE,C:\WINDOWS\help\iisHelp\common\403-8.htm
       403,9,FILE,C:\WINDOWS\help\iisHelp\common\403-9.htm
       403,10,FILE,C:\WINDOWS\help\iisHelp\common\403-10.htm
       403,11,FILE,C:\WINDOWS\help\iisHelp\common\403-11.htm
```

```
403,12,FILE,C:\WINDOWS\help\iisHelp\common\403-12.htm
403,13,FILE,C:\WINDOWS\help\iisHelp\common\403-13.htm
403,15,FILE,C:\WINDOWS\help\iisHelp\common\403-15.htm
403,16,FILE,C:\WINDOWS\help\iisHelp\common\403-16.htm
403,17,FILE,C:\WINDOWS\help\iisHelp\common\403-17.htm
403,18,FILE,C:\WINDOWS\help\iisHelp\common\403.htm
403,19,FILE,C:\WINDOWS\help\iisHelp\common\403.htm
403,20,FILE,C:\WINDOWS\help\iisHelp\common\403-20.htm
404,*,FILE,C:\WINDOWS\help\iisHelp\common\404b.htm
404,2,FILE,C:\WINDOWS\help\iisHelp\common\404b.htm
404,3,FILE,C:\WINDOWS\help\iisHelp\common\404b.htm
405,*,FILE,C:\WINDOWS\help\iisHelp\common\405.htm
406,*,FILE,C:\WINDOWS\help\iisHelp\common\406.htm
407,*,FILE,C:\WINDOWS\help\iisHelp\common\407.htm
412,*,FILE,C:\WINDOWS\help\iisHelp\common\412.htm
414,*,FILE,C:\WINDOWS\help\iisHelp\common\414.htm
415,*,FILE,C:\WINDOWS\help\iisHelp\common\415.htm
500,12,FILE,C:\WINDOWS\help\iisHelp\common\500-12.htm
500,13,FILE,C:\WINDOWS\help\iisHelp\common\500-13.htm
500,15,FILE,C:\WINDOWS\help\iisHelp\common\500-15.htm
500,16,FILE,C:\WINDOWS\help\iisHelp\common\500.htm
500,17,FILE,C:\WINDOWS\help\iisHelp\common\500.htm
500,18,FILE,C:\WINDOWS\help\iisHelp\common\500.htm
500,19,FILE,C:\WINDOWS\help\iisHelp\common\500.htm"
```

The preceding HttpErrors property uses the MULTISZ data type, allowing multiple string values to be specified with spaces (or line breaks) in between.

```
IIs5IsolationModeEnabled="FALSE"
InProcessIsapiApps="C:\WINDOWS\system32\inetsrv\httpext.dll
    C:\WINDOWS\system32\inetsrv\httpodbc.dll
    C:\WINDOWS\system32\inetsrv\ssinc.dll
    C:\WINDOWS\system32\msw3prt.dll"
LogExtFileFlags="LogExtFileDate | LogExtFileTime |
LogExtFileClientIp | LogExtFileUserName | LogExtFileServerIp |
LogExtFileMethod | LogExtFileUriStem | LogExtFileUriQuery |
LogExtFileHttpStatus | LogExtFileWin32Status | LogExtFileServerPort |
LogExtFileUserAgent | LogExtFileHttpSubStatus"
LogFileDirectory="C:\WINDOWS\system32\LogFiles"
LogFilePeriod="1"
```

You might guess that the preceding property indicates that IIS create a new log file every day, and you'd be right! But if you guessed a value of "7" will create a new log every week, you're wrong—the correct value to do this is "2" instead. Check the Metabase Reference for more information.

```
LogFileTruncateSize="20971520"
LogInUTF8="FALSE"
LogOdbcDataSource="HTTPLOG"
LogOdbcPassword="4963446260000000120000004000000003b15b816fb4caa69023de4e
5afdaf5f6d2f301003dd46796d884d5328d3aeb83e532e6d4dc4a109b082b6e3c69dc9ce65
7d7983e7f9a6665f59a5a2d0ec64cc9ea511f0ad8da79cbb410ddec24fc8d7e9525f6b5b011
0028"
LogOdbcTableName="InternetLog"
LogOdbcUserName="InternetAdmin"
LogPluginClsid="{FF160663-DE82-11CF-BC0A-00AA006111E0}"
LogType="1"
MaxConnections="4294967295"
MaxGlobalBandwidth="4294967295"
MinFileBytesPerSec="240"
PasswordChangeFlags="AuthChangeDisable | AuthAdvNotifyDisable"
ScriptMaps=".asp,C:\WINDOWS\system32\inetsrv\asp.dll,5,GET,HEAD,POST,TRACE
       .cer,C:\WINDOWS\system32\inetsrv\asp.dll,5,GET,HEAD,POST,TRACE
       .cdx,C:\WINDOWS\system32\inetsrv\asp.dll,5,GET,HEAD,POST,TRACE
       .asa,C:\WINDOWS\system32\inetsrv\asp.dll,5,GET,HEAD,POST,TRACE
       .idc,C:\WINDOWS\system32\inetsrv\httpodbc.dll,5,GET,POST
       .shtm,C:\WINDOWS\system32\inetsrv\ssinc.dll,5,GET,POST
       .shtml,C:\WINDOWS\system32\inetsrv\ssinc.dll,5,GET,POST
       .stm,C:\WINDOWS\system32\inetsrv\ssinc.dll,5,GET,POST"
```

The preceding ScriptMaps property identifies which file extensions are associated with different script processors such as asp.dll for Active Server Pages, httpodbc.dll for Internet Database Connector, and so on. The property also defines which HTTP verbs are allowed for each scriptmap.

```
WAMUserName="IWAM_ESRV220B"
WAMUserPass="4963446270000000220000004000000003b15b816a44c8069473dc0e596dad5f
6b4f3e3f149bfa43ffe435ab06bdd9f2f6c0b00000100010025232161330 07f603a05bcc6099
a11fec6f0e92ebae05501fb713a5ce6b074aa4fe70b8995f2ca9d57c94b909621b04235acf97
87ab7fc5b83466cbc38c51335"
WebSvcExtRestrictionList="0,*.dll
       0,*.exe
       0,C:\WINDOWS\system32\inetsrv\asp.dll,0,ASP,Active Server Pages
       0,C:\WINDOWS\system32\inetsrv\httpodbc.dll,0,HTTPODBC,Internet Data
       Connector
       0,C:\WINDOWS\system32\inetsrv\ssinc.dll,0,SSINC,Server Side Includes
       0,C:\WINDOWS\system32\inetsrv\httpext.dll,0,WEBDAV,WebDAV"
```

The preceding WebSvcExtRestrictionList property represents the current settings of the Web Service Extensions (WSE) node in IIS Manager.

That's the closing bracket of the <IIsWebService> tag that started several pages ago!

```
<Custom
       Name="UnknownName_2166"
```

```
        ID="2166"
        Value="1"
        Type="DWORD"
        UserType="IIS_MD_UT_SERVER"
        Attributes="NO_ATTRIBUTES"
    />
```

Unfortunately, I have no idea what the preceding Custom property represents because a lot of metabase settings are still undocumented by Microsoft.

```
<Custom
        Name="UnknownName_9202"
        ID="9202"
        Value="4294967295"
        Type="DWORD"
        UserType="IIS_MD_UT_SERVER"
        Attributes="NO_ATTRIBUTES"
    />
</IIsWebService>
```

That's the end of the IIsWebService key representing configuration settings for the WWW service and global settings for all websites running on IIS.

Now let's look at the key for a particular website, namely, the Default Web Site:

```
<IIsWebServer      Location ="/LM/W3SVC/1"
        AppPoolId="DefaultAppPool"
        DefaultDoc="Default.htm,Default.asp,index.htm,iisstart.htm"
        ServerBindings=":80:"
        ServerComment="Default Web Site"
        ServerSize="1"
    >
</IIsWebServer>
```

The preceding key was short and sweet because of properties inheritance.

```
<IIsFilters      Location ="/LM/W3SVC/1/Filters"
```

AdminACL="49634462f0000000a4000000400000003b15b816894cdce9ee3d88e550da92f6d2
f3baf166bf973fc44300b048ddcb2f6c0bf739aca29375ad73f07d24a27bc9ffe2ae30ec615c
d08d8b8813ff2353ddb5a48b8c6bcaee802d2b2cfad02fc3563513639dc23e5c7dcc38710955
bed070ca3459b5d1d056d816b5c731532d7edaad3c8aea36a105537c4eb0771b9bf8bfc3d080
9f81ba6fd34d6c58b8e1becdf18aa94c32f3f07334c21f5f12fcaf40a8d48f9c5157d28e11aa
5df74eaa898ae62ffee384f1715e30109d0709c597c46c0a8be018453a9ab2c73d1822a44a71
67d3932f0ec20d12d7328b760c148afb0857cccdd292a53884"
```
    >
</IIsFilters>
```

```
<IIsCertMapper      Location ="/LM/W3SVC/1/IIsCertMapper"
    >
</IIsCertMapper>
```

Although the IIsWebServer key a few lines back contained configuration information for the Default Web Site, here is another key relating to this site that specifies application settings and the location home directory for the site. Note the location of this key "/LM/W3SVC/1/ROOT" within the metabase hierarchy.

```
<IIsWebVirtualDir      Location ="/LM/W3SVC/1/ROOT"
        AccessFlags="AccessRead | AccessScript"
        AppFriendlyName="Default Application"
        AppIsolated="2"
```

You'd be right if you thought "0" meant in-process, "1" out of process, and "2" pooled process. Or did you get 1 and 2 reversed? This property is probably here only for backward compatibility reasons as websites can no longer run in-process on IIS 6. Looking up this property in IIS Help reveals that you should consider it read-only and should not try to configure it manually.

```
            AppPoolId="DefaultAppPool"
            AppRoot="/LM/W3SVC/1/ROOT"
            Path="c:\inetpub\wwwroot"
    >
</IIsWebVirtualDir>
```

Settings for the following IIsApplicationPools key apply to all application pools running on the IIS machine:

```
<IIsApplicationPools      Location ="/LM/W3SVC/AppPools"
```

```
AdminACL="49634462f0000000a4000000400000003b15b816894cdce9ee3d88e550da92f6d2
f3baf166bf973fc44300b048ddcb2f6c0bf739a7a29375ad73f07d24a27bc9ffe2ae30ec615c
d0868b8813ff2353ddb5a48b8c6bcaee802d2b2cfadb2fc3563513639dc23e5c7dcc38710955
bed070ca3459b5d1d056d816b5c731532d7edaad3c8aea36a105537c4eb0771b9bf8bfc3d080
9f81ba6fd34d6c58b8e1becdf18aa94c32f3f07334c21f5f12fcaf40a8d48f9c5157d28e11fa
36354cf9e4a0252865d4169694e9a718803cee803d0ca0d0b45fe6b447a3f7f069e83296d7f5
86eef4bde1e87a465253bbe5e8f69553c432a7b85e09452f6b"
```

```
            AppPoolIdentityType="2"
            AppPoolQueueLength="1000"
```

Here's where you can configure request queuing limits for the HTTP Listener, also called the Universal Listener. Exceeding this number of queued requests will cause an HTTP 503 error to be returned to clients.

```
            CPULimit="0"
```

There's where you can configure the maximum amount (in thousandths of a percent) of CPU time that worker processes can consume, also called *CPU throttling*, as we discussed in Chapter 12, "Performance Tuning and Monitoring." A value of "0" means CPU throttling is disabled, which it is by default.

```
CPUResetInterval="5"
DisallowOverlappingRotation="FALSE"
```

The preceding setting can be modified to enable overlapping recycling of worker processes, which is disabled by default.

```
DisallowRotationOnConfigChange="FALSE"
IdleTimeout="20"
LoadBalancerCapabilities="2"
LogEventOnRecycle="AppPoolRecycleTime | AppPoolRecycleMemory |
        AppPoolRecyclePrivateMemory"
MaxProcesses="1"
OrphanWorkerProcess="FALSE"
PeriodicRestartMemory="0"
PeriodicRestartPrivateMemory="0"
PeriodicRestartRequests="0"
PeriodicRestartTime="1740"
PingInterval="30"
PingResponseTime="90"
PingingEnabled="TRUE"
RapidFailProtection="TRUE"
RapidFailProtectionInterval="5"
RapidFailProtectionMaxCrashes="5"
SMPAffinitized="FALSE"
SMPProcessorAffinityMask="4294967295"
```

Specific worker processes can be assigned to specific CPUs on an SMP machine using the preceding two properties, a feature called CPU affinity, as discussed earlier.

```
ShutdownTimeLimit="90"
StartupTimeLimit="90"
    >
</IIsApplicationPools>
```

Now you have a key for a specific application pool, the DefaultAppPool. Note that this key has no properties other than Location because, by default, it inherits all its settings from the IIsApplicationPools node above it.

```
<IIsApplicationPool     Location ="/LM/W3SVC/AppPools/DefaultAppPool"
    >
```

```
</IIsApplicationPool>
<IIsFilters     Location ="/LM/W3SVC/Filters"

AdminACL="49634462f0000000a4000000400000003b15b816894cdce9ee3d88e550da92f6d2
f3baf166bf973fc44300b048ddcb2f6c0bf739aca29375ad73f07d24a27bc9ffe2ae30ec615c
d08d8b8813ff2353ddb5a48b8c6bcaee802d2b2cfad02fc3563513639dc23e5c7dcc38710955
bed070ca3459b5d1d056d816b5c731532d7edaad3c8aea36a105537c4eb0771b9bf8bfc3d080
9f81ba6fd34d6c58b8e1becdf18aa94c32f3f07334c21f5f12fcaf40a8d48f9c5157d28e11aa
5df74eaa898ae62ffee384f1715e30109d0709c597c46c0a8be018453a9ab2c73d1822a44a71
67d3932f0ec20d12d7328b760c148afb0857cccdd292a53884"
        FilterLoadOrder=""
   >
</IIsFilters>
<IIsFilter     Location ="/LM/W3SVC/Filters/Compression"
   >
</IIsFilter>
<IIsCompressionScheme     Location ="/LM/W3SVC/Filters/Compression/deflate"
        HcCompressionDll="%windir%\system32\inetsrv\gzip.dll"
        HcCreateFlags="0"
        HcDoDynamicCompression="TRUE"
        HcDoOnDemandCompression="TRUE"
        HcDoStaticCompression="FALSE"
        HcDynamicCompressionLevel="0"
        HcFileExtensions="htm
            html
            txt"
        HcOnDemandCompLevel="10"
        HcPriority="1"
        HcScriptFileExtensions="asp
            dll
            exe"
   >
</IIsCompressionScheme>
<IIsCompressionScheme     Location ="/LM/W3SVC/Filters/Compression/gzip"
        HcCompressionDll="%windir%\system32\inetsrv\gzip.dll"
        HcCreateFlags="1"
        HcDoDynamicCompression="TRUE"
        HcDoOnDemandCompression="TRUE"
        HcDoStaticCompression="TRUE"
        HcDynamicCompressionLevel="0"
        HcFileExtensions="htm
            html
            txt"
```

```
                HcOnDemandCompLevel="10"
                HcPriority="1"
                HcScriptFileExtensions="asp
                        dll
                        exe"
        >
</IIsCompressionScheme>
<IIsCompressionSchemes        Location ="/LM/W3SVC/Filters/Compression/Parameters"
                HcCacheControlHeader="maxage=86400"
                HcCompressionBufferSize="8192"
                HcCompressionDirectory="%windir%\IIS Temporary Compressed Files"
                HcDoDiskSpaceLimiting="FALSE"
                HcDoDynamicCompression="FALSE"
                HcDoOnDemandCompression="TRUE"
                HcDoStaticCompression="FALSE"
                HcExpiresHeader="Wed, 01 Jan 1997 12:00:00 GMT"
                HcFilesDeletedPerDiskFree="256"
                HcIoBufferSize="8192"
                HcMaxDiskSpaceUsage="100000000"
                HcMaxQueueLength="1000"
                HcMinFileSizeForComp="1"
                HcNoCompressionForHttp10="TRUE"
                HcNoCompressionForProxies="TRUE"
                HcNoCompressionForRange="FALSE"
                HcSendCacheHeaders="FALSE"
        >
</IIsCompressionSchemes>
```

The following key contains more settings global to all websites running on IIS:

```
<IIsWebInfo       Location ="/LM/W3SVC/Info"
```

```
AdminACL="49634462a0000000580000004000000003b15b816894cdce95a3d88e584da92f6d2
f3baf166bf973fc4434cb04dddcb2f6c0bfb398ca29775ad70f07d24a27bc9cce2ae30cc6348
d007898813fe2253d895a48b895fc8ee802c2908fa5b2fc3531416639de23c5c7874cdc802d1
6f5faac05cafeba90944485c56bad32d7c36da2e0b7a2661dfecb6d0b431041e1b74fa75d5f5
6df4e802eeeffbafd80de2429a8e08b33e54108184"
```

```
                CustomErrorDescriptions="400,0,Bad Request,,0
                        401,1,Unauthorized,Logon failed,1
                        401,2,Unauthorized,Logon failed due to server configuration,1
                        401,3,Unauthorized,Unauthorized due to ACL on resource,1
                        401,4,Unauthorized,Authorization failed by filter,1
                        401,5,Unauthorized,Authorization failed by ISAPI/CGI app,1
                        401,7,Unauthorized,Denied due to URL Authorization policy,0
```

```
403,1,Forbidden,Execute access denied,0
403,2,Forbidden,Read access denied,0
403,3,Forbidden,Write access denied,0
403,4,Forbidden,SSL required,0
403,5,Forbidden,SSL128 required,0
403,6,Forbidden,IP address rejected,0
403,7,Forbidden,Client certificate required,0
403,8,Forbidden,Site access denied,0
403,9,Forbidden,Too many users,0
403,10,Forbidden,Invalid Configuration,0
403,11,Forbidden,Password Change,0
403,12,Forbidden,Mapper Denied Access,0
403,13,Forbidden,Client certificate revoked,0
403,14,Forbidden,Directory Listing Denied,0
403,15,Forbidden,Client Access Licenses Exceeded,0
403,16,Forbidden,Client certificate untrusted or ill-formed,0
403,17,Forbidden,Client certificate has expired or is not yet valid,0
403,18,Forbidden,Cannot execute request from this application pool,0
403,19,Forbidden,CGI Access denied,0
403,20,Forbidden,Passport Login failed,0
404,0,Not Found,,0
404,2,Not Found,Denied due to Lockdown Policy,0
404,3,Not Found,Denied due to MIMEMAP Policy,0
405,0,Method Not Allowed,,0
406,0,Not Acceptable,,0
407,0,Proxy Authentication Required,,1
412,0,Precondition Failed,,0
414,0,Request-URI Too Long,,0
415,0,Unsupported Media Type,,0
500,0,Internal Server Error,,0
500,12,Internal Server Error,Application restarting,0
500,13,Internal Server Error,Server too busy,0
500,15,Internal Server Error,Direct requests for GLOBAL.ASA forbidden,0
500,16,Internal Server Error,UNC Access Error,0
500,17,Internal Server Error,URL Authorization store not found,0
500,18,Internal Server Error,URL Authorization store cannot be opened,0
500,19,Internal Server Error,Bad file metadata,0
500,100,Internal Server Error,ASP error,0
```

```
        501,0,Not Implemented,,0
        502,0,Bad Gateway,,1"
    LogModuleList="NCSA Common Log File Format,Microsoft IIS Log File Format,W3C
    Extended Log File Format,ODBC Logging"
    MD_SERVER_CAPABILITIES="129983"
    MD_SERVER_PLATFORM="1"
    MajorIIsVersionNumber="6"
    MinorIIsVersionNumber="0"
  >
</IIsWebInfo>
```

Here are some keys used for legacy compatibility; don't change anything in them:

```
<IIsConfigObject      Location ="/LM/W3SVC/Info/Templates"
    >
</IIsConfigObject>
<IIsWebServer      Location ="/LM/W3SVC/Info/Templates/Public Web Site"
        ServerComment="Allows all users to browse static and dynamic content."
    >
</IIsWebServer>
<IIsWebVirtualDir      Location ="/LM/W3SVC/Info/Templates/Public Web Site/Root"
        AccessFlags="AccessRead | AccessScript"
        AuthFlags="AuthAnonymous"
        IPSecurity=""
    >
</IIsWebVirtualDir>
<IIsWebServer      Location ="/LM/W3SVC/Info/Templates/Secure Web Site"
        ServerComment="Allows users with a Windows account to view static and dynamic
content."
    >
</IIsWebServer>
<IIsWebVirtualDir      Location ="/LM/W3SVC/Info/Templates/Secure Web Site/Root"
        AccessFlags="AccessRead | AccessScript"
        AuthFlags="AuthBasic | AuthNTLM | AuthMD5"
        IPSecurity=""
    >
</IIsWebVirtualDir>
```

And that's the end of metabase properties. The XML document now ends with two closing tags to complete the elements defined at the beginning of the file.

```
</MBProperty>
</configuration>
```

And that completes our tour of the XML metabase!

Modifying the MetaBase.xml File Using IIS Manager

Let's make a significant change to the metabase by creating a new website using IIS Manager. Create a new site having the name New Site with IP address 172.16.11.221 and home directory C:\stuff. Leave the rest of the settings in the Web Site Creation Wizard at their defaults.

Now right-click the *servername* node in IIS Manager, and select All Tasks and then Save Configuration To Disk. This writes the changes made to the in-memory metabase to the metabase configuration file MetaBase.xml. Now open Metabase.xml using Notepad, search for "New Site," and you'll discover that three new keys have been added to the metabase:

```
<IIsWebServer      Location ="/LM/W3SVC/388907640"
```

The new key is located as a child node of the W3SVC node in the LM namespace. The key is uniquely identified by a number randomly generated by IIS and assigned to the new website.

```
            AuthFlags="0"
            ServerAutoStart="TRUE"
            ServerBindings="172.16.11.221:80:"
            ServerComment="New Site"
     >
</IIsWebServer>
<IIsFilters      Location ="/LM/W3SVC/388907640/filters"

AdminACL="49634462f0000000a400000040000000a9002a570dc9357e6d84f3ae0e023613af
861eebb31cab956b85e79c6da1187cf9815cfe906e003f40451e6d38093390e60d74a2b7e5f8
435d4446613bb1af1d7733d1421669a15a1222f65c08fcb6b39414fc88b9625675273685b507
1a7b466bf6d67b5ece76505e59b7ceca0d14fe36815866d42ac94258895db4dba1c23cfafcc0
db2d2ab69aa2785aaff31482b5817982836c645b7baf337685ffd8311fd2faabd50068dbd0aa
5df74eaa898ae62ffee384f1715e30109d0709c597c46c0a8be018453a9ab2c73d1822a44a71
67d3932f0ec20d12d7328b760c148afb0857cccdd292a53884"
     >
</IIsFilters>
<IIsWebVirtualDir      Location ="/LM/W3SVC/388907640/root"
```

Interestingly, the location for this key has "root" in lowercase, while the Default Web Site uses "ROOT" instead. A bug or a "feature"?

```
            AccessFlags="AccessRead | AccessScript"
            AppFriendlyName="Default Application"
            AppIsolated="2"
```

```
        AppRoot="/LM/W3SVC/388907640/Root"
        AuthFlags="AuthAnonymous | AuthNTLM"
        DirBrowseFlags="DirBrowseShowDate | DirBrowseShowTime |
        DirBrowseShowSize | DirBrowseShowExtension | DirBrowseShowLongDate |
        EnableDefaultDoc"
        Path="C:\stuff"
    >
</IIsWebVirtualDir>
```

Summary of MetaBase.xml Structure

I'll conclude my overview of the logical structure of the metabase configuration file by summarizing the hierarchical nature of this structure two ways: by the KeyType property of metabase keys and by the Location attribute of the keys. I'll use the updated version of your MetaBase.xml file that contains information about the new website you just created.

Key Hierarchy

First, here is a representation of the hierarchy of keys found in your sample MetaBase.xml file, omitting all XML except for the elements at the start and end of the document. Repeated keys are indicated by ellipses ("...").

```
<?xml version ="1.0"?>
<configuration xmlns="urn:microsoft-catalog:XML_Metabase_V54_0">
<MBProperty>
IIS_Global
IIS_ROOT
IIsComputer
IIsConfigObject
IIsConfigObject...
IIsLogModules
IIsCustomLogModule
IIsCustomLogModule...
IIsLogModule
IIsLogModule...
IIsMimeMap
IIsWebService
IIsWebServer
IIsFilters
IIsCertMapper
IIsWebVirtualDir
IIsWebServer
IIsFilters
IIsWebVirtualDir
IIsApplicationPools
```

```
IISApplicationPool
IIsFilters
IIsFilter
IIsCompressionScheme
IIsCompressionScheme
IIsCompressionSchemes
IIsWebInfo
IIsConfigObject
IIsWebServer
IIsWebVirtualDir
IIsWebServer
IIsWebVirtualDir
</MBProperty>
</configuration>
```

That's not very informative, but it does give you a general map of keys in the metabase and where they're located with respect to each other, so it may be useful to refer to it on occasion. Besides, it's not very hierarchical because, apart from the first two XML elements, there is no nesting of keys in the metabase.

Location Hierarchy

The real hierarchy for the metabase is the namespace of Location attributes for keys, and following is a representation of this hierarchy:

```
.
/
/LM
/LM/IISADMIN
/LM/IISADMIN/EXTENSIONS
/LM/IISADMIN/EXTENSIONS/DCOMCLSIDS
/LM/IISADMIN/PROPERTYREGISTRATION
/LM/Logging
/LM/Logging/Custom Logging
/LM/Logging/Custom Logging/Date
/LM/Logging/Custom Logging/Extended Properties
/LM/Logging/Custom Logging/Extended Properties/Bytes Received
/LM/Logging/Custom Logging/Extended Properties/Bytes Sent
/LM/Logging/Custom Logging/Extended Properties/Client IP Address
/LM/Logging/Custom Logging/Extended Properties/Cookie
/LM/Logging/Custom Logging/Extended Properties/Host
/LM/Logging/Custom Logging/Extended Properties/Method
/LM/Logging/Custom Logging/Extended Properties/Protocol Status
/LM/Logging/Custom Logging/Extended Properties/Protocol Substatus
```

```
/LM/Logging/Custom Logging/Extended Properties/Protocol Version
/LM/Logging/Custom Logging/Extended Properties/Referer
/LM/Logging/Custom Logging/Extended Properties/Server IP
/LM/Logging/Custom Logging/Extended Properties/Server Name
/LM/Logging/Custom Logging/Extended Properties/Server Port
/LM/Logging/Custom Logging/Extended Properties/Service Name
/LM/Logging/Custom Logging/Extended Properties/Time Taken
/LM/Logging/Custom Logging/Extended Properties/URI Query
/LM/Logging/Custom Logging/Extended Properties/URI Stem
/LM/Logging/Custom Logging/Extended Properties/User Agent
/LM/Logging/Custom Logging/Extended Properties/User Name
/LM/Logging/Custom Logging/Extended Properties/Win32 Status
/LM/Logging/Custom Logging/Time
/LM/Logging/Microsoft IIS Log File Format
/LM/Logging/NCSA Common Log File Format
/LM/Logging/ODBC Logging
/LM/Logging/W3C Extended Log File Format
/LM/MimeMap
/LM/W3SVC
/LM/W3SVC/1
/LM/W3SVC/1/Filters
/LM/W3SVC/1/IIsCertMapper
/LM/W3SVC/1/ROOT
/LM/W3SVC/388907640
/LM/W3SVC/388907640/filters
/LM/W3SVC/388907640/root
/LM/W3SVC/AppPools
/LM/W3SVC/AppPools/DefaultAppPool
/LM/W3SVC/Filters
/LM/W3SVC/Filters/Compression
/LM/W3SVC/Filters/Compression/deflate
/LM/W3SVC/Filters/Compression/gzip
/LM/W3SVC/Filters/Compression/Parameters
/LM/W3SVC/Info
/LM/W3SVC/Info/Templates
/LM/W3SVC/Info/Templates/Public Web Site
/LM/W3SVC/Info/Templates/Public Web Site/Root
/LM/W3SVC/Info/Templates/Secure Web Site
/LM/W3SVC/Info/Templates/Secure Web Site/Root
</MBProperty>
</configuration>
```

This representation is much easier to read than the previous one that used KeyType. Here you can clearly see where the settings for the Default Web Site and New Site are located and get a clear idea of the hierarchical nature of the metabase. The big picture of the metabase is gained by combining the two structures developed in the preceding sections—I'll leave that as an exercise for you to try.

THE METABASE SCHEMA FILE

Our discussion of the metabase schema file MBSchema.xml will be brief because modifying the schema is rarely needed and requires advanced understanding of XML syntax. The purpose of the schema is to define the properties that can be used in the metabase configuration file MetaBasd.xml and also to enforce the data type for such in-schema properties.

Like MetaBase.xml, the schema is written to memory when IIS starts and periodically flushed to disk whenever changes occur in either file. The format for the schema is different, however, and consists of a number of containers called *collections* that contain configuration objects defining metabase properties. Here is a small portion of the collection named IIsConfigObject showing a single property called AnonymousUserName (IIsConfigObject has more than 100 such properties):

```
<Collection     InternalName ="IIsConfigObject"
                MetaFlagsEx="NOTABLESCHEMAHEAPENTRY"
                MetaFlags="HASUNKNOWNSIZES | HIDDEN
                >
...
<Property       InternalName ="AnonymousUserName"
                ID="6020"
                Type="STRING"
                UserType="IIS_MD_UT_FILE"
                Attributes="INHERIT"
                MetaFlagsEx="CACHE_PROPERTY_MODIFIED"
                DefaultValue=""
                >
...
</Collection>
```

For more information on the metabase schema and how to interpret and extend it, see IIS Help.

MANAGING THE METABASE

Now that you can navigate your way around the metabase, you may think you're ready to start editing it using Notepad. But what if you make a mistake and cause the metabase to become corrupt so that IIS no longer starts? Before you start messing around with the metabase, it's important to have a rollback plan in case something goes wrong.

So, before I discuss how to modify the metabase, we'll first look at several issues regarding metabase management, including flushing the in-memory metabase to disk, backing up the metabase, and restoring the metabase from history files or backups. Next, we'll look at how to edit and repair the metabase, and I'll close this chapter with a look at metabase import and export.

Saving Changes to Disk

The in-memory metabase is flushed to disk whenever the following happens:

- IIS is stopped or restarted gracefully with IIS Manager or using net stop, iisadmin, or iisreset /stop from the command line. If, however, IIS stops suddenly and unexpectedly (for example, due to a power failure when no UPS is configured) then any metabase edits pending in-memory will be lost.

- IIS automatically restarts itself due to abnormal termination of the IIS Admin service for some reason. This depends on whether the Automatic Restart feature of IIS is enabled (which it is by default) or disabled (which occurs when you type **iisreset /disable** in a command-prompt window running locally on your IIS machine).

- Changes have been made to IIS Manager properties sheets and All Tasks | Save Configuration to Disk has been selected for the *servername* node.

- Changes have been made to IIS Manager properties sheets and sufficient time has elapsed for IIS to automatically flush the metabase to disk (see the earlier section in "Automatic Flushing" for a detailed description of how this process works).

- Iiscnfg /save is used at the command line (see the next section, "iiscnfg.vbs").

- IIS configuration information is backed up using IIS Manager or running the command iisback /backup at the command line.

"Flushing" the metabase means that IIS overwrites the MetaBase.xml and MBSchema.xml files in the \System32\Inetsrv folder with the contents of the in-memory metabase. Whenever the metabase is flushed to disk, a new pair of history files is also created in the \System32\Instsrv\History folder.

A few notes concerning IIS Help on the subject of metabase flushing:

- If IIS Manager is simply opened and then closed without any property sheet settings being modified, the metabase is flushed to disk and new history files are created. This behavior is not described in IIS Help and may be a bug.

- If IIS is stopped or restarted while metabase edits are pending in-memory but edit-while-running is disabled, IIS Help says that the pending edits will be lost. This does not seem to be the case, however, so again, it's either a bug or the Help file is wrong.

If you make a lot of changes to the metabase using IIS Manager, it may be a good idea to use Save Configuration to Disk immediately afterward to ensure these changes are persisted to disk. That way, if the power suddenly goes off and you discover your UPS battery is dead, you haven't lost your work.

iiscnfg.vbs

Iiscnfg.vbs is another WMI script that can be used to manage certain aspects of IIS from the command line. For a full discussion of IIS command-line administration, see Chapter 11, "Working from the Command Line."

Iiscnfg.vbs can perform the following tasks:

- Save configurations to disk
- Export configurations
- Import configurations
- Copy configurations

I'll discuss the first of these options here and the rest in later sections. Here's an example of how to save the configuration (flush the in-memory metabase to disk) of an IIS machine using this command:

```
C:\>iiscnfg /save
Connecting to server ...Done.
Metadata successfully flushed to disk.
```

If you're working from a remote computer, you could do the same thing like this:

```
C:\>iiscnfg /save /s 172.16.11.220
```

You could also add specific credentials, like this:

```
C:\>iiscnfg /save /s server16 /u MTIT\Administrator /p ********
```

NOTE   The message "Metadata successfully flushed to disk" doesn't necessarily mean the metabase has been flushed. If no changes are pending in the in-memory metabase, the metabase is *not* flushed even though the command responds by saying that flushing has occurred. This is not a bug but a poorly coded script that doesn't check afterward to see if a flush actually occurred.

Backing Up the Metabase

While IIS automatically creates metabase backups in the form of history files, you can also manually back up the metabase to ensure you can recover from a problem or disaster. Let's now look at some of the ways you can do this.

NOTE The following procedures back up IIS configuration information only, not website content. A good disaster recovery plan should involve regular backups of all server data including system state information. To do this, use Windows Backup or a third-party tool like Backup Exec from Veritas.

Initial Configuration Backup

When IIS is first installed, it automatically creates an initial configuration backup and saves it in the \System32\Inetsrv\MetaBack folder (Figure 14-2). You can use this backup to restore IIS to its immediate post-installation state if this is ever required.

Using IIS Manager

To manually back up the metabase using IIS Manager, right-click the *servername* node and select All Tasks and then Backup/Restore Configuration. This opens the Configuration Backup/Restore dialog box (Figure 14-3).

This dialog box shows all metabase backups that have been made to date, including:

- The automatic initial configuration backups saved in the \Inetsrv\MetaBack folder
- Manually created backups, also saved in the \Inetsrv\MetaBack folder
- History files saved in the \Inetsrv\History folder

The list of backups displayed in the Configuration Backup/Restore dialog box is therefore a merging of the contents of the History and MetaBack folders. Now click the Create Backup button and specify an informative name for your backup set (Figure 14-4). Click OK to create the new backup, which consists of an *.MD0 and *.SC0 file in the MetaBack folder.

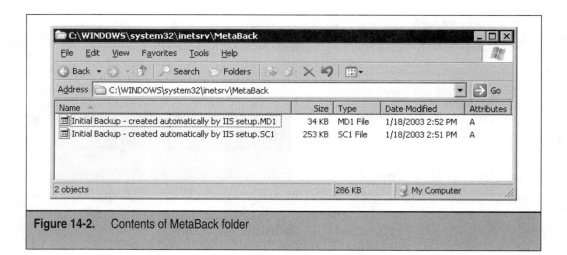

Figure 14-2. Contents of MetaBack folder

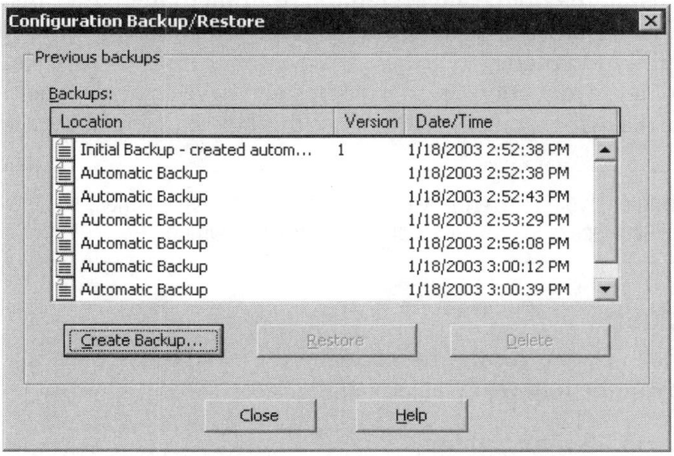

Figure 14-3.   Backing up the metabase

Note that you can also specify that your backup be encrypted using a password you supply. This is important because only backups that have been encrypted can be restored to a different machine running IIS or to the current machine after Windows Server 2003 has been reinstalled on it. The initial configuration backup created automatically when IIS is installed is *not* encrypted and is therefore no use if your server fatally crashes and

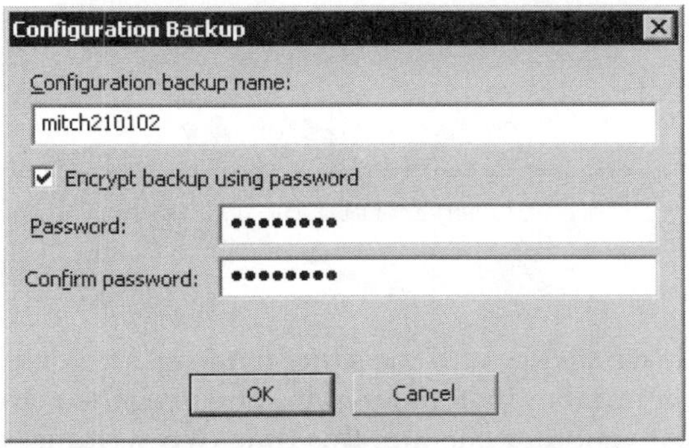

Figure 14-4.   Naming a metabase backup set

you have to reinstall the operating system on it. Immediately after installing the IIS components on your machine, you should manually create a *second* configuration backup and make sure it's encrypted.

You can also delete any unnecessary backups you have created using the Configuration Backup/Restore dialog box, but you cannot use this box to delete history files.

NOTE Creating encrypted backups takes longer than unencrypted ones, and the metabase is locked during the backup process to prevent modifications from occurring.

Using iisback.vbs

You can also back up your configuration using the WMI script iisback.vbs, which can be used to perform the following tasks:

- Backing up IIS configurations
- Restoring IIS configurations
- Deleting IIS configurations
- Listing IIS configurations

Let's try this out. First, create another backup with the same name as the previous one (imagine you're creating them both on the same day):

```
C:\>iisback /backup /b mitch210102 /e password
Connecting to server ...Done.
Backup mitch210102 version NEXT_VERSION has been CREATED.
```

To see what happened, list all the backups (note that this lists only backups in the MetaBack folder and not history files in the History folder, as in Figure 14-3):

```
C:\>iisback /list
Connecting to server ...Done.
Backup Name                          Version #      Date/Time
======================================================================
Initial Backup - created automatically by IIS setup 1 1/18/2003 2:52:38 PM
mitch210102                          0              1/21/2003 4:04:28 PM
mitch210102                          1              1/21/2003 4:14:22 PM
```

Because you made a backup with the same name as an existing backup, the new backup has its version number incremented by one over the previous backup of the same name. Now create another backup, this time overwriting version 1:

```
C:\>iisback /backup /b mitch210102 /v 1 /overwrite /e password
Connecting to server ...Done.
Backup mitch210102 version NEXT_VERSION has been CREATED.
```

Verify the result:

```
C:\>iisback /list
Connecting to server ...Done.
Backup Name                              Version #      Date/Time
=======================================================================
Initial Backup - created automatically by IIS setup 1 1/18/2003 2:52:38 PM
mitch210102                          0               1/21/2003 4:04:28 PM
mitch210102                          1               1/21/2003 4:15:41 PM
```

Note that the timestamp for mitch210102 version 1 has changed. Now delete this backup:

```
C:\>iisback /delete /b mitch210102 /v 1
Connecting to server ...Done.
Backup mitch210102 version 1 has been DELETED.
```

And verify:

```
C:\>iisback /list
Connecting to server ...Done.
Backup Name                              Version #      Date/Time
=======================================================================
Initial Backup - created automatically by IIS setup 1 1/18/2003 2:52:38 PM
mitch210102                          0               1/21/2003 4:04:28 PM
```

TIP You can also use ADSI or WMI to programmatically back up IIS configurations and Scheduled Tasks to automate running iisback.vbs commands.

Restoring the Metabase

You have a choice of two ways of restoring configuration information:

- **Restoring from backup files** This method is more powerful as you can restore to a different machine or to the same machine after reinstalling Windows Server 2003. However, you must ensure that your backup is encrypted in order to perform a restore on anything other than the current installation on your IIS machine.

- **Restoring from history files** This method allows you to restore your configuration only to the same IIS machine. If you reinstall Windows Server 2003 on your IIS machine, you will not be able to restore history files created before the reinstallation.

I'll focus first on restoring configurations to the same machine and then at how to restore them to different machines later in this chapter in the section entitled "Exporting the Metabase."

NOTE Restoring a backup created on an earlier version of IIS isn't supported.

Restoring from Backup Files

To restore from backup files using IIS Manager, follow these steps:

1. Create a new website called Test Site on your IIS machine in the usual way.
2. Create a backup called Test Backup of your configuration using IIS Manager.
3. Delete the website you just created.
4. Save your configuration to disk to make sure that all trace of Test Site is removed from the metabase.
5. Restore your configuration from the backup you created by right-clicking the *servername* node in IIS Manager and selecting All Tasks | Backup/Restore Configuration.
6. Select the backup you created in step 2 and click Restore.
7. Click Yes and wait while IIS stops and configuration information is restored from the backup files. When IIS restarts, you'll be informed of the result.
8. Use IIS Manager to verify that Test Site has been restored.

Now do the same thing with iisback.vbs. Because you already have Test Site on your machine, you can omit the preceding first step and proceed as follows:

1. Create a backup called Another Test Backup of your configuration using iisback /backup as described in the preceding section.
2. Delete Test Site from your machine.
3. Save your configuration to disk.
4. Restore your configuration from your backup by typing the following at a command-prompt window on the IIS machine:

```
iisback /restore /b "Another Test Backup"
```

5. Refresh IIS Manager to verify that Test Site has been restored.

Restoring from History Files

Now you'll try a similar walkthrough, but this time you'll restore your configuration from a history file on your system. First, use IIS Manager to perform the restore:

1. Delete Test Site from your system.

2. Save your configuration to disk to flush the metabase to disk.

3. Right-click the *servername* node in IIS Manager and select All Tasks | Backup/Restore Configuration.

4. Select the *second most recent* history file by reviewing the timestamps of files named Automatic Backup. Why the second most recent file? Because the most recent one was created when you saved your configuration to disk, and this was done *after* you deleted Test Site!

5. Click Yes and wait while IIS stops and configuration information is restored from the backup files. When IIS restarts, you'll be informed of the result.

6. Refresh IIS Manager and verify that Test Site has been restored.

What if you can't use IIS Manager to restore from a history file? For example, if you edit the metabase manually using Notepad and make an error in XML syntax that results in metabase corruption, IIS Manager may not be able to enumerate the metabase and hence will not be able to start. If you don't have any recent backups in the \MetaBack folder to restore from, you may think you're out of luck because the iisback /restore command cannot be used to restore a history file, only a backup file. Fortunately, however, there is a procedure you can follow to restore the metabase from a history file, even when IIS Manager won't start:

1. Save your configuration to disk to create a history file with information about Test Site. Then delete Test Site with IIS Manager and save your configuration to disk again to flush the metabase.

2. Open a command prompt on your server and type **iisreset /stop** to stop all IIS services.

3. Type **cd C:\Windows\System32\Inetsrv** to change your current directory and then make backup copies of your current metabase files with **copy MetaBase.xml MetaBase.old** and **copy MBSchema.xml MBSchema.old**, just in case something else goes wrong.

4. Type **cd History** to make the \History folder your current directory, and type **dir** to display the history files.

5. Determine which pair of history files you want to restore for the metabase configuration and schema, for example, using the **find** or **findstr** commands to search for the string "Test Site" within the history files.

6. Copy and overwrite the pair of history files you select over the schema files using the copy command, for example,

```
copy /y MetaBase_0000000081_0000000000.xml ..\MetaBase.xml
copy /y MBSchema_0000000081_0000000000.xml ..\MBSchema.xml
```

7. Type **iisreset /start** to restart all IIS services. Open IIS Manager and verify that Test Site has been restored.

Editing the Metabase

Before editing the metabase directly, make sure that you back up your IIS configuration using the methods described in the previous sections. There are two ways you can edit the metabase manually in IIS 6:

- **Stop all IIS services first**   This was the approach used in previous versions of IIS, but it has the disadvantage of your having to disconnect users from your server and take the server offline while you make your changes to the metabase.

- **Enable edit-while-running**   Also called direct metabase edit, this feature lets you make changes to the metabase while IIS services are still running. This new method increases the availability of IIS by reducing downtime for maintenance.

I'll focus in this section on the direct metabase edit approach.

NOTE   Even if you enable edit-while-running on your IIS machine, you can't directly edit the MBSchema.xml file using a text editor. You can only edit the MBSchema.xml file programmatically using ADSI, and only when IIS is stopped.

Enabling Direct Metabase Edit

Direct metabase edit is disabled by default on IIS and can be enabled by opening the properties sheet for the *servername* node and selecting the appropriate check box (Figure 14-5).

You can also enable direct metabase edit from the command line as follows:

1. Open a command prompt on the server and type **iisreset /stop** to stop all IIS services on the machine.

2. Open the MetaBase/xml file using Notepad or some other text editor, search for the EnableEditWhileRunning property, and change the value of this property from 0 to 1.

3. Save your changes and type **iisreset /start** from the command line.

NOTE   For the direct metabase edit feature to work, the history feature must be enabled on IIS and the MaxHistoryFiles property be set to at least 10. By default the history feature is enabled and MaxHistoryFiles has the value 10.

How Direct Metabase Edit Works

When direct metabase edit is enabled, you can open the MetaBase.xml file in the \Inetsrv folder and edit it directly using Notepad, or you can programmatically modify the file

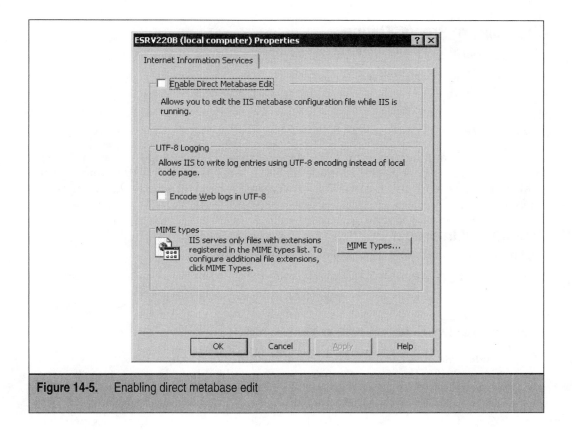

Figure 14-5.   Enabling direct metabase edit

using scripts. When using Notepad, for example, you would typically make a number of changes and then save the file to write the changes to MetaBase.xml. When you save the file, the Windows file change notification service detects that the MetaBase.xml file has changed on disk. A short time later, IIS copies the MetaBase.xml file to the in-memory metabase, so there's a slight delay between modifying the metabase on disk and seeing the changes take effect. The response time of the file change notification service is independent of how many changes have been made to the file.

Examples of Editing the Metabase

Let's now try editing the metabase directly and test the result. First, you'll make some changes properly, and then I'll have you deliberately make some mistakes and see what that effect is. Be sure to make backups of your metabase before each walkthrough so you can recover afterward if something goes wrong.

Examples of Proper Editing

Open MetaBase.xml using Notepad and change the line

```
ServerComment="Default Web Site"
```

to

```
ServerComment="Default Webbie Site"
```

Save the file and quickly refresh IIS Manager to see if the change has taken effect. You should see the change almost immediately. If you check the \History folder, you will see that a new history file pair was also created when you saved your changes to Metabase.xml.

Example of Improper Editing

Open MetaBase.xml using Notepad and change the line

```
ServerComment="Default Webbie Site"
```

to

```
ServerComment=Default Webbie Site
```

Removing the quotes ruins the syntax of the XML for this line. When you save your changes, refresh IIS Manager and you will see that nothing has changed. This is because improper XML syntax makes the modified MetaBase.xml file invalid, and as a result IIS automatically restores MetaBase.xml from the most recent history file. To verify this, close Notepad (do not click F5 to refresh Notepad—it doesn't work) and reopen the MetaBase.xml file in Notepad, and you'll see that the line again reads

```
ServerComment="Default Webbie Site"
```

If you check the \History file, you'll see a file named MetaBaseError_0000000000.xml. If you open this file in Notepad, you'll find the line

```
ServerComment=Default Webbie Site
```

The metabase error file contains the bad version of the MetaBase.xml file you just created. By comparing the error file with the current MetaBase.xml file using the comp command, you can retrace your steps and determine what went wrong.

An even quicker way of finding out what went wrong is by reviewing event logs on the server. Open the Event Viewer console from Administrative Tools and display the contents of the System Log (Figure 14-6).

Note the three errors whose source is IIS Config—these are generated by the IIS Admin service trying to parse the metabase and write the changes to the in-memory metabase. Open the first of these errors to view its event properties (Figure 14-7). Note the detailed explanation of the problem.

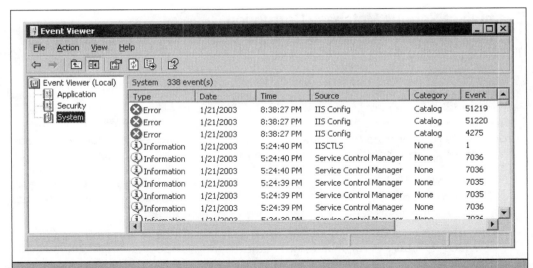

Figure 14-6. Metabase errors in Event Viewer

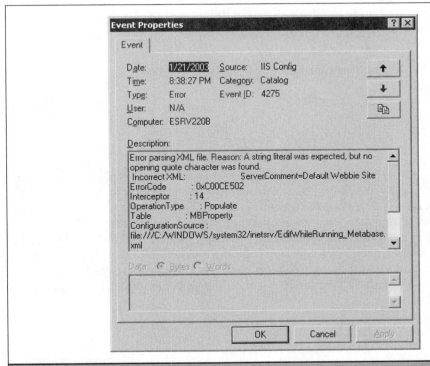

Figure 14-7. Details of a metabase error event

Example of Serious Metabase Corruption

Let's really try to wreck the metabase. Open the MetaBase.xml file using Notepad and delete the following line:

```
</IIS_Global>
```

What you've done here is wreck the XML of the metabase by deleting the closing tag for the IIS_Global key. This is fairly serious, but, interestingly enough, IIS is able to automatically recover from this problem. If you immediately open the \Inetsrv folder in Windows Explorer, you'll probably see two things:

- A file named EditWhileRunning_Metabase.xml, which is generated by IIS during the process of repairing the XML syntax of the metabase configuration file and which vanishes as soon as the repair process is complete.

- A file named something like IIS Config_0000000001.log or something similar, which contains a permanent record of the diagnosis and repair process performed by IIS.

Once the EditWhileRunning_Metabase.xml file disappears, open MetaBase.xml in Notepad and you should see that the </IIS_Global> tag has been restored.

Now try something more drastic. Delete the following lines from MetaBase.xml and save the changes:

```
<IIsComputer     Location ="/LM"
        EnableEditWhileRunning="1"
        EnableHistory="1"
        MaxBandwidth="4294967295"
        MaxHistoryFiles="10"
    >
</IIsComputer>
```

This is too much metabase corruption for the automatic repair process to handle. If you refresh IIS Manager, you'll find that your server is in a fatal error state (Figure 14-8).

The solution here is to restore the metabase manually from your backup files in the \MetaBack folder. First, open a command prompt and type **iisreset /stop**. Then open the \Inetsrv folder in Windows Explorer and rename MetaBase.xml as MetaBase.bad. Switch to the \Inetsrv\MetaBack folder and copy the most recent *.MD0 file to \Inetsrv and rename it MetaBase.xml. Return to your command-prompt window and type **iisreset /start**. Now open IIS Manager, and it should connect to your server and display your sites as expected.

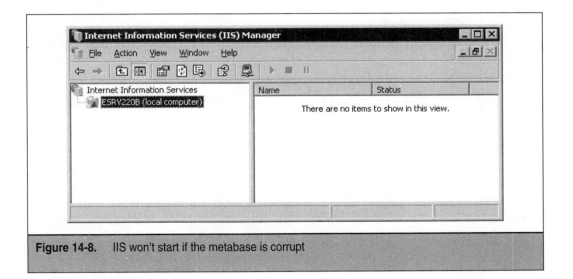

Figure 14-8. IIS won't start if the metabase is corrupt

Exporting the Metabase

My final topics are how to export and import portions of the metabase. Exporting lets you save portions of the metabase such as the configuration info for a particular website or virtual directory (or even the configuration of all websites on your machine) as an XML file that can later be imported back into your server or onto another Windows Server 2003 machine with IIS installed. The export feature can also create a metabase template file that will copy or "clone" website configurations to multiple IIS machines so they all have the same settings.

Note that metabase export is not the same as metabase backup and should not be used to replace proper backups of the metabase. The differences are as follows:

- Metabase export files do not include encrypted properties present in metabase backup files.
- Metabase export can only be used to back up the metabase configuration file and not the metabase schema file.

There are two ways to export metabase information to a file:

- Using IIS Manager
- Using the iiscnfg.vbs script

Using IIS Manager

First, you'll use IIS Manager to export the configuration of the Default Web Site (actually the Default Webbie Site, if you've been performing the walkthroughs in this chapter). Do the following:

1. Right-click the Default Webbie Site and select All Tasks | Save Configuration to a File.

2. Specify a name for your export file and select the encryption option so you can later try importing the file into a different IIS 6 machine (Figure 14-9).

3. Click OK

Find your export file in the \Inetsrv folder and open it using Notepad. Here's a condensed version of what it should look like, replacing properties of keys with ellipses:

```
<?xml version ="1.0"?>
<configuration xmlns="urn:microsoft-catalog:XML_Metabase_V54_0">
<MBProperty>
<IIS_Global...>
</IIS_Global>
<IIsWebServer...>
</IIsWebServer>
<IIsFilters...>
</IIsFilters>
<IIsCertMapper...>
</IIsCertMapper>
<IIsWebVirtualDir...>
</IIsWebVirtualDir>
<IIsInheritedProperties...>
</IIsInheritedProperties>
</MBProperty>
</configuration>
```

Using iiscnfg.vbs

Now you'll create another export file for the Default Webbie Site, but this time you'll use the iiscnfg.vbs script to perform the action from the command line. Here's an example of what your command-line session might look like:

```
C:\>iiscnfg /export /f export_test_2.xml /sp /lm/w3svc/1 /inherited
/children
Connecting to server ...Done.
Configuration exported from /lm/w3svc/1 to file export_test_2.xml.
```

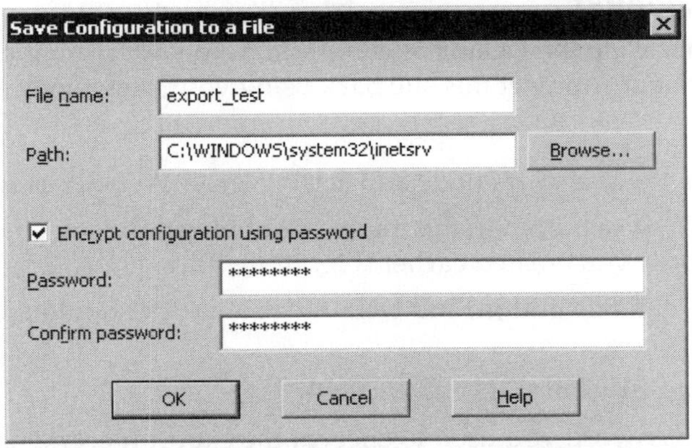

Figure 14-9.   Exporting a website configuration using IIS Manager

The syntax of this command is as follows:

- /f *filename*.xml is the name of the export file, which is saved by default in the root of the C: drive unless a path is explicitly specified.

- /sp *location* specifies the topmost metabase node to export. /lm/w3svc/1 is the location of the Default Web Site (or, here, the "Default Webbie Site") in the metabase hierarchy.

- /inherited specifies that properties inherited by the location node from its parent node should explicitly be included in the export file.

- /children specifies that subkeys should be recursively added to the export file.

TIP   To export the entire configuration of an IIS machine, specify location as / (a slash) in the preceding command.

Importing the Metabase

Now you can try importing your first export file. You'll import it first to the same machine and then later to a different machine, which is more complicated.

To the Same Machine

Open IIS Manager, delete the Default Webbie Site from your machine, and save your configuration to disk. To import this site back using your previously created export file, do the following:

1. Right-click the Web Sites node and select New | Web Site (From File).
2. Click the Browse button in the Import Configuration dialog box, and select the export file you created earlier (Figure 14-10).
3. Click the Read File button, and Default Webbie Site should appear in the Location listbox.
4. Select Default Webbie Site and click OK.
5. Enter the password you used to encrypt the export file, and click OK.
6. The Default Webbie Site should appear in IIS Manager in a stopped state. Start it and test it by browsing http://localhost.

Now repeat the preceding walkthrough using the iiscnfg.vbs script instead of IIS Manager. Delete the Default Webbie Site again, save your configuration to disk, open a command prompt and type:

```
C:\>iiscnfg /import /f C:\export_test_2.xml /sp /lm/w3svc/1 /dp /lm/w3svc/1
/children /inherited
Connecting to server ...Done.
Configuration imported from /lm/w3svc/1 in file
C:\export_test_2.xml to /lm/w3svc/1 in the Metabase.
```

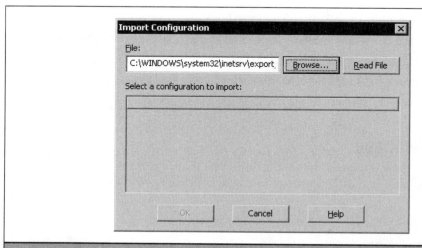

Figure 14-10.   Importing a previously exported configuration file

Refresh IIS Manger, and note that this time the Default Webbie Site is restored and already started.

TIP The iiscnfg /import command has some additional options such as /merge that can be used for advanced tasks like merging a virtual directory with a website or importing good metabase data over corrupt or damaged data. See IIS Help for more info on these options.

To Another Machine

Before you can import a configuration file exported from one IIS 6 machine into another, you have to do a little extra work first. Specifically, you need to:

- Change or remove any machine-specific information from the export file.

- Create any necessary folders on the target machine, for example, the home directories for each website being imported.

Examples of machine-specific information you may have to modify or delete include

- Modifying any file system paths in metabase properties such as Path="c:\inetpub\wwwroot" if these are different on the target machine.

- Deleting any properties referencing IUSR or IWAM accounts (they will be different on the target computer).

- Deleting any AdminACL properties (they are machine specific and cannot be hand modified).

- Deleting any properties specifying passwords (they are machine specific and cannot be hand modified).

Copying Configurations

Another useful command to explore is iiscnfg /copy, which can be used to copy the entire metabase configuration and the schema files from one IIS 6 machine to another in a single step. (This is particularly useful for creating web server farms in enterprise environments by cloning a fully configured IIS machine.) While this command removes machine-specific information from the metabase, unfortunately it doesn't adjust directory paths that might need modifying, so you may still need to manually edit the metabase on the target machine afterward to make things work. The iiscnfg /copy command replaces IISSync.vbs and IISRepl.vbs, which were used for a similar purpose in IIS 5.

Also, the IIS 6 Migration Tool can be used to copy entire IIS configurations with website content from one IIS 6 machine to another, or from earlier IIS 4 or IIS 5 machines to IIS 6. This tool is currently in Beta 1 version at the time of writing and should be available soon from Microsoft.

Try making the necessary changes to your export file and then importing it into another IIS 6 machine on which the Default Web Site has been deleted to see if you can successfully re-create the Default Webbie Site on that machine. Use either IIS Manager or iiscnfg.vbs to import the file, and then test the final result to make sure everything works.

CHECKLIST: MANAGING THE METABASE

Check off each of the following administrative tasks involving the metabase after you become familiar with how to perform them:

- ☐ Modifying the metabase using IIS Manager.
- ☐ Modifying the metabase using a text editor such as Notepad.
- ☐ Forcing pending in-memory metabase updates to be flushed to disk using IIS Manager.
- ☐ Forcing pending in-memory metabase updates to be flushed to disk using iiscnfg /save.
- ☐ Backing up the metabase using IIS Manager.
- ☐ Backing up the metabase using iisback /backup.
- ☐ Restoring the metabase using IIS Manager.
- ☐ Restoring the metabase from backup files using IIS Manager.
- ☐ Restoring the metabase from backup files using iisback /restore.
- ☐ Restoring the metabase from history files using IIS Manager.
- ☐ Restoring the metabase from history files manually from the command line.
- ☐ Enabling the direct metabase edit feature.
- ☐ Exporting the metabase using IIS Manager.
- ☐ Exporting the metabase using iiscnfg /export.
- ☐ Importing the metabase using IIS Manager.
- ☐ Importing the metabase using iiscnfg /export.
- ☐ Copying metabase configuration and schema using iiscnfg /copy.

CHAPTER 15

SMTP and NNTP

W hile the primary purpose of IIS is to provide a platform for deploying web applications and hosting websites, IIS also includes other application-layer TCP/IP services including the Simple Mail Transfer Protocol (SMTP) and Network News Transfer Protocol (NNTP) services. These two services are the focus of this chapter.

THE SMTP SERVICE

The SMTP service is included as a component of IIS for three basic purposes:

- To enable IIS machines to function as RFC 821/822–compliant SMTP hosts that can be used by service providers for forwarding e-mail across the Internet. While most service providers rely heavily on Sendmail, the standard SMTP server application for UNIX/Linux platforms, IIS is a viable alternative to Sendmail for this purpose.

- To enable an IIS machine running SMTP to act as a buffer between a corporate e-mail server running Microsoft Exchange and a Sendmail host at the company's ISP. This provides an extra layer of security to protect Exchange servers from attack and misuse.

- To provide ASP developers with a tool for sending e-mail from their applications, for example, in response to a user submitting a form on a web page.

The SMTP service is thus designed for sending outgoing mail and forwarding incoming mail to mail servers or other SMTP hosts. The SMTP service is *not* designed to handle incoming mail and provide mailboxes so users can receive messages. Incoming mail is generally handled by mail servers like Microsoft Exchange that support the POP3 and IMAP protocols for message delivery and storage.

Another way of saying this is that SMTP is a mail forwarding protocol, not a mail delivery protocol. SMTP can only be used to forward mail from one SMTP host to another and cannot deliver mail directly to a client. Mail clients like Outlook Express use SMTP for sending mail and POP3 (or IMAP) for receiving mail.

NOTE Windows Server 2003 now includes a POP3 service that can be used for handling incoming mail and setting up mailboxes for users. The POP3 service is *not* a component of IIS 6, however, but a separate component of Windows Server 2003, so it's not covered in this book. For information on how to set up and manage POP3, use the Help and Support Center on your server.

Installing the SMTP and NNTP Services

To use IIS as an SMTP host, you need to install the SMTP service component of IIS first, as it is not installed by default on Standard or Enterprise Editions of Windows Server 2003 (SMTP is installed by default on Web Edition, however).

To install the SMTP and NNTP services, first insert your Windows Server 2003 product CD-ROM into your CD-ROM drive. Then click Start, select Control Panel, and open Add Or Remove Programs. Click the Add/Remove Windows Components button, select Application Server, click Details, select Internet Information Services (IIS), click Details again, and select the check boxes for SMTP Service and NNTP Service. Click OK several times to return to the wizard, and the components will be installed.

To verify your installation, open IIS Manager and make sure you have nodes for Default SMTP Virtual Server and Default NNTP Virtual Server in the console tree (Figure 15-1). You can use IIS Manager to perform the following SMTP administration tasks:

- Create and configure SMTP virtual servers and start, stop, and pause them independent of one another.
- Configure connection, delivery, message, security, authentication, relay, and other settings for SMTP virtual servers.
- Create and configure new SMTP alias and remote domains.
- Display current sessions and terminate selected (or all) connections.

Message Store Directory Structure

When the SMPT service is installed on IIS, a directory structure is created with root folder \Inetpub\Mailroot on the local machine. This directory structure represents the message store for the service and consists of the following folders:

- **Badmail**   Messages that can't be delivered to their intended recipients after a configured number of attempts and that can't be returned to the sender are

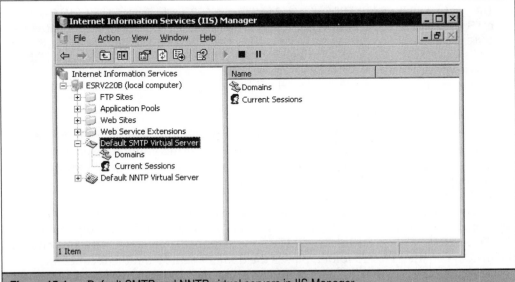

Figure 15-1.   Default SMTP and NNTP virtual servers in IIS Manager

placed in this folder so they can be examined later by an administrator to determine what went wrong.

- **Drop**   All incoming messages addressed to local domains managed by the SMTP service are "dropped" into this folder regardless of their intended recipient, and there they wait. Note that the SMTP service does not have individual mailboxes for users, only a catch-all \Drop folder instead. If you need mailboxes for users, install the POP3 component of Windows Server 2003 or use a full-featured messaging platform like Microsoft Exchange.

- **Pickup**   Messages placed in this folder are "picked up" by the SMTP service and processed as outbound messages. For example, you can create a message by hand using Notepad, including the necessary SMTP message headers addressing it, and then place it in this directory, and the SMTP service will try to deliver it to its intended recipient. Alternatively, you could write an application that creates a message and places it in this directory for delivery. If the destination domain in the To: header of the message is a local domain managed by the SMTP service, the message is moved to the \Drop folder.

- **Queue**   If a message in the \Pickup folder cannot be delivered immediately because of some reason such as the connection to the remote host being down or busy, the message is moved to the \Queue folder, where the SMTP service tries to deliver it again at regular intervals.

- **Mailbox, Route, and SortTemp**   Relics of the code base for the legacy Microsoft Commercial Internet System (MCIS), these folders are actually not used in IIS 6 and can be deleted if desired.

TIP   If you are a developer and want to mail-enable your ASP application to use the SMTP service of IIS, consider using Collaboration Data Objects for Windows 2000 (CDOSYS), which replaces the earlier Collaboration Data Objects for Windows NT Server (CDONTS) library. CDONTS was used for mail-enabling applications in IIS 4 and was supported for backward compatibility reasons in IIS 5, but is no longer supported in Windows Server 2003.

How Mail Is Processed

The SMTP service (smtpsvc.dll) runs in-process within the host main IIS process Inetinfo.exe and continually monitors TCP port 25 for incoming messages and the \Pickup directory for outgoing messages. When a message comes in addressed to a user belonging to a local domain managed by the SMTP service, the message is placed in the \Drop folder and delivery is done.

To send an outgoing message to a user belonging to some other DNS domain, an ASP application running on IIS can use CDOSYS to create and place the outgoing message in the \Pickup folder. The SMTP service immediately detects the presence of the message in the \Pickup folder, parses the domain name from the recipient's e-mail address (for example, the mtit.com in mitch@mtit.com), and then performs a DNS lookup using TCP port 53 on the configured name server to determine the name of the SMTP host that handles mail for the remote domain. This is done by looking up the MX record for the remote domain.

Once the fully qualified domain name (FQDN) of the remote SMTP host has been identified (for example, smtp.mtit.com), the SMTP service tries to establish a connection with the remote host on TCP port 25, the standard SMTP communication port for message transfer. Depending on how the remote host is configured, credentials may need to be provided to establish the connection and transfer the message.

If the remote host accepts the connection attempt, the message is transferred to the remote host, which forwards it to the POP3 or IMAP server where the recipient's mailbox resides. The next time the recipient opens their mail client program (such as Outlook Express or Eudora), the client connects to the POP3/IMAP server and downloads the message.

If the remote host rejects the connection attempt, the SMTP service tries to return a nondelivery report (NDR) to its original sender, for example, a mail-enabled application running on the IIS machine. If the service is unable to return the message to its original sender, the message is moved to the \Badmail directory and can be retrieved there later by the administrator to troubleshoot the delivery problem.

If the SMTP service is unable to communicate with the remote SMTP host, the message is placed in the \Queue folder, where it waits for a configurable interval of time while the service periodically tries to send the message. If the maximum time limit is exceeded, the service tries to return the message to the sender with an NDR. If it can't return the NDR to the sender after a configurable time interval, the message is moved to the \Badmail folder.

As an alternative to direct delivery to the SMTP host managing the intended recipient's DNS domain, the SMTP service can be configured to forward the message to an intermediate host called an *SMTP relay*. The relay host receives the message forwarded from the SMTP service, and in turn forwards it to the destination host (or to another relay for further forwarding).

Configuring the Default SMTP Virtual Server

When the SMTP service is installed, a Default SMTP Virtual Server is created that can immediately be used for sending mail from e-mail clients like Outlook Express and receiving mail from other SMTP hosts such as Sendmail hosts on the Internet. You can create additional SMTP virtual servers, but usually the default is sufficient and can be renamed if desired.

Like FTP sites, discussed in Chapter 9, "Creating and Configuring FTP Sites," SMTP virtual servers are uniquely identified by their IP address and port number. If you want to add additional SMTP virtual servers to your IIS machine, you should first bind additional IP addresses to your network interface. In theory, you could have two virtual servers with the same address on the same machine if they had different port numbers, but in reality all virtual servers need to use the same port 25, or they won't be able to send or receive mail with other SMTP hosts.

Although the default settings for the Default SMTP Virtual Server may suffice for some environments, it's important to understand the various configuration settings for reasons of security, reliability, and performance. To configure these settings, right-click the Default SMTP Virtual Server node in IIS Manager and select Properties. The next several sections examine various aspects of configuring SMTP on your IIS machine.

General Tasks

There are several general tasks you should perform to begin configuring the Default SMTP Virtual Server. These tasks are performed using the General tab of the Default SMTP Virtual Server properties sheet (Figure 15-2):

- **IP Address**   By default, a virtual server (or server, as I'll call them from now on) is configured to listen on port 25 to all unassigned IP addresses on the machine. If your machine has two IP addresses, 172.16.11.220 and 172.16.11 221, and a remote host attempts to establish a connection on port 25 with either of these addresses, the server will respond. If you have a larger pool of addresses on your server and you only want your SMTP server to listen to a few of them, change the All Unassigned setting to a specific address, click Advanced, and specify other addresses the server should use to assign your server multiple identities.

- **Enable Logging**   IIS can log SMTP commands received from other SMTP hosts trying to communicate with it. It's a good idea to do this for maintenance and troubleshooting reasons. SMTP logging works the same way web logging does. In fact, when logging is enabled, SMTP writes events to the same log files used by the WWW and FTP services (unless those services have been configured to use a different logging format than SMTP uses). The only difference is that if W3C Extended Log File Format is selected, then initially no log options are selected and you have to specify which options to log using the Advanced tab on the Logging Properties sheet. For more information on how to enable and configure IIS logging, see Chapter 13, "Maintenance and Troubleshooting."

Incoming Connections

Incoming connections are those established when a remote SMTP host tries to connect to your SMTP server to send a message to your server. There are two settings you can configure on the General tab (see Figure 15-2 again) to control how incoming connections are managed by servers:

- **Limit Number of Connections To**   By default SMTP is configured to accept an unlimited number of simultaneous inbound connections from other hosts, but this is not always a good idea because it leaves your server susceptible to a denial-of-service (DoS) attack. This occurs when an attacker continually attempts to establish new connections with your server until no more TCP ports are available, resulting in legitimate clients being unable to access services on your machine. By limiting the number of connections to a value sufficient for the ordinary needs of your server, you can lessen the effect of this type of attack.

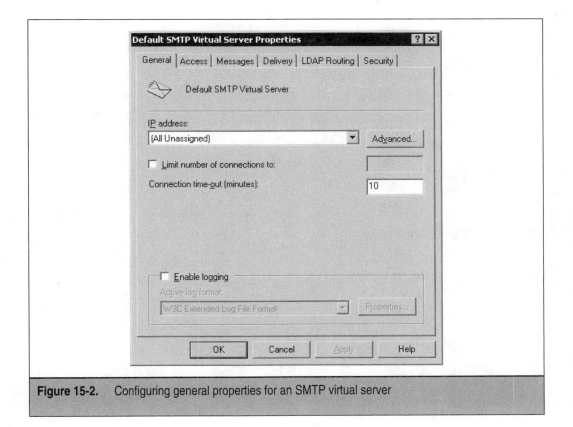

Figure 15-2.   Configuring general properties for an SMTP virtual server

- **Connection Timeout**   By default, if a remote host establishes a connection with a server and then generates no activity for 10 minutes, the connection is automatically terminated by the server. This timeout value can be lowered to further lessen the effects of a DoS attack.

Outgoing Connections

Outgoing connections are those established when your SMTP server tries to connect to a remote SMTP host to send mail to that host. Administrators familiar with the SMPT service in IIS 5 will notice immediately that the connection settings have changed their location in this version of IIS. In the previous version, a Connection button on the General tab opened a dialog box that let you configure *both* incoming and outgoing connections. In IIS 6, however, the connection settings on the General tab are for configuring incoming connections *only* (though there is no label to that effect, which is confusing), while outgoing connections are configured using the Outbound Connections button on the Delivery tab (Figure 15-3).

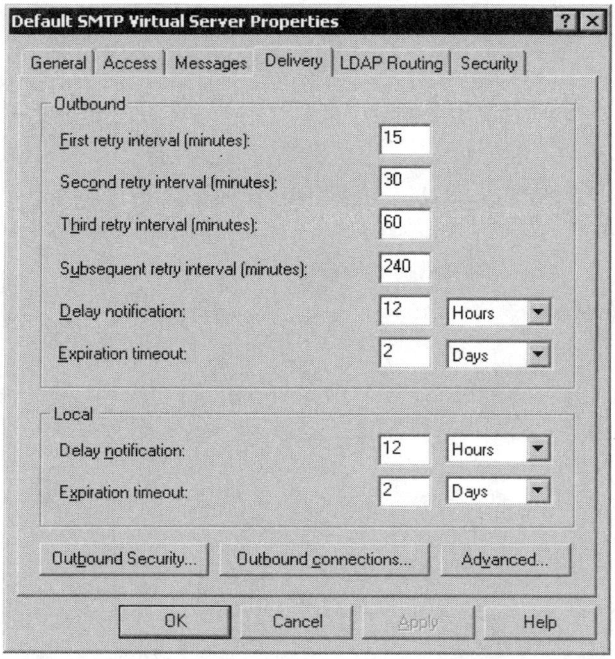

Figure 15-3. Delivery tab on properties sheet

Configuring outgoing connections is slightly more complicated than inbound ones. When you click the Outbound Connections button, an Outbound Connections dialog box appears (Figure 15-4) allowing you to configure the following settings:

- **Limit Number of Connections To**   This specifies the total number of simultaneous outbound connections that the server can establish with remote hosts, regardless of their domain. The default limit is 1000 outbound connections, but this can be set to Unlimited by clearing the check box.

- **Timeout**   When a connection is idle for the indicated time interval, it is terminated to free up network resources. The default timeout interval is 10 minutes, just as for inbound connections.

- **Limit Number of Connections per Domain**   By default, the maximum number of simultaneous connections SMTP can establish with a single remote domain for sending messages is 100 connections. If you have multiple remote domains configured on your server, this setting, if configured properly, prevents any one domain from being starved of resources by other domains.

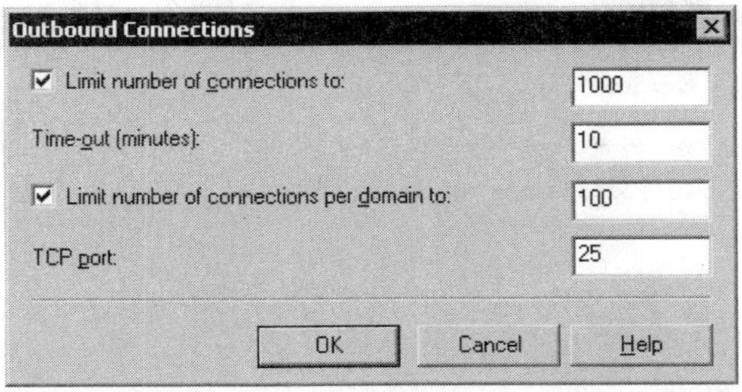

Figure 15-4. Configuring outbound connections

- **TCP Port** As I've mentioned, the default port for establishing outgoing connections is port 25, and this is almost always sufficient, unless you are trying to operate some kind of "stealth" SMTP server network using nonstandard ports for communicating. If you want your server to communicate with other SMTP hosts on the Internet, however, make sure you leave this set to port 25.

Security and Authentication

Ensuring the secure operation of your SMTP server is essential in today's high-risk networking environment, and there are a number of configuration settings relating to security and authentication. Most security settings are on the Access tab (Figure 15-5).

The first security setting you can configure is the authentication method your server will require when remote hosts try to establish incoming connections with your server. To configure authentication for incoming connections, click the Authentication button on the Access tab. This opens the Authentication properties sheet, which allows you to specify which methods will authenticate incoming connections (Figure 15-6).

NOTE Again, there is no label for this button specifically identifying that it applies to incoming connections as opposed to outbound ones, which can be confusing.

There are three authentication methods supported for inbound connections, whether from clients like Outlook Express trying to send mail through your server or from remote SMTP hosts trying to deliver mail to or relay mail through your server. These authentication methods are the same as their counterparts for the WWW Service and were discussed in detail in Chapter 10, "Securing IIS." You can enable one, two, or all three of these authentication methods.

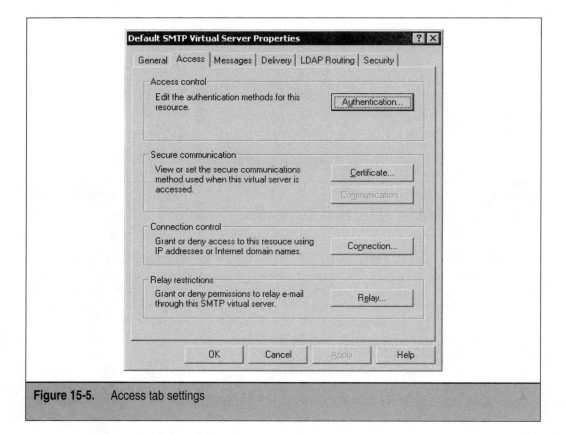

Figure 15-5.   Access tab settings

The three methods supported by SMTP for inbound connections are

*   **Anonymous Access**   Selecting this method essentially disables authentication and allows anyone to send mail to your server. You might think you should disable this method to prevent this from happening; but if your server is connected to the Internet, you should leave it enabled so that SMTP hosts around the world can send mail to your server. If anonymous access is not enabled, these SMTP hosts will have no idea what credentials you require and will be unable to forward mail to your server. So leave anonymous access enabled for inbound connections, unless your server is used for internal company use only.

*   **Basic Authentication**   This method transfers credentials in clear text, which is not secure. However, the advantage of using Basic Authentication is that it is an Internet standard that is supported by the widest number of clients. To make Basic Authentication secure, you can require TLS encryption to be used for

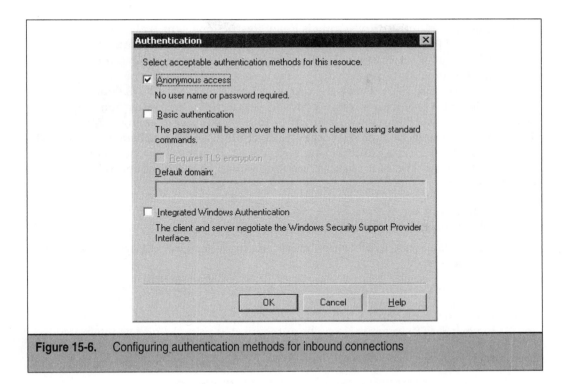

Figure 15-6. Configuring authentication methods for inbound connections

encrypting the connection. TLS is a standardized version of SSL and is almost identical to SSL, which I discussed in Chapter 10. If you plan to enable Basic Authentication, consider enabling TLS as well. However, you'll first have to install a certificate on your server to create the key pair necessary for TLS to work. To install a certificate, click the Certificate button on the Access tab and follow the prompts of the wizard.

- **Integrated Windows Authentication** This method requires incoming connections to provide a Windows account name and password to be authenticated. If your SMTP server will be used for sending mail to recipients on the Internet, you should enable this authentication method to ensure that only your users can access the server for sending mail.

Another security setting you can configure is Connection Control (see Figure 15-5 again), which lets you specify which computers (SMTP clients such as Outlook Express and/or remote SMTP hosts) are allowed to access your server. These computers can be specified by IP address, network ID and subnet mask, or DNS domain name, and you can either allow or deny access based on any of these methods. This feature is similar in operation to the one for the WWW Service discussed in Chapter 10.

Another important security setting is Relay Restrictions, which allows or denies computers (SMTP clients and/or remote SMTP hosts) the ability to use your server as an SMTP relay for forwarding mail to users in domains other than your own. By default, the server is configured to deny relay access to all hosts except those that are authenticated (Figure 15-7). This is the proper setting because it allows your users' Outlook clients to relay mail through your server to recipients in other domains but prevents remote SMTP hosts from doing the same. By denying relaying to remote SMTP hosts, you prevent malicious users from sending spam (unsolicited commercial e-mail) through your server and causing recipients to blame you for this activity.

The best combination of authentication for inbound connections and relay restrictions is to:

- Enable both anonymous access and Windows Integrated Authentication for inbound connections.

- Deny relay access to all computers except those that are properly authenticated by your server.

When your server is configured this way, here's what happens:

- Users on your company network can use Outlook or Outlook Express to connect to your SMTP server, they can be authenticated using Windows Integrated

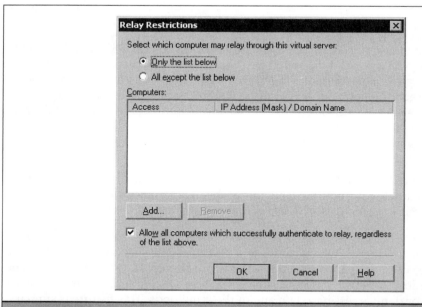

Figure 15-7.   Configuring relay restrictions

Authentication, and their messages are then relayed to recipients in a remote domain.

- SMTP hosts on the Internet trying to send mail to your users are "authenticated" using anonymous access (in reality, no authentication occurs), and the mail is delivered to your SMTP server and "popped" into users' mailboxes on your POP3 server.

- SMTP hosts trying to relay spam through your server to users in other domains are prevented from doing so because they have not been properly authenticated (because anonymous access does not constitute authentication but an absence of authentication).

Another security setting you can configure is the authentication methods used for outbound connections. This is configured by clicking the Outbound Security button on the Delivery tab (see Figure 15-3 again), which opens the Outbound Security properties sheet (Figure 15-8).

The options for outbound authentication are essentially the same as for inbound, with the addition that you can select a user account to specify the credentials that will be sent to remote SMTP hosts for authenticating your outbound connections to them. You can select such an account for either Basic or Integrated Windows Authentication,

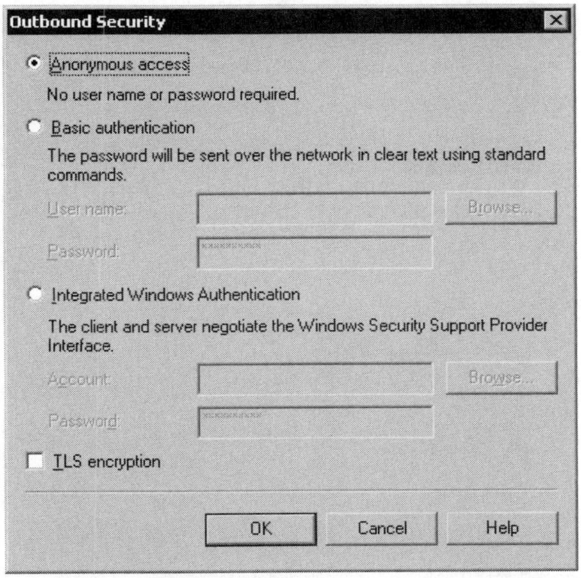

Figure 15-8. Configuring authentication methods for outbound connections

and the account you select can be either a local account (on a stand-alone server) or a domain account (in a domain environment).

The last security setting is on the Security tab (Figure 15-9), where you can specify which users and groups are assigned operator permissions to allow them to configure the properties of the selected virtual server. By default, only members of the local Administrators group on a stand-alone server have these permissions (plus the built-in special identities LocalService and NetworkService). You can add additional users and groups to this list if desired.

Message and Delivery Settings

The last group of settings you can configure for your SMTP servers are message and delivery settings. Message settings are configured on the Messages tab (Figure 15-10) and allow you to specify the following:

- **Maximum incoming message size**   Anything over 2MB is rejected by default.

- **Maximum session size**   The maximum amount of incoming data that can be transmitted in message bodies during the life of the connection.

- **Maximum number of messages sent per connection**   If this number is exceeded, the server will open additional outgoing connections as necessary.

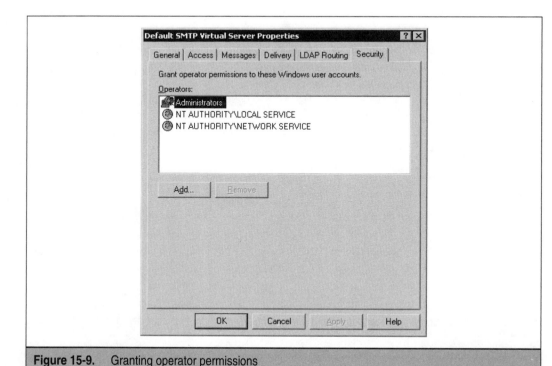

Figure 15-9.   Granting operator permissions

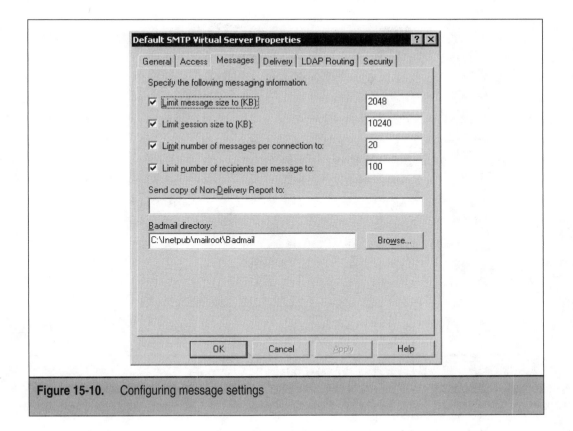

Figure 15-10.   Configuring message settings

- **Maximum number of recipients per message**   If this number is exceeded, the server will open additional outgoing connections as needed to send the message to any remaining recipients.

Note that the first two settings deal with incoming connections and the second two with outgoing. You can tune the performance of your SMTP server by adjusting these settings through judicious experimentation.

On this tab, you can also change the location of the \Badmail folder, and you can specify an e-mail address to which copies of all NDRs will be sent (typically, an account used by the mail administrator).

Delivery settings are configured on the Delivery tab (Figure 15-11) and allow you to specify the following:

- **Outbound delivery settings**   These include retry intervals for attempting to retransmit messages waiting in the \Queue folder. If delivery fails after all attempts, message delivery is considered to have failed. Other outbound delivery settings include Delay Notification, to allow for delays caused by

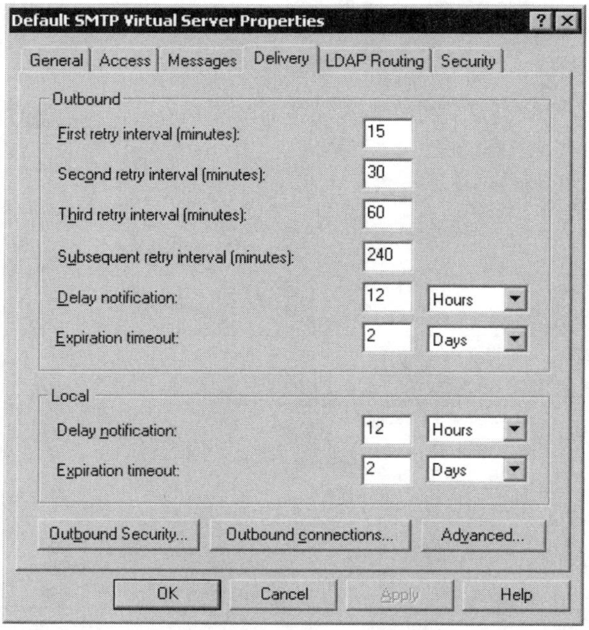

Figure 15-11. Configuring delivery settings

network congestion, and Expiration Timeout, to specify a final grace period before the server returns an NDR to the sender.

- **Inbound delivery settings** These are a subset of the outbound settings and include only Delay Notification and Expiration Timeout values.

By clicking the Advanced button, you can open the Advanced Delivery dialog box (Figure 15-12), where you can configure additional delivery options such as

- **Maximum Hop Count** The maximum number of remote SMTP hosts allowed to relay an outgoing message as it travels toward its destination. If this number is exceeded, delivery fails and an NDR is returned.

- **Masquerade Domain** This replaces the local domain in the From: line of outgoing messages with something different to hide the source domain. This only occurs on the first hop the message traverses.

- **Fully-Qualified Domain Name** The FQDN for the SMTP server is obtained automatically from the Computer Name tab of System in Control Panel, but it can also be configured as something different (you need to do this, for example, on a stand-alone SMTP server). Your SMTP server must also have a resolvable

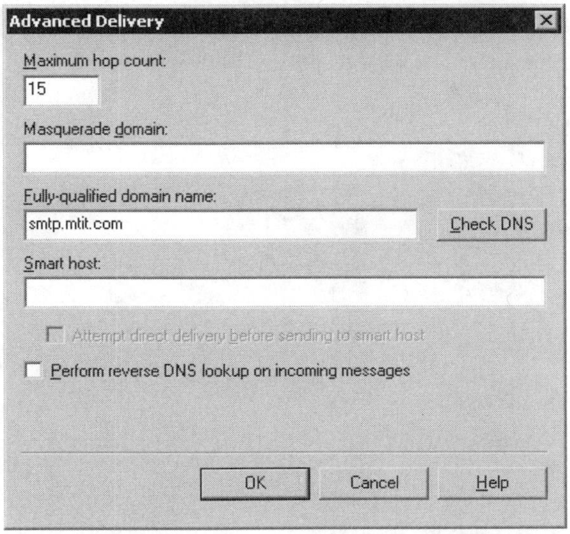

Figure 15-12.   Configuring advanced delivery options

FQDN (one that can be resolved by a name lookup on a DNS name server), or it will be unable to receive incoming mail. This includes both an A record and an MX record in the database on the name server. Contact your company's ISP to ensure their DNS administrator updates their name server's database with these two records for your SMTP server.

- **Smart Host**   This is another SMTP host through which outgoing messages are routed (unless a remote domain has been configured to override this setting for that remote domain). You can also configure your server to attempt direct delivery to the remote host before trying the smart host instead. You can specify a smart host using either its FQDN or IP address, but if you use an IP address, be sure to enclose it with square brackets (as in [204.63.144.8]), or your outgoing mail will end up in the \Badmail folder!

- **Perform Reverse DNS Lookup on Incoming Messages**   Reverse DNS lookup ensures that incoming messages are coming from real domains and not fake domains that have been forged by spammers. However, this is a costly process that significantly slows the performance of your SMTP server and it's generally not a good idea to enable this setting.

The final delivery settings you can configure are on the LDAP Routing tab (Figure 15-13). With these settings you can configure your SMTP server to contact a directory service such as Active Directory to try and resolve e-mail addresses from

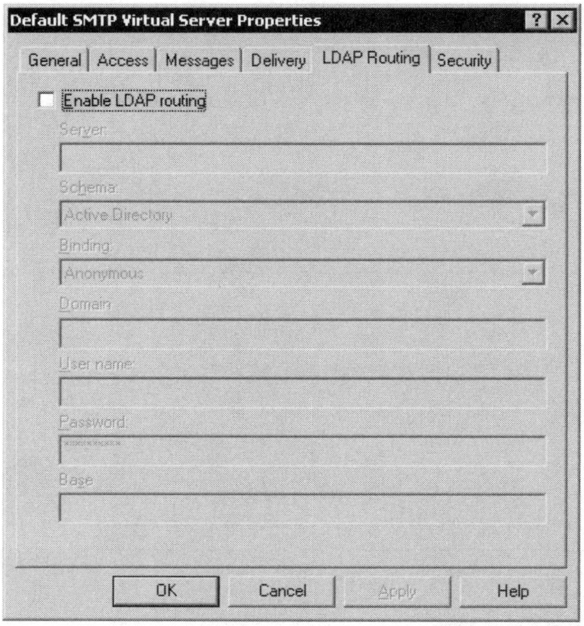

Figure 15-13. Configuring LDAP routing settings

names of senders and recipients. For example, if you wanted to send a message to user Bob Smith in the mcgraw-hill.com domain, you would normally have to address your message to something like bsmith@mcgraw-hill.com. By enabling LDAP routing for your server, however, you can address your message to Bob Smith instead and have Active Directory (or some other LDAP directory service) resolve the name Bob Smith into its associated e-mail address bsmith@mcgraw-hill.com. For more details on how to configure this tab, see IIS Help.

SMTP Domains

SMTP domains, also called "service domains," are DNS domains that organize messages for delivery. When you install the SMTP service, the Default SMTP Virtual Server has a single domain called the *default domain* (Figure 15-14). The default domain is a local domain that cannot be deleted, and it stamps incoming messages from addresses that don't have a domain. The name of the default domain is generated automatically from the Computer Name tab of System in Control Panel, but you can rename it by right-clicking it in IIS Manager and selecting Rename.

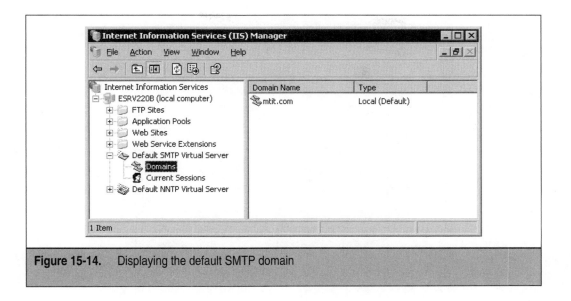

Figure 15-14.   Displaying the default SMTP domain

To configure the default domain, right-click it and select Properties (Figure 15-15). This properties sheet lets you view or modify the location of the \Drop folder for your server, which is the location where incoming mail for your domain (here, mtit.com) is deposited. By selecting the check box for Enable Drop Directory Quota, you can limit the size of the \Drop directory to ten times the maximum message size allowed, or 20MB by default.

Local vs. Remote Domains

I just mentioned that the default domain is a local domain. The SMTP service uses two types of domains:

- **Local domain**   DNS domains that can receive incoming messages addressed to the domain and place them in the \Drop folder. In Figures 15-14 and 15-15, the domain mtit.com is a local domain serviced by the Default SMTP Virtual Server.

- **Remote domain**   DNS domains managed by specific remote SMTP hosts. An example is the server smtp.mcgraw-hill.com, which manages SMTP forwarding for the mcgraw-hill.com DNS domain. By default, when you install the SMTP service on IIS, the Default SMTP Virtual Server has no remote domains configured. We'll look at why and how to create and configure remote domains in a moment.

Alias Domains

In addition to the default domain (of which there can only be one per SMTP virtual server), the other type of local domain you can create is an *alias domain*. Creating alias domains

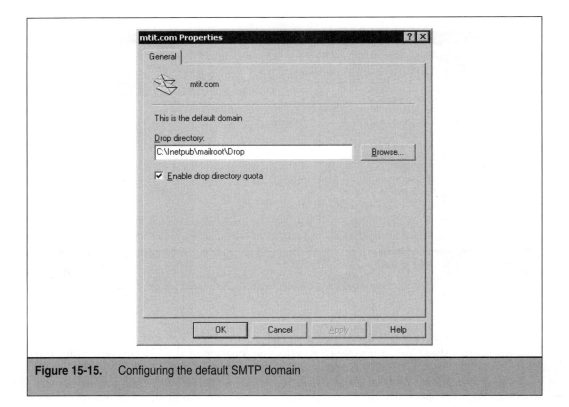

Figure 15-15. Configuring the default SMTP domain

lets you create secondary domains that point to your default domain and use the same \Drop directory. Incoming messages addressed to an alias domain are stamped with the name of the default domain. This way, for example, incoming messages addressed to recipients in the mtitworld.com (alias) domain can be accepted by the server and placed in the \Drop folder for the mtit.com (default) domain. This allows your SMTP server to receive mail addressed to recipients in more than one DNS domain.

Creating and Configuring Domains

To create a new domain, right-click the Domains node under Default SMTP Virtual Server and select New | Domain. This starts the New SMTP Domain Wizard (Figure 15-16), which can create either alias or remote domains.

To create an alias domain, select Alias, click Next, specify the DNS name (such as mtitworld.com) of the additional domain you want your default domain to handle incoming messages for, and click Finish. Don't bother opening the properties sheet for your alias domain, as it has no settings to configure.

Creating a remote domain is almost as easy, but why would you want to? The main reason is that you can override some of the default delivery settings for your SMTP virtual server and specify additional advanced delivery settings by creating and then

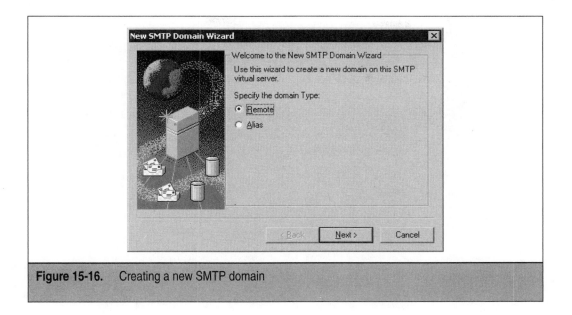

Figure 15-16. Creating a new SMTP domain

configuring remote domains. For example, you might do this for specific DNS names you frequently send messages to.

Now you'll create a remote domain for the domain mcgraw-hill.com, pretending that you (like I do) frequently send messages to users in that domain. In the wizard, select Remote, click Next, specify mcgraw-hill.com as the name of the remote domain, and click Finish. Now open the properties sheet for the remote domain to see the delivery settings you can configure (Figure 15-17).

Using the General tab for your remote domain you can:

- Click the Outbound Security button and configure authentication methods for outbound messages being sent to this remote domain that are different from those methods configured at the virtual server level.

- Override the default no relay setting at the virtual server level and allow relaying of incoming messages addressed to this domain.

- Begin an SMTP communications session using the HELO command instead of EHLO. This allows your server to tell an SMTP host in the remote domain that it supports ESMTP (SMTP Extensions), an advanced form of SMTP that has additional features beyond RFCs 821 and 822.

- Specify the routing method for sending messages to the remote domain. You can either configure the remote domain so that messages sent to it by your server use DNS to look up the SMTP host servicing the remote domain so it can forward the messages directly to the host, or configure it to use a designated smart host if this provides more expedited delivery.

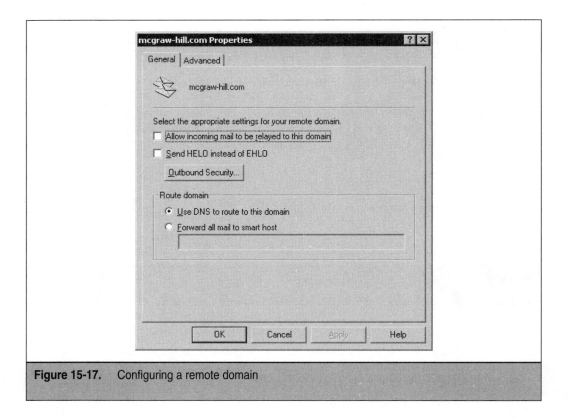

Figure 15-17. Configuring a remote domain

In addition, selecting the Advanced tab of the remote domain properties sheet allows you to configure your SMTP server to hold mail for the SMTP host servicing the remote domain. This is useful if the host connects to the Internet only occasionally (for example, using a modem) to download mail addressed to users in its domain. In this case, the host first establishes an Internet connection and then issues an ATRN command to your SMTP server to say, "I'm online! Start delivering any messages you've queued up for my domain!" The remote host must also be configured to supply suitable credentials in this kind of situation.

Testing the SMTP Service

I'll finish this discussion of the SMTP service by having you test to see if you can send messages successfully. You'll try this two ways:

- Composing a message using Notepad and saving it directly into the \Pickup folder of your Default STMP Virtual Server.

- Using a Telnet client to connect directly to the server on TCP port 25 and type the message line by line until it's finished and sent.

Creating and Sending Messages Manually Using Notepad

First, open Windows Explorer and select the C:\Inetpub\mailroot\Queue folder in the left pane to view the contents of the folder, which should be empty initially. Then open Notepad and create a text file similar to the following. Where info@mtit.com occurs in the message, you should replace it with a valid e-mail address of your own. Note the blank line between the message headers and message body: this is required.

```
x-sender: bob@nowhere.com
x-receiver: info@mtit.com
From: bob@nowhere.com
To: info@mtit.com
Subject: Just a test

Hi there, hope you had a great vacation!
```

Now select File | Save and save your message as test.txt in the C:\Inetpub\mailroot\Pickup directory on your IIS machine. Immediately switch to Windows Explorer and you should see something like this in the \Pickup folder:

```
NTFS_984b42365c005401aad550001.EML
```

If you open this file in Notepad, it will look something like this:

```
Received: from mail pickup service by esrv220b with Microsoft SMTPSVC;
    Thu, 23 Jan 2003 02:01:21 -0600
From: bob@nowhere.com
To: info@mtit.com
Subject: Just a test
Message-ID: <ESRV220BC8wSA1XvpFV00000009@esrv220b>
X-OriginalArrivalTime: 23 Jan 2003 08:01:21.0035 (UTC)
FILETIME=[9DB1F5B0:01C2C2B5]
Date: 23 Jan 2003 02:01:21 -0600

Hi there, hope you had a great vacation!
```

In a few moments, the file should leave the queue and be forwarded to the SMTP host that manages the mtit.com domain (or whatever domain your e-mail address belongs to). Open your mail client; you should see the message in your Inbox.

Creating and Sending Messages Manually Using Telnet

Open a command prompt on your server, type **telnet**, and press ENTER to start your Telnet session. (Be sure to type **set localecho** so you can see your keystrokes.) Then type **open localhost 25** to connect to port 25 (the SMTP service) on your server, which should respond with something like

```
220 smtp.mtit.com Microsoft ESMTP MAIL Service, Version: 6.0.3718.0 ready at
Thu, 23 Jan 2003 02:15:30 -0600
```
Now type **helo me** to begin submitting a message, and the server will respond
with250 smtp.mtit.com Hello [127.0.0.1]

Type **mail from:bob@mtit.com** to create the From: header for your message, and the server will respond with

```
250 2.1.0 bob@mtit.com....Sender OK
```

Type **rcpt to:info@mtit.com** to create the To: header for your message, and the server will respond with

```
250 2.1.5 info@mtit.com
```

Type **data,** and the response will be

```
354 Start mail input; end with <CRLF>.<CRLF>
```

Type the following lines:

```
Subject:Another test
Hi Mitch:

I'm coming back to work tomorrow, had a great vacation!

Bob
```

To indicate to the server that this is the end of your message, press ENTER, type . (a period), and press ENTER a second time. The server will respond with something like

```
250 2.6.0 <ESRV220BoYAPNXRPmca0000000b@smtp.mtit.com> Queued mail for delivery
```

Type **quit** to end your Telnet session with the server, and check the Inbox of your mail client to see if the message has arrived. If you want to learn more about SMTP commands such as HELO, DATA, and QUIT, read RFCs 821 and 822, which define the SMTP specification.

TIP　As an additional exercise, try composing and sending a message to a nonexistent domain and see what your SMTP server does with it!

THE NNTP SERVICE

The NNTP service is included as a component of IIS for the purpose of hosting discussion groups similar to USENET newsgroups. These discussion groups can be used by companies for internal use on corporate intranets, for customer help and support, and other purposes. Authentication can be required for users to read and post items to newsgroups, or the service can be configured to allow anyone access.

NOTE The NNTP component of IIS is a lightweight implementation intended mainly for the uses just described. For a fuller implementation of this protocol, including the ability to create and configure newsfeeds with USENET servers, you can use Microsoft Exchange.

Installing the NNTP Service

To use IIS as an NNTP host, you need to install the NNTP service component of IIS first; it is not installed by default on any edition of Windows Server 2003. If you haven't done this yet, follow the procedure outlined earlier in the section entitled "Installing the SMTP and NNTP Services" before proceeding further in this chapter.

To verify your installation, open IIS Manager and make sure you have a node called Default NNTP Virtual Server in the console tree (see Figure 15-1, earlier). You can use IIS Manager to perform the following NNTP administration tasks:

- Create and configure NNTP virtual servers and start, stop, and pause them independent of each other.
- Configure authentication, security, connection, posting, and newsgroup settings for NNTP virtual servers.
- Create and configure new newsgroups (including moderated ones), and post and reply to messages on them.
- Display current sessions and terminate selected (or all) connections.
- Rebuild an NNTP virtual server.

NNTP Directory Structure

When the NNTP service is installed on IIS, a directory structure is created with root folder \Inetpub\nntpfile on the local machine (Figure 15-18). This directory structure represents the article store for the service and consists of the following folders:

- **_temp.files_** A temporary folder used by the NNTP service while processing postings.
- **Drop** All incoming postings are "dropped" into this folder, regardless of the newsgroup they are being posted to, until the NNTP service can process them and post them to the appropriate newsgroup.

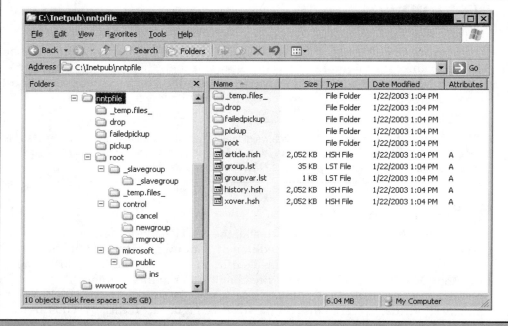

Figure 15-18. Directory structure associated with NNTP service

- **Failedpickup** Postings that are improperly formatted for NNTP are moved to this directory so they can be examined by the administrator.

- **Pickup** Text files placed manually or programmatically into this file will be "picked up" and moved to the \drop folder, from which they will be posted to the appropriate newsgroup (if properly formatted) or moved to the \failedpickup (if improperly formatted).

- **Root** This is the parent folder for all newsgroup folders in which articles reside; it is discussed in the next two sections.

Default Newsgroups

There are four newsgroups created by default when the NNTP service is installed (Figure 15-19):

- Control.cancel
- Control.newgroup
- Control.rmgroup
- Microsoft.public.ins

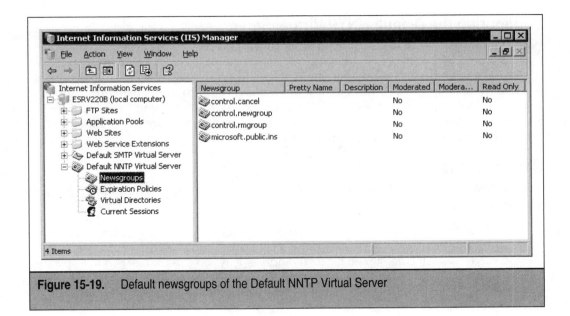

Figure 15-19. Default newsgroups of the Default NNTP Virtual Server

The control.* newsgroups are used for control messages sent by NNTP clients and other NNTP servers for communicating with the NNTP service on IIS. Do not delete any of these newsgroups or the NNTP service may fail. Also, do not delete any messages posted to them unless you have thorough knowledge of how the NNTP protocol works and you are troubleshooting communication between your server and other NNTP clients or hosts.

The Microsoft.public.ins newsgroup is a sample newsgroup containing a welcome message that you can use for posting test messages to your NNTP server to see if they are displayed by your NNTP client. You'll learn how to post to newsgroups later in this chapter.

Newsgroup Directory Structure

Associated with the newsgroups described in the preceding section is a directory structure beneath the \Inetpub\nntpfile\root folder (see Figure 15-18 again). The first two folders (_slavegroup and _temp.files_) are used internally for the operation of the NNTP service. The remaining folders map to the four default newsgroups of the Default NNTP Virtual Server.

As an example of how newsgroups map to file system folders on IIS, consider the Microsoft.public.ins newsgroup, whose content folder is \root\microsoft\public\ins under \Inetpub\nntpfile. Note that the DNS structure of the newsgroup maps piece by piece to the hierarchy of folders starting with \microsoft. If you create a new newsgroup called mtit.public.buysell, the associated folder structure would be \root\mtit\public\buysell, and messages posted to this group would be stored in the \buysell folder. I'll show you how to test this later in the chapter.

Configuring the Default NNTP Virtual Server

When you install the NNTP service on IIS, a Default NNTP Virtual Server is created that can immediately create new newsgroups and receive articles posted by NNTP clients like the Outlook Newsreader. You can create additional NNTP virtual servers if needed—for example, if you want to host discussion groups for more than one company. You can also rename the Default NNTP Virtual Server to something friendlier like Help Desk News Server. As you'll see later in this chapter, there are many similarities between configuring NNTP and SMTP virtual servers in IIS.

General Tasks

General tasks for NNTP virtual server (or NNTP server) configuration (Figure 15-20) include:

- **IP Address**   Each NNTP server must be assigned a unique identity in the form of a combination of IP address and TCP port number. As usual, the default server has All Unassigned for its IP address, but you can change this to a specific address. You can also add additional IP addresses to assign multiple identities to your server so it can listen to several addresses in the same way as SMTP

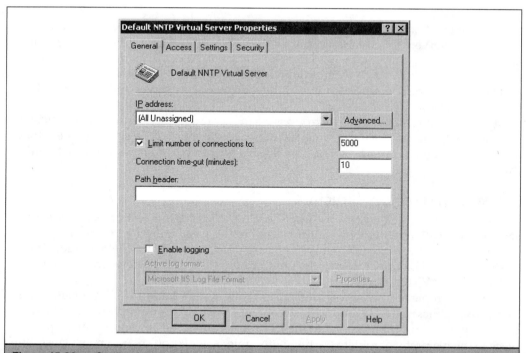

Figure 15-20.   Configuring general settings of an NNTP virtual server

servers discussed previously. By default, NNTP uses port 119 for ordinary connections and 563 for encrypted SSL connections, and you should generally leave the default ports as assigned.

- **Connection limits and timeout values**   These settings are configured similar to those for SMTP servers and apply to inbound connections from both NNTP clients and other NNTP servers. There are no configurable settings for outbound connections with other NNTP servers.

- **Logging**   You can enable logging and specify a logging format in the same way as for SMTP discussed previously.

- **Path Header**   This is the only setting on the General tab for NNTP servers that is different from those on the General tab for SMTP servers. You can specify a string here for the path line in each news posting. Path statements are generated by NNTP to record the path a news message takes to reach its destination. The string specified here will be added to the path line generated by the NNTP server in the message header.

NOTE   Do not use periods in the path header string you specify. For more information on how NNTP path statements are generated, refer to RFC 1036.

Security and Authentication Settings

The settings for authentication, secure SSL communication, connection control, and operator permissions are essentially identical for NNTP as for SMTP discussed previously. The only differences are for authentication (Figure 15-21):

- When you enable anonymous access on NNTP, you can specify which user account on your Windows machine (for stand-alone NNTP servers) or domain account (when using Active Directory) will control access by anonymous users to newsgroup content. By default, the Everyone built-in group and ANONYMOUS LOGON system identity has Full Control permission on the \Inetpub\nntpfile\ root folder and all its subfolders—in other words, on all newsgroup content. If no user account is specified here, the ANONYMOUS LOGON identity is used by default.

- Unlike SMTP servers, no domain needs to be specified when enabling Basic Authentication for NNTP servers.

- While SSL (specifically TLS) can only be enabled for Basic Authentication for SMTP servers, you can enable SSL for any authentication method (anonymous, Basic, or Integrated Windows) for NNTP servers. Additionally, if NNTP client computers have SSL client certificates installed and mapped to user accounts, you can configure NNTP servers to use client certificates for authenticating the NNTP clients.

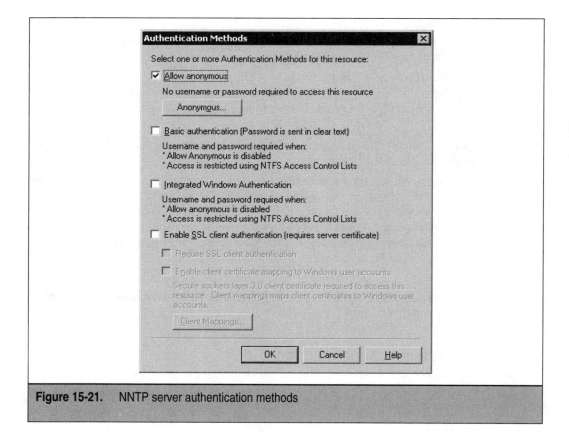

Figure 15-21. NNTP server authentication methods

Posting and Newsfeed Settings

The Settings tab of an NNTP server properties sheet configures settings for message posting and newsfeeds (Figure 15-22). The various configuration options include:

- **Allow Client Posting**   You can enable or disable posting of articles by NNTP clients to your server (enabled by default), limit the size of posted messages to prevent your server from being overwhelmed (1MB per message, by default), and limit the amount of data posted during a client session (20MB, by default).

- **Allow Feed Posting**   You can enable or disable downloading of newsfeeds pulled from other NNTP hosts (such as USENET hosts) and limit the message size and total size of the feeds.

- **Allow Servers To Pull Articles From This Server**   You can allow other NNTP hosts to pull newsfeeds from your NNTP server (disabled by default).

- **Allow Control Messages**   Checking this causes your NNTP server to automatically process any NNTP control messages sent to it from another NNTP server and also to log these messages in the transaction log. Leaving it unchecked prevents control messages from being processed but logs them regardless. Note that enabling control messages can pose a threat to your newsgroups and should be done only by experienced NNTP administrators.

- **SMTP Server for Moderated Groups**   If you have moderated newsgroups on your server, you must specify the FQDN of an SMTP server that the NNTP server can use for sending messages to the moderator you've designated for that server. Or, instead of an FQDN, you can specify a local directory on your server to deliver such messages to.

- **Default Moderator Domain**   Specify the DNS name of the domain to which moderator messages will be sent for moderated newsgroups. For example, if you specify mtit.com here, moderator messages for the moderated newsgroup mtit.private.accounting will be sent to the e-mail address mtit.private.accounting @mtit.com.

- **Administrator E-mail Account**   If a message is sent to the moderator of a moderated newsgroup but can't be delivered, an NDR will be generated and sent to the e-mail address specified here. Note, however, that such NDRs are only generated if you create the following DWORD Registry key on your IIS machine and assign it a value of 1:

```
HKLM\System\CurrentControlSet\Services\NntpSvc\Parameters\MailFromHeader
```

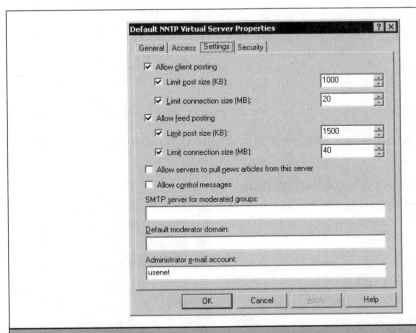

Figure 15-22.   Configuring posting and newsfeed settings

Note on Newsfeeds

At the time of writing this book, it is unclear if the newsfeeds feature of NNTP in IIS 6 actually works or not. Newsfeeds are the flow of information from one NNTP server to another and are used in USENET to replicate content among Internet NNTP hosts located around the world. Newsfeeds can either be outbound (pulled from your server to a remote NNTP host) or inbound (pulled from a remote host to your server). The options Allow Feed Posting and Allow Servers to Pull News Articles from This Server were included on the Settings tab of NNTP server properties in the earlier IIS 5 platform, but they didn't work, and there's currently no documentation on how to make this work in IIS 6, so it may not work in this platform either. Consult the latest documentation for Windows Server 2003 to determine the status of this feature.

Administering NNTP Servers

In addition to the usual tasks of stopping, starting, and pausing NNTP servers, administrators can perform the following tasks:

- Create new newsgroups and configure them.
- Create and configure expiration policies for newsgroups.
- Create and configure new virtual directories for newsgroup content.
- Restrict access to newsgroups for groups of users.
- Create additional NNTP virtual servers.
- Rebuild NNTP virtual servers.
- Limit which type and how many newsgroups are displayed in IIS Manager.

IIS also has several admin scripts included for managing different aspects of NNTP servers.

Creating and Configuring Newsgroups

You can use the New Newsgroup Wizard to create a new newsgroup on your NNTP server and then configure it by opening the properties sheet for the newsgroup. To create a newsgroup called mtit.public.buysell on the Default NNTP Virtual Server:

1. Open IIS Manager and expand the Default NNTP Virtual Server node in the console tree to expose the Newsgroups node beneath it.
2. Right-click Newsgroups and select New | Newsgroup to open the wizard.
3. Type **mtit.public.buysell** and click Next.
4. Type a description and a Pretty Name (short description displayed by some NNTP clients) and click Finish.

Refresh the view in IIS Manager by pressing F5, and you should see your new newsgroup listed in the details pane. You'll test posting to this newsgroup in a moment, but first I'll go over what other configuration tasks you can perform. Right-click mtit.public.buysell to open the properties sheet for the newsgroup (Figure 15-23).

In addition to the Description and Pretty Name fields specified previously, there are two other settings that are specifically related to moderating the newsgroup:

- **Read Only**   Select this check box to allow only the moderator for the newsgroup to post articles to the group. This is useful for newsgroups that publish information such as product updates or the latest sales figures.

- **Moderated**   Select this check box and specify the moderator's e-mail address if you want this to be a moderated newsgroup. A moderated newsgroup is one where articles that are posted are first sent to the moderator, who then decides whether each article should be accepted or not. Moderation is generally based on the relevance of the content and proper newsgroup etiquette. To use moderating, you need to also specify the relevant settings on the Settings tab of the NNTP server properties sheet, as discussed earlier.

You can also rename or delete newsgroups in the usual way.

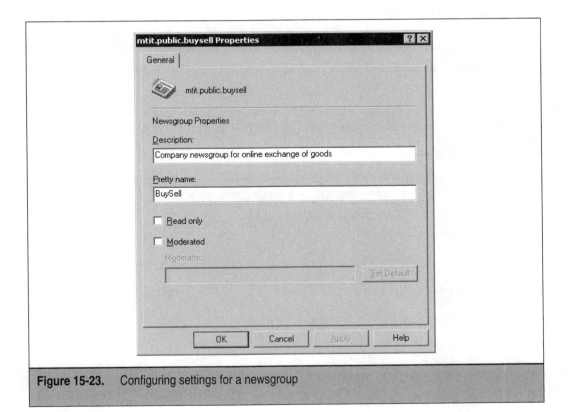

Figure 15-23.   Configuring settings for a newsgroup

Creating and Configuring Expiration Policies

An expiration policy defines how long posted articles remain in newsgroups before they are automatically deleted by the server. Expiration policies can apply to individual newsgroups, several newsgroups, or all newsgroups on the server. You can create as many expiration policies as you desire, and none are created by default. If you fail to create expiration policies for heavily used newsgroups, your server's disk may become full and the NNTP service may shut down until you delete some of the articles manually.

To create an expiration policy for the mtit.public.buysell newsgroup you created earlier follow these steps:

1. Open IIS Manager and expand the Default NNTP Virtual Server node in the console tree to expose the Expiration Policies node beneath it.

2. Right-click Expiration Policies and select New | Expiration Policy.

3. Type **Expiration Policy for mtit.public.* newsgroups** and click Next.

4. By default, the expiration policy applies to * (an asterisk), meaning all newsgroups on the server. Click the Remove button to remove this setting, and click Add to open the Add Newsgroup dialog box (Figure 15-24).

5. Leave the Include option selected, type **mtit.public.*** in the Newsgroup text box, and click OK to close the dialogbox.

6. Click Next, and specify how long news articles should remain on the server before being deleted (the default is 168 hours or 1 week).

7. Click Finish, and verify that your new expiration policy is displayed in the details pane.

You can further configure your new policy by opening its properties sheet and changing the time interval or which newsgroups it applies to. You can also rename or delete the policy.

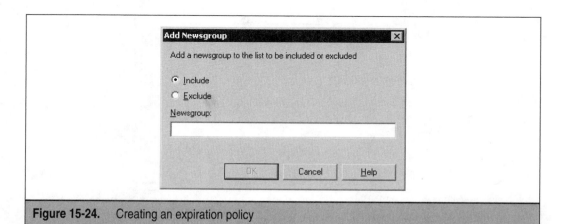

Figure 15-24. Creating an expiration policy

Creating and Configuring Virtual Directories

NNTP virtual directories specify where content for newsgroups is located, and like WWW virtual directories, this can be either a folder on the local machine or a shared folder on a network file server. Select the Virtual Directories node under the Default NNTP Virtual Server node to see what virtual directories are defined on your server (Figure 15-25).

By default, IIS creates two virtual directories for hosting the content of the Default NNTP Virtual Server:

- **Default**   This alias maps to the C:\Inetpub\nntpfile\root folder. New newsgroups you create will have their content folder subtrees located within this folder.

- **Control**   This alias maps to the C:\Inetpub\nntpfile\root\control folder. This is used for the control.* newsgroups utilized internally by the NNTP service.

You can configure several aspects of these virtual directories by opening their properties sheets. Look at the settings for the Default virtual directory (Figure 15-26):

- **Contents**   Click this button to specify a different folder on the local machine to map to the virtual directory alias, or to specify the UNC path to a remote network share and the credentials needed to access this share.

- **Secure**   Click this button to enable or disable SSL for newsgroups associated with this virtual directory and whether to use 40- or 128-bit encryption.

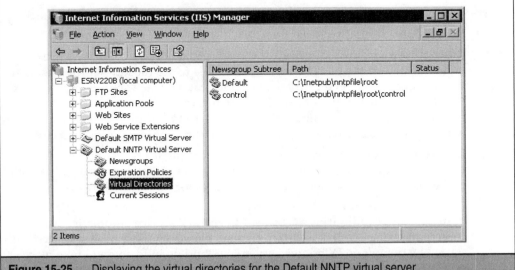

Figure 15-25.   Displaying the virtual directories for the Default NNTP virtual server

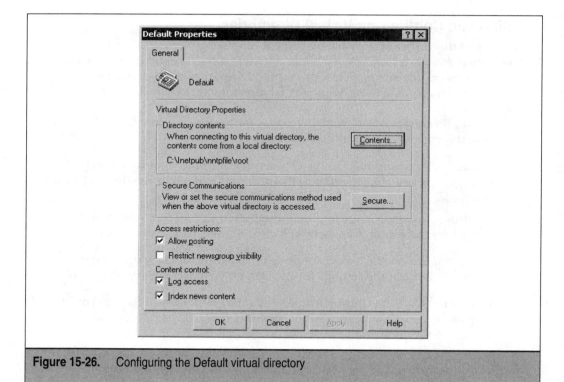

Figure 15-26. Configuring the Default virtual directory

- **Allow Posting** Configure this setting to allow or deny users to post articles to newsgroups using the virtual directory.

- **Restrict Newsgroup Visibility** If this is checked, only users who are authenticated by the NNTP server will be able to see the newsgroups using the virtual directory when they try to list (enumerate) the newsgroups on the server. This feature makes it possible for administrators to "hide" some or all of their newsgroups from anonymous users. Don't select this option unless you require it; it adds processing overhead to the server and can slow performance.

- **Log Access** Lets you enable or disable IIS logging for newsgroups using the virtual directory. Logging must still be turned on globally on the General tab of the NNTP virtual server's properties sheets for it to work, however.

- **Index News Content** Like the WWW Service discussed in Chapter 7, "Creating and Configuring Websites," the NNTP service automatically enables content indexing on all newsgroup content. However, the Indexing service is *not* started by default on Windows Server 2003, and no indexing will take place unless the Indexing service is started using Services in Control Panel.

You can also create new virtual directories to host your newsgroup content. For example, to create a new virtual directory for mtit.private.* newsgroups, which you could create later for the company intranet, do this:

1. Right-click the Virtual Directories node, and select New | Virtual Directory to open the New NNTP Virtual Directory Wizard.

2. Start the wizard, type **mtit.private** as the newsgroup subtree that will use this virtual directory, and click Next.

3. Select either File System or Remote to specify the location for the virtual directory's contents, and complete the wizard.

Now create a new newsgroup called mtit.private.accounts and verify that a folder called "accounts" has been created in your virtual directory's location as the content location for this newsgroup. Your new virtual directory may be in a disable state, and you may need to restart your NNTP virtual server after you create your first newsgroup for this virtual directory to make it work.

Creating New Virtual Servers

You can create additional NNTP virtual servers similar to the way you created SMTP virtual servers earlier in this chapter. When you create a new NNTP virtual server, however, you are prompted to specify two paths—one for the NNTP server's internal files and the other for the newsgroup content. The folder for internal files must be local to the server, while the newsgroup content can be located either locally or on a remote network share. For comparison, the location of the internal files for the Default NNTP Virtual Server is \Inetpub\nntpfile, and the content directory is \Inetpub\nntpfile\root.

Restricting Access to Newsgroups

In addition to hiding newsgroups as discussed previously, you can also control access to newsgroups by configuring suitable permissions on the content folders for your newsgroups. Setting permissions at the \root folder level will apply to all newsgroups that use this folder. Alternatively, you can set permissions at sublevels to control access to specific subtrees of newsgroups or individual newsgroups. If you restrict access to newsgroups this way, you should also disable anonymous access to your NNTP server. The LocalSystem account should always have Full Control permission on all newsgroup folders.

Limiting Newsgroup Enumeration

You can filter which newsgroups will be displayed when you select the Newsgroups node in IIS Manager. This is useful if you have thousands of newsgroups hosted on your machine. To do this, right-click Newsgroups and select Limit Groups Enumeration.

By default, all newsgroups (indicated by an asterisk) are enumerated on the server (Figure 15-27). To change this so that only newsgroups such as mtit.public.buysell and mtit.public.announcements are displayed, type **mtit.public.*** in the text box. You can also specify the maximum number of newsgroups displayed in the results pane; the default is 100. Note that hiding newsgroups here in IIS Manager does not hide them from NNTP clients!

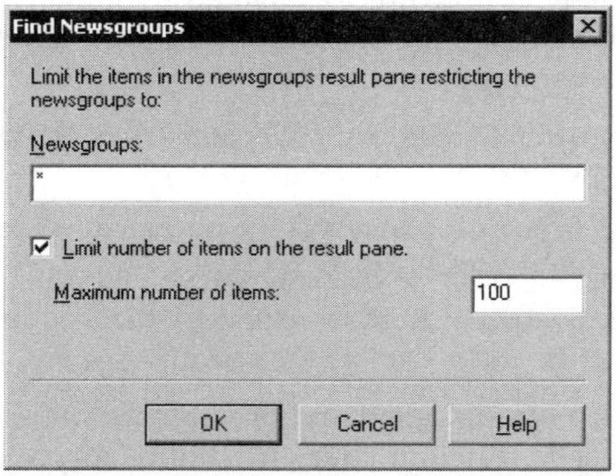

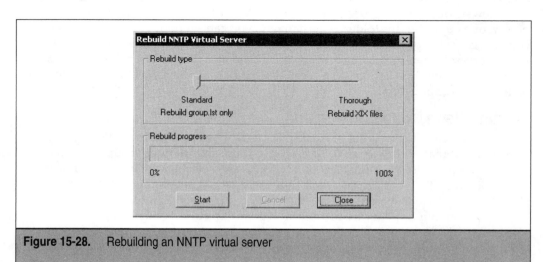

Figure 15-27. Limiting newsgroup enumeration

Rebuilding an NNTP Virtual Server

If files become corrupted on your NNTP server and newsgroups or messages are not displayed, you can rebuild your server to correct the problem. This action will update the indexes and hash tables that keep track of the articles posted to your server. To rebuild a server, follow these steps:

1. Stop the NNTP virtual server you want to rebuild by right-clicking it and selecting Stop.

2. Right-click the virtual server again, and select All Tasks | Rebuild Server (Figure 15-28).

Figure 15-28. Rebuilding an NNTP virtual server

3. Try a Standard rebuild first, restart your virtual server, and test. If the problem has not been resolved, repeat the process and try a Thorough rebuild.

4. If a rebuild fails to correct the problem, consult the Knowledge Base on the Microsoft Product Support Services (PSS) website at support.microsoft.com for further information on troubleshooting NNTP service problems on IIS.

NNTP Admin Scripts

IIS 6 also includes several admin scripts for managing certain aspects of the NNTP service:

- **Rexpire.vbs**   Adds, deletes, or modifies expiration policies. For example, to enumerate the expiration policies on the Default NNTP Virtual Server (whose ID is 1), do this:

```
C:\>cd C:\Windows\system32\inetsrv
C:\WINDOWS\system32\inetsrv>rexpire -t e -v 1
Expire ID: 1
Name: Expiration policy for mtit.public.* newsgroups
Time horizon: 168
Newsgroups: mtit.public.*
```

- **Rgroup.vbs**   Creates, deletes, or modifies newsgroups. For example, to create the newsgroup mtit.public.announcements, do this:

```
C:\WINDOWS\system32\inetsrv>rgroup -t a -g
mtit.public.announcements
Newsgroup: mtit.public.announcements
Description:
Moderator:
Read only: False
Prettyname:
Creation time: 1/24/2003 4:46:00 PM
```

- **Rsess.vbs**   Enumerates and terminates NNTP client sessions with your server. For example, to enumerate all active sessions, do this:

```
C:\WINDOWS\system32\inetsrv>rsess -t e
Number of sessions: 0
```

- **Rfeed.vbs**   Configures newsfeeds with other NNTP hosts. This feature is still not documented at the time of writing, apart from that you type **rfeed /?** at the command prompt. Consult the latest Windows Server 2003 documentation for more information on this feature.

Testing the NNTP Service

I'll end this chapter by performing a simple test to see if you can post a message to a newsgroup on your NNTP server. You can use any NNTP client you are familiar with; I'll use the newsreader included with Microsoft Outlook 2000 for illustration.

Posting Messages with Outlook Newsreader

Post a message to the mtit.public.announcements group you created earlier using the Rgroup.vbs script or to any other newsgroup on your server:

1. Open Microsoft Outlook and select View | Go To | News to open the Outlook Newsreader.

2. Select Tools | Accounts to open the Internet Accounts box.

3. Click the Add button, and select News to open the Internet Connection Wizard.

4. Follow the wizard, and specify the IP address of the Default NNTP Virtual Server on your IIS machine until the wizard completes.

5. Close the Internet Accounts dialog box, and click OK when a message displays asking if you would like to download a list of newsgroups from the server.

6. A dialog box called Newsgroup Subscripts should display the newsgroups on your IIS machine. Double-click the mtit.public.announcements group to subscribe to the group, and click the Go To button to display the messages in that group in the Outlook Newsreader (there won't be any yet).

7. Click the New Post button on the newsreader and try posting a test message to the group. Click the Send/Recv button to ensure the message has been sent, and then click the Headers button to download headers for new messages on the server.

NOTE You can also use Telnet to test NNTP servers. This is similar to what you did earlier in this chapter to test SMTP with Telnet. To learn about the various Telnet commands used for NNTP, see RFC 997.

CHALLENGE

Use the Help and Support Center on Windows Server 2003 to find out more about the new POP3 service included in this platform. Now that Windows server platforms include both SMTP and POP3 services, why would you need to deploy Microsoft Exchange for your company? What messaging and collaboration features does Microsoft Exchange include that the default SMTP and POP3 services can't provide? In what circumstances would the SMTP and POP3 services be sufficient, and when would Exchange be needed instead? If you are not familiar with the features of Microsoft Exchange, see www.microsoft.com/exchange for more information.

The message you posted should be displayed in Outlook Newsreader. The NNTP service on IIS stores messages as text files with the extension *.nws in the folder mapped to the name of the newsgroup. For example, the test message you posted to mtit.public .announcements is in the folder \Inetpub\nntpfile\root\mtit\public\announcements.

Because this is the first message posted to this group, the name of the message will be 1000000.nws. If you open this file in Notepad, it should look something like this (depending on how you've configured your account for the NNTP server):

```
From: "Mitch Tulloch" <info@NOSPAMmtit.com>
Subject: test
Date: Fri, 24 Jan 2003 17:04:31 -0600
Lines: 8
X-Priority: 3
X-MSMail-Priority: Normal
X-Newsreader: Microsoft Outlook Express 5.50.4920.2300
X-MimeOLE: Produced By Microsoft MimeOLE V5.50.4920.2300
Message-ID: <4TiXbz$wCHA.2096@esrv220b>
Newsgroups: mtit.public.announcements
Path: esrv220b
Xref: esrv220b mtit.public.announcements:1
NNTP-Posting-Host: 172.16.11.44

This is just a test.
```

CHECKLIST: ADMINISTERING SMTP AND NNTP

Check off each of the following check boxes when you've become familiar with how to perform the associated administrative tasks concerning the SMTP and NNTP services.

- ☐ Install the SMTP service.
- ☐ Describe the message store directory structure for the SMTP service.
- ☐ Configure the identity of an SMTP virtual server.
- ☐ Configure multiple identities for an SMTP virtual server.
- ☐ Enable and configure logging for an SMTP virtual server.
- ☐ Configure incoming connections limits and timeouts for an SMTP virtual server.
- ☐ Configure outgoing connections settings an SMTP virtual server.
- ☐ Configure security and authentication settings for an SMTP virtual server.
- ☐ Configure message and delivery settings for an SMTP virtual server.
- ☐ Create and configure alias domains for an SMTP virtual server.
- ☐ Create and configure remote domains for an SMTP virtual server.

☐ Test the SMTP service by creating a properly formatted FRC 821/822 text message and placing it in the \Pickup folder.

☐ Test the SMTP service with Telnet.

☐ Install the NNTP service.

☐ Describe the directory structure of the NNTP service.

☐ Explain the purpose of the default newsgroups created when the NNTP service is installed.

☐ Configure the identity for an NNTP virtual server.

☐ Configure multiple identities for an NNTP virtual server.

☐ Configure inbound connection limits and timeout values for an NNTP virtual server.

☐ Enable and configure logging for an NNTP virtual server.

☐ Specify a path header for an NNTP virtual server.

☐ Configure security and authentication settings for an NNTP virtual server.

☐ Configure posting and newsfeed settings for an NNTP virtual server.

☐ Create and configure newsgroups on an NNTP virtual server.

☐ Create and configure expiration policies on an NNTP virtual server.

☐ Create and configure virtual directories for newsgroup content on an NNTP virtual server.

☐ Restrict newsgroup access on an NNTP virtual server.

☐ Create and configure additional NNTP servers.

☐ Rebuild an NNTP virtual server.

☐ Configure newsgroup enumeration for an NNTP virtual server.

☐ Manage the NNTP service using scripts.

☐ Test the NNTP service using Outlook Newsreader or Outlook Express.

CHAPTER 16

Publishing with IIS

The final chapter of this book deals with the topic of publishing content to IIS using WebDAV and FrontPage Server Extensions (FPSE). It also covers managing various aspects of web content including redirection, content expiration, and content ratings.

WEBDAV

WebDAV is a method for publishing to web servers that lets you publish and manage any content including HTML files, graphics, ASP pages, scripts, and executables. WebDAV stands for Web Distributed Authoring and Versioning, and is a proposed extension of the HTTP/1.1 protocol described in RFCs 2518 and 3253.

The traditional way of publishing and managing content on web servers is using the File Transfer Protocol (FTP), which we discussed in Chapter 9, "Creating and Configuring FTP Sites." One disadvantage of using FTP is that it requires additional ports to be opened on your firewall. Another disadvantage is that FTP has no file locking mechanism to prevent two users from trying to simultaneously upload files to a web server. Finally, to modify web content using FTP you have to download the content to your client machine, modify it, and then upload it again to the web server.

WebDAV, on the other hand, is designed to use the same port used by HTTP itself (TCP port 80), thus reducing the number of open ports required on your firewall. WebDAV also supports a locking mechanism that lets multiple users read files concurrently but allows only one user at a time to modify files. WebDAV additionally lets you manage resources on a remote web server transparently as if the files were located on your local client machine, including dragging and dropping files to copy or move them on the server, searching for text within files, and modifying the properties of files.

How WebDAV Works

WebDAV works by using standard HTTP/1.1 verbs like GET and PUT and also by implementing an extended set of HTTP verbs including the LOCK, and PROPFIND methods. To use WebDAV for publishing web content, you need a WebDAV-enabled web server such as IIS and a WebDAV client such as Windows XP Professional or Windows Server 2003, both of which have integrated WebDAV clients. Then you must set up a publishing directory on your IIS machine and assign appropriate NTFS and web permissions to this directory, and users with suitable permissions will be able to publish and manage content. I'll walk you through these procedures next.

Enabling WebDAV

Unlike earlier versions of IIS, WebDAV is neither installed nor enabled by default in IIS 6. To install WebDAV, use Add or Remove Programs in Control Panel to add the WebDAV Publishing component, a subcomponent of the WWW Publishing Service (Figure 16-1).

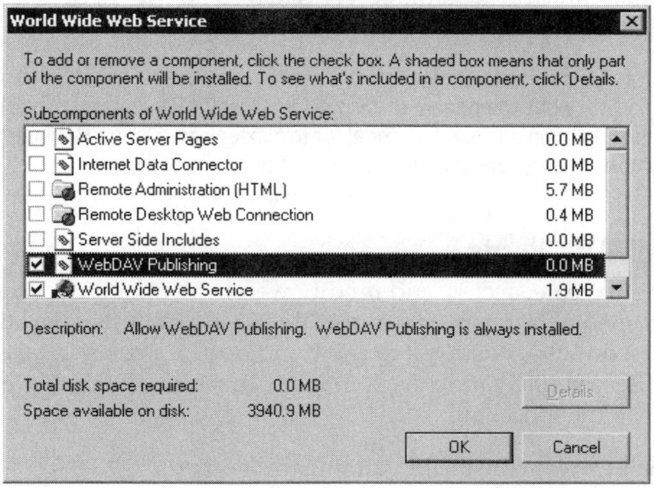

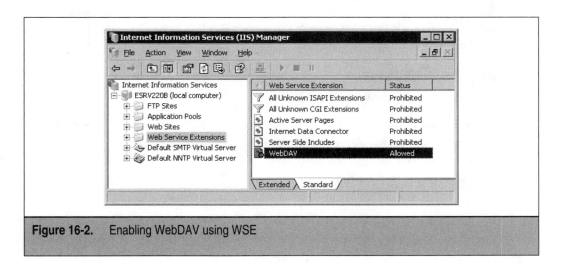

Figure 16-1.   Installing WebDAV

After installing WebDAV, you need to enable it. To do this, open IIS Manager and select the Web Service Extensions (WSE) node to display the list of service extensions installed on your server. Then right-click WebDAV in the results pane and select Allow to enable the extension (Figure 16-2). Note that this globally enables WebDAV for all

Figure 16-2.   Enabling WebDAV using WSE

websites and virtual directories on the server. There is no way in IIS 6 to enable or disable WebDAV on a per-site or per-directory basis.

TIP   You can find out what component of IIS provides WebDAV support by double-clicking the WebDAV extension to open a properties sheet for this extension. On the Required Files tab, you'll see that WebDAV support is provided through httpext.dll.

Enabling WebDAV Clients

To use WebDAV to create, access, and modify web content on Internet servers, you also need to enable the client to support WebDAV. To fully take advantage of WebDAV support on IIS 6, you need to use Windows XP Professional or a member of the Windows Server 2003 family as your client machine. To enable WebDAV on these platforms, do the following:

1. Open the Services console in Administrative Tools.
2. Scroll down and find the WebClient service in the console.
3. If this service is Disabled, double-click it to open the properties sheet for the service.
4. Change the Startup Type setting from Disabled to Automatic if you plan to use the machine regularly for publishing content.
5. Click Apply and then click Start to start the WebClient service on the client machine.

TIP   In addition to Windows XP and Windows Server 2003, WebDAV is supported to various degrees by Windows 2000 machines with Internet Explorer 5 or higher installed and by Office 2000 and Office XP. Consult the documentation for these products to see which WebDAV features are supported.

Configuring WebDAV

The main issues in configuring WebDAV are

-   Creating a virtual directory for publishing WebDAV content on the server
-   Configuring web permissions so clients can publish and manage different types of content
-   Configuring NTFS permissions to control which users can use WebDAV

Enterprise Content Management

In an enterprise environment, it's generally not a good idea to publish content directly to a production web server using WebDAV or any other mechanism. A better practice is to first create or edit your content on a development server with WebDAV or FrontPage Server Extensions enabled. Once this content has been approved, it can then be moved to a staging server such as Microsoft Application Center, which can then publish the changed content to the product server or web farm. For more information on this procedure, see the *Microsoft Application Center Resource Kit*.

Creating a WebDAV Virtual Directory

Begin by creating a target virtual directory for publishing content to the Default Web Site on your IIS machine. To do this, right-click the Default Web Site and select New | Virtual Directory to start the new Virtual Directory Wizard. Create a new virtual directory with alias "Test" that maps to a folder C:\stuff on your hard drive. If necessary, refer back to Chapter 7, "Creating and Configuring Websites," for more information on how to create virtual directories on IIS.

NOTE   Use the default Virtual Directory Access permissions when creating the virtual directory because you will configure these later in the section "Configuring Web Permissions."

Configuring NTFS Permissions

It's extremely important that NTFS permissions be properly configured for the folder mapped to your WebDAV virtual directory. This is because to use WebDAV, you must enable Write web permission and this constitutes a security risk on your IIS machine unless NTFS permissions prevent unauthorized users from writing to the virtual directory.

To view the current NTFS permissions on the C:\stuff folder mapped to your \test directory, right-click the Test virtual directory under the Default Web Site in IIS Manager and select Permissions (Figure 16-3).

The important permissions are those for the Users group because you generally want to control WebDAV publishing for ordinary users on your network. The default

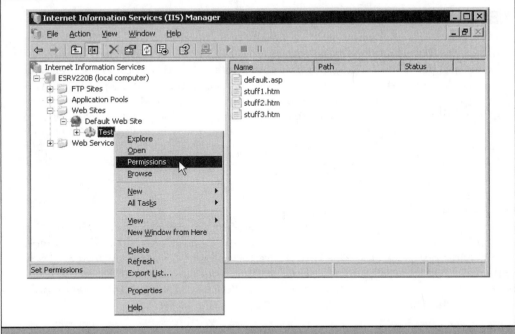

Figure 16-3.   Open NTFS permissions for the Test virtual directory

permissions configured for Users and how they affect users access to IIS using WebDAV are as follows (Figure 16-4):

- **Read**   Lets users read the contents of a file using WebDAV.
- **Read & Execute**   Lets users read files and run scripts or CGI executables using WebDAV.
- **List Folder Contents**   Lets users view the contents of your WebDAV directory.

TIP   If you have a special group set up for employees whose job is updating websites, you can set up corresponding permissions for this group and restrict the permissions for Users. This is a more secure setup than enabling WebDAV access to all users on your network.

If you scroll down the Permissions list box. you'll see that Special Permissions is allowed for Users. To view these Special Permissions, click the Advanced button on the properties sheet (as shown in Figure 16-3) to open the Advanced Security Settings properties sheet for the \stuff folder. Select the Special Permission entry for Users in

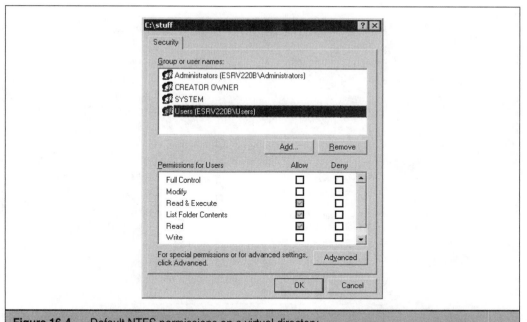

Figure 16-4.   Default NTFS permissions on a virtual directory

this list and click Edit to open the Permission Entry properties sheet (Figure 16-5). Note the two special permissions assigned to the Users group in this list:

- Create Files/Write Data
- Create Folders/Append Data

These two permissions are required for Users to be able to write content to the \stuff folder using WebDAV.

SECURITY ALERT   If your website is a public one that allows anonymous users to access its content, you should also add the Internet guest account (IUSR_*servername*) to the NTFS permissions for Users (as shown in Figure 16-3) and assign this account the single permission Deny Write. This will prevent anonymous users from being able to publish or modify content on your server using WebDAV.

Configuring Web Permissions

Once you've configured NTFS permissions properly on the \stuff folder to prevent unauthorized users from using WebDAV on the folder, you still need to configure

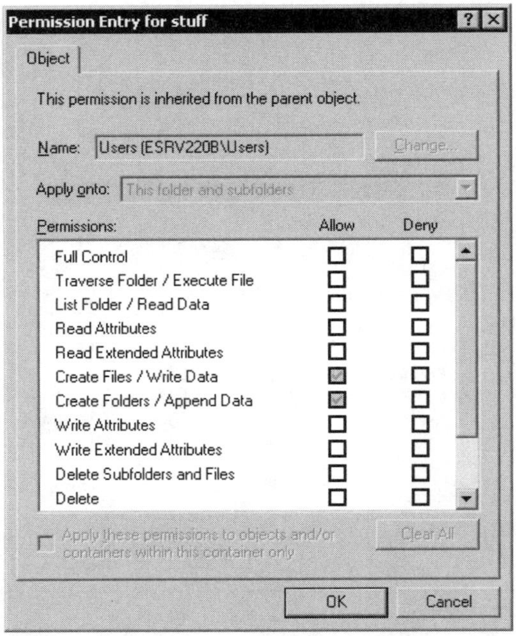

Figure 16-5. Special permissions for Users on a virtual directory

web permissions for the Test virtual directory to which \stuff is mapped. How you configure these web permissions depends on what sort of actions you want users to be able to perform using WebDAV.

Web permissions are configured on the Virtual Directory tab of the properties sheet for the virtual directory (Figure 16-6). The settings to configure here are

- **Read**   Allows users to read files in the directory, provided the NTFS permissions also allow them.

- **Write**   Allows users to write files to the directory subject to NTFS permissions.

- **Directory Browsing**   Allows users to list files in the directory subject to NTFS permissions.

In addition, the following two settings are important to how WebDAV works:

- **Index This Resource**   Allows users to search for text within files in the directory subject to NTFS permissions, provided the Indexing service has been enabled on the server.

- **Script Source Access**   Together with Write permission, allows users to modify ASP pages and other script-mapped files in the directory.

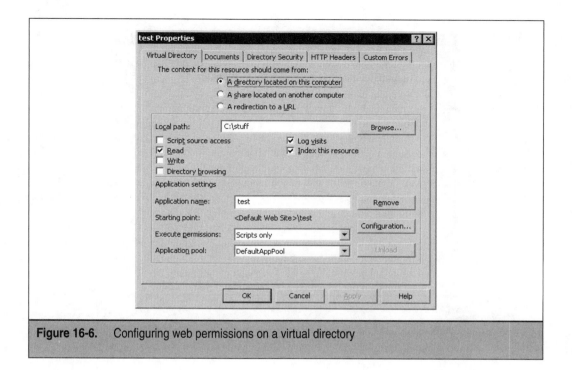

Figure 16-6.   Configuring web permissions on a virtual directory

For purposes of testing WebDAV later, make sure Read, Write, and Directory Browsing are all enabled for your Test virtual directory. This will allow users to display a list of files in the directory; publish additional files to the directory; and manipulate files in the directory by moving, copying, or modifying them.

NOTE   The Indexing service is enabled by default on IIS, but its startup type is set to manual instead of automatic. To start this service, type **net start cisvc** at the command prompt. This will initiate the process of building a catalog file for virtual directories on which indexing is enabled. These catalog files are required to perform text searches using this service.

Publishing Using WebDAV

Now you can test publishing to your WebDAV-enabled virtual directory from another machine. Open Internet Explorer on the Windows XP or Windows Server 2003 machine from which you want to publish content. Select File | Open from the menu and type the URL **http://***servername***/test**, where *servername* is the IP address or NetBIOS name of the IIS machine where Test resides (or the DNS name if you are using Active Directory). Be sure to select the check box labeled Open As Web Folder, and click OK. This will open a web folder showing the contents of the virtual directory on the remote web server (Figure 16-7).

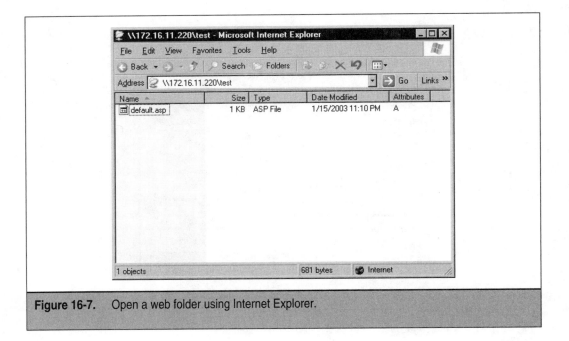

Figure 16-7.   Open a web folder using Internet Explorer.

Now create some HTML files on your client computer that you will publish to your IIS machine. For example, create three files: stuff1.htm, stuff2.htm, and stuff3.htm in the C:\morestuff folder on the local machine (Figure 16-8).

With both the web folder *servername*\test (Figure 16-7) and local folder \morestuff (Figure 16-8) open on your client machine, you can publish these files by dragging and dropping them from the local folder to the web folder. You may need to press F5 to refresh the web folder afterward to see the published files. Try viewing one of the published files using Internet Explorer, for example, by opening the URL http://*servername*/test/stuff1.htm on the client machine.

Now try modifying the file you just opened. Return to the web folder on the client, right-click the stuff.htm file, and select Open With | Notepad. Make some changes to the HTML in the file, save the file, and try opening it again using Internet Explorer. You've now used WebDAV to publish and modify files on your remote IIS machine!

TIP   Add the web folder URL to your Favorites list on Internet Explorer so you can more easily open it in the future.

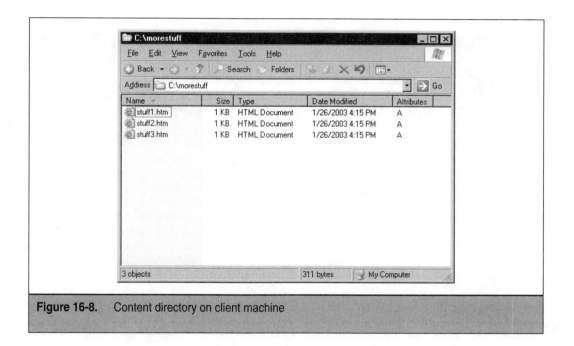

Figure 16-8. Content directory on client machine

Another way of publishing using WebDAV is to create a shortcut to the web folder in My Network Places. To do this, perform the following steps:

1. Open Windows Explorer and select My Network Places.

2. Double-click Add Network Place to open the New Network Place Wizard, and click Next.

3. Select the option Choose Another Network Location and click Next.

4. Type **http://*servername*/test** and click Next.

5. Specify a friendly name for the new shortcut or accept the suggested name, and click Next.

The new shortcut to your web folder should now be visible in My Network Places (Figure 16-9). To create a shortcut to this web folder on your desktop for easy drag-and-drop publishing, right-click it and select Send To | Desktop.

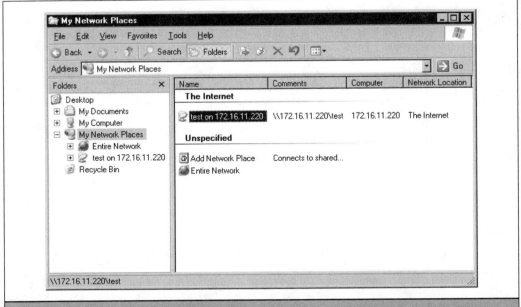

Figure 16-9. Adding a web folder to My Network Places

FRONTPAGE SERVER EXTENSIONS (FPSE)

Another way of publishing and managing web content on IIS is using Microsoft FrontPage, the web authoring tool included as part of Microsoft Office. To support FrontPage on the server end, IIS 6 includes an optional component called *FrontPage Server Extensions 2002 (FPSE 2002)*, which allows client computers to use FrontPage to open connections with the web server and create, delete, or modify web content directory on the server. FrontPage also allows multiple users to administer the same site in a shared authoring environment.

Our discussion of FrontPage and FPSE in this chapter will be limited because, unfortunately, the subject requires an entire book of its own to do it justice. I'll discuss only setting up FPSE on the server, extending websites to support FrontPage, and testing content publishing using FrontPage. For a full discussion of FrontPage Server Extensions, SharePoint Team Services (a superset of FrontPage Server Extensions), and related topics, see the following URL on Microsoft's website:

```
www.microsoft.com/technet/prodtechnol/sharepnt/proddocs/admindoc/ows000.asp
```

NOTE A website or virtual directory on IIS cannot support both WebDAV and FrontPage as publishing methods; but if both methods are enabled, then FrontPage is used by default, and any WebDAV commands issued by the client are ignored.

Enabling FPSE

Before users can use FrontPage to author and manage content on IIS, FrontPage Server Extensions (FPSE) must be installed on the server. These extensions must first be installed as an optional IIS component, and then enabled globally for all websites using WSE. Finally, the specific virtual servers (websites) you want to support FrontPage must be extended. Extending a website configures the permissions and directory structure of the server to support authoring by clients running FrontPage.

To install the FPSE component of IIS, use Add Or Remove Programs in Control Panel to add the FrontPage 2002 Server Extensions component of Internet Information Services (IIS). You'll need your Windows Server 2003 CD-ROM on hand for this procedure. After FPSE is installed, open IIS Manager, select the WSE node, and allow FrontPage Server Extensions 2002 (Figure 16-10). This action will also extend any existing websites on the server, enabling them to support FrontPage clients.

NOTE   You can also use Manage Your Server to add support for FPSE when you add the Application Server role to your Windows Server 2003 machine to install IIS.

If you then create additional websites on the machine, you must extend these sites manually if you want them to support FrontPage. For example, create a site called Test whose home directory is C:\docs. Right-click Test in IIS Manager and select All Tasks | Configure Server Extensions 2002. This opens the HTML administration tool for managing FPSE on the selected website (Figure 16-11).

Click the Submit button to extend your Test website and configure FPSE to work on this website. The main administration page for managing FPSE appears (Figure 16-12). By clicking various links on this page, you can view and configure the current FPSE settings globally and for each site on your server.

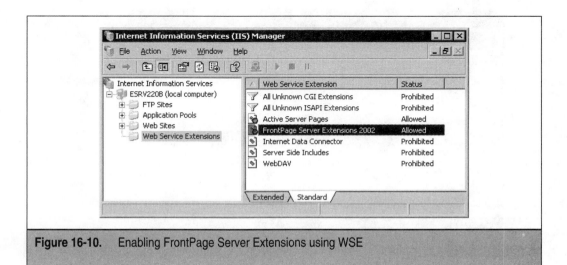

Figure 16-10.   Enabling FrontPage Server Extensions using WSE

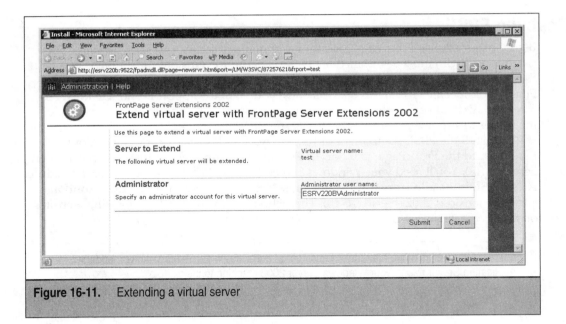

Figure 16-11.   Extending a virtual server

You can also access this site for administering FPSE any time by selecting the
Microsoft SharePoint Administrator node in IIS Manager (Figure 16-13). This node
is created when the FrontPage 2002 Server Extensions component is added to IIS.

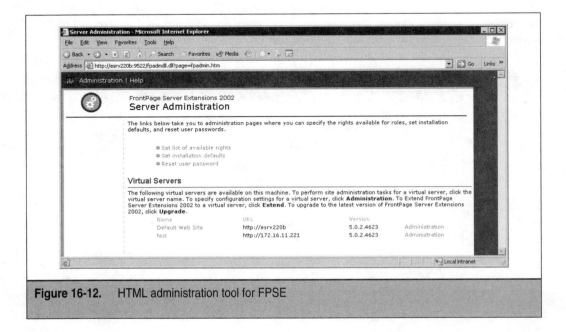

Figure 16-12.   HTML administration tool for FPSE

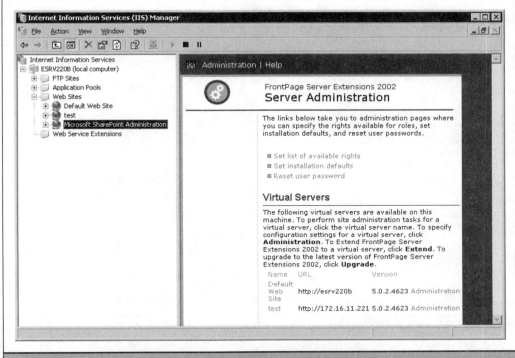

Figure 16-13.   Opening the FPSE admin tool from IIS Manager

In addition, extending a website to support FPSE adds an extra tab called Server Extensions 2002 to the properties sheet for the website in IIS Manager (Figure 16-14). By clicking the Settings button on this tab, you can configure various aspects of how FPSE works on your site, including enabling or disabling authoring, specifying an SMTP server for use by forms created using FrontPage, tuning the performance of FrontPage authoring on the site, specifying the type of client scripting supported by the site, and configuring advanced security settings.

Testing FrontPage Authoring

To test publishing content to IIS using FrontPage, you'll need a copy of FrontPage installed on your client machine. If you have this installed, do the following:

1. Open FrontPage on your client machine.

2. Select File | Open Web and specify http://*IP_address*, where *IP_address* is the address of the remote IIS machine where you created the Test website.

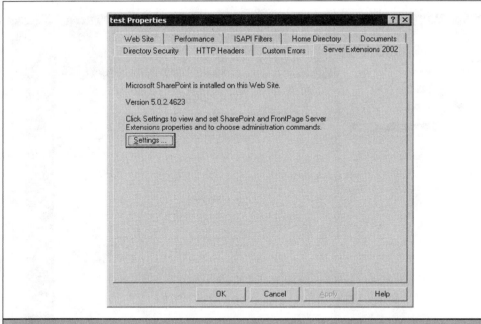

Figure 16-14.   Server Extensions 2002 tab on a website properties sheet

3. When prompted for credentials, for purposes of this test, use those of the administrator on the remote IIS machine.

4. The website should now open in FrontPage. If you are familiar with this authoring tool, try creating a web page named default.htm, save the result to publish the page to the Test site, and then open http://*servername* in Internet Explorer to review the result.

REDIRECTION

Sometimes when you are managing a website, you may need to move content to some other location to reorganize your site or for some other purpose. As a result, clients who try to access this content using URLs saved in their Favorites folder will receive "HTTP 404—File Not Found." Fortunately, you can use *redirection* to prevent such errors. Redirection is a way of having IIS tell web browsers that the content they are requesting has moved to a different location by having IIS provide the browser with the new URL for the moved content. The browser responds by automatically trying to open the new location without any intervention by the user.

There are several ways you can redirect client requests for files in a directory on your web server. For example, you can redirect such requests:

- To a different directory on the same site to which the content has been moved. In this case, all requests such as http://site/olddir/anyfile.abc will be redirected to http://site/newdir/anyfile.abc, regardless of the name of the file requested.

- To an entirely different website to which the content has been moved. In this case, all requests such as http://site/olddir/anyfile.abc will be redirected to http://othersite/anyfile.abc for any filename.

- To go to a specific file in any directory on the site, for example, a file that displays the message "We're reorganizing our site, please come back soon," no matter what page is requested. In this case, all requests such as http://site/olddir/anyfile.abc will be redirected to http://site/otherdir/message.htm, regardless of what file is requested.

- To go to a specific URL that can be anything on any site on the Internet. In this case, all requests such as http://site/olddir/anyfile.abc will be redirected to http://redirect_URL, regardless of what file is requested.

Configuring Redirection

To configure redirection for a website or virtual directory, open the properties sheet for that site or directory and select the Home Directory or Virtual Directory tab. For example, you can redirect requests to content in the root of the Default Web Site to a specific page message.htm in the root of the Test website created earlier. To do this, first use Notepad to create a file named message.htm that has a short message in it, and then save this file in the C:\ folder on the IIS machine. Now do the following:

1. Open the properties sheet for the Default Web Site in IIS Manager and select the Home Directory tab.

2. Select the option A Redirection to a URL.

3. The Home Directory tab now changes to display redirection settings (Figure 16-15).

4. Select the check box labeled The Exact URL Entered Above, and type **http://IP_address/message.htm**, where *IP_address* is the address for the Test website on the IIS machine.

5. Click OK to close the properties sheet and apply the changes.

6. Now right-click the Default Web Site in IIS Manager and select Browse, and the message.htm file should be displayed in the results pane.

Other things you can try:

- Redirect the root directory on your Default Web Site to http://www.yahoo.com/index.html (redirection to a page on the Internet).

- Move the content from your Default Web Site to your Test site, leave the check box The Exact URL Entered Above selected, and type **http://IP_address**, where *IP_address* is the address for the Test website on the IIS machine. This should redirect a request for anyfile.abc in the root of the Default Web Site to anyfile.abc in the root of the Test website.

- Select the check box A Directory Below URL Entered to Redirect Requests to the Root Directory of the Site to Virtual Directory Beneath It. For example, if you move the content of the Test website to the Temp virtual directory below it, you can type **\Temp** in the Redirect To text box to accomplish the redirection.

- Select the check box A Permanent Redirection for This Resource to indicate that the content has been moved permanently, and not temporarily. Doing this changes the HTTP status message IIS sends during redirection from "HTTP 302—Temporary Redirect" to "HTTP 301—Permanent Redirect." If supported, when your web browser receives this message, it will update any favorite or bookmark associated with its request so that next time the user opens it, the browser will open the new URL and no redirection will occur.

TIP   You can also configure redirection on FTP sites, virtual directories, and files.

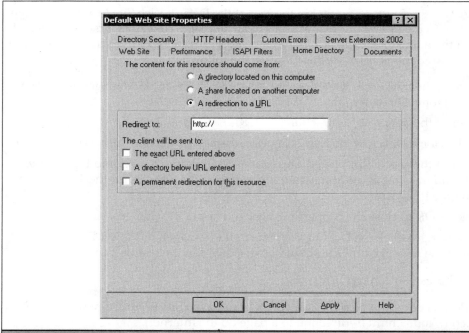

Figure 16-15.   Configuring redirection

CONTENT EXPIRATION

Sometimes your website will have time-sensitive content that is updated frequently, such as the latest football scores on a sports site. In this case, it's not useful for web browsers to cache such content because the next time users access the site, the content will be changed and will have to be downloaded anew. Content expiration is a feature of IIS that allows you to specify to the client when content should expire on the server. This works by caching the page the first time the browser visits it, and, the next time the browser visits the page, comparing the timestamp on the cached page to the content expiration information received from the server in the HTTP headers. If the content has passed its expiration date or time interval, the page is requested anew; otherwise, the page is fetched from the cache.

You can configure content expiration at the site, virtual directory, or file level. For example, to configure content expiration for a page named realtimescores.asp in your Default Web Site, open the properties sheet for the site and select the HTTP Headers tab. Select the check box to enable content expiration, and choose the Expire Immediately option for a page that dynamically displays the latest sports scores (Figure 16-16). Other options include defining a specific date when content on the page expires or a specific time interval in days, minutes, or hours until expiration.

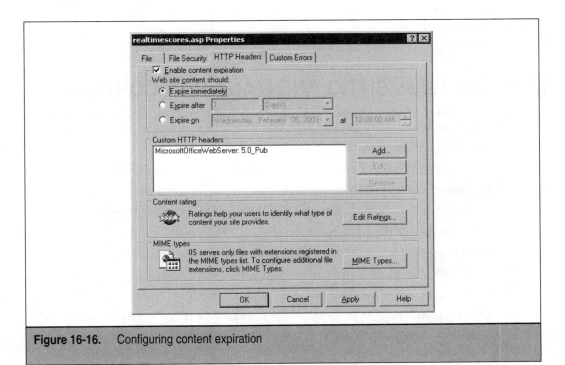

Figure 16-16. Configuring content expiration

CONTENT RATINGS

Content Ratings (see Figure 16-16 again) are used to enable users to block sites from being viewed that display offensive or adult content. This feature was developed by the Recreational Software Advisory Council (RSAC) and uses the Platform for Internet Content Selection (PICS) rating system that rates content based on the level of violence, nudity, sexual content, or offensive language present on the site. Unfortunately, for this feature to work, the user must also enable and configure the Content Advisor on their Internet Explorer web browser, and there's little guarantee that users will do this because most users use the default settings on their software almost exclusively. For more information about content ratings, see IIS Help.

CHALLENGE

You are planning on deploying a corporate network for your company using IIS 6 and have selected an individual in each department to be responsible for updating content on each department's virtual directory. How would you go about deploying this network? Would you employ FTP, WebDAV, or FrontPage for publishing content? Give reasons for your choices that relate to ease of use, administrative overhead, and security.

CHECKLIST: PUBLISHING AND MANAGING CONTENT

Check off each of the following administrative tasks after you become familiar with using them for publishing and managing content on IIS:

- ☐ Installing and enabling WebDAV on IIS.
- ☐ Configuring WebDAV security using NTFS and web permissions.
- ☐ Publishing content to IIS using WebDAV.
- ☐ Installing and enabling FrontPage 2002 Server Extensions (FPSE) on IIS.
- ☐ Opening the HTML administration tool for FPSE on IIS.
- ☐ Publishing content to IIS using FrontPage.
- ☐ Configuring redirection for a site, virtual directory, or file.
- ☐ Enabling content expiration for a site, virtual directory, or file.
- ☐ Using content rating to block offensive content on a site, virtual directory, or file.

PART V

Appendixes

APPENDIX A

Comparison of IIS 5 and 6

The following table compares the features of IIS 5 and 6 by highlighting some of the key *differences* between the two platforms. For example, while both platforms support 32-bit processor architecture, only IIS 6 supports 64-bit Itanium processors, so only this difference is highlighted.

Feature	IIS 5	IIS 6
ACLs on web content		IUSR account has Deny Write
Application model	In-process, pooled process, or isolated processes	Multiple application pools
ASP.NET		New
Passport authentication		New
CDONTS		Replaced by CDOSYS
Clustering	IISsynch.exe	Windows clustering
Fortezza		Removed
Hardware architecture		Supports 64-bit
Host process	DLLhost.exe	w3wp.exe
HTTP routing	Inetinfo.exe	Http.sys
Isolation mode	IIS 5	Worker process and IIS 5
Metabase	Binary	XML
Sample content		Found in IIS 6 Reskit
Script engines		Disabled by default
Security	IIS Lockdown Wizard	Web Service Extensions
Timeouts and Limits	Aggressive to repel DoS	
Web gardens		New
Web permissions		Script source access (new)
WMI support		New

APPENDIX B

Useful IIS Resources

The following is a list of some popular Internet resources that can be useful for those who deploy, administer, and troubleshoot IIS.

- **IISFAQ (www.iisfaq.com)** Managed by MVP Chris Crowe, this popular site is an essential resource for those who deploy, administer, and troubleshoot IIS. Chris also haunts the IIS newsgroups on news.microsoft.com, offering advice and answering questions.

- **IIS Answers (www.iisanswers.com)** Managed by Brett Hill, this site has IIS news, articles, FAQs, events, and more. Has an e-mail newsletter you can subscribe to for keeping up with the latest.

- **IIS Training (www.iistraining.com)** Also managed by Brett Hill, on this site he offers training seminars in IIS administration and security using courseware he has developed.

- **IIS Lists (www.iislists.com)** A variety of IIS-related mailing lists moderated by Brett Hill.

- **IIS Modules (www.iismodules.com)** Lots of articles, tutorials, and other info on IIS, ISAPI, ASP, and more. Also has links to third-party IIS add-ons and other useful products.

- **Port80 Software (www.port80software.com)** This site features useful add-on modules for improving IIS security and performance.

- **Windows Web Solutions (www.windowswebsolutions.com)** Part of the Windows and .NET Magazine Network, this site has lots of tutorials, tips, news on IIS, and web-enabled Microsoft technologies. Also has a good newsletter and popular discussion forums.

- **IIS-Resources.com (www.iis-resources.com)** Managed by Jeff Tindillier, this site has articles, downloads, forums, and lots more of interest to IIS admins.

- **IIS Community Center (www.microsoft.com/windows2000/community/ centers/iis)** A site from Microsoft on which you can access the latest technical information, FAQs, and IIS newsgroups.

- **IIS on TechNet (www.microsoft.com/technet/prodtechnol/iis)** A clearinghouse of resources for deploying, maintaining, and supporting all versions of IIS. Includes tips, downloads, hotfixes, and more.

- **IIS Insider (www.microsoft.com/technet/columns/insider)** This popular monthly column has frequently asked IIS questions from customers with answers by Brett Hill.

- **IIS Support Center (support.microsoft.com/default.aspx?scid= fh;EN-US;iis50)** This site currently focuses on resources for IIS 5, but this should change to IIS 6 by the time this book is in print.

- **IIS 6 Product Documentation (www.microsoft.com/technet/prodtechnol/ windowsnetserver/proddocs/server/iiswelcome.asp)** You can access the full product documentation for IIS 6 here on the Microsoft TechNet site.

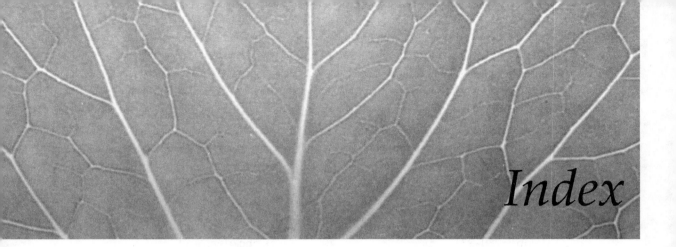

Index

K

O

P

❖ S

❖ **T**

U

 V

W

INTERNATIONAL CONTACT INFORMATION

AUSTRALIA
McGraw-Hill Book Company Australia Pty. Ltd.
TEL +61-2-9900-1800
FAX +61-2-9878-8881
http://www.mcgraw-hill.com.au
books-it_sydney@mcgraw-hill.com

CANADA
McGraw-Hill Ryerson Ltd.
TEL +905-430-5000
FAX +905-430-5020
http://www.mcgraw-hill.ca

GREECE, MIDDLE EAST, & AFRICA
(Excluding South Africa)
McGraw-Hill Hellas
TEL +30-210-6560-990
TEL +30-210-6560-993
TEL +30-210-6560-994
FAX +30-210-6545-525

MEXICO (Also serving Latin America)
McGraw-Hill Interamericana Editores S.A. de C.V.
TEL +525-117-1583
FAX +525-117-1589
http://www.mcgraw-hill.com.mx
fernando_castellanos@mcgraw-hill.com

SINGAPORE (Serving Asia)
McGraw-Hill Book Company
TEL +65-6863-1580
FAX +65-6862-3354
http://www.mcgraw-hill.com.sg
mghasia@mcgraw-hill.com

SOUTH AFRICA
McGraw-Hill South Africa
TEL +27-11-622-7512
FAX +27-11-622-9045
robyn_swanepoel@mcgraw-hill.com

SPAIN
McGraw-Hill/Interamericana de España, S.A.U.
TEL +34-91-180-3000
FAX +34-91-372-8513
http://www.mcgraw-hill.es
professional@mcgraw-hill.es

UNITED KINGDOM, NORTHERN,
EASTERN, & CENTRAL EUROPE
McGraw-Hill Education Europe
TEL +44-1-628-502500
FAX +44-1-628-770224
http://www.mcgraw-hill.co.uk
computing_europe@mcgraw-hill.com

ALL OTHER INQUIRIES Contact:
McGraw-Hill/Osborne
TEL +1-510-596-6600
FAX +1-510-596-7600
http://www.osborne.com
omg_international@mcgraw-hill.com